Oh! 1001 Homemade Casserole Recipes

(Oh! 1001 Homemade Casserole Recipes - Volume 1)

Julia Nedd

Content

4

CHAPTER 4: HAMBURGER CASSEROLE RECIPES

CHAPTER 5: ITALIAN CASSEROLES RECIPES

CHAPTER 7: PORK CASSEROLE RECIPES

14

Chapter 1: Baked Macaroni And Cheese Recipes

***

---

1. Baked Mac & Cheese

Serving: 4 | Prep: | Cook: 25mins | Ready in:

Ingredients

- 3 tablespoons plain dry breadcrumbs, (see Tip)
- 1 teaspoon extra-virgin olive oil
- ¼ teaspoon paprika
- 1 16-ounce or 10-ounce package frozen spinach, thawed
- 1¾ cups low-fat milk, divided
- 3 tablespoons all-purpose flour
- 2 cups shredded extra-sharp Cheddar cheese
- 1 cup low-fat cottage cheese
- ⅛ teaspoon ground nutmeg
- ¼ teaspoon salt
- Freshly ground pepper, to taste
- 8 ounces (2 cups) whole-wheat elbow macaroni, or penne

Direction

- Add water in a large pot and let it boil. Prepare the oven by preheating to 450°F. Use cooking spray to coat an 8-inch square (2-qt.) baking dish.
- In a small bowl, combine paprika, oil and breadcrumbs. In a fine-mesh sieve, put the spinach and press out extra moisture.
- In a large, heavy saucepan over medium-high heat, place 1 1/2 cups milk and heat until steaming. In a small bowl, whisk flour and remaining 1/4 cup milk until it turns smooth;

pour to the hot milk and cook for 2 to 3 minutes, stirring constantly, until the sauce thickens and simmers. Turn off heat and mix in cheddar until dissolved. Add in the pepper, salt, nutmeg and cottage cheese.
- Cook pasta for 4 minutes, or until not quite soft. (It will keep on cooking in the oven.) Strain and put to the cheese sauce; blend well. In a prepared baking dish, spread half of the pasta mixture. Add the spinach on top using spoon. Add the remaining pasta. Dust with the breadcrumb mixture.
- Place casserole in the preheated oven and bake for 25-30 minutes until golden and bubbly.

Nutrition Information

- Calories: 584 calories;
- Sodium: 907
- Fiber: 9
- Cholesterol: 65
- Sugar: 9
- Protein: 38
- Saturated Fat: 13
- Total Carbohydrate: 60
- Total Fat: 24

---

2. Baked Mac & Cheese For Two

Serving: 2 servings. | Prep: 20mins | Cook: 20mins | Ready in:

Ingredients

- 1/2 cup uncooked spiral pasta
- 1 tablespoon butter
- 1 tablespoon all-purpose flour
- 1 cup 2% milk
- 1/8 teaspoon salt
- 1/8 teaspoon pepper
- 1/8 teaspoon ground mustard
- 1/8 teaspoon Worcestershire sauce

- Dash ground nutmeg
- 1/2 cup shredded cheddar cheese
- 1/4 cup process cheese (Velveeta), cubed

Direction

- Cook pasta following the package instructions. Heat butter in a big saucepan, mix in flour until smooth. Slowly pour in milk, mix in nutmeg, Worcestershire sauce, mustard, pepper, and salt. Boil it, cook while stirring until thickened, about 1-2 minutes. Mix in cheeses until melted.
- Strain the pasta, mix in the cheese sauce. Remove into a non-oiled 2-cup baking dish. Bake without a cover at 350° until bubbly, about 10-15 minutes.

Nutrition Information

- Calories: 351 calories
- Protein: 16g protein.
- Total Fat: 20g fat (13g saturated fat)
- Sodium: 602mg sodium
- Fiber: 1g fiber)
- Total Carbohydrate: 27g carbohydrate (8g sugars
- Cholesterol: 66mg cholesterol

3. Baked Mac And Cheese

Serving: 8 servings. | Prep: 20mins | Cook: 30mins | Ready in:

Ingredients

- 1 package (16 ounces) uncooked elbow macaroni
- 1/3 cup plus 1/4 cup butter, divided
- 3/4 cup finely chopped onion
- 6 tablespoons all-purpose flour
- 1 teaspoon ground mustard
- 3/4 teaspoon salt
- 1/4 teaspoon pepper

- 4-1/2 cups 2% milk
- 4 cups shredded sharp cheddar cheese
- 3/4 cup dry bread crumbs

Direction

- Start preheating oven to 350°. Cook macaroni following the package instructions for al dente, then drain.
- Heat 1/3 cup of butter in a Dutch oven over medium heat. Sauté the onion until tender. Whisk in seasonings and flour until blended; stir in milk gradually. Bring to a boil, stirring constantly. Cook while stirring until thickened. Mix in cheese until melted. Mix in macaroni. Place into an oiled 13x9-in. baking dish.
- Melt the remaining butter in a microwave; toss with the bread crumbs. Add over top of casserole. Bake, uncovered, about 30 to 35 mins or until heated through.

Nutrition Information

- Calories: 689 calories
- Total Carbohydrate: 62g carbohydrate (10g sugars
- Cholesterol: 104mg cholesterol
- Protein: 28g protein.
- Total Fat: 37g fat (22g saturated fat)
- Sodium: 834mg sodium
- Fiber: 3g fiber)

4. Baked Three Cheese Macaroni

Serving: 12 servings (3/4 cup each). | Prep: 20mins | Cook: 30mins | Ready in:

Ingredients

- 1 package (16 ounces) elbow macaroni or fusilli pasta
- 6 tablespoons butter, cubed
- 1/2 cup all-purpose flour
- 4 cups 2% milk, warmed

- 4 cups shredded Gruyere cheese
- 2 cups shredded extra-sharp cheddar cheese
- 2 teaspoons salt
- 3/4 teaspoon freshly ground pepper
- 1/4 teaspoon freshly ground nutmeg
- 1-1/2 cups panko (Japanese) bread crumbs
- 1/2 cup grated Parmesan cheese
- 2 tablespoons butter, melted

Direction

- Set oven to 350° to preheat. In a 6-quart stockpot, cook macaroni until al dente as directed on package. Drain off water; pour back into the pot.
- Melt 6 tablespoons butter in a large saucepan over medium heat. Mix in flour until smooth; stir in warmed milk. Bring the mixture to a boil; stirring often; stir and cook until thickened, or for 2 to 3 minutes.
- Put off the heat; mix in nutmeg, pepper, salt, Cheddar cheese, and Gruyere cheese. Mix in macaroni; toss well to coat.
- Pour the pasta mixture into an oiled 13x9-inch baking dish. Combine bread crumbs with melted butter and Parmesan cheese and toss; scatter over the casserole. Baking without covering until bubbles appear and surface has turned golden brown, or for 30 to 40 minutes.

Nutrition Information

- Calories: 487 calories
- Protein: 27g protein.
- Total Fat: 24g fat (14g saturated fat)
- Sodium: 515mg sodium
- Fiber: 2g fiber)
- Total Carbohydrate: 41g carbohydrate (6g sugars
- Cholesterol: 76mg cholesterol

5. Broccoli Mac & Cheese Bake

Serving: 12 servings. | Prep: 25mins | Cook: 20mins | Ready in:

Ingredients

- 3 cups uncooked elbow macaroni
- 4 cups fresh broccoli florets
- 1/2 cup butter, cubed
- 3 tablespoons all-purpose flour
- 1/2 teaspoon garlic powder
- 1/2 teaspoon onion powder
- 1/4 teaspoon pepper
- 1/8 teaspoon salt
- 2 cans (12 ounces each) evaporated milk
- 2-1/2 cups shredded cheddar cheese, divided
- 1/2 cup crushed cornbread-flavored crackers (about 6 crackers)

Direction

- Cook the macaroni as the package directions say and place in broccoli at the final 3-4 minutes; drain it.
- Melt butter in a big saucepan. Mix in flour, onion powder, garlic powder, salt, and pepper until it is smooth and slowly mix in the evaporated milk. Bring it up to a boil and cook and mix it until it gets thick for about 2 minutes. Take it off the heat and mix in 2 cups of cheese.
- Put half of the broccoli and macaroni into a greased baking dish that's 13x9 inches. Top it with half of cheese sauce and repeat the layers. Sprinkle some cracker crumbs and the leftover cheese on top.
- Bake it at 375°F without a cover until it's bubbly for about 20-25 minutes.

Nutrition Information

- Calories: 335 calories
- Total Carbohydrate: 25g carbohydrate (7g sugars
- Cholesterol: 61mg cholesterol
- Protein: 13g protein.

- Total Fat: 21g fat (12g saturated fat)
- Sodium: 331mg sodium
- Fiber: 1g fiber)

6. Cheeseburger Macaroni

Serving: 6 servings | Prep: 30mins | Cook: | Ready in:

Ingredients

- 1 lb. lean ground beef
- 3 cups water
- 1/3 cup HEINZ Tomato Ketchup
- 1 tsp. onion powder
- 1 cup elbow macaroni, uncooked
- 1/2 lb. (8 oz.) VELVEETA®, cut into 1/2-inch cubes

Direction

- In a large skillet, brown the meat; drain. Place meat back to skillet. Add onion powder, ketchup and water; mix well. Let come to boil, stirring frequently.
- Mix in macaroni; simmer on medium-low heat for around 10 minutes till tender, stirring occasionally.
- Add VELVEETA; cook for approximately 3 to 5 minutes till mixture blends well and VELVEETA melts completely, stirring frequently.

Nutrition Information

- Calories: 320
- Saturated Fat: 7 g
- Sodium: 690 mg
- Fiber: 1 g
- Total Carbohydrate: 23 g
- Cholesterol: 70 mg
- Total Fat: 14 g
- Sugar: 4 g
- Protein: 23 g

7. Cheesy Mac & Cheese

Serving: 8 servings. | Prep: 20mins | Cook: 30mins | Ready in:

Ingredients

- 2 cups uncooked elbow macaroni
- 1 tablespoon all-purpose flour
- 1 cup heavy whipping cream
- 1 cup half-and-half cream
- 1/4 cup sour cream
- 1 large egg
- 1/2 teaspoon ground mustard
- 1/2 teaspoon cayenne pepper
- 1/4 teaspoon salt
- 1/4 teaspoon pepper
- 1/8 teaspoon ground nutmeg
- 8 ounces Monterey Jack cheese, cubed
- 8 ounces cheddar cheese, cubed
- 2 cups shredded cheddar cheese

Direction

- Follow package instructions to cook macaroni. At the same time, whisk nutmeg, pepper, salt, cayenne, mustard, egg, sour cream, half-and-half, cream, and flour in a big bowl until smooth.
- Drain pasta. Move to an oiled 2-1/2-quart baking dish. Mix in cubed cheeses. Arrange cream mixture over top. Sprinkle shredded cheese on top.
- Bake at 350 degrees without cover for 30-40 minutes or until golden brown and bubbly.

Nutrition Information

- Calories: 563 calories
- Protein: 25g protein.
- Total Fat: 43g fat (28g saturated fat)
- Sodium: 648mg sodium
- Fiber: 1g fiber)
- Total Carbohydrate: 18g carbohydrate (2g sugars

- Cholesterol: 172mg cholesterol

8. Chicken Ranch Mac & Cheese

Serving: 8 servings. | Prep: 20mins | Cook: 60mins | Ready in:

Ingredients

- 3 cups uncooked elbow macaroni
- 3 tablespoons butter
- 2 tablespoons all-purpose flour
- 1/2 teaspoon salt
- 1/4 teaspoon pepper
- 1 cup 2% milk
- 1-1/2 cups shredded cheddar cheese
- 1/2 cup grated Parmesan cheese
- 1/2 cup shredded Swiss cheese
- 3/4 cup ranch salad dressing
- 1 cup coarsely chopped cooked chicken
- TOPPING:
- 1/3 cup seasoned bread crumbs
- 2 tablespoons butter, melted
- 10 bacon strips, cooked and crumbled
- 1 tablespoon minced fresh parsley

Direction

- Start preheating the oven to 350°F. In a 6-quart stockpot, using the package directions, cook the macaroni for al dente; drain the water and return it to the pot.
- Over medium heat melt butter in a medium pot. Mix in flour, pepper, and salt until smooth; gradually incorporate milk. Heat to a boil, cook and stir constantly until thick about 1-2 minutes. Mix in cheeses until fully blended. Mix in the dressing.
- Toss to combine the chicken and sauce in the macaroni. To a greased 13 x 9-inch pan, transfer the macaroni.
- Add in bread crumbs with melted butter; sprinkle on the macaroni. Top it with bacon. Bake it uncovered until the top is golden brown about 30-35 mins. Top it with parsley.

Freeze option: Prepare recipe as indicated, increase the milk to 1-1/3 cups. Let the unbaked casserole cool; cover and put in freezer. To serve, let it partly thaw overnight in the refrigerator. Remove the casserole from the refrigerator 30 minutes before baking. Heat the oven to 350°F. Cover casserole with foil and bake for 30 minutes. Remove cover; then continue baking as indicated or until it is cooked through and a thermometer poked in middle reads 165°F.

Nutrition Information

- Calories: 586 calories
- Cholesterol: 84mg cholesterol
- Protein: 25g protein.
- Total Fat: 37g fat (15g saturated fat)
- Sodium: 889mg sodium
- Fiber: 2g fiber)
- Total Carbohydrate: 40g carbohydrate (4g sugars

9. Chili Mac & Cheese

Serving: 8 servings. | Prep: 30mins | Cook: 20mins | Ready in:

Ingredients

- 2 packages (7-1/4 ounces each) macaroni and cheese dinner mix
- 2 pounds ground beef
- 1 small onion, chopped
- 1 can (14-1/2 ounces) diced tomatoes, undrained
- 1 can (10 ounces) diced tomatoes and green chilies, undrained
- 1 can (8 ounces) tomato sauce
- 2 tablespoons chili powder
- 1 teaspoon garlic salt
- 1/2 teaspoon ground cumin
- 1/4 teaspoon crushed red pepper flakes
- 1/4 teaspoon pepper

- 2 cups (16 ounces) sour cream
- 1-1/2 cups shredded Mexican cheese blend, divided

Direction

- Set the oven at 350° to preheat. Put the cheese packets aside from the dinner mixes. Boil 2 quarts water in a large saucepan. Put in macaroni, then cook until softened, 8-10 minutes.
- Meanwhile, over medium heat, cook while stirring onion and beef in a Dutch oven until the beef is no longer pink, for 8-10 minutes; let drain. Stir in seasonings, tomato sauce, green chilies, and tomatoes. Allow the macaroni to drain; then put into the beef mixture. Stir in 1 cup cheese, sour cream, and the contents of cheese packets.
- Transfer to an oiled 13x9-in. baking dish; lay remaining cheese on top. Uncover and bake until bubbly, for 20-25 minutes.

Nutrition Information

- Calories: 631 calories
- Total Fat: 35g fat (17g saturated fat)
- Sodium: 1286mg sodium
- Fiber: 3g fiber)
- Total Carbohydrate: 22g carbohydrate (10g sugars
- Cholesterol: 105mg cholesterol
- Protein: 35g protein.

10. Company Mac And Cheese

Serving: 6-8 servings. | Prep: 15mins | Cook: 15mins | Ready in:

Ingredients

- 1 package (7 ounces) elbow macaroni
- 6 tablespoons butter, divided
- 3 tablespoons all-purpose flour
- 2 cups whole milk

- 1 package (8 ounces) cream cheese, cubed
- 2 cups shredded cheddar cheese
- 2 teaspoons spicy brown mustard
- 1/2 teaspoon salt
- 1/4 teaspoon pepper
- 3/4 cup dry bread crumbs
- 2 tablespoons minced fresh parsley

Direction

- Prepare the oven by preheating to 400°F. Cook macaroni based on the package directions. In the meantime, put 4 tablespoons butter in a big saucepan to dissolve. Mix in flour until it becomes smooth. Slowly stir in milk. Let it boil then stir and cook for 2 minutes.
- Lower the heat then add in pepper, salt, mustard and cheeses. Mix until cheese is dissolved and the sauce becomes smooth. Strain macaroni then stir in to the cheese sauce to coat.
- Place in a shallow 3-qt.baking dish that is greased. Dissolve remaining butter then mix with parsley and breadcrumbs. Spread it over the macaroni. Place in the preheated oven and bake for 15-20 minutes or until golden brown.

Nutrition Information

- Calories: 453 calories
- Cholesterol: 92mg cholesterol
- Protein: 15g protein.
- Total Fat: 30g fat (19g saturated fat)
- Sodium: 623mg sodium
- Fiber: 1g fiber)
- Total Carbohydrate: 32g carbohydrate (4g sugars

11. Crab Macaroni & Cheese

Serving: 10 servings. | Prep: 45mins | Cook: 15mins | Ready in:

Ingredients

- 1 package (16 ounces) elbow macaroni
- 6 baby portobello mushrooms
- 2 green onions, sliced
- 1 tablespoon plus 1/4 cup butter, divided
- 1/4 cup all-purpose flour
- 1 teaspoon ground mustard
- 1 teaspoon pepper
- 1/2 teaspoon salt
- 1/4 teaspoon paprika
- 2-1/2 cups half-and-half cream
- 1-1/2 cups shredded part-skim mozzarella cheese, divided
- 1-1/2 cups shredded medium cheddar cheese, divided
- TOPPING:
- 1/2 cup panko (Japanese) bread crumbs
- 3 tablespoons butter, melted
- 1 tablespoon dried basil
- 1-1/2 pounds cooked snow crab legs, meat removed
- 4 thin slices Swiss cheese
- 1/4 cup grated Parmesan cheese

Direction

- Cook the macaroni following directions on the packaging. Drain, rinse pasta under cold water.
- Meanwhile, sauté onions and mushrooms with 1 tablespoon of butter in a big skillet until tender; put aside.
- Melt remaining butter in a big saucepan. Stir in paprika, salt, pepper, mustard and flour until the mixture is smooth; put in cream gradually. Boil; cook while stirring for 2 minutes or until the mixture is thickened. Mix in 3/4 cup of each cheddar cheese and mozzarella cheese until they are blended. Take the saucepan away from heat; fold in the . macaroni.
- Set the oven at 350° and start preheating. Mix basil, butter and bread crumbs in a small bowl. Pour 1/2 macaroni mixture into a 13x9-inch baking dish coated with cooking spray. Put reserved mushroom mixture, leftover macaroni mixture, mozzarella and cheddar cheeses on top. Then, put crab and Swiss

cheese on top. Scatter with crumb mixture and parmesan cheese.
- Bake the dish for 15 to 20 minutes or until it has a golden-brown color. Allow it to rest for 5 minutes before you serve it.

Nutrition Information

- Calories: 535 calories
- Sodium: 534mg sodium
- Fiber: 2g fiber)
- Total Carbohydrate: 42g carbohydrate (4g sugars
- Cholesterol: 118mg cholesterol
- Protein: 25g protein.
- Total Fat: 29g fat (18g saturated fat)

12. Creamy Baked Macaroni

Serving: 4-6 servings. | Prep: 20mins | Cook: 25mins | Ready in:

Ingredients

- 1-2/3 cups uncooked elbow macaroni
- 1 can (10-3/4 ounces) condensed cream of chicken soup, undiluted
- 1 cup milk
- 1 tablespoon minced chives
- 1/2 teaspoon ground mustard
- 1/4 teaspoon hot pepper sauce
- 1-1/2 cups (6 ounces) Gouda or cheddar cheese (1/2-inch cubes)
- 2 tablespoons dry bread crumbs
- 1 tablespoon butter, melted

Direction

- Cook macaroni following the package instructions; strain. Mix hot pepper sauce, mustard, chives, milk, and soup together in a big bowl. Mix in cheese and macaroni.
- Ladle into a shallow 2-quart baking dish coated with cooking spray. Mix together

butter and bread crumbs, sprinkle the mixture onto the top. Bake without a cover at 400° until bubbly and fully heated, about 25-30 minutes.

Nutrition Information

- Calories: 272 calories
- Total Fat: 15g fat (8g saturated fat)
- Sodium: 678mg sodium
- Fiber: 1g fiber)
- Total Carbohydrate: 23g carbohydrate (4g sugars
- Cholesterol: 47mg cholesterol
- Protein: 13g protein.

13. Creamy Cavatappi & Cheese

Serving: 10 servings. | Prep: 30mins | Cook: 20mins | Ready in:

Ingredients

- 6 cups uncooked cavatappi or spiral pasta
- 3 garlic cloves, minced
- 1/3 cup butter
- 1/4 cup all-purpose flour
- 1 tablespoon hot pepper sauce
- 4 cups 2% milk
- 6 cups shredded sharp cheddar cheese
- 1 cup cubed process cheese (Velveeta)
- 3 green onions, chopped
- TOPPINGS:
- 1/2 cup panko (Japanese) bread crumbs
- 3 thick-sliced bacon strips, cooked and coarsley crumbled
- 1 tablespoon butter, melted
- 1 green onion, chopped
- Coarsely ground pepper, optional

Direction

- Cook cavatappi following instruction of the package.

- In the meantime, in a Dutch oven, sauté garlic in butter. Mix in pepper sauce and flour till blended; put in milk gradually. Let come to a boil; cook and stir for around 2 minutes till thicken.
- Mix in cheeses till melted; add green onions. Drain cavatappi; stir into cheese mixture.
- Place to a greased baking dish of 13x9-inch. Combine the melted butter, bacon and bread crumbs; sprinkle over top.
- Bake at 350° with no cover for approximately 20 to 25 minutes till bubbly. Scatter green onion (and pepper if you want) over.

Nutrition Information

- Calories: 706 calories
- Total Carbohydrate: 60g carbohydrate (8g sugars
- Cholesterol: 110mg cholesterol
- Protein: 32g protein.
- Total Fat: 38g fat (21g saturated fat)
- Sodium: 782mg sodium
- Fiber: 3g fiber)

14. Creamy Ham 'n' Macaroni

Serving: 6 servings. | Prep: 20mins | Cook: 20mins | Ready in:

Ingredients

- 2 cups uncooked elbow macaroni
- 1/4 cup butter, cubed
- 1/4 cup all-purpose flour
- 2 cups 2% milk
- 4 teaspoons chicken bouillon granules
- 1/4 teaspoon pepper
- 2 cups shredded cheddar cheese, divided
- 1-1/2 cups cubed fully cooked ham
- 1/4 cup grated Parmesan cheese

Direction

- Following package instructions to cook macaroni. Drain and put aside. In a big saucepan over low heat, melt butter; beat in flour until smooth. Blend in pepper, bouillon, and milk. Heat to a boil; stir and cook for 2 minutes or until thickened. Take away from heat. Mix in macaroni, Parmesan cheese, ham, and 1 cup cheddar cheese.
- Move to an oiled 2-quart baking dish. Sprinkle the rest of cheddar cheese over top. Bake at 350 degrees without cover for 20-25 minutes or until bubbly. Let it sit for 5 minutes then serve.

Nutrition Information

- Calories: 434 calories
- Sodium: 1414mg sodium
- Fiber: 1g fiber)
- Total Carbohydrate: 29g carbohydrate (5g sugars
- Cholesterol: 93mg cholesterol
- Protein: 22g protein.
- Total Fat: 26g fat (16g saturated fat)

15. Creamy Macaroni And Cheese

Serving: 10 | Prep: | Cook: | Ready in:

Ingredients

- 1 tablespoon salt
- 1 pound elbow, shell or other bite-size shaped pasta
- 2 (12 fluid ounce) cans evaporated milk
- 1 cup chicken broth
- 3 tablespoons butter
- 1/3 cup flour
- 1 1/2 tablespoons Dijon mustard
- 1/2 cup grated Parmesan cheese
- Freshly ground black pepper
- 1 pound grated extra-sharp cheddar cheese

Direction

- In a big soup kettle, place 2-qt. of water and make it boil. Stir in the pasta and salt. Cook until it's al dente, following the package directions. Strain. To avoid sticking, strain and quickly place on a big lipped baking sheet and allow to cool while making the sauce.
- In the meantime, put chicken broth and milk in a bowl or 4-cup Pyrex measuring cup and microwave until steamy and hot (not boiling). Dissolve butter in the empty pasta pot; mix in flour, next the hot milk mixture. Keep on stirring for 3-4 minutes until bubbly and thick. Mix in pepper, Parmesan and mustard. Turn heat off, mix in cheddar until dissolved.
- Stir drained pasta to sauce, until all is well blended on low heat. Whisk to heat through and add a bit of water to thin if the sauce is very thick. Serve while hot.

Nutrition Information

- Calories: 529 calories;
- Total Fat: 26.5
- Sodium: 1203
- Total Carbohydrate: 47.1
- Cholesterol: 82
- Protein: 25.1

16. Creamy Makeover Macaroni And Cheese

Serving: 10 servings. | Prep: 30mins | Cook: 25mins | Ready in:

Ingredients

- 1 package (16 ounces) elbow macaroni
- 2 tablespoons butter
- 1/3 cup all-purpose flour
- 2 cups fat-free half-and-half
- 2 cups fat-free milk
- 1/2 teaspoon garlic powder
- 1/2 teaspoon pepper
- 1/4 teaspoon salt

- 3 cups shredded reduced-fat sharp cheddar cheese
- TOPPING:
- 1 medium onion, chopped
- 2 tablespoons butter
- 5 cups cubed bread
- 1/2 cup shredded reduced-fat cheddar cheese

Direction

- Cook the macaroni following the package instructions. In the meantime, melt the butter in a big saucepan on medium heat. Mix the half-and-half and flour and stir it into the pan. Add seasonings and milk, then gently boil. Take it out of the heat. Mix in cheese until it melts. Drain the macaroni and add it to the cheese sauce and mix until coated.
- Move to a cooking spray coated 13x9-inch baking dish. Sauté the onion in butter in a big frying pan until it becomes tender, then add the bread; sauté for additional 2-3 minutes. Sprinkle cheese and bread mixture on top of the macaroni mixture. Let it bake for 25 to 30 minutes at 350 degrees without a cover or until heated through.

Nutrition Information

- Calories: 432 calories
- Sodium: 526mg sodium
- Fiber: 2g fiber)
- Total Carbohydrate: 55g carbohydrate (10g sugars
- Cholesterol: 41mg cholesterol
- Protein: 21g protein.
- Total Fat: 15g fat (9g saturated fat)

17. Deluxe Baked Macaroni And Cheese

Serving: 12 servings. | Prep: 30mins | Cook: 25mins | Ready in:

Ingredients

- 1 package (16 ounces) elbow macaroni
- 1/4 cup all-purpose flour
- 2 cups 2% milk
- 1/2 cup heavy whipping cream
- 1 package (8 ounces) process cheese (Velveeta), cubed
- 1 cup shredded cheddar cheese
- 2/3 cup whipped cream cheese
- 1/4 cup grated Parmesan cheese
- 1 can (14-1/2 ounces) diced tomatoes, drained
- 1-1/2 cups cubed fully cooked ham
- 1 cup (8 ounces) sour cream
- 1 teaspoon Dijon mustard
- TOPPING:
- 1-1/2 cups soft bread crumbs
- 1/4 cup grated Parmesan cheese
- 2 tablespoons butter, melted

Direction

- Set the oven at 350° to preheat. Cook macaroni following the package directions. Whisk cream, milk, and flour in a Dutch oven until smooth. Boil; cook and stir until thickened, for 2 minutes.
- Stir in cheeses until melted. Add mustard, sour cream, ham, and tomatoes. Drain the macaroni; then place to the cheese mixture and toss to coat.
- Transfer to a greased 13x9-in. baking dish. Mix the topping ingredients in a small bowl; dust over the top. Uncover and bake until bubbly and the bread crumbs are lightly browned, for 25-30 minutes.

Nutrition Information

- Calories: 441 calories
- Protein: 19g protein.
- Total Fat: 23g fat (14g saturated fat)
- Sodium: 734mg sodium
- Fiber: 2g fiber)
- Total Carbohydrate: 39g carbohydrate (7g sugars
- Cholesterol: 85mg cholesterol

18. Deluxe Macaroni 'n' Cheese

Serving: 8-10 servings. | Prep: 15mins | Cook: 25mins | Ready in:

Ingredients

- 2 cups 4% cottage cheese
- 1 cup sour cream
- 1 large egg, lightly beaten
- 3/4 teaspoon salt
- Garlic salt and pepper to taste
- 2 cups shredded sharp cheddar cheese
- 1 package (7 ounces) elbow macaroni, cooked and drained
- Paprika, optional

Direction

- Mix pepper, salt, garlic, salt, egg, sour cream and cottage cheese in a big bowl. Place in cheddar cheese; stir well. Put in the macaroni and mix until coated.
- Place in a 2-1/2-qt. baking dish that is greased. Bake in the oven for 25 to 20 minutes, without a cover, at 350°F or until heated through. Dust with paprika if you want.

Nutrition Information

- Calories: 255 calories
- Cholesterol: 71mg cholesterol
- Protein: 14g protein.
- Total Fat: 13g fat (9g saturated fat)
- Sodium: 492mg sodium
- Fiber: 1g fiber)
- Total Carbohydrate: 18g carbohydrate (3g sugars

19. Double Jack Mac

Serving: 6 servings. | Prep: 25mins | Cook: 25mins | Ready in:

Ingredients

- 1 pound small pasta shells
- 1/4 cup chopped onion
- 1/4 cup butter, cubed
- 2 garlic cloves, minced
- 1/4 cup all-purpose flour
- 2-1/2 cups 2% milk
- 4 ounces cream cheese, cubed
- 1 cup shredded Monterey Jack cheese
- 1 cup shredded pepper Jack cheese
- 1 cup shredded sharp cheddar cheese
- 1 teaspoon salt
- 1 teaspoon ground cumin
- 1/8 teaspoon pepper
- 1 can (15 ounces) black beans, rinsed and drained
- 8 bacon strips, cooked and crumbled
- 2 tablespoons minced fresh cilantro
- 1/2 cup shredded Mexican cheese blend
- Additional minced fresh cilantro

Direction

- Follow package instructions to cook shells.
- At the same time, in a Dutch oven, in butter, sauté onion. Put in garlic and cook for 1 more minute. Mix in flour until combined; slowly pour in milk. Heat to a boil; stir and cook for 2 minutes or until thickened.
- Add pepper, cumin, salt, cheddar cheese, pepper Jack cheese, Monterey Jack cheese, and cream cheese; stir and cook until cheese melts.
- Drain pasta. Place pasta, cilantro, bacon, and beans into cheese sauce. Move to an oiled 13x9-inch baking dish. Sprinkle Mexican cheese blend over top.
- Bake at 375 degrees without cover for 25-30 minutes or until golden brown and bubbly. Put more cilantro to garnish.

Nutrition Information

- Calories: 837 calories
- Protein: 37g protein.
- Total Fat: 41g fat (24g saturated fat)
- Sodium: 1283mg sodium
- Fiber: 6g fiber)
- Total Carbohydrate: 79g carbohydrate (8g sugars
- Cholesterol: 123mg cholesterol

20. Five Cheese Macaroni With Prosciutto Bits

Serving: 12 servings. | Prep: 25mins | Cook: 20mins | Ready in:

Ingredients

- 1 package (16 ounces) elbow macaroni
- 1/3 cup unsalted butter, cubed
- 1 medium onion, halved and thinly sliced
- 1 garlic clove, minced
- 1/3 cup all-purpose flour
- 1/2 cup white wine or reduced-sodium chicken broth
- 4 cups heavy whipping cream
- 1 teaspoon white pepper
- 1/4 teaspoon salt
- 5 ounces fresh goat cheese, crumbled
- 5 ounces white cheddar cheese, shredded
- 5 ounces Swiss cheese, shredded
- 3 ounces smoked Gouda cheese, shredded
- 3/4 cup grated Parmesan cheese
- 1/2 cup panko (Japanese) bread crumbs
- 4 ounces thinly sliced prosciutto, chopped

Direction

- Cook macaroni following the package instructions until al dente.
- In the meantime, melt butter in a Dutch oven over medium-high heat. Add onion, stir and cook until turning golden brown, about 4-6 minutes. Add garlic, cook for another 1

minute. Mix in flour until combined, slowly whisk in the wine. Add salt, pepper, and cream; boil it, whisking continually. Stir and cook until thickened, about 2 minutes.
- Lower the heat to medium-low. Add goat cheese, lightly whisk until melted. Slowly whisk in the rest of the cheeses, cook until melted. Take away from the heat.
- Strain the macaroni, mix into the sauce. Remove into a 13x9-inch baking dish coated with cooking spray. Sprinkle bread crumbs over. Bake without a cover at 375° until turning light brown, about 15-20 minutes.
- In the meantime, cook prosciutto in a small nonstick frying pan over medium heat until crunchy, about 5-7 minutes, whisking often. Right before eating, sprinkle over the macaroni.

Nutrition Information

- Calories: 667 calories
- Fiber: 2g fiber)
- Total Carbohydrate: 37g carbohydrate (4g sugars
- Cholesterol: 155mg cholesterol
- Protein: 21g protein.
- Total Fat: 48g fat (30g saturated fat)
- Sodium: 558mg sodium

21. Guilt Free Macaroni And Cheese

Serving: 8 servings. | Prep: 20mins | Cook: 10mins | Ready in:

Ingredients

- 3 cups uncooked elbow macaroni
- 1/3 cup all-purpose flour
- 2 teaspoons ground mustard
- 1/4 teaspoon pepper
- 1 can (12 ounces) fat-free evaporated milk
- 1-1/4 cups fat-free milk

- 1/2 cup minced onion
- 10 ounces reduced-fat process cheese (Velveeta), cut into 1/4-inch cubes
- 1/2 cup shredded reduced-fat sharp cheddar cheese
- 1/2 cup crumbled cooked bacon

Direction

- Preheat oven to 400°. Cook macaroni following instruction of the package.
- In the meantime, in a large saucepan, whisk milks, seasonings and flour; mix in onion. Let come to a boil, stirring constantly; cook and stir for around 1 to 2 minutes till thicken. Take away from heat; mix in process cheese till melted. Drain macaroni; place to a baking dish of 13x9-inch covered with cooking spray. Pour sauce over macaroni; mix to coat, scatter cheddar cheese over. Bake with no cover for approximately 10 to 15 minutes till cheese melts. Scatter bacon over.

Nutrition Information

- Calories: 343 calories
- Protein: 21g protein. Diabetic Exchanges: 2-1/2 starch
- Total Fat: 12g fat (5g saturated fat)
- Sodium: 765mg sodium
- Fiber: 1g fiber)
- Total Carbohydrate: 39g carbohydrate (12g sugars
- Cholesterol: 35mg cholesterol

22. Ham Mac And Cheese

Serving: 4 servings. | Prep: 30mins | Cook: 35mins | Ready in:

Ingredients

- 1 package (7-1/4 ounces) macaroni and cheese dinner mix
- 3/4 cup soft bread crumbs

- 2 tablespoons grated Parmesan cheese
- 1 tablespoon minced fresh parsley
- 1 tablespoon butter, melted
- 1 cup cubed fully cooked ham
- 1 cup (8 ounces) cream-style cottage cheese
- 1/2 cup sour cream
- 2 tablespoons sliced green onion
- 1 tablespoon diced pimientos, optional
- 1/4 teaspoon salt
- 1/4 teaspoon ground mustard

Direction

- Prepare cheese and macaroni following the package directions. In the meantime, combine butter, parsley, Parmesan cheese, and bread crumbs in a small bowl; set aside.
- Combine mustard, salt, pimientos (if desired), green onion, sour cream, cottage cheese, ham, cheese and macaroni in a large bowl. Pour into a greased 1-1/2 qt. baking dish. Then dust with bread crumb mixture.
- Bake without cover for 35-40 minutes at 350°, or until heated through.

Nutrition Information

- Calories: 534 calories
- Fiber: 1g fiber)
- Total Carbohydrate: 43g carbohydrate (7g sugars
- Cholesterol: 96mg cholesterol
- Protein: 26g protein.
- Total Fat: 28g fat (17g saturated fat)
- Sodium: 1472mg sodium

23. Hearty Ham Mac And Cheese

Serving: 10 servings. | Prep: 30mins | Cook: 20mins | Ready in:

Ingredients

- 6 slices white bread

- 3 tablespoons cold butter, cubed
- 1 package (16 ounces) uncooked elbow macaroni
- 6 tablespoons butter, cubed
- 1 garlic clove, minced
- 1 teaspoon water
- 1 teaspoon ground mustard
- 1/4 teaspoon cayenne pepper
- 6 tablespoons all-purpose flour
- 1 can (14-1/2 ounces) reduced-sodium chicken broth
- 2 cans (12 ounces each) evaporated milk
- 1 cup 2% milk
- 4 cups shredded Colby cheese
- 2 cups shredded cheddar cheese
- 1/2 teaspoon salt
- 1/8 teaspoon coarsely ground pepper
- 3 cups cubed fully cooked ham (1/2-in. cubes)

Direction

- Grease a baking dish of 13-x9-inch; leave aside.
- For bread crumbs, in a food processor, pulse bread and cold butter for about 20 to 25 pulses till crumbs are fine; leave aside.
- Cook pasta following instruction of the package. In the meantime, in a Dutch oven, melt butter over medium heat. Whisk in the water, garlic, cayenne and mustard for nearly 30 seconds. Stir in flour till blended; cook and stir for around 2 to 3 minutes till it has golden brown color. Whisk in broth and milk gradually. Cook and stir for an addition of 4 to 5 minutes till mixture starts to thicken.
- Take away from the heat; stir in pepper, salt and cheeses. Drain pasta; add to cheese mixture. Fold in ham. In prepared baking dish, pour the mixture; scatter bread crumbs over.
- Bake with no cover at 375° for approximately 20 to 25 minutes till crumbs have golden brown color. Allow to rest for nearly 5 minutes before serving.

Nutrition Information

- Calories:
- Total Fat:
- Sodium:
- Fiber:
- Total Carbohydrate:
- Cholesterol:
- Protein:

24. Herbed Macaroni N Cheese

Serving: 4 servings. | Prep: 10mins | Cook: 30mins | Ready in:

Ingredients

- 1 tablespoon butter
- 3 tablespoons all-purpose flour
- 2 cups fat-free milk
- 3/4 to 1 teaspoon dried marjoram
- 1/2 teaspoon dried thyme
- 1/8 teaspoon ground nutmeg
- 1/8 teaspoon paprika
- 1 tablespoon Dijon mustard
- 1/2 cup grated Parmesan cheese, divided
- 1 package (7 ounces) elbow macaroni, cooked and drained
- 1 cup (8 ounces) 1% cottage cheese

Direction

- Dissolve butter in a big saucepan. Mix in flour until it turns smooth. Slowly add milk, whisking constantly. Let it boil over medium heat; boil for 2 minutes until thick. Put in the paprika, nutmeg, thyme and marjoram; whisk until combined. Separate the pan from heat.
- Mix in 1/3 cup Parmesan cheese and mustard; stir well. Mix in the cottage cheese and macaroni; whisk until coated.
- Place into an 8-inch square baking dish sprayed with cooking spray. Place in the oven and bake for 30 minutes at 350°F, without cover, or until golden brown on top.

Nutrition Information

- Calories: 372 calories
- Protein: 23g protein. Diabetic Exchanges: 3 starch
- Total Fat: 9g fat (0 saturated fat)
- Sodium: 615mg sodium
- Fiber: 0 fiber)
- Total Carbohydrate: 50g carbohydrate (0 sugars
- Cholesterol: 50mg cholesterol

25. Herbed Macaroni And Cheese

Serving: 6 servings. | Prep: 20mins | Cook: 15mins | Ready in:

Ingredients

- 1 package (7 ounces) uncooked elbow macaroni
- 2 tablespoons butter
- 2 tablespoons all-purpose flour
- 1/2 teaspoon Italian seasoning
- 1/4 teaspoon onion powder
- Salt and pepper to taste
- 1 cup milk
- 1/4 cup sour cream
- 3/4 cup shredded cheddar cheese, divided
- 1/2 cup cubed Havarti or Muenster cheese
- 2 tablespoons grated Parmesan cheese
- 2 tablespoons Italian-style seasoned bread crumbs

Direction

- Cook macaroni as directed on package; drain off water. Put drained pasta into a 1 1/2-quart casserole and set to one side.
- In the meantime, melt butter over medium heat in a large saucepan. Mix in seasonings and flour; slowly pour in milk. Bring to a boil; cook for 2 minutes, stirring, until mixture thickens. Put the pan off the heat; add Havarti

cheese, 1/2 cup Cheddar cheese, and sour cream. Whisk until cheeses are melted.
- Stream cheese sauce over macaroni; stir until well coated. Mix together the remaining Cheddar cheese, bread crumbs, and Parmesan cheese; scatter over casserole. Bake for 15 to 20 minutes at 350° until thoroughly heated.

Nutrition Information

- Calories: 315 calories
- Sodium: 279mg sodium
- Fiber: 1g fiber)
- Total Carbohydrate: 31g carbohydrate (4g sugars
- Cholesterol: 49mg cholesterol
- Protein: 13g protein.
- Total Fat: 15g fat (10g saturated fat)

26. Home Style Mac 'N' Cheese

Serving: 4-6 servings. | Prep: 15mins | Cook: 20mins | Ready in:

Ingredients

- 2 cups uncooked elbow macaroni
- 1 small onion, chopped
- 1 tablespoon butter
- 2 cups cubed fully cooked ham
- 2 cups Cheddar Cheese Sauce
- Salt and pepper to taste
- 1/2 cup shredded cheddar cheese

Direction

- Cook macaroni following instruction of the package; drain. In a large saucepan, sauté onion in butter till soften. Add the ham, macaroni, cheese sauce, pepper and salt. In a greased baking dish of 2-quart, pour the mixture. Scatter cheese over. Bake with cover at 350° for around 20 to 25 minutes till heated through.

Nutrition Information

- Calories:
- Protein:
- Total Fat:
- Sodium:
- Fiber:
- Total Carbohydrate:
- Cholesterol:

27. Homey Mac & Cheese

Serving: 8 servings. | Prep: 20mins | Cook: 25mins | Ready in:

Ingredients

- 2-1/2 cups uncooked elbow macaroni
- 1/4 cup butter, cubed
- 1/4 cup all-purpose flour
- 1/2 teaspoon salt
- 1/4 teaspoon pepper
- 3 cups 2% milk
- 5 cups shredded sharp cheddar cheese, divided
- 2 tablespoons Worcestershire sauce
- 1/2 teaspoon paprika

Direction

- Ready the oven by preheating to 350°F. Then based on the directions given on the package, cook the macaroni until well-done, yet firm when bitten.
- In the meantime, heat butter on medium heat, in a large pot. Mix in the pepper, salt and flour until it becomes smooth; gently add in milk. Allow to boil, whisking continuously; stir and cook for about 2-3 minutes or until it becomes thick. Lower the heat. Mix in the Worcestershire sauce and 3 cups of cheese, stirring until cheese is dissolved.
- Strain the macaroni, and mix into the sauce. Then pour into a 10-inch ovenproof pan that is greased. Bake in the preheated oven for about

20 minutes, uncovered. Add the remaining cheese on top; drizzle paprika as well. Then bake for about 5-10 minutes until the cheese is dissolved and bubbly.

Nutrition Information

- Calories: 447 calories
- Total Carbohydrate: 28g carbohydrate (6g sugars
- Cholesterol: 97mg cholesterol
- Protein: 22g protein.
- Total Fat: 28g fat (20g saturated fat)
- Sodium: 701mg sodium
- Fiber: 1g fiber)

28. Italian Three Cheese Macaroni

Serving: 12 servings (1 cup each). | Prep: 30mins | Cook: 50mins | Ready in:

Ingredients

- 4 cups uncooked elbow macaroni
- 1/2 cup butter, cubed
- 1/4 cup all-purpose flour
- 2 teaspoons Italian seasoning
- 1 teaspoon salt
- 1 teaspoon pepper
- 4 cups 2% milk
- 2 cups shredded cheddar cheese
- 1/2 cup grated Parmesan cheese
- 2 cans (14-1/2 ounces each) diced tomatoes, undrained
- 2 cups shredded part-skim mozzarella cheese
- 1/2 cup dry bread crumbs
- 2 tablespoons butter, melted

Direction

- Cook macaroni following the package instructions.
- In the meantime, start preheating oven to 350°. Melt butter in a small saucepan. Mix in

pepper, salt, Italian seasoning and flour until smooth; gradually pour in milk. Bring to a boil; cook while stirring until thickened, or about 2 minutes. Discard from the heat; whisk in Parmesan and cheddar cheeses until they are melted. Drain the macaroni.

- Spread one cup of the cheese sauce in an oiled 13x9-in. baking pan. Layer with 1/2 of the macaroni, tomatoes and the cheese sauce. Repeat the layers. Top with the mozzarella cheese. Mix butter and bread crumbs; dust over the top.
- Bake, covered, for 40 minutes. Uncover and bake until bubbly and golden brown, or about 10 to 15 minutes more. Allow to stand for 5 minutes. Serve.

Nutrition Information

- Calories: 402 calories
- Protein: 17g protein.
- Total Fat: 23g fat (13g saturated fat)
- Sodium: 763mg sodium
- Fiber: 2g fiber)
- Total Carbohydrate: 33g carbohydrate (8g sugars
- Cholesterol: 66mg cholesterol

29. Mac 'n' Cheese For A Bunch

Serving: 36 servings (1 cup each). | Prep: 30mins | Cook: 35mins | Ready in:

Ingredients

- 3 packages (two 16 ounces, one 7 ounces) elbow macaroni
- 1-1/4 cups butter, divided
- 3/4 cup all-purpose flour
- 2 teaspoons salt
- 3 quarts milk
- 3 pounds sharp cheddar cheese, shredded
- 1-1/2 cups dry bread crumbs

Direction

- Cook macaroni following the package directions until almost softened.
- In the meantime, set the oven at 350° to preheat. Melt 1 cup butter in a large stockpot. Add flour and salt, stir until smooth. Then stir in milk gradually. Bring to a boil; cook, stir until thickened, for 2 minutes. Then reduce the heat. Add cheese and keep stirring until melted. Drain macaroni, then stir into the sauce.
- After that, transfer to 3 greased 13x9-in. baking dishes. Next, melt the leftover butter and toss with bread crumbs. Dust over the casseroles.
- Uncover and bake until golden brown, for 35-40 minutes.

Nutrition Information

- Calories: 395 calories
- Sodium: 510mg sodium
- Fiber: 1g fiber)
- Total Carbohydrate: 32g carbohydrate (5g sugars
- Cholesterol: 68mg cholesterol
- Protein: 17g protein.
- Total Fat: 23g fat (14g saturated fat)

30. Macaroni & Cheese Bake

Serving: 8 servings. | Prep: 20mins | Cook: 35mins | Ready in:

Ingredients

- 2-1/2 cups uncooked elbow macaroni
- 1/4 cup butter, cubed
- 1 can (12 ounces) evaporated milk
- 3 large eggs, lightly beaten
- 5 slices process American cheese, chopped
- 1 cup (8 ounces) sour cream
- 3/4 cup process cheese sauce

- 3/4 teaspoon onion powder
- 1/2 teaspoon seasoned salt
- 1/8 teaspoon pepper
- 2-1/2 cups shredded cheddar cheese, divided

Direction

- Cook macaroni following the package instructions.
- In the meantime, melt butter in a big saucepan. Mix in seasonings, cheese sauce, sour cream, process cheese, eggs, and milk. Stir and cook over medium heat until the cheese melts, about 3-4 minutes. Strain the macaroni, mix with 2 cups cheddar cheese.
- Remove into a 13x9-inch baking dish coated with cooking spray. Add the sauce mixture and stir thoroughly. Sprinkle the leftover cheddar cheese over. Bake without a cover at 350° until bubbly and turning golden brown, about 35-40 minutes.

Nutrition Information

- Calories: 507 calories
- Total Fat: 34g fat (23g saturated fat)
- Sodium: 989mg sodium
- Fiber: 1g fiber)
- Total Carbohydrate: 27g carbohydrate (7g sugars
- Cholesterol: 189mg cholesterol
- Protein: 22g protein.

31. Macaroni 'n' Cheese Italiano

Serving: 6 servings. | Prep: 20mins | Cook: 25mins | Ready in:

Ingredients

- 2 cups uncooked elbow macaroni
- 3/4 cup chopped onion
- 1/4 cup chopped celery
- 1/4 cup chopped green pepper

- 2 teaspoons olive oil
- 1/2 cup meatless spaghetti sauce
- 1/2 teaspoon dried basil
- 1/2 teaspoon dried oregano
- 2 tablespoons all-purpose flour
- 1/2 teaspoon salt
- 1/4 teaspoon ground nutmeg
- 1/8 teaspoon cayenne pepper
- 2 cups fat-free milk
- 1-1/4 cups shredded reduced-fat cheddar cheese
- 1/2 cup shredded part-skim mozzarella cheese
- 2 tablespoons grated Parmesan cheese
- 2 plum tomatoes, seeded and sliced

Direction

- Cook pasta following the package instructions until cooked, but firm. In the meantime, sauté green pepper, celery, and onion with oil in a big nonstick frying pan until soft. Mix in oregano, basil, and spaghetti sauce. Boil it. Lower the heat; simmer without a cover for 5 minutes. Strain the macaroni, mix into the sauce. Remove into a greased 2-quart baking dish; put aside.
- Mix cayenne, nutmeg, salt, and flour together in a saucepan. Slowly mix in milk until smooth. Boil over medium heat, cook while stirring until thickened, about 2 minutes. Lower the heat; mix in mozzarella and cheddar cheeses until melted.
- Add onto the macaroni mixture. Put tomatoes and Parmesan cheese on top. Bake without a cover at 350° until turning golden brown and bubbling, about 25-30 minutes. Allow sit before eating, about 5 minutes.

Nutrition Information

- Calories: 262 calories
- Sodium: 406mg sodium
- Fiber: 2g fiber)
- Total Carbohydrate: 31g carbohydrate (0 sugars
- Cholesterol: 25mg cholesterol

- Protein: 16g protein. Diabetic Exchanges: 2 lean meat
- Total Fat: 9g fat (5g saturated fat)

32. Macaroni 'n' Cheese For Two

Serving: 2 servings. | Prep: 5mins | Cook: 25mins | Ready in:

Ingredients

- 1/3 cup sour cream
- 1/3 cup whole milk
- 1 cup shredded sharp cheddar cheese
- 3/4 cup elbow macaroni, cooked and drained
- 2 tablespoons chopped onion, optional
- Paprika

Direction

- Combine milk and sour cream in a bowl. Mix in macaroni, cheese, and onion (if wanted). Pour mixture into an oiled 2 1/2-cup baking dish; scatter top with paprika. Bake, covered for 25 minutes at 325°, or until thoroughly heated.

Nutrition Information

- Calories: 405 calories
- Fiber: 1g fiber)
- Total Carbohydrate: 26g carbohydrate (4g sugars
- Cholesterol: 92mg cholesterol
- Protein: 18g protein.
- Total Fat: 25g fat (18g saturated fat)
- Sodium: 381mg sodium

33. Macaroni And Cheese

Serving: | Prep: 20 | Cook: 1 | Ready in:

Ingredients

- 1 pound Elbow macaroni
- 4 tablespoons Butter
- 3 cups Milk
- 16 ounces Cheddar Cheese
- 2 teaspoons Flour
- 1/4 cup Water
- 1/2 cup Italian Bread Crumbs

Direction

- In a pan, put butter, cheese, and milk on medium heat. Stir often until the butter and cheese melt.
- Boil a pot of salted water in a second pan. Put in the elbow macaroni.
- Make a paste with water and flour once the cheese is melted. Temper the paste with the cheese sauce, place in the pan. Increase the heat to medium high, then stir until the cheese sauce is thickened; turn off the heat.
- Allow the cooked macaroni to drain and put in a 13x9 pan. Pour over macaroni with the cheese sauce and stir to combine.
- Scatter bread crumbs to cover the top of the cheese and macaroni; place for 30-45 minutes in 350° oven. The sauce should be browned lightly on top and bubbler on the sides.

Nutrition Information

34. Macaroni And Cheese Casserole

Serving: 8 | Prep: 15mins | Cook: 25mins | Ready in:

Ingredients

- 1 (8 ounce) package uncooked elbow macaroni
- 1 pound processed cheese, cubed
- 1 (15 ounce) can mixed vegetables, drained
- 1 (10.75 ounce) can condensed cream of mushroom soup
- 1 pound kielbasa sausage, sliced

Direction

- Prepare the oven by preheating to 350°F (175°C).
- Place lightly salted water in a big pot and make it boil. Put in the macaroni and cook for 8-10 minutes or until al dente; strain.
- Mix in a big bowl the sausage, 1/2 of a soup can of water, mushroom soup, mixed vegetables, processed cheese and macaroni. Place to a 9x13 inch baking dish.
- Place in the preheated oven and bake for 20-25 minutes, cover with aluminum foil.

Nutrition Information

- Calories: 525 calories;
- Total Carbohydrate: 33.9
- Cholesterol: 83
- Protein: 22.8
- Total Fat: 32.8
- Sodium: 1595

35. Macaroni And Cheese Deluxe

Serving: 6 servings. | Prep: 5mins | Cook: 30mins | Ready in:

Ingredients

- 1 package (7-1/2 ounces) macaroni and cheese
- 1 pound diced fully cooked ham
- 3 cups frozen chopped broccoli, thawed and drained
- 1 can (10-3/4 ounces) condensed cream of celery soup, undiluted

Direction

- Cook macaroni and cheese based on the package directions. Mix in soup, broccoli and ham; place into a 2-qt.baking dish that is greased. Bake in the oven, covered, for 30-45 minutes at 350°F or until bubbly.

Nutrition Information

- Calories:
- Fiber:
- Total Carbohydrate:
- Cholesterol:
- Protein:
- Total Fat:
- Sodium:

36. Macaroni And Cheese With Garlic Bread Cubes

Serving: 12 servings. | Prep: 50mins | Cook: 30mins | Ready in:

Ingredients

- 1 pound uncooked spiral pasta
- 2 tablespoons butter, melted
- BREAD CUBES:
- 1 garlic clove, minced
- 3 tablespoons butter
- 4 cups cubed French bread (1/2-inch cubes)
- 1/4 teaspoon seasoned salt
- SAUCE:
- 1 small onion, finely chopped
- 3 tablespoons butter
- 1 garlic clove, minced
- 3 tablespoons all-purpose flour
- 3 cups half-and-half cream
- 1 package (8 ounces) process cheese (Velveeta), cubed
- 1/2 teaspoon sugar
- 1/2 teaspoon seasoned salt
- 1/2 teaspoon ground mustard
- 1/4 teaspoon hot pepper sauce
- 1/8 teaspoon pepper
- 1 cup shredded fontina cheese
- 1 cup shredded cheddar cheese
- 1/2 cup shredded Swiss cheese
- 1/2 cup grated Parmesan cheese
- 1/4 teaspoon paprika

Direction

- Follow directions on package for cooking pasta. After draining the pasta, put it in a 13x9-in. greased pan. Melt the butter and mix in with the pasta. Put some butter in a frying pan and sauté garlic until tender. In a separate bowl place, the bread cubes. Pour the butter mixture over bread cubes and shake on the seasoned salt; mix well. Sauté onion with butter in the same frying pan. Put in the garlic and cook for 1 more minute. Whisk in flour until blended. Slowly add cream. Stirring constantly, heat to a boil, and cook until thick, 2 minutes. Mix in seasoned salt, processed cheese, pepper, sugar, pepper sauce, and mustard. Continue to stir until the cheese is completely melted. In a separate bowl, mix Swiss cheeses, cheddar, and fontina. Put 2 cups of the cheese mixture in the sauce. Stir until the 2 cups of cheese are melted. Pour the mixture over the pasta and mix to combine. Spread the rest of the cheese mixture on top. Sprinkle Parmesan cheese, bread cubes, and paprika on top. Bake in a 350-degree oven until cheese is bubbling and the bread cubes are slightly brown, 30-35 minutes.

Nutrition Information

- Calories: 0
- Sodium: 687 mg sodium
- Fiber: 2 g fiber
- Total Carbohydrate: 41 g carbohydrate
- Cholesterol: 91 mg cholesterol
- Protein: 19 g protein.
- Total Fat: 27 g fat (17 g saturated fat)

37. Makeover Creamy Mac & Cheese

Serving: 10 servings. | Prep: 30mins | Cook: 25mins | Ready in:

Ingredients

- 1 package (16 ounces) elbow macaroni
- 1/3 cup all-purpose flour
- 1/2 teaspoon garlic powder
- 1/2 teaspoon pepper
- 1/4 teaspoon salt
- 2 cups fat-free half-and-half
- 2 tablespoons butter
- 2 cups fat-free milk
- 3 cups shredded reduced-fat sharp cheddar cheese
- OPTIONAL TOPPING:
- 2 tablespoons butter
- 1 medium onion, chopped
- 5 cups cubed bread
- 1/2 cup shredded reduced-fat cheddar cheese

Direction

- Set oven to heat to 350 degrees. Follow directions on package for cooking macaroni. Drain water from macaroni. In the meantime, stir until smooth half-and-half, flour, and seasonings in a mixing bowl. With the stove set to medium heat, melt butter in large pot. Whisk in the half-and-half/flour mixture. Stir in milk. Keep stirring and heat to a rolling boil. Immediately move away from heat. Stir in the cheese until it melts. Add macaroni and mix well. Place in a 13x9-in. grease pan. If topping is desired, place butter in a frying pan on medium-high heat. Put the onion in and stir constantly until soft. Mix in the cubes of bread and stir for another 2 minutes. Spread evenly over macaroni and sprinkle cheese on top. Do not cover; bake until heated, 25-30 minutes.

Nutrition Information

- Calories: 343 calories
- Protein: 18g protein.
- Total Fat: 11g fat (6g saturated fat)
- Sodium: 354mg sodium
- Fiber: 2g fiber)
- Total Carbohydrate: 45g carbohydrate (8g sugars

- Cholesterol: 31mg cholesterol

---

38. Makeover Creamy Macaroni And Cheese

Serving: 7 servings. | Prep: 20mins | Cook: 35mins | Ready in:

Ingredients

- 2 cups uncooked elbow macaroni
- 1/4 cup butter, cubed
- 1/3 cup all-purpose flour
- 1-1/2 cups fat-free milk
- 1/4 cup reduced-sodium chicken broth
- 1 cup (8 ounces) fat-free sour cream
- 1/2 pound reduced-fat process cheese (Velveeta), cubed
- 1/4 cup grated Parmesan cheese
- 1/2 teaspoon ground mustard
- 1/2 teaspoon pepper
- 2 cups shredded reduced-fat cheddar cheese
- Minced chives, optional

Direction

- Cook the macaroni following the package instructions. In the meantime, melt the butter in a big saucepan, then mix in flour until it becomes smooth. Slowly add the broth and milk, then boil. Let it cook and stir for 2 minutes or until it becomes thick.
- Lower the heat and stir in the pepper, mustard, Parmesan, process cheese and sour cream until it becomes smooth.
- Drain the macaroni and mix in the cheddar cheese. Move to a cooking spray coated 13x9-inch baking dish, then add the cream sauce and stir well. Let it bake for 35 to 40 minutes at 350 degrees without a cover or until it becomes bubbly. If preferred, sprinkle chives on top.

Nutrition Information

- Calories: 394 calories
- Protein: 23g protein.
- Total Fat: 18g fat (11g saturated fat)
- Sodium: 842mg sodium
- Fiber: 1g fiber)
- Total Carbohydrate: 37g carbohydrate (9g sugars
- Cholesterol: 61mg cholesterol

---

39. Makeover Sloppy Joe Mac And Cheese

Serving: 12 servings. | Prep: 60mins | Cook: 30mins | Ready in:

Ingredients

- 1 package (16 ounces) elbow macaroni
- 3/4 pound lean ground turkey
- 1/2 cup finely chopped celery
- 1/2 cup shredded carrot
- 1 can (14-1/2 ounces) diced tomatoes, undrained
- 1 can (6 ounces) tomato paste
- 1/2 cup water
- 1 envelope sloppy joe mix
- 1 small onion, finely chopped
- 1 tablespoon butter
- 1/3 cup all-purpose flour
- 1 teaspoon ground mustard
- 3/4 teaspoon salt
- 1/4 teaspoon pepper
- 4 cups 2% milk
- 1 tablespoon Worcestershire sauce
- 8 ounces reduced-fat process cheese (Velveeta), cubed
- 2 cups shredded cheddar cheese, divided

Direction

- Cook the macaroni following the package instructions. In the meantime, cook the carrot, celery and turkey in a big nonstick frying pan on medium heat until no visible pink color in the meat and the vegetables become tender, then drain. Add the sloppy joe mix, water, tomato paste and tomatoes, then boil. Lower the heat, put a cover and let it simmer for 10 minutes, stirring from time to time.

- Drain the macaroni, then put it aside. Sauté the onion in butter in a big saucepan until it becomes tender. Stir in pepper, salt, mustard and flour until it becomes smooth. Slowly add the Worcestershire sauce and milk, then boil. Let it cook and stir for 1 to 2 minutes or until it becomes thick. Take it out of the heat. Mix in the process cheese until it melts, then add 1 cup cheddar cheese and macaroni; stir well.
- In a 13x9-inch baking dish coated with cooking spray, spread 2/3 of the macaroni mixture. Spread turkey mixture to within 2-inch of the edges, then spoon the leftover macaroni mixture around the edges of the pan. Put a cover and let it bake for 30 to 35 minutes at 375 degrees or until it becomes bubbly. Sprinkle the leftover cheddar cheese on top. Put a cover and allow it to stand until the cheese melts.

Nutrition Information

- Calories: 390 calories
- Total Carbohydrate: 45g carbohydrate (10g sugars
- Cholesterol: 55mg cholesterol
- Protein: 23g protein.
- Total Fat: 14g fat (7g saturated fat)
- Sodium: 923mg sodium
- Fiber: 3g fiber)

40. Mom's Macaroni And Cheese

Serving: 8 | Prep: | Cook: 30mins | Ready in:

Ingredients

- 1 pound elbow macaroni
- 1/2 cup vegetable oil
- 2 cups all-purpose flour

- 2 quarts milk
- 1/2 teaspoon ground black pepper
- 1 pound American cheese, cubed
- 1 (28 ounce) can crushed tomatoes
- 3/4 cup seasoned dry bread crumbs

Direction

- Set the oven to 230°C or 450°F to preheat. Bring lightly salted water in a big pot to a boil. Put in pasta and cook just until less than al dente, or for 5-7 minutes, then drain.
- Heat oil in a big saucepan on medium heat. Put in flour, all at once, and stir vigorously until mixed. Put in milk, a little at a time, while stirring continuously until all milk is blended and sauce is smooth. Stir in tomatoes, American cheese and pepper, then stir until cheese has melted and the mixture is smooth (in case cheese begins to stick, lower the heat). Put macaroni into a 15"x10" baking dish, then place cheese mixture on top and sprinkle with bread crumbs.
- Bake until top turns golden, or for 15 minutes.

Nutrition Information

- Calories: 869 calories;
- Total Carbohydrate: 94.9
- Cholesterol: 73
- Protein: 35.3
- Total Fat: 38.8
- Sodium: 1274

41. Mushroom Swiss Mac & Cheese

Serving: 8 servings. | Prep: 40mins | Cook: 25mins | Ready in:

Ingredients

- 1 package (16 ounces) mini penne pasta
- 1/2 pound baby portobello mushrooms, chopped
- 1 small onion, finely chopped

- 2 tablespoons butter
- 1 tablespoon olive oil
- 1 garlic clove, minced
- SAUCE:
- 5 tablespoons butter
- 1 package (8 ounces) cream cheese, cubed
- 1-1/4 cups whole milk
- 1-1/4 cups half-and-half cream
- 2-1/2 cups shredded Swiss cheese
- 1-1/4 cups grated Parmesan and Romano cheese blend
- 1/4 teaspoon salt
- 1/4 teaspoon pepper
- 6 bacon strips, cooked and crumbled
- TOPPING:
- 1/3 cup panko (Japanese) bread crumbs
- 2 tablespoons minced fresh parsley
- 2 tablespoons butter, melted

Direction

- Cook pasta as directed on package. In the meantime, sauté onion and mushrooms in butter and oil in a large skillet until tender. Add garlic; sauté for another minute. Put to one side.
- To make the sauce: melt butter in a large saucepan. Mix in cream cheese until no lumps remain. Slowly pour in cream and milk; cook until thoroughly heated. Mix in pepper, salt, and cheeses until well combined. Add bacon; stir well. Strain pasta; mix with sauce and mushroom mixture. Pour pasta mixture into an oiled 13x9-inch baking dish. Mix melted butter, parsley, and bread crumbs together; scatter over the top of pasta mixture. Bake without covering for 25 to 30 minutes at 375°, or until top turns golden brown.

Nutrition Information

- Calories: 750 calories
- Fiber: 3g fiber)
- Total Carbohydrate: 51g carbohydrate (6g sugars
- Cholesterol: 143mg cholesterol

- Protein: 32g protein.
- Total Fat: 47g fat (28g saturated fat)
- Sodium: 808mg sodium

42. Old Fashioned Macaroni And Cheese

Serving: 12-16 servings. | Prep: 15mins | Cook: 45mins | Ready in:

Ingredients

- 3-1/2 cups uncooked elbow macaroni (about 12 ounces)
- 1/4 cup butter, cubed
- 1/4 cup all-purpose flour
- 1 teaspoon salt
- 3/4 teaspoon ground mustard
- 1/2 teaspoon pepper
- Few dashes hot pepper sauce
- 3-1/2 cups whole milk
- 5 cups shredded cheddar cheese, divided

Direction

- Put the macaroni in a pot with boiling water and boil until just about tender. Drain water off macaroni. In the meantime, melt the butter in a Dutch oven. Stir in pepper sauce, mustard, flour, salt, and pepper until smooth. Cook until bubbling, about 1 minute. Mix in 4 cups of cheese, macaroni, and milk. Place in a 13x9-in. pan that is not greased. Cover; bake in a 350-degree oven until bubbling, 45-50 minutes. Remove cover and put the rest of the cheese on top. Let it cool for 5 minutes before enjoying.

Nutrition Information

- Calories: 249 calories
- Protein: 12g protein.
- Total Fat: 15g fat (10g saturated fat)
- Sodium: 416mg sodium

- Fiber: 1g fiber)
- Total Carbohydrate: 17g carbohydrate (3g sugars
- Cholesterol: 52mg cholesterol

- Cholesterol: 161mg cholesterol
- Protein: 20g protein.
- Total Fat: 33g fat (20g saturated fat)
- Sodium: 550mg sodium
- Fiber: 2g fiber)
- Total Carbohydrate: 51g carbohydrate (6g sugars

43. Over The Top Mac 'n' Cheese

Serving: 7 servings. | Prep: 15mins | Cook: 40mins | Ready in:

Ingredients

- 1 package (16 ounces) elbow macaroni
- 1/2 cup shredded Muenster cheese
- 1/2 cup shredded mild cheddar cheese
- 1/2 cup shredded sharp cheddar cheese
- 1/2 cup shredded Monterey Jack cheese
- 1/2 cup plus 1 tablespoon butter, divided
- 2 cups half-and-half cream
- 2 large eggs, lightly beaten
- 1 cup cubed process cheese (Velveeta)
- 1/4 teaspoon seasoned salt
- 1/8 teaspoon pepper

Direction

- Set oven to 350° to preheat. Cook macaroni as directed on package. In the meantime, combine Monterey Jack cheese, Cheddar cheese, and Muenster cheese together; put to one side.
- Melt 1/2 cup butter in a large saucepan over medium heat. Mix in 1 1/2 cups of cheese mixture, seasonings, process cheese, eggs, and cream. Strain macaroni; add to cheese mixture and mix to coat.
- Pour pasta mixture into an oiled 2 1/2-quart baking dish. Scatter top with the rest of cheese mixture and dot with the remaining butter. Bake without covering for 40 to 45 minutes or until a thermometer achieves 160°.

Nutrition Information

- Calories: 585 calories

44. Philly Style Mac And Cheese

Serving: 6 servings. | Prep: 30mins | Cook: 25mins | Ready in:

Ingredients

- 2 cups uncooked elbow macaroni
- 1/2 pound sliced fresh mushrooms
- 1 medium onion, chopped
- 1 medium green pepper, chopped
- 1/4 cup butter, cubed
- 1/4 cup all-purpose flour
- 1 cup 2% milk
- 1 cup beef broth
- 2 cups shredded provolone cheese
- 2 cups shredded part-skim mozzarella cheese
- 1 teaspoon garlic powder
- 1 teaspoon Montreal steak seasoning
- 1/2 teaspoon onion powder
- 1 package (10-1/2 ounces) frozen Steak-umm sliced steaks, browned
- 1/2 cup French-fried onions

Direction

- Cook macaroni following the package instructions.
- In the meantime, sauté green pepper, onion, and mushrooms with butter in a big frying pan until soft. Mix in flour until combined; slowly pour in broth and milk. Boil it, cook while stirring until thickened, about 2 minutes. Lower the heat. Mix in onion powder, steak seasoning, garlic powder, and cheeses.
- Strain the macaroni, put on the sauce mixture. Mix in steak. Remove into a non-oiled 13x9-

inch baking dish, sprinkle over the top with fried onions. Bake without a cover at 350° until bubbling, about 25-30 minutes.

Nutrition Information

- Calories: 635 calories
- Cholesterol: 106mg cholesterol
- Protein: 34g protein.
- Total Fat: 41g fat (22g saturated fat)
- Sodium: 921mg sodium
- Fiber: 2g fiber)
- Total Carbohydrate: 33g carbohydrate (7g sugars

45. Pizza Mac & Cheese

Serving: 6 servings. | Prep: 30mins | Cook: 30mins | Ready in:

Ingredients

- 1 package (7-1/4 ounces) macaroni and cheese dinner mix
- 6 cups water
- 1 pound ground beef
- 1 medium onion, chopped
- 1 small green pepper, chopped
- 1-1/2 cups shredded part-skim mozzarella cheese, divided
- 1-1/2 cups shredded cheddar cheese, divided
- 1 jar (14 ounces) pizza sauce
- 1/2 cup sliced pepperoni

Direction

- Put the cheese packet from dinner mix aside. Bring water to a boil in a saucepan. Add in macaroni; cook for 8-10 minutes, until softened.
- In the meantime, cook the green pepper, onion and beef in a large skillet on medium heat until no longer pink; drain.

- Drain macaroni; and stir in the contents of cheese packet. Transfer to a round 2-1/2-qt. baking dish coated with grease. Sprinkle with 1/2 cup cheddar cheese and 1/2 cup mozzarella cheese. Put the pepperoni, pizza sauce, beef mixture, and leftover cheeses on top.
- Bake without a cover for 30-35 minutes at 350°, until well heated.

Nutrition Information

- Calories: 512 calories
- Fiber: 2g fiber)
- Total Carbohydrate: 32g carbohydrate (9g sugars
- Cholesterol: 104mg cholesterol
- Protein: 35g protein.
- Total Fat: 27g fat (14g saturated fat)
- Sodium: 1038mg sodium

46. Pizza Macaroni & Cheese

Serving: 12 servings. | Prep: 30mins | Cook: 25mins | Ready in:

Ingredients

- 2 packages (14 ounces each) deluxe macaroni and cheese dinner mix
- 1/2 cup sour cream
- 1 can (14-1/2 ounces) petite diced tomatoes, drained
- 1 can (15 ounces) pizza sauce
- 1 small green pepper, chopped
- 1 small sweet red pepper, chopped
- 2 cups shredded Italian cheese blend
- 2 ounces sliced pepperoni

Direction

- Prepare the oven by preheating to 350°F. Cook macaroni based on the package directions until al dente. Strain and put back into the pan. Mix in the sour cream and the contents of cheese packets. Place in a 13x9-inch baking dish that is greased.

- Mix pizza sauce and tomatoes in a small bowl then drop spoonfuls over the macaroni. Put pepperoni, cheese and peppers on top. Bake in the preheated oven for 25-30 minutes, without cover, until bubbly.

Nutrition Information

- Calories: 340 calories
- Sodium: 927mg sodium
- Fiber: 3g fiber)
- Total Carbohydrate: 37g carbohydrate (5g sugars
- Cholesterol: 37mg cholesterol
- Protein: 14g protein.
- Total Fat: 14g fat (7g saturated fat)

47. Porcini Mac & Cheese

Serving: 6 servings. | Prep: 30mins | Cook: 35mins | Ready in:

Ingredients

- 1 package (1 ounce) dried porcini mushrooms
- 1 cup boiling water
- 1 package (16 ounces) small pasta shells
- 6 tablespoons butter, cubed
- 1 cup chopped baby portobello mushrooms
- 1 shallot, finely chopped
- 1 garlic clove, minced
- 3 tablespoons all-purpose flour
- 2-1/2 cups 2% milk
- 1/2 cup pumpkin or amber ale
- 2 cups shredded sharp white cheddar cheese
- 1 cup shredded fontina cheese
- 1 teaspoon salt
- 1 cup soft bread crumbs

Direction

- Start preheating the oven to 350°. Mix boiling water and dried mushrooms together in a small bowl; allow to sit until the mushrooms are tender, about 15-20 minutes. Using a slotted spoon, take the mushrooms out; rinse and chop finely. Remove the liquid. Cook pasta following the package instructions until al dente.
- In the meantime, heat butter in a Dutch oven over medium-high heat. Add shallot and portobello mushrooms, cook while stirring until soft, about 2-3 minutes. Add garlic, cook for another 1 minute. Mix in flour until combined; slowly mix in beer and milk. Boil it, whisking continually, cook while stirring until thickened a bit, about 3-4 minutes. Mix in the saved mushrooms, salt, and cheeses.
- Strain the pasta, put into the mushroom mixture and mix to blend. Remove into a 13x9-inch baking dish coated with cooking spray. Put bread crumbs on top. Bake without a cover until turning golden brown, about 35-40 minutes.

Nutrition Information

- Calories: 723 calories
- Protein: 30g protein.
- Total Fat: 33g fat (19g saturated fat)
- Sodium: 968mg sodium
- Fiber: 4g fiber)
- Total Carbohydrate: 74g carbohydrate (9g sugars
- Cholesterol: 97mg cholesterol

48. Rich 'n' Cheesy Macaroni

Serving: 6-8 servings. | Prep: 30mins | Cook: 30mins | Ready in:

Ingredients

- 2-1/2 cups uncooked elbow macaroni
- 6 tablespoons butter, divided

- 1/4 cup all-purpose flour
- 1 teaspoon salt
- 1 teaspoon sugar
- 2 cups whole milk
- 8 ounces process cheese (Velveeta), cubed
- 1-1/3 cups 4% cottage cheese
- 2/3 cup sour cream
- 2 cups shredded sharp cheddar cheese
- 1-1/2 cups soft bread crumbs

Direction

- Cook macaroni following the package directions; allow to drain. Arrange in a greased 2-1/2-qt. baking dish. Melt 4 tablespoons butter in a saucepan. Stir in sugar, salt, and flour until smooth. Stir in milk gradually. Boil; cook while stirring until thickened, for 2 minutes.
- Lower the heat; then put in American cheese and stir until melted. Continue to stir in sour cream and cottage cheese. Pour over the macaroni. Dust with cheddar cheese. Then melt the leftover butter, toss with bread crumbs, and dust over the top.
- Bake without cover at 350° for a half-hour, or until golden brown.

Nutrition Information

- Calories: 508 calories
- Total Carbohydrate: 33g carbohydrate (9g sugars
- Cholesterol: 101mg cholesterol
- Protein: 23g protein.
- Total Fat: 31g fat (20g saturated fat)
- Sodium: 1109mg sodium
- Fiber: 1g fiber)

49. Sicilian Mac & Cheese

Serving: 8 servings. | Prep: 45mins | Cook: 20mins | Ready in:

Ingredients

- 4 Johnsonville® Mild Italian Sausage Links (4 ounces each)
- 1/2 cup water
- 1 package (16 ounces) elbow macaroni
- 4 large eggs
- 2 cups half-and-half cream
- 1/2 cup butter, melted
- 2 cups shredded part-skim mozzarella cheese
- 2 cups grated Parmesan cheese
- 2 cups loosely packed basil leaves, chopped
- 2 tablespoons fennel seed, toasted
- 2 garlic cloves, minced
- 1 teaspoon salt
- 1/2 teaspoon pepper
- 1 cup shredded Romano cheese
- Additional chopped fresh basil

Direction

- Preheat the oven to 350°. Put the sausages in a big skillet and let it cook for about 5 minutes until it is evenly browned on every side. Lower the heat setting to medium-low heat then pour in the water. Cover the skillet and let the mixture cook for 10-15 minutes or until a poked thermometer into the sausage indicates a temperature of 160°. Remove the cooked sausage from the skillet and slice it into bite-size pieces. Follow the package instructions in cooking the pasta to al dente.
- While waiting for the pasta to cook, beat the cream, butter and eggs together in a big bowl until well-combined. Add in the garlic, sliced cooked sausage, basil, salt, mozzarella cheese, pepper, fennel seed and Parmesan cheese and mix everything together. Drain the cooked pasta and put it into the prepared cheese mixture right away; toss well until evenly coated.
- Coat eight 10-ounce ramekins with oil then distribute the prepared pasta mixture evenly among each of the ramekins. Top it off with Romano cheese. Place the filled ramekins onto baking sheets. Put it in the preheated oven and let it bake without cover for 20-25 minutes or

until a poked thermometer into the mixture indicates a temperature of 160°. Top it off with extra basil.

Nutrition Information

- Calories:
- Total Fat:
- Sodium:
- Fiber:
- Total Carbohydrate:
- Cholesterol:
- Protein:

50. Three Cheese Spirals

Serving: 8 servings. | Prep: 15mins | Cook: 30mins | Ready in:

Ingredients

- 1 package (16 ounces) spiral pasta
- 1 large egg
- 1-1/2 cups (12 ounces) sour cream
- 1-1/2 cups 4% cottage cheese
- 1 pound process cheese (Velveeta), cubed
- 2 cups shredded cheddar cheese

Direction

- Cook the pasta following the directions on the package. While it cooks, blend egg, cottage cheese, and sour cream in a blender until it's smooth. Move it to a large bowl and add in the cheddar and American cheeses. Drain out the pasta and mix it into the cheese bowl until every piece of pasta is coated.
- Move it to a greased shallow 3-quart baking dish. Bake it for 15 minutes without a cover at 350 degrees. Mix it and then bake it for another 15-20 minutes until the edges are getting brown or bubbly.

Nutrition Information

- Calories: 658 calories
- Protein: 32g protein.
- Total Fat: 34g fat (22g saturated fat)
- Sodium: 1141mg sodium
- Fiber: 2g fiber)
- Total Carbohydrate: 52g carbohydrate (10g sugars
- Cholesterol: 145mg cholesterol

51. Triple Cheese Macaroni

Serving: 6 servings. | Prep: 20mins | Cook: 25mins | Ready in:

Ingredients

- 1 package (16 ounces) elbow macaroni
- 2 large eggs
- 1 can (12 ounces) evaporated milk
- 1/4 cup butter, melted
- 2 tablespoons prepared mustard
- 1 teaspoon seasoned salt
- 1 teaspoon pepper
- 8 ounces process cheese (Velveeta), melted
- 2 cups shredded mild cheddar cheese, divided
- 2 cups shredded sharp cheddar cheese, divided

Direction

- Follow directions on package to cook the macaroni. In the meantime, whisk milk, mustard, seasoned salt, eggs, and pepper in a large mixing bowl. Mix in 1-1/2 cups of both cheddar cheeses and the processed cheese. Drain the macaroni and combine with cheese mixture. Dump into a 3-qt. greased dish. Place the rest of the cheeses on top. Preheat oven to 350 degrees and bake uncovered until sides are bubbling and cheese is melted, 25-30 minutes.

Nutrition Information

- Calories: 830 calories
- Sodium: 1368mg sodium
- Fiber: 3g fiber)
- Total Carbohydrate: 67g carbohydrate (11g sugars
- Cholesterol: 213mg cholesterol
- Protein: 39g protein.
- Total Fat: 45g fat (30g saturated fat)

52. Tuna Mac And Cheese Bake

Serving: 8 servings. | Prep: 15mins | Cook: 30mins | Ready in:

Ingredients

- 1 package (7-1/4 ounces) macaroni and cheese dinner mix
- 1 can (12 ounces) light water-packed tuna, drained and flaked
- 1 can (10-3/4 ounces) condensed cream of mushroom soup, undiluted
- 1-1/3 cups 2% milk
- 2 packages (9 ounces each) frozen peas and pearl onions
- 1 can (4 ounces) mushroom stems and pieces, drained
- 1 can (2.8 ounces) French-fried onions, divided

Direction

- Prepare cheese and macaroni following the package directions. Stir in 1/2 of the fried onions, mushrooms, peas, milk, soup, and tuna.
- Arrange in a greased 11x7-in. baking dish. Uncover and bake for 25 minutes at 325°. Sprinkle with the leftover fried onions, then continue to bake until heated through, or for another 5 minutes.

Nutrition Information

- Calories: 359 calories

- Total Carbohydrate: 35g carbohydrate (7g sugars
- Cholesterol: 37mg cholesterol
- Protein: 20g protein.
- Total Fat: 15g fat (7g saturated fat)
- Sodium: 976mg sodium
- Fiber: 3g fiber)

53. Zippy Macaroni And Cheese

Serving: 4 servings. | Prep: 20mins | Cook: 25mins | Ready in:

Ingredients

- 1-1/3 cups uncooked elbow macaroni
- 1 cup 4% cottage cheese
- 1 cup shredded part-skim mozzarella cheese
- 1/2 cup shredded cheddar cheese
- 1 teaspoon cornstarch
- 1 cup whole milk
- 1 small onion, grated
- 1/4 cup finely chopped green pepper
- 1 teaspoon Dijon mustard
- 1/2 teaspoon salt
- 1/4 to 1/2 teaspoon crushed red pepper flakes
- 1/2 cup crushed cornflakes
- 1 tablespoon butter, melted

Direction

- Set oven to 350 degrees and start preheating. Follow package directions to cook the macaroni. Drain water from the macaroni. Mix in cheddar, cottage, and mozzarella cheeses and put aside. Mix milk and cornstarch until smooth in a large pot. Mix in pepper flakes, onion, mustard, green pepper, and salt. Heat to boiling. Stirring constantly, cook until thick, about 2 minutes. Pour mixture over macaroni mixture; carefully stir to cover. Place in a 2-qt. greased pan. Mix butter and cornflakes and spread on top. Do not cover; bake until top is turning golden brown and bubbling, 25-30 minutes.

Nutrition Information

- Calories:
- Protein:
- Total Fat:
- Sodium:
- Fiber:
- Total Carbohydrate:
- Cholesterol:

Chapter 2: Gratin Casserole Recipes

***

---
54. Artichoke, Potato, And Portobello Mushroom Casserole

Serving: Makes 8 servings | Prep: | Cook: | Ready in:

Ingredients

- 4 tablespoons extra-virgin olive oil
- 4 large artichokes
- 2 pounds Yukon Gold potatoes, thinly sliced
- 4 large portobello mushroom caps, thinly sliced
- 6 ounces soft fresh goat cheese
- 3 garlic cloves, minced
- 3 tablespoons freshly grated Parmesan cheese
- 1/2 cup dry white wine

Direction

- Heat the oven to 425° F. Brush a tablespoon of oil on a glass, 13x9x2-inch baking dish. To clip artichoke, put juice from a lemon half into one big bowl with cold water. Slice off stem of artichoke; rub another half of lemon on cut side. Remove all leaves. Slice off top-an-inch artichoke. Scoop out fibrous choke from the middle with spoon that has a serrated edge. Rub lemon on the entire artichoke and plunge in lemon water. Strain prior to using.
- Cut the artichoke hearts. Place 1/2 the potatoes into the dish, fully covering the base. Put on top with 1/2 the artichoke hearts and 1/2 of the mushrooms. Break 1/2 goat cheese coarsely on top. Scatter salt, pepper and 1/2 of garlic, over, then a tablespoon of the Parmesan. Sprinkle with a tablespoon of oil. Top with the rest of mushrooms to cover, then the artichokes, the goat cheese, the garlic, a tablespoon of the Parmesan, and a tablespoon of the oil. Put the rest of potatoes on top. Add wine on top; sprinkle leftover tablespoon of oil over. Use foil to cover the dish. Bake, about 40 minutes. Lower the oven heat to 400°F. Scatter leftover 1 tablespoon of Parmesan on top. Bake with no cover for 25 minutes to soften the potatoes and brown the surface. Partially cool to serve.

Nutrition Information

- Calories: 263
- Saturated Fat: 4 g(22%)
- Sodium: 178 mg(7%)
- Fiber: 7 g(28%)
- Total Carbohydrate: 31 g(10%)
- Cholesterol: 12 mg(4%)
- Protein: 9 g(18%)
- Total Fat: 12 g(19%)

---
55. Artichoke Prosciutto Gratin

Serving: Makes12 first-course servings | Prep: | Cook: | Ready in:

Ingredients

- 2 14-ounce cans artichoke hearts, drained, quartered

- 6 ounces thinly sliced prosciutto
- 1 cup whipping cream
- 1 1/2 cups crumbled Gorgonzola cheese
- 1/2 cup pine nuts (about 2 ounces), toasted
- 1/4 cup grated Parmesan cheese
- 1 teaspoon chopped fresh sage

Direction

- Pat dry quartered artichoke hearts using paper towels. Crosswise cut each prosciutto slice in half. In halved prosciutto slice to wrap every artichoke heart quarter; put wrapped artichoke hearts in 13x9x2-in. glass baking dish in 1 layer. Put cream over; sprinkle sage, parmesan, pine nuts and gorgonzola. Bake for 25 minutes till sauce thickens and gratin is bubbly. Serve warm.

Nutrition Information

- Calories: 216
- Total Fat: 16 g(25%)
- Saturated Fat: 8 g(40%)
- Sodium: 669 mg(28%)
- Fiber: 4 g(15%)
- Total Carbohydrate: 9 g(3%)
- Cholesterol: 46 mg(15%)
- Protein: 11 g(23%)

56. Barley Casserole

Serving: Serves 6 | Prep: | Cook: | Ready in:

Ingredients

- 1/2 pound mushrooms
- 4-5 tablespoons butter
- 1 large onion, chopped very fine
- 1 cup pearl barley
- Salt, pepper
- 2-3 cups beef or chicken broth

Direction

- Cut the mushroom caps and slice the stems. In a skillet, heat butter and put the chopped onion. Cook for 3-4 minutes and put in the mushrooms. Cook, tossing sometimes, about another 4 minutes. Put in barley and lightly brown it, thoroughly stirring with the mushrooms and onions. Use pepper and salt to season to taste and add to a casserole coated with butter. Cover the mixture by 1/2 inch above with enough boiling broth. Tightly put a cover on the casserole and bake in the oven at 350°F, about 25 minutes. Test if the barley is done by tasting it. Pour in more broth if needed, and keep cooking until the barley is soft and the liquid has incorporated. Enjoy with squab, goose, game, and duck and any other types of poultry, wherever you use wild rice.
- Variations: Just before eating, add to the barley with finely slivered buttered almonds.
- Add chicken gizzards to well-seasoned broth to cook. Cook the barley with the broth. In the final minute, add thin slices of the gizzards.
- Just before eating, add to the barley casserole with some chopped fresh parsley and sautéed chicken livers.
- You can use 1/2 cup finely chopped green onions instead of the onion and add 3/4 cup thinly sliced water chestnuts and 1/4 cup finely chopped celery. Use several dashes of soy sauce to season the broth. Sprinkle chopped parsley over the top of this oriental version of barley casserole and enjoy.

Nutrition Information

- Calories: 239
- Protein: 8 g(16%)
- Total Fat: 11 g(16%)
- Saturated Fat: 6 g(30%)
- Sodium: 475 mg(20%)
- Fiber: 6 g(24%)
- Total Carbohydrate: 30 g(10%)
- Cholesterol: 26 mg(9%)

57. Beef Potpies With Yorkshire Pudding Crusts

Serving: Serves 6 | Prep: | Cook: | Ready in:

Ingredients

- 5 cups 1/2-inch pieces cooked rare roast beef (about 2 pounds)
- a 10-ounce package frozen peas, thawed
- 1 pound boiling potatoes (about 4), cooked and cut into 1/2-inch pieces
- 1 onion, sliced thin
- 1 tablespoon unsalted butter, plus 2 tablespoons unsalted butter, melted (or 2 tablespoons roast beef drippings, heated)
- 1 garlic clove, minced
- 1 tablespoon Worcestershire sauce
- 1 1/2 teaspoons bottled horseradish
- 1/4 cup heavy cream
- 2 large eggs
- 1/2 teaspoon salt
- 1 cup all-purpose flour
- 1 cup milk
- 1 large egg white at room temperature

Direction

- Mix together the potatoes, peas and roast beef in a big bowl. Cook the onion in a frypan with 1 tbsp. of unmelted butter over medium-low heat, mixing from time to time, until it becomes soft, then put the garlic and cook the mixture for 3 minutes. Mix in the cream, horseradish and Worcestershire sauce and cook the mixture, mixing, until it becomes thick. Put the sauce into the roast beef mixture, then sprinkle with pepper and salt to season the mixture and blend it well. Distribute the mixture among the six 1 1/2 cup gratin dishes.
- Pour the melted butter around the gratin dishes' edges and heat the pot pies for 2 minutes in the center of a 450 degrees F preheated oven. Pour 1/3 cup of the Yorkshire pudding batter around each gratin dish's edges and bake the potpies for 15 minutes (avoid opening the oven door). Lower the heat to 400 degrees F and bake the potpies for another 10-15 minutes or until the pudding turns brown and puffed.
- Making the Yorkshire pudding better: Blend the milk, flour, salt and eggs in a blender for half a minute and chill the mixture in the fridge for half an hour with a cover. Beat the egg white in a small bowl, until soft peaks are formed, then fold it into the mixture.

Nutrition Information

- Calories: 580
- Total Carbohydrate: 40 g(13%)
- Cholesterol: 198 mg(66%)
- Protein: 42 g(84%)
- Total Fat: 27 g(42%)
- Saturated Fat: 12 g(61%)
- Sodium: 418 mg(17%)
- Fiber: 5 g(18%)

58. Blue Cheese Potato Gratin

Serving: Makes 6 to 8 servings | Prep: | Cook: | Ready in:

Ingredients

- 2 tablespoons olive oil
- 1 pound onions (3 medium), halved lengthwise, then thinly sliced crosswise
- 2 pounds russet (baking) potatoes (about 4)
- 2 cups heavy cream
- 1/4 pound Maytag Blue cheese, crumbled (1 cup)
- 1/4 pound whole-milk mozzarella, coarsely grated (1 cup)
- 1/2 teaspoon salt
- 1/2 teaspoon black pepper
- a Japanese Benriner or other adjustable-blade slicer

Direction

- Set oven to 375 degrees F and start preheating.
- In a 12-in. heavy skillet on moderately high heat, heat oil until hot yet not smoking. Add onions and sauté for 4 minutes while mixing from time to time until onions start to brown. Decrease to moderate heat, cook onions for 12 minutes while mixing from time to time until golden brown.
- Peel potatoes, use a slicer to slice paper-thin crosswise (approximately less than 1/16-inch thick). In a 2-qt. heavy saucepan, combine cream and potatoes (cream may not fully cover the potatoes on top); heat to a boil. Take away from heat; let it cool for 30 minutes to warm.
- Using a slotted spoon, bring 1/3 potatoes to a lightly greased 3-qt. shallow baking dish (save any cream in the pan), arranging them to make an even layer, evenly sprinkle with 1/2 onions and 1/3 of each cheese. Season with 1/4 teaspoon pepper and 1/4 teaspoon salt. Follow the same manner, make an additional layer with each of onions, potatoes, and cheeses and seasoning; top with the rest of cheeses and the rest of potatoes (do not season the top layer). Evenly spread reserved cream over top, tightly cover with foil.
- Bake for 45 minutes in the middle of the oven. Raise oven temperature to 400 degrees F, take out foil and bake for 12-15 minutes longer till golden brown in top. Let it sit for 15 minutes then serve.

Nutrition Information

59. Braised Belgian Endive Gratin

Serving: Serves 8 | Prep: | Cook: | Ready in:

Ingredients

- 8 Belgian endives (about 2 pounds), trimmed, leaving the root ends intact, and halved lengthwise
- 1 1/2 tablespoons fresh lemon juice
- 3 tablespoons unsalted butter, cut into bits
- 1/2 teaspoon salt
- 2 teaspoons sugar
- 3/4 cup chicken broth
- 2/3 cup finely grated Gruyère
- 1 1/3 cups dry bread crumbs

Direction

- Arrange the endives in a heavy kettle in 2 layers, cut-sides down, and toss in salt, broth, butter, lemon juice, and sugar. Use a buttered round of wax paper to cover the mixture. Cover the paper with the lid. Bring the mixture to a boil. Simmer the mixture while covered for 20-30 minutes until the endives are extremely tender. Use a slotted spoon to transfer the endives into the buttered gratin dish (large enough to hold everything in 1 layer), cut-sides down. Mix the bread crumbs and Gruyere in a small bowl and sprinkle the mixture all over the endives. Position the gratin under the preheated broiler 4-inches away from the heat source and broil for 3-4 minutes until the cheese has melted and the topping is golden.

Nutrition Information

- Calories: 185
- Sodium: 390 mg(16%)
- Fiber: 4 g(16%)
- Total Carbohydrate: 19 g(6%)
- Cholesterol: 24 mg(8%)
- Protein: 7 g(14%)
- Total Fat: 9 g(14%)
- Saturated Fat: 5 g(26%)

60. Bread Pudding With Cheese And Apples

Serving: Makes 8 to 10 dessert or brunch servings | Prep: 45mins | Cook: 2hours | Ready in:

Ingredients

- 3 cups water
- 1/2 cup fresh orange juice
- 3/4 cup packed dark brown sugar
- 1 tablespoon mild molasses
- 1 (4- by 1-inch) strip fresh lemon zest
- 1 (4- by 1-inch) strip fresh orange zest
- 2 whole cloves
- 1/2 stick (1/4 cup) unsalted butter
- 12 slices firm cinnamon-raisin sandwich bread
- 3 Golden Delicious apples (1 1/2 lb)
- 8 oz Monterey Jack cheese, coarsely grated (2 cups)
- 3 tablespoons pine nuts, lightly toasted

Direction

- Preheat the oven to 350°F.
- In 2-quart saucepan, boil cloves, zests, molasses, brown sugar, orange juice and water, mixing till sugar melts. Lower heat and let syrup simmer for 20 minutes, with no cover, then throw cloves and zests.
- Meanwhile, in a nonstick, 12-inch skillet, heat a tablespoon of butter on medium heat till froth settles, then working in 3 batches, brown slices of bread, putting a tablespoon of butter in every batch.
- Peel apples and grate coarsely. In shallow, 2-quart buttered baking dish, put 4 slices of bread in single layer. Put pine nuts, 1/3 of apples and cheese on top. Redo piling two more times with the rest of the pine nuts, cheese, apples and bread. Evenly add syrup over and scatter the leftover tablespoon bits of butter on top.
- Let pudding bake for 40 minutes in center of the oven till golden brown and puffed. Serve while warm.

Nutrition Information

- Calories: 433
- Total Carbohydrate: 57 g(19%)
- Cholesterol: 45 mg(15%)
- Protein: 13 g(25%)
- Total Fat: 18 g(28%)
- Saturated Fat: 9 g(46%)
- Sodium: 404 mg(17%)
- Fiber: 4 g(16%)

61. Broccoli Cheddar Corn Bread Leblanc

Serving: | Prep: | Cook: |Ready in:

Ingredients

- 3 cups coarsely chopped broccoli (about 10 ounces)
- 1 cup all-purpose flour
- 1 cup yellow cornmeal
- 4 teaspoons double-acting baking powder
- 4 large eggs, beaten lightly
- 1 cup finely chopped onion
- 2 cups grated extra-sharp Cheddar
- 1 stick (1/2 cup) unsalted butter, cut into bits

Direction

- Blanch the broccoli for 2 minutes in a large saucepan of boiling salted water; let drain well and pat to dry between several thicknesses of paper towels. Whisk flour, baking powder, and cornmeal in a bowl, dust pepper and salt to taste; put in the eggs, and continue to whisk until it is just blended. (The batter will be very thick.) Stir in the Cheddar, broccoli, and onion. In a preheated 400 degrees F oven, heat the butter in a 9-inch square baking pan until it is hot (not smoking), scoop and evenly spread the batter into the pan. In the middle of the oven, bake the cornbread for 25 to 30 minutes, or until the tester comes out clean. Enjoy the cornbread as an accompaniment to soup.

Nutrition Information

- Calories: 269
- Saturated Fat: 9 g(45%)
- Sodium: 276 mg(12%)
- Fiber: 2 g(7%)
- Total Carbohydrate: 22 g(7%)
- Cholesterol: 102 mg(34%)
- Protein: 10 g(19%)
- Total Fat: 16 g(25%)

62. Butternut Squash Gratin With Rosemary Breadcrumbs

Serving: Makes 10 servings | Prep: | Cook: | Ready in:

Ingredients

- 1/4 cup (1/2 stick) unsalted butter
- 4 cups thinly sliced onions (about 1 pound)
- 2 1/2 pounds butternut squash, peeled, seeded, cut into 1/2-inch cubes
- 1 teaspoon sugar
- 1/2 teaspoon salt
- 1/2 teaspoon ground black pepper
- 3/4 cup canned low-salt chicken broth
- 2 cups fresh breadcrumbs made from soft white bread
- 2 cups (packed) grated sharp white cheddar cheese
- 1 1/2 tablespoons chopped fresh rosemary
- 1/2 teaspoon dried thyme

Direction

- Set oven to 350 degrees F and start preheating. Brush butter on a 13x9x2-in. glass baking dish. In a big and heavy skillet, melt butter on medium-high heat. Add in onions, sauté for 8 minutes until light golden. Add in squash and sauté for 4 minutes. Sprinkle the vegetables with pepper, salt, and sugar; sauté for 5 minutes until squash and onions start to caramelize.
- Place vegetable mixture into the prepared dish; spread chicken broth over top. Tightly cover with foil then bake for 45 minutes. (You can make the squash mixture 1 day in advance. Let cool, cover, and put in the fridge. Reheat in 350 degrees F oven for 10 minutes until heated through.)
- Raise oven temperature to 400 degrees F. In a medium bowl, combine thyme, rosemary, cheese, and breadcrumbs. Arrange over the top of gratin. Bake for 30 minutes without cover, until top is crisp and golden brown.

Nutrition Information

- Calories: 292
- Protein: 10 g(21%)
- Total Fat: 14 g(21%)
- Saturated Fat: 8 g(38%)
- Sodium: 432 mg(18%)
- Fiber: 4 g(16%)
- Total Carbohydrate: 34 g(11%)
- Cholesterol: 35 mg(12%)

63. Butternut Squash And Hazelnut Lasagne

Serving: Makes 6 servings | Prep: 1.5hours | Cook: 2.5hours | Ready in:

Ingredients

- 1 large onion, chopped
- 3 tablespoons unsalted butter
- 3 lb butternut squash, peeled, seeded, and cut into 1/2-inch pieces
- 1 teaspoon minced garlic
- 1 teaspoon salt
- 1/4 teaspoon white pepper
- 2 tablespoons chopped fresh flat-leaf parsley
- 4 teaspoons chopped fresh sage

- 1 cup hazelnuts (4 oz), toasted , loose skins rubbed off with a kitchen towel, and coarsely chopped
- 1 teaspoon minced garlic
- 3 tablespoons unsalted butter
- 5 tablespoons all-purpose flour
- 5 cups milk
- 1 bay leaf (not California)
- 1 teaspoon salt
- 1/8 teaspoon white pepper
- 1/2 lb fresh mozzarella, coarsely grated (2 cups)
- 1 cup finely grated Parmigiano-Reggiano (3 oz)
- 12 (7- by 3 1/2-inch) sheets no-boil lasagne (1/2 lb)

Direction

- Filling: In a 12-in. heavy deep skillet, cook onion in butter on medium heat, occasionally mixing, for 10 minutes till golden. Add white pepper, salt, garlic and squash. Cook, occasionally mixing, for 15 minutes till squash is just tender. Take off heat. Mix nuts, sage and parsley in. Cool the filling.
- While squash cooks, make sauce. In a heavy 3-qt. saucepan, cook garlic in butter on medium low heat for 1 minute, mixing. Whisk flour in and cook roux for 3 minutes, whisking. In a stream, add milk, whisking. Put bay leaf. Boil, constantly whisking. Lower heat. Simmer for 10 minutes, occasionally whisking. Whisk white pepper and salt in. Take off heat. Throw bay leaf. Use wax paper to cover sauce surface if you aren't using it right away.
- Lasagna: Preheat the oven to 425°F.
- Toss the cheeses together. In a buttered 13x9x2-in. glass baking dish/shallow 30qt. baking dish, spread 1/2 cup sauce. Use 3 pasta sheets to cover. Leave spaces between the sheets. Spread 1/3 of filling and 2/3 cup sauce. Sprinkle a heaping 1/2 cup of cheese on top. Layer two more times, starting with pasta sheets then finish with cheese. Put leftover 3 pasta sheets, the rest of the sauce and leftover cheese on top.

- Use buttered foil to cover baking dish tightly. In middle of oven, bake lasagna for 30 minutes. Discard foil. Bake for 10-15 more minutes till bubbly and golden. Before serving, let lasagna stand for 15-20 minutes.
- Sauce and filling can be made a day in advance, kept separately, chilled and covered. Before assembling, bring to room temperature.

Nutrition Information

- Calories: 796
- Fiber: 9 g(36%)
- Total Carbohydrate: 78 g(26%)
- Cholesterol: 90 mg(30%)
- Protein: 31 g(62%)
- Total Fat: 43 g(66%)
- Saturated Fat: 19 g(97%)
- Sodium: 1307 mg(54%)

64. Cauliflower Cheddar Gratin With Horseradish Crumbs

Serving: Makes 8 servings | Prep: 45mins | Cook: 55mins | Ready in:

Ingredients

- 3 lb cauliflower (1 large head), cut into 1 1/2- to 2-inch florets
- 1/2 stick (1/4 cup) unsalted butter
- 2 tablespoons all-purpose flour
- 1 1/2 cups whole milk
- 6 oz sharp Cheddar, coarsely grated (2 cups)
- 1/2 cup finely chopped scallion greens
- 1/2 teaspoon salt
- 1/2 teaspoon black pepper
- 20 (2-inch) square saltine crackers
- 2 tablespoons drained bottled horseradish

Direction

- Preheat an oven to 450°F. Butter the 2-qt. shallow baking dish.

- In 5-6-qt. pot with boiling salted water, cook cauliflower for 6-8 minutes till just tender. In a colander, drain cauliflower well. Put into baking dish.
- As cauliflower cooks, melt 2 tablespoons butter in 3-4-qt. heavy saucepan on medium low heat; whisk flour in. Cook roux for 3 minutes, whisking. In a slow stream, add milk, whisking; boil, frequently whisking. Lower heat. Simmer sauce, occasionally whisking, for 8 minutes. Take off heat; add pepper, salt, scallion greens and cheese, whisking till cheese melts. Put cheese sauce on cauliflower; gently mix to combine.
- Crumble coarsely crackers in a bowl. Melt leftover 2 tablespoons butter in small saucepan. Take off heat. Mix horseradish in. Put on crumbs; toss till coated.
- Evenly sprinkle crumb topping on cauliflower.
- Bake gratin for 10 minutes till topping is golden brown.

Nutrition Information

- Calories: 176
- Saturated Fat: 6 g(31%)
- Sodium: 329 mg(14%)
- Fiber: 3 g(10%)
- Total Carbohydrate: 15 g(5%)
- Cholesterol: 27 mg(9%)
- Protein: 6 g(12%)
- Total Fat: 11 g(16%)

65. Cauliflower And Horseradish Gratin

Serving: Serves 8 to 10 | Prep: | Cook: |Ready in:

Ingredients

- 3 1/2 pounds cauliflower, trimmed, cut into florets (about 8 cups)
- 6 tablespoons unsalted butter
- 3 tablespoons all purpose flour
- 2 cups half and half
- 7 tablespoons prepared white horseradish
- 1 teaspoon white wine vinegar
- Ground nutmeg
- 1 cup packed grated Fontina cheese (about 4 ounces)
- 1/2 tablespoon Dijon mustard
- 2 cups fresh French breadcrumbs

Direction

- Preheat an oven to 375°F. Steam cauliflower for 9 minutes till crisp-tender. Put in 13x9x2-in. glass baking dish. In heavy big saucepan, melt 3 tbsp. butter on medium heat. Put flour; mix for 2 minutes, don't brown. Whisk half and half in slowly. Cook for 4 minutes, constantly whisking, till sauce thickens and boils. Mix vinegar and 5 tbsp. horseradish in. Season with pepper, salt and nutmeg to taste. Put sauce on cauliflower; mix to coat. Sprinkle on cheese. Can be done 1 day ahead, chilled and covered.
- In heavy medium skillet, melt 3 tbsp. butter on medium heat. Mix leftover 2 tbsp. horseradish and mustard in. Add breadcrumbs; mix for 9 minutes till crumbs are golden brown. Sprinkle on cauliflower.
- Bake for 25 minutes till cauliflower heats through.

Nutrition Information

- Calories: 384
- Protein: 13 g(27%)
- Total Fat: 22 g(34%)
- Saturated Fat: 13 g(66%)
- Sodium: 462 mg(19%)
- Fiber: 6 g(23%)
- Total Carbohydrate: 36 g(12%)
- Cholesterol: 62 mg(21%)

66. Cauliflower Leek Kugel With Almond Herb Crust

Serving: Makes 8 servings | Prep: | Cook: | Ready in:

Ingredients

- 8 cups cauliflower florets (from 2 medium heads of cauliflower)
- 6 tablespoons olive oil, divided
- 4 cups coarsely chopped leeks (white and pale green parts; from 3 large)
- 6 tablespoons unsalted matzo meal
- 3 large eggs
- 1/2 cup chopped fresh parsley, divided
- 1/2 cup chopped fresh dill, divided
- 1 1/2 teaspoons salt
- 1/2 teaspoon coarsely ground black pepper
- 1/3 cup almonds, toasted, chopped

Direction

- Cook cauliflower in a big pot with boiling salted water for 10 minutes till tender; drain. Put into big bowl; coarsely mash using potato masher.
- Heat 3 tbsp. oil on medium high heat in big heavy skillet. Add leeks; sauté for 5 minutes till starting to color and tender. Put leek mixture in cauliflower; stir in matzo meal. Beat pepper, salt, 1 tbsp. dill, 1 tbsp. parsley and eggs to blend in small bowl; mix into the cauliflower mixture.
- Brush 1 tbsp. oil on 11x7-in. baking dish; evenly spread cauliflower mixture in prepped dish. Mix 2 tbsp. oil, 7 tbsp. dill, leftover 7 tbsp. parsley and almonds to blend in a medium bowl. Evenly sprinkle on kugel. You can make it 8 hours ahead. Cover; chill.
- Preheat an oven to 350°F; bake the kugel, uncovered, for 35 minutes till starting to brown on top and set in center. Allow to for 10 minutes.

Nutrition Information

- Calories: 217
- Cholesterol: 70 mg(23%)
- Protein: 7 g(13%)
- Total Fat: 15 g(24%)
- Saturated Fat: 2 g(12%)
- Sodium: 450 mg(19%)
- Fiber: 4 g(16%)
- Total Carbohydrate: 16 g(5%)

67. Chard, Tomato And Cheese Casserole

Serving: 8 TO 10 SIDE-DISH SERVINGS | Prep: | Cook: | Ready in:

Ingredients

- 2 tablespoons olive oil
- 2 bunches Swiss chard, washed, center ribs cut away, coarsely chopped (about 8 cups) or three 10-ounce packages frozen chopped, thawed, squeezed dry
- 3 red bell peppers, chopped
- 1 large onion, chopped
- 2 cups packed grated Monterey Jack cheese (about 8 ounces)
- 1/2 cup grated Parmesan cheese
- 2 large tomatoes, thinly sliced

Direction

- Grease a 13x9x2-inch glass baking dish. In a heavy large Dutch oven, heat 1 tablespoon oil over high heat. Add chard and sauté for about 3 minutes, or until wilted. Move the chard to a colander and allow to drain well, release the liquid by pressing chard on with the back of a spoon.
- In a heavy large saucepan, heat the remaining 1 tablespoon oil over medium heat. Put in onion and bell peppers, sauté for about 8 minutes, until soft. Mix in the chard, then toss to combine. Next, mix in 1/2 of each cheese. Then season with pepper and salt and to taste. Scoop into the prepared dish. Overlap tomato slices atop vegetable mixture, covering

completely. Dust with pepper and salt to season the tomatoes. Sprinkle over with the remaining cheeses. Wrap up with foil. (This can be prepared 2 hours in advance. Allow to sit at room temperature.)

- Set the oven at 350°F to preheat. Bake casserole for about 40 minutes, or until heated through. Uncover and continue to bake for about 10 minutes longer or until the top starts to brown.

Nutrition Information

- Calories: 205
- Total Fat: 14 g(22%)
- Saturated Fat: 7 g(35%)
- Sodium: 423 mg(18%)
- Fiber: 3 g(11%)
- Total Carbohydrate: 9 g(3%)
- Cholesterol: 30 mg(10%)
- Protein: 12 g(23%)

68. Cheesy Potato And Kale Gratin With Rye Croutons

Serving: 6–8 servings | Prep: 50mins | Cook: 2hours40mins | Ready in:

Ingredients

- 4 slices seeded rye bread
- 1 large bunch kale (preferably Tuscan; about 12 ounces), ribs removed, leaves torn into 3" pieces
- 6 ounces good-quality Gruyère, grated on the large holes of a food processor blade or box grater (about 2 cups)
- 2 ounces good-quality Parmesan, grated on the large holes of a food processor blade or box grater (about 1/2 cup)
- 2 pounds yellow-fleshed potatoes (such as Yukon Gold), unpeeled, cut crosswise into 1/8"-thick slices (see Cooks' Note), divided
- 1 teaspoon dried thyme, divided
- Kosher salt, freshly ground pepper

- 2 1/2 cups heavy cream
- 2 garlic cloves, finely grated or pressed
- 3 tablespoons extra-virgin olive oil, divided
- A 13x9x2" or 3-quart baking dish

Direction

- Put rack in middle of oven; preheat it to 350°F. Put bread slices on rimmed baking sheet; bake, flipping halfway through once, for 15-20 minutes till lightly toasted and dry. Cool. Put into resealable plastic bag; break to irregular 1/2-1-in. pieces. Put into medium bowl; put aside.
- Meanwhile, wash kale then spin-dry; layer between big kitchen towel/paper towels. Pat dry.
- In a medium bowl, mix parmesan and gruyere. In 3-4 rows, shingle 1/4 potatoes, slightly overlapping, on bottom of baking dish then sprinkle 1/8 tsp. pepper, 1/4 thyme and 1/4 tsp. salt. Put 2 cups kale then 1/4 cheese mixture over; repeat twice more. Shingle leftover potatoes on cheese; top with leftover thyme, 1/8 tsp. pepper and 1/4 tsp. salt. Reserve leftover cheese and kale.
- In liquid measuring cup, mix 1/8 tsp. pepper, 1/4 tsp. salt, garlic and cream; evenly put on potatoes.
- Bake gratin for 40 minutes. Use foil to cover; bake for 35-45 minutes till potatoes are tender when a paring knife pierces them and cream is thick and bubbly.
- Meanwhile, in a medium bowl, toss 2 tbsp. oil with reserved croutons. Toss leftover 1 tbsp. oil with leftover kale. Top gratin with kale, leftover cheese then croutons, letting kale pieces peek through. Bake gratin for 15 minutes till exposed kale edges crisp well and croutons are golden brown. Cool for 10 minutes minimum; serve.
- You can roast bread 3 days ahead; keep at room temperature in airtight container.
- You can tear, wash and pat dry kale 3 days ahead. In paper towels, wrap. Put into resealable plastic bag; chill.

- You can make gratin 1 day ahead; cool. Tightly wrap in plastic; chill. Bring it to room temperature; cover using foil. Warm in 300°F oven for 15-20 minutes till heated through. Uncover; warm to re-crisp exposed kale edges and croutons for 5 minutes.
- To cut potatoes quickly to uniform-sized pieces, use a mandolin. Reheat casserole: Bring it to room temperature and cover with foil; warm in 300°F oven for 15-20 minutes till heated through. Uncover; warm to re-crisp exposed kale edges and croutons for 5 minutes.

Nutrition Information

- Calories: 736
- Sodium: 741 mg(31%)
- Fiber: 4 g(15%)
- Total Carbohydrate: 32 g(11%)
- Cholesterol: 188 mg(63%)
- Protein: 20 g(40%)
- Total Fat: 60 g(92%)
- Saturated Fat: 32 g(161%)

69. Chicken Divan

Serving: 6 | Prep: 25mins | Cook: 30mins | Ready in:

Ingredients

- 2 1/2 cups cooked chopped broccoli
- 2 cups shredded, cooked chicken meat
- 2 (4.5 ounce) cans mushrooms, drained
- 1 (8 ounce) can water chestnuts, drained (optional)
- 2 (10.75 ounce) cans condensed cream of chicken soup
- 1 cup mayonnaise
- 1 teaspoon lemon juice
- 1/4 teaspoon curry powder
- 1 tablespoon melted butter
- 1/2 cup shredded Cheddar cheese

Direction

- Set the oven to 350°F (175°C) for preheating. Grease the 3-qt casserole dish.
- Place the cooked broccoli into the prepared baking dish. Arrange the chicken over the broccoli. Add the water chestnuts and mushrooms.
- Mix the lemon juice, melted butter, curry powder, soup, and mayonnaise in a medium-sized bowl. Drizzle sauce mixture over the vegetables and chicken. Sprinkle the top with cheese. Bake it inside the preheated oven for 30-45 minutes until the cheese is golden brown and the casserole is bubbling.

Nutrition Information

- Calories: 524 calories;
- Total Fat: 42.2
- Sodium: 1164
- Total Carbohydrate: 18
- Cholesterol: 72
- Protein: 20

70. Chicken Normande With Mashed Apples And Potatoes

Serving: 4 to 6 servings | Prep: | Cook: | Ready in:

Ingredients

- 3 cups canned low-salt chicken broth
- 1 cup apple cider or apple juice
- 8 ounces parsnips, peeled, cut into 1/2-inch cubes
- 1 3/4 pounds Yukon Gold potatoes, peeled, cut into 1/2-inch cubes
- 3/4 pound Golden Delicious apples (about 2 large), peeled, cored, cut into 1/2-inch cubes
- 5 tablespoons butter
- 8 skinless boneless chicken thighs, cut into 1-inch pieces
- 6 teaspoons minced fresh thyme

- 2 tablespoons all purpose flour
- 1 cup frozen peas, thawed
- 1/3 cup brandy
- 1/3 cup whipping cream

Direction

- Boil initial 3 ingredients in big heavy pot. Lower heat to medium; cover. Simmer for 5 minutes till parsnips are tender. Put parsnips into small bowl using slotted spoon. Add apples and potatoes in same pot; cover. Simmer for 20 minutes till very tender. Take off heat. Put apples and potatoes in big bowl using slotted spoon; add 3 tbsp. butter. Mash till nearly smooth. Season with pepper and salt. Put broth mixture from the pot into medium bowl; put pot aside.
- Sprinkle 4 tsp. thyme, pepper and salt on chicken; dust using flour. Melt leftover 2 tbsp. butter in reserved pot on medium high heat. Add 1/2 chicken; sauté, turning with tongs, for 5 minutes till cooked through and brown. Put sautéed chicken into 11x7x2-in. glass baking dish using slotted spoon. Repeat with leftover chicken. Top with peas, leftover 2 tsp. thyme and parsnips. Put broth mixture in same pot; add whipping cream and brandy. Boil on medium high heat, scraping browned bits up, for 3 minutes till sauce reduces to 1 1/4 cups. Season with pepper and salt; put on chicken. Use potato-apple mixture to cover. You can prep it 1 day ahead. Refrigerate till cold. Cover; keep refrigerated.
- Preheat an oven to 350°F. Bake casserole while uncovered for 35 minutes, 45 minutes if refrigerated, till chicken filling heats through and potato topping is crusty.

Nutrition Information

- Calories: 1229
- Saturated Fat: 27 g(135%)
- Sodium: 362 mg(15%)
- Fiber: 11 g(44%)
- Total Carbohydrate: 75 g(25%)
- Cholesterol: 352 mg(117%)

- Protein: 61 g(121%)
- Total Fat: 72 g(111%)

71. Chicken And Mushroom Pie With Phyllo Parmesan Crust

Serving: Makes 6 servings | Prep: | Cook: | Ready in:

Ingredients

- 1 1/2-ounce package dried porcini mushrooms
- 1 cup hot water
- 9 tablespoons butter, divided
- 1 pound assorted fresh mushrooms (such as crimini, stemmed shiitake, and button mushrooms), sliced
- 3 garlic cloves, minced
- 2 cups low-salt chicken broth
- 3/4 cup Riesling or other fruity white wine
- 2 ounces thin prosciutto slices, cut into thin strips
- 2 teaspoons grated lemon peel
- 2 teaspoons chopped fresh thyme
- 1 teaspoon salt
- 1/2 teaspoon ground black pepper
- 3 tablespoons cornstarch mixed with 1/2 cup water
- 12 sheets fresh phyllo pastry or frozen, thawed
- 2 pounds skinless boneless chicken thighs, excess fat removed, thighs quartered
- 2 tablespoons chopped fresh Italian parsley
- 1/2 cup finely grated Parmesan cheese

Direction

- Mix 1 cup of hot water and dried porcini in a small bowl; stand for 20 minutes till porcini are soft. Drain porcini; keep liquid.
- Melt 3 tbsp. of butter in a big heavy pot on medium high heat then add garlic and fresh mushrooms; sauté for 8 minutes till mushrooms are browned. Add 1/2 tsp. of pepper, 1 tsp. of salt, thyme, lemon peel, prosciutto, wine, broth, porcini soaking liquid

(leave sediment behind) and porcini. Lower heat to medium low; simmer for 20 minutes to merge flavors, uncovered. Whisk cornstarch mixture to mix. Add to skillet; mix for 1 1/2 minutes till mixture slightly thickens. Season sauce with extra salt and pepper to taste (optional). You can make this 1 day ahead; slightly cool then refrigerate, covered.

- Preheat an oven to 425°F. In a small saucepan, melt 6 tbsp. of butter; take off from heat. On a work surface, put 1 phyllo sheet; use plastic wrap sheet then damp towel to cover leftover sheet. Brush some melted butter on phyllo sheet; scrunch buttered phyllo sheet gently into a loose ball, 2 1/2-3-in. in diameter, with both hands. Put on a work surface. Repeat using leftover melted butter and phyllo sheets.
- Boil mushroom sauce; mix in parsley and chicken. Put mixture in a 13x9x2-in. ceramic or glass baking dish; use phyllo balls to cover hot filling. Sprinkle with parmesan; bake for 15 minutes. Lower oven temperature to 350°F and bake for 20 more minutes till chicken cooks through and phyllo is golden.
- You scrunch the phyllo pastry dough to make pretty biscuits over the pot pie.

Nutrition Information

- Calories: 740
- Saturated Fat: 20 g(102%)
- Sodium: 1065 mg(44%)
- Fiber: 3 g(10%)
- Total Carbohydrate: 34 g(11%)
- Cholesterol: 207 mg(69%)
- Protein: 39 g(77%)
- Total Fat: 49 g(75%)

72. Chile And Chorizo Cornbread

Serving: Makes 6 to 8 servings | Prep: | Cook: |Ready in:

Ingredients

- 1/2 pound Chorizo, removed from casing
- 1 cup yellow cornmeal
- 1 tablespoon baking powder
- 1/2 teaspoon salt
- 2 eggs, lightly beaten
- 1 cup sour cream or yogurt
- 1 (8-ounce) can creamed corn
- 4 fresh Anaheim chiles, fire-roasted, peeled, and chopped
- 1 fresh jalapeno chile, seeded and finely chopped or 1 (4-ounce) can green chiles chopped
- 2 cups grated sharp Cheddar cheese

Direction

- Preheat an oven to 350 degrees F.
- Over medium-high heat, crumble and fry Chorizo for 5 minutes in a heavy skillet to render some fat. In a large bowl, place Put 3 tablespoons of the fat and the sausage meat. Add 1 1/4 cups of cheese, cornmeal, salt, corn, eggs, baking powder, sour cream, and chiles. Combine all the ingredients well.
- Generously coat a 10-inch heavy skillet or 1 1/2 quart casserole or a 9 by 9-inch baking dish with butter. Scoop in cornbread batter. Drizzle the remaining 3/4 cup of cheese on top. Bake for about 45 to 55 minutes until cornbread smells nice and turns golden. Serve while still hot.

Nutrition Information

- Calories: 557
- Protein: 24 g(48%)
- Total Fat: 37 g(57%)
- Saturated Fat: 18 g(89%)
- Sodium: 1004 mg(42%)
- Fiber: 2 g(10%)
- Total Carbohydrate: 32 g(11%)
- Cholesterol: 145 mg(48%)

73. Contemporary Cassoulet

Serving: Makes 8 to 10 servings | Prep: | Cook: | Ready in:

Ingredients

- 4 bacon slices, coarsely chopped
- 3 pounds fully cooked smoked sausages (such as kielbasa), cut crosswise into 3/4-inch-thick rounds
- 2 medium onions, chopped
- 6 garlic cloves, chopped
- 1 tablespoon chopped fresh rosemary
- 1 tablespoon chopped fresh thyme
- 1/2 teaspoon dried crushed red pepper
- 1/2 cup brandy
- 3 15-ounce cans Great Northern beans, drained
- 2 14 1/2-ounce cans diced tomatoes in juice
- 1 10-ounce package frozen baby lima beans, thawed
- 1 cup (or more) canned low-salt chicken broth
- 3 tablespoons tomato paste
- 1/2 teaspoon ground allspice
- 1/4 cup olive oil
- 4 cups coarse fresh breadcrumbs made from crustless French bread
- 1/2 cup freshly grated Parmesan cheese
- 1/4 cup chopped fresh parsley

Direction

- Set oven to 350 degrees F and start preheating.
- In a heavy and big ovenproof pot, cook bacon for 4 minutes on medium-high heat, until crisp and brown. Transfer bacon to the bowl with a slotted spoon.
- To drippings in the pot, add sausages; sauté for 15 minutes until brown.
- Bring to the bowl with bacon. Pour off all apart from 1/4 cup drippings from the pot. To the pot, add garlic and onions, sauté for 10 minutes until just softened. Mix in crushed red pepper, thyme, and rosemary. Add in brandy; allow simmering for 3 minutes until mostly evaporated. Mix in allspice, tomato paste, 1 cup broth, lima beans, tomatoes with juices,

and canned beans. Bring bacon and sausages back to the pot. Season the cassoulet with pepper and salt. Heat to a boil.

- Put cover on the pot, put in the preheated oven and bake for 30 minutes. (This dish can be prepared up to 2 days in advance. Remove cover and let cool for 1 hour. Keep with no cover in the fridge till it is cold; put on cover and keep refrigerated. Just before continuing, put on cover and rewarm in the oven for 40 minutes at 350 degrees F, pouring in additional broth if dry.)
- Raise oven temperature to 400 degrees F. In a big nonstick skillet, heat oil on medium heat.
- Put in breadcrumbs, sauté 4 minutes until light golden. Move to a small bowl. Blend in Parmesan cheese; use pepper and salt as seasoning. Arrange over the warm cassoulet. Bake about 20 minutes till breadcrumb topping turns deep golden. Sprinkle parsley over the cassoulet; serve.

Nutrition Information

- Calories: 1228
- Fiber: 27 g(109%)
- Total Carbohydrate: 106 g(35%)
- Cholesterol: 97 mg(32%)
- Protein: 55 g(109%)
- Total Fat: 68 g(104%)
- Saturated Fat: 24 g(121%)
- Sodium: 2317 mg(97%)

74. Corn Pudding

Serving: 6 | Prep: | Cook: 20mins | Ready in:

Ingredients

- 2 cups fresh corn kernels, (about 2 large ears), divided (see Tip)
- 2 tablespoons all-purpose flour
- 3 large eggs
- 3 large egg whites

- 1 cup nonfat evaporated milk
- 1 teaspoon salt
- ¼ teaspoon freshly ground pepper
- 1 teaspoon butter
- 2 tablespoons plain dry breadcrumbs

Direction

- Set the oven to 325 degrees F to preheat. Use cooking spray to grease a 1 1/2- or 2-qt. soufflé or baking dish.
- In a blender or food processor, mix flour and 1 cup of corn together, then process until the mixture is smooth. In a big bowl, whisk egg whites and eggs together, then stir in pepper, salt, evaporated milk, leftover 1 cup kernels and pureed corn. Transfer the mixture into prepped dish and bake about half an hour.
- In the meantime, in a small saucepan, melt butter on low heat and cook for a half minute to 4 minutes depending on your stove, until butter has a light and nutty brown color. Put in breadcrumbs and cook for 1 to 1 1/2 minutes while stirring often, until crumbs darken a bit.
- Sprinkle breadcrumbs on top of pudding once it has baked for half an hour, then keep on baking for 25-35 minutes longer, until a knife stuck near the center exits clean. Serve instantly.

Nutrition Information

- Calories: 143 calories;
- Total Fat: 4
- Fiber: 1
- Cholesterol: 96
- Saturated Fat: 1
- Sodium: 523
- Total Carbohydrate: 18
- Sugar: 8
- Protein: 10

75. Creamy Chicken Noodle Casserole With Spinach And Mushrooms

Serving: Makes 6 servings | Prep: | Cook: | Ready in:

Ingredients

- 1pound skinless boneless chicken breast halves
- 1 1/2 cups (about) water
- 2 large garlic cloves, minced
- 1 bay leaf
- 1/3 cup all purpose flour
- 2 tablespoons cornstarch
- 2 cups low-fat (1%) milk
- 1 teaspoon dried tarragon
- 1 teaspoon salt
- 1/8 teaspoon ground nutmeg
- 1/4 cup dry white wine
- 1 10-ounce package frozen spinach, thawed, squeezed dry
- 8 ounces spinach fettuccine
- 8 ounces mushrooms, sliced
- 1 1/2 teaspoons olive oil
- 3/4 cup coarse fresh breadcrumbs from French bread
- 1/4 cup freshly grated Parmesan cheese

Direction

- In a big saucepan, combine bay leaf, garlic, 1 cup water and chicken. Cover; allow to simmer 15 minutes, turning once, just until chicken has been cooked through. Remove chicken to a plate; let it cool. Shred chicken. Transfer cooking liquid to a measuring cup, adding additional water if needed to measure 1 cup. Save cooking liquid.
- In a big and heavy saucepan, combine cornstarch and flour. Pour in 1 cup milk; beat until smooth. Mix in 1 cup of reserved chicken cooking liquid, nutmeg, salt, tarragon and 1 cup milk. Stir 5 minutes on medium heat, till the mixture boils and thickens. Pour in wine; mix 2 more minutes till the mixture is very thick. Take away from heat. Mix in spinach

and shredded chicken. (Can be prepared 1 day in advance. Cover and keep chilled. Before continuing, reheat on medium-low heat, mixing frequently.)

- Set oven to 400°F and start preheating. Brush oil on an 11x7x2-in. glass baking dish. In a big pot with boiling water, cook fettuccine until just tender but still firm to bite; drain. Bring back to the pot. Put in chicken mixture and mushrooms; toss. Season with pepper and salt. Remove to the prepared baking dish.
- In a small nonstick skillet on medium-high heat, heat oil. Add breadcrumbs and mix 1 minutes. Scatter over casserole. Bake 20 minutes until breadcrumbs are golden and casserole bubbles. Allow to rest 10 minutes. Sprinkle Parmesan atop.

Nutrition Information

- Calories: 425
- Saturated Fat: 3 g(16%)
- Sodium: 665 mg(28%)
- Fiber: 4 g(14%)
- Total Carbohydrate: 54 g(18%)
- Cholesterol: 67 mg(22%)
- Protein: 31 g(63%)
- Total Fat: 9 g(13%)

76. Crusted Chicken And Black Beans

Serving: Makes 6 servings | Prep: | Cook: | Ready in:

Ingredients

- One 3-pound cooked chicken (boiled or roasted)
- 1 medium-size ripe tomato, peeled and chopped (juices included)
- One 15 1/4-ounce can black beans, drained
- 1 1/2 cups bottled salsa
- 6 ounces Monterey Jack cheese, shredded
- 1 tablespoon chopped fresh cilantro leaves

- 1/2 teaspoon ground cumin
- Salt and black pepper to taste
- Four 8-inch flour tortillas, cut into quarters
- 2 tablespoons corn oil

Direction

- Preheat an oven to 350°F then grease 2 1/2-qt. casserole; put aside.
- Remove then discard bones and skin from chicken; shred meat. Put in big mixing bowl. Add 3/4 cheese, cumin, cilantro, salsa, beans and tomato; season with pepper and salt. Mix till blended well; scrape into prepped casserole. Overlapping each other, put tortilla quarters on top; sprinkle oil then cover. Bake for 30 minutes.
- Uncover; evenly sprinkle leftover cheese over. Bake for 10-15 minutes till top is crust and golden.

Nutrition Information

- Calories: 556
- Saturated Fat: 8 g(42%)
- Sodium: 1089 mg(45%)
- Fiber: 8 g(30%)
- Total Carbohydrate: 35 g(12%)
- Cholesterol: 122 mg(41%)
- Protein: 48 g(95%)
- Total Fat: 25 g(38%)

77. Dulce De Leche Fruit Gratin

Serving: Makes 4 servings | Prep: 10mins | Cook: 15mins | Ready in:

Ingredients

- 6 tablespoons dulce de leche*
- 1 1/2 cups blueberries (7 1/2 oz)
- 4 ripe small plums, quartered and pitted
- 2 tablespoons hazelnuts (with skin), chopped
- 4 (6- by 4-inch) flameproof gratin dishes

Direction

- Preheat the broiler.
- On base of every gratin dish, evenly scatter 1 1/2 tablespoons of dulce de leche, then distribute blueberries equally between dishes. Set 4 quarters of plum in every dish.
- On baking sheet, place the gratin dishes and let broil 4- to 6-inch away from heat for 4 minutes till dulce de leche starts to bubble, then scatter nuts evenly and broil for 1 to 2 minutes longer till nuts turn brown. Serve warm.

Nutrition Information

---

78. Eggplant Cannelloni With Pine Nut Romesco Sauce

Serving: Serves 6 | Prep: | Cook: | Ready in:

Ingredients

- 2 large eggplants, peeled and sliced lengthwise 1/2-inch thick
- 2–3 tablespoons water
- 2 medium red bell peppers, seeded and coarsely chopped
- 1 medium onion, coarsely chopped
- 1 cup chopped carrots
- 1/2 cup chopped celery
- 4 cloves garlic
- 8 ounces baby spinach
- No-salt seasoning blend, adjusted to taste, or 1 tablespoons Dr. Fuhrman's VegiZest
- 1 cup cooked quinoa, Kamut, barley, spelt, or brown rice
- 2 cups no-salt-added or low-sodium pasta sauce
- 3 ounces nondairy, mozzarella-type cheese, shredded
- 1/2 cup onion, chopped
- 2 cloves garlic, chopped
- 1/2 tomato, chopped
- 1 teaspoon ancho chili powder
- 1/2 cup roasted red peppers
- 2 tablespoons water
- 2 tablespoons pine nuts (see Note)
- 2 tablespoons nutritional yeast

Direction

- Preheat an oven to 350°F; oil a nonstick baking pan lightly. In 1 layer, put eggplant in pan; bake till eggplant is flexible to easily roll up for 20 minutes. Put aside.
- Heat 2 tbsp. water in a big pan then add garlic, celery, carrots, onion and bell pepper; sauté, adding extra water if needed, till just tender. Add VegiZest/other no-salt seasoning blend and spinach; cook till spinach wilts. Add cooked quinoa.
- Put in a mixing bowl; mix all shredded cheese and 2-3 tbsp. pasta sauce in. Spread 1/4 cup pasta sauce in a baking pan. On each eggplant slice, put some veggie mixture; roll up. Put in a pan; put leftover sauce on eggplant rolls. Bake till heated through for 20 minutes.
- Romesco sauce: Sauté tomatoes, garlic and onions in little water/white wine till onions are translucent then add chili powder; sauté for 1 minute. Place onion mixture and leftover ingredients in high-powered blender; puree till smooth. Serve eggplant with a drizzle of romesco sauce.
- You can use raw almonds for Mediterranean pine nuts.

Nutrition Information

- Calories: 285
- Total Carbohydrate: 41 g(14%)
- Cholesterol: 16 mg(5%)
- Protein: 14 g(28%)
- Total Fat: 10 g(15%)
- Saturated Fat: 3 g(16%)
- Sodium: 537 mg(22%)
- Fiber: 14 g(57%)

79. Eggplant, Potato And Pepper Casserole

Serving: Serves 8 | Prep: | Cook: | Ready in:

Ingredients

- 2 1 1/4-pound eggplants, thinly sliced crosswise
- 1 1/2 tablespoons olive oil
- 1 large onion, chopped
- 5 large garlic cloves, chopped
- 1 28-ounce can Italian-style tomatoes
- 2 large fresh thyme sprigs
- olive oil (for frying)
- 3 pounds russet potatoes, peeled, thinly sliced
- 3 green bell peppers, cored, thinly sliced
- 5 tablespoons minced fresh thyme

Direction

- Put the slices of eggplant onto two baking sheets. Salt both sides of eggplant lightly. Allow to rest for an hour. Blot eggplant dry with paper towels, wiping off the salt.
- In a big skillet, heat 1 1/2 tablespoons of oil over moderate heat. Put in garlic and onion, sauté for 10 minutes, till golden. Put in thyme sprigs and tomatoes including the juices; boil. Lower the heat and simmer for 20 minutes till mixture is cooked down to 2 1/2 cups, crumbling tomatoes using back of a spoon. Use pepper and salt to season the sauce. Throw the thyme sprigs away.
- Heat the oven to 350°F. Into two big skillets, put oil reaching quarter-inch depth. Heat over moderately-high heat. Put the eggplant into skillets in batches and cook till golden in color, 5 minutes on each side, putting additional oil into skillets as need be. Turn onto paper towels to drain. Put the potatoes into skillets in batches, cook till golden in color, for 3 minutes on each side. Turn the potatoes onto paper towels. In the same skillet, put the green peppers; sauté for 5 minutes, till nearly soft. Turn onto paper towels.

- In a glass, 15x10x2-inch baking dish, layer 1/2 of eggplant. Scatter with a tablespoon of thyme. Scoop half cup of sauce on top. Put 1/2 of potatoes over. Add pepper and salt to season. Place a tablespoon of thyme over top. Scoop half cup of the sauce on top. Top with all slices of pepper. Add pepper and salt to season. Put a tablespoon of thyme on top. Scoop half cup of sauce on top. Put the rest of eggplant over top. Put a tablespoon of thyme on top. Scoop half cup of sauce over the top. Place the leftover potatoes over top. Add pepper and salt to season. Put a tablespoon of thyme and half cup of the sauce on top.
- Bake for 40 minutes with no cover to soften the vegetables. Allow to rest for 15 minutes prior to serving.

Nutrition Information

- Calories: 867
- Saturated Fat: 11 g(53%)
- Sodium: 130 mg(5%)
- Fiber: 9 g(38%)
- Total Carbohydrate: 47 g(16%)
- Protein: 7 g(13%)
- Total Fat: 76 g(116%)

80. Fettuccine Meatball Lasagne

Serving: Makes 8 to 10 servings | Prep: 1.5hours | Cook: 2.25hours | Ready in:

Ingredients

- 3 tablespoons olive oil
- 1 medium onion, finely chopped
- 3 garlic cloves, minced
- 1/2 teaspoon dried oregano, crumbled
- 2 (28-ounce) cans whole tomatoes in juice, drained, reserving juice, and finely chopped
- 1 tablespoon tomato paste
- 1 Turkish or 1/2 California bay leaf
- 1 teaspoon salt

62

- 1 1/2 cups coarse fresh bread crumbs (from an Italian or French loaf)
- 1/3 cup whole milk
- 1 pound meatloaf mix (1/3 pound each of ground pork, ground chuck, and ground veal)
- 2 garlic cloves, minced
- 1 ounce finely grated Pecorino Romano (1/2 cup)
- 1 large egg, lightly beaten
- 1/4 cup finely chopped fresh flat-leaf parsley
- 1/2 teaspoon salt
- 1/4 teaspoon black pepper
- 1 cup vegetable oil
- 1 pound ricotta (preferably fresh)
- 1 large egg, lightly beaten
- 1 ounce finely grated Pecorino Romano (1/2 cup)
- 1/4 cup chopped fresh flat-leaf parsley
- 1/4 teaspoon salt
- 3/4 pound dried egg fettuccine
- 1/2 pound chilled fresh mozzarella, coarsely grated

Direction

- In a 5- to 6-quart heavy pot over moderately high heat, heat oil until hot but not smoking; sauté onion in heated oil for 6 minutes, stirring sometimes, or until golden. Add oregano and garlic; sauté and stir for another minute. Add salt, bay leaf, tomato paste, tomatoes with reserved juice; simmer without a cover for 30 to 35 minutes, stirring occasionally, or until thickened. Remove bay leaf from the mixture.
- Shape and fry meatballs: combine milk and bread crumbs together in a large bowl; allow to stand for 10 minutes. Add pepper, salt, parsley, egg, cheese, garlic, and meat; mix until just incorporated using your hands (avoid overmixing). Shape 1/2-teaspoon pieces into meatballs, making about 135 meatballs in total.
- In a 10-inch heavy skillet over moderate heat, heat oil until hot but not smoking. Working in 5 batches (do not crowd), fry meatballs in heated oil until evenly browned and thoroughly cooked, turning sometimes, about

2 minutes for each batch. Remove cooked meatballs to paper towels using a slotted spoon.
- For filling: combine all filling ingredients until incorporated well.
- Boil and bake pasta: position oven rack in the middle of the oven and set oven to 425°F to preheat.
- In a 6- to 8-quart pot, cook pasta in boiling salted water without covering until al dente. Transfer to a colander to drain; wash with cold water and drain once more.
- Distribute 2 cups sauce in a 3-quart or 13x9-inch ceramic or glass baking dish; place 1/3 of fettuccine over the sauce. Arrange meatballs atop pasta. Repeat layering with 2 cups sauce, 1/3 of fettuccine; distribute the filling all over pasta layer. Top with the rest of pasta, and then the rest of sauce. Sprinkle top with mozzarella evenly.
- Loosely cover with foil and bake for 10 minutes. Uncover and bake for 20 minutes longer or until cheese turns golden and sauce is bubbling. Remove the baking pan to a rack and allow to cool for about 20 minutes.
- The sauce can be prepared 3 days in advance, let cool entirely, uncovered, and let chill until with a cover.

Nutrition Information

- Calories: 948
- Saturated Fat: 17 g(87%)
- Sodium: 1155 mg(48%)
- Fiber: 7 g(27%)
- Total Carbohydrate: 58 g(19%)
- Cholesterol: 177 mg(59%)
- Protein: 40 g(80%)
- Total Fat: 63 g(97%)

81. Four Onion Gratin

Serving: Serves 8 | Prep: | Cook: | Ready in:

Ingredients

- 1/4 cup (1/2 stick) butter
- 6 leeks (white and pale green parts only), sliced
- 2 large onions, cut into eighths
- 8 shallots, halved
- 2 garlic cloves, minced
- 1 1/2 10-ounce bags frozen baby onions, thawed, drained
- 2 cups whipping cream
- 2 tablespoons dry breadcrumbs
- 2 tablespoons chopped fresh parsley

Direction

- In a big heavy skillet, melt butter on medium heat. Add garlic, shallots, big onions and leeks. Sauté for 20 minutes until all are tender. Add baby onions. Cook for 10 more minutes, occasionally stirring. Mix 2 cups whipping cream in. boil for 10 minutes until cream thickens to a sauce consistency. Put veggie-cream mixture in a shallow 6-cup baking dish. Can be made 1 day ahead, covered and refrigerated. Bring the mixture to room temperature prior to continuing.
- Preheat the oven to 425 degrees F. On onion mixture, sprinkle breadcrumbs. Bake for 20 minutes until onion mixture bubbles and breadcrumbs become golden brown. Sprinkle parsley on top.

Nutrition Information

- Calories: 349
- Fiber: 5 g(21%)
- Total Carbohydrate: 30 g(10%)
- Cholesterol: 82 mg(27%)
- Protein: 6 g(11%)
- Total Fat: 25 g(38%)
- Saturated Fat: 15 g(76%)
- Sodium: 65 mg(3%)

82. French's Green Bean Casserole

Serving: 6 servings | Prep: 5mins | Cook: 40mins | Ready in:

Ingredients

- 1 can (10 1/2 oz.) Campbell's® Condensed Cream of Mushroom Soup
- 3/4 cup milk
- 1/8 tsp. black pepper
- 4 cups cooked cut green beans or 2 cans (14.5oz each) any style Del Monte® Green Beans, drained
- 1 1/3 cups French's® Crispy Fried Onions, divided

Direction

- In a 1 1/2 -qt. baking dish, mix pepper, milk and soup. Stir in 2/3 cup Crispy Fried Onions and beans.
- Bake at 350°F until hot, for a half-hour. Stir well.
- Lay the remaining 2/3 cup onions on top. Bake until the onions are golden, for 5 minutes.

Nutrition Information

- Calories: 202
- Total Carbohydrate: 23 g(8%)
- Cholesterol: 3 mg(1%)
- Protein: 4 g(8%)
- Total Fat: 11 g(17%)
- Saturated Fat: 3 g(17%)
- Sodium: 747 mg(31%)
- Fiber: 3 g(10%)

83. Garnet Yams With Blis Maple Syrup And Maple Sugar Streusel

Serving: Makes 10 servings | Prep: | Cook: | Ready in:

Ingredients

- 3 1/2 pounds slender garnet yams or other yams (red-skinned sweet potatoes; about 2 1/2 inches in diameter)
- 1/4 cup Blis maple syrup or other pure maple syrup
- 1/4 cup (1/2 stick) unsalted butter
- 1 tablespoon apple cider vinegar
- 1 teaspoon coarse kosher salt
- 3/4 teaspoon freshly ground black pepper
- 1 cup all purpose flour
- 1/2 cup maple sugar* (scant 3 ounces)
- 1/3 cup (packed) golden brown sugar
- 3/4 teaspoon ground cinnamon
- 6 tablespoons (3/4 stick) unsalted butter, melted

Direction

- Yams: Butter a 13x9x2-in. glass baking dish and peel yams; cut 1-in. off the ends. Grate coarsely enough of yam ends to get 1/2 cup; put aside for streusel. Throw leftover ends; cut leftover whole yams to 1/3-in. thick rounds. In 4 lengthwise overlapping rows, put yam rounds in prepped baking dish.
- Boil cider vinegar, butter, maple syrup and 1/2 cup water in a small saucepan; mix 3/4 tsp. pepper and 1 tsp. coarse salt in. Put maple syrup mixture on yams; tightly cover baking dish using a foil.
- Streusel: In a small bowl, mix initial 4 ingredients. Add melted butter; rub in using fingertips till you make moist clumps. Mix leftover 1/2 cup grated yams in; you can make streusel and yams 6 hours ahead, separately covered, refrigerated. Stand yams for 1 hour prior to baking at room temperature.
- Preheat an oven to 375°F; bake the yams for 40 minutes till nearly tender, covered. Put oven temperature on 400°F; sprinkle top with streusel. Bake for 35 minutes more till streusel is slightly crisp and golden and yams are very tender, uncovered. Serve warm.

Nutrition Information

- Calories: 359
- Saturated Fat: 7 g(37%)
- Sodium: 281 mg(12%)
- Fiber: 5 g(21%)
- Total Carbohydrate: 61 g(20%)
- Cholesterol: 31 mg(10%)
- Protein: 4 g(8%)
- Total Fat: 12 g(18%)

84. Goat Gratin

Serving: Makes 6 to 8 servings | Prep: | Cook: |Ready in:

Ingredients

- 3 pounds boneless goat shoulder, cubed
- 1/2 quart goat's milk
- 1 pound gold potatoes, sliced 1/2 inch thick
- Salt and pepper
- 1/4 tablespoon extra-virgin olive oil
- 2 1/2 pounds yellow onions, sliced thin
- 1 tablespoon chopped garlic
- 1 small bunch parsley, chopped
- 1 small bunch thyme, chopped
- 1/4 cup white wine
- 3 cups bread crumbs or 2 cups panko
- Capricious cheese or any dry goat cheese you like, grated

Direction

- In goat's milk, soak goat meat in the fridge overnight. Slice meat thin; put milk aside. Aside from goat, soak potatoes in the goat's milk for 1 hour. Pat dry goat; season to taste with pepper and salt. Brown meat in olive oil in a big sauté pan. Remove meat. In same pan, sauté onions till golden slightly; add thyme, parsley and garlic. Cook for 10 minutes; put aside. Deglaze pan using wine.
- Use 1/2 onion mixture to layer bottom of casserole dish; put goat over then, in a layer, potatoes. Finish using leftover onions. Nearly fully cover top layer using deglazing liquid

from pan and goat's milk. Mix goat cheese and breadcrumbs; sprinkle on gratin.

- Cover; cook for 1 1/2 hours in 350°F oven. Uncover; cook till breadcrumbs and cheese are toasted while liquid are bubbling for 20 minutes.

Nutrition Information

- Calories: 672
- Sodium: 1503 mg(63%)
- Fiber: 8 g(33%)
- Total Carbohydrate: 76 g(25%)
- Cholesterol: 138 mg(46%)
- Protein: 61 g(122%)
- Total Fat: 12 g(19%)
- Saturated Fat: 5 g(23%)

85. Gratin Of Scallops With Porcini And Chives

Serving: 4 Appetizer servings | Prep: | Cook: | Ready in:

Ingredients

- 1 ounce dried porcini mushrooms
- 1 cup hot water
- 1 tablespoon olive oil
- 1 large garlic clove, minced
- 1/4 cup brandy
- 12 large sea scallops, halved horizontally
- 3 tablespoons chopped fresh chives
- 1/4 cup fresh white breadcrumbs

Direction

- In medium size bowl, put porcini. Add hot water on top. Rest for 30 minutes, till porcini are soft. Take off from water; press any water back into the bowl. Cut porcini. Set soaking water aside.
- Preheat the broiler. In big heavy skillet, heat the oil on moderately-high heat. Put in the garlic; mix for 10 seconds. Put in the porcini

and half cup of reserved soaking water, retaining any residue in bowl base. Put in the brandy; simmer for 3 minutes till nearly all liquid vaporizes. Put in chives and scallops; sauté for 2 minutes till scallops are nearly cooked completely. Add pepper and salt to season.

- Turn mixture of scallop into round 9-inch gratin dish. Scatter with breadcrumbs. Broil for 3 minutes till breadcrumbs turn golden, keeping an eye to prevent excessive browning. Serve while hot.

Nutrition Information

- Calories: 195
- Total Carbohydrate: 15 g(5%)
- Cholesterol: 29 mg(10%)
- Protein: 16 g(32%)
- Total Fat: 4 g(7%)
- Saturated Fat: 1 g(4%)
- Sodium: 524 mg(22%)
- Fiber: 1 g(5%)

86. Gratineed Mustard Creamed Onions

Serving: Makes 8 servings | Prep: 45mins | Cook: 1.5hours | Ready in:

Ingredients

- 2 pound white pearl onions
- 2 tablespoons unsalted butter
- 2 tablespoons all-purpose flour
- 1 cup whole milk
- 3 tablespoons cream Sherry
- 1 tablespoon grainy mustard
- 1 tablespoon Dijon mustard
- 1/4 teaspoon grated nutmeg
- 1/2 cup grated Parmigiano-Reggiano
- Equipment: a 2-qt shallow gratin or other flameproof baking dish (2 inches deep)

Direction

- Cook onions in big heavy pot with boiling salted water, 4-qt water to 2 tsp. salt, for 25-30 minutes till tender. Put 1 cup cooking water aside. Drain; put pot aside. Cool onions to warm; peel.
- Melt butter on medium heat in dry pot. Add flour; cook, mixing, for 2 minutes. Whisk in Sherry, milk and reserved cooking water; cook, frequently whisking, for 8 minutes till it is thick. Whisk in 1/2 tsp. each of pepper and salt, nutmeg and mustards. Put onions in sauce; simmer for 5 minutes.
- Preheat a broiler.
- Put cream onions into baking dish; evenly sprinkle cheese. Broil 4-5-in. from heat for 3 minutes till top is bubbly and golden brown.
- You can make, not gratineed, creamed onions without cheese 1 day ahead. Chill till cool, uncovered. Cover. Bring it to room temperature. Reheat for 20 minutes in 400°F oven. Sprinkle cheese; broil.

Nutrition Information

- Calories: 136
- Sodium: 157 mg(7%)
- Fiber: 2 g(9%)
- Total Carbohydrate: 15 g(5%)
- Cholesterol: 15 mg(5%)
- Protein: 5 g(10%)
- Total Fat: 6 g(9%)
- Saturated Fat: 4 g(18%)

87. Green Bean Casserole

Serving: 4 | Prep: 5mins | Cook: 30mins |Ready in:

Ingredients

- 1 (14.5 ounce) can French style green beans, drained

- 1 (10.75 ounce) can condensed cream of mushroom soup
- 1 (6 ounce) can French-fried onions

Direction

- Preheat the oven to 175 degrees C (350 degrees F).
- In a small casserole dish, combine the soup and green beans.
- Bake in the preheated oven for around 10-15 minutes. Remove from the oven and lay onions on top. Continue to bake for 10 minutes more and enjoy.

Nutrition Information

- Calories: 352 calories;
- Cholesterol: 0
- Protein: 2.1
- Total Fat: 25.5
- Sodium: 1187
- Total Carbohydrate: 26.6

88. Greens And Bulgur Gratin

Serving: Serves 4 as a main course or 6 as a side dish | Prep: | Cook: |Ready in:

Ingredients

- 1/2 cup coarse bulgur*
- 2 pounds assorted greens such as kale, collard, escarole, spinach,Swiss chard, and/or mustard greens
- 6 large garlic cloves, minced
- 3 tablespoons olive oil
- 1/4 cup freshly grated Parmesan (about 1 ounce)
- 6 ounces chilled whole-milk or part-skim mozzarella, grated coarse
- 1/2 cup fine fresh bread crumbs
- 1 tablespoon olive oil

- *available at natural foods stores and specialty foods shops

Direction

- In a heatproof bowl, pour over bulgur with enough boiling water to cover by 1 inch. Use a plate to cover the bowl in order to keep the steam; allow to stand for 20 minutes. Let the bulgur drain in a large fine sieve, press out the excess liquid, then transfer to a bowl.
- Place each variety of green separate, and tear them into bite-size pieces, removing the stems. Still keep the veggies separate, dunk in a sinkful of water to wash thoroughly and transfer to a colander to drain.
- Next, put coarser greens (collard or kale) in a 4 1/2 to 5-quart kettle, cover and steam over moderate heat in the water clinging to leave for about 4 minutes, occasionally stirring, until wilted. Put in the delicate greens (Swiss chard, spinach, escarole, and/or mustard), cover and continue to steam for 3-4 minutes, stirring occasionally, just until wilted. Allow the greens to drain in a colander, press out the excess liquid.
- Over moderate heat, cook while stirring garlic in oil in a large heavy skillet until tender but not golden. Stir in bulgur and greens, generously season with pepper and salt. Stir in Parmesan and remove the skillet from the heat.
- Set the oven at 400°F to preheat and lightly grease a shallow baking dish or a 1 1/2-quart gratin dish.
- In a dish, spread 1/2 of the greens mixture and evenly dust with mozzarella. Next, spread over mozzarella with the remaining greens mixture and make the top smooth using a rubber spatula. Gratin can be prepared up to this point 8 hours ago, covered and chilled.
- To make the topping: Use a fork to stir bread crumbs and oil together in a small bowl until the crumbs are moistened evenly.
- Sprinkle over greens mixture with the topping and bake for a half-hour in the middle of the oven, or until bubbling and the top is lightly browned.

Nutrition Information

- Calories: 359
- Total Carbohydrate: 38 g(13%)
- Cholesterol: 9 mg(3%)
- Protein: 15 g(30%)
- Total Fat: 19 g(29%)
- Saturated Fat: 4 g(20%)
- Sodium: 265 mg(11%)
- Fiber: 10 g(41%)

89. Gujarti Eggplant And Sweet Potato "Lasagna" With Kadi Sauce

Serving: Serves 6 as an entrée | Prep: | Cook: |Ready in:

Ingredients

- A Tomato Masala
- 1 pound sweet potatoes, peeled
- 1/2 pound eggplant, unpeeled, ends trimmed
- 3/4 pound zucchini, ends trimmed
- 1/2 large red bell pepper (4 ounces)
- 1/2 large green bell pepper (4 ounces)
- 1/4 cup canola oil
- 1/2 cup chopped unsalted roasted peanuts
- 1 teaspoon salt
- 1 cup gram flour (besan)
- 3 cups water
- 1 teaspoon finely chopped fresh ginger
- 1/2 teaspoon finely chopped fresh Thai green chile
- 1/2 teaspoon ground turmeric
- 1 tablespoon whole-milk yogurt
- 2 teaspoons salt
- 1/4 teaspoon citric acid powder (see Note)
- Cooking spray
- Kadi Sauce, for serving

Direction

- For the filling: Have the tomato masala ready and put aside.
- Have the vegetables ready for the filling, separating them.
- Slice sweet potatoes into cubes, 1/2-in. each.
- Slice eggplant into cubes, 1/2-in. each.
- Slice zucchini crosswise in half. Put 1 half to stand upright and slice four 1/2-in. flesh slices from around the seeds in the middle. Dice the flesh into 1/2-in. cubes (remove the seeds). Continue with the remaining half.
- Slice bell peppers into squares, 1/2-in. each.
- Heat oil in a big frying pan over medium-high heat until it is glistening. Mix in sweet potatoes and sauté for 5 minutes until par-cooked and remaining slightly crispy, mixing sometimes. Mix in eggplant and cook for 4 minutes, mixing often. Add zucchini and cook for 5 minutes until the zucchini is tender. Add bell peppers and sauté for 1 minute. Remove the vegetables to a big bowl. Add salt, tomato masala, and peanuts and stir thoroughly.
- For the "lasagna" sheets: Prepare a wide expanse of really clean counter space.
- Stir together water and gram flour in a medium-sized saucepan until smooth. Add citric acid, salt, yogurt, turmeric, green chile, and ginger. Cook over medium heat for 9-10 minutes until the batter has fully thickened, using a wooden spoon or a silicone spatula to whisk continually. (It should look like cream puff dough or thick pastry cream).
- Invert the dough onto the counter. Quickly spread into a really thin (1/8-in. thick), approximately 24x20-in. rectangular sheet using an offset spatula. Cut the rectangle into an 18-in. square with a paring knife. (Dispose the trimmings or enjoy as a snack). And then, slice the square into 4 squares, exactly 9-in. each square. The dough will set and cool fast so you can easily remove the 4 squares from the counter when using.
- Turn the oven to 375°F to preheat. Spray cooking spray over a 9-in. square baking dish to coat.
- To assemble the "lasagna": Turn the oven to 375°F to preheat. Spray cooking spray over a 9-in. square baking dish to coat.
- In the bottom of the pan, evenly spread 1/4 of the vegetable mixture; gently press with the back of a spoon onto the mixture to move it to the corners and tighten it instead of loosening.
- Put 1 of the lasagna sheets on the vegetables to precisely fit it into the pan. Continue with the leftover 3 lasagna sheets and 3 vegetables portions, finishing with a lasagna sheet.
- Put a 9-in. parchment paper square on the lasagna to cover, and then use foil to cover the dish. Put it on a baking sheet and bake for 40 minutes.
- In the meantime, reheat (or make) the kadi sauce.
- For serving, slice the lasagna into 6 rectangles. In big pasta bowls, put the lasagna, add kadi sauce on top of each portion and enjoy.

Nutrition Information

- Calories: 344
- Total Carbohydrate: 33 g(11%)
- Cholesterol: 0 mg(0%)
- Protein: 9 g(19%)
- Total Fat: 21 g(32%)
- Saturated Fat: 2 g(10%)
- Sodium: 864 mg(36%)
- Fiber: 7 g(30%)

90. Hamburger Pie

Serving: 6 | Prep: 15mins | Cook: 45mins | Ready in:

Ingredients

- 4 potatoes
- 1 pound lean ground beef
- 1 onion, chopped
- 2 (10.75 ounce) cans condensed tomato soup
- 1 (15 ounce) can green beans, drained
- 1 cup shredded Cheddar cheese

Direction

- Preheat the oven to 175 degrees C (350 degrees F).
- Boil the big pot of the salted water. Skin and cut the potatoes into 4 equal pieces, and put into the boiling water; cook for roughly 15 minutes or till softened. Drain off and smash. Put aside.
- In the big skillet on medium-high heat, cook the onion and ground beef till the beef turns brown. Drain off. Whisk in the green beans and tomato soup. Add to the 9x13-inch baking plate. Mound the mashed potatoes in the ring around meat mixture but don't cover the meat. Drizzle the potatoes with the shredded cheese.
- Bake in the preheated oven till the potatoes turn golden or for half an hour.

Nutrition Information

- Calories: 424 calories;
- Cholesterol: 66
- Protein: 22.6
- Total Fat: 18.3
- Sodium: 927
- Total Carbohydrate: 43.4

91. Hungarian Blintz Loaf (Palacsinta Felfujt)

Serving: Makes 6 to 8 servings | Prep: | Cook: | Ready in:

Ingredients

- 1/2 cup all-purpose flour
- 3 large eggs
- 3/4 cup sour cream
- 1/4 cup orange juice
- 1/4 cup (1/2 stick) unsalted butter or margarine, softened
- 3 tablespoons sugar
- 1 teaspoon vanilla extract
- 1 teaspoon double-acting baking powder
- 1/4 teaspoon salt
- 1 cup (8 ounces) small-curd cottage or ricotta cheese
- 4 ounces cream cheese, softened
- 1 large egg yolk
- 2 tablespoons sugar
- 1/2 teaspoon vanilla extract
- 1/2 teaspoon fresh lemon juice or ground cinnamon (optional)

Direction

- Set the oven to 350°F to preheat (325°F if using a glass pan). Grease a 9-inch square baking pan.
- For the batter: whip together all the batter ingredients in a blender, food processor, or a big bowl, until smooth.
- For the filling: Mix all the filling ingredients.
- Put half of the batter into the greased pan, put the filling by heaping tablespoonfuls on top of the batter, then top with the leftover batter carefully (the layers will blend a bit).
- It can be covered and chilled for up to 1 day. Put back to room temperature before baking.
- Bake for 50-60 minutes until slightly brown and puffed. Serve warm with fresh fruit or a fruit sauce (optional).

Nutrition Information

- Calories: 385
- Fiber: 0 g(1%)
- Total Carbohydrate: 23 g(8%)
- Cholesterol: 199 mg(66%)
- Protein: 11 g(22%)
- Total Fat: 28 g(43%)
- Saturated Fat: 16 g(80%)
- Sodium: 310 mg(13%)

92. Jessica Alba's Chicken Enchiladas

Serving: Makes 4 servings | Prep: | Cook: | Ready in:

Ingredients

- 4 cups chicken stock
- 4 boneless, skinless chicken breasts (about 5 oz each), cut into strips
- 1 jalapeño pepper
- 1 clove garlic
- 1 jar (12 oz) salsa
- 1 cup shredded lowfat cheddar
- 1/2 cup shredded lowfat Monterey Jack
- 1/2 cup chopped fresh cilantro
- 1 can (2.25 oz) sliced black olives, drained
- 1 can (16 oz) traditional enchilada sauce
- 1 can (16 oz) green chile enchilada sauce
- Mexican hot sauce
- Cayenne pepper
- Vegetable-oil cooking spray
- 8 corn tortillas (6 inches across)

Direction

- Heat the oven to 425°. Boil garlic, jalapeño, chicken and stock in a medium pot for 15 minutes till chicken is cooked through. Strain the chicken, run cold water over it then shred into a bowl. Stir in salsa and reserve. Mix olives, cilantro, a quarter cup Monterey Jack and cheddar in another bowl; reserve. Mix enchilada sauces and put in cayenne and Mexican hot sauce to taste in a big pot over medium heat. Mix till simmering. Reserve. With nonstick spray, coat an 11x13 inch casserole pan. Microwave the tortillas for 20 seconds. Put small handfuls of chicken and cheese mixture in middle of every tortilla, roll up and put in pan, seam side facing down. Scatter leftover cheese mixture over. Ladle over sauce, then put in leftover a quarter cup Monterey Jack. Allow to bake for 20 minutes. Serve with leftover sauce alongside.

Nutrition Information

93. Kartoffel Kugel (Ashkenazic Potato Pudding)

Serving: 6–8 servings | Prep: | Cook: | Ready in:

Ingredients

- 1/2 cup schmaltz or vegetable oil
- 6 medium or 4 large russet potatoes (about 2 pounds), peeled
- 2 medium yellow onions, chopped (about 1 cup)
- 3 large eggs, lightly beaten
- About 1 teaspoon salt
- Ground black pepper to taste
- 1/4 cup gribenes (poultry cracklings) or grated carrot, optional
- About 1/3 cup matza meal or all-purpose flour

Direction

- Start preheating the oven to 375°F. Put an 8-9-in. square baking dish in the oven to heat.
- Brush 1/4 cup of oil or schmaltz over the sides and bottom of the baking dish and put back into the oven for 15 minutes until fully hot.
- In a big bowl, put potatoes with lightly salted cold water. (This will prevent the potatoes from discoloring). Grate the potatoes into the onions, tossing to blend.
- Mix in carrot or gribenes (if you want), pepper, salt, the leftover 1/4 cup oil or schmaltz, and eggs. Add a sufficient amount of flour or matza meal to hold the batter together.
- Add to the heated dish and bake for 60 minutes until turning golden brown. Enjoy the dish warm will be best, you can enjoy the leftovers at room temperature.

Nutrition Information

- Calories: 327
- Fiber: 2 g(9%)
- Total Carbohydrate: 29 g(10%)
- Cholesterol: 93 mg(31%)

- Protein: 7 g(13%)
- Total Fat: 21 g(33%)
- Saturated Fat: 2 g(10%)
- Sodium: 430 mg(18%)

94. Lamb Moussaka With Currants

Serving: Serves 8 | Prep: | Cook: | Ready in:

Ingredients

- 5 tablespoons olive oil
- 3 large green bell peppers, seeded, cut into 1/2-inch pieces
- 1 1/2 pounds ground lamb
- 2 cups chopped onion
- 2/3 cup dry red wine
- 1 teaspoon cayenne pepper
- 2 28-ounce cans Italian-style tomatoes, drained, chopped
- 1/2 cup dried currants
- 2 tablespoons tomato paste
- Pinch of ground nutmeg
- 2 large eggplants (about 2 1/4 pounds total), cut lengthwise into 1/4-inch-thick slices
- 2 teaspoons sea salt
- Olive oil
- 1 pound russet potatoes (about 2 medium), peeled
- 3 cups plain yogurt (do not use low-fat or nonfat)
- 3 large egg yolks

Direction

- In a big, heavy Dutch oven, heat 2 tablespoons oil over medium-high heat. Add peppers and sauté for 8 minutes until starting to color and softened. Remove the peppers to a bowl. In the same Dutch oven, heat the leftover 3 tablespoons oil over medium-high heat. Add lamb and sauté for 6 minutes until fully cooked, use the back of a spoon to crumble. Add onion and sauté for 6 minutes until the onion is soft. Add cayenne pepper and wine

and cook for 2 minutes. Mix in nutmeg, tomato paste, currants, and tomatoes. Lower the heat to medium. Put a cover on and simmer for 70 minutes until the sauce decreases to 6 cups and fully thick, whisking sometimes. Use pepper and salt to season to taste.
- In the meantime, line foil into a big baking sheet. On the prepared sheet, place layers of eggplant slices, sprinkling sea salt over each layer. Let sit for 30 minutes at room temperature.
- Turn on the broiler to preheat. Line foil into a separate big baking sheet. Pat dry eggplant slices using paper towels. On the second prepared sheet, place 1 layer of some of the eggplant slices. Lightly brush over both sides with olive oil. Broil for 4 minutes each side until turning golden brown. Remove to a platter. Do again with the rest of the eggplant.
- In a big pot, boil potatoes in salted water for 5 minutes. Strain. Let cool. Slice the potatoes into slices with 1/4-in. thickness.
- Turn the oven to 400°F to preheat. Grease a 13x9x2-in glass baking dish using oil. In the bottom of the dish, place the potatoes. Arrange over the potatoes with 1/2 of the eggplant slices. Add 1/2 of the sauce on top. Arrange over the sauce with the sautéed peppers. Arrange over the peppers with the leftover eggplant. Add the leftover sauce on top.
- Bake the moussaka for 45 minutes until the edges are bubbly. Scoop out any excess grease. Press the back of a spoon onto the moussaka to tighten the layers. In a medium-sized bowl, stir together egg yolks and yogurt to combine. Add to the moussaka to fully cover. Bake for 15 minutes until the yogurt topping softly sets. Remove the baking dish to a rack and let sit for 20 minutes. (You can prepare this 1 day in advance. Let cool. Put a cover on and chill. Reheat in an oven at 400°F for 30 minutes until fully heated). Scoop the moussaka on dishes.

Nutrition Information

- Calories: 668
- Cholesterol: 143 mg(48%)
- Protein: 24 g(49%)
- Total Fat: 44 g(68%)
- Saturated Fat: 14 g(70%)
- Sodium: 837 mg(35%)
- Fiber: 12 g(49%)
- Total Carbohydrate: 46 g(15%)

95. Lamb And Eggplant Potpie With Feta Potato Crust

Serving: Serves 8 | Prep: | Cook: | Ready in:

Ingredients

- two 1-pound eggplants, cut into 1/2-inch cubes (about 8 cups)
- 5 tablespoons vegetable oil
- 1 large onion, chopped
- 1 tablespoon minced garlic
- 2 pounds ground lamb
- 1 1/4 teaspoons cinnamon
- 2 teaspoons crumbled dried mint
- 1 1/4 teaspoons crumbled dried oregano
- 1/2 teaspoon ground allspice
- a 35-ounce can Italian plum tomatoes, drained, reserving 1 cup of the juice, and chopped
- 2 tablespoons tomato paste
- 1/4 cup freshly grated Parmesan
- 3 pounds russet (baking) potatoes (about 6)
- 2 tablespoons unsalted butter
- 1/3 cup freshly grated Parmesan
- 1/3 pound grated Feta
- 1 tablespoon unsalted butter

Direction

- Prepare lamb mixture: sprinkle salt on eggplant in colander and drain it for half an hour. Heat 4 tablespoons olive oil in a big skillet on medium heat, pat eggplant dry, let it cook in it for 15 minutes, in batches, mixing, till tender yet still keeps its form, and use a slotted spoon to turn onto bowl. Heat leftover 1 tablespoon of oil in skillet on medium heat and cook onion, mixing, till soften. Put in garlic and let the mixture cook for a minute while mixing. Put in lamb and let mixture cook, mixing and crumbling any lumps, till lamb is not pink anymore. Drain off any extra fat from skillet, put in allspice, orégano, mint and cinnamon, and let the mixture cook for a minute, mixing. Put in pepper and salt to taste, tomatoes including the reserved juice and tomato paste, and let mixture cook for 15 minutes, mixing, or till thicken. Turn mixture onto a big bowl and mix Parmesan in. Lamb mixture enhances in flavor if prepared up to this part and kept in refrigerator overnight with cover. Put to lamb mixture with eggplant, stir mixture thoroughly, and scatter it in 3-quart shallow gratin dish that's buttered.
- Prepare topping: peel potatoes, and slice into an-inch portions then in a big saucepan mix them with sufficient cold water to soak by an-inch, boil the water, and let potatoes simmer till tender, for 10 to 15 minutes. Let potatoes drain, put them back to pan, and cook on medium heat for half a minute, shaking pan, to vaporize any extra liquid. Press potatoes through a food mill medium disk or a ricer into bowl, put in pepper and salt to taste, Feta, Parmesan and butter, and combine the mixture till thoroughly blended and butter melts.
- Top the lamb mixture with scoop of topping, scattering it to fully coat lamb mixture, and scatter bits of butter on top. Let potpie bake for 35 to 40 minutes in the center of a prepped 400°F. oven, or till slightly browned.

Nutrition Information

- Calories: 708
- Cholesterol: 117 mg(39%)
- Protein: 30 g(61%)
- Total Fat: 46 g(71%)
- Saturated Fat: 19 g(96%)
- Sodium: 406 mg(17%)

- Fiber: 9 g(35%)
- Total Carbohydrate: 44 g(15%)

96. Mashed Potato And Turnip Gratin

Serving: Makes 6 servings | Prep: | Cook: | Ready in:

Ingredients

- 2 pounds Yukon Gold potatoes (about 5 medium)
- 1 3/4 pounds turnips (about 5 medium)
- 1/4 cup (1/2 stick) butter
- 1/2 cup grated pecorino Romano cheese, divided
- Pinch of ground nutmeg

Direction

- Wipe an 11x7x2-in. ceramic or glass baking plate with butter. In a big, heavy pot, cook turnips and potatoes in hot salted water for 35 minutes until soft. Strain. Let the vegetables cool briefly and remove the skin. Slice into big pieces and put in a food processor. Add butter and process, scraping down the sides of the bowl sometimes, until smooth. Add 1/4 pinch of ground nutmeg and cup cheese, toss lightly. Sprinkle pepper and salt over the puree to season. Transfer to the prepared plate. Use the leftover 1/4 cup cheese to sprinkle. (You can make the gratin 1 day in advance. Put a cover on and refrigerate).
- Start preheating the oven to 425°F. Bake the gratin without a cover for 25 minutes until the top turns golden and the vegetables are tender.

Nutrition Information

- Calories: 264
- Sodium: 256 mg(11%)
- Fiber: 6 g(23%)

- Total Carbohydrate: 35 g(12%)
- Cholesterol: 32 mg(11%)
- Protein: 8 g(16%)
- Total Fat: 11 g(17%)
- Saturated Fat: 7 g(34%)

97. Mexican Chicken And Vegetable Casserole

Serving: Serves 4 to 8 | Prep: | Cook: | Ready in:

Ingredients

- 1 teaspoon ground cumin
- 1 teaspoon chili powder
- 1/2 teaspoon cinnamon
- 2 teaspoons white-wine vinegar
- 3 garlic cloves
- 3 tablespoons vegetable oil
- 8 chicken thighs (about 2 pounds)
- 1 large onion, sliced thin
- 2 tomatoes, chopped coarse
- 4 zucchini (about 1 1/2 pounds), scrubbed, quartered lengthwise, and cut crosswise into 3/4-inch pieces
- 1/4 cup chicken broth
- 1 to 2 tablespoons drained minced pickled jalapeño pepper (wear rubber gloves)
- 1 red bell pepper, cut into 1/2-inch pieces
- 1 cup fresh or thawed frozen corn
- 1/4 teaspoon dried orégano, crumbled
- 1/2 cup coarsely grated Monterey Jack

Direction

- Whisk pepper and salt to taste, 1 tbsp. of oil, minced and mashed to a paste with a pinch of salt, 1garlic clove, vinegar, cinnamon, chili powder, and cumin together in a small bowl. Coat the chicken with the spice paste. In a greased ridged grill pan set over moderately high heat, or on a greased grill set about 6 inches over glowing coals, grill the chicken for 12 to 15 minutes per side, flipping once, until cooked through.

- While cooking the chicken, over moderate heat, cook the onion in the leftover 2 tablespoons oil in a skillet, stirring infrequently, until lightly golden. Add tomatoes and the remaining minced 2 garlic cloves; over moderately low heat, cook the mixture for 5 minutes, stirring occasionally. Add pepper and salt to taste, oregano, corn, bell pepper, jalapeño, broth, and zucchini; then bring the mixture to a simmer for 20 minutes, stirring infrequently, or until the bell pepper and zucchini are softened.
- Combine chicken and the zucchini mixture in a large flameproof shallow casserole, dust over the top with Monterey Jack, then broil for 1 minute under a preheated broiler about 6 inches from the heat, or until the cheese is bubbling.

Nutrition Information

- Calories: 403
- Cholesterol: 114 mg(38%)
- Protein: 23 g(47%)
- Total Fat: 29 g(44%)
- Saturated Fat: 8 g(38%)
- Sodium: 193 mg(8%)
- Fiber: 3 g(12%)
- Total Carbohydrate: 14 g(5%)

98. Mexican Style Cheese And Sausage Casserole

Serving: 4 Main-course servings | Prep: | Cook: |Ready in:

Ingredients

- 1 pound bulk pork sausage
- 1 4-ounce can chopped mild green chilies
- 4 tablespoons chopped fresh cilantro
- 1/4 teaspoon hot pepper sauce (such as Tabasco)
- 1 1/2 cups grated cheddar cheese
- 1 cup grated Monterey Jack cheese
- 12 6-inch-diameter flour or corn tortillas

Direction

- Set oven to 350 degrees F and start preheating. In a big and heavy skillet, sauté sausage on medium-high heat for 7 minutes while using the back of a spoon to break up clumps, until brown. Transfer sausage to an 8x8x2-in. ovenproof pan or glass baking dish, using slotted spoon. Blend hot sauce, 3 tablespoons cilantro, and chopped green chilies into the sausage. Sprinkle sausage mixture with remaining tablespoon cilantro, Monterey Jack cheese, and cheddar cheese. Bake the casserole for 10 minutes.
- Use foil to wrap tortillas tightly. Put in the oven alongside the sausage casserole; heat through. Keep baking casserole for 10 more minutes, till sausage mixture has been heated through and cheeses are bubble.
- Serve cheese mixture and sausage with warm tortillas.

Nutrition Information

- Calories: 790
- Cholesterol: 152 mg(51%)
- Protein: 40 g(81%)
- Total Fat: 55 g(84%)
- Saturated Fat: 23 g(117%)
- Sodium: 1354 mg(56%)
- Fiber: 5 g(20%)
- Total Carbohydrate: 37 g(12%)

99. Mixed Vegetable Gratin

Serving: Serves 8 | Prep: | Cook: |Ready in:

Ingredients

- 2 1/2 pounds russet potatoes
- 3 large celery stalks, cut into 1/2-inch pieces

- 3 large carrots, peeled, cut into 1/2-inch pieces
- 1 large green bell pepper, cut into 1/2-inch pieces
- 2 tablespoons minced garlic
- 2 tablespoons chopped fresh basil or 2 teaspoons dried, crumbled
- 2 teaspoons chopped fresh rosemary or 1/2 teaspoon dried, crumbled
- 1/4 cup (1/2 stick) butter
- 1 1/2 cups grated Monterey Jack or Fontina cheese (optional)

Direction

- Set the oven to 400 degrees F to preheat. In a big bowl, mix the first seven ingredients together, then pour butter over mixture and toss to coat well. Use pepper and salt to season. Move the vegetable mixture to a 13"x9"x2" glass baking dish. Use aluminum foil to cover and bake for 40 minutes. Take off foil and bake for about half an hour more while stirring sometimes, until vegetables are starting to brown and softened.
- Preheat broiler. Use cheese to sprinkle over the mixture and broil for about 4 minutes, until cheese starts to brown and melts.

Nutrition Information

- Calories: 185
- Sodium: 47 mg(2%)
- Fiber: 3 g(14%)
- Total Carbohydrate: 31 g(10%)
- Cholesterol: 15 mg(5%)
- Protein: 4 g(8%)
- Total Fat: 6 g(9%)
- Saturated Fat: 4 g(19%)

100. Mushroom And Onion Gratins

Serving: Serves 6 as a first course | Prep: | Cook: | Ready in:

Ingredients

- 1 pound mushrooms, sliced thin
- 1/2 stick (1/4 cup) unsalted butter
- 1/4 cup all-purpose flour
- 2 large onions (about 1 3/4 pounds), sliced very thin
- 6 tablespoons heavy cream
- 1 cup grated Gruyère
- 1/4 cup fresh fine bread crumbs

Direction

- Cook mushrooms in 2 1/2 tbsp. butter in a skillet on moderately low heat till most liquid given off evaporates and mushrooms are soft while mixing. Mix in flour; cook mixture for 3 minutes while mixing.
- Layer onions, the rest of butter, cut into bits, mushroom mixture and pepper and salt to taste in each of the six 1 1/2-cup gratin dishes, starting and finishing with the onion layers. Put 1 tbsp. cream over each gratin. Mix breadcrumbs and Gruyere well in a small bowl; sprinkle mixture on top of cream. Or, gratin, layered the same way, can be prepped in one 2-qt. gratin dish. Bake gratins in center of the preheated 325°F oven till tops are golden and onions are tender or for 50-60 minutes. You can prep gratins 3 hours ahead, kept chilled, covered, then reheated for 5 minutes inside a preheated 400°F oven till heated through.

Nutrition Information

- Calories: 311
- Saturated Fat: 13 g(63%)
- Sodium: 205 mg(9%)
- Fiber: 3 g(12%)
- Total Carbohydrate: 21 g(7%)
- Cholesterol: 65 mg(22%)
- Protein: 12 g(23%)
- Total Fat: 21 g(32%)

101. Mustard Chicken And Orzo Casserole With Dill And Capers

Serving: Makes 4 to 6 servings | Prep: 45mins | Cook: 1.75hours | Ready in:

Ingredients

- 3 cups chicken broth
- 1 3/4 lb skinless boneless chicken breast halves
- 3 tablespoons unsalted butter
- 3 tablespoons all-purpose flour
- 3/4 cup heavy cream
- 2 tablespoons Dijon mustard
- 2 tablespoons coarse-grain mustard
- 3 tablespoons drained bottled capers, rinsed
- 1/2 teaspoon salt
- 1/4 teaspoon black pepper
- 1/8 teaspoon freshly grated nutmeg
- 1/4 to 1/2 cup chopped fresh dill
- 1/4 cup sour cream
- 6 celery ribs, cut diagonally into 1/4-inch-thick slices
- 1 cup orzo (rice-shaped pasta)
- a 2 1/2- to 3-quart flameproof gratin dish or shallow casserole dish (1 1/2 to 2 inches deep; not glass)

Direction

- In a heavy 4-quart saucepan, simmer broth on medium heat. Put in chicken and simmer very gently for 6 minutes in all, flipping once. Take pan off heat and put cover, then rest for 15 minutes till chicken is barely cooked completely. To cool the chicken, turn it onto a plate and slightly cover to retain broth's warmth.
- In a heavy 2- to 3-quarts saucepan, liquify the butter on low heat, then put in flour and let roux cook for 3 minutes, mixing. Put in warm broth all together, mixing, and gently simmer for 10 minutes, mixing from time to time. Mix in cream and let simmer for 5 minutes, mixing from time to time. Take off from heat and mix in dill, nutmeg, pepper, salt, capers and mustards to taste.
- Turn half cup of sauce onto one small bowl and to create topping, mix in sour cream.
- Using your fingers, pull chicken apart and in a big bowl, mix along with leftover sauce.
- Preheat the oven to 350°F.
- In a big pot with salted boiling water, let celery cook for 8 minutes till soft. Using a slotted spoon, turn onto a bowl with cold water to end the cooking and bring cooking water back to boil. In colander, let celery drain and put to mixture of chicken. In the same boiling water, let orzo cook till barely soft, then let drain in sieve.
- Into the mixture of chicken, mix orzo, then turn the mixture into gratin dish, scattering equally. Over the top, scoop sour cream topping and scatter equally. In center of oven, bake with foil as cover, till heated completely and sauce is bubbling surrounding edges, for 25 minutes to half an hour.
- Preheat the broiler.
- Take foil off dish and broil for 3 to 5 minutes, approximately 3-inch away from heat till top is speckled with brown patches.
- Note: Casserole may be prepared, yet not broiled or baked, 6 hours in advance and cool with no cover, then refrigerate with foil as cover. Rest for 15 minutes at room temperature prior to baking.

Nutrition Information

- Calories: 701
- Cholesterol: 242 mg(81%)
- Protein: 56 g(111%)
- Total Fat: 36 g(56%)
- Saturated Fat: 19 g(96%)
- Sodium: 1030 mg(43%)
- Fiber: 3 g(11%)
- Total Carbohydrate: 35 g(12%)

102. Noodle Less Zucchini Lasagna

Serving: Serves 8 | Prep: | Cook: | Ready in:

Ingredients

- 1 pound 93% lean ground beef
- 1 1/4 teaspoons kosher salt
- 1 teaspoon olive oil
- 1/2 large onion, chopped
- 3 garlic cloves, minced
- 1 (28-ounce) can crushed tomatoes
- 2 tablespoons chopped fresh basil
- Freshly ground black pepper
- 3 medium zucchini
- Cooking spray or oil mister
- 1 1/2 cups part-skim ricotta cheese
- 1/4 cup grated Parmigiano-Reggiano cheese
- 1 large egg
- 4 cups shredded part-skim mozzarella cheese (16 ounces)

Direction

- Heat a big, deep nonstick frying pan on high heat. Add meat, use 1/2 teaspoon of the salt to season, and cook for 4-5 minutes, crumble the meat into small pieces with a wooden spoon as it browns. Drain the meat in a colander and clean the frying pan using a paper towel.
- Place the frying pan on medium heat. Add onion and olive oil and cook for 3-4 minutes until tender, tossing. Add garlic and cook for 1 minute. Put the meat back into the pan; add black pepper, 1/4 teaspoon of the salt to taste, basil, and tomatoes. Lower the heat to low, put a cover on and simmer for 5 minutes, tossing sometimes. Remove the lid, simmer uncovered until thickened, about 10 minutes.
- In the meantime, using a mandolin, cut zucchini lengthwise into slices, about 1/8-inch thick each slice. (You should have a minimum of 30-35 long zucchini ribbons). Lightly salt the zucchini with the leftover 1/2 teaspoon salt and put aside, about 15 minutes. Tap dry zucchini using paper towels.
- Start preheating a grill to medium heat (or preheat a grill pan to medium heat).
- Spray cooking spray over the grill pan or grease the grill grates to prevent sticking. Grill the zucchini for 2-3 minutes per side until turning light brown and cooked. Remove onto a paper towel-lined dish and press to absorb the excess moister.
- Start preheating the oven to 375°.
- Mix egg, Parmesan, and ricotta together in a medium-sized bowl. Spread over the bottom of a 9×13×2 1/2-in. baking dish with 1/2 cup of the meat sauce. Cover the bottom of the dish with a layer of the zucchini over the sauce. Spread over the zucchini with 1/2 cup of the ricotta mixture and sprinkle 1 cup of the mozzarella over. Put on zucchini in another layer, put 1 cup mozzarella, 1/2 cup ricotta mixture, and 1 1/2 cups meat sauce on top. Repeat the layers with the rest of the ingredients until you have 3 layers in total. Complete the lasagna with meat sauce and the leftover zucchini on top. Use a foil to cover the dish.
- Bake for 30 minutes, take away the foil and bake without a cover for 20 minutes. Add the leftover 1 cup mozzarella and bake without a cover until bubbly and the cheese melts, about another 10 minutes. Allow to sit for 5-10 minutes, and then slice into 8 pieces.

Nutrition Information

103. Penne And Vegetable Gratin

Serving: Serves 4 as main course or 6 as a side dish | Prep: | Cook: | Ready in:

Ingredients

- 1/2 pound penne or other tubular pasta (about 2 1/2 cups)

- 2 medium zucchini, quartered lengthwise and cut crosswise into 1/2-inch-thick slices
- 3/4 pound vine-ripened tomatoes, seeded and chopped (about 1 1/3 cups)
- 1 cup coarsely grated chilled Fontina cheese (preferably Italian, about 1/4 pound)
- 1/2 cup packed fresh basil leaves, washed well, spun dry, and chopped
- 1/3 cup packed fresh parsley leaves, washed well, spun dry, and chopped
- 2 large garlic cloves, minced
- 1/4 teaspoon dried hot red pepper flakes
- 2 tablespoons unsalted butter
- 1/2 pound mushrooms, sliced (about 3 1/2 cups)
- 1 tablespoon all-purpose flour
- 2 tablespoons tomato paste
- 2 cups milk
- 1/4 teaspoon freshly grated nutmeg
- 1/2 cup fine fresh bread crumbs
- 1 tablespoon olive oil

Direction

- Bring 3-qt of salted water in a 4-qt kettle to a boil. Add the pasta and cook for 8 minutes while occasionally stirring it. (The pasta will be finished cooking when baked.) Drain the pasta in a colander and wash it with cold water. Drain the pasta and spread it in a 2-2 1/2-qt gratin dish or shallow baking dish. Toss it with tomatoes, herbs, zucchini, and Fontina.
- Set the oven to 400°F for preheating.
- For the sauce, cook the red pepper flakes and garlic in a large heavy saucepan with butter over moderately low heat for 2 minutes while stirring. Add the mushrooms and salt to taste. Cook and stir over moderate heat until the mushrooms turn tender and release all of their liquid. Add the flour and cook and stir for 2 minutes. Add the nutmeg, tomato paste, milk, and salt and pepper to taste. Bring the mixture to a boil while stirring it. Simmer the sauce while stirring it for 30 seconds.
- Spread the sauce all over the pasta mixture evenly. Gently shake the gratin dish until the pasta is well coated with the sauce.

- For the topping, stir the bread crumbs and oil in a small bowl using the fork until the crumbs are well moistened.
- Sprinkle the pasta mixture with the topping. Bake it inside the middle of the oven for 30 minutes. Allow the gratin to cool for 10 minutes before serving it.

Nutrition Information

- Calories: 640
- Sodium: 500 mg(21%)
- Fiber: 6 g(22%)
- Total Carbohydrate: 76 g(25%)
- Cholesterol: 66 mg(22%)
- Protein: 27 g(54%)
- Total Fat: 26 g(40%)
- Saturated Fat: 13 g(66%)

104. Poblano Potato Gratin

Serving: Makes 8 (side dish) servings | Prep: 45mins | Cook: 2.5hours | Ready in:

Ingredients

- 1 1/2 pounds fresh poblano chiles (about 5)
- 1 pound onions, cut lengthwise into 1/4-inch strips
- 1 tablespoon vegetable oil
- 3 pounds large Yukon Gold potatoes
- 1 1/2 cups heavy cream
- 3/4 cup whole milk
- Equipment: an adjustable-blade slicer

Direction

- Preparing to roast the chiles and make the rajas: On the racks of the gas burners, roast the chiles on their sides on high for about 10 minutes, flipping it using tongs, until the skins become blackened all over. Move to a bowl right away and allow it to stand for 10 minutes, tightly covered.

- Once the chiles are cool enough to touch, rub or peel off the skin. Slit the chiles lengthwise, take off the seed and stem, then devein. Slice it lengthwise into thin strips.
- In a 12-inch heavy frying pan, cook the onions with 1 tsp salt in oil on medium-low heat for about 8 minutes, stirring from time to time, until it turns golden. Mix in chiles and take out the rajas from heat. For the topping, set aside 1/2 cup of the rajas.
- Making the gratin: Set an oven to preheat to 400 degrees F and place the rack in the middle. Butter a 3-qt. shallow baking dish liberally.
- Take off the skin from the potatoes and use a slicer to slice it crosswise into 1/16-inch thick pieces. Move to a small heavy pot. Add 1 tsp salt, milk and cream, then bring just a boil on medium heat, stirring from time to time (the liquid will get thick). Mix in rajas, then evenly pour the mixture into the baking dish. Sprinkle the top with the reserved 1/2 cup of rajas.
- Let it bake for 45 minutes to 1 hour, until the potatoes become tender. Allow it to stand for 15 minutes prior to serving.
- Cook's notes: The chiles can be roasted, turning, for 8-10 minutes by broiling on a broiler pan and place it 2 inches from the heat source.
- The rajas can be prepared 3 days in advance and chilled in the fridge.
- The gratin can be prepared 1 day in advance and chilled in the fridge. Bring to room temperature and rewarm for about 30 minutes in a 350 degrees F oven with cover.

Nutrition Information

- Calories: 371
- Fiber: 6 g(24%)
- Total Carbohydrate: 45 g(15%)
- Cholesterol: 63 mg(21%)
- Protein: 7 g(15%)
- Total Fat: 20 g(30%)
- Saturated Fat: 11 g(55%)
- Sodium: 47 mg(2%)

---

105.   Popover Pudding With Irish Bacon

Serving: Serves 8 | Prep: | Cook: | Ready in:

Ingredients

- 2 cups whole milk
- 4 large eggs
- 1 3/4 cups all-purpose flour
- 1 1/4 teaspoons salt
- 1 large bunch fresh chives
- 1 pound sliced Irish bacon*
- about 1/2 cup vegetable oil
- *available at many supermarkets

Direction

- Blend salt, flour, eggs and milk till smooth in a blender; put batter into bowl. Chop enough chives finely to get 1/2 cup; whisk into batter. Chill the batter for 1 hour – 1 day, covered.
- Preheat an oven to 400°F.
- From bacon, trim fat; cook fat in a big nonstick skillet on low heat till solids are golden brown and most fat is rendered, occasionally mixing. Discard solids; put heat on medium high. Heat rendered fat till hot yet not smoking; in batches, sauté bacon for 1 minute per side till just golden. Put bacon as cooked on paper towels; drain. Put referred fat in measuring cup; add extra oil to get 1/2 cup total.
- Heat oil mixture for 5 minutes in center of oven in 13x9x2-in. glass baking dish/12x2-in. 3 1/2-qt. enameled cast-iron casserole. Evenly put bacon in baking dish/casserole quickly; put batter over. Bake pudding for 50 minutes till golden brown and puffed in center of oven.

Nutrition Information

- Calories: 533
- Protein: 15 g(30%)

- Total Fat: 41 g(63%)
- Saturated Fat: 10 g(52%)
- Sodium: 438 mg(18%)
- Fiber: 1 g(3%)
- Total Carbohydrate: 25 g(8%)
- Cholesterol: 137 mg(46%)

106.   Potato Fennel Gratin

Serving: Makes 8 servings | Prep: 15mins | Cook: 1.25hours |Ready in:

Ingredients

- 1 (1 pound) fennel bulb with fronds
- 2 pounds boiling potatoes
- 4 tablespoons (1/4 cup) unsalted butter, melted
- 1 cup coarsely grated Gruyère cheese (3 ounces)
- a handheld adjustable-blade slicer

Direction

- Place rack in the bottom third of the oven then preheat to 450 degrees F. Spread butter on a 2-qt shallow baking dish or flameproof gratin pan. Do not use glass dishes.
- Slice the fronds from the fennel then chop just enough to make a 1 tbsp.; set aside. Cut and get rid of the stalks. Slice the fennel lengthwise in quarters then use a slicer to thinly cut on a big bowl.
- Skin the potatoes then use a slicer to thinly cut on a big bowl. Toss in a quarter teaspoon pepper, 3/4 tsp. salt and butter to coat.
- Evenly spread the vegetables on a gratin dish; tightly cover with foil.
- Bake for half an hour then lower the heat to 350 degrees F. Bake for another 20-25 minutes until the vegetables are tender.
- Take it out of the oven then uncover; evenly sprinkle cheese on top of the gratin.

- Preheat the broiler then broil for 4-5 minutes about four to five inches from heat until the cheese is pale golden.
- Let it sit for 5 minutes then serve.

Nutrition Information

107.   Potato Gratin With Goat Cheese And Garlic

Serving: Makes 4 to 6 servings | Prep: | Cook: |Ready in:

Ingredients

- 1 cup whole milk
- 1 cup whipping cream
- 1 cup crumbled soft fresh goat cheese (such as Montrachet; about 5 ounces)
- 1 garlic clove, minced
- 1 1/2 teaspoons salt
- 3/4 teaspoon ground black pepper
- 1/8 teaspoon ground nutmeg
- 2 pounds Yukon Gold potatoes, peeled, thinly sliced

Direction

- Preheat an oven to 400°F. Butter an 11x7x2-inch glass baking dish generously. Whisk initial 7 ingredients to blend in a medium bowl. Place 1/3 of the potatoes on bottom of the prepared dish, slightly overlapping and completely covering. Put 1/3 cream mixture on. Repeat layering cream mixture and potatoes twice more. Bake for 1 hour 15 minutes, uncovered, till top is golden brown in spots and potatoes are tender. Serve while hot.

Nutrition Information

- Calories: 508
- Total Carbohydrate: 45 g(15%)
- Cholesterol: 93 mg(31%)

- Protein: 16 g(32%)
- Total Fat: 30 g(46%)
- Saturated Fat: 19 g(97%)
- Sodium: 916 mg(38%)
- Fiber: 5 g(21%)

108. Potato Gratin With Juniper

Serving: Makes 4 to 6 side-dish servings | Prep: 20mins | Cook: 1.5hours | Ready in:

Ingredients

- 1 1/2 teaspoons juniper berries*
- 1 cup heavy cream
- 3/4 stick (6 tablespoons) unsalted butter, melted
- 1 1/4 teaspoons salt
- 3/4 teaspoon black pepper
- 2 lb russet (baking) potatoes (about 4)
- an electric coffee/spice grinder; an adjustable-blade slicer; a 2-qt flameproof shallow baking dish

Direction

- Position oven rack in center place and preheat the oven to 375°F.
- In grinder, grind juniper berries finely.
- In a big bowl, whip pepper, salt, 1 1/4 teaspoons of ground juniper (throw the rest), butter and cream together till blended. Remove potatoes skin and slice into 1/8-inch-thick pieces. Into the mixture of cream, fold pieces of potato and turn into the baking dish, evenly spreading. Tightly cover in foil and bake for 50 to 60 minutes, till potatoes are extremely soft.
- Preheat the broiler.
- Take off foil and let potatoes broil for 6 minutes, 2- to 3-inch away from heat till golden.
- Rest for 10 minutes prior to serving.

Nutrition Information

- Calories: 539
- Fiber: 5 g(21%)
- Total Carbohydrate: 42 g(14%)
- Cholesterol: 127 mg(42%)
- Protein: 7 g(13%)
- Total Fat: 40 g(61%)
- Saturated Fat: 25 g(124%)
- Sodium: 775 mg(32%)

109. Potato Gratin With Mushrooms And Gruyère

Serving: Makes 8 to 10 servings | Prep: 1hours | Cook: 2hours | Ready in:

Ingredients

- 1/4 cup olive oil
- 4 cups finely chopped leeks (white and pale green parts only; about 3 large)
- 1 1/2 pounds 1/2-inch cubes assorted mushrooms (such as crimini and stemmed shiitake; about 10 cups)
- 2 garlic cloves, minced
- 3 pounds Yukon Gold potatoes, peeled, cut into 1/8-inch-thick slices
- 2 cups heavy whipping cream
- 1 teaspoon (or more) salt
- 1/2 teaspoon (or more) freshly ground black pepper
- 1 cup coarsely grated Gruyère cheese

Direction

- In a big frying pan, heat 1/4 cup oil over medium-high heat. Add leeks, sauté for 10-12 minutes until turning light brown and tender. Add mushrooms, sprinkle pepper and salt over, and sauté for 7-8 minutes until tender and the liquid has evaporated. Add garlic, sauté for 1 minute. Use pepper and salt to season. Put aside. You can prepare this 4 days in advance. Allow to sit at room temperature.

- Start preheating the oven to 375°F. Using a kitchen towel, pat the potato slices dry. In a big pot, mix together 1/2 teaspoon pepper, 1 teaspoon salt, and cream. Add potatoes. Boil it, lower the heat to medium and simmer with a cover on, whisking sometimes, about 10 minutes. Uncover, simmer for 3 minutes until the potatoes have slightly cooked and the cream has decreased by approximately 1/2, whisking frequently and watching carefully to make sure the mixture doesn't burn. Use pepper and salt to season.
- Brush oil over a 13x9x2-in. ceramic or glass baking dish. Remove 1/2 of the potato mixture to the dish, spreading out into an even layer. Spoon over 1 even layer of the mushroom mixture. Spoon the leftover potato mixture over, spreading into an even layer. Sprinkle with cheese. Use a foil to cover, tenting in the middle so the cheese doesn't stick to the foil. Bake for 30 minutes. Remove the cover, bake for 20-25 minutes more until the top turns brown and the potatoes are soft. Allow sit before serving, about 10 minutes.

Nutrition Information

- Calories: 746
- Sodium: 472 mg(20%)
- Fiber: 5 g(22%)
- Total Carbohydrate: 43 g(14%)
- Cholesterol: 198 mg(66%)
- Protein: 16 g(31%)
- Total Fat: 61 g(93%)
- Saturated Fat: 32 g(161%)

110.   Potato Torta

Serving: Makes 8 servings | Prep: | Cook: | Ready in:

Ingredients

- 6 tablespoons extra-virgin olive oil
- 4 pounds waxy potatoes, peeled

- 2 cups fresh bread crumbs
- Salt and freshly ground black pepper
- 1/2 cup finely chopped Italian parsley
- 1 cup freshly grated pecorino romano

Direction

- Set the oven to 350 degrees F to preheat. Grease using 2 tablespoons of olive oil a baking dish or 2-3 quart, 2-3 inch deep earthenware casserole.
- In a large bowl, place the 1/4 inch thick sliced potatoes and toss with 1/2 cup of bread crumbs. Season well with pepper and salt. Mix the remaining 1 1/2 cups bread crumbs with the parsley, pecorino and the remaining 1/4 cup olive oil in a small bowl.
- In the bottom of the casserole, spread a layer of potatoes and sprinkle with the cheese mixture and 3-4 tablespoons of bread crumbs. Continue to layer, finishing with the breadcrumb cheese mixture.
- Bake until the top turns golden brown in color and the potatoes are soft or for 1 hour. Serve while hot.

Nutrition Information

- Calories: 438
- Fiber: 7 g(26%)
- Total Carbohydrate: 60 g(20%)
- Cholesterol: 17 mg(6%)
- Protein: 14 g(27%)
- Total Fat: 16 g(25%)
- Saturated Fat: 5 g(23%)
- Sodium: 663 mg(28%)

111.   Potato And Fennel Gratin With Gorgonzola, Olives And Tomato Marjoram Sauce

Serving: Makes 6 servings | Prep: | Cook: | Ready in:

Ingredients

- 1 garlic clove, peeled, flattened
- 4 1/2 tablespoons butter, cut into pieces
- 2 pounds Yukon Gold potatoes or white-skinned potatoes, unpeeled, cut into 1/8-inch-thick rounds
- 1/4 cup oil-cured black olives, pitted, chopped
- 1 1/4 cups crumbled Gorgonzola cheese (about 5 ounces)
- 2 medium fennel bulbs, trimmed, cored, cut into 1/4-inch-wide strips (about 3 cups)
- 1 teaspoon dried marjoram
- 1/2 cup hot whole milk
- 6 oil-cured black olives, pitted, halved
- Tomato-Marjoram Sauce

Direction

- Preheat an oven to 375°F. Rub a garlic clove inside 9x9x2-in. metal baking pan. Rub 1/2 tbsp. butter on pan. Use 1/4 potatoes to cover bottom, slightly overlapping. Sprinkle 1/3 chopped olives then 1/4 cheese. Put 1/3 fennel over; sprinkle 1/3 marjoram, pepper and salt. Dot using 1 tbsp. butter. Repeat the layers twice. Put leftover potatoes over then leftover 1/2 cheese; dot with leftover 1 tbsp. butter. Put milk on top; put halves olives over. Sprinkle pepper and salt; use foil to cover pan.
- Bake gratin for 50 minutes till veggies are nearly tender. Remove foil; sprinkle leftover cheese. Bake for 25 minutes till potatoes are golden and tender, uncovered. You can make it 2 hours ahead; stand in room temperature. Rewarm for 20 minutes till heated through in 350°F oven. Stand gratin for 15 minutes then serve it with tomato-marjoram sauce.

Nutrition Information

- Calories: 261
- Sodium: 386 mg(16%)
- Fiber: 4 g(17%)
- Total Carbohydrate: 20 g(7%)
- Cholesterol: 43 mg(14%)
- Protein: 8 g(17%)
- Total Fat: 17 g(26%)
- Saturated Fat: 10 g(52%)

112. Potato And Macaroni Gratin

Serving: Serves 6 | Prep: | Cook: | Ready in:

Ingredients

- 1 12-ounce russet potato, peeled, cut into 1/2-inch pieces (about 2 cups)
- 8 ounces small elbow macaroni
- 2 tablespoons (1/4 stick) butter
- 1 pound onions (about 3 medium), sliced
- 3/4 cup whipping cream
- 3/4 cup milk (do not use low-fat or nonfat)
- 1 1/2 cups grated Swiss cheese (about 6 ounces)

Direction

- Set the oven to 350 degrees F to preheat. Coat an 8"x8"x2" baking dish with butter. In a big pot of boiling salted water, cook potato for about 10 minutes, until tender. Move potato to a big bowl with a slotted spoon. Put into the same pot of boiling water the macaroni and cook until just tender yet still firm to bite. Drain macaroni and put into the bowl with potato.
- In the meantime, in a heavy big skillet, melt 2 tbsp. of butter on moderately high heat. Put in sliced onions and sauté for about 15 minutes while stirring frequently, until browned and softened.
- Put into the potato mixture the cheese, milk, cream and onions. Use pepper and salt to season to taste. Move to prepped dish and bake for about 20 minutes, until cheese is melted, and mixture is heated through. Allow to cool for 5 minutes, then serve hot.

Nutrition Information

- Calories: 452

- Fiber: 3 g(12%)
- Total Carbohydrate: 47 g(16%)
- Cholesterol: 72 mg(24%)
- Protein: 16 g(32%)
- Total Fat: 23 g(35%)
- Saturated Fat: 14 g(70%)
- Sodium: 51 mg(2%)

113. Potato And Poblano Chile Gratin

Serving: Makes 10 to 12 servings | Prep: | Cook: | Ready in:

Ingredients

- 3 pounds red-skinned potatoes
- 1 tablespoon olive oil
- 5 fresh poblano chiles, seeded, peeled, chopped (about 4 cups)
- 1 medium onion, sliced
- 2 cups whipping cream
- 1 cup whole milk
- 1 large garlic clove
- 2 1/2 cups (packed) grated Gruyère cheese (about 10 ounces)

Direction

- Preheat the oven to 350°F. Butter a glass 13x9x2-in. baking dish. In pot with boiling salted water, cook potatoes for 25 minutes till tender. In colander, drain potatoes. Completely cool. Peel then cut potatoes to 1/2-in. thick rounds. Put into big bowl. Sprinkle pepper and salt on potatoes.
- In a heavy big skillet, heat oil on medium high heat. Add onion and chiles. Sauté for 15 minutes till onion is very soft. Put chile mixture into food processor. Put garlic, milk and cream. Blend to make a thick sauce. Season to taste with pepper and salt. Put sauce on potatoes. Gently mix to coat. In bottom of prepped dish, overlap 1/2 potatoes with sauce. Sprinkle 1/2 cheese on. Put leftover

potatoes and sauce on top followed by leftover cheese. Bake gratin for 30 minutes till brown on top and heated through.

Nutrition Information

- Calories: 411
- Total Fat: 26 g(41%)
- Saturated Fat: 15 g(77%)
- Sodium: 242 mg(10%)
- Fiber: 4 g(15%)
- Total Carbohydrate: 32 g(11%)
- Cholesterol: 87 mg(29%)
- Protein: 14 g(28%)

114. Potato And Porcini Gratin

Serving: Serves 8 | Prep: | Cook: | Ready in:

Ingredients

- 1 ounce dried porcini mushrooms (about 1 cup)
- 1 cup warm water
- 5 large russet (baking) potatoes (about 3 pounds)
- 3 garlic cloves, minced
- 1 tablespoon unsalted butter
- 2 cups milk
- 1 cup heavy cream
- 2 tablespoons minced fresh chives
- 1 teaspoon salt

Direction

- Soak porcini in warm water in a bowl until softened, for 30 minutes. Through a fine sieve lined with a double thickness of rinsed and squeezed cheesecloth or with a coffee filter, slowly filter the soaking liquid into a small saucepan, being careful to keep the last tablespoon (including sediment) in a bowl. Bring the soaking liquid to a boil until reduced to about half cup.

- Set the oven at 350°F to preheat.
- Rinse porcini under cold water to discard any grit and pat dry. Cut the porcini coarse. Next, peel potatoes and chop into 1/8 inch thick. Over moderate heat, cook garlic and porcini in butter in a large (4-quart) saucepan for 2 minutes, stirring. Add 4 teaspoons chives, cream, milk, reduced porcini liquid, potatoes, and salt; bring the liquid to boiling, stirring.
- Transfer the mixture to a greased 2-quart gratin dish and bake until the potatoes are softened, for 60 minutes. Sprinkle with the leftover 2 teaspoons chives and gratin.

Nutrition Information

- Calories: 255
- Saturated Fat: 9 g(45%)
- Sodium: 338 mg(14%)
- Fiber: 3 g(12%)
- Total Carbohydrate: 27 g(9%)
- Cholesterol: 51 mg(17%)
- Protein: 5 g(11%)
- Total Fat: 15 g(22%)

115. Potato And Portobello Mushroom Gratin

Serving: Makes 10 servings | Prep: | Cook: | Ready in:

Ingredients

- 1 1/2 cups hot water
- 1 1/2-ounce package dried porcini mushrooms*
- 1 1/2 pounds portobello mushrooms
- 12 tablespoons olive oil
- 4 garlic cloves, minced
- 4 pounds Yukon Gold potatoes or white-skinned potatoes, peeled, cut into 1/8-inch-thick slices
- 1/4 cup chopped fresh parsley
- 1 tablespoon chopped fresh thyme
- 1 tablespoon chopped fresh rosemary
- 2 teaspoons salt
- 1 teaspoon ground black pepper

Direction

- In a small bowl, mix together porcini and 1 1/2 cups hot water. Allow to sit for 30 minutes until the mushrooms are tender. Strain, saving 2/3 cup soaking liquid. Cut the porcini, put aside. Discard and cut the stems from the portobellos, put in a big bowl. Scrape away the dark gills from the portobellos with a small spoon. Cut the portobello caps into pieces, about 1/2-in each piece; add to the bowl.
- In a big heavy frying pan, heat 3 tablespoons olive over medium-high heat. Add the chopped Portobello caps and stems and sauté for 4 minutes. Mix in the saved reserved porcini and garlic and sauté for 10 minutes until the mushrooms are soft. Use pepper and salt to season. Take away from heat.
- Start preheating the oven to 375°F. Brush 1 tablespoon oil over two 13x9x2-in. glass baking dishes to coat. In a big bowl, mix together pepper, salt, rosemary, thyme, parsley, potatoes, and the leftover 7 tablespoons oil; mix to blend. In each prepared dish, place 1/6 of the potato mixture (there should not be enough to overlap slices). Put 1/4 of the mushroom mixture on top of the potatoes on each dish. Add to the potatoes in each dish with 1/3 cup reserved porcini soaking liquid. Use foil to cover each dish.
- Bake the gratins for 45 minutes. Remove the cover and bake for another 40 minutes until the potatoes are soft and the tops turn brown. (You can prepare 2 hours in advance. Let sit at room temperature. Use foil to cover and reheat in the oven for 20 minutes at 350°F).

Nutrition Information

- Calories: 240
- Saturated Fat: 2 g(12%)
- Sodium: 480 mg(20%)
- Fiber: 4 g(14%)
- Total Carbohydrate: 22 g(7%)

- Protein: 4 g(8%)
- Total Fat: 17 g(26%)

116.   Potato And Turnip Gratin

Serving: Makes 12 servings | Prep: | Cook: | Ready in:

Ingredients

- 4 cups heavy whipping cream
- 2 cups low-salt chicken broth
- 6 large fresh thyme sprigs
- 4 large fresh sage sprigs
- 2 large fresh rosemary sprigs
- 2 large garlic cloves, pressed
- 1 Turkish bay leaf
- 1 tablespoon coarse kosher salt
- 1 teaspoon ground black pepper
- 1/4 teaspoon ground nutmeg
- 1/4 teaspoon cayenne pepper
- 3 1/2 pounds russet potatoes
- 2 pounds turnips
- 1 cup freshly grated Parmesan cheese

Direction

- Put the oven rack in the top third of the oven and start preheating the oven to 350°F. Add the first eleven ingredients to a big saucepan and boil. Lower the heat and simmer for 35 minutes until the mixture decreases to 3/4 cups. Drain the cream mixture into a big bowl.
- Remove the skin from the potatoes, slice into rounds, about 1/8-in. thick, immediately adding to the mixture to avoid discoloration. Remove the skin from the turnips, slice into rounds, about 1/8-in. thick. Add to the potato mixture, mix to blend.
- In a 15x10x2-in. glass baking plate, add the vegetable mixture and press to make the layer even. Use foil to cover the plate. Bake for 1 hour. Take away the over, use cheese so sprinkle. Bake for another 25 minutes until nearly all of the cream mixture has reduced,

potatoes are soft, and the top turns golden brown.

Nutrition Information

- Calories: 772
- Saturated Fat: 39 g(196%)
- Sodium: 724 mg(30%)
- Fiber: 5 g(20%)
- Total Carbohydrate: 38 g(13%)
- Cholesterol: 246 mg(82%)
- Protein: 14 g(27%)
- Total Fat: 67 g(104%)

117.   Potato, Leek, Gruyère And Oyster Mushroom Gratin

Serving: Serves 10 | Prep: | Cook: | Ready in:

Ingredients

- 4 tablespoons (1/2 stick) butter
- 1 pound oyster mushrooms, halved if large
- 1 tablespoon minced garlic
- 4 cups thinly sliced leeks (white and pale green parts only; about 4 large)
- 1 tablespoon minced fresh thyme
- 1 3/4 cups canned low-salt chicken broth
- 1 3/4 cups whipping cream
- 1/4 cup dry white wine
- 1 teaspoon salt
- 1/2 teaspoon ground black pepper
- 3 3/4 pounds russet potatoes, peeled, thinly sliced into rounds (about 8 cups)
- 2 1/2 cups grated Gruyère cheese (about 10 ounces)

Direction

- Preparation: Put 2 tbsp. of butter in a heavy large skillet and melt it over medium-high heat. Put in the mushrooms and sauté for 5 minutes, or until almost tender. Add the garlic and sauté for 3 more minutes, or until the mushrooms are golden and tender. Pour the mushroom mixture into a bowl. Put the remaining 2 tbsp. of butter in the same skillet and melt it over medium-high heat. Add the thyme and leeks. Sauté for 8 minutes, or until the leeks soften and start to brown. Pour the leek mixture into the bowl with mushrooms. (This can be prepared 1 day ahead. Just keep it covered and chilled.)

- Set the oven to 400°F for preheating. Grease a 13x9x2-inches baking dish. In a large bowl, mix the cream, 1 tsp. of salt, broth, 1/2 tsp. of pepper, and wine until blended. Layer the bottom of the greased dish with 1/3 of the potatoes. Spread half of the mushroom-leek mixture on top of the potatoes. Sprinkle it with 3/4 cup of cheese. Place 1/2 of the remaining potatoes on top. Spread the top with 1/2 of the cream mixture. Pour the remaining mushroom-leek mixture on top, and then top it with 3/4 cup of cheese. Cover them with the remaining potatoes. Spread remaining cream mixture all over the potatoes. Sprinkle the dish with the remaining cheese.
- Let it bake uncovered inside the oven for 1 hour and 20 minutes, or until the sauce thickly bubbles and the potatoes are tender. Allow the gratin to stand for half an hour. Serve.

Nutrition Information

- Calories: 423
- Sodium: 484 mg(20%)
- Fiber: 3 g(14%)
- Total Carbohydrate: 32 g(11%)
- Cholesterol: 90 mg(30%)
- Protein: 15 g(30%)
- Total Fat: 27 g(42%)
- Saturated Fat: 17 g(83%)

118.   Potato, Zucchini, And Tomato Gratin

Serving: Makes 10 servings | Prep: | Cook: | Ready in:

Ingredients

- 2 3/4 pounds medium tomatoes (about 10), halved, cored, seeded
- 3/4 cup olive oil, divided, plus 2 tablespoons
- 1 pound medium Yukon Gold potatoes, peeled, cut into 1/4-inch-thick rounds
- 1 pound large zucchini, trimmed, cut diagonally into 1/4-inch-thick slices
- 2 teaspoons fresh thyme leaves
- 1/2 cup finely grated Parmesan cheese

Direction

- Preheat the oven to 250 degrees F. Put parchment paper on a rimmed baking sheet; put in tomato halves with the cut-side up on the prepare sheet. Drizzle a half cup of olive oil on the tomatoes; add salt. Roast for an hour in the oven until soft; slightly cool. Remove the skins of the tomato halves with your fingertips; set the tomatoes aside. Turn the oven temperature to 375 degrees F.
- Put parchment paper on another rimmed baking sheet. In a medium bowl, mix a quarter cup olive oil and the potato slices; toss and sprinkle with pepper and salt to coat. In one layer, put the potatoes on the prepared sheet; drizzle with any oil from the bowl. Roast for 25 minutes until soft and starting to brown; cool.
- On medium-high heat, heat 2 tbsp. oil in a big non-stick pan. Sprinkle pepper and salt over the zucchini. Sauté zucchini in batches for a minute per side until light brown; drain on paper towels then cool.
- Grease a 13-in by 9-in by 2-in glass or ceramic baking dish lightly. Starting from the outer edges of the baking dish and working toward the middle of the baking dish, alternate slices of potato, zucchini, and tomato halves, slightly overlapping. Sprinkle pepper, salt, Parmesan,

and thyme leaves. You can prepare this a day in advance; cover and refrigerate.

- Preheat the oven to 350 degrees F. Bake gratin without cover for 35 minutes until the juices bubble at the edges and the cheese melts.

Nutrition Information

- Calories: 254
- Sodium: 91 mg(4%)
- Fiber: 3 g(12%)
- Total Carbohydrate: 14 g(5%)
- Cholesterol: 4 mg(1%)
- Protein: 5 g(9%)
- Total Fat: 21 g(32%)
- Saturated Fat: 4 g(18%)

---

119. Roasted Winter Vegetable Baklava

Serving: 6 servings | Prep: 45mins | Cook: 1.75hours | Ready in:

Ingredients

- 1/2 cup walnuts (2 ounces), toasted
- 1/4 cup fine dry plain bread crumbs
- 1 pound Yukon Gold potatoes
- 2 medium fennel bulbs, trimmed, reserving fronds, bulbs halved and sliced lengthwise 1/4 inch thick
- 3/4 pound parsnips (3 medium), sliced diagonally 1/3 inch thick
- 1/2 pound carrots (3 medium), sliced diagonally 1/3 inch thick
- 1 large onion, halved and sliced
- 3/4 cup olive oil, divided
- 2/3 cup water
- 1/3 cup chopped dill
- 8 (17-by 12-inch) phyllo sheets, thawed if frozen
- Equipment: a shallow 3-quart oval or rectangular baking dish

Direction

- Preheat an oven with racks in lower and upper thirds to 425°F.
- Pulse breadcrumbs and walnuts till nuts are chopped finely, not ground, in a food processor.
- Peel potatoes; cut 1/4-in. thick. Divide all veggies among 2 big 4-sided sheet pans; toss each pan of veggies with 1/2 tsp. pepper, 1/2 tsp. salt and 3 tbsp. oil.
- Roast veggies for 35-40 minutes till golden brown in spots and soft, mixing and switching pan positions halfway through; with 1 rack in center, leave oven on.
- To each pan of veggies, add 1/3 cup water; mix and scrape brown bits from bottom. Chop 1/4 cup of fennel fronds; mix all veggies in 1 pan. Toss with dill and fennel fronds.
- Brush some leftover olive oil on baking dish. Use plastic wrap and a damp kitchen towel to cover phyllo sheet stack; keep leftover phyllo covered. Put 1 sheet on a work surface, working quickly. Brush with some oil gently; sprinkle 2 rounded tbsp. walnut mixture. Put another phyllo sheet over; repeat brushing then sprinkling. Put 3rd sheet over; brush using oil.
- In 1/2 of baking dish, drape phyllo stack; press up the side and into bottom gently, leaving an overhang. Create another stack using leftover walnut mixture, extra oil and 3 extra phyllo sheets. Drape into other 1/2 of dish; the phyllo will overlap in middle of dish.
- Put veggies in phyllo shell and fold overhang toward middle over the filling, it won't cover veggies; brush oil on edge. Brush leftover oil on leftover 2 phyllo sheets; tear in half and crumple. Put over filling.
- Bake for 20-25 minutes till phyllo is deep golden brown in middle of oven; before serving, cool for 5 minutes.

Nutrition Information

- Calories: 545
- Sodium: 235 mg(10%)

- Fiber: 10 g(39%)
- Total Carbohydrate: 53 g(18%)
- Protein: 8 g(15%)
- Total Fat: 35 g(55%)
- Saturated Fat: 5 g(24%)

120. Root Vegetable Gratin

Serving: 8 | Prep: | Cook: 30mins | Ready in:

Ingredients

- 3 pounds assorted root vegetables, peeled (see Tip) and cut into ⅛-inch-thick slices
- 3 tablespoons extra-virgin olive oil, divided
- 1 cup thinly sliced shallots
- 1⅓ cups low-fat milk, divided
- 3 tablespoons all-purpose flour
- 1½ cups finely shredded Gruyère cheese, divided
- 1 tablespoon chopped fresh thyme, or 1 teaspoon dried
- ½ teaspoon salt
- ¼ teaspoon freshly ground pepper
- 1 cup fresh whole-wheat breadcrumbs, (see Tip)

Direction

- Preheat an oven to 400°F. Use cooking spray to coat a 9x13-in. baking dish.
- For parsnips, quarter lengthwise; remove woody core. Cut to 1/8-inch thick slices. In a big pot with boiling water, cook vegetables for 5 minutes till barely tender; drain.
- Heat 2 tablespoons of oil in a medium saucepan on medium heat. Add shallots; cook, occasionally mixing, for 3-4 minutes till light brown. Add 1 cup of milk; simmer. Mix leftover 1/3 cup of milk and flour to make a smooth paste in a small bowl. Mix into hot milk; cook, constantly whisking, for 1-2 minutes till sauce thickens and bubbles. Take off heat; mix pepper, salt, thyme and 3/4 cup of cheese.

- Mix 1 tablespoon of oil, leftover 3/4 cup of cheese and breadcrumbs in a bowl.
- Layer vegetable slices in the prepared baking dish. Put cheese sauce on top; put breadcrumb mixture on top.
- Bake gratin for 30-40 minutes till top is golden and bubbly. Cool for 10 minutes; serve.

Nutrition Information

- Calories: 285 calories;
- Total Fat: 13
- Saturated Fat: 5
- Cholesterol: 24
- Sugar: 12
- Sodium: 427
- Fiber: 6
- Total Carbohydrate: 33
- Protein: 12

121. Root Vegetable Gratin With Blue Cheese

Serving: Serves 10 | Prep: | Cook: | Ready in:

Ingredients

- 1 1/2 pounds parsnips
- 1 1/2 pounds carrots
- 1 1/2 pounds rutabagas
- 2 1/2 cups whipping cream
- 1 cup chicken stock or canned broth
- 4 garlic cloves, minced
- 1 teaspoon minced fresh thyme or 1/4 teaspoon dried, crumbled
- 3/4 cup crumbled Gorgonzola or other blue cheese (about 3 ounces)

Direction

- Preheat oven to 425 degrees F. Butter a 9x13x2-in. baking dish.
- Peel carrots and parsnips. Cut to 1/4-in. thick slices. Peel rutabagas and halve. Cut to 1/4-in.

thick half rounds. Boil thyme, garlic, stock, and cream in a big saucepan. Add rutabagas. Simmer, covered, for 10 minutes. Add in parsnips and carrots. Simmer for 5 minutes more. Generously season with pepper and salt.

- Put cream and veggie mixture in the prepped dish. Bake for 35 minutes, uncovered, until liquid thickens and veggies are tender. Sprinkle cheese on top. Bake for 10 more minutes. Cool for 15 minutes prior to serving. You can make this a day ahead, covered and kept in the fridge. Reheat for 20 minutes in covered dish in 350 degrees F oven.

Nutrition Information

- Calories: 319
- Cholesterol: 73 mg(24%)
- Protein: 6 g(12%)
- Total Fat: 22 g(33%)
- Saturated Fat: 13 g(66%)
- Sodium: 214 mg(9%)
- Fiber: 7 g(27%)
- Total Carbohydrate: 28 g(9%)

122.   Roquefort Potato Gratin

Serving: Serves 12 | Prep: | Cook: | Ready in:

Ingredients

- 5 1/4 pounds russet potatoes, peeled, cut into 1/8-inch-thick slices
- 2 cups whipping cream
- 5 ounces Roquefort cheese, crumbled
- 1/2 cup dry breadcrumbs
- 1 1/2 teaspoons crumbled dried rosemary
- 1/4 cup (1/2 stick) butter, cut into small pieces

Direction

- Preheat an oven to 425°F. Butter a 15x10x2-in. glass baking dish, in prepped dish, layer potatoes, sprinkling pepper and salt on each

layer. Boil cream in medium heavy saucepan; lower heat to medium. Put Roquefort in cream; whisk till cheese melts. Put cream mixture on potatoes; use foil to cover. Bake for 1 hour till potatoes are tender.

- Preheat a broiler. In small bowl, mix rosemary and breadcrumbs; sprinkle on potatoes. Dot using butter. Broil, closely watching, for 4 minutes till crumb mixture gets golden brown and butter melts; stand for 10 minutes then serve warm.

Nutrition Information

- Calories: 369
- Cholesterol: 65 mg(22%)
- Protein: 8 g(17%)
- Total Fat: 20 g(31%)
- Saturated Fat: 13 g(63%)
- Sodium: 271 mg(11%)
- Fiber: 3 g(11%)
- Total Carbohydrate: 41 g(14%)

123.   Sausage And White Bean "Cassoulet"

Serving: Serves 2 | Prep: | Cook: | Ready in:

Ingredients

- 4 sweet Italian sausage links (about 10 ounces total), skins pricked all over with a fork
- 1 teaspoon olive oil
- 2 medium onions, halves and sliced thin lengthwise (about 1 1/2 cups)
- 2 garlic cloves, chopped fine
- 1 1/2 teaspoon mixed chopped fresh herbs such as rosemary, thyme, and/or sage or 3/4 teaspoon mixed dried herbs, crumbled
- 1 bay leaf
- 1/2 cup chopped scallion greens or fresh parsley (wash and dry before chopping)
- a 14 1/2-ounce can diced tomatoes including juice

- 19-ounce can white beans such as cannellini, navy, or Great Northern, drained and rinsed
- 1 tablespoon olive oil
- 2 slices firm white sandwich bread, crusts discarded, cut into 1/4-inch dice
- 1 small garlic clove, chopped fine
- 2 tablespoons finely chopped fresh parsley leaves (wash and dry before chopping)

Direction

- Over moderate heat, cook sausages in oil in a medium skillet, flipping, for about 8 minutes, until all sides are browned and cooked through; move to paper towels to drain.
- Cook, stir garlic and onions in the remaining fat in the skillet until golden; then stir in tomatoes with juice, scallions or parsley, herbs (including bay leaf), add pepper and salt to taste. Boil the mixture, keep stirring for 5 minutes. Cut the sausage into 1/4-inch-thick slices. Add beans and the sausage to the tomato mixture and continue to cook, stir until heated through. Then discard the bay leaf, cover and keep the "cassoulet" warm.
- To prepare the topping: over moderately high heat, heat oil in a small skillet until hot but not smoking, then sauté the bread until pale golden. Stir in parsley, garlic, add pepper and salt to taste, continue to sauté and stir for 1 minute.
- Transfer the "cassoulet" to a 1-quart serving dish and evenly cover with the topping.

Nutrition Information

- Calories: 690
- Sodium: 2100 mg(87%)
- Fiber: 15 g(61%)
- Total Carbohydrate: 71 g(24%)
- Cholesterol: 50 mg(17%)
- Protein: 48 g(96%)
- Total Fat: 25 g(38%)
- Saturated Fat: 7 g(35%)

124.   Scalloped Potatoes

Serving: 5 | Prep: 10mins | Cook: 30mins | Ready in:

Ingredients

- 5 potatoes, peeled and sliced
- 1 (8 ounce) package Cheddar cheese, cubed
- 1/2 cup butter
- 1 cup milk
- 2 teaspoons cooking sherry
- 1 cup cornflakes cereal crumbs

Direction

- Preheat the oven to 175 degrees C (350 degrees F).
- Boil a large pot of salted water. Add potatoes and cook for about 15 minutes, until soft. Allow to drain and arrange in a 2-quart casserole plate.
- Combine milk, butter, and cheese in a microwave-safe dish. Microwave until the butter and cheese are melted; then stir in the sherry. Pour the cheese mixture over the potatoes and dust the cornflakes crumbs on top.
- Next, bake for 15 to 30 minutes in the preheated oven, or until heated through.

Nutrition Information

- Calories: 555 calories;
- Total Carbohydrate: 46.4
- Cholesterol: 100
- Protein: 16.6
- Total Fat: 34.4
- Sodium: 491

125.   Scalloped Potatoes And Parsnips

Serving: | Prep: | Cook: | Ready in:

Ingredients

- 1 large red onion
- 2 tablespoons water
- 2 parsnips (about 1/2 pound)
- 2 small russet (baking) potatoes (about 3/4 pound total)
- 1 1/4 cups low-fat (1%) milk
- 3/4 cup chicken broth
- 1 1/2 tablespoons all-purpose flour
- a pinch freshly grated nutmeg

Direction

- Slice onion in half lengthwise and cut crosswise to make quarter-inch-thick pieces. Cook onion in water for 5 minutes in a big saucepan while covering, over moderate heat, mixing occasionally, or till softened. Uncover and let onion cook till all liquid in saucepan is evaporated.
- Preheat the oven to 425 °F.
- Peel potatoes and parsnips. Grate the parsnips coarse and slice potatoes crosswise to make 1/8-inch-thick pieces. Beat together flour, broth and milk in a bowl or a 2-cup measure till mixed thoroughly. Put the milk mixture into the onion along with salt to taste, nutmeg, potatoes and parsnips, and simmer for a minute, mixing often.
- Into a 1 1/2-quart shallow baking dish, carefully transfer the vegetable mixture and let it bake for 45 minutes in lower third of oven, or till surface turns golden brown and potatoes are soft once pricked with knife.

Nutrition Information

126.   Scalloped Potatoes With Goat Cheese And Herbes De Provence

Serving: Serves 8 | Prep: | Cook: | Ready in:

Ingredients

- 1 1/2 cups whipping cream
- 1 1/2 cups canned chicken broth
- 1 cup dry white wine
- 1/2 cup minced shallots
- 1 tablespoon minced garlic
- 4 teaspoons herbes de Provence*
- 3/4 teaspoon salt
- 1 10 1/2- to 11-ounce log soft fresh goat cheese, crumbled
- 4 pounds russet potatoes, peeled, thinly sliced
- *A dried herb mixture available at specialty foods stores and some supermarkets.

Direction

- Set oven to 400 degrees F and start preheating. Add butter on a 13x9x2-in. glass baking dish. In a big pot, combine the first 7 ingredients. Simmer on medium high heat. Put in 1/2 cheese; beat until smooth. Chill the rest of cheese. Place potatoes in the pot; heat to simmer.
- Move potato mixture to the prepared dish, arranging evenly. Use foil to cover then bake for 15 minutes. Remove cover and bake for 50 minutes, until liquid bubbles thickly and potatoes are very tender.
- Dot remaining cheese over potatoes. Bake for 5 minutes till cheese is softened. Cool for 15 minutes then serve.

Nutrition Information

- Calories: 440
- Total Carbohydrate: 46 g(15%)
- Cholesterol: 67 mg(22%)
- Protein: 13 g(27%)
- Total Fat: 22 g(34%)
- Saturated Fat: 14 g(72%)
- Sodium: 604 mg(25%)
- Fiber: 4 g(15%)

127. Scalloped Yukon Gold And Sweet Potato Gratin With Fresh Herbs

Serving: Makes 12 servings | Prep: | Cook: | Ready in:

Ingredients

- 1 1/2 pounds medium Yukon Gold potatoes
- 1 1/2 pounds medium red-skinned sweet potatoes (yams)
- 2 cups heavy whipping cream
- 1/4 cup (1/2 stick) butter
- 2 garlic cloves, minced
- 1 tablespoon minced fresh Italian parsley
- 1 tablespoon minced fresh rosemary
- 1 tablespoon minced fresh sage
- 1 tablespoon minced fresh thyme
- 1 1/2 teaspoons fine sea salt
- 3/4 teaspoon freshly ground black pepper
- 1 1/4 cups (packed) coarsely grated Gruyére cheese (about 5 ounces)

Direction

- Fill a big bowl using cold water. One by one, peel then cut 1 Yukon gold potato into 1/8-in. thick rounds; put in bowl with water. Repeat using sweet potatoes. Simmer garlic, butter and cream in a medium saucepan. Take off from heat. In a small bowl, mix all herbs. Mix black pepper and sea salt in a separate small bowl.
- Butter a 13x9x2-in. glass baking dish. Drain the potatoes; use kitchen towels to pat dry. Put 1/2 potatoes in a prepped baking dish; evenly spread and distribute with hands. Sprinkle 1/2 pepper-salt mixture then 1/2 herb mixture. Sprinkle 1/2 cheese; repeat with leftover cheese, herb mixture, salt-pepper mixture and potatoes. Put cream on gratin; lightly press to submerge the potato mixture as much as you can. You can make it 6 hours ahead, chilled, covered in plastic wrap. Before baking, remove plastic wrap.
- Preheat an oven to 400°F. Tightly cover gratin with foil; bake for 30 minutes. Uncover; bake

for 25 minutes more till most of the liquid is absorbed and top of gratin becomes golden. Let stand for 10 minutes. Serve

Nutrition Information

- Calories: 473
- Sodium: 437 mg(18%)
- Fiber: 3 g(14%)
- Total Carbohydrate: 25 g(8%)
- Cholesterol: 143 mg(48%)
- Protein: 8 g(17%)
- Total Fat: 40 g(61%)
- Saturated Fat: 23 g(117%)

128. Seafood Cannelloni

Serving: Makes 6 servings | Prep: 1.75hours | Cook: 3.5hours | Ready in:

Ingredients

- 1/3 cup finely chopped shallot
- 2 tablespoons finely chopped carrot
- 2 tablespoons finely chopped celery
- 1 lb medium shrimp in shells (31 to 35 per lb), peeled, reserving shells, and deveined
- 1 lb sea scallops, tough muscle removed from side of each and reserved
- 5 tablespoons unsalted butter, softened
- 1 teaspoon tomato paste
- 1 cup dry white wine
- 3 cups water
- 1 tablespoon seafood glaze* (optional)
- 2 fresh flat-leaf parsley sprigs
- 3 tablespoons all-purpose flour
- 1 cup heavy cream
- 1/2 teaspoon fresh lemon juice, or to taste
- 1 1/2 teaspoons salt
- 1/2 teaspoon black pepper
- 2 tablespoons Cognac
- 1/2 cup finely chopped fresh chives
- 14 (6- by 3-inch) flat fresh or no-boil lasagne noodles (without curly edges)

94

- a 3-quart flameproof rectangular casserole dish (about 13 by 9 inches; not glass)

Direction

- For the sauce, cook the carrot, reserved scallop muscles, reserved shrimp shells, celery, and shallot in a 2-3-qt heavy saucepan with 3 tbsp. of butter over moderately low heat for 5 minutes, uncovered and stirring for some time until the vegetables are pale golden and softened. Add the tomato paste. Cook and stir the mixture for 1 minute. Add the wine. Boil the mixture over high heat for 6-8 minutes while occasionally stirring it until it is reduced to 1/4 cup. Add the water, parsley sprigs, and seafood glaze, if using. Cover the mixture and simmer for 30 minutes.
- Discard the parsley. Working in 2 batches, puree the stock and shrimp shells in a blender (be careful in blending hot liquids). Transfer the mixture into a bowl through the fine-mesh sieve. Make sure to press the solids and discard it after.
- In a clean saucepan, melt leftover 2 tbsp. of butter over moderately low heat. Add the flour and cook and stir over low heat for 3 minutes. Add all the warm seafood stock while stirring the mixture. Bring the mixture to a boil while stirring it. Add 1/2 cup of the cream. Simmer the sauce gently for 10 minutes, stirring it for some time. Mix in 1/4 tsp. of pepper, 1/2 tsp. of salt, and lemon juice.
- Pour 1/2 cup of the sauce into a bowl that is set over a larger bowl. Fill the larger bowl with ice and cold water to cool the filling.
- For the seafood filling, get 1/3 of the scallops and 1/3 of the shrimp. Slice them into 1/4-inch pieces. Toss the slices with 1/4 tsp. of salt. In a food processor, puree the remaining scallops and shrimp together with the cooled 1/2 cup of sauce, Cognac, leftover 1/4 tsp. of pepper, and leftover 3/4 tsp. of salt. Pour in 1/2 cup of cream. Pulse the mixture until just combined. Pour the mousse into a large bowl. Mix in chives and shrimp and scallop slices.
- Cook the pasta and start assembling the cannelloni. Set the oven to 375°F for preheating.
- In a large pot, boil the lasagna noodles, a few at a time, together with salted water for 2 minutes for fresh noodles while 6 minutes for no-boil, stirring the noodles to separate until al dente. Use tongs and a slotted spatula to transfer the noodles into a large bowl with cold water. Allow the noodles to stop cooking. Lift the noodles out, shaking off any excess water, and then lay the noodles flat onto the dry kitchen towels (do not use terry cloth). Drizzle each noodle with 1/3 cup of the mousse. Make sure to leave a 1/2-inch border on all of the short ends. Roll each noodle up loosely, starting from the short end.
- Pour 1/2 cup of the sauce onto the bottom of the casserole dish. Arrange the cannelloni onto the dish snugly in 1 layer, seam-sides down. Drizzle over the remaining sauce. Cover the cannelloni with foil and bake it inside the middle of the oven for 25-30 minutes until the filling is cooked through and the sauce is bubbling. (To test the doneness of the filling, insert a metal skewer into the cannelloni and let it stay there for 5 seconds. Remove the skewer and bring it against your bottom lip, pressing it to your lip of bottom. If the metal is already warm, the filling is already cooked and the casserole is heated through.)
- Set the broiler to preheating.
- Remove the foil and position the cannelloni inside the broiler 3-inches away from the heat. Broil for 3-5 minutes until brown spots appear. Allow it to stand for 10 minutes; serve.
- Note: Ingredients are available in some specialty foods shops or supermarkets.
- Also, the casserole can be assembled 4 hours ahead (not yet baked or broiled). Just let it chilled and covered with a foil. Before baking the casserole, let it stand first at room temperature for 20 minutes.

Nutrition Information

- Calories: 598
- Total Fat: 26 g(41%)
- Saturated Fat: 16 g(78%)
- Sodium: 1003 mg(42%)
- Fiber: 3 g(10%)
- Total Carbohydrate: 54 g(18%)
- Cholesterol: 193 mg(64%)
- Protein: 29 g(58%)

129.　　Serrano Ham And Poblano Corn Pudding

Serving: Makes 12 servings | Prep: | Cook: | Ready in:

Ingredients

- 2 large poblano chiles*
- 2 cups fresh corn kernels (from 2 large ears) or frozen, thawed, divided
- 2 large eggs
- 1/2 cup (1 stick) butter, melted, slightly cooled
- 1 teaspoon salt
- Large pinch of baking powder
- 1 cup sour cream
- 1/2 cup instant corn masa mix (Maseca)**
- 4 ounces 1/4-inch-thick slices Serrano ham or prosciutto, cut into 1/4-inch cubes (about 1 cup)
- 1 cup coarsely grated Manchego cheese (about 4 1/2 ounces)

Direction

- Char chiles in broiler/above gas flame till all sides are blackened. Enclose in paper bag for 15 minutes. Peel then seed chiles; lengthwise cut to 1/4-in. wide strips.
- Preheat an oven to 350°F. Butter 13x9x2-in. glass baking dish lightly. Blend eggs, 1 1/2 cups corn and next 3 ingredients till nearly smooth in blender; put mixture in big bowl. Add Maseca and sour crema; mix till blended. Mix leftover 1/2 cup corn, chiles, cheese and ham in; put mixture in prepped baking dish.

Bake for 40 minutes till golden brown in spots on the top and corn pudding is puffed.

Nutrition Information

- Calories: 226
- Cholesterol: 79 mg(26%)
- Protein: 8 g(16%)
- Total Fat: 17 g(26%)
- Saturated Fat: 10 g(48%)
- Sodium: 401 mg(17%)
- Fiber: 1 g(4%)
- Total Carbohydrate: 12 g(4%)

130.　　Sparerib, Rice And Chick Pea Casserole

Serving: Serves 6 | Prep: | Cook: | Ready in:

Ingredients

- 2 1/2 pounds country-style spareribs
- 1 large onion, chopped
- 4 large garlic cloves, chopped
- 2 14 1/2-ounce cans beef broth
- 2 cups long-grain white rice
- 1 15- to 16-ounce can chick-peas (garbanzo beans), drained
- 2/3 cup water
- 1/3 cup red wine vinegar
- 2 tablespoons chopped fresh cilantro
- 1 tablespoon paprika
- 1 tablespoon dried oregano, crumbled
- 1 4-ounce jar sliced pimientos, drained

Direction

- Start preheating the oven to 350°F. Add pepper and salt to season spareribs. In heavy large Dutch oven, brown spareribs over high heat. Place ribs on plate. Put onion and garlic into pot; sauté for 5 minutes or until onion turns translucent. Put all the remaining ingredients except pimientos into pot. Bring to a boil, scraping up any browned bits. Put the ribs with all the collected juices into pot. Push the ribs into the rice mixture. Add pepper and salt to season. Evenly spread the pimientos on top. Bake, with cover, for 50 minutes or until all the liquids are absorbed and rice and meat become tender.

Nutrition Information

- Calories: 892
- Total Fat: 47 g(72%)
- Saturated Fat: 15 g(73%)
- Sodium: 824 mg(34%)
- Fiber: 6 g(24%)
- Total Carbohydrate: 73 g(24%)
- Cholesterol: 151 mg(50%)
- Protein: 41 g(82%)

131.   Spiced Sweet Potato And Parsnip Tian

Serving: 8–10 servings | Prep: 45mins | Cook: 2.5hours | Ready in:

Ingredients

- 4 cups apple cider
- 1/2 cup (1 stick) unsalted butter
- 2 tablespoons thyme leaves
- 1 tablespoon plus 2 teaspoons Aleppo pepper
- 4 teaspoons kosher salt, divided
- 6 1/2 pounds sweet potatoes (about 8 medium), peeled, sliced into 1/8"-thick rounds
- 2 pounds parsnips (about 3 extra-large), peeled, sliced into 1/8"-thick rounds
- A 4-quart casserole dish or braiser, preferably round

Direction

- In the center of oven, place rack and preheat the oven to 325 °F. In a big saucepan, boil cider over medium-high heat. Lower the heat to

low, put in 2 teaspoon salt, Aleppo, thyme and butter, and let it cook, mixing, till butter is melted. Allow to slightly cool.
- In a big bowl, put parsnips and potatoes. Transfer cider mixture on top and coat by tossing. Stack a handful of slices approximately 3-inch high, then vertically put in the casserole dish. Maintain slices standing up with a small bowl or measuring cup as you proceed, working surrounding the perimeter and then into the middle, making concentric circles. In pan, keep setting slices till securely packed, you may have a few remaining. Add cider mixture to reach midway up the dish sides; throw away leftover cider mixture. Scatter the leftover 2 teaspoon salt and cover securely using foil.
- Let it bake with a cover for an hour. Take off the foil and using a pastry brush, brush over slices surfaces with pan juices. Raise oven temperature to 425 °F and let it bake without a cover for 35 to 40 minutes longer, till golden brown on surface.
- After the first round of baking at 325° F, allow to cool, then refrigerate up to 2 days. Let it come to room temperature, then bake without a cover for 40 to 50 minutes at 425 °F.
- Note: use mandoline to slice parsnips and sweet potatoes if available, it will make them thinner, more equal slices in shorter time compared to using hand. The quantity of parsnips and potatoes needed to fill casserole dish will vary on their width, better to have extra just in case, and try look for parsnips whose width is as close to the sweet potatoes.

Nutrition Information

132.   Spinach And Bechamel Gratin

Serving: Serves 4 | Prep: | Cook: | Ready in:

Ingredients

- 3 10-ounce packages frozen chopped spinach, thawed
- 5 tablespoons butter
- 2 tablespoons flour
- 1/2 cup whipping cream
- 1/2 cup milk
- Pinch of ground nutmeg
- Pinch of ground cloves
- 2/3 cup grated manchego or Parmesan cheese

Direction

- Set the oven at 375°F and start preheating. Coat an 8- or 9-inch glass pie dish lightly with butter. Squeeze spinach very dry. Place a heavy, medium skillet on medium-high heat and melt 3 tablespoons of butter. Include in the spinach; sauté for 3 minutes. Season with pepper and salt. Evenly spread the spinach in the prepared pie dish.
- Place a heavy, medium saucepan on medium heat and melt the remaining 2 tablespoons of butter. Include in flour and whisk for 2 minutes; do not allow the mixture to turn brown. Slowly include in cream, then milk; whisk till smooth. Cook while whisking frequently till the sauce thicken, around 6 minutes. Include in cloves and nutmeg. Season with pepper and salt.
- Spoon the sauce over the spinach. Sprinkle with cheese. Bake for around 15 minutes, or till the sauce bubbles and the cheese turns golden.

Nutrition Information

- Calories: 370
- Saturated Fat: 19 g(94%)
- Sodium: 453 mg(19%)
- Fiber: 5 g(19%)
- Total Carbohydrate: 14 g(5%)
- Cholesterol: 87 mg(29%)
- Protein: 15 g(30%)
- Total Fat: 30 g(47%)

133. Spinach And Roasted Red Pepper Gratin

Serving: Makes 8 servings | Prep: | Cook: | Ready in:

Ingredients

- 4 10-ounce bags fresh spinach leaves
- 3 red bell peppers
- 1 1/2 tablespoons butter
- 1 1/2 tablespoons olive oil
- 3 medium leeks (white and pale green parts only), thinly sliced (about 3 cups)
- 1 large shallot, chopped (about 1/4 cup)
- 3 garlic cloves, minced
- 1 cup whipping cream
- 4 large eggs
- 1 cup part-skim ricotta cheese
- 1/2 cup grated Swiss cheese
- 1/4 cup grated Parmesan cheese
- 1 1/2 teaspoons salt
- 1/2 teaspoon ground black pepper

Direction

- Heat a deep big nonstick skillet on medium high heat; 10 cups at a time, sauté fresh spinach in batches in dry skillet for about 2 minutes per batch till wilted and bright green. Put spinach into a strainer; squeeze dry spinach, rolling in kitchen towel to get rid of excess water.
- Char peppers directly above gas flame or in broiler till all sides are blackened. In paper bag, enclose; stand for 10 minutes. Peel then seed peppers; cut into 1/4-in. wide strips.
- Melt oil and butter in a big heavy skillet on medium heat. Add garlic, shallot and leeks; cook for about 5 minutes till soft. Take off the heat. Whisk eggs and cream to blend in a big bowl; whisk in pepper, salt and all cheeses. Mix in 2/3 of roasted red peppers (keep 1/3 of peppers for topping), leek mixture and spinach. You can make it 1 day ahead, refrigerated, covered.

- Preheat an oven to 350°F and butter a 13x9x2-in. baking dish generously. Put spinach mixture into a prepped dish; bake gratin for approximately 50 minutes till an inserted knife in the middle exits clean. Decoratively put the leftover red pepper strips on top of gratin; serve.

Nutrition Information

- Calories: 319
- Saturated Fat: 13 g(64%)
- Sodium: 679 mg(28%)
- Fiber: 5 g(18%)
- Total Carbohydrate: 14 g(5%)
- Cholesterol: 156 mg(52%)
- Protein: 15 g(31%)
- Total Fat: 24 g(37%)

134. Stilton Potato Gratin

Serving: Serves 6 | Prep: | Cook: | Ready in:

Ingredients

- 2 1/2 pounds russet potatoes (about 5 medium), peeled, thinly sliced
- 8 ounces Stilton cheese or other blue cheese, crumbled
- 1 1/3 cups canned low-salt chicken broth
- 2 tablespoons (1/4 stick) butter, cut into small pieces

Direction

- Set an oven to preheat to 350 degrees F. Grease a 13x9x2-inch glass baking dish with butter. In the bottom of the pan, lay 1/3 of the potato slices, overlapping it a bit. Sprinkle 1/2 of the cheese on top of the potatoes, then sprinkle with pepper and salt. Lay 1/2 of the leftover slices of potato on top of the cheese, overlapping a bit. Sprinkle the leftover cheese on top, then sprinkle with pepper and salt. Decoratively lay the leftover slices of potato on

top of the cheese, then pour the broth on top. Sprinkle pepper and salt on top. Dot butter over the potatoes.
- Bake the potatoes for about an hour and 40 minutes, until the liquid becomes thick, the potatoes become tender and the top turns golden brown, tilting the pan from time to time to baste broth mixture on the top layer of the potatoes.
- Move the pan to a rack and allow to stand for 5 minutes. Serve while still hot.

Nutrition Information

- Calories: 325
- Fiber: 2 g(10%)
- Total Carbohydrate: 36 g(12%)
- Cholesterol: 39 mg(13%)
- Protein: 13 g(26%)
- Total Fat: 15 g(23%)
- Saturated Fat: 10 g(48%)
- Sodium: 459 mg(19%)

135. Sweet Potato, Onion, And Apple Gratin

Serving: Makes 6 servings | Prep: | Cook: | Ready in:

Ingredients

- 4 pounds red-skinned sweet potatoes (yams), peeled, cut into 1/4-inch-thick rounds, divided
- 1 large onion, halved, thinly sliced, divided
- 3 large Granny Smith apples (about 1 1/2 pounds), peeled, cored, cut into 1/4-inch-thick slices, divided
- 2 tablespoons fresh lime juice, divided
- 2 tablespoons (packed) dark brown sugar, divided
- 1 cup whipping cream, divided
- 3 tablespoons butter, divided

Direction

- Preheat an oven to 400°F. Butter then flour a 15x10x2-in. baking dish; on bottom of the dish, spread 1/3 potato slices. Put 1/2 onion slices then 1/2 apple slices on top; sprinkle 1/3 cup cream, 1 tbsp. sugar and 1 tbsp. lime juice. Dot using 1 tbsp. butter; sprinkle pepper and salt. Repeat the layers. Put leftover potato slices over; drizzle with leftover 1/3 cup cream. Use leftover 1 tbsp. butter to dot potatoes; sprinkle pepper and salt.
- Use foil to cover the dish; bake for 45 minutes till apples and potatoes are tender. Put oven temperature on 500°F; remove the foil. Bake for 10 minutes till potatoes are golden brown.

Nutrition Information

- Calories: 515
- Total Fat: 18 g(28%)
- Saturated Fat: 11 g(57%)
- Sodium: 184 mg(8%)
- Fiber: 12 g(49%)
- Total Carbohydrate: 83 g(28%)
- Cholesterol: 59 mg(20%)
- Protein: 6 g(13%)

---

136. Sweet Potato, Swiss Chard, And Quinoa Gratin

Serving: Serves 6 | Prep: | Cook: |Ready in:

Ingredients

- 1 1/2 pounds sweet potatoes (about 3)
- 1 cup quinoa*
- 4 tablespoons olive oil
- 2 cups coarse fresh breadcrumbs
- 2 1/2 pounds Swiss chard, washed well and stems trimmed, removed, and reserved
- 3 tablespoons minced garlic (about 6 cloves), or to taste
- *available at natural foods stores and specialty foods shops

Direction

- Preheat an oven to 450 °F and with butter, grease a shallow baking dish, 2 quarts in size.
- With fork, puncture every potato thrice and in center of the oven, let bake for an hour on sheet, or till extremely soft.
- Meanwhile, rinse quinoa in a bowl in a minimum of 5 replaces of cold water, massaging grains and allowing to set prior to removing most of water, till the water runs clear and drain in a fine sieve.
- Mix 2 cups of salted water and quinoa in a saucepan and boil. Let quinoa simmer with a cover for 15 minutes, till entire liquid is soaked in, and take off lid.
- Heat a tablespoon of oil in a skillet over medium heat and let bread crumbs cook till golden brown. Add pepper and salt to crumbs to season.
- Meanwhile, slice reserved stems of Swiss chard finely and roughly slice the leaves, store both individually. Heat leftover 3 tablespoons of oil in heavy deep 12 inches kettle heat over medium heat and let stems cook for 5 minutes till soft. Mix in leaves, one handful at a time, and mix in the garlic, tossing. Let leaves cook for 4 minutes till barely wilted. Take the kettle off heat and mix in the quinoa till incorporated thoroughly. Add pepper and salt to the mixture to season.
- Lower temperature to 350° F.
- Once potatoes are cool enough to touch, remove skin and crush using a fork. Add pepper and salt to potatoes to season.
- In a baking dish using big spoon, drop piles of Swiss chard mixture and potatoes, alternate them in a decorative manner to cover base, and level the surface. Put bread crumbs over gratin.
- In center of oven, let gratin bake for 30 minutes, or till hot. Allow gratin to cool 5 minutes prior to serving.

Nutrition Information

- Calories: 464

- Saturated Fat: 2 g(10%)
- Sodium: 731 mg(30%)
- Fiber: 10 g(40%)
- Total Carbohydrate: 75 g(25%)
- Protein: 14 g(28%)
- Total Fat: 13 g(20%)

137.   Sweet Potato Gratins

Serving: Makes 12 servings | Prep: | Cook: | Ready in:

Ingredients

- 1 tablespoon unsalted butter, at room temperature
- 2 large sweet potatoes, peeled and thinly sliced (use a sharp knife, a mandoline, or a food processor with the slicing disc attached)
- 1/2 large Idaho potato, peeled and thinly sliced
- 1 cup heavy cream
- 1 pinch ground nutmeg
- 1 pinch freshly ground black pepper
- Kosher salt to taste
- 3 ounces Gruyère, grated (about 1 cup)

Direction

- Preheat an oven to 400 °F. Butter a 12-capacity muffin pan.
- Toss together salt, pepper, nutmeg, cream, Idaho potato and sweet potatoes in a big bowl.
- Set slices of potato in every muffin cup till 3/4 full, then put any leftover cream to top the muffin cups. Scatter some of cheese on every gratin. With tinfoil, loosely cover the pan and let bake for 20 minutes.
- Uncover and continue to bake for 10 to 15 minutes longer till cheese turn golden brown and potatoes are easily prick with fork. Take out and cool for 5 minutes prior to serving.

Nutrition Information

- Calories: 158
- Saturated Fat: 7 g(36%)
- Sodium: 173 mg(7%)
- Fiber: 1 g(5%)
- Total Carbohydrate: 9 g(3%)
- Cholesterol: 42 mg(14%)
- Protein: 4 g(9%)
- Total Fat: 12 g(18%)

138.   Swiss Chard Gratin

Serving: Makes 6 servings | Prep: 1.25hours | Cook: 1.75hours | Ready in:

Ingredients

- 5 tablespoons unsalted butter
- 1 cup fresh white bread crumbs
- 3 oz Tomme de Savoie or Gruyère cheese, grated (1 cup)
- 1 garlic clove, halved lengthwise, germ removed if green, and garlic finely chopped
- 1 tablespoon finely chopped mixed fresh herbs (preferably chives, tarragon, and flat-leaf parsley)
- 1/8 teaspoon freshly grated nutmeg
- 1 cup low-sodium chicken broth
- 1/2 cup heavy cream
- 1 tablespoon all-purpose flour
- 1 medium onion, finely chopped
- 3 lb Swiss chard, leaves and stems separated and both cut into 1-inch pieces
- 1 lb spinach, coarse stems discarded, leaves coarsely chopped

Direction

- Melt 2 tbsp. butter; toss with pepper and salt to taste, 1/2 of nutmeg, herbs, garlic, cheese and bread crumbs in a bowl.
- In a small saucepan, boil broth till reduced by half then add cream; keep warm.
- In a heavy small saucepan, melt 1 tbsp. butter on moderate heat; mix in flour. Cook the roux for 1 minute, whisking. Whisk in broth

mixture; boil for 1 minute, whisking. Season sauce using pepper and salt.

- Preheat an oven to 400°F.
- Cook onion in the leftover 2 tbsp. butter in an 8-qt. heavy wide pot on moderately low heat till soft while mixing. Add pepper and salt to taste, the leftover nutmeg and chard stems; cook for approximately 8 minutes till veggies are tender but not brown while mixing.
- Put heat on moderately high. By big handfuls, add spinach and chard leaves, mixing, till all greens get wilted. Season with pepper and salt.
- To drain well, put veggies into a colander; use back of a big spoon to press out liquid. Toss cream sauce and veggies; put into a 2-qt. shallow baking pan or buttered 12-in. oval gratin, evenly spreading.
- Put breadcrumbs on veggies; bake in center of oven for about 20 minutes till topping is golden and bubbly.
- You can prep gratin 4 hours ahead without baking, covered, chilled. Before baking, bring to room temperature.
- For the gratin to not get wet, drain as much liquid as you can from the veggies.

Nutrition Information

- Calories: 395
- Fiber: 6 g(26%)
- Total Carbohydrate: 28 g(9%)
- Cholesterol: 77 mg(26%)
- Protein: 17 g(34%)
- Total Fat: 26 g(40%)
- Saturated Fat: 15 g(76%)
- Sodium: 854 mg(36%)

139.   Tarragon Scallop Gratins

Serving: 2 Servings; Can be doubled | Prep: | Cook: | Ready in:

Ingredients

- 8 ounces bay scallops
- 2 tablespoons olive oil
- 2 tablespoons dry white wine or vermouth
- 1 large shallot, chopped
- 1 tablespoon chopped fresh tarragon or 1 teaspoon dried
- 1/3 cup fresh breadcrumbs

Direction

- Begin preheating the oven to 450 degrees F. In a medium bowl, mix tarragon, chopped shallot, olive oil, white wine, olive oil and scallops together. Add pepper and salt to season. Combine until blended. Distribute the mixture into 2 small gratin plates. Add on each an equal sprinkle of fresh breadcrumbs.
- Bake for about 15 minutes until crumbs turn golden and scallops are opaque and just heated through.

Nutrition Information

- Calories: 312
- Cholesterol: 27 mg(9%)
- Protein: 17 g(35%)
- Total Fat: 15 g(23%)
- Saturated Fat: 2 g(11%)
- Sodium: 583 mg(24%)
- Fiber: 2 g(9%)
- Total Carbohydrate: 24 g(8%)

140.   Tortilla Pie

Serving: Makes 4 main-course servings | Prep: 20mins | Cook: 35mins | Ready in:

Ingredients

- 1 (15-oz) can black beans, drained and rinsed
- 1 (10-oz) package frozen corn kernels, thawed
- 1 cup mild tomato salsa
- 1 (8-oz) can tomato sauce

- 6 oz pepper Jack cheese, coarsely grated (2 cups)
- 1/2 cup chopped fresh cilantro
- 2 scallions, thinly sliced
- 1/2 teaspoon ground cumin
- 4 (10-inch) flour tortillas (burrito-size)
- 1 tablespoon olive oil
- Accompaniment: sour cream

Direction

- To make the preparation: Position the oven rack in lower third of oven and preheat oven to 450 degrees F.
- In a big bowl, mix cumin, scallions, cilantro, cheese, tomato sauce, salsa, corn and beans.
- Heat one 12-in. heavy skillet on high heat till smoking. Brush both sides of each tortilla using oil and fry, flipping one time, for roughly 1 minute or till puffed and golden in spots.
- Add one tortilla into a well-oiled 15x10-in. shallow baking pan, and then spread with 1 1/3 cups of filling. Repeat the layers two times, and then add the leftover tortillas on top, pushing lightly to help layers adhere.
- Bake for roughly 12 minutes or till filling is thoroughly heated. Move using a big metal spatula to a platter, then chop the pie into wedges using a serrated knife.

Nutrition Information

- Calories: 679
- Cholesterol: 59 mg(20%)
- Protein: 30 g(60%)
- Total Fat: 29 g(44%)
- Saturated Fat: 14 g(70%)
- Sodium: 1260 mg(53%)
- Fiber: 11 g(46%)
- Total Carbohydrate: 76 g(25%)

141.   Turkey Tetrazzini

Serving: 6 | Prep: 25mins | Cook: 25mins | Ready in:

Ingredients

- 2 (8 ounce) packages angel hair pasta
- 1/4 cup butter
- 2/3 cup sliced onion
- 1/4 cup all-purpose flour
- 2 cups milk
- 1 teaspoon salt
- 1/4 teaspoon ground white pepper
- 1/2 teaspoon poultry seasoning
- 1/4 teaspoon ground mustard
- 1 cup shredded sharp Cheddar cheese, divided
- 2 tablespoons chopped pimento peppers (optional)
- 1 (4.5 ounce) can sliced mushrooms
- 1 pound cooked turkey, sliced

Direction

- Preheat oven to 200 °C or 400 °F. In a big pot, let lightly salted water boil. Put pasta and cook until almost tender or for 4 minutes. Drain it.
- Over medium heat, melt butter in a saucepan. Put onion, then cook and stir until tender. Mix the flour in until blended. Stir milk in gradually to avoid lumps from forming. Use mustard, poultry seasoning, pepper and salt to season. Over medium heat, cook it until the mixture thickens, stirring constantly. Move it away from heat and add pimento and 2/3 cup of cheese. Keep on stirring until cheese melts. In cheese sauce, put undrained mushrooms.
- At the bottom of 9x13 inch baking dish, put a layer of pasta. Put a layer of turkey to cover and put a layer of cheese sauce. Repeat the layers. Over top, sprinkle remaining 1/3 cup of cheese.
- In the preheated oven, bake for about 25 minutes until cheese on top is toasted and until sauce is bubbly.

Nutrition Information

- Calories: 604 calories;
- Cholesterol: 113
- Protein: 38.9
- Total Fat: 26.4
- Sodium: 914
- Total Carbohydrate: 52.1

142. Vegetable Casserole With Tofu Topping

Serving: Makes 6 to 8 side-dish servings | Prep: | Cook: | Ready in:

Ingredients

- 2 tablespoons olive oil
- 2 medium onions, halved lengthwise and thinly sliced lengthwise
- 1 lb cabbage, cored and cut crosswise into 1/3-inch-thick slices (4 cups)
- 1 lb kale, stems and center ribs removed and leaves coarsely chopped (12 cups)
- 1/2 lb carrots, cut into 1/4-inch-thick matchsticks
- 1/2 cup water
- 2 tablespoons soy sauce
- 1/2 teaspoon salt
- 1 1/2 cups fine fresh or dried bread crumbs, preferably whole wheat
- 7 oz firm tofu
- 1 oz finely grated Parmigiano-Reggiano (1/2 cup)
- 1/3 cup olive oil
- 2 teaspoons dried basil, crumbled
- 1 1/2 teaspoons dried oregano, crumbled
- 1 teaspoon paprika
- 1 garlic clove, chopped
- 1/4 teaspoon salt

Direction

- Sauté vegetables: In middle position, put oven rack and set the oven at 350°F.
- Over moderately high heat, heat oil in a deep 12- to 14-inch heavy skillet until hot (but not

smoking); add onion and sauté for about 5 minutes, stirring often, until tender and starting to brown. Reduce the heat to moderate, then add carrots, kale, cabbage, salt, soy sauce, and water. (The skillet will be full, but the volume will reduce once the vegetable is steamed.) Cover and cook for 10 to 15 minutes, stirring often, or until the greens are just tender. Then transfer to a 13- by 9-inch glass baking dish.
- To make the topping: In a food processor, pulse all topping ingredients until well combined. Alternatively, in a large bowl, use a potato masher to mash the ingredients together. In a baking dish, sprinkle over the vegetables with the tofu mixture; bake without cover for 15 to 20 minutes, or until the greens are heated through and the topping is golden brown.

Nutrition Information

- Calories: 422
- Saturated Fat: 4 g(18%)
- Sodium: 709 mg(30%)
- Fiber: 11 g(44%)
- Total Carbohydrate: 48 g(16%)
- Cholesterol: 3 mg(1%)
- Protein: 15 g(30%)
- Total Fat: 22 g(34%)

143. Vegetarian Cassoulet

Serving: 8 | Prep: 20mins | Cook: 9hours | Ready in:

Ingredients

- 2 tablespoons olive oil
- 1 onion
- 2 carrots, peeled and diced
- 1 pound dry navy beans, soaked overnight
- 4 cups mushroom broth
- 1 cube vegetable bouillon
- 1 bay leaf

- 4 sprigs fresh parsley
- 1 sprig fresh rosemary
- 1 sprig fresh lemon thyme, chopped
- 1 sprig fresh savory
- 1 large potato, peeled and cubed

Direction

- In a skillet, heat a little oil over medium heat. In oil, cook and stir carrots and onion until tender.
- Combine bay leaf, bouillon, mushroom broth, onion, carrots, and beans in a slow cooker. Add water to cover ingredients if needed. Tie savory, thyme, rosemary, and parsley together, put into the pot. Choose Low setting, cook for 8 hours.
- Mix in potato, keep cooking 1 more hour. Take away herbs then serve.

Nutrition Information

- Calories: 279 calories;
- Sodium: 141
- Total Carbohydrate: 47.2
- Cholesterol: 0
- Protein: 15.3
- Total Fat: 4.4

144. Winter Greens Gratin

Serving: Makes 8 to 10 servings | Prep: | Cook: | Ready in:

Ingredients

- 1 tablespoon unsalted butter plus more for dish
- 2 pounds kale, center ribs and stems removed, torn into large pieces, or two 10-ounce bags trimmed, chopped kale (about 24 cups)
- Kosher salt
- 2 1/2 pounds mustard greens, center ribs and stems removed, torn into large pieces
- 1/4 cup extra-virgin olive oil
- 3 cups coarse fresh breadcrumbs
- 1/2 cup finely grated Parmesan
- 2 teaspoons fresh thyme leaves, divided, plus 7 sprigs thyme
- 2 shallots, sliced into 1/4"-thick rounds (about 1 cup)
- 1 cup heavy cream
- 1 cup whole milk
- 7 garlic cloves, smashed
- 1/8 teaspoon freshly ground nutmeg
- Freshly ground black pepper
- 1 cup coarsely grated Gruyère

Direction

- Lightly brush over a 3-qt. baking dish with butter. Working in batches, blanch kale in a pot with boiling lightly salted water for 3 minutes until barely tender. Remove the kale into a big bowl with ice water using a slotted spoon; allow to cool, and then strain. Using your hands; extract as much excess liquid as you can and remove the kale onto a work surface.
- Do the same with mustard greens, blanching for 2 minutes each batch. Cut all the greens coarsely and mix in a big bowl (you should prepare 6 cups tightly packed of greens). Using your hands, separate loosen chopped leaves and clumps.
- In a 12-in. frying pan, heat oil over medium heat. Add breadcrumbs and cook for 8-10 minutes until crunchy and turning golden, tossing often. Remove into a big bowl; mix in 1 teaspoon thyme leaves and Parmesan. You can prepare the breadcrumbs and greens 2 days in advance. Put a cover on the greens and refrigerate. Preserve the breadcrumbs airtight at room temperature.
- In a medium-sized saucepan, melt 1 tablespoon butter over medium-high heat. Add shallots, cook for 5 minutes until turning light golden and tender a bit, tossing frequently. Transfer the shallots to the greens in the bowl. Add thyme sprigs, garlic, milk, and cream to the same saucepan; simmer it.

Cook for 10-12 minutes until the mixture has decreased to 1 1/2 cups and thickened. Remove the garlic and thyme sprigs, mix in nutmeg. Use pepper and salt to season.

- Add cream mixture to the bowl with the greens and to mix to evenly blend in the sauce, use pepper and salt to season to taste. Transfer the greens mixture into the prepared baking dish; sprinkle with Gruyère. Put breadcrumbs on top. Use a foil to cover the dish. You can assemble the gratin 1 day in advance.
- Start preheating the oven to 400°F. Bake for 25 minutes until the filling is hot. Remove the cover and bake for another 10-20 minutes until the breadcrumbs turn golden brown, the edges are bubbly, and the cheese melts. Use the leftover 1 teaspoon thyme leaves to garnish.

Nutrition Information

- Calories: 561
- Saturated Fat: 14 g(71%)
- Sodium: 946 mg(39%)
- Fiber: 11 g(45%)
- Total Carbohydrate: 52 g(17%)
- Cholesterol: 71 mg(24%)
- Protein: 24 g(48%)
- Total Fat: 31 g(48%)

---

145.   Yellow Squash And Bell Pepper Torte

Serving: Makes 6 (side dish) servings | Prep: 40mins | Cook: 8hours | Ready in:

Ingredients

- 4 yellow bell peppers, halved lengthwise, stemmed, and seeded
- 5 to 6 tablespoons olive oil, divided
- 6 garlic cloves, thinly sliced
- 2 pounds yellow squash (4 medium), sliced diagonally 1/2 inch thick, divided

- 1 pound red onions (2 medium), cut crosswise into 1/3-inch-thick rounds
- 3 tablespoons red-wine vinegar
- 1/2 cup grated Parmigiano-Reggiano
- 1/3 cup chopped basil
- Equipment: an 8- to 9-inch springform pan
- Garnish: Parmigiano-Reggiano shavings and basil leaves

Direction

- Put the rack in the center of the oven and preheat the oven to 425°F.
- In a 17x11-in. sheet pan with 4 sides, combine bell peppers with 1/4 teaspoon pepper, 1/2 teaspoon salt, and 1 tablespoon oil. Roast for 25-30 minutes until tender, turning 1 time.
- As the bell peppers are roasting, in a 12-in. heavy frying pan, heat garlic with 3 tablespoons oil over medium heat until the oil is hot. Add 1/3 the squash with 1/4 teaspoon pepper and 1/4 teaspoon pepper salt and cook for 6-8 minutes in total until barely soft, turning 1 time (make sure to not overcook). Using a slotted spoon, remove the garlic with the cooked squash to a tray. Repeat in 2 batches with the rest of the squash with pepper and salt, using extra 1 tablespoon oil if needed and removing the squash to the tray.
- Add 1 tablespoon oil to the frying pan and cook onions with 1/2 teaspoon pepper and 1/2 teaspoon salt for 16-18 minutes until barely soft, tossing sometimes. Add vinegar and quickly simmer until the liquid evaporates. Allow to cool to room temperature.
- Invert the bottom of a springform pan to turn the lip down (this will make the torte slide off more easily), then secure in place. Briefly oil the pan. In the pan, lay 1/3 squash and the garlic, partially overlapping. Sprinkle some of the basil and grated cheese over. Place over the squash with 1/2 bell peppers, and then 1/2 onions and extra cheese and basil. Continue with all of the leftover onions and 1/2 of the leftover squash, and all of the leftover bell peppers, sprinkling the leftover

basil and cheese over. Put on top with the last layer of squash.

- In a small baking pan, put the springform pan and use plastic wrap to cover the springform. Top the vegetables with a small dish (the dish should fit inside springform just right), and then put on 2-3 heavy cans (15-19- ounces) to weigh down. Refrigerate for a minimum of 6 hours until chilled (the torte will release liquid).
- Take away the plastic wrap, plate, and weights. Take the torte out of the pan and put on a dish. Tap dry any excess liquid. Let the torte warm to room temperature and slice into wedges.
- Note: You can refrigerate the torte in the pan for a maximum of 2 days (remove the weights once the torte has chilled for 12 hours).

Nutrition Information

- Calories: 277
- Saturated Fat: 3 g(17%)
- Sodium: 141 mg(6%)
- Fiber: 5 g(19%)
- Total Carbohydrate: 32 g(11%)
- Cholesterol: 6 mg(2%)
- Protein: 7 g(14%)
- Total Fat: 15 g(24%)

146. Yukon Gold Potato Gratin With Horseradish & Parmesan

Serving: Makes 10 (side-dish) servings | Prep: | Cook: | Ready in:

Ingredients

- 1 bunch fresh thyme
- 1 tablespoon black peppercorns
- 1 dried bay leaf

- 3 pounds boiling potatoes, such as Yukon Gold, peeled and cut crosswise into 1/8-inch slices
- 2 tablespoons sea salt
- 5 garlic cloves, peeled and smashed with back of knife
- 4 cups heavy cream
- 1/4 cup fresh horseradish, grated
- 1 1/2 cups Parmesan cheese, coarsely grated

Direction

- Put rack in middle position. Preheat an oven to 400°F.
- Butter a 2 1/2 - 3-qt. gratin dish/other shallow baking dish generously.
- Wrap bay leaf, peppercorns and thyme in a 6-in. cheese cloth square and secure with kitchen string to make a bouquet garni.
- Mix cream, garlic cloves, salt, bouquet garni and potatoes in a heavy 6-qt. saucepan on medium heat; boil. Lower heat to low; simmer for 10 minutes, uncovered, till potatoes can get pierced with a fork. Remove garlic and bouquet garni with a slotted spoon; discard. Mix horseradish in.
- In buttered dish, spread potato mixture. Sprinkle with cheese. Bake for 30-40 minutes till potatoes are tender and top is golden brown. Before serving, let stand for 15 minutes.

Nutrition Information

- Calories: 453
- Protein: 10 g(19%)
- Total Fat: 40 g(61%)
- Saturated Fat: 25 g(124%)
- Sodium: 432 mg(18%)
- Fiber: 2 g(8%)
- Total Carbohydrate: 16 g(5%)
- Cholesterol: 142 mg(47%)

147. Yukon Gold Potato And Wild Mushroom Gratin

Serving: Makes 8 servings | Prep: | Cook: | Ready in:

Ingredients

- 6 tablespoons (3/4 stick) butter
- 12 ounces assorted fresh wild mushrooms, sliced
- 3 pounds Yukon Gold potatoes
- 1 1/2 teaspoons salt
- 3/4 teaspoon ground black pepper
- 2 cups heavy whipping cream

Direction

- Start preheating the oven to 375°F. In a big, heavy frying pan, heat butter over medium-high heat. Put in mushrooms and sauté for 6 minutes until tender and turning brown. Liberally brush over an 11x7x2-inch baking dish with butter. Peel the skin and slice the potatoes into slices, about 1/8-in. thick each slice. In the prepared dish, arrange the potatoes into 2 layers. Spoon over the potatoes with 1/3 of the mushrooms. Sprinkle 1/4 teaspoon pepper and 1/2 teaspoon salt over. Continue layering the potatoes, the mushrooms, and pepper, salt until having 2 more layers. Add cream to the potatoes. Use a foil to cover and bake for 45 minutes (You can prepare 2 hours in advance. Allow to sit at room temperature). Remove the cover and keep baking for another 20 minutes until set and turning golden brown (for 30 minutes if at room temperature). Allow to sit before eating, about 10 minutes.

Nutrition Information

- Calories: 664
- Fiber: 5 g(22%)
- Total Carbohydrate: 37 g(12%)
- Cholesterol: 203 mg(68%)
- Protein: 8 g(16%)
- Total Fat: 57 g(88%)

- Saturated Fat: 34 g(168%)
- Sodium: 491 mg(20%)

148. Zucchini Lasagna

Serving: 12 | Prep: 30mins | Cook: 1hours | Ready in:

Ingredients

- 9 lasagna noodles
- 3 cubes chicken bouillon
- 2 cups boiling water
- 1/2 cup butter
- 1 large onion, finely chopped
- 2 teaspoons minced garlic
- 1/2 cup all-purpose flour
- 1 teaspoon salt
- 1 1/2 cups milk
- 6 ounces cream cheese, cubed
- 2 large carrots, finely chopped
- 1/2 cup chopped fresh basil
- 1/2 teaspoon ground black pepper
- 2 cups small curd cottage cheese, divided
- 1 large zucchini, cut into 1/8-inch thick rounds
- 1 cup grated Parmesan cheese, divided
- 2 cups shredded mozzarella cheese, divided

Direction

- Let oven warm up to 350°F or to 175°C. Prepare a 9x13-inch baking sheet and coat with grease.
- Let a pot of salted water boil then cook lasagna noodles one by one. Over medium heat, slowly stir noodles to restrain from sticking to each other. Let it boil for 8 to 9 minutes until al dente. Use strainer to drain and let it set in the sink.
- In the boiling water, melt bouillon cube and put aside.
- Dissolve butter in a big skillet over medium fire then stir onion and garlic until brown for ten minutes. Lower down heat if needed to refrain burning the vegetables. In the same skillet, mix in flour and then add chicken

bouillon mixture then add milk little by little while stirring to make the sauce smooth. Mix in cream cheese then stir until it melts and combines into the sauce. Mix in black pepper, basil and carrots; lower heat and let it simmer until just under a boil. Take off from the heat.

- Even out one cup of sauce into the bottom of the baking dish. On top, arrange 3 lasagna noodles. Even out one cup of cottage cheese and then pour one more cup of the sauce. Halve the sliced zucchini and then spread on top of the sauce. Dash it with 1/3 cup of parmesan cheese. Dash 2/3 cup of mozzarella cheese. Create two more layers and finish it off with 3 lasagna noodles, a cup of sauce and remaining 1/3 Parmesan cheese and 2/3 cup mozzarella cheese. Then wrap dish with a foil.

- Let bake in a warmed up oven until it becomes hot and forms bubbles for about 35 minutes. Take off foil and put it back inside the oven. Allow it to bake for another 15 minutes until cheese becomes golden brown. Wait for 10 minutes to cool and then serve.

Nutrition Information

- Calories: 349 calories;
- Total Fat: 20.4
- Sodium: 975
- Total Carbohydrate: 24.4
- Cholesterol: 62
- Protein: 17.7

---

149.   Zucchini And Sausage Casserole

Serving: Makes 10 (side dish) or 6 (main dish) servings | Prep: | Cook: | Ready in:

Ingredients

- 2 pounds zucchini or yellow squash, coarsely grated
- 3/4 pound sage sausage
- 3/4 pound hot sausage
- 2 onions, chopped
- 3 garlic cloves, chopped
- 1 cup heavy cream
- 1 cup fresh bread crumbs
- 5 large eggs, lightly beaten
- 2 to 3 cups grated sharp cheddar cheese
- 2 cups chopped pecans
- Salt
- Freshly ground pepper
- Hot sauce
- 6 tablespoons butter, melted
- 3/4 cup fresh bread crumbs
- 3/4 cup chopped pecans
- 1/2 cup grated cheddar cheese

Direction

- Start preheating the oven to 350°F. Spray nonstick spray over or grease a wide, a 2-qt. baking dish.
- Strain zucchini in a colander for approximately 30 minutes or you can use a clean tea towel to wrap the zucchini and lightly squeeze it to extract the excess liquid. In a big mixing bowl, put the zucchini.
- Heat a big frying pan and add hot sausage and sage sausage. Cook until the sausage begins to turn brown, tossing to crumble it. Reserve 3 tablespoons grease and discard the rest. Put in onions and cook for 5 minutes until tender. Mix in garlic and cook for another 1 minute. Mix the zucchini with the onions and sausage.
- Mix in 2 cups pecans, 2-3 cups cheese, eggs, 1 cup bread crumbs, and cream. Add hot sauce, pepper, and salt to taste. Add the mixture to the baking dish. At this stage, you can chill the casserole for a maximum of 2 days or frozen for a maximum of 3 months.
- To prepare the topping, mix together 3/4 cup pecans, 3/4 cup bread crumbs, and butter. Evenly sprinkle the mixture over the casserole. Bake without a cover for 30 minutes until fully hot. Sprinkle 1/2 cup cheese over the top and put back into the oven until the cheese turns light brown and melts.

Nutrition Information

- Calories: 823
- Fiber: 5 g(21%)
- Total Carbohydrate: 26 g(9%)
- Cholesterol: 226 mg(75%)
- Protein: 29 g(58%)
- Total Fat: 69 g(107%)
- Saturated Fat: 25 g(123%)
- Sodium: 914 mg(38%)

Chapter 3: Chicken Casserole Recipes

***

---

150.   2 For 1 Chicken Tetrazzini

Serving: 2 casseroles (3-4 servings each). | Prep: 30mins | Cook: 20mins | Ready in:

Ingredients

- 1 package (12 ounces) spaghetti
- 1/3 cup butter, cubed
- 1/3 cup all-purpose flour
- 3/4 teaspoon salt
- 1/4 teaspoon white pepper
- 1 can (14-1/2 ounces) chicken broth
- 1-1/2 cups half-and-half cream
- 1 cup heavy whipping cream
- 4 cups cubed cooked chicken
- 3 cans (4 ounces each) mushroom stems and pieces, drained
- 1 jar (4 ounces) sliced pimientos, drained
- 1/2 cup grated Parmesan cheese

Direction

- Follow the package instructions to cook spaghetti. Meanwhile, melt butter in a Dutch oven. Mix in pepper, salt and flour till smooth. Slowly put in whipping cream, half-and-half and broth. Boil the mixture; cook while stirring till thicken, 2 minutes.
- Take away from the heat. Mix in pimientos, mushrooms and chicken. Strain the spaghetti; put into the chicken mixture; toss to coat.
- Transfer into two 11x7-inch baking sheets coated with grease. Sprinkle cheese on top. Freeze one casserole with a cover for up to 2 months. Bake the second casserole without a cover, at 350°, till heated through, 20-25 minutes.
- To use the frozen casserole: Place in the refrigerator to thaw overnight. Bake with a cover at 350° for 30 minutes. Remove cover and bake till heated through, 15-20 more minutes. Mix before serving.

Nutrition Information

- Calories: 572 calories
- Total Carbohydrate: 40g carbohydrate (4g sugars
- Cholesterol: 150mg cholesterol
- Protein: 31g protein.
- Total Fat: 31g fat (17g saturated fat)
- Sodium: 746mg sodium
- Fiber: 2g fiber)

---

151.   Artichoke Chicken Casserole

Serving: 4 | Prep: 15mins | Cook: 30mins | Ready in:

Ingredients

- 1 cup grated Parmesan cheese
- 1 cup light mayonnaise
- 1 pinch garlic powder, or to taste
- 4 (4 ounce) skinless, boneless chicken breast halves

- 1 (14 ounce) can artichoke hearts, drained
- 1 (8 ounce) package crimini mushrooms, sliced

Direction

- Preheat oven to 350° F (175° C).
- In a bowl, mix garlic powder, mayonnaise, and Parmesan cheese together.
- In a 9x13-inch baking dish, place the chicken breasts; top with crimini mushrooms and artichoke hearts. Scatter cheese mixture over the mushroom and artichoke layer.
- In the preheated oven, bake for around 30 minutes until the chicken has no pink left in the center and the juices flow out clear. An instant-read thermometer pinned into the middle should reach no less than 165° F (74° C).

Nutrition Information

- Calories: 457 calories;
- Total Fat: 28.3
- Sodium: 1152
- Total Carbohydrate: 14.2
- Cholesterol: 103
- Protein: 36.4

---

152.   Artichoke Ratatouille Chicken

Serving: 6 servings. | Prep: 25mins | Cook: 60mins | Ready in:

Ingredients

- 3 Japanese eggplants (about 1 pound)
- 4 plum tomatoes
- 1 medium sweet yellow pepper
- 1 medium sweet red pepper
- 1 medium onion
- 1 can (14 ounces) water-packed artichoke hearts, drained and quartered
- 2 tablespoons minced fresh thyme

- 2 tablespoons capers, drained
- 2 tablespoons olive oil
- 2 garlic cloves, minced
- 1 teaspoon Creole seasoning, divided
- 1-1/2 pounds boneless skinless chicken breasts, cubed
- 1 cup white wine or chicken broth
- 1/4 cup grated Asiago cheese
- Hot cooked pasta, optional

Direction

- Set the oven to 350° and start preheating. Slice onion, peppers, tomatoes and eggplants into pieces of 3/4 inches; place into a large bowl. Mix in 1/2 teaspoon of Creole seasoning, garlic, oil, capers, thyme and artichoke hearts.
- Sprinkle the remaining Creole seasoning over chicken. Place the chicken in a 13-inx9-in. baking dish sprayed with cooking spray; spoon the vegetable mixture on top. Drizzle wine over vegetables.
- Bake with cover for half an hour. Remove the cover; bake for 30-45 more minutes or until the vegetables are tender while the chicken is no longer pink. Sprinkle cheese on top. Serve with pasta if desired.

Nutrition Information

- Calories: 252 calories
- Protein: 28g protein. Diabetic Exchanges: 3 lean meat
- Total Fat: 9g fat (2g saturated fat)
- Sodium: 468mg sodium
- Fiber: 4g fiber)
- Total Carbohydrate: 15g carbohydrate (4g sugars
- Cholesterol: 67mg cholesterol

153. Artichoke And Chicken Casserole

Serving: 6 servings. | Prep: 20mins | Cook: 25mins | Ready in:

Ingredients

- 2 cups uncooked bow tie pasta
- 2 cups cubed cooked chicken
- 1 can (14 ounces) water-packed artichoke hearts, rinsed, drained and chopped
- 1 can (10-3/4 ounces) condensed cream of chicken soup, undiluted
- 1 cup shredded Parmesan cheese
- 1 cup mayonnaise
- 1/3 cup 2% milk
- 1 garlic clove, minced
- 1/2 teaspoon onion powder
- 1/2 teaspoon pepper
- 1 cup onion and garlic salad croutons, coarsely crushed

Direction

- Set the oven at 350° and start preheating. Follow the package instructions to cook pasta. Meanwhile, mix pepper, onion powder, garlic, milk, mayonnaise, cheese, soup, artichokes and chicken in a large bowl. Strain the pasta; include into the chicken mixture.
- Transfer into a 2-quart baking sheet coated with grease. Spread croutons on top. Bake without a cover till heated through, 25-30 minutes.

Nutrition Information

- Calories: 614 calories
- Protein: 26g protein.
- Total Fat: 41g fat (9g saturated fat)
- Sodium: 1085mg sodium
- Fiber: 2g fiber)
- Total Carbohydrate: 33g carbohydrate (2g sugars
- Cholesterol: 70mg cholesterol

154. Asparagus Chicken Divan

Serving: 6-8 servings. | Prep: 20mins | Cook: 25mins | Ready in:

Ingredients

- 1 pound boneless skinless chicken breasts
- 2 pounds fresh asparagus, trimmed
- 1 can (10-3/4 ounces) condensed cream of chicken soup, undiluted
- 1 teaspoon Worcestershire sauce
- 1/4 teaspoon ground nutmeg
- 1 cup grated Parmesan cheese, divided
- 1/2 cup heavy whipping cream, whipped
- 3/4 cup mayonnaise

Direction

- Broil both sides of the chicken 4-6 inches from the heat until juices run clear for 6-8 minutes. In the meantime, boil 1/2 in. of water in a large skillet. Put in asparagus. Lower the heat; simmer for 3-5 minutes or until crisp-tender, covered. Drain and put onto a shallow 2-1/2-qt. greased baking dish. Slice chicken into thin cuts.
- In a small bowl, combine the nutmeg, Worcestershire sauce and soup. Layer half atop the asparagus. Sprinkle 1/3 cup Parmesan cheese over. Place chicken on top. Layer the rest of the soup mixture atop the chicken; use 1/3 cup Parmesan cheese to sprinkle.
- Bake at 400°, uncovered, for 20 minutes. Fold the whipped cream into the mayonnaise; layer on top. Scatter the rest of the Parmesan cheese over. Broil 4-6 in. from the heat until golden brown for about 2 minutes.

Nutrition Information

- Calories: 356 calories
- Cholesterol: 70mg cholesterol
- Protein: 18g protein.

- Total Fat: 29g fat (9g saturated fat)
- Sodium: 634mg sodium
- Fiber: 1g fiber)
- Total Carbohydrate: 6g carbohydrate (2g sugars

155. Asparagus Enchiladas

Serving: 12 servings. | Prep: 30mins | Cook: 30mins | Ready in:

Ingredients

- 1/3 cup vegetable oil
- 1 dozen flour tortillas (8 inches each)
- 1/2 cup butter
- 1/2 cup all-purpose flour
- 2 cans (15 ounces each) chicken broth
- 1 cup sour cream
- 1/2 cup green taco sauce
- 3 cups shredded Monterey Jack cheese, divided
- 3 cups cooked shredded chicken
- 1/2 cup chopped green onions, divided
- 2 pounds fresh asparagus, trimmed
- 1/3 cup grated Parmesan cheese
- 1/4 cup sliced ripe olives

Direction

- Heat oil in a skillet over medium-high heat. Put tortillas into the hot oil to soften, for 30 seconds each side. Put on a paper towel to strain; cool.
- Melt butter in a big saucepan over medium heat. Mix in flour. Stir in chicken broth, stir and cook until thickened. Take away from the heat. Mix in taco sauce and sour cream. Keep warm without boiling. Distribute over the 12 tortillas with all the onions (minus 2 tablespoons), 2 1/2 cups Monterey Jack cheese, and the chicken. Arrange over the filling with asparagus, the tips should extend over the tortillas. Put 2 tablespoons sauce on top each. Roll up and put in a 13x9-inch

baking dish with the seam side facing down. Put Parmesan cheese and the leftover sauce on top.
- Bake at 400° until bubbly, or for 25 minutes. Sprinkle the leftover Monterey Jack cheese over and put back into the oven just until melted. Use the saved onions and olives to garnish. Enjoy with extra green taco sauce.

Nutrition Information

- Calories: 526 calories
- Total Carbohydrate: 33g carbohydrate (2g sugars
- Cholesterol: 92mg cholesterol
- Protein: 25g protein.
- Total Fat: 32g fat (15g saturated fat)
- Sodium: 797mg sodium
- Fiber: 1g fiber)

156. Asparagus, Chicken, Wild Rice Casserole

Serving: 6 servings. | Prep: 10mins | Cook: 01hours15mins | Ready in:

Ingredients

- 1 cup uncooked wild rice, rinsed
- 2 cups chicken broth
- 1 can (4 ounces) mushroom stems and pieces, undrained
- 6 tablespoons butter, divided
- 6 boneless skinless chicken breast halves
- 2 tablespoons onion soup mix
- 1 can (10-3/4 ounces) condensed cream of mushroom soup, undiluted
- 1-1/2 pounds fresh asparagus, trimmed

Direction

- Spread rice in a 13x9-in. baking dish coated with cooking spray. Put in the mushrooms and broth; dot with 2 tablespoons of butter.

Place chicken in the middle of dish; sprinkle onion soup mix on top. Pour mushroom soup over top.

- Bake without cover for 1 hour at 350°. Place asparagus around edges of the dish. Melt the rest of butter, then brush onto asparagus and sprinkle paprika over. Bake for 15 to 20 minutes more or until asparagus is soft.

Nutrition Information

- Calories:
- Total Carbohydrate:
- Cholesterol:
- Total Fat:
- Fiber:
- Protein:
- Sodium:

---

157. Avocado Chicken Casserole

Serving: 6 servings. | Prep: 25mins | Cook: 20mins | Ready in:

Ingredients

- 1/4 cup butter, cubed
- 1/4 cup all-purpose flour
- 1/2 teaspoon salt
- 1/4 teaspoon each garlic powder, onion powder, dried basil, marjoram and thyme
- 1-1/2 cups 2% milk
- 1 cup half-and-half cream
- 8 ounces medium egg noodles, cooked and drained
- 3 medium ripe avocados, peeled and sliced
- 3 cups cubed cooked chicken
- 2 cups shredded cheddar cheese

Direction

- Melt the butter in a big saucepan; mix seasonings and flour till becoming smooth.

Slowly pour in milk and cream. Boil; cook and stir till becoming thick or for 2 minutes. Take out of the heat.

- In one greased 13x9-in. baking dish, layer with 1/2 of the noodles, avocados, chicken, white sauce and cheese. Repeat the layers.
- Keep it covered and baked at 350 degrees for 20 to 25 minutes. Uncover it; bake till becoming bubbly or for 5 minutes more.

Nutrition Information

- Calories:
- Sodium:
- Fiber:
- Total Carbohydrate:
- Cholesterol:
- Protein:
- Total Fat:

---

158. Bacon Swiss Penne

Serving: 10 servings. | Prep: 35mins | Cook: 30mins | Ready in:

Ingredients

- 12 ounces uncooked penne pasta
- 13 bacon strips
- 1-1/2 pounds boneless skinless chicken breasts, cut into 1-inch cubes
- 3 tablespoons butter
- 6 green onions, chopped
- 3 tablespoons all-purpose flour
- 4 cups 2% milk
- 3 cups shredded cheddar cheese
- 1-1/2 cups shredded Swiss cheese
- 1-1/2 cups frozen peas, thawed
- 3/4 teaspoon pepper
- 1/2 teaspoon dried thyme
- TOPPING:
- 3/4 cup dry bread crumbs
- 2 tablespoons butter, melted

Direction

- Follow the package instructions to cook penne.
- Meanwhile, cook bacon in a large skillet on medium heat till crisp, working in batches. Transfer onto paper towels; strain, reserving 4 teaspoons of the drippings. Crumble the bacon; set aside.
- Sauté chicken in the drippings and butter till not pink anymore. Put in onions; cook for 1 more minute. Mix in flour till blended; slowly pour in milk. Let the mixture come to a boil; cook while stirring till thicken, 2 minutes. Mix in bacon, thyme, pepper, peas and cheeses.
- Strain penne; put into the chicken mixture; toss to coat. Move into a 13x9-inch baking sheet coated with grease. Mix butter and bread crumbs in a small bowl; spread over the top. Bake without a cover at 350° till golden brown, 30-35 minutes.

Nutrition Information

- Calories: 614 calories
- Total Fat: 32g fat (18g saturated fat)
- Sodium: 651mg sodium
- Fiber: 3g fiber)
- Total Carbohydrate: 43g carbohydrate (8g sugars
- Cholesterol: 124mg cholesterol
- Protein: 39g protein.

---

159. Barbecue Chicken Casserole

Serving: 4-6 servings. | Prep: 25mins | Cook: 50mins | Ready in:

Ingredients

- 1 cup all-purpose flour
- 1 broiler/fryer chicken (3 to 4 pounds), cut up
- 2 tablespoons canola oil
- 1 cup chopped onion
- 1 cup chopped green pepper
- 1 cup thinly sliced celery
- 1 cup ketchup
- 1/2 cup water
- 3 tablespoons brown sugar
- 3 tablespoons Worcestershire sauce
- 1/2 teaspoon salt
- 1/4 teaspoon pepper
- 1 package (16 ounces) frozen corn, thawed

Direction

- Start preheating the oven to 350°. In a big resealable plastic bag, put flour. Add chicken, several pieces each time, and shake to blend. Brown chicken with oil in a big frying pan; remove into a non-oiled 13x9-inch baking dish.
- Strain the frying pan, saving 2 tablespoons drippings. Sauté celery, green pepper, and onion in the drippings until soft. Mix pepper, salt, Worcestershire sauce, brown sugar, water, and ketchup together in a small bowl; add to the vegetables. Boil it. Add to the chicken.
- Put a cover on and bake for 30 minutes. Sprinkle corn over. Bake until the corn is soft and the chicken juices run clear, about another 18-20 minutes.

Nutrition Information

- Calories: 522 calories
- Cholesterol: 88mg cholesterol
- Protein: 33g protein.
- Total Fat: 20g fat (5g saturated fat)
- Sodium: 854mg sodium
- Fiber: 4g fiber)
- Total Carbohydrate: 55g carbohydrate (15g sugars

160. Beef Or Chicken Enchiladas

Serving: 6 servings. | Prep: 30mins | Cook: 20mins | Ready in:

Ingredients

- 1 tablespoon butter
- 2 medium onions, chopped
- 1 garlic clove, minced
- 2 tablespoons all-purpose flour
- 1 cup chicken broth
- 1 cup whole milk
- 2 cans (4 ounces each) chopped green chilies
- 1/4 teaspoon salt
- 1/4 teaspoon ground cumin
- 12 flour or corn tortillas
- 1-1/2 cups shredded cooked beef or chicken
- 1 cup shredded Monterey Jack cheese
- 1 cup shredded cheddar cheese
- 2 green onions with tops, thinly sliced
- Sour cream
- Salsa

Direction

- In the sauce pan, melt the butter on medium heat. Sauté the garlic and onion till the onion softens. Blend in the flour. Whisk in the cumin, salt, chilies, milk and broth. Cook and stir till bubbly and thicken. Lower the heat; let simmer for 5 minutes, whisking once in a while. Put aside.
- Grease a 13x9-inch baking dish. Scoop small amount of the sauce in the middle of every tortilla; spread to the edges. Add roughly 2 tablespoons of the meat down each tortilla middle. Mix the cheeses; scatter 1 to 2 tablespoons over the meat. Roll the tortillas up and put into baking dish, with seam-side facing downward. Add the rest of the sauce on top. Scatter the rest of the cheese and green onions over. Bake, with no cover, at 350 degrees till bubbly and hot or for 20 to 30 minutes. Serve along with salsa and sour cream.

Nutrition Information

- Calories: 450 calories
- Total Fat: 21g fat (9g saturated fat)
- Sodium: 1123mg sodium
- Fiber: 2g fiber)
- Total Carbohydrate: 38g carbohydrate (5g sugars
- Cholesterol: 73mg cholesterol
- Protein: 28g protein.

161. Biscuit Nugget Chicken Bake

Serving: 4-6 servings. | Prep: 20mins | Cook: 10mins | Ready in:

Ingredients

- 3 cups cubed cooked chicken
- 1 can (10-3/4 ounces) condensed cream of chicken soup, undiluted
- 1 cup milk
- 1 jar (4-1/2 ounces) sliced mushrooms, drained
- 1/2 teaspoon dill weed
- 1/2 teaspoon paprika
- TOPPING:
- 1/4 cup grated Parmesan cheese
- 1 tablespoon dried minced onion
- 1 teaspoon dried parsley flakes
- 1/2 teaspoon paprika
- 1 tube (12 ounces) refrigerated buttermilk biscuits

Direction

- Mix the first 6 ingredients together in a big saucepan. Cook while stirring over medium heat for until fully heated, about 5-7 minutes; keep warm.
- Mix paprika, parsley, onion, and cheese together in a big resealable plastic bag. Divide

biscuits and cut into 4 portions, put in the bag and shake to blend. Put on a non-oiled cookie sheet. Bake for 5 minutes at 400°.

- Remove the chicken mixture into an 8-inch square baking dish coated with cooking spray, put biscuits on top. Bake without a cover until bubbly and the biscuits turn golden brown, about 10-13 minutes.

Nutrition Information

- Calories:
- Protein:
- Total Fat:
- Sodium:
- Fiber:
- Total Carbohydrate:
- Cholesterol:

162. Biscuit Topped Lemon Chicken

Serving: 15 servings (30 biscuits). | Prep: 40mins | Cook: 35mins |Ready in:

Ingredients

- 2 large onions, finely chopped
- 4 celery ribs, finely chopped
- 1 cup butter, cubed
- 2 garlic cloves, minced
- 8 green onions, thinly sliced
- 2/3 cup all-purpose flour
- 8 cups 2% milk
- 12 cups cubed cooked chicken
- 2 cans (10-3/4 ounces each) condensed cream of chicken soup, undiluted
- 1/2 cup lemon juice
- 2 tablespoons grated lemon peel
- 2 teaspoons pepper
- 1 teaspoon salt
- CHEDDAR BISCUITS:
- 5 cups self-rising flour
- 2 cups 2% milk

- 2 cups shredded cheddar cheese
- 1/4 cup butter, melted

Direction

- In a Dutch oven, sauté celery and onions in butter. Put in garlic; cook for 1 more minutes. Put in green onions. Mix in flour till blended; gradually put in milk. Allow to boil; cook while stirring till thickened, or for 2 minutes.
- Mix in salt, pepper, lemon juice and peel, soup and chicken; heat through. Transfer into two greased 13x9-in. baking dishes; set aside.
- Set the oven at 350° and start preheating. In a large bowl, mix biscuit ingredients just till moistened. Turn onto a lightly floured surface; knead 8 to 10 times. Roll out or pat to 3/4-in. thickness. Cut out 30 biscuits with a floured 2 1/2-in. biscuit cutter.
- Arrange over the chicken mixture. Bake without a cover till golden brown, or for 35-40 minutes.

Nutrition Information

- Calories: 687 calories
- Cholesterol: 180mg cholesterol
- Protein: 47g protein.
- Total Fat: 34g fat (19g saturated fat)
- Sodium: 1224mg sodium
- Fiber: 2g fiber)
- Total Carbohydrate: 47g carbohydrate (10g sugars

163. Black Bean & Chicken Enchilada Lasagna

Serving: 8 servings. | Prep: 30mins | Cook: 25mins |Ready in:

Ingredients

- 2 cans (10 ounces each) enchilada sauce
- 12 corn tortillas (6 inches)

- 2 cups coarsely shredded rotisserie chicken
- 1 small onion, chopped
- 1 can (15 ounces) black beans, rinsed and drained
- 3 cans (4 ounces each) whole green chilies, drained and coarsely chopped
- 3 cups crumbled queso fresco or shredded Mexican cheese blend
- 2 medium ripe avocados
- 2 tablespoons sour cream
- 2 tablespoons lime juice
- 1/2 teaspoon salt
- Chopped fresh tomatoes and cilantro

Direction

- Set oven temperature to 350 degrees and leave aside to preheat. Grease a 13x9-inch baking tray and distribute 1/2 cup of enchilada sauce evenly to layer as follows; 4 tortillas at the bottom, followed by 1 cup of chicken, 1/4 cup of onion, 1/3 cup of green chilies, and 1 cup of cheese. Continue layering in this arrangement. Splash 1/2 a cup of enchilada sauce and finish the stacking with the remainder of the ingredients. Bake for 25-30 minutes while uncovered until the cheese has melted or bubbles appear. Sit dish aside for 10 minutes before consumption. In the meantime, remove skin and scoop out an avocado; place into food processor. Mix in lime juice, sour cream, and salt, and pulse until blended evenly. Remove skin and scoop out the remaining avocado, cutting them into small cubed pieces. Top off lasagna with cilantro, cubed avocadoes, and tomatoes. It is ready to serve with the avocado sauce.

Nutrition Information

- Calories: 407 calories
- Cholesterol: 64mg cholesterol
- Protein: 28g protein.
- Total Fat: 18g fat (7g saturated fat)
- Sodium: 857mg sodium
- Fiber: 8g fiber)

- Total Carbohydrate: 39g carbohydrate (4g sugars

164. Black Bean Chicken Casserole

Serving: 10 servings. | Prep: 25mins | Cook: 35mins | Ready in:

Ingredients

- 1 large onion, chopped
- 1 small green pepper, chopped
- 1 tablespoon canola oil
- 2 garlic cloves, minced
- 1 can (14-1/2 ounces) diced tomatoes, undrained
- 1/2 cup salsa
- 1 teaspoon ground cumin
- 1/2 teaspoon salt
- 1/2 teaspoon dried oregano
- 1/4 teaspoon pepper
- 2 cans (15 ounces each) black beans, rinsed and drained
- 3 cups cubed cooked chicken breast
- 8 corn tortillas (6 inches)
- 1-1/2 cups shredded reduced-fat Monterey Jack or Mexican cheese blend, divided
- Fat-free sour cream, chopped green onions and sliced ripe olives, optional

Direction

- Combine green pepper and onion in a large saucepan, sauté in oil until softened. Add garlic and cook for another 1 minute. Stir in pepper, oregano, salt, cumin, salsa and tomatoes. Add chicken and beans; heat through.
- Coat a 13x9 inch baking dish with cooking spray, spread 1/3 of the mixture into the prepared baking dish. Arrange on top four tortillas, 1/3 of the chicken mixture and 1 cup cheese in layers. Repeat with remaining

chicken mixture and tortillas until there is no leftover.

- Bake, covered, for 25 to 30 minutes at 350° or until heated through. Uncover and add remaining cheese on top. Bake for an additional 8 to 10 minutes or until cheese is completely melted. Serve with olives, green onions and sour cream if desired.

Nutrition Information

- Calories: 283 calories
- Total Carbohydrate: 27g carbohydrate (4g sugars
- Cholesterol: 50mg cholesterol
- Protein: 24g protein. Diabetic Exchanges: 3 lean meat
- Total Fat: 9g fat (4g saturated fat)
- Sodium: 664mg sodium
- Fiber: 6g fiber)

165. Broccoli Chicken Bake

Serving: 6 servings. | Prep: 25mins | Cook: 35mins | Ready in:

Ingredients

- 4 cups uncooked egg noodles
- 1 medium onion, chopped
- 4 teaspoons butter
- 5 tablespoons all-purpose flour
- 1/2 teaspoon salt
- 1/2 teaspoon pepper
- 1 can (14-1/2 ounces) reduced-sodium chicken broth
- 1 cup fat-free milk
- 3 cups cubed cooked chicken breast
- 3 cups frozen chopped broccoli, thawed and drained
- 1 cup shredded reduced-fat cheddar cheese

Direction

- Cook noodles following the package instructions. In the meantime, in a big nonstick frying pan, cook onion with butter over medium heat until soft. Mix in pepper, salt, and flour until combined. Slowly mix in milk and broth. Boil it, cook while stirring until thickened, about 1-2 minutes.
- Take away from heat. Strain the noodles, put in a greased 2-quart baking dish. Mix in 1 cup sauce. Then lay the chicken, and broccoli, then leftover sauce.
- Put a cover on and bake for 30 minutes at 350°. Remove the cover, sprinkle cheese over. Bake until fully heated and the cheese melts, about another 5-10 minutes.

Nutrition Information

- Calories: 354 calories
- Cholesterol: 102mg cholesterol
- Protein: 34g protein. Diabetic Exchanges: 4 lean meat
- Total Fat: 10g fat (5g saturated fat)
- Sodium: 601mg sodium
- Fiber: 3g fiber)
- Total Carbohydrate: 33g carbohydrate (6g sugars

166. California Chicken

Serving: 4 | Prep: | Cook: | Ready in:

Ingredients

- 4 skinless, boneless chicken breasts
- 1 teaspoon olive oil
- 1/2 teaspoon onion powder
- 1 pinch salt
- 1 pinch ground black pepper
- 2 avocados - peeled, pitted and sliced
- 2 ripe tomatoes, sliced
- 1 (8 ounce) package Monterey Jack cheese, cut into 10 slices

119

Direction

- Prepare the oven by preheating to 350°F (175°C).
- Put oil in a skillet to warm and put onion and chicken. Then cook for 15 minutes or until chicken is browned and just about done. Season with pepper and salt.
- On a cookie sheet, put the chicken and place 1 to 2 slices of tomato and 2 to 3 slices of cheese on top of each breast. Put in the preheated oven for 10 to 15 minutes, until cheese has melted. Take out of the oven, top each breast with 2 to 3 slices of avocado, and serve right away.

Nutrition Information

- Calories: 541 calories;
- Cholesterol: 122
- Protein: 42.8
- Total Fat: 36.7
- Sodium: 373
- Total Carbohydrate: 12.1

167.   Cashew Chicken Bake

Serving: 4 | Prep: 25mins | Cook: 55mins | Ready in:

Ingredients

- cooking spray
- 1/2 cup brown rice
- 1 cup diced celery
- 1 red bell pepper, diced
- 1 green bell pepper, diced
- 3 skinless, boneless chicken breasts, cut into 1-inch pieces
- 1 cup water
- 2 tablespoons gluten-free soy sauce (tamari)
- 1 tablespoon rice vinegar
- 1 tablespoon minced garlic
- 1 1/2 teaspoons minced ginger
- 1/2 teaspoon ground cumin

- 1/2 teaspoon ground black pepper
- 1/4 teaspoon salt
- 1 (8 ounce) can sliced water chestnuts, drained
- 1 cup cashews

Direction

- Preheat the oven to 190 °C or 375 °F. With cooking spray, grease a big casserole dish.
- Scatter brown rice at the base of the casserole dish. Arrange green pepper, red bell pepper and celery over. Atop with chicken.
- In a small bowl, combine salt, pepper, cumin, ginger, garlic, rice vinegar, soy sauce and water. Put over chicken. Put water chestnuts over.
- In the prepped oven, bake for 45 minutes till chicken is soft. Put cashews. Keep baking till browned, for 10 minutes longer.

Nutrition Information

- Calories: 428 calories;
- Cholesterol: 44
- Protein: 26
- Total Fat: 18.6
- Sodium: 937
- Total Carbohydrate: 41.8

168.   Cashew Chicken With Broccoli

Serving: 4 servings. | Prep: 10mins | Cook: 45mins | Ready in:

Ingredients

- 1 pound boneless skinless chicken breasts, cut into 1-inch cubes
- 1 medium onion, chopped
- 2 cups frozen broccoli cuts
- 1-3/4 cups boiling water
- 1 cup uncooked long grain rice
- 1 jar (6 ounces) sliced mushrooms, drained

- 1 tablespoon chicken bouillon granules
- 1/2 to 1 teaspoon ground ginger
- Pepper to taste
- 3/4 cup salted cashews, divided

Direction

- Pu together the first 9 ingredients in a big bowl. Put to a shallow 1-1/2-qt. greased baking dish.
- Put cover and bake at 375° for 45 to 55 minutes or till rice is soft and chicken is not pink anymore. Mix in half cup of cashews. Scatter remaining cashews over.

Nutrition Information

- Calories:
- Total Fat:
- Sodium:
- Fiber:
- Total Carbohydrate:
- Cholesterol:
- Protein:

169.   Cheddar Chicken Potpie

Serving: 6 servings. | Prep: 30mins | Cook: 40mins | Ready in:

Ingredients

- CRUST:
- 1 cup all-purpose flour
- 1/2 teaspoon salt
- 5 tablespoons cold butter, cubed
- 3 tablespoons cold water
- FILLING:
- 1-1/2 cups chicken broth
- 2 cups peeled cubed potatoes
- 1 cup sliced carrots
- 1/2 cup sliced celery
- 1/2 cup chopped onion
- 1/4 cup all-purpose flour

- 1-1/2 cups whole milk
- 2 cups shredded sharp cheddar cheese
- 4 cups cubed cooked chicken
- 1/4 teaspoon poultry seasoning
- Salt and pepper to taste

Direction

- To make crust, mix salt and flour in a small bowl. Cut in the butter until the mixture is coarse crumbs. Mixing carefully with a fork, slowly add water. Form a ball. Put plastic wrap on top and place in refrigerator for 30 minutes or more. For the filling, in a Dutch oven add broth and heat to boiling on high heat. Mix in veggies. Decrease heat and simmer until veggies are tender, 10-15 minutes. Mix flour and milk in a small bowl; whisk into the broth mixture. Stirring constantly, cook on medium heat until bubbling and slightly thick. Stir in poultry seasoning, pepper, cheese, salt, and chicken. Continue heating until cheese is melted. Put into a 2-1/2 to 3-qt. or 10-in. dish. Set it aside. Roll out the crust to fit top of dish on a lightly floured surface. Trim edges to fit. Put over the dish covering filling. Make sure to seal the edges. To let steam escape, cut several slits in the middle of the crust. Bake in 425-degree oven until golden brown, 40 minutes.

Nutrition Information

- Calories: 603 calories
- Sodium: 902mg sodium
- Fiber: 3g fiber)
- Total Carbohydrate: 38g carbohydrate (6g sugars
- Cholesterol: 161mg cholesterol
- Protein: 42g protein.
- Total Fat: 31g fat (18g saturated fat)

170. Cheesy Chicken And Broccoli

Serving: 4 servings. | Prep: 10mins | Cook: 20mins | Ready in:

Ingredients

- 1 package (10 ounces) frozen broccoli with cheese sauce
- 1 package (6-1/2 ounces) broccoli au gratin rice mix
- 1 cup cubed cooked chicken
- 1/2 cup cubed process cheese (Velveeta)

Direction

- Prepare broccoli following the instruction of the package. In a large saucepan, prepare rice mix following the package instructions. Blend in the process cheese, chicken and broccoli. Cook till cheese melts.

Nutrition Information

- Calories: 323 calories
- Fiber: 2g fiber)
- Total Carbohydrate: 35g carbohydrate (6g sugars
- Cholesterol: 40mg cholesterol
- Protein: 20g protein.
- Total Fat: 12g fat (5g saturated fat)
- Sodium: 1007mg sodium

171. Chicken & Dumpling Casserole

Serving: 8 servings. | Prep: 30mins | Cook: 40mins | Ready in:

Ingredients

- 1/2 cup chopped onion
- 1/2 cup chopped celery
- 1/4 cup butter, cubed
- 2 garlic cloves, minced
- 1/2 cup all-purpose flour
- 2 teaspoons sugar
- 1 teaspoon salt
- 1 teaspoon dried basil
- 1/2 teaspoon pepper
- 4 cups chicken broth
- 1 package (10 ounces) frozen green peas
- 4 cups cubed cooked chicken
- DUMPLINGS:
- 2 cups biscuit/baking mix
- 2 teaspoons dried basil
- 2/3 cup 2% milk

Direction

- Set oven to preheat at 350°. In a large saucepan, sauté celery and onion until tender in butter. Add the garlic; cook for 1 more minute. Mix in pepper, basil, salt, sugar and flour until well mixed. Add broth gradually; heat until boiling. Cook and stir until thickened, or for 1 minute; lower the heat. Put in peas and cook for 5 minutes, stir continuously. Mix in chicken. Transfer into a 13x9-in. greased baking dish.
- To make dumplings, combine basil and baking mix in a small bowl. Mix in milk using a fork until moistened. Drop the dumplings over chicken mixture into mounds by tablespoonfuls.
- Bake for 30 minutes uncovered. Cover and bake for 10 more minutes or until an inserted toothpick exits clean from a dumpling.

Nutrition Information

- Calories: 393 calories
- Cholesterol: 80mg cholesterol
- Protein: 27g protein.
- Total Fat: 17g fat (7g saturated fat)
- Sodium: 1313mg sodium
- Fiber: 3g fiber)
- Total Carbohydrate: 33g carbohydrate (6g sugars

172. Chicken & Egg Noodle Casserole

Serving: 8 servings. | Prep: 20mins | Cook: 30mins | Ready in:

Ingredients

- 6 cups uncooked egg noodles (about 12 ounces)
- 2 cans (10-3/4 ounces each) condensed cream of chicken soup, undiluted
- 1 cup (8 ounces) sour cream
- 3/4 cup 2% milk
- 1/4 teaspoon salt
- 1/4 teaspoon pepper
- 3 cups cubed cooked chicken breasts
- 1 cup crushed Ritz crackers (about 20 crackers)
- 1/4 cup butter, melted

Direction

- Preheat oven to 350°. Cook noodles as stated on package directions for al dente; let drain.
- In a big bowl, whisk pepper, salt, milk, sour cream, and soup up to blended. Mix in noodles and chicken. Move into a greased 13x9-inch baking dish. In a small bowl, stir butter and crushed crackers together; dust over top. Bake for 30-35 minutes or till bubbly.

Nutrition Information

- Calories: 446 calories
- Protein: 23g protein.
- Total Fat: 22g fat (10g saturated fat)
- Sodium: 820mg sodium
- Fiber: 2g fiber)
- Total Carbohydrate: 37g carbohydrate (4g sugars
- Cholesterol: 107mg cholesterol

173. Chicken & Spaghetti Squash

Serving: 5 servings. | Prep: 45mins | Cook: 20mins | Ready in:

Ingredients

- 1 medium spaghetti squash (4 pounds)
- 1 can (14-1/2 ounces) diced tomatoes, undrained
- 2 tablespoons prepared pesto
- 1/2 teaspoon garlic powder
- 1/2 teaspoon Italian seasoning
- 1/4 cup dry bread crumbs
- 1/4 cup shredded Parmesan cheese
- 1 pound boneless skinless chicken breasts, cut into 1/2-inch cubes
- 1 tablespoon plus 1 teaspoon olive oil, divided
- 1/2 pound sliced fresh mushrooms
- 1 medium onion, chopped
- 1 garlic clove, minced
- 1/2 cup chicken broth
- 1/3 cup shredded cheddar cheese

Direction

- Lengthwise, halve squash; discard seeds. Put squash on microwave-safe plate, cut side down. Microwave on high, uncovered, till tender for 14-16 minutes.
- Meanwhile, process Italian seasoning, garlic powder, pesto and tomatoes in a blender, covered, till blended. Put aside. Mix parmesan cheese and breadcrumbs in small bowl; put aside.
- Cook chicken in 1 tbsp. oil in big skillet till not pink; remove then keep warm. Sauté onion and mushrooms in leftover oil in same skillet till tender. Add garlic; cook for a minute. Mix reserved tomato mixture, chicken and broth in; boil. Lower heat; simmer for 5 minutes, uncovered.
- Use fork to separate strands when squash is cool to handle. Layer 1/2 of reserved crumb mixture, chicken mixture and squash in big ovenproof skillet then repeat layers.

- Bake for 15 minutes at 350° till heated through, uncovered. Sprinkle cheddar cheese; broil it 3-4-in. away from heat till cheese is golden brown and melted for 5-6 minutes.

Nutrition Information

- Calories: 348 calories
- Fiber: 7g fiber)
- Total Carbohydrate: 32g carbohydrate (6g sugars
- Cholesterol: 63mg cholesterol
- Protein: 27g protein.
- Total Fat: 14g fat (5g saturated fat)
- Sodium: 493mg sodium

174. Chicken & Sweet Potato Potpie

Serving: 6 servings. | Prep: 40mins | Cook: 10mins | Ready in:

Ingredients

- 2 teaspoons olive oil
- 1/2 pound sliced fresh mushrooms
- 1 small onion, chopped
- 1 large sweet potato, cubed
- 1 cup chopped sweet red pepper
- 1/2 cup chopped celery
- 2 cups reduced-sodium chicken broth, divided
- 1/3 cup all-purpose flour
- 1/2 cup 2% milk
- 1 skinned rotisserie chicken, shredded
- 2 tablespoons sherry or reduced-sodium chicken broth
- 3/4 teaspoon minced fresh rosemary
- 1/2 teaspoon salt
- 1/2 teaspoon dried thyme
- 1/4 teaspoon pepper
- 5 sheets phyllo dough (14x9-in. size)
- Butter-flavored cooking spray

Direction

- Set oven to 425 degrees and start preheating. In a big skillet on medium-high heat, heat oil. Add onions and mushrooms; cook and stir 3 to 4 minutes until tender. Mix in celery, red pepper, and sweet potato; cook for 5 more minutes. Pour in 1/4 cup broth. Lower the heat and cook without cover on medium-low heat for 6-8 minutes, until the vegetables are tender.
- Scatter flour on vegetables; stir and cook for 1 minute. Slowly add the remaining broth and milk. Heat to a boil; stir and cook 1-2 minutes until thickened. Mix in seasonings, sherry, and chicken. Move to an 11x7-inch baking dished coated with cooking spray. Bake for 10-15 minutes without cover, until heated through.
- At the same time, stack all 5 sheets of phyllo dough. Roll up lengthways, slice crosswise into 1/2-inch-wide strips. Toss strips in a bowl to separate; use butter-flavored spray to spritz. Arrange on an unoiled baking tray; spritz again. Bake for 4 to 5 minutes until golden brown. Place over the chicken mixture.

Nutrition Information

- Calories: 329 calories
- Cholesterol: 75mg cholesterol
- Protein: 30g protein. Diabetic Exchanges: 4 lean meat
- Total Fat: 10g fat (2g saturated fat)
- Sodium: 517mg sodium
- Fiber: 3g fiber)
- Total Carbohydrate: 30g carbohydrate (10g sugars

175. Chicken & Swiss Casserole

Serving: 8 servings. | Prep: 30mins | Cook: 10mins | Ready in:

Ingredients

- 5-1/2 cups uncooked egg noodles (about 1/2 pound)
- 3 tablespoons olive oil
- 3 shallots, chopped
- 3 small garlic cloves, minced
- 1/3 cup all-purpose flour
- 2 cups chicken broth
- 3/4 cup 2% milk
- 1-1/2 teaspoons dried thyme
- 3/4 teaspoon grated lemon peel
- 1/2 teaspoon salt
- 1/4 teaspoon ground nutmeg
- 1/4 teaspoon pepper
- 5 cups cubed rotisserie chicken
- 1-1/2 cups frozen peas
- 2 cups shredded Swiss cheese
- 3/4 cup dry bread crumbs
- 2 tablespoons butter, melted

Direction

- Preheat and set oven to 350 degrees. Follow directions on package to cook the noodles. Drain water from noodles. Place oil in large frying pan and heat on medium. Add garlic and shallots to the frying pan and stir constantly for 45 seconds. Mix in flour and continue stirring for 1 minute. Mix in thyme, nutmeg, broth, salt, milk, pepper, and lemon peel. Add the peas and chicken and heat through. Mix in cheese and noodles and dump into a 13x9-in. greased pan. In a separate bowl, mix together butter and bread crumbs. Sprinkle bread crumb mixture on top. Bake until top is brown, 8-10 minutes.

Nutrition Information

- Calories: 551 calories
- Total Carbohydrate: 38g carbohydrate (4g sugars
- Cholesterol: 136mg cholesterol
- Protein: 41g protein.
- Total Fat: 25g fat (10g saturated fat)
- Sodium: 661mg sodium
- Fiber: 3g fiber)

176.   Chicken 'n' Chilies Casserole

Serving: 6-8 servings. | Prep: 15mins | Cook: 01hours15mins | Ready in:

Ingredients

- 1 cup sour cream
- 1 cup half-and-half cream
- 1 cup chopped onion
- 1 can (4 ounces) chopped green chilies
- 1 teaspoon salt
- 1/2 teaspoon pepper
- 1 package (2 pounds) frozen shredded hash brown potatoes
- 2-1/2 cups cubed cooked chicken
- 2-1/2 cups shredded cheddar cheese, divided
- Chopped fresh cilantro, optional

Direction

- Mix pepper, salt, chilies, onion, half-and-half cream, and sour cream in a big bowl. Mix in 2 cups of cheese, chicken and potatoes.
- Add into one greased 13x9-in. baking dish. Bake, while uncovered, at 350 degrees till becoming golden brown in color or for 1-1/4 hours. Drizzle with leftover cheese prior to serving. Drizzle with chopped cilantro if you want.

Nutrition Information

- Calories: 410 calories
- Fiber: 2g fiber)
- Total Carbohydrate: 25g carbohydrate (4g sugars
- Cholesterol: 111mg cholesterol
- Protein: 26g protein.
- Total Fat: 21g fat (14g saturated fat)
- Sodium: 647mg sodium

177.   Chicken 'n' Chips

Serving: 4-6 servings. | Prep: 10mins | Cook: 25mins | Ready in:

Ingredients

- 1 can (10-3/4 ounces) condensed cream of chicken soup, undiluted
- 1 cup sour cream
- 2 tablespoons taco sauce
- 1/4 cup chopped green chilies
- 3 cups cubed cooked chicken
- 12 slices process American cheese
- 4 cups crushed tortilla chips

Direction

- Mix chilies, taco sauce, sour cream and soup in a big bowl. In one ungreased shallow 2-qt. baking dish, layer 1/2 of the chicken, soup mixture, cheese and tortilla chips. Repeat the layers.
- Bake, while uncovered, at 350 degrees till becoming bubbly or for 25 to 30 minutes.

Nutrition Information

- Calories: 575 calories
- Total Fat: 32g fat (15g saturated fat)
- Sodium: 1186mg sodium
- Fiber: 2g fiber)
- Total Carbohydrate: 36g carbohydrate (4g sugars
- Cholesterol: 120mg cholesterol
- Protein: 33g protein.

178.   Chicken 'n' Hash Brown Bake

Serving: 8-10 servings. | Prep: 10mins | Cook: 50mins | Ready in:

Ingredients

- 1 package (32 ounces) frozen cubed hash brown potatoes, thawed
- 1 teaspoon salt
- 1/4 teaspoon pepper
- 4 cups diced cooked chicken
- 1 can (4 ounces) mushroom stems and pieces, drained
- 1 cup sour cream
- 2 cups chicken broth or stock
- 1 can (10-3/4 ounces) condensed cream of chicken soup, undiluted
- 2 teaspoons chicken bouillon granules
- 2 tablespoons finely chopped onion
- 2 tablespoons finely chopped sweet red pepper
- 1 garlic clove, minced
- Paprika
- 1/4 cup sliced almonds

Direction

- In an ungreased baking dish of 13- x 9-inch, spread potatoes. Use salt and pepper to sprinkle over. Sprinkle over the top with mushrooms and chicken. Combine the broth, sour cream, bouillon, soup, onion, garlic and red pepper; pour over mushrooms.
- Have paprika and almonds to sprinkle over. Bake with no cover at 350° for around 50 to 60 minutes till heated through.

Nutrition Information

- Calories: 274 calories
- Total Carbohydrate: 22g carbohydrate (2g sugars
- Cholesterol: 68mg cholesterol
- Protein: 21g protein.
- Total Fat: 11g fat (4g saturated fat)
- Sodium: 955mg sodium
- Fiber: 3g fiber)

179. Chicken 'n' Rice Hot Dish

Serving: 4 servings. | Prep: 15mins | Cook: 30mins | Ready in:

Ingredients

- 1/2 cup uncooked instant brown rice
- 1/4 cup boiling water
- 1 package (10 ounces) frozen chopped spinach, thawed and squeezed dry
- 1 tablespoon butter
- 3 tablespoons all-purpose flour
- 1/2 teaspoon curry powder
- 1/4 teaspoon salt
- Dash pepper
- Dash garlic powder
- 3/4 cup reduced-sodium chicken broth
- 3/4 cup fat-free milk
- 1/4 cup reduced-fat mayonnaise
- 3 cups cubed cooked chicken breast
- 1/3 cup shredded Parmesan cheese

Direction

- Blend water and rice together; move into an 11x7-inch baking dish sprayed with cooking spray. Put spinach on top.
- In a nonstick saucepan sprayed with cooking spray, melt butter. Mix in the garlic powder, pepper, salt, curry, and flour up to blended. Slowly whisk in milk and broth till smooth. Set to a boil; cook and mix for about 2 minutes, or till condense.
- Take away from the heat; stir in mayonnaise till blended. Top spinach with half of the sauce. Top with the remaining sauce and chicken.
- Bake with cover at 350° for 25 minutes. Uncover; scatter with Parmesan cheese. Bake for 5-10 minutes more, or till heated through and rice soften.

Nutrition Information

- Calories: 325 calories
- Fiber: 3g fiber)
- Total Carbohydrate: 20g carbohydrate (3g sugars
- Cholesterol: 81mg cholesterol
- Protein: 31g protein. Diabetic Exchanges: 3 lean meat
- Total Fat: 13g fat (5g saturated fat)
- Sodium: 659mg sodium

180. Chicken Amandine

Serving: 8 servings. | Prep: 35mins | Cook: 30mins | Ready in:

Ingredients

- 1/4 cup chopped onion
- 1 tablespoon butter
- 1 package (6 ounces) long grain and wild rice
- 2-1/4 cups chicken broth
- 3 cups cubed cooked chicken
- 2 cups frozen french-style green beans, thawed
- 1 can (10-3/4 ounces) condensed cream of chicken soup, undiluted
- 3/4 cup sliced almonds, divided
- 1 jar (4 ounces) diced pimientos, drained
- 1 teaspoon pepper
- 1/2 teaspoon garlic powder
- 1 bacon strip, cooked and crumbled

Direction

- Sauté onion in butter in a large saucepan till tender. Put in rice with broth and contents of the seasoning packet. Boil the mixture. Lower the heat; simmer with a cover till the liquid is absorbed, 25 minutes. Uncover and set aside to cool.
- In a large bowl, mix together garlic powder, pepper, pimientos, 1/2 cup of almonds, soup, green beans and chicken. Mix in rice.
- Transfer into a 2 1/2-quart baking sheet coated with grease. Sprinkle with the remaining almonds and bacon. Bake with a cover at 350° till heated through, 30-35 minutes.

Nutrition Information

- Calories: 297 calories
- Sodium: 912mg sodium
- Fiber: 3g fiber)
- Total Carbohydrate: 24g carbohydrate (3g sugars
- Cholesterol: 54mg cholesterol
- Protein: 22g protein.
- Total Fat: 13g fat (3g saturated fat)

---

181. Chicken Artichoke Casserole

Serving: 8 | Prep: 40mins | Cook: 1hours | Ready in:

Ingredients

- 3 bone-in chicken breasts
- 1 cup mayonnaise
- 2 (10.5 ounce) cans cream of chicken soup
- 2 teaspoons lemon juice
- 1 teaspoon curry powder
- salt and ground black pepper to taste
- 1 (6.5 ounce) jar marinated artichoke hearts, liquid reserved
- 4 cups cubed bread
- 1 cup shredded extra-sharp Cheddar cheese
- 4 tablespoons butter

Direction

- Boil a big pot with water. In boiling water, cook chicken breasts for 30 minutes till juices are clear and not pink at the bone. An inserted instant-read thermometer near bone should register 74°C/165°F.
- As chicken boils, mix pepper, salt, curry powder, lemon juice, cream of chicken soup and mayonnaise in a bowl. Put aside.
- Slice cooked chicken meat to bite-sized pieces. Put into a bottom of 9x13-in. casserole dish. Slice artichoke hearts to bite-sized pieces.

Scatter on chicken. Sprinkle 1 tbsp. Reserved liquid from artichoke jars on artichoke and chicken mixture. Put soup on artichokes and chicken. Scatter cheddar cheese over.
- Preheat oven to 175°C/350°F.
- In a skillet, melt butter on medium heat. Stir and cook bread cubes in melted butter till browned. Sprinkle croutons on entire casserole.
- In preheated oven, bake casserole for 30 minutes till top is bubbling.

Nutrition Information

- Calories: 639 calories;
- Protein: 43.5
- Total Fat: 42.5
- Sodium: 1076
- Total Carbohydrate: 20.7
- Cholesterol: 143

---

182. Chicken Biscuit Bake

Serving: 6 | Prep: 15mins | Cook: 40mins | Ready in:

Ingredients

- 1 (10.75 ounce) can condensed cream of chicken soup, undiluted
- 2/3 cup mayonnaise*
- 2 teaspoons Worcestershire sauce
- 4 cups cubed cooked chicken
- 3 cups cooked chopped broccoli
- 1 medium onion, chopped
- 1 cup shredded Cheddar cheese
- 2 (12 ounce) packages refrigerated buttermilk biscuits
- 2 eggs
- 1/2 cup sour cream
- 2 teaspoons celery seed
- 1 teaspoon salt

Direction

- In a bowl, combine the Worcestershire sauce, mayonnaise and soup. Mix in onion, broccoli and chicken. Put into a 13-in. x 9-in. x 2-in. greased baking dish. Sprinkle cheese on top. Bake at 375°F, covered, for 20 minutes.
- Separate the biscuits; slice each one in half. Layer them onto the hot chicken mixture, with the cut side down. In a bowl, mix together the rest of the ingredients; add on top of the biscuits. Bake, uncovered, until golden brown, or for another 20 minutes.

Nutrition Information

Nutrition Information

- Calories: 269 calories
- Cholesterol: 65mg cholesterol
- Protein: 24g protein.
- Total Fat: 10g fat (5g saturated fat)
- Sodium: 743mg sodium
- Fiber: 2g fiber)
- Total Carbohydrate: 19g carbohydrate (2g sugars

183.   Chicken Broccoli Bake

Serving: 8 servings. | Prep: 5mins | Cook: 40mins | Ready in:

Ingredients

- 2 packages (6.2 ounces each) broccoli au gratin rice mix
- 2-1/4 cups water
- 1 can (10-3/4 ounces) condensed cream of chicken soup, undiluted
- 1 to 2 tablespoons Dijon mustard
- 1-1/2 pounds boneless skinless chicken breasts, cut into 1-inch cubes
- 4 cups frozen broccoli florets, thawed
- 1 cup shredded cheddar cheese

Direction

- In a greased baking dish of 13x9-inch, spread rice evenly from rice packages. In a bowl, combine the contents of sauce packets from the rice, water, soup and mustard; pour half over rice. Layer with broccoli and chicken. Pour over top with the rest of sauce.
- Bake with no cover at 375° for around 30 to 40 minutes till rice is tender and chicken juices run clear. Use cheese to sprinkle. Bake for an addition of 10 minutes till cheese melts.

184.   Chicken Casserole

Serving: | Prep: 20mins | Cook: 1hours | Ready in:

Ingredients

- 2 cups Wild Rice (cooked)
- 2 tablespoons Olive Oil
- 1 Onion [diced]
- 2 Sweet Potatoes [peeld, cut into small cubes]
- 1/2 pound Brussel Sprouts [trimmed and quartered]
- 1 teaspoon Thyme
- 1 teaspoon Paprika
- 1/4 teaspoon Salt
- 1/8 teaspoon Pepper
- 1/4 cup Chicken Broth
- 1 1/2 pounds Boneless Chicken Breasts
- 1/2 cup Cranberries [dried]
- 1/2 cup Almonds [sliced]

Direction

- Preparation:
- Start preheating the oven at 350° and grease a 9x13-inch baking dish.
- Make the chicken: In a large skillet, heat 1 tablespoon of olive oil. Flavor chicken all over with pepper and salt. Put the chicken in the skillet and cook for about 6 to 8 minutes each side until cooked thoroughly. Allow to rest for

10 minutes, then slice each breast into bite-sized pieces.

- Mix in cranberries, cooked chicken and prepared rice. Place the mixture to the baking dish, sprinkle with sliced almonds, and bake for 20 minutes.

Nutrition Information

┌─────────────────────────────────────┐
│ **185.   Chicken Casserole**   │
│   **Supreme**   │
└─────────────────────────────────────┘

Serving: 6 servings. | Prep: 40mins | Cook: 20mins | Ready in:

Ingredients

- 1 cup reduced-sodium chicken broth
- 1 medium apple, peeled and chopped
- 1/2 cup golden raisins
- 1 tablespoon butter
- 1 package (6 ounces) reduced-sodium stuffing mix
- 1 pound boneless skinless chicken breasts, cubed
- 1/4 teaspoon salt
- 1/4 teaspoon pepper
- 1 cup sliced fresh mushrooms
- 1 small onion, chopped
- 1 tablespoon olive oil
- 3 garlic cloves, minced
- 1-1/2 cups (12 ounces) fat-free sour cream
- 1 can (10-3/4 ounces) reduced-fat reduced-sodium condensed cream of mushroom soup, undiluted
- 4 cups frozen broccoli florets, thawed

Direction

- Combine raisins, apple and broth in a large saucepan. Boil. Lower heat; simmer for 3-4 minutes, uncovered, or until apple becomes

tender. Mix in stuffing mix and butter. Put off the heat; let sit, covered, for 5 minutes.

- Sprinkle chicken with pepper and salt. Cook onion, mushrooms and chicken in oil in a large skillet over medium heat until chicken is not pink anymore. Add in garlic; cook for 1 more minute. Put off the heat. Mix in soup and sour cream.
- Put into a cooking spray-coated 13x9-in. baking dish. Layer with broccoli and the stuffing mixture. Bake at 350°, uncovered, until heated through for 20-25 minutes.

Nutrition Information

- Calories: 390 calories
- Fiber: 3g fiber)
- Total Carbohydrate: 52g carbohydrate (19g sugars
- Cholesterol: 59mg cholesterol
- Protein: 26g protein.
- Total Fat: 8g fat (2g saturated fat)
- Sodium: 771mg sodium

┌─────────────────────────────────────┐
│ **186.   Chicken Cheddar Stuffing** │
│   **Casserole**   │
└─────────────────────────────────────┘

Serving: 2 casseroles (6 servings each). | Prep: 15mins | Cook: 30mins | Ready in:

Ingredients

- 2 packages (6 ounces each) chicken stuffing mix
- 2 cans (10-3/4 ounces each) condensed cream of mushroom soup, undiluted
- 1 cup 2% milk
- 4 cups cubed cooked chicken
- 2 cups frozen corn
- 2 cans (8 ounces each) mushroom stems and pieces, drained
- 4 cups shredded cheddar cheese

Direction

- Follow the package instructions to prepare stuffing mixes. Meanwhile, mix milk and soup in a large bowl; set aside. Spread the stuffing into two 8-inch square baking sheets coated with grease. Layer with chicken, then corn, mushrooms, the soup mixture and finally cheese.
- Freeze one casserole with a cover for up to 3 months. Bake the second casserole with a cover at 350° till the cheese melts, 30-35 minutes.
- To use the frozen casserole: take out of freezer half an hour before baking (do not thaw). Bake for 1 1/2 hours at 350°. Remove cover and bake till heated through, 10-15 more minutes.

Nutrition Information

- Calories: 373 calories
- Total Carbohydrate: 21g carbohydrate (3g sugars
- Cholesterol: 96mg cholesterol
- Protein: 26g protein.
- Total Fat: 21g fat (12g saturated fat)
- Sodium: 822mg sodium
- Fiber: 1g fiber)

---

187. Chicken Cheese Enchiladas

Serving: 6 servings. | Prep: 25mins | Cook: 50mins | Ready in:

Ingredients

- 2 cups (16 ounces) sour cream
- 1 can (10-3/4 ounces) condensed cream of chicken soup, undiluted
- 1 can (4 ounces) chopped green chilies
- 1 can (2-1/4 ounces) sliced ripe olives, drained
- 4 cups cubed cooked chicken
- 3 cups shredded Monterey Jack cheese, divided
- 3 cups shredded cheddar cheese, divided

- 12 flour tortillas (6 inches), warmed
- 4 green onions, thinly sliced

Direction

- Mix olives, chilies, soup, and sour cream together in a big bowl. Put 1 1/2 cups aside to use for topping. Add 2 cups cheddar cheese, 2 cups Monterey Jack cheese, and chicken to the leftover soup mixture.
- Down the middle of each tortilla, spoon approximately 1/2 cup chicken mixture; roll up tightly. Put in a 13x9-inch baking dish coated with grease with the seam side facing down. Put the saved soup mixture on top.
- Bake without a cover at for 40 minutes at 350°. Sprinkle the leftover cheese over, put onions on top. Bake until the cheese melts, or for another 10-15 minutes.

Nutrition Information

- Calories: 992 calories
- Cholesterol: 251mg cholesterol
- Protein: 63g protein.
- Total Fat: 63g fat (35g saturated fat)
- Sodium: 1765mg sodium
- Fiber: 1g fiber)
- Total Carbohydrate: 36g carbohydrate (4g sugars

---

188. Chicken Cheese Strata

Serving: 8 servings. | Prep: 15mins | Cook: 15mins | Ready in:

Ingredients

- 3/4 pound boneless skinless chicken breasts, cut into 1/2-inch cubes
- 4 tablespoons butter, divided
- 3 cups frozen broccoli florets, thawed
- 1/2 teaspoon onion salt
- 1/2 teaspoon dried thyme
- 1/2 teaspoon dried rosemary, crushed

- 1/4 teaspoon pepper
- 6 cups cubed French bread
- 2 large eggs
- 3/4 cup 2% milk
- 2/3 cup condensed cream of onion soup, undiluted
- 1 cup shredded Colby-Monterey Jack cheese

Direction

- Preheat oven to 400°. In an ovenproof, 10-inch skillet sauté chicken in 2 tablespoons butter till no longer pink. Put in onion, broccoli, thyme, salt, pepper and rosemary; heat through. Take out of skillet and keep warm.
- Toast bread cubes in leftover butter in the same skillet till brown lightly. In a small bowl, combine soup, milk and eggs; pour over bread cubes. Mix in chicken mixture. Scatter cheese over.
- Bake with no cover for approximately 15 to 20 minutes till a knife pinned in the center comes out clean. Allow 5 minutes to rest before cutting.

Nutrition Information

- Calories: 570 calories
- Sodium: 1282mg sodium
- Fiber: 4g fiber)
- Total Carbohydrate: 77g carbohydrate (6g sugars
- Cholesterol: 108mg cholesterol
- Protein: 30g protein.
- Total Fat: 16g fat (8g saturated fat)

189.   Chicken Chili Enchiladas

Serving: 2 servings. | Prep: 20mins | Cook: 20mins | Ready in:

Ingredients

- 1 medium onion, thinly sliced
- 1 tablespoon butter

- 3 ounces cream cheese, cubed
- 2 tablespoons canned chopped green chilies
- 1/8 teaspoon salt
- 4 flour tortillas (8 inches)
- 2 tablespoons canola oil
- 3/4 cup shredded cooked chicken
- 1 tablespoon 2% milk
- 1 cup shredded Monterey Jack cheese
- Chopped green onions and sliced ripe olives, optional

Direction

- Sauté onion in butter in a small frying pan till softened. Take it away from the heat. Mix in salt, chilies and cream cheese until thoroughly blended.
- In another frying pan over medium heat, cook both sides of tortillas in oil till lightly browned and warmed. Drain on paper towels. Spoon a quarter of cream cheese mixture down the center of each tortilla. Top with chicken. Roll up, then arrange seam side-down in an 8-inch square baking dish greased with cooking spray.
- Bake while uncovered at 350° for about 15 minutes. Brush the tops with milk; dust with cheese. Bake for 5-10 minutes more or until cheese becomes melted. Top with olives and green onions if wanted.

Nutrition Information

- Calories: 877 calories
- Fiber: 2g fiber)
- Total Carbohydrate: 61g carbohydrate (6g sugars
- Cholesterol: 145mg cholesterol
- Protein: 44g protein.
- Total Fat: 52g fat (23g saturated fat)
- Sodium: 1261mg sodium

190. Chicken Church Casserole

Serving: 4 casseroles (12 servings each). | Prep: 35mins | Cook: 60mins | Ready in:

Ingredients

- 20 cups cubed cooked chicken
- 1 package (2 pounds) elbow macaroni, cooked and drained
- 6 jars (6 ounces each) sliced mushrooms, drained
- 2 jars (4 ounces each) diced pimientos, drained
- 2 large onions, chopped
- 2 large green peppers, chopped
- 4 cans (10-3/4 ounces each) condensed cream of celery soup, undiluted
- 4 cans (10-3/4 ounces each) condensed cream of mushroom soup, undiluted
- 2 pounds process cheese (Velveeta), cubed
- 1-1/3 cups milk
- 4 teaspoons dried basil
- 2 teaspoons lemon-pepper seasoning
- 2 cups crushed cornflakes
- 1/4 cup butter, melted

Direction

- Mix in a several large bowls the peppers, onions, pimientos, mushrooms, macaroni and chicken. Mix the lemon-pepper, basil, milk, cheese and soups in a separate big bowl; then put to chicken mixture.
- Put about 12 cups mixture in each of four 13x9-inch baking dishes that are greased. Keep in the refrigerator for overnight, covered.
- Take from refrigerator 30 minutes prior baking. Mix butter and cornflakes; dust over the casseroles. Then bake for 45 minutes at 350°F, covered. Then remove the cover and bake for 15-20 minutes longer or until bubbly.

Nutrition Information

- Calories: 271 calories

- Total Carbohydrate: 20g carbohydrate (3g sugars
- Cholesterol: 65mg cholesterol
- Protein: 23g protein.
- Total Fat: 11g fat (5g saturated fat)
- Sodium: 423mg sodium
- Fiber: 1g fiber)

191. Chicken Crescent Amandine

Serving: 8 servings. | Prep: 15mins | Cook: 20mins | Ready in:

Ingredients

- 1 can (10-3/4 ounces) condensed cream of chicken soup, undiluted
- 2/3 cup Miracle Whip
- 1/2 cup sour cream
- 2 tablespoons dried minced onion
- 3 cups cubed cooked chicken
- 1 can (8 ounces) sliced water chestnuts, drained
- 1 can (4 ounces) mushroom stems and pieces, drained
- 1/2 cup chopped celery
- 1 tube (8 ounces) refrigerated crescent rolls
- TOPPING:
- 2/3 cup shredded Swiss or American cheese
- 1/2 cup slivered almonds
- 2 tablespoons butter, melted

Direction

- Combine onion, sour cream, Miracle Whip, and soup in a large saucepan. Mix in celery, mushrooms, water chestnuts, and chicken; cook mixture over medium heat until bubbly and hot. Transfer to an unoiled 13x9-inch baking dish. Unroll crescent dough and divide into 2 separate rectangles, cutting of excess dough to fit the dish. Arrange dough rectangles over the hot chicken mixture.

Combine almonds and cheese; scatter over the dough. Drizzle butter over top.

- Bake without covering for 20 to 25 minutes at 375°, or until crust has a deep golden brown color. Serve right away.

Nutrition Information

- Calories: 528 calories
- Protein: 23g protein.
- Total Fat: 38g fat (11g saturated fat)
- Sodium: 778mg sodium
- Fiber: 2g fiber)
- Total Carbohydrate: 21g carbohydrate (5g sugars
- Cholesterol: 82mg cholesterol

192. Chicken Deep Dish Potpie

Serving: 6 servings. | Prep: 25mins | Cook: 50mins | Ready in:

Ingredients

- 2 cups all-purpose flour
- 1/4 teaspoon salt
- 2/3 cup cold butter, cubed
- 1/4 cup cold water
- FILLING:
- 2-1/2 cups cubed cooked chicken
- 2 cups fresh or frozen peas
- 2 medium potatoes, peeled and cubed
- 3 medium carrots, thinly sliced
- 2 celery ribs, finely chopped
- 1/4 cup finely chopped onion
- 3 tablespoons butter
- 3 tablespoons all-purpose flour
- 1 to 2 tablespoons chicken bouillon granules
- 1-1/2 teaspoons dried tarragon
- Pepper to taste
- 1 cup milk
- 1/2 cup chicken broth

- Additional milk

Direction

- Mix salt and flour in a large bowl; cut in butter till crumbly. Slowly put in water; use a fork to toss till a ball form. Set aside 1/3 of the dough. Unroll the remaining dough to fit a 2 1/2-quart baking sheet. Move the pastry to the baking sheet; trim even with edge; set aside.
- To make filling, mix together the onion, celery, carrots, potatoes, peas and chicken in a large bowl; set aside. Melt butter in a large saucepan. Mix in pepper, tarragon, bouillon and flour till smooth. Slowly mix in broth and milk. Boil the mixture; cook while stirring till thicken, 2 minutes. Mix into the chicken mixture; scoop into the crust.
- Unroll the reserved dough to fit the top of the pie. Create cutouts in the pastry. Place over the filling; trim, seal and flute the edges. Brush more milk over the pastry.
- Bake at 375° till the filling is bubbly and the crust turns golden brown, 50-60 minutes.

Nutrition Information

- Calories: 634 calories
- Cholesterol: 128mg cholesterol
- Protein: 28g protein.
- Total Fat: 32g fat (18g saturated fat)
- Sodium: 957mg sodium
- Fiber: 6g fiber)
- Total Carbohydrate: 58g carbohydrate (9g sugars

193. Chicken Divine

Serving: 6 servings. | Prep: 25mins | Cook: 0mins | Ready in:

Ingredients

- 6 boneless skinless chicken breast halves (4 ounces each)

- Dash pepper
- 3 cups frozen chopped broccoli, thawed
- 2 medium carrots, julienned
- 2 tablespoons water
- 1-3/4 cups three-cheese spaghetti sauce
- 2 tablespoons sherry or chicken broth
- 1/8 teaspoon ground nutmeg
- Hot cooked noodles

Direction

- In an 11x7-inch microwave-safe dish coated with grease, put chicken; sprinkle with pepper. Use waxed paper to cover. Microwave on high till the juices run clear, 4-6 minutes.
- Mix water, carrots and broccoli in a microwave-safe bowl. Microwave with a cover on high till crisp-tender, 2-3 minutes; strain. Spoon over the chicken.
- Mix nutmeg, sherry and spaghetti sauce together in a small bowl; transfer over the vegetables and chicken. Cook with a cover on high till heated through, 2-3 minutes. Serve along with noodles.

Nutrition Information

- Calories:
- Sodium:
- Fiber:
- Total Carbohydrate:
- Cholesterol:
- Protein:
- Total Fat:

---

194. Chicken Dressing Casserole

Serving: 6 servings. | Prep: 10mins | Cook: 50mins | Ready in:

Ingredients

- 1 can (14-1/2 ounces) reduced-sodium chicken broth
- 1 can (10-3/4 ounces) reduced-fat reduced-sodium condensed cream of chicken soup, undiluted
- 1 can (10-3/4 ounces) reduced-fat reduced-sodium condensed cream of mushroom soup, undiluted
- 1 package (6 ounces) reduced-sodium stuffing mix
- 2 cups cubed cooked chicken breast
- 1-1/2 cups frozen mixed vegetables, thawed
- 1/2 cup soft whole wheat bread crumbs
- 1 tablespoon butter, melted

Direction

- Mix soups and broth in a bowl; set aside. Layer half of stuffing mix, 1 cup of chicken, 3/4 cup of mixed vegetables and half of the soup mixture into a 2-quart baking dish greased with cooking spray. Repeat the layers. (The dish will be full.) Bake with a cover for 30 minutes at 350°. Bake without a cover for 15 minutes. Mix butter and bread crumbs in a small bowl. Scatter over the casserole. Bake till heated through and the topping turns golden brown, 5-10 more minutes. Allow to sit for 5 minutes before serving.

Nutrition Information

- Calories: 303 calories
- Protein: 21g protein. Diabetic Exchanges: 2-1/2 starch
- Total Fat: 6g fat (2g saturated fat)
- Sodium: 930mg sodium
- Fiber: 3g fiber)
- Total Carbohydrate: 39g carbohydrate (7g sugars
- Cholesterol: 49mg cholesterol

195.   Chicken Dumplings Meal

Serving: 8 servings. | Prep: 40mins | Cook: 60mins | Ready in:

Ingredients

- 1 broiler/fryer chicken (2-1/2 to 3 pounds), cut up
- 3 cups water
- 1 cup chopped onion
- 4 celery ribs, sliced
- 3 medium carrots, sliced
- 1 teaspoon celery seed
- 2 teaspoons rubbed sage, divided
- 1/4 teaspoon pepper
- 3 cups biscuit/baking mix
- 3/4 cup plus 2 tablespoons milk
- 1 tablespoon minced fresh parsley

Direction

- In a Dutch oven, put water and chicken. Boil it. Lower the heat, put a cover on and cook for 30 minutes until the chicken is soft.
- Take the chicken out of the kettle, remove the bone and dice. Put the chicken back into the kettle together with pepper, 1 teaspoon sage, celery seed, carrots, celery, and onion. Put a cover on and simmer until the vegetables are soft, about 45-60 minutes.
- To prepare the dumplings, mix together the leftover sage, parsley, milk, and biscuit mix to make a stiff batter. Into the simmering chicken mixture, drop the batter by tablespoonfuls. Put a cover on and simmer, about 15 minutes. Enjoy immediately.

Nutrition Information

- Calories: 276 calories
- Protein: 20g protein. Diabetic Exchanges: 2 starch
- Total Fat: 9g fat (0 saturated fat)
- Sodium: 284mg sodium
- Fiber: 0 fiber)

- Total Carbohydrate: 30g carbohydrate (0 sugars
- Cholesterol: 29mg cholesterol

196.   Chicken Enchilada Casserole

Serving: 6 servings. | Prep: 30mins | Cook: 30mins | Ready in:

Ingredients

- 1 large onion, chopped
- 1 medium green pepper, chopped
- 1 teaspoon butter
- 3 cups shredded cooked chicken breast
- 2 cans (4 ounces each) chopped green chilies
- 1/4 cup all-purpose flour
- 1-1/2 to 2 teaspoons ground coriander
- 2-1/2 cups reduced-sodium chicken broth
- 1 cup (8 ounces) reduced-fat sour cream
- 1 cup (4 ounces) reduced-fat Monterey Jack or reduced-fat Mexican cheese blend, divided
- 12 corn tortillas (6 inches), warmed

Direction

- Sauté green pepper and onion with butter in a small skillet until soft. Mix onion mixture, green chilies, and chicken together in a big bowl.
- Mix coriander and flour together in a small saucepan. Pour in broth, whisking until smooth. Stir and cook over medium heat until the mixture boils. Stir and cook until thickened, about another 1-2 minutes. Take away from heat, then mix in 1/2 cup cheese and sour cream. Mix into the chicken mixture with 3/4 cup sauce.
- Down the middle of each tortilla, put 1/3 cup chicken mixture. Roll up and put in a greased 13x9-inch baking dish with the seam side turning down. Add the leftover sauce on top and sprinkle the leftover cheese over. Bake

without a cover at 350° until fully heated, about 30-35 minutes.

Nutrition Information

- Calories: 383 calories
- Sodium: 710mg sodium
- Fiber: 5g fiber)
- Total Carbohydrate: 37g carbohydrate (5g sugars
- Cholesterol: 82mg cholesterol
- Protein: 33g protein. Diabetic Exchanges: 4 lean meat
- Total Fat: 12g fat (6g saturated fat)

197.   Chicken Enchiladas

Serving: Serves 8 | Prep: | Cook: | Ready in:

Ingredients

- 1 16-ounce container light sour cream
- 1 7-ounce can diced green chilies
- 4 large green onions, chopped
- 1/2 cup chopped fresh cilantro
- 1 1/2 teaspoons ground cumin
- 2 cups diced cooked chicken
- 2 cups packed grated sharp cheddar cheese (about 8 ounces)
- 8 8-inch-diameter flour tortillas
- 1 8-ounce package light cream cheese, cut lengthwise into 8 strips
- 1 1/2 16-ounce bottles mild picante sauce or salsa
- Additional chopped fresh cilantro (optional)

Direction

- Coat a 13x9x2-inch glass baking dish with butter. In a large bowl, combine 1 3/4 cups of sour cream, 1/2 cup of cilantro, chilies, cumin and green onions. Stir in one cup of cheddar cheese and chicken. Season the filling with pepper and salt.

- Generously scoop half cup of filling down the middle of each tortilla. Add cream cheese strip on top of the filling. Wrap the filling by rolling up each tortilla. Spread the enchiladas in the prepared dish with seam side down. (You can make three hours ahead and then chill while covered).
- Preheat the oven to 350 degrees F. Spread picante sauce on top of enchiladas. Cover and then bake for about 45 minutes until the enchiladas are heated through and the sauce bubbles. Remove cover, drizzle with the remaining one cup of cheddar cheese and then bake for about 5 minutes until the cheese has melted.
- Add the remaining sour cream on top. If desired, stud with cilantro.

Nutrition Information

- Calories: 533
- Saturated Fat: 16 g(80%)
- Sodium: 1327 mg(55%)
- Fiber: 3 g(14%)
- Total Carbohydrate: 39 g(13%)
- Cholesterol: 106 mg(35%)
- Protein: 25 g(51%)
- Total Fat: 32 g(49%)

198.   Chicken Feed

Serving: 6-8 servings. | Prep: 15mins | Cook: 45mins | Ready in:

Ingredients

- 1 small onion, sliced
- 2 cups fresh mushrooms, sliced
- 1 garlic clove, minced
- 1/2 teaspoon dried thyme, divided
- 1 tablespoon butter
- 4 cups cubed leftover cooked chicken
- 4 cups leftover gravy
- 1 chicken bouillon cube, crushed

- Dash pepper
- 3 cups mashed potatoes

Direction

- Sauté 1/4 teaspoon thyme, garlic, mushrooms, and onion with butter in a frying pan. Mix in pepper, bouillon, gravy, and chicken; transfer into a 3-quart casserole coated with cooking spray. Mix together the leftover thyme and potatoes, add to the mixture. Bake without a cover for 45 minutes at 350°.

Nutrition Information

- Calories:
- Total Fat:
- Sodium:
- Fiber:
- Total Carbohydrate:
- Cholesterol:
- Protein:

199. Chicken Flowerpot Pie

Serving: 6 servings. | Prep: 01hours15mins | Cook: 30mins | Ready in:

Ingredients

- PASTRY:
- 2 cups all-purpose flour
- 1 teaspoon salt
- 3/4 cup cold butter, cut into thin slices
- 3 tablespoons shortening
- 1/3 cup ice water
- FILLING:
- 1 broiler/fryer chicken (3 to 4 pounds), cut up
- 2 quarts water
- 1 bay leaf
- 1 garlic clove, minced
- 1-1/2 cups fresh or frozen cut green beans
- 1-1/2 cups thinly sliced carrots
- 1 cup diced peeled potatoes
- 1/2 teaspoon dried basil
- 1/2 cup sliced fresh mushrooms
- 1 package (10 ounces) frozen peas
- 1 can (14-1/2 ounces) diced tomatoes, drained
- 1/4 cup butter, cubed
- 1/4 cup all-purpose flour
- 2 large egg yolks
- 1 cup heavy whipping cream
- Salt and pepper to taste
- GLAZE:
- 1 large egg yolk
- 1 tablespoon cold water
- OTHER MATERIALS NEEDED:
- 6 new clay flowerpots (4-inch diameter)
- Canola oil
- Aluminum foil
- Decorative seed packets glued onto wooden craft sticks

Direction

- Combine salt and flour in a large bowl. Cut in shortening and butter until mixture becomes coarse crumbs. Slowly pour in water, stirring using a fork until dough becomes a ball; flatten the ball into a circle. Chill in the fridge for at least 3 hours or overnight.
- To make filling: Arrange garlic, bay leaf, water, and chicken in a Dutch oven. Bring to a boil. Lower heat; cook, covered until chicken is tender, about 30 to 40 minutes. Take chicken out; and debone chicken; put to one side. Ladle off fat. Add basil, potatoes, carrots, and beans to the broth. Simmer, covered until vegetables are tender, about 12 to 15 minutes. Mix in tomatoes, peas, and mushrooms; simmer, covered for 3 to 5 minutes. Strain vegetables, save the broth; put to one side. Melt butter in another large kettle. Stir in flour until no lumps remain. Pour in 1 1/2 cups of the saved stock. Bring to a boil. Cook while stirring until thickened, about 2 minutes. Combine cream and egg yolks in a small bowl. Stir into the sauce; turn off the heat. Add pepper and salt to season. Gently mix in vegetables and the reserved chicken.

- To make flowerpots, brush oil over the outsides of pots. Line a 15x12-inch piece of aluminum foil over each pot; gently press the foil down into the pot and make sure not to tear it. Pour about 1 1/2 cups of filling into each pot, leaving approximately 1/2-inch headspace; put to one side.
- Roll pastry to a thickness of 1/8-inch; cut 6 circles with 6 inches in diameter. Arrange one circle on each flowerpot, turn down the edges and flute. In the center of each pastry, cut three vents. Lightly whisk glaze ingredients in a small bowl; brush glaze mixture over per crust. Arrange flowerpots on a baking sheets. Bake for 30 to 35 minutes at 425°, or until the filling is bubbly and the crust turns golden brown. Garnish each flowerpot with a seed packet on a stick just before serving.

Nutrition Information

- Calories: 1000 calories
- Fiber: 6g fiber)
- Total Carbohydrate: 56g carbohydrate (9g sugars
- Cholesterol: 330mg cholesterol
- Protein: 40g protein.
- Total Fat: 68g fat (34g saturated fat)
- Sodium: 988mg sodium

200.   Chicken Livers Royale

Serving: 4 servings. | Prep: 20mins | Cook: 25mins | Ready in:

Ingredients

- 1/2 cup seasoned croutons
- 1 pound chicken livers, cut into bite-size pieces
- 2 tablespoons olive oil, divided
- 1 cup sliced fresh mushrooms
- 1/2 cup chopped onion
- 1 garlic clove, minced
- 16 pitted ripe olives, halved, optional
- 4 bacon strips, cooked and crumbled
- 1/2 cup spaghetti sauce
- 4 large eggs
- 1 cup shredded mozzarella cheese
- 1/4 cup chopped fresh parsley

Direction

- Grease four individual 10-ounce custard cups or ramekins with cooking spray. Separate croutons among dishes; put aside.
- Sauté chicken livers in 1 tablespoon of oil in a large skillet for 8 minutes until the outsides are lightly browned and the centers still look slightly pink. Take them out of the pan with a slotted spoon and arrange over croutons. Remove the drippings from the skillet.
- Sauté olives (if wanted), garlic, onion, and mushrooms in the same skillet in the remaining oil until vegetables seem tender. Use a slotted spoon to take them out of the pan and put over chicken livers. Scatter bacon over; pour with spaghetti sauce on top. Crack an egg into individual dish, then top with cheese.
- Bake, without covering, at 325° for about 25 to 30 minutes until whites are totally firm and the yolks start to thicken. Top with parsley. Serve immediately.

Nutrition Information

- Calories: 454 calories
- Fiber: 1g fiber)
- Total Carbohydrate: 14g carbohydrate (4g sugars
- Cholesterol: 739mg cholesterol
- Protein: 36g protein.
- Total Fat: 27g fat (9g saturated fat)
- Sodium: 579mg sodium

201. Chicken Noodle Delight

Serving: 6 servings. | Prep: 25mins | Cook: 35mins | Ready in:

Ingredients

- 4 cups uncooked egg noodles
- 1 can (10-3/4 ounces) condensed cream of chicken soup, undiluted
- 1 package (8 ounces) cream cheese, cubed
- 1 cup (8 ounces) sour cream
- 1/4 cup whole milk
- 3 tablespoons minced fresh parsley or 1 tablespoon dried parsley flakes
- 1 teaspoon salt
- 1 teaspoon onion salt
- 2 cups cubed cooked chicken
- 1-1/4 cups crushed saltines (about 35 crackers)
- 1/2 cup butter, melted

Direction

- Follow directions on package to cook noodles. In the meantime, mix cream cheese, onion salt, soup, parsley, sour cream, salt, and milk in a big bowl. Stir the chicken in. Drain water from noodles and mix with chicken mixture. Place in a 2-qt. greased dish. Mix butter and cracker crumbs; spread over dish. Do not cover; bake in a 350-degree oven until golden brown, 35-40 minutes.

Nutrition Information

- Calories: 653 calories
- Protein: 25g protein.
- Total Fat: 44g fat (25g saturated fat)
- Sodium: 1635mg sodium
- Fiber: 2g fiber)
- Total Carbohydrate: 36g carbohydrate (4g sugars
- Cholesterol: 180mg cholesterol

202. Chicken Nugget Casserole

Serving: 4-6 servings. | Prep: 5mins | Cook: 30mins | Ready in:

Ingredients

- 1 package (13-1/2 ounces) frozen chicken nuggets
- 1/3 cup grated Parmesan cheese
- 1 can (26-1/2 ounces) spaghetti sauce
- 1 cup shredded part-skim mozzarella cheese
- 1 teaspoon Italian seasoning

Direction

- In a greased 11x7-in. baking dish, add the chicken nuggets. Sprinkle Parmesan cheese on top. Then, layer the spaghetti sauce, mozzarella cheese, Italian seasoning.
- Cover and bake at 350° until cheese is melted and chicken is heated through, about 30-35 minutes.

Nutrition Information

- Calories: 355 calories
- Sodium: 1118mg sodium
- Fiber: 2g fiber)
- Total Carbohydrate: 22g carbohydrate (8g sugars
- Cholesterol: 59mg cholesterol
- Protein: 19g protein.
- Total Fat: 21g fat (8g saturated fat)

203. Chicken Parmesan Stuffed Shells

Serving: 12 servings. | Prep: 10mins | Cook: 15mins | Ready in:

Ingredients

- 1 package (12 ounces) uncooked jumbo pasta shells
- 2 tablespoons olive oil
- FILLING:
- 1 pound boneless skinless chicken breasts, cut into 1/2-inch cubes
- 1-1/2 teaspoons Italian seasoning
- 1 teaspoon salt, divided
- 1/2 teaspoon pepper, divided
- 1 tablespoon olive oil
- 2 tablespoons butter
- 1/3 cup seasoned bread crumbs
- 3 cups part-skim ricotta cheese
- 1 cup shredded part-skim mozzarella cheese
- 1/2 cup grated Parmesan cheese
- 1/2 cup 2% milk
- 1/4 cup chopped fresh Italian parsley
- ASSEMBLY:
- 4 cups meatless pasta sauce
- 1/4 cup grated Parmesan cheese
- 8 ounces fresh mozzarella cheese, thinly sliced and halved

Direction

- Set oven to 375° to preheat. Prepare shells following package directions for al dente; strain. Stir with oil; put onto a baking tray evenly.
- To make the filling, stir 1/4 teaspoon pepper, 1/2 teaspoon salt and Italian seasoning with chicken. Heat oil in a big skillet on medium-high heat; sauté chicken for about 2 mins until browned lightly. Turn the heat down to medium; mix butter in until melted. Mix in breadcrumbs; cook for 2 to 3 mins until crumbs are toasted slightly, mixing from time to time. Let cool a bit.
- Stir pepper and the remaining salt, parsley, milk and cheeses in a big bowl. Fold chicken in.
- Put 2 cups pasta sauce into a greased 13x9-inch baking tray. Stuff each shell with 2-1/2 tablespoons ricotta mix; put on top of the sauce. Put remaining sauce and cheeses on top (the tray will be full).

- Bake for half an hour, covered with greased foil; uncover, then bake for 10 to 15 mins until thoroughly heated.

Nutrition Information

- Calories: 431 calories
- Fiber: 2g fiber)
- Total Carbohydrate: 36g carbohydrate (8g sugars
- Cholesterol: 71mg cholesterol
- Protein: 28g protein.
- Total Fat: 19g fat (10g saturated fat)
- Sodium: 752mg sodium

204. Chicken Penne Casserole

Serving: 4 servings. | Prep: 35mins | Cook: 45mins | Ready in:

Ingredients

- 1-1/2 cups uncooked penne pasta
- 1 tablespoon canola oil
- 1 pound boneless skinless chicken thighs, cut into 1-inch pieces
- 1/2 cup chopped onion
- 1/2 cup chopped green pepper
- 1/2 cup chopped sweet red pepper
- 1 teaspoon dried basil
- 1 teaspoon dried oregano
- 1 teaspoon dried parsley flakes
- 1/2 teaspoon salt
- 1/2 teaspoon crushed red pepper flakes
- 3 garlic cloves, minced
- 1 can (14-1/2 ounces) diced tomatoes, undrained
- 3 tablespoons tomato paste
- 3/4 cup chicken broth
- 2 cups shredded part-skim mozzarella cheese
- 1/2 cup grated Romano cheese

Direction

- Prepare the oven by preheating to 350 degrees. Follow directions on package to cook the pasta. While cooking pasta, heat oil in a large pot on medium heat. Sauté chicken, seasonings, peppers, and onion until the meat of the chicken is not pink. Mix in garlic and heat 1 more minute. Pulse tomato paste and tomatoes until blended in blender with cover on. Add tomato mixture to pot with chicken. Mix in the broth and boil on medium heat. Cover, decrease heat, simmer for 10-15 minutes until somewhat thick. Drain water from pasta and toss with chicken and tomato mixture. Spread half the mixture into a 2-qt. greased baking pan. Put on half the cheese and repeat the layers. Bake, uncovered, for 30 minutes at 350 degrees. Make sure it is heated through may take an additional 15-20 minutes.

Nutrition Information

- Calories: 579 calories
- Sodium: 1357mg sodium
- Fiber: 4g fiber)
- Total Carbohydrate: 36g carbohydrate (9g sugars
- Cholesterol: 128mg cholesterol
- Protein: 47g protein.
- Total Fat: 28g fat (12g saturated fat)

205. Chicken Potato Delight

Serving: 6 servings. | Prep: 10mins | Cook: 60mins | Ready in:

Ingredients

- 1 can (10-3/4 ounces) condensed cream of chicken soup, undiluted
- 3/4 cup sour cream
- 1/4 cup whole milk
- 1 cup cubed cooked chicken
- 2-1/2 cups shredded cheddar cheese, divided

- 2-1/2 cups frozen shredded hash brown potatoes, thawed
- 1 can (2.8 ounces) french-fried onions
- 1 cup sour cream and onion potato chips

Direction

- Combine 1-1/4 cups cheese, chicken, milk, sour cream, and soup in a bowl. In a greased 2-qt. baking dish, spread out 3/4 of the mixture. Sprinkle over the top with hash browns and lightly press down. Then spread with the leftover soup mixture.
- Sprinkle with the remaining cheese, potato chips, and onions. Bake without cover for 1 hour at 350°, or until bubbly. Allow to sit for 5-10 minutes before serving.

Nutrition Information

- Calories:
- Protein:
- Total Fat:
- Sodium:
- Fiber:
- Total Carbohydrate:
- Cholesterol:

206. Chicken Potpie

Serving: 6 | Prep: | Cook: 15mins | Ready in:

Ingredients

- Filling
- 3 teaspoons canola oil, divided
- 1 cup frozen pearl onions, thawed
- 1 cup peeled baby carrots
- 10 ounces cremini mushrooms, halved
- 2½ cups reduced-sodium chicken broth, divided
- ¼ cup cornstarch
- 2½ cups diced cooked chicken, or turkey
- 1 cup frozen peas, thawed

- ¼ cup reduced-fat sour cream
- ¼ teaspoon salt
- Freshly ground pepper, to taste
- Biscuit topping
- ¾ cup whole-wheat pastry flour, (see Ingredient Note)
- ¾ cup all-purpose flour
- 2 teaspoons sugar
- 1¼ teaspoons baking powder
- ½ teaspoon baking soda
- ½ teaspoon salt
- 1 teaspoon dried thyme
- 1½ tablespoons cold butter, cut into small pieces
- 1 cup nonfat buttermilk, (see Tip)
- 1 tablespoon canola oil

Direction

- Prepare filling: Heat 1 tsp. oil in a Dutch oven/big skillet over medium-high heat. Add carrots and onions; cook and stir for 7 minutes till tender and golden brown. Put into a bowl. Heat leftover 2 tsp. oil in pan over medium-high heat then add mushrooms; cook while stirring often for 5-7 minutes till liquid evaporates and brown. Put carrots and onions back in the pan. Add 2 cups of broth; boil. Lower heat to simmer. Mix leftover 1/2 cup broth with cornstarch; add to pan. Cook, stirring till sauce thickens. Mix in pepper, salt, sour cream, peas and turkey/chicken; put filling into 2-qt. baking dish.
- Biscuit topping and bake potpie: Preheat an oven to 400°F. Whisk the thyme, salt, baking soda, baking powder, sugar, all-purpose flour and whole-wheat flour in a big bowl; cut butter into dry ingredients till crumbly with 2 knives/your fingertips. Add oil and buttermilk; mix just till combined. Drop dough in 6 even portions onto filling; put baking dish onto a baking sheet.
- Bake potpie for 30-35 minutes till filling is bubbling and topping is golden; cool for 10 minutes. Serve.

Nutrition Information

- Calories: 363 calories;
- Saturated Fat: 3
- Cholesterol: 59
- Sugar: 7
- Protein: 27
- Total Carbohydrate: 40
- Total Fat: 11
- Sodium: 849
- Fiber: 4

207.   Chicken Potpie Galette With Cheddar Thyme Crust

Serving: 8 servings. | Prep: 45mins | Cook: 30mins | Ready in:

Ingredients

- 1-1/4 cups all-purpose flour
- 1/2 cup shredded sharp cheddar cheese
- 2 tablespoons minced fresh thyme
- 1/4 teaspoon salt
- 1/2 cup cold butter, cubed
- 1/4 cup ice water
- FILLING:
- 3 tablespoons butter
- 2 large carrots, sliced
- 1 celery rib, diced
- 1 small onion, diced
- 8 ounces sliced fresh mushrooms
- 3 cups julienned Swiss chard
- 3 garlic cloves, minced
- 1 cup chicken broth
- 3 tablespoons all-purpose flour
- 1/2 teaspoon salt
- 1/4 teaspoon pepper
- 2 cups shredded cooked chicken
- 1/2 teaspoon minced fresh oregano
- 2 tablespoons minced fresh parsley

Direction

- Mix together salt, flour, thyme, and cheese; cut in the butter until it is crumbly. Slowly add the ice water, use a fork to mix until the dough stays together when pressed. Form into a disk; place in refrigerator for 1 hour.
- For the filling, on medium-high heat melt butter in a big pot. Add onion, carrots, and celery; stir and cook for 5-7 minutes or until a little soft. Add the mushrooms; cook for 3 more minutes. Add garlic and Swiss chard; cook 2-3 minutes or until wilted.
- Stir together pepper, flour, broth, and salt; gradually pour on veggies, stir continually. Cook 2-3 minutes until thick. Stir in oregano and chicken.
- Set oven to 400 degrees and start preheating. On a sheet of parchment paper with flour, roll the dough until it is a 12-in. circle. Move to a cookie sheet. Put the filling on the pastry spread close to edges, within 2 inches. Fold the pastry edges over the filling, making pleats, but leaving the middle uncovered. Put on a lower oven rack; bake 30-35 minutes or until filling is bubbling and crust is golden brown. Let it stand for 15 minutes before cutting. Sprinkle on parsley.

Nutrition Information

- Calories: 342 calories
- Sodium: 594mg sodium
- Fiber: 2g fiber)
- Total Carbohydrate: 22g carbohydrate (2g sugars
- Cholesterol: 81mg cholesterol
- Protein: 16g protein.
- Total Fat: 21g fat (12g saturated fat)

208.   Chicken Potpie With Cheddar Biscuit Topping

Serving: 9 servings. | Prep: 20mins | Cook: 45mins | Ready in:

Ingredients

- 4 cups cubed cooked chicken
- 1 package (12 ounces) frozen broccoli with cheese sauce
- 1 can (10-3/4 ounces) condensed cream of chicken and mushroom soup, undiluted
- 1 can (10-3/4 ounces) condensed cream of chicken soup, undiluted
- 2 medium potatoes, cubed
- 3/4 cup chicken broth
- 2/3 cup sour cream
- 1/2 cup frozen peas
- 1/4 teaspoon pepper
- TOPPING:
- 1-1/2 cups biscuit/baking mix
- 3/4 cup shredded sharp cheddar cheese
- 3/4 cup 2% milk
- 3 tablespoons butter, melted

Direction

- In a Dutch oven, combine the first nine ingredients; let boil. Place to a greased baking dish of 13x9-inch.
- In a small bowl, combine the topping ingredients; spoon over top. Bake with no cover at 350° for nearly 40 to 45 minutes till bubbly and topping has golden brown color. Allow 10 minutes to rest before serving.

Nutrition Information

- Calories: 457 calories
- Fiber: 2g fiber)
- Total Carbohydrate: 32g carbohydrate (4g sugars
- Cholesterol: 98mg cholesterol
- Protein: 27g protein.
- Total Fat: 24g fat (11g saturated fat)
- Sodium: 1181mg sodium

Serving: 6 servings. | Prep: 20mins | Cook: 15mins | Ready in:

Ingredients

- 2 cups frozen peas and carrots
- 1/2 cup chopped onion
- 1 can (4 ounces) mushroom pieces, drained
- 1/4 cup butter, cubed
- 1/3 cup all-purpose flour
- 1/2 teaspoon salt
- 1/4 teaspoon rubbed sage
- 1/8 teaspoon pepper
- 2 cups hot water
- 3/4 cup milk
- 3 teaspoons chicken bouillon granules
- 3 cups cubed cooked chicken or turkey
- 1 jar (2 ounces) diced pimientos, drained
- 1/4 cup minced fresh parsley
- Pastry for double-crust pie

Direction

- Follow the package instructions to cook frozen vegetables. Strain; set aside. Sauté mushrooms and onion in butter in a large saucepan till tender. Mix in pepper, sage, salt and flour till blended. Mix together bouillon, milk and water. Gradually put into the saucepan, stirring constantly.
- Boil the mixture. Cook while stirring till bubbly and thicken, 2 minutes. Mix in the reserved carrots and peas, parsley, pimientos and chicken. Spoon into six individual baking sheets.
- Roll and cut the pastry into circles 1 inch smaller than the top of the casseroles; put one circle on each. Bake at 425° till the crust turns light brown, 12-15 minutes.

Nutrition Information

- Calories: 605 calories
- Protein: 27g protein.
- Total Fat: 33g fat (15g saturated fat)
- Sodium: 1145mg sodium
- Fiber: 3g fiber)
- Total Carbohydrate: 50g carbohydrate (8g sugars
- Cholesterol: 101mg cholesterol

Serving: 4 servings. | Prep: 15mins | Cook: 01hours05mins | Ready in:

Ingredients

- 1 broiler/fryer chicken (3 to 4 pounds), cut up
- 1 tablespoon canola oil
- 1-1/2 cup chopped onion
- 3 garlic cloves, minced
- 2 cans (15-1/2 ounces each) great northern beans, rinsed and drained
- 1 can (29 ounces) diced tomatoes, undrained
- 3 medium carrots, sliced 1/4 inch thick
- 1 tablespoon chicken bouillon granules
- 1 teaspoon dried thyme
- 1/2 teaspoon dried oregano
- 1/2 teaspoon pepper

Direction

- In a large skillet, brown chicken in oil; take out and leave aside.
- Sauté garlic and onion in drippings until soften. Mix in the rest of ingredients.
- Spoon into a baking dish of 3-quart; place chicken pieces on top. Bake with cover at 350° for approximately 65 to 75 minutes till chicken juices run clear.

Nutrition Information

- Calories: 580 calories
- Fiber: 11g fiber)
- Total Carbohydrate: 37g carbohydrate (14g sugars
- Cholesterol: 132mg cholesterol

- Protein: 50g protein.
- Total Fat: 25g fat (6g saturated fat)
- Sodium: 1277mg sodium

---

211. Chicken Rice Casserole With Toasted Almonds

Serving: 10 servings. | Prep: 30mins | Cook: 50mins | Ready in:

Ingredients

- 2 cups uncooked long grain rice
- 2 cans (14-1/2 ounces each) reduced-sodium chicken broth
- 1/2 cup water
- 2 cans (10-3/4 ounces each) reduced-fat reduced-sodium condensed cream of chicken soup, undiluted
- 2 cups fat-free milk
- 1 tablespoon dried minced onion
- 1 teaspoon Worcestershire sauce
- 1/2 teaspoon salt
- 4 cups cubed cooked chicken breast
- 2 cups chopped celery
- 3/4 cup sliced almonds, toasted, divided

Direction

- Boil water, broth and rice in a large saucepan. Lower heat; simmer, covered, for 15-18 minutes or until rice is tender and liquid is absorbed.
- In the meantime, combine salt, Worcestershire sauce, onion, milk and soup in a large bowl. Mix in the rice, 1/2 cup almonds, celery and chicken. Place into a cooking spray-coated 13x9-in. baking dish.
- Bake at 350° for 45 minutes, covered. Take off the cover; sprinkle the rest of the almonds on top. Bake for 5-10 more minutes or until well heated.

Nutrition Information

- Calories: 334 calories
- Sodium: 660mg sodium
- Fiber: 2g fiber)
- Total Carbohydrate: 41g carbohydrate (5g sugars
- Cholesterol: 49mg cholesterol
- Protein: 25g protein. Diabetic Exchanges: 3 starch
- Total Fat: 7g fat (1g saturated fat)

---

212. Chicken Rice Casserole With Veggies

Serving: 6 servings. | Prep: 20mins | Cook: 25mins | Ready in:

Ingredients

- 6 boneless skinless chicken breast halves (1-1/2 pounds)
- 1 tablespoon canola oil
- 3/4 cup chopped sweet red pepper
- 3/4 cup chopped green pepper
- 1/2 cup chopped onion
- 1/2 cup chopped fresh mushrooms
- 1 garlic clove, minced
- 2 cups uncooked instant brown rice
- 2 cups chicken broth
- 1-1/2 cups frozen corn, thawed
- 1/4 teaspoon salt
- 1/8 teaspoon pepper
- 1/4 cup slivered almonds, toasted
- 2 tablespoons minced parsley

Direction

- Brown chicken in oil in a large skillet till a thermometer reads 170°, 4 minutes per side. Take away; keep warm. Sauté mushrooms, onion and peppers in the same skillet till tender. Put in garlic; cook for 1 more minutes. Mix in pepper, salt, corn, broth and rice; boil the mixture.
- Move onto an 11x7-inch baking sheet greased with cooking spray. Place chicken on top. Bake

at 350°, with cover, 20 minutes. Continue baking without a cover till heated through, 5 more minutes. Sprinkle parsley and almonds on top.

Nutrition Information

- Calories: 351 calories
- Total Carbohydrate: 37g carbohydrate (0 sugars
- Cholesterol: 66mg cholesterol
- Protein: 33g protein. Diabetic Exchanges: 3 lean meat
- Total Fat: 8g fat (1g saturated fat)
- Sodium: 493mg sodium
- Fiber: 4g fiber)

---

213.   Chicken Rice Dinner

Serving: 5 servings. | Prep: 20mins | Cook: 60mins | Ready in:

Ingredients

- 1/2 cup all-purpose flour
- 1 teaspoon salt
- 1/2 teaspoon pepper
- 10 bone-in chicken thighs (about 3-3/4 pounds)
- 3 tablespoons canola oil
- 1 cup uncooked long grain rice
- 1/4 cup chopped onion
- 2 garlic cloves, minced
- 1 can (4 ounces) mushroom stems and pieces, undrained
- 2 teaspoons chicken bouillon granules
- 2 cups boiling water
- Minced fresh parsley, optional

Direction

- Combine pepper, salt and flour together in a large resealable plastic bag. Insert the chicken thighs in one by one and toss to coat. In a big

skillet over medium heat, cook the chicken in oil until browned.
- In an ungreased 13-inch by 9-inch baking dish, then sprinkle with garlic and onion and top off with mushrooms. Insert the bouillon in boiling water until it dissolves then pour it over the baking dish. Place the chicken atop everything and cover it up. Bake at 350°F until the rice is tender, about 1 hour. It is ready when a thermometer reads 180°F. Garnish with parsley if desired.

Nutrition Information

- Calories:
- Total Fat:
- Sodium:
- Fiber:
- Total Carbohydrate:
- Cholesterol:
- Protein:

---

214.   Chicken Salad Casserole

Serving: 4 servings. | Prep: 10mins | Cook: 30mins | Ready in:

Ingredients

- 2 cups diced cooked chicken
- 1 can (10-3/4 ounces) condensed cream of chicken soup, undiluted
- 2 celery ribs, finely chopped
- 1/2 cup mayonnaise
- 1 can (4 ounces) mushroom stems and pieces, drained
- 2 tablespoons finely chopped onion
- 1/2 cup crushed butter-flavored crackers (about 12 crackers)
- 1/2 cup crushed potato chips
- 1/2 cup sliced almonds, toasted

Direction

- Combine the onion, mushrooms, mayonnaise, celery, soup and chicken in a big bowl then stir the cracker crumbs in. Grease a 1-1/2 quart baking dish and spoon the mixture in. Leave it uncovered and bake at 375°F for 15 minutes. Scatter almonds and potato chips over it. Continue baking until lightly browned and bubbly, about 15 minutes more.

Nutrition Information

- Calories: 578 calories
- Total Carbohydrate: 21g carbohydrate (3g sugars
- Cholesterol: 78mg cholesterol
- Protein: 27g protein.
- Total Fat: 43g fat (7g saturated fat)
- Sodium: 1044mg sodium
- Fiber: 3g fiber)

215.   Chicken Stuffing Bake

Serving: 6 servings. | Prep: 5mins | Cook: 45mins | Ready in:

Ingredients

- 6 boneless skinless chicken breast halves (6 ounces each)
- 6 slices Swiss cheese
- 1 can (10-3/4 ounces) condensed cream of chicken soup, undiluted
- 1/3 cup white wine or chicken broth
- 3 cups seasoned stuffing cubes
- 1/2 cup butter, melted

Direction

- In a greased baking dish of 13- x 9-inch, place chicken; place cheese on top. In a small bowl, combine wine and soup; spoon over cheese.
- In a small bowl, combine butter and stuffing cubes; sprinkle over soup. Bake with no cover at 350° for around 45 to 55 minutes till a thermometer measure 170°.

Nutrition Information

- Calories: 402 calories
- Fiber: 2g fiber)
- Total Carbohydrate: 22g carbohydrate (2g sugars
- Cholesterol: 86mg cholesterol
- Protein: 16g protein.
- Total Fat: 27g fat (15g saturated fat)
- Sodium: 947mg sodium

216.   Chicken Stuffing Casserole

Serving: 6-8 servings. | Prep: 15mins | Cook: 40mins | Ready in:

Ingredients

- 2 large potatoes, peeled and cubed
- 2 medium carrots, coarsely chopped
- 1 package (8 ounces) crushed corn bread stuffing
- 1/2 cup butter, melted
- 3 cups cubed cooked chicken
- 1 can (10-3/4 ounces) condensed cream of chicken soup, undiluted
- 1 can (10-3/4 ounces) condensed cream of celery soup, undiluted
- 1 cup chicken broth

Direction

- In a saucepan, place 1 inch of water; put in carrots and potatoes. Let boil. Lessen heat; simmer with cover for around 5 to 7 minutes until crisp-tender. Let drain and leave aside.
- Toss the butter and stuffing; in a greased baking dish of 13- x 9-inch, spread half of butter mixture. Have chicken to top. In a large bowl, combine the broth, soups, carrots and potatoes; spread over chicken evenly. Have the rest of stuffing mixture to sprinkle over.

Bake with no cover at 350° for nearly 40 to 45 minutes till heated through.

Nutrition Information

- Calories: 455 calories
- Sodium: 1170mg sodium
- Fiber: 4g fiber)
- Total Carbohydrate: 46g carbohydrate (4g sugars
- Cholesterol: 82mg cholesterol
- Protein: 22g protein.
- Total Fat: 20g fat (9g saturated fat)

217.   Chicken Supreme

Serving: 6 servings. | Prep: 15mins | Cook: 30mins | Ready in:

Ingredients

- 1/2 cup dry bread crumbs
- 1/2 cup grated Parmesan cheese
- 2 tablespoons minced fresh parsley
- 1 garlic clove, minced
- 1/4 teaspoon pepper
- 3 egg whites
- 6 boneless skinless chicken breast halves (4 ounces each)
- 1/4 cup sliced almonds
- Refrigerated butter-flavored spray

Direction

- Mix the initial 5 ingredients in shallow bowl. Whip egg whites in a separate shallow bowl. Dunk the chicken into the egg whites, then place in crumb mixture and coat. Place in a baking dish of 13x9-inch covered with cooking spray.
- Use almonds to sprinkle over chicken. Spray with butter-flavored spray. Bake with no cover at 350° for around 30 minutes till a thermometer registers 170°.

Nutrition Information

- Calories: 224 calories
- Protein: 33g protein. Diabetic Exchanges: 3-1/2 lean meat
- Total Fat: 6g fat (2g saturated fat)
- Sodium: 304mg sodium
- Fiber: 1g fiber)
- Total Carbohydrate: 8g carbohydrate (0 sugars
- Cholesterol: 71mg cholesterol

218.   Chicken Taco Pie

Serving: 6 servings. | Prep: 20mins | Cook: 30mins | Ready in:

Ingredients

- 1 tube (8 ounces) refrigerated crescent rolls
- 1 pound ground chicken
- 1 envelope taco seasoning
- 1 can (4 ounces) chopped green chilies
- 1/2 cup water
- 1/2 cup salsa
- 1/2 cup shredded Mexican cheese blend
- 1 cup shredded lettuce
- 1 small sweet red pepper, chopped
- 1 small green pepper, chopped
- 1 medium tomato, seeded and chopped
- 1 green onion, thinly sliced
- 2 tablespoons pickled jalapeno slices
- Sour cream and additional salsa

Direction

- Heat the oven to 350°F. Get the crescent dough and unroll it. Make sure to separate the dough into individual triangles. Grease a 9-inch pie plate. Press dough in the bottom to make a crust. Make sure to seal the seams. Bake until it's golden brown, 18-20 minutes.
- In the meantime, put a big skillet on medium heat and cook the chicken in it. When cooking crumble chicken, continue cooking until the meat is not pink anymore, 6-8 minutes. Drain

grease. Put in salsa, water, green chilies, and taco seasoning. Let it boil.

- Use a spoon to place mixture on the crust, then get cheese and sprinkle it on top. Put it back in the oven and let it bake until the cheese melts, 8-10 minutes.
- Use pickled jalapeno, green onion, tomato, peppers, and lettuce as toppings. The pizza can be served with a side of additional salsa and sour cream.

Nutrition Information

- Calories: 328 calories
- Fiber: 1g fiber)
- Total Carbohydrate: 25g carbohydrate (5g sugars
- Cholesterol: 58mg cholesterol
- Protein: 17g protein.
- Total Fat: 17g fat (6g saturated fat)
- Sodium: 1122mg sodium

219.   Chicken Tetrazzini

Serving: 8 | Prep: | Cook: | Ready in:

Ingredients

- 8 chicken tenderloins
- salt and pepper to taste
- 3/4 cup fresh sliced mushrooms
- 1 red bell pepper, chopped
- 1/2 yellow bell pepper, chopped
- 1 (8 ounce) package uncooked spaghetti
- 1/4 cup butter
- 1/4 cup all-purpose flour
- 1 cup chicken broth
- 1 cup half-and-half
- 1 teaspoon garlic salt
- ground black pepper to taste
- 1/2 cup shredded Swiss cheese
- 1/3 cup grated Parmesan cheese
- 1/4 cup grated Parmesan cheese for topping (optional)

Direction

- Sauté the tenderloins in a large non-skillet. Season to taste with pepper and salt. Add yellow bell peppers, red bell peppers, and mushrooms; cook until the greens are tender.
- Cook the spaghetti following the package directions. Let drain and put aside.
- Melt margarine or butter in a large saucepan, then blend in flour. Stir in half-and-half and the chicken broth gradually. Over medium-low heat, cook until the sauce starts to thicken, stirring constantly. Add ground black pepper and garlic salt to taste. Blend in the Parmesan and Swiss cheeses, then continue to heat until the cheeses melt, stirring constantly.
- Stir in the vegetable/chicken mixture and heat thoroughly. Then toss with the cooked pasta; if desired, put grated Parmesan cheese on top.

Nutrition Information

- Calories: 329 calories;
- Sodium: 421
- Total Carbohydrate: 27.7
- Cholesterol: 70
- Protein: 22.3
- Total Fat: 14

220.   Chicken Wild Rice Casserole

Serving: 6-8 servings. | Prep: 15mins | Cook: 30mins | Ready in:

Ingredients

- 1 package (6 ounces) long grain and wild rice mix
- 3 tablespoons plus 1 teaspoon cornstarch
- 1 teaspoon salt
- Dash black pepper
- 1 can (12 ounces) evaporated skim milk
- 12 ounces chicken broth

- 1/4 cup chopped onion
- 2 tablespoons butter
- 5 cups cubed cooked chicken
- 1/4 cup diced pimientos
- 1/4 cup minced fresh parsley

Direction

- Prepare the rice following package directions, omitting butter; put aside.
- Mix the broth, milk, pepper, salt and cornstarch in a big saucepan until smooth. Put in butter and onion. Boil. Cook and mix for two minutes or until thickened.
- In a 2-quart baking tray, mix the reserved rice, sauce, parsley, pimientos and chicken. Bake at 375°, uncovered, for half an hour or until thoroughly heated.

Nutrition Information

- Calories: 336 calories
- Total Fat: 12g fat (6g saturated fat)
- Sodium: 895mg sodium
- Fiber: 1g fiber)
- Total Carbohydrate: 24g carbohydrate (5g sugars
- Cholesterol: 99mg cholesterol
- Protein: 31g protein.

---

221. Chicken Zucchini Casserole

Serving: 6 servings. | Prep: 20mins | Cook: 45mins |Ready in:

Ingredients

- 1 package (6 ounces) stuffing mix
- 3/4 cup butter, melted
- 3 cups diced zucchini
- 2 cups cubed cooked chicken breast
- 1 can (10-3/4 ounces) condensed cream of chicken soup, undiluted

- 1 medium carrot, shredded
- 1/2 cup chopped onion
- 1/2 cup sour cream

Direction

- In a big bowl, combine butter and stuffing mix together. Leave a half cup aside for topping. Put the sour cream, onion, carrot, soup, chicken and zucchini into the leftover stuffing mixture.
- Move to a greased 11x7-inch baking dish. Top with the reserved stuffing mixture. Let bake while uncovered at 350° for around 40-45 minutes, or until bubbly and golden brown.

Nutrition Information

- Calories: 481 calories
- Sodium: 1174mg sodium
- Fiber: 2g fiber)
- Total Carbohydrate: 27g carbohydrate (6g sugars
- Cholesterol: 115mg cholesterol
- Protein: 21g protein.
- Total Fat: 31g fat (18g saturated fat)

---

222. Chicken And Cheddar Enchiladas

Serving: 4-6 servings. | Prep: 15mins | Cook: 20mins |Ready in:

Ingredients

- 4 cups shredded cooked chicken
- 2 cups shredded cheddar cheese, divided
- 1 can (10-3/4 ounces) condensed cream of mushroom soup, undiluted
- 1/3 cup chopped onion
- 1 teaspoon salt
- 1/4 teaspoon pepper
- 3 cans (8 ounces each) tomato sauce
- 1 tablespoon chili powder

- 1/4 teaspoon ground cumin
- 1 can (2-1/4 ounces) sliced ripe olives, drained
- 10 flour tortillas (8 inches)
- 1/2 cup shredded Monterey Jack cheese

Direction

- In a bowl, combine 1 cup cheddar cheese, chicken, onion, soup, pepper and salt; leave aside. In a saucepan, combine chili powder, tomato sauce, olives and cumin. Uncover and simmer for around 5 to 10 minutes.
- In the meantime, on each tortilla, spoon 1/3 to 1/2 cup of chicken mixture down the center. Roll up; in a greased baking dish that's 13x9 inches in size, place tortillas seam side down. Place the tomato sauce mixture on top; sprinkle with the rest of the cheddar cheese and Monterey Jack cheese. Uncover and bake at 350° for approximately 20 to 25 minutes till heated through.

Nutrition Information

- Calories: 660 calories
- Total Fat: 29g fat (13g saturated fat)
- Sodium: 1802mg sodium
- Fiber: 2g fiber)
- Total Carbohydrate: 52g carbohydrate (2g sugars
- Cholesterol: 133mg cholesterol
- Protein: 47g protein.

223. Chicken And Dressing Dish

Serving: 8 servings. | Prep: 15mins | Cook: 55mins | Ready in:

Ingredients

- 1 cup chopped onion
- 1 cup chopped celery
- 1/4 cup butter, cubed

- 2 cups chicken broth
- 1-1/2 teaspoons dried thyme
- 1 teaspoon poultry seasoning
- 1/2 teaspoon salt
- 1/2 teaspoon pepper
- 1/4 teaspoon ground nutmeg
- 2 large eggs, lightly beaten, or 1/2 cup egg substitute
- 1 package (12 ounces) unseasoned stuffing cubes
- 1/4 cup minced fresh parsley
- 3 cups cubed cooked chicken
- 1 can (10-3/4 ounces) condensed cream of chicken or mushroom soup, undiluted
- 1/3 cup water

Direction

- In a large saucepan, sauté celery and onion until tender in butter; take off the heat. Mix in the eggs, seasonings and broth. Add parsley and bread cubes; coat by tossing.
- Add to a 13-in. x 9-in. greased baking dish. Place chicken on top. Combine water and soup; use a spoon to add on top the chicken. Let it sit for 10 minutes.
- Bake at 350°, covered for 50 minutes. Take off the cover; bake for another 5-10 minutes or until a thermometer reads 160°.

Nutrition Information

- Calories: 390 calories
- Protein: 26g protein. Diabetic Exchanges: 2-1/2 starch
- Total Fat: 13g fat (0 saturated fat)
- Sodium: 572mg sodium
- Fiber: 0 fiber)
- Total Carbohydrate: 41g carbohydrate (0 sugars
- Cholesterol: 48mg cholesterol

224.   Chicken And Ham Roll Ups

Serving: 4-6 servings. | Prep: 15mins | Cook: 10mins | Ready in:

Ingredients

- 3 cups cooked rice
- 1-1/2 cups chopped cooked chicken
- 1 can (10-3/4 ounces) condensed cream of chicken soup, undiluted, divided
- 1/4 cup finely chopped celery
- 1 green onion, thinly sliced
- 1/4 teaspoon pepper, divided
- 6 slices fully cooked ham
- 1/4 cup sour cream or plain yogurt
- 1/4 cup milk
- 1/4 teaspoon dried thyme
- 1/2 cup shredded Swiss or part-skim mozzarella cheese
- Paprika or additional chopped green onion

Direction

- In an 11x7-inch microwave-safe baking dish coated with cooking spray, spread rice; put aside. Mix 1/8 teaspoon pepper, onion, celery, 1/3 cup soup, and chicken together in a medium-sized bowl. On each slice of ham, put 1/4 cup and roll up. If needed, use a toothpick to keep in place. Put the ham rolls on top of the rice with the seam side facing down.
- Mix together the leftover pepper and soup, thyme, milk, and sour cream; add to the rolls. Put a cover on and microwave on high for 6-10 minutes until fully heated, turning the dish 1/2 through the cooking time. Sprinkle paprika or onion and cheese over. Put a cover on and let sit for 5 minutes. Discard the toothpicks before enjoying.

Nutrition Information

- Calories:
- Sodium:
- Fiber:
- Total Carbohydrate:
- Cholesterol:
- Protein:
- Total Fat:

225.   Chicken And Rice

Serving: 6 | Prep: 5mins | Cook: 15mins | Ready in:

Ingredients

- 2 cups instant rice
- 1 (5 ounce) can chicken chunks, drained
- 1 (10.75 ounce) can condensed cream of chicken soup

Direction

- Prepare rice as directed on package.
- Once rice is ready, add chicken; keep stirring over low heat. Stir in soup; keep cooking until thoroughly heated.

Nutrition Information

- Calories: 205 calories;
- Total Fat: 5.3
- Sodium: 456
- Total Carbohydrate: 29.4
- Cholesterol: 19
- Protein: 8.6

226.   Chicken And Rice Dinner

Serving: 6 servings. | Prep: 15mins | Cook: 55mins | Ready in:

Ingredients

- 1 broiler/fryer chicken (3-1/2 to 4 pounds), cut up
- 1/4 to 1/3 cup all-purpose flour

- 2 tablespoons canola oil
- 2-1/3 cups water
- 1-1/2 cups uncooked long grain rice
- 1 cup milk
- 1 teaspoon salt
- 1 teaspoon poultry seasoning
- 1/2 teaspoon pepper
- Minced fresh parsley

Direction

- Coat chicken with flour. Cook chicken in oil in a large skillet over medium heat until evenly browned on all sides. Combine pepper, poultry seasoning, salt, milk, rice, and water in a large bowl. Transfer mixture into an oiled 13x9-inch baking dish. Place chicken over the mixture.
- Bake, covered for 55 minutes at 350° or until juices run clear. Top with parsley before serving.

Nutrition Information

- Calories: 541 calories
- Sodium: 504mg sodium
- Fiber: 1g fiber)
- Total Carbohydrate: 43g carbohydrate (2g sugars
- Cholesterol: 108mg cholesterol
- Protein: 38g protein.
- Total Fat: 23g fat (6g saturated fat)

---

227.   Chicken And Spinach Supper

Serving: 8 servings. | Prep: 20mins | Cook: 40mins | Ready in:

Ingredients

- 4 packages (10 ounces each) frozen chopped spinach, thawed and well drained
- 1/4 teaspoon ground nutmeg

- 1 teaspoon salt, divided, optional
- 4 cups diced cooked chicken
- 1/4 cup butter
- 1/4 cup all-purpose flour
- 1/4 teaspoon pepper
- 1/8 teaspoon paprika
- 2 cups chicken broth
- 1 tablespoon lemon juice
- 1/2 teaspoon dried rosemary, crushed
- TOPPING:
- 1 tablespoon butter, melted
- 1/2 cup bread crumbs
- 1/3 cup grated Parmesan cheese

Direction

- Mix together the optional 1/2 teaspoon salt, nutmeg, and spinach. Push in the bottom of a 13x9-in. greased pan. Put chicken on top. In a pot, melt butter. Add paprika, pepper, flour, and the rest of the optional salt. Stir until a smooth paste is formed. Slowly add rosemary, broth, and lemon juice while stirring continually. Heat to a boil. Cook until thick, about 1 minute. Dump over chicken. Mix the ingredients for the topping and spread on top. Do not cover; bake in a 350-degree oven until bubbling, 40-45 minutes.

Nutrition Information

- Calories: 298 calories
- Fiber: 0 fiber)
- Total Carbohydrate: 14g carbohydrate (0 sugars
- Cholesterol: 73mg cholesterol
- Protein: 31g protein. Diabetic Exchanges: 4 lean meat
- Total Fat: 12g fat (0 saturated fat)
- Sodium: 307mg sodium

228. Chicken And Wild Rice Bake

Serving: 10 servings. | Prep: 60mins | Cook: 50mins | Ready in:

Ingredients

- 3 cups water
- 1 cup uncooked wild rice
- 2-1/2 teaspoons salt, divided
- 1/4 cup butter, cubed
- 1 pound sliced fresh mushrooms
- 1 medium onion, chopped
- 3 cups diced cooked chicken
- 1 jar (2 ounces) chopped pimiento, drained
- 1/4 cup minced fresh parsley
- 1/4 teaspoon pepper
- 1 cup chicken broth
- 1 cup heavy whipping cream
- 1/4 cup grated Parmesan cheese
- 3/4 cup slivered almonds

Direction

- Bring water in a large sauce to a boil. Mix in 1 teaspoon salt and rice. Lower heat; cover and simmer for 45 to 50 minutes until kernels have puffed open. Drain any excess liquid.
- Turn oven to 350° to preheat. Melt butter over medium-high heat in a 6-quart stockpot. Sauté onion and mushrooms in melted butter for 5 minutes. Mix in the remaining salt, cream, broth, pepper, parsley, pimiento, chicken, and rice.
- Pour mixture into a 13x9-inch baking dish. Sprinkle top with almonds and cheese. Bake without covering for 50 to 60 minutes until heated through.

Nutrition Information

- Calories: 332 calories
- Sodium: 809mg sodium
- Fiber: 3g fiber)
- Total Carbohydrate: 18g carbohydrate (3g sugars

- Cholesterol: 79mg cholesterol
- Protein: 19g protein.
- Total Fat: 21g fat (10g saturated fat)

229. Chicken In Every Pot Pie

Serving: 8 | Prep: | Cook: | Ready in:

Ingredients

- 4 cups cubed, cooked chicken meat
- 1 1/2 cups chicken broth
- 1 1/2 cups frozen green peas
- 4 carrots, sliced
- 1 (10.75 ounce) can condensed cream of mushroom soup
- 1/4 teaspoon salt
- 1/4 teaspoon ground black pepper
- 2 cups baking mix
- 1 1/4 cups milk
- 1 teaspoon garlic powder
- 1/2 teaspoon celery seed
- 1/4 teaspoon paprika

Direction

- Combine pepper, salt, soup, carrots, peas, broth and chicken in a saucepan. Boil, stirring occasionally.
- In the meantime, combine celery seed, garlic powder, milk and the biscuit mix (the mixture will be thin).
- Transfer the hot chicken mixture to the 9x13 oiled oven proof dish. Evenly spoon the biscuit mixture over top of chicken mixture immediately. Top with the paprika.
- Bake, uncovered, for 30 to 35 mins at 350°F (175°C), until the topping turns golden brown.

Nutrition Information

- Calories: 305 calories;
- Sodium: 1147
- Total Carbohydrate: 33.9

- Cholesterol: 56
- Protein: 26.2
- Total Fat: 6.7

---

230. Chili Chicken

Serving: 12 | Prep: 10mins | Cook: 20mins | Ready in:

Ingredients

- 2 tablespoons honey
- 5 tablespoons sweet chili sauce
- 3 tablespoons soy sauce
- 12 chicken drumsticks, skin removed

Direction

- Combine sweet chili sauce, soy sauce, and honey in a big bowl. Put a small dish of marinade aside for basting. Put drumsticks in a bowl and cover with remaining marinade. Cover; place in refrigerator for at least 1 hour.
- Start an outdoor grill and preheat for medium-high heat.
- Put a little oil on the grill grate. Place drumsticks on grill. Grill until juices are clear, 10 minutes a side. During the last 5 minutes, use the reserved marinade to baste often.

Nutrition Information

- Calories: 142 calories;
- Total Carbohydrate: 5.9
- Cholesterol: 62
- Protein: 19.6
- Total Fat: 4.1
- Sodium: 353

231. Colorful Chicken Casserole

Serving: 2 casseroles (4 servings each). | Prep: 25mins | Cook: 30mins | Ready in:

Ingredients

180°

- 1 cup chopped celery
- 1 cup chopped green pepper
- 3/4 cup chopped onion
- 2 tablespoons butter
- 1 cup chicken broth *chicken gravy*
- 1 cup frozen corn
- 1 cup frozen peas
- 1 teaspoon salt, optional
- 1/4 teaspoon pepper
- 3 cups cubed cooked chicken
- 1 package (7 ounces) elbow macaroni, cooked and drained
- 1 jar (4-1/2 ounces) sliced mushrooms, drained
- 1 cup shredded cheddar cheese

Direction

- Stir-fry in butter in a large skillet the onion, green pepper and celery until tender. Stir in the salt, peas, corn, broth, if wished, and pepper; heat through.
- Mix in macaroni and chicken.
- Split between 2 11x7 inch baking dishes that is coated with cooking spray. Sprinkle cheese and mushrooms on top.
- Cover one casserole and freeze for up to 3 months. Place the second casserole in the oven and bake for 20 minutes at 350°F, covered. Remove cover and bake for 10 minutes longer or until heated through.
- To consume frozen casserole: Take from the freezer 30 minutes prior to baking. Place in the oven and bake for 35 minutes at 350°F. Remove cover and bake for 15 minutes longer or until heated through.

Nutrition Information

- Calories: 295 calories
- Protein: 25g protein. Diabetic Exchanges: 3 lean meat
- Total Fat: 9g fat (4g saturated fat)
- Sodium: 334mg sodium
- Fiber: 3g fiber)
- Total Carbohydrate: 30g carbohydrate (4g sugars
- Cholesterol: 62mg cholesterol

232. Colorful Chicken And Rice

Serving: 6-8 servings. | Prep: 20mins | Cook: 25mins | Ready in:

Ingredients

- 1 can (10-3/4 ounces) condensed cream of chicken soup, undiluted
- 1 cup (8 ounces) sour cream
- 1/2 cup 4% cottage cheese
- 3 ounces cream cheese, cubed
- 3 cups cubed cooked chicken
- 3 cups cooked rice
- 1-1/2 cups shredded Monterey Jack cheese
- 1 can (4 ounces) chopped green chilies
- 1 can (2-1/4 ounces) sliced ripe olives, drained
- 1/8 teaspoon garlic salt
- 1-1/2 cups crushed corn chips
- 2 cups shredded lettuce
- 2 medium tomatoes, chopped

Direction

- Mix cream cheese, cottage cheese, sour cream and soup in a blender; keep it covered and process till becoming smooth. Move into a big bowl. Mix in garlic salt, olives, chilies, Monterey Jack cheese, rice and chicken.
- Add to one greased 2-qt. baking dish. Bake, while uncovered, at 350 degrees till thoroughly heated or for 25 to 30 minutes. Just prior to serving, add tomatoes, lettuce and corn chips on top.

Nutrition Information

- Calories: 497 calories
- Protein: 28g protein.
- Total Fat: 24g fat (12g saturated fat)
- Sodium: 836mg sodium
- Fiber: 3g fiber)
- Total Carbohydrate: 40g carbohydrate (4g sugars
- Cholesterol: 103mg cholesterol

233. Comforting Chicken

Serving: 4 servings. | Prep: 15mins | Cook: 45mins | Ready in:

Ingredients

- 1 medium onion, sliced and separated into rings
- 1/2 cup butter, cubed
- 1 broiler/fryer chicken (3 to 4 pounds), cut up
- 4 medium potatoes, peeled and quartered
- 4 medium carrots, quartered widthwise
- 1 cup heavy whipping cream
- 1 tablespoon minced fresh parsley
- 1/2 teaspoon salt
- 1/4 teaspoon pepper

Direction

- Put butter in a large frying pan and sauté onion until soft. Use a slotted spoon to remove onion and set it aside. In the same frying pan, add the chicken pieces and brown on all sides. Put the onion back in and add carrots and potatoes. Cover; cook on medium-low until veggies are tender and chicken juices are clear, 30 minutes. Mix in pepper, parsley, salt, and cream. Do not cover, decrease heat, and simmer until a slightly thick, 15 minutes.

Nutrition Information

- Calories: 941 calories
- Protein: 47g protein.
- Total Fat: 66g fat (34g saturated fat)
- Sodium: 689mg sodium
- Fiber: 5g fiber)
- Total Carbohydrate: 40g carbohydrate (10g sugars
- Cholesterol: 274mg cholesterol

234.   Cordon Bleu Casserole

Serving: 6 servings. | Prep: 25mins | Cook: 25mins | Ready in:

Ingredients

- 2 cups cubed fully cooked ham
- 4 cups cubed cooked turkey
- 1 cup shredded Swiss cheese
- 1 large onion, chopped
- 1/3 cup butter, cubed
- 1/3 cup all-purpose flour
- 1/8 teaspoon ground mustard
- 1/8 teaspoon ground nutmeg
- 1-3/4 cups whole milk
- TOPPING:
- 1-1/2 cups soft bread crumbs
- 1/2 cup shredded Swiss cheese
- 1/4 cup butter, melted

Direction

- Cook ham in a big nonstick frying pan until turning brown, about 4-5 minutes; strain and tap dry. In a 2-quart baking dish coated with cooking spray, place ham, cheese, and turkey; put aside.
- Sauté onion with butter in a big saucepan until soft. Mix in nutmeg, mustard, and flour until combined. Slowly whisk in milk. Boil it, cook while stirring until thickened, about 2 minutes. Add over the ham.
- Mix together the topping ingredients, sprinkle onto the top. Bake without a cover at 350° until

bubbly and turning golden brown, about 25-30 minutes.

Nutrition Information

- Calories: 601 calories
- Cholesterol: 178mg cholesterol
- Protein: 48g protein.
- Total Fat: 37g fat (20g saturated fat)
- Sodium: 1008mg sodium
- Fiber: 1g fiber)
- Total Carbohydrate: 18g carbohydrate (6g sugars

235.   Creamed Chicken 'n' Veggies

Serving: 6 servings. | Prep: 5mins | Cook: 15mins | Ready in:

Ingredients

- 2 cups frozen mixed vegetables
- 2 cups frozen broccoli cuts
- 2 tablespoons olive oil
- 4 cups cubed cooked chicken
- 1 jar (16 ounces) roasted garlic Parmesan Alfredo sauce
- 1/2 teaspoon salt
- 1/4 teaspoon pepper
- Hot cooked rice

Direction

- Sauté broccoli and mixed vegetables in oil until tender in a large skillet. Stir in pepper, salt, Alfredo sauce and chicken; heat through. Serve with rice.

Nutrition Information

- Calories:
- Total Fat:
- Sodium:

- Fiber:
- Total Carbohydrate:
- Cholesterol:
- Protein:

236.   Creamy Buffalo Chicken Enchiladas

Serving: 6 servings. | Prep: 15mins | Cook: 25mins | Ready in:

Ingredients

- 3 cups shredded rotisserie chicken
- 1 can (10 ounces) enchilada sauce
- 1/4 cup Buffalo wing sauce
- 1-1/4 cups shredded Monterey Jack or cheddar cheese, divided
- 12 corn tortillas (6 inches), warmed
- 1 can (10-3/4 ounces) condensed cream of celery soup, undiluted
- 1/2 cup blue cheese salad dressing
- 1/4 cup 2% milk
- 1/4 teaspoon chili powder
- Optional toppings: sour cream, thinly sliced green onions and additional Buffalo wing sauce

Direction

- Preheat the oven at 350°. Mix wing sauce, enchilada sauce and chicken in a big bowl. Mix 3/4 cup cheese in.
- On every tortilla, put 1/4 cup chicken mixture off center. Roll up. Put in, seam side down, 13x9-in. greased baking dish.
- Mix milk, salad dressing and soup in a small bowl. Put on enchiladas. Sprinkle leftover cheese on. Put chili powder on top.
- Bake for 25-30 minutes or heated through and cheese melts, uncovered. Put toppings as you want. Freezing: Freeze unbaked casserole, covered. Use: Partially thaw in refrigerator overnight prior to use. 30 minutes before baking, remove it from the fridge. Preheat the oven to 350°. As directed, bake casserole; add more time as needed to let heat through. An inserted thermometer in the middle should read 165°.

Nutrition Information

- Calories: 477 calories
- Sodium: 1195mg sodium
- Fiber: 5g fiber)
- Total Carbohydrate: 31g carbohydrate (3g sugars
- Cholesterol: 92mg cholesterol
- Protein: 31g protein.
- Total Fat: 27g fat (8g saturated fat)

237.   Creamy Chicken Enchiladas

Serving: 6 | Prep: 40mins | Cook: | Ready in:

Ingredients

- ½ pound skinless, boneless chicken breasts
- 4 cups torn fresh spinach or ½ of one 10-ounce package frozen chopped spinach, thawed and well-drained
- ¼ cup green onions, thinly sliced
- 1 (8 ounce) carton light dairy sour cream
- ¼ cup plain fat-free yogurt
- 2 tablespoons all-purpose flour
- ¼ teaspoon ground cumin
- ¼ teaspoon salt
- ½ cup fat-free milk
- 1 (4 ounce) can diced green chiles, drained
- 6 (7 inch) flour tortillas
- ⅓ cup reduced-fat Cheddar or MontereyJack cheese (1- ½ ounces)
- Chopped tomato or salsa (optional)
- Thinly sliced green onion (optional)

Direction

- Put the chicken in a 3-qt. saucepan and add an enough amount of water to cover. Boil it, lower the heat. Put a cover on and simmer until the chicken is not pink anymore, or for about 15 minutes. Take the chicken out of the saucepan. Once cool enough to handle, shred the chicken into bite-size pieces with a fork. (You should prepare approximately 1 1/2 cups). Put aside.
- If you use fresh spinach, in a steamer basket over boiling water, put the spinach. Lower the heat. Put a cover on and steam until soft or for 3 – 5 minutes. (Alternatively, cook in a small amount of boiling water with a cover on, for 3-5 minutes). Strain thoroughly.
- Mix green onions, spinach, and chicken together in a big bowl; put aside. Mix salt, cumin, flour, yogurt, and sour cream together in a bowl. Mix in chili peppers and milk. Split the sauce into two equal portions. Put 1 portion aside.
- To prepare the filling, mix the spinach-chicken mixture with 1 portion of the sauce. Distribute the filling between the tortillas. Roll up the tortillas. In a non-oiled 2-qt. rectangular baking dish, put the tortillas with the seam-side facing down.
- Spoon over the tortillas with the leftover portion of the sauce. Bake without a cover in the oven at 350°F until thoroughly heated, or for about 25 minutes. Sprinkle cheese over, let it sit for 5 minutes. Remove into a serving platter. For serving, if you want, use extra green onion, salsa or chopped tomato to garnish.

Nutrition Information

- Calories: 287 calories;
- Fiber: 3
- Total Carbohydrate: 21
- Cholesterol: 51
- Sugar: 2
- Protein: 17
- Total Fat: 15
- Saturated Fat: 8
- Sodium: 560

238.   Creamy Chicken Potpie

Serving: 4 | Prep: | Cook: 25mins | Ready in:

Ingredients

- 4 teaspoons extra-virgin olive oil, divided
- 1 pound boneless, skinless chicken breast, trimmed, cut into ½-inch cubes
- 1 cup sliced shallots
- 1 10- or 12-ounce bag frozen mixed vegetables (2-2½ cups), thawed
- ¼ teaspoon dried thyme
- 2 cups reduced-sodium chicken broth, divided
- ¼ cup cornstarch
- ¼ cup reduced-fat sour cream
- ¼ teaspoon salt
- ¼ teaspoon freshly ground pepper
- 6 sheets 9-by-14-inch phyllo dough, defrosted (follow package directions)
- Cooking spray (olive oil or canola oil)

Direction

- Set the oven at 425°F to preheat.
- In a large nonstick skillet, heat 2 teaspoons of oil over medium-high heat. Add chicken, then cook for 2-3 minutes, stirring often, until it turns white. Remove to a dish. Next, add shallots and the remaining 2 teaspoons of oil, reduce the heat to medium, continue to cook and stir for 2-3 minutes more, until slightly softened. Stir in thyme and the vegetables; cook until hot, stirring infrequently, for 2-4 minutes. Add 1 3/4 cups of broth and boil. In a small bowl, whisk cornstarch and the leftover 1/4 cup of broth and pour to the pan. Then return to a boil and continue to cook for about 1 minute, until thickened. Turn off the heat, stir in pepper, salt, sour cream, and chicken. In four 12-ounce ovenproof baking plates, distribute the mixture.

- Make 2 stacks, each stack has 3 sheets of phyllo; before stacking, lightly coat each sheet using cooking spray. Cut the stacks in 2 parts crosswise. Next, drape over each baking dish with 1 half. Fold in any overhanging edges.
- Arrange the potpies on a baking sheet. Bake for 18-20 minutes, until the filling is bubbly and the tops are golden.

Nutrition Information

- Calories: 387 calories;
- Fiber: 4
- Cholesterol: 68
- Sugar: 2
- Total Fat: 11
- Saturated Fat: 3
- Sodium: 667
- Total Carbohydrate: 40
- Protein: 30

---

239.   Creamy Chicken Tetrazzini Casserole

Serving: 6 servings. | Prep: 30mins | Cook: 30mins | Ready in:

Ingredients

- 12 ounces uncooked spaghetti
- 1 small onion, chopped
- 1 celery rib, chopped
- 1/4 cup butter, cubed
- 1 can (14 ounces) chicken broth
- 1-1/2 cups half-and-half cream
- 1 package (8 ounces) cream cheese, cubed
- 2 cups cubed cooked chicken
- 1 can (4 ounces) mushroom stems and pieces, drained
- 2 to 4 tablespoons sliced pimientos
- 1/2 teaspoon salt
- 1/4 teaspoon pepper
- 1/2 cup sliced almonds, toasted
- 1/4 cup grated Parmesan cheese

- 1/4 cup crushed potato chips

Direction

- Cook the spaghetti following the package instructions. In the meantime, sauté celery and onion in a big pan with butter until tender. Mix in cream cheese, cream, and broth; cook and stir until the cheese melts. Take off heat.
- Mix in pepper, chicken, salt, pimentos, and mushrooms. Drain the spaghetti then toss into the chicken mixture to coat. Move to a greased 13-in by 9-in baking dish.
- Bake for 20mins in a 350 degrees oven without cover; top with chips, Parmesan cheese, and almonds. Bake for another 10-15mins until the topping is golden brown and completely heated.

Nutrition Information

- Calories: 668 calories
- Sodium: 865mg sodium
- Fiber: 4g fiber)
- Total Carbohydrate: 51g carbohydrate (5g sugars
- Cholesterol: 138mg cholesterol
- Protein: 30g protein.
- Total Fat: 37g fat (19g saturated fat)

---

240.   Creamy Green Chili Chicken Cobbler

Serving: 8 servings. | Prep: 25mins | Cook: 45mins | Ready in:

Ingredients

- 2 cups all-purpose flour
- 1/2 cup grated Parmesan cheese
- 2 teaspoons baking powder
- 6 tablespoons cold butter, cubed
- 3/4 cup plus 2 tablespoons heavy whipping cream

- 3 ounces cream cheese, softened
- 1/2 cup sour cream
- 1 can (10-1/2 ounces) condensed cream of chicken soup, undiluted
- 1 can (10 ounces) green enchilada sauce
- 2 cans (4 ounces each) chopped green chilies
- 2-1/2 cups shredded rotisserie chicken (about 10 ounces)
- 1-1/2 cups shredded Colby-Monterey Jack cheese

Direction

- Preheat the oven to 450°. Crumb topping: whisk baking powder, cheese, and flour. Cut butter in till mixture looks like coarse crumbs. Put cream and mix till moistened. Crumble mixture into 1/2 to 1-in. pieces on a 15x10x1-in. lightly greased pan.
- Bake on upper oven rack for 8-10 minutes or till light golden brown. Lower oven setting down to 350°.
- Mix sour cream and cream cheese till smooth in a big bowl. Mix chicken, green chilies, enchilada sauce, and soup in. Put onto an 11x7-in. baking dish then sprinkle with cheese. Put crumb topping (it will be full).
- On a baking sheet, put the dish. Bake on lower oven rack, uncovered, for 35-40 minutes or till filling is bubbly and topping is deep golden brown.

Nutrition Information

- Calories: 581 calories
- Total Carbohydrate: 33g carbohydrate (3g sugars
- Cholesterol: 132mg cholesterol
- Protein: 25g protein.
- Total Fat: 39g fat (22g saturated fat)
- Sodium: 1076mg sodium
- Fiber: 2g fiber)

241. Creamy Skinny Pasta Casserole

Serving: 6 servings. | Prep: 20mins | Cook: 10mins | Ready in:

Ingredients

- 12 ounces uncooked whole wheat penne pasta
- 1 pound lean ground chicken
- 1 small onion, finely chopped
- 1 teaspoon garlic powder, divided
- 1 teaspoon Italian seasoning
- 1/2 teaspoon salt
- 1/4 teaspoon pepper
- 1 can (14-1/2 ounces) diced tomatoes, undrained
- 3 ounces reduced-fat cream cheese
- 1/2 cup reduced-fat sour cream
- 1 cup shredded part-skim mozzarella cheese, divided
- Minced fresh parsley and crushed red pepper flakes, optional

Direction

- Turn oven to 400° to preheat. Cook pasta until al dente as directed on package. Drain pasta, saving 1/3 cup pasta cooking liquid; pour all back into the pot.
- In the meantime, cook and crumble chicken with the remaining seasonings, 1/2 teaspoon garlic powder, and onion over medium-high heat in a large skillet until chicken is no longer pink, for 5 to 7 minutes. Mix in tomatoes; bring to a boil. Add mixture to drained pasta; stir well until combined. Pour pasta mixture into a 13x9-inch baking dish greased with cooking spray.
- Mix together the remaining garlic powder, 1/2 cup mozzarella cheese, sour cream, and cream cheese. Drop mixture by tablespoonfuls atop pasta. Scatter on top with the leftover of mozzarella cheese.
- Bake without covering for 8 to 10 minutes until cheese is melted. Garnish with pepper flakes and parsley, if desired.

Nutrition Information

- Calories: 445 calories
- Total Fat: 13g fat (6g saturated fat)
- Sodium: 559mg sodium
- Fiber: 7g fiber)
- Total Carbohydrate: 49g carbohydrate (6g sugars
- Cholesterol: 78mg cholesterol
- Protein: 33g protein.

242. Crowd Pleasing Rice Bake

Serving: 18 servings. | Prep: 45mins | Cook: 30mins | Ready in:

Ingredients

- 9 cups chicken broth
- 3 packages (2-1/2 ounces each) chicken noodle soup mix
- 2 cups uncooked long grain rice
- 1 pound Jones No Sugar Pork Sausage Roll sausage
- 1-1/2 cups sliced celery
- 2 large onions, chopped
- 2 medium green peppers, chopped
- 1 can (10-3/4 ounces) condensed cream of mushroom soup, undiluted
- 6 cups cubed cooked chicken
- 1/2 cup slivered almonds, toasted

Direction

- Boil broth in a large saucepan. Mix in soup mixes; simmer for 10 minutes. Include in rice; simmer for 15 minutes. Take away from the heat; set aside.
- Place a large skillet on medium heat; brown while crumbling sausage till not pink anymore. Using a slotted spoon, take out and set aside.

- Discard all but 1 tablespoon of the drippings. Sauté peppers, onions and celery in drippings till tender. Mix in the rice mixture, chicken, mushroom soup and the sausage till well combined.
- Transfer into two 2 1/2-quart baking dishes coated with grease. Bake with a cover at 350° till the rice turns tender, 30 minutes. Sprinkle almonds on top.

Nutrition Information

- Calories: 279 calories
- Sodium: 875mg sodium
- Fiber: 2g fiber)
- Total Carbohydrate: 25g carbohydrate (3g sugars
- Cholesterol: 53mg cholesterol
- Protein: 19g protein.
- Total Fat: 11g fat (3g saturated fat)

243. Crunchy Chicken Casserole

Serving: 8 | Prep: 15mins | Cook: 30mins | Ready in:

Ingredients

- 2 cooked skinless, boneless chicken breast halves, cubed
- 1 cup mayonnaise
- 1 cup sour cream
- 1 (10.75 ounce) can condensed cream of chicken soup
- 2 cups cooked white rice
- 1/4 cup slivered almonds
- 2 cups shredded mozzarella cheese
- 2 cups shredded Cheddar cheese
- 2 cups crushed potato chips

Direction

- Preheat an oven to 175°C/350°F.

- Mix condensed cream of chicken soup, mozzarella cheese, almonds, rice, sour cream, mayonnaise and chicken in a big casserole dish. Layer on cheddar cheese. Put potato chips on top.
- In preheated oven, bake for 35 minutes till golden brown and bubbly.

Nutrition Information

- Calories: 688 calories;
- Protein: 26.4
- Total Fat: 53.8
- Sodium: 868
- Total Carbohydrate: 25.4
- Cholesterol: 95

244.   Cupid's Chicken 'n' Stuffing

Serving: 8 servings. | Prep: 15mins | Cook: 50mins | Ready in:

Ingredients

- 1 package (6 ounces) seasoned stuffing mix
- 8 boneless skinless chicken breast halves (4 ounces each)
- 1 teaspoon canola oil
- 1/4 teaspoon salt
- 1/4 teaspoon pepper
- 4 Swiss cheese slices (2 ounces), halved
- 2 tablespoons butter
- 1 can (10-3/4 ounces) condensed cream of chicken soup, undiluted
- 1/4 cup water

Direction

- Follow package directions to prepare stuffing mix. Remove to a 9-inch x13-inch baking dish coated with grease. Brown chicken in a big skillet with oil, then sprinkle pepper and salt

over. Put on top of stuffing and place cheese on top. Use butter to drizzle over.
- Mix water and soup, then scoop over stuffing. Place a cover and bake at 350 degrees about 40 minutes. Uncover and bake until juices from chicken run clear, about 10 to 15 more minutes.

Nutrition Information

- Calories: 331 calories
- Sodium: 734mg sodium
- Fiber: 0 fiber)
- Total Carbohydrate: 19g carbohydrate (3g sugars
- Cholesterol: 92mg cholesterol
- Protein: 29g protein.
- Total Fat: 14g fat (7g saturated fat)

245.   Curried Chicken And Grits Casserole

Serving: 8 servings. | Prep: 25mins | Cook: 50mins | Ready in:

Ingredients

- 1 cup water
- 1-1/2 cups chicken broth, divided
- 1/4 teaspoon salt
- 1/2 cup quick-cooking grits
- 2 large eggs, beaten
- 2 cups shredded cheddar cheese, divided
- 3 tablespoons butter, cubed
- 1 can (10-3/4 ounces) condensed cream of chicken and mushroom soup, undiluted
- 1-1/2 cups mayonnaise
- 2 teaspoons curry powder
- 1 package (16 ounces) frozen broccoli-cauliflower blend
- 2 cups cubed cooked chicken
- 2 cups refrigerated diced potatoes with onion

Direction

- In a large saucepan, boil salt, 1 cup broth, and water. Gradually whisk in grits. Lessen heat; cook and mix for 5-6 minutes or till thicken. Take away from heat; whisk a bit of grits into eggs. Transfer all back to the pan while frequently stirring. Put in 1 and a half cups of cheese and butter; mix until melted.
- Preheat oven to 350°. In a large bowl, blend the leftover broth, curry powder, mayonnaise and soup. Put in potatoes, chicken and vegetable blend; toss to cover. Move into a greased 13x9-inch baking dish. Put grits on top; dust with the rest of cheese.
- Bake with no cover for 50-55 minutes, or till heated through.

Nutrition Information

- Calories: 629 calories
- Total Carbohydrate: 16g carbohydrate (1g sugars
- Cholesterol: 137mg cholesterol
- Protein: 21g protein.
- Total Fat: 53g fat (14g saturated fat)
- Sodium: 1094mg sodium
- Fiber: 2g fiber)

---

246.   Curried Chicken And Rice

Serving: 4 servings | Prep: 30mins | Cook: | Ready in:

Ingredients

- 1 Tbsp. oil
- 1 lb. boneless skinless chicken breast s, cut into bite-size pieces
- 1 clove garlic , minced
- 1/2 cup fat-free reduced-sodium chicken broth
- 1/4 cup chopped chutney
- 3 Tbsp. raisins
- 1-1/2 tsp. curry powder
- 1 Tbsp. chopped fresh cilantro

- 1/4 tsp. pepper
- 3 cups hot cooked long-grain white rice
- 1/4 cup BAKER'S ANGEL FLAKE Coconut

Direction

- In a large nonstick skillet, heat oil over medium-high heat. Sauté garlic and chicken in heated oil for 5 to 6 minutes or until meat is no longer pink.
- Add curry powder, raisins, chutney, and chicken broth to the skillet; stir well to combine. Simmer for 5 minutes over medium-low heat, stirring sometimes. Mix in pepper and cilantro.
- Ladle rice into a large bowl. Spoon chicken mixture over rice; mix gently. Sprinkle top with coconut before serving.

Nutrition Information

- Calories: 450
- Total Fat: 9 g
- Saturated Fat: 3.5 g
- Total Carbohydrate: 60 g
- Cholesterol: 65 mg
- Protein: 28 g
- Sodium: 310 mg
- Fiber: 2 g
- Sugar: 19 g

---

247.   Curried Chicken With Asparagus

Serving: 4 servings. | Prep: 20mins | Cook: 25mins | Ready in:

Ingredients

- 1 can (10-3/4 ounces) condensed cream of chicken soup, undiluted
- 1/3 cup mayonnaise
- 1 teaspoon lemon juice
- 1/2 teaspoon curry powder

- 1/8 teaspoon pepper
- 1 package (10 ounces) frozen asparagus spears, thawed
- 1 pound boneless skinless chicken breasts, cut into 1/2-inch pieces
- 2 tablespoons canola oil
- 1/4 cup shredded cheddar cheese

Direction

- Combine pepper, curry, lemon juice, mayonnaise, and soup together in a large mixing bowl; put aside.
- Arrange 1/2 of the asparagus on a greased 8x8-inch baking dish. Spread with 1/2 of the soup mixture.
- Sauté chicken in oil in a large skillet until no longer pink. Layer chicken over soup mixture. Place the leftover of asparagus atop chicken and top with the leftover of soup mixture.
- Bake, covered for 20 minutes at 375°. Remove cover; sprinkle on top with cheese. Continue to bake until cheese is melted, or for an additional of 5 to 8 minutes.

Nutrition Information

- Calories: 426 calories
- Protein: 29g protein.
- Total Fat: 31g fat (6g saturated fat)
- Sodium: 779mg sodium
- Fiber: 2g fiber)
- Total Carbohydrate: 8g carbohydrate (2g sugars
- Cholesterol: 83mg cholesterol

248.   Curry Chicken Casserole

Serving: 6 | Prep: 20mins | Cook: 45mins | Ready in:

Ingredients

- 2 1/2 cups broccoli florets
- 2 cups fresh green beans, trimmed

- 1 pound cooked chicken breast, cut into bite-sized pieces
- 1 1/2 cups shredded Cheddar cheese
- 2 cups chicken broth
- 1/3 cup all-purpose flour
- 1 cup plain yogurt
- 1 tablespoon fish sauce
- 1 tablespoon lime juice
- 1 tablespoon curry powder
- salt and ground black pepper to taste
- 1/2 cup shredded Cheddar cheese

Direction

- Position the steamer insert into the sauce pan and fill with the water to just below steamer's bottom. Boil the water. Put in the green beans and broccoli, keep covered and steam 2-6 minutes till becoming soft.
- Preheat the oven to 175 degrees C (350 degrees F).
- Add the green beans and broccoli into the 9x13-in. baking dish. Cover with 1.5 cups of the Cheddar cheese and chicken.
- Heat the chicken broth on medium heat in the sauce pan till nearly boiling. Whisk a little broth along with the flour in the bowl to make a paste; stir the paste to the rest of the chicken broth till becoming thick. Whisk in the curry powder, lime juice, fish sauce and yogurt. Use the pepper and salt to season. Add the curry mixture on top of the chicken. Drizzle with the leftover half cup of the Cheddar cheese.
- Bake in the preheated oven 30-45 minutes till becoming bubbly.

Nutrition Information

- Calories: 325 calories;
- Total Fat: 17.3
- Sodium: 491
- Total Carbohydrate: 14.6
- Cholesterol: 80
- Protein: 28.1

249.   Easy Cheddar Chicken Potpie

Serving: 6 servings. | Prep: 20mins | Cook: 25mins | Ready in:

Ingredients

- 1 package (16 ounces) frozen vegetables for stew, thawed and coarsely chopped
- 1 jar (12 ounces) chicken gravy
- 2 cups shredded cheddar cheese
- 2 cups cubed cooked chicken
- 2 cups biscuit/baking mix
- 1 teaspoon minced fresh or 1/4 teaspoon dried thyme
- 2 large eggs
- 1/4 cup 2% milk

Direction

- Combine gravy and vegetables in a large saucepan. Bring to a boil. Lower heat; mix in chicken and cheese. Cook while stirring until cheese melts. Transfer mixture to an oiled 11x7-inch baking dish. In a small bowl, combine thyme and biscuit mix. Stir together milk and eggs in another bowl; mix into dry ingredients until just moistened. Drop the biscuit mixture by tablespoonfuls over the chicken mixture; distribute gently.
- Bake without covering for 23 to 27 minutes at 375°, or until top is golden brown. Allow to sit for 5 minutes before serving.

Nutrition Information

- Calories: 481 calories
- Protein: 29g protein.
- Total Fat: 22g fat (10g saturated fat)
- Sodium: 977mg sodium
- Fiber: 2g fiber)
- Total Carbohydrate: 41g carbohydrate (3g sugars
- Cholesterol: 146mg cholesterol

250.   Easy Chicken Divan

Serving: 4-6 servings. | Prep: 15mins | Cook: 20mins | Ready in:

Ingredients

- 3 cups cubed cooked chicken
- 1/2 teaspoon salt
- 1/4 teaspoon pepper
- 4 cups frozen broccoli florets, thawed
- 2 cans (10-3/4 ounces each) condensed cream of chicken soup, undiluted
- 1/3 cup mayonnaise
- 1/4 cup 2% milk
- 2 cups shredded Mexican cheese blend or cheddar cheese, divided

Direction

- Combine the pepper, salt and chicken in a greased shallow 2-1/2-qt. baking dish. Place broccoli on top. In a large bowl, combine the 1-1/2 cups cheese, milk, mayonnaise and soup; pour over broccoli. Sprinkle with the rest of the cheese.
- Bake at 375°, uncovered, until heated through for 20-25 minutes.

Nutrition Information

- Calories:
- Total Carbohydrate:
- Cholesterol:
- Protein:
- Total Fat:
- Sodium:
- Fiber:

251.   Easy Chicken Enchiladas

Serving: 6 | Prep: 20mins | Cook: 30mins | Ready in:

Ingredients

- 1 (8 ounce) package cream cheese
- 1 cup salsa
- 2 cups chopped cooked chicken breast meat
- 1 (15.5 ounce) can pinto beans, drained
- 6 (6 inch) flour tortillas
- 2 cups shredded Colby-Jack cheese

Direction

- Preheat an oven to 175 degrees C (350 degrees F). Coat a 9x13 inch baking dish lightly with grease.
- Over medium heat, mix salsa and cream cheese in a small saucepan. Cook while stirring until melted and blended well. Mix in pinto beans and chicken. Fill the tortillas with the mixture, roll and transfer to the prepared baking dish. Add cheese all over the top. Cover using aluminum foil.
- Bake for about 30 minutes or until heated through. Garnish with toppings you love like sour cream or tomatoes and lettuce.

Nutrition Information

- Calories: 565 calories;
- Sodium: 1166
- Total Carbohydrate: 32.8
- Cholesterol: 120
- Protein: 32.6
- Total Fat: 34.1

---

252. Easy Creamy Chicken Enchiladas

Serving: 5 | Prep: 20mins | Cook: | Ready in:

Ingredients

- 1 (10 ounce) can Old El Paso® Red Enchilada Sauce
- 2 1/2 cups shredded deli rotisserie chicken

- 1 1/2 cups shredded Cheddar cheese
- 1 (8 ounce) package cream cheese, cut into 1/2-inch cubes
- 1 (1 ounce) package fajita seasoning mix*
- 10 Old El Paso® flour tortillas for soft tacos & fajitas (6 inch)

Direction

- Start preheating the oven to 375°F. Spray cooking spray over a 13x9-in. (3-qt.) baking dish. Spread onto the bottom of the baking dish with 1/4 cup of the enchilada sauce.
- Combine seasoning mix, cream cheese, 1 cup of the Cheddar cheese, and chicken in a medium-sized bowl using a spoon, crumble the cream cheese cubes. Onto each tortilla, spoon slightly less than 1/2 cup filling. Roll up each tortilla tightly, put in the baking dish with the seam-side facing down. Drizzle the leftover enchilada sauce over. Sprinkle the leftover 1/2 cup Cheddar cheese over.
- Use foil to cover, bake for 15 minutes. Remove the cover and bake until turning light brown and bubbly, or for another 15 minutes.

Nutrition Information

- Calories: 644 calories;
- Protein: 34
- Total Fat: 41.1
- Sodium: 1412
- Total Carbohydrate: 31.9
- Cholesterol: 139

---

253. Easy Divan Chicken

Serving: 4 servings. | Prep: 10mins | Cook: 30mins | Ready in:

Ingredients

- 1 package (10 ounces) frozen broccoli spears, thawed and drained
- 3 chicken breast halves, cooked and sliced

- 1 can (10-3/4 ounces) condensed cream of broccoli soup, undiluted
- 1/2 cup mayonnaise
- 1 teaspoon lemon juice
- 1 teaspoon butter, melted
- 1/4 cup soft bread crumbs
- 1/4 cup shredded Swiss cheese

Direction

- Arrange spears of broccoli in an oiled 8x8-inch baking dish. Place chicken over broccoli. Mix together lemon juice, mayonnaise, and soup; distribute all over chicken. Toss bread crumbs and butter together; add cheese. Scatter crumb mixture over the sauce. Bake without a cover for 30 to 35 minutes at 350° or until bubbly.

Nutrition Information

- Calories: 311 calories
- Fiber: 0 fiber)
- Total Carbohydrate: 15g carbohydrate (0 sugars
- Cholesterol: 65mg cholesterol
- Protein: 25g protein. Diabetic Exchanges: 3 lean meat
- Total Fat: 13g fat (0 saturated fat)
- Sodium: 510mg sodium

254.   Easy Enchiladas

Serving: 10 | Prep: 15mins | Cook: 30mins | Ready in:

Ingredients

- 2 (16 ounce) jars prepared salsa
- 1 pound ground beef
- 1 (15.5 ounce) jar prepared salsa con queso
- 20 (8 inch) flour tortillas
- 1 (8 ounce) package shredded Cheddar-Monterey Jack cheese blend

Direction

- Preheat an oven to 350°F (175°C). Grease a baking dish that's 9x13 inches in size, then pour the salsa into the bottom. Leave aside.
- In a frying pan, cook and stir the ground beef over medium heat for 10 minutes till meat is crumbly and browned. Drain the grease from the beef, then add the salsa con queso to the frying pan, stir to mix well. On each tortilla, place about 2 tablespoons of the beef mixture down the center, roll the tortillas; in the baking dish, place them seam side down on top of the salsa. Drizzle the shredded cheese on top of the enchiladas.
- In the preheated oven, bake for approximately 15 to 20 minutes till the enchiladas are hot and bubbling and the cheese is browned.

Nutrition Information

- Calories: 595 calories;
- Sodium: 1757
- Total Carbohydrate: 68.3
- Cholesterol: 54
- Protein: 24.3
- Total Fat: 25.8

255.   Easy Vegetable Casserole

Serving: 4-6 servings. | Prep: 5mins | Cook: 50mins | Ready in:

Ingredients

- 2 cups cubed cooked chicken
- 8 ounces frozen small onions, thawed and drained
- 1 package (10 ounces) frozen mixed vegetables, thawed and drained
- 1 can (4 ounces) mushroom stems and pieces, drained
- 1 can (10-3/4 ounces) condensed cream of chicken soup, undiluted
- 1/2 teaspoon dried thyme
- 1 cup crushed potato chips

Direction

- In a bowl, blend thyme, soup, mushrooms, mixed vegetables, onions and chicken together. Transfer into a greased 8-inch square baking dish. Scatter with chips. Bake with no cover at 350° for around 50-55 minutes, or till bubbly.

Nutrition Information

- Calories: 231 calories
- Protein: 18g protein.
- Total Fat: 10g fat (3g saturated fat)
- Sodium: 568mg sodium
- Fiber: 4g fiber)
- Total Carbohydrate: 18g carbohydrate (5g sugars
- Cholesterol: 46mg cholesterol

---

256. Fast Chicken Divan

Serving: 4-6 servings. | Prep: 5mins | Cook: 30mins | Ready in:

Ingredients

- 8 cups frozen broccoli florets or chopped broccoli
- 3 cups cubed cooked chicken
- 2 cans (10-3/4 ounces each) condensed cream of chicken soup, undiluted
- 1 cup mayonnaise
- 1 teaspoon lemon juice
- 1 cup shredded sharp cheddar cheese
- 3/4 cup dry bread crumbs
- 3 tablespoons butter, melted
- 1 tablespoon sliced pimientos, optional

Direction

- Cook broccoli in a big saucepan with boiling water, about 1 minute; strain. Remove into an 11x7-inch baking dish coated with cooking spray, put the chicken on top. Mix together

lemon juice, mayonnaise, and soup; put on the chicken to spread. Sprinkle cheese over. Mix together butter and bread crumbs; sprinkle onto the top.

- Bake without a cover at 325° until turning golden brown and bubbly, about 30 minutes. Let sit before eating, about 10 minutes. Use pimientos to garnish if you want.

Nutrition Information

- Calories: 629 calories
- Protein: 28g protein.
- Total Fat: 49g fat (14g saturated fat)
- Sodium: 944mg sodium
- Fiber: 2g fiber)
- Total Carbohydrate: 16g carbohydrate (1g sugars
- Cholesterol: 115mg cholesterol

---

257. Favorite Company Casserole

Serving: 8 servings. | Prep: 15mins | Cook: 45mins | Ready in:

Ingredients

- 1 package (6 ounces) wild rice, cooked
- 3 cups frozen chopped broccoli, thawed
- 1-1/2 cups cubed cooked chicken
- 1 cup cubed cooked ham
- 1 cup shredded cheddar cheese
- 1 jar (4-1/2 ounces) sliced mushrooms, drained
- 1 cup mayonnaise
- 1 teaspoon prepared mustard
- 1/2 to 1 teaspoon curry powder
- 1 can (10-3/4 ounces) condensed cream of mushroom soup, undiluted
- 1/4 cup grated Parmesan cheese

Direction

- Preheat oven to 350°. In a greased 2-quart baking dish, orderly layer the first six ingredients as listed. Mix soup, curry, mustard and mayonnaise. Scatter over top. Dust with Parmesan cheese.
- Bake with no cover for 45-60 minutes, or till top becomes light golden brown.

Nutrition Information

- Calories: 405 calories
- Cholesterol: 61mg cholesterol
- Protein: 18g protein.
- Total Fat: 32g fat (8g saturated fat)
- Sodium: 872mg sodium
- Fiber: 2g fiber)
- Total Carbohydrate: 11g carbohydrate (1g sugars

---

258. Fiesta Chicken 'N' Stuffing

Serving: 4 servings. | Prep: 10mins | Cook: 10mins | Ready in:

Ingredients

- 3 eggs
- 3/4 cup milk
- 2 cups crushed stuffing mix
- 1-1/2 cups cubed cooked chicken
- 1 large tomato, chopped
- 3 tablespoons chopped green chilies
- 3 tablespoons chopped green onions
- Sour cream and salsa, optional

Direction

- Mix milk and eggs in a big bowl. Mix in onions, chilies, tomato, chicken and stuffing mix.
- Move to a greased microwave-safe 9-in. pie dish. Microwave, while covered, on high for 2

minutes; mix. Microwave for 2 more minutes; mix.
- Cook for 1-1/2 to 2 minutes longer or till becoming set and a thermometer reaches 160 degrees. Allow to rest for 5 minutes prior to serving. If you want, use salsa and sour cream to decorate.

Nutrition Information

- Calories: 306 calories
- Fiber: 1g fiber)
- Total Carbohydrate: 25g carbohydrate (7g sugars
- Cholesterol: 212mg cholesterol
- Protein: 26g protein.
- Total Fat: 10g fat (3g saturated fat)
- Sodium: 656mg sodium

---

259. Garlic Chicken Enchiladas

Serving: 6 servings. | Prep: 50mins | Cook: 20mins | Ready in:

Ingredients

- 1 pound boneless skinless chicken breasts
- 1/2 cup water
- 5 teaspoons minced garlic, divided
- 1 cup finely chopped onion
- 3 tablespoons butter
- 2 cans (4 ounces each) chopped green chilies
- 1 tablespoon chili powder
- 1-1/2 teaspoons salt
- 1/2 teaspoon each ground cumin and dried oregano
- 1/4 teaspoon pepper
- 1/2 cup all-purpose flour
- 1 cup chicken broth
- 1 cup heavy whipping cream
- 2 cups shredded Monterey Jack cheese, divided
- 1/3 cup vegetable oil

- 12 corn tortillas (6 inches)
- 1 cup sliced green onion, divided

Direction

- Boil 2 teaspoons of garlic, water, and chicken in a saucepan. Turn down the heat; put a cover on and bring to a simmer until the chicken is not pink anymore, 15-20 minutes. Take the chicken out and save the liquid. Slice the chicken into thin strips. Then, put aside.
- Sauté onion in butter in a skillet until it becomes tender. Put in the remaining garlic, sauté for a minute. Add seasoning and chilies and sauté for a minute. Add flour and stir until combined. Put in the saved liquid, cream, and chicken broth gradually and stir. Boil on medium heat; stir and cook until thick, 2 minutes. Take away from the heat. Add a cup of cheese and stir until it melts. Mix chicken and a cup of cheese sauce and put aside.
- Heat the oil in a large skillet. Plunge tortillas, one at a time, in the heated oil for 5 seconds per side until just limp. Drain with paper towels. Add approximate 1/4 cup of the chicken mixture on the center of each tortilla; dust with a tablespoon of green onion. Roll the tortillas up and arrange in a 13x9-inch baking dish coated with cooking spray, seam sides down. Evenly top tortillas with the remaining sauce. Put a cover on and bake at 400 degrees until bubbly and cooked thoroughly, 20-25 minutes. Dust with the remaining cheese and bake until the cheese melts, 3-4 more minutes. Add the remaining green onions on top to decorate.

Nutrition Information

- Calories: 706 calories
- Protein: 32g protein.
- Total Fat: 48g fat (22g saturated fat)
- Sodium: 1289mg sodium
- Fiber: 5g fiber)
- Total Carbohydrate: 40g carbohydrate (0 sugars
- Cholesterol: 149mg cholesterol

---

260.   Greek Chicken Nachos

Serving: 12 servings. | Prep: 20mins | Cook: 10mins | Ready in:

Ingredients

- 2 packages (10 ounces each) lemon-pepper marinated chicken breast fillets
- 2 cans (15 ounces each) garbanzo beans or chickpeas, rinsed and drained
- 1/2 cup Italian salad dressing
- 4 cups coarsely crushed tortilla chips
- 1 package crumbled tomato and basil feta cheese
- 1 cup chopped tomatoes
- 1 cup Greek olives, chopped
- 2 cups shredded part-skim mozzarella cheese

Direction

- On an indoor grill, cook chicken in batches for 6 to 8 minutes or until juices run clear.
- In the meantime, in a food processor, combine salad dressing and garbanzo beans; process, covered, until smooth. Dice chicken. Arrange half of the bean mixture, tortilla chips, chicken, feta cheese, tomatoes, olives and mozzarella cheese in layers in an ungreased 13x9 inch baking dish. Repeat layering with remaining ingredients.
- Bake, uncovered, for 8 to 10 minutes at 325° or until cheese is fully melted.

Nutrition Information

- Calories: 300 calories
- Fiber: 4g fiber)
- Total Carbohydrate: 20g carbohydrate (3g sugars
- Cholesterol: 39mg cholesterol
- Protein: 19g protein.
- Total Fat: 15g fat (4g saturated fat)
- Sodium: 1030mg sodium

261.   Greek Spaghetti With Chicken

Serving: 10 servings. | Prep: 25mins | Cook: 25mins | Ready in:

Ingredients

- 1 package (16 ounces) spaghetti, broken into 2-inch pieces
- 4 cups cubed cooked chicken breast
- 2 packages (10 ounces each) frozen chopped spinach, thawed and squeezed dry
- 2 cans (10-3/4 ounces each) condensed cream of chicken soup, undiluted
- 1 cup mayonnaise
- 1 cup (8 ounces) sour cream
- 3 celery ribs, chopped
- 1 small onion, chopped
- 1/2 cup chopped green pepper
- 1 jar (2 ounces) diced pimientos, drained
- 1/2 teaspoon lemon-pepper seasoning
- 1 cup shredded Monterey Jack cheese
- 1/2 cup soft bread crumbs
- 1/2 cup shredded Parmesan cheese

Direction

- Cook spaghetti following the instruction of the package; let drain. Place spaghetti back to saucepan. Blend in the spinach, chicken, mayonnaise, soup, celery, sour cream, green pepper, onion, lemon-pepper and pimientos.
- Place to a greased baking dish of 13x9-inch (dish can be full). Place Parmesan cheese, bread crumbs and Monterey Jack cheese on top. Bake with no cover at 350° for nearly 25 to 30 minutes till heated through.

Nutrition Information

- Calories: 601 calories
- Sodium: 850mg sodium

- Fiber: 4g fiber)
- Total Carbohydrate: 44g carbohydrate (4g sugars
- Cholesterol: 85mg cholesterol
- Protein: 31g protein.
- Total Fat: 32g fat (10g saturated fat)

262.   Ham Chicken Casserole

Serving: 6 servings. | Prep: 15mins | Cook: 25mins | Ready in:

Ingredients

- 1 package (6 ounces) long grain and wild rice mix
- 2 cups cubed cooked chicken
- 1 cup cubed fully cooked ham
- 1 can (10-3/4 ounces) condensed cream of chicken soup, undiluted
- 1 can (12 ounces) evaporated milk
- 1 cup shredded Colby cheese
- 1/8 teaspoon pepper
- 1/4 cup grated Parmesan cheese

Direction

- Follow the package instructions to cook rice mix. Transfer into a 2-quart baking dish coated with grease. Top with ham and chicken.
- Mix pepper, Colby cheese, milk and soup together in a large bowl; transfer over the chicken mixture. Sprinkle Parmesan cheese over.
- Bake without a cover at 350° till bubbly, 25-30 minutes.

Nutrition Information

- Calories: 428 calories
- Sodium: 1333mg sodium
- Fiber: 1g fiber)
- Total Carbohydrate: 30g carbohydrate (7g sugars

- Cholesterol: 97mg cholesterol
- Protein: 31g protein.
- Total Fat: 19g fat (10g saturated fat)

263. Hash Brown Breakfast Casserole

Serving: 4 servings. | Prep: 10mins | Cook: 40mins | Ready in:

Ingredients

- 4 cups frozen shredded hash brown potatoes, thawed
- 1-1/2 cups egg substitute
- 1 cup finely chopped cooked chicken breast
- 1/2 teaspoon garlic powder
- 1/2 teaspoon pepper
- 3/4 cup shredded reduced-fat cheddar cheese

Direction

- Mix together the pepper, garlic powder, chicken, egg substitute and hash browns in a big bowl. Move to a cooking spray coated 8-inch square baking dish, then sprinkle cheese on top.
- Let it bake for 40 to 45 minutes at 350 degrees without cover or until an inserted knife in the middle exits clean. Prior to serving, allow to stand for 5 minutes.

Nutrition Information

- Calories: 220 calories
- Protein: 26g protein. Diabetic Exchanges: 3 lean meat
- Total Fat: 6g fat (3g saturated fat)
- Sodium: 355mg sodium
- Fiber: 1g fiber)
- Total Carbohydrate: 16g carbohydrate (3g sugars
- Cholesterol: 42mg cholesterol

264. Haunted Potpie

Serving: 12 servings. | Prep: 30mins | Cook: 50mins | Ready in:

Ingredients

- 4 cups cubed cooked chicken
- 4 cups frozen cubed hash brown potatoes, thawed
- 1 package (16 ounces) frozen mixed vegetables, thawed and drained
- 1 can (10-3/4 ounces) condensed cream of chicken soup, undiluted
- 1 can (10-3/4 ounces) condensed cream of onion soup, undiluted
- 1 cup (8 ounces) sour cream
- 2/3 cup milk
- 2 tablespoons all-purpose flour
- 1/2 teaspoon salt
- 1/2 teaspoon pepper
- 1/4 teaspoon garlic powder
- 3 slices rye bread
- 1 sheet frozen puff pastry, thawed

Direction

- Mix the initial 11 ingredients in a big bowl; put into a 13x9-in. greased baking dish. Process bread to make crumbs in a food processor, covered; sprinkle over chicken mixture. Bake till bubbly for 40-45 minutes at 350°.
- Meanwhile, unfold pastry sheet on a lightly floured surface; cut 12 ghosts out with a ghost-shaped, small floured cookie cutter. Put onto an ungreased baking sheet. Take off potpie from oven; put aside. Keep warm. Bake the ghosts till golden brown and puffy for 10 minutes at 400°; put a ghost on top of each serving. Immediately serve.

Nutrition Information

- Calories: 366 calories
- Total Fat: 15g fat (5g saturated fat)

- Sodium: 668mg sodium
- Fiber: 5g fiber)
- Total Carbohydrate: 37g carbohydrate (4g sugars
- Cholesterol: 61mg cholesterol
- Protein: 20g protein.

265.   Home Style Chicken Potpie

Serving: 10-12 servings. | Prep: 60mins | Cook: 25mins | Ready in:

Ingredients

- 3/4 cup cold butter, cubed
- 2 cups all-purpose flour
- 1 cup shredded cheddar cheese
- 1/4 cup cold water
- FILLING:
- 2-1/2 cups halved baby carrots
- 3 celery ribs, sliced
- 6 tablespoons butter, cubed
- 7 tablespoons all-purpose flour
- 1 teaspoon salt
- 1/4 teaspoon coarsely ground pepper
- 2-1/2 cups chicken broth
- 1 cup heavy whipping cream
- 4 cups cubed cooked chicken
- 1 cup frozen pearl onions, thawed
- 1 cup frozen peas, thawed
- 3 tablespoons minced chives
- 3 tablespoons minced fresh parsley
- 2 teaspoons minced fresh thyme or 1/2 teaspoon dried thyme
- 1 large egg, lightly beaten

Direction

- Cut butter into flour in a large bowl, until crumbled. Blend in cheese. Slowly pour in water, use a fork to toss until the dough shapes into a ball. Cover and let cool in the refrigerator for a minimum of 1 hour.

- Cook celery and carrots in a small amount of water in a large saucepan until tender and crisp; drain and put aside.
- In a different saucepan, melt butter. Combine and whisk in pepper, salt, and flour, until smooth. Slowly mix in cream and broth. Heat to a boil; cook and stir for 2 minutes until thick. Blend in thyme, parsley, chives, peas, onions, chicken, and carrot mixture; heat thoroughly. Place in a greased 13x9-inch baking dish.
- Flour a surface, and roll the dough on it to fit the top of dish; slice out vents. Arrange the dough over filling; trim and flute edges. Coat with egg. Bake for about 25 to 30 minutes at 400°, until bubbly and crust turns to golden brown. Allow to stand in 10 minutes prior to using.

Nutrition Information

- Calories:
- Total Carbohydrate:
- Cholesterol:
- Protein:
- Total Fat:
- Sodium:
- Fiber:

266.   Hot Chicken Salad

Serving: 11 | Prep: 10mins | Cook: 25mins | Ready in:

Ingredients

- 2 1/2 cups chopped, cooked chicken meat
- 2 cups chopped celery
- 1/2 cup chopped salted almonds
- 1/4 cup chopped green bell pepper
- 2 tablespoons minced onion
- 2 tablespoons chopped pimento peppers
- 3/4 teaspoon salt
- 2 tablespoons lemon juice
- 1/2 cup mayonnaise

- 1/3 cup shredded Swiss cheese
- 3 cups crushed potato chips

Direction

- Preheat an oven to 175°C/350°F.
- Mix mayonnaise, lemon juice, salt, pimento, onion, bell pepper, almonds, celery and chicken well; put into 1 1/2-qt. casserole dish.
- Put crushed potato chips and grated cheese over; bake till cheese melts for 25 minutes.

Nutrition Information

- Calories: 288 calories;
- Total Fat: 21.1
- Sodium: 363
- Total Carbohydrate: 13.3
- Cholesterol: 31
- Protein: 12.6

267. Individual Chicken Potpies

Serving: 4 servings. | Prep: 40mins | Cook: 25mins | Ready in:

Ingredients

- 1/4 cup chopped onion
- 2 tablespoons chopped green pepper
- 1/4 cup butter, cubed
- 1/3 cup all-purpose flour
- 1 can (14-1/2 ounces) chicken broth
- 1 cup whole milk
- 1 cup fresh broccoli florets
- 1/2 cup fresh cauliflowerets
- 1/2 cup thinly sliced celery
- 1/2 cup thinly sliced carrot
- 1 cup shredded Swiss cheese
- 2 cups cubed cooked chicken
- PASTRY:
- 1-1/3 cups all-purpose flour
- 1/2 teaspoon salt

- 1/2 teaspoon paprika
- 1/2 cup shortening
- 3 to 4 tablespoons cold water

Direction

- In a big saucepan, sauté green pepper and onion in butter till onion soften. Put in flour till blended. Mix in the carrot, celery, cauliflower, broccoli, milk and broth. Set to a boil; cook and mix for 2 minutes or up to thicken. Take away from the heat. Mix in cheese. Distribute chicken among 4 ungreased 1-and-a-half-cup baking dishes. Top with vegetable mixture.
- For pastry, in a bowl, combine the paprika, salt and flour; cut in shortening till crumbly. Slowly pour in water, use a fork to toss to form a dough ball. Split into 4 portions; roll out each into 1/8-inch thickness. Position pastry over vegetable mixture. Trim pastry to half-inch beyond edge of dish; flute edges. Slice slits in top. Bake at 350° for around 30-40 minutes or till golden brown.

Nutrition Information

- Calories: 811 calories
- Protein: 38g protein.
- Total Fat: 51g fat (21g saturated fat)
- Sodium: 1021mg sodium
- Fiber: 3g fiber)
- Total Carbohydrate: 49g carbohydrate (8g sugars
- Cholesterol: 126mg cholesterol

268. Lemon Chicken And Rice

Serving: 4 servings. | Prep: 20mins | Cook: 10mins | Ready in:

Ingredients

- 2 tablespoons butter

- 1 pound boneless skinless chicken breasts, cut into strips
- 1 medium onion, chopped
- 1 large carrot, thinly sliced
- 2 garlic cloves, minced
- 1 tablespoon cornstarch
- 1 can (14-1/2 ounces) chicken broth
- 2 tablespoons lemon juice
- 1/2 teaspoon salt
- 1 cup frozen peas
- 1-1/2 cups uncooked instant rice

Direction

- Heat butter in a big skillet on medium-high heat; sauté garlic, carrot, onion and chicken for 5 to 7 mins until the meat is no longer pink.
- Stir salt, lemon juice, broth and cornstarch in a small bowl until smooth. Put into the skillet slowly; boil. Cook and mix for 1 to 2 mins until thickened.
- Mix peas in; put back to a boil. Mix rice in. Take it away from heat; cover and let sit for 5 minutes.

Nutrition Information

- Calories: 370 calories
- Protein: 29g protein.
- Total Fat: 9g fat (4g saturated fat)
- Sodium: 893mg sodium
- Fiber: 3g fiber)
- Total Carbohydrate: 41g carbohydrate (4g sugars
- Cholesterol: 80mg cholesterol

269. Lemon Curry Chicken Casserole

Serving: 6 servings. | Prep: 20mins | Cook: 40mins | Ready in:

Ingredients

- 2 packages (12 ounces each) frozen cut asparagus, thawed and drained
- 4 boneless skinless chicken breast halves, cut into 1/2-inch strips
- Salt and pepper to taste
- 3 tablespoons butter
- 1 can (10-3/4 ounces) condensed cream of chicken soup, undiluted
- 1/2 cup mayonnaise
- 1/4 cup lemon juice
- 1 teaspoon curry powder
- 1/4 teaspoon ground ginger
- 1/8 teaspoon pepper
- 1/2 cup sliced almonds, toasted

Direction

- In a greased baking dish of 11x7-inch, place asparagus; leave aside. Use pepper and salt to sprinkle chicken
- In a large skillet, sauté chicken in butter for around 10 to 14 minutes till juices run clear. Place over asparagus. Combine mayonnaise, soup, curry powder, lemon juice, pepper and ginger together; spoon over chicken.
- Bake with no cover at 350° for nearly 35 minutes. Have almonds to sprinkle and return to the oven for approximately 5 minutes.

Nutrition Information

- Calories: 373 calories
- Total Carbohydrate: 8g carbohydrate (2g sugars
- Cholesterol: 68mg cholesterol
- Protein: 20g protein.
- Total Fat: 29g fat (7g saturated fat)
- Sodium: 583mg sodium
- Fiber: 3g fiber)

270. Lemony Chicken & Rice

Serving: 2 casseroles (4 servings each). | Prep: 15mins | Cook: 55mins | Ready in:

Ingredients

- 2 cups water
- 1/2 cup reduced-sodium soy sauce
- 1/4 cup lemon juice
- 1/4 cup olive oil
- 2 garlic cloves, minced
- 2 teaspoons ground ginger
- 2 teaspoons pepper
- 16 bone-in chicken thighs, skin removed (about 6 pounds)
- 2 cups uncooked long grain rice
- 4 tablespoons grated lemon peel, divided
- 2 medium lemons, sliced

Direction

- Mix the initial seven ingredients in a large resealable plastic bag. Put in chicken; seal bag and turn to coat. Allow 4 hours or overnight to cool in refrigerator.
- Preheat oven to 325°. In each of two greased baking dishes of 13x9-inch, spread 1 cup rice. Place half of the marinade, 8 chicken thighs and1 tablespoon lemon peel on top of each. Place sliced lemons on top.
- Cover and bake for around 40 minutes. Uncover and bake for an addition of 15 to 20 minutes till a thermometer pinned in chicken measures 180°. Use the rest lemon peel to sprinkle over.

Nutrition Information

- Calories: 624 calories
- Total Fat: 26g fat (6g saturated fat)
- Sodium: 754mg sodium
- Fiber: 1g fiber)
- Total Carbohydrate: 41g carbohydrate (1g sugars
- Cholesterol: 173mg cholesterol
- Protein: 53g protein.

271.   Love Me Tender Chicken Bake

Serving: 8 servings. | Prep: 25mins | Cook: 20mins | Ready in:

Ingredients

- 2 medium onions, chopped
- 6 celery ribs, chopped
- 1/2 cup butter, cubed
- 5 cups cubed cooked chicken
- 3/4 cup water
- 2 cans (10-3/4 ounces each) condensed cream of mushroom soup, undiluted
- 1 cup (8 ounces) sour cream
- 2 cans (8 ounces each) sliced water chestnuts, drained
- 1 cup sliced almonds, toasted
- 1 cup crushed butter-flavored crackers

Direction

- Put butter in a big frying pan and sauté celery and onion until tender. Mix in water and chicken; cook through. Take away from heat. Add and stir almonds, sour cream, soup, and water chestnuts. Dump into eight 1-1/2-c. greased dishes. Sprinkle cracker crumbs on. Do not cover; bake in a 400-degree oven until bubbling, 20-25 minutes.

Nutrition Information

- Calories: 519 calories
- Fiber: 4g fiber)
- Total Carbohydrate: 22g carbohydrate (6g sugars
- Cholesterol: 130mg cholesterol
- Protein: 31g protein.
- Total Fat: 34g fat (14g saturated fat)
- Sodium: 596mg sodium

272. Makeover Chicken A La King Casserole

Serving: 8 servings. | Prep: 10mins | Cook: 30mins | Ready in:

Ingredients

- 8 ounces uncooked wide egg noodles
- 1 can (10-3/4 ounces) reduced-fat reduced-sodium condensed cream of chicken soup, undiluted
- 2/3 cup fat-free evaporated milk
- 6 ounces cubed reduced-fat process cheese (Velveeta)
- 2 cups cubed cooked chicken breast
- 1 cup sliced celery
- 1/4 cup chopped green pepper
- 1 jar (2 ounces) diced pimientos, drained
- 1/3 cup dry bread crumbs
- 1 tablespoon butter, melted
- 1/4 cup slivered almonds

Direction

- Cook the noodles following the package instructions. In the meantime, mix together the milk and soup in a big saucepan. Let it cook and stir for 2 minutes on medium heat. Lower the heat and mix in the cheese until it melts. Add the pimientos, green pepper, celery and chicken.
- Drain the noodles then add it to the chicken mixture and stir well. Move to a cooking spray coated shallow 2-quart baking dish. Put cover and let it bake for 20 minutes at 400 degrees.
- Toss the butter and breadcrumbs, then sprinkle it on top. Sprinkle almonds on top. Let it bake for 10 to 15 minutes without cover or until it turns golden and heated through.

Nutrition Information

- Calories: 306 calories
- Sodium: 405mg sodium
- Fiber: 2g fiber)
- Total Carbohydrate: 31g carbohydrate (0 sugars
- Cholesterol: 72mg cholesterol
- Protein: 24g protein. Diabetic Exchanges: 2 starch
- Total Fat: 9g fat (3g saturated fat)

273. Makeover Chicken Artichoke Bake

Serving: 6 servings. | Prep: 25mins | Cook: 45mins | Ready in:

Ingredients

- 3 tablespoons all-purpose flour
- 1 teaspoon sodium-free chicken bouillon granules
- 1-1/3 cups fat-free milk
- 1 can (10-3/4 ounces) reduced-fat reduced-sodium condensed cream of celery soup, undiluted
- 1 cup (8 ounces) plain yogurt
- 1/3 cup reduced-fat mayonnaise
- 3 cups cubed cooked chicken breast
- 1 can (14 ounces) water-packed artichoke hearts, rinsed, drained and chopped
- 1 can (8 ounces) sliced water chestnuts, drained
- 1 package (6 ounces) long grain and wild rice mix
- 1 cup sliced fresh mushrooms
- 1 medium onion, finely chopped
- 1 celery rib, finely chopped
- 1 jar (2 ounces) diced pimientos, drained
- 1/4 teaspoon pepper
- 1 cup seasoned stuffing cubes

Direction

- Mix together the milk, bullion and flour in a small saucepan until it becomes smooth, then boil on medium heat, stirring continuously. Let it cook and stir for 1 to 2 minutes more until it becomes thick, then move to a big bowl.

- Stir in the mayonnaise, yogurt and soup until combined. Stir in the pepper, pimientos, celery, onion, mushrooms, rice mix with contents of seasoning packet, water chestnuts, artichokes and chicken.
- Move to a cooking spray coated 2 1/2-quart baking dish. Sprinkle stuffing cubes on top. Let it bake for 45 to 55 minutes at 350 degrees without a cover or until the rice becomes tender and the edges become bubbly.

Nutrition Information

- Calories: 431 calories
- Sodium: 1240mg sodium
- Fiber: 3g fiber)
- Total Carbohydrate: 52g carbohydrate (9g sugars
- Cholesterol: 67mg cholesterol
- Protein: 31g protein.
- Total Fat: 11g fat (3g saturated fat)

274. Makeover Chicken Cheese Enchiladas

Serving: 6 servings. | Prep: 25mins | Cook: 45mins | Ready in:

Ingredients

- 1-1/2 cups (12 ounces) reduced-fat sour cream
- 1 can (10-3/4 ounces) reduced-fat reduced-sodium condensed cream of chicken soup, undiluted
- 1 can (4 ounces) chopped green chilies
- 1 can (2-1/4 ounces) sliced ripe olives, drained
- 4 cups cubed cooked chicken breast
- 1 cup shredded reduced-fat Monterey Jack or Mexican cheese blend, divided
- 1 cup shredded reduced-fat cheddar cheese, divided
- 12 fat-free flour tortillas (6 inches), warmed

- 4 green onions, thinly sliced

Direction

- Mix together the olives, chilies, soup and sour cream in a big bowl, then reserve 1 1/2 cups for the topping. Add 1/2 cup cheddar cheese, 1/2 cup Monterey Jack cheese and chicken into the leftover soup mixture.
- Scoop approximately 1/3 cup chicken mixture down the middle of each tortilla, then roll it up tightly. Put it seam side down in a cooking spray coated 13x9-inch baking dish. Put the reserved soup mixture on top.
- Let it bake for 35 minutes at 350 degrees without a cover. Sprinkle it with leftover cheeses, then put onions on top. Let it bake for 10-15 minutes more or until the cheese melts.

Nutrition Information

- Calories: 508 calories
- Protein: 46g protein.
- Total Fat: 18g fat (11g saturated fat)
- Sodium: 1164mg sodium
- Fiber: 2g fiber)
- Total Carbohydrate: 40g carbohydrate (6g sugars
- Cholesterol: 123mg cholesterol

275. Makeover Hot Chicken Salad

Serving: 6 servings. | Prep: 25mins | Cook: 30mins | Ready in:

Ingredients

- 1-1/2 teaspoons all-purpose flour
- 1/2 cup fat-free milk
- 1/2 cup plain yogurt
- 1/4 cup reduced-fat mayonnaise
- 1/4 cup reduced-fat sour cream
- 1 tablespoon lemon juice

- 2 teaspoons grated onion
- 1/2 teaspoon salt
- 3 cups cubed cooked chicken breast
- 1 cup chopped celery
- 1 can (8 ounces) sliced water chestnuts, drained and coarsely chopped
- 1 cup seasoned salad croutons
- 1/4 cup slivered almonds, chopped and toasted
- 1 cup soft bread crumbs
- 1 tablespoon reduced-fat butter, melted
- 3/4 cup shredded reduced-fat cheddar cheese

Direction

- Whisk the milk and flour in a small saucepan until it becomes smooth, then boil on medium heat. Let it cook and stir for 2 minutes or until it becomes thick. Take it out of the heat.
- Whisk the salt, onion, lemon juice, sour cream, mayonnaise and yogurt in a big bowl until it becomes smooth. Whisk in the milk mixture, then stir in almonds, croutons, water chestnuts, celery and chicken.
- Spoon into a cooking spray coated 2-quart baking dish. Put a cover and let it bake for 25 minutes at 350 degrees.
- Mix together the butter and breadcrumbs, then mix in cheese. Sprinkle on top of the casserole. Let it bake for 5 to 10 minutes more without a cover or until the cheese melts and heated through.

Nutrition Information

- Calories: 323 calories
- Protein: 29g protein. Diabetic Exchanges: 4 lean meat
- Total Fat: 15g fat (5g saturated fat)
- Sodium: 592mg sodium
- Fiber: 2g fiber)
- Total Carbohydrate: 19g carbohydrate (5g sugars
- Cholesterol: 78mg cholesterol

276. Makeover Poppy Seed Chicken

Serving: 6 servings. | Prep: 10mins | Cook: 30mins | Ready in:

Ingredients

- 3 cups cubed cooked chicken breast
- 2 cans (10-3/4 ounces each) reduced-fat reduced-sodium condensed cream of chicken soup, undiluted
- 1 cup (8 ounces) reduced-fat sour cream
- 2 teaspoons poppy seeds
- 1 cup crushed reduced-fat butter-flavored crackers (about 25 crackers)
- 3 tablespoons reduced-fat butter, melted
- 1/3 cup grated Parmesan cheese

Direction

- Set an oven to preheat to 350 degrees. Mix together the poppy seeds, sour cream, soup and chicken in a big bowl. Mix together the butter and cracker crumbs in a small bowl, then reserve 1/2 cup for the topping. Mix in leftover crumbs into the chicken mixture.
- Move to a cooking spray coated 11x7-inch baking dish. Put the reserved crumbs on top and sprinkle it with cheese. Let it bake for 30 to 35 minutes without cover or until it becomes bubbly.

Nutrition Information

- Calories: 332 calories
- Fiber: 0 fiber)
- Total Carbohydrate: 23g carbohydrate (5g sugars
- Cholesterol: 87mg cholesterol
- Protein: 27g protein.
- Total Fat: 13g fat (6g saturated fat)
- Sodium: 705mg sodium

277. Marvelous Chicken Enchiladas

Serving: 6 enchiladas. | Prep: 30mins | Cook: 25mins | Ready in:

Ingredients

- 1 pound boneless skinless chicken breasts, cut into thin strips
- 4 teaspoons chili powder
- 2 teaspoons olive oil
- 2 tablespoons all-purpose flour
- 1-1/2 teaspoons ground coriander
- 1 teaspoon baking cocoa
- 1 cup fat-free milk
- 1 cup frozen corn, thawed
- 4 green onions, chopped
- 1 can (4 ounces) chopped green chilies, drained
- 1/2 teaspoon salt
- 1/2 cup minced fresh cilantro, divided
- 6 whole wheat tortillas (8 inches)
- 1/2 cup salsa
- 1/2 cup tomato sauce
- 1/2 cup shredded reduced-fat cheddar cheese

Direction

- Use chili powder to sprinkle onto chicken. In a large greased nonstick frying pan, cook chicken in oil over medium heat till not pink anymore. Sprinkle with cocoa, coriander and flour; stir till blended.
- Stir in milk gradually. Allow to boil; cook and stir for approximately 2 minutes till thickened. Mix in the onions, corn, salt and chilies; cook and stir for an additional 2 minutes till heated through. Take away from the heat. Mix in 1/4 cup cilantro.
- On each tortilla, spread 2/3 cup filling down the center. Roll up and arrange in a 13x9-inch baking dish coated with cooking spray, seam side down.
- In a small bowl, combine the rest of the cilantro, tomato sauce and salsa; pour mixture over enchiladas. Drizzle cheese over. Cover

while baking at 375° for around 25 minutes till heated through.

Nutrition Information

- Calories: 336 calories
- Fiber: 4g fiber)
- Total Carbohydrate: 37g carbohydrate (5g sugars
- Cholesterol: 49mg cholesterol
- Protein: 25g protein. Diabetic Exchanges: 3 lean meat
- Total Fat: 9g fat (2g saturated fat)
- Sodium: 749mg sodium

278. Meaty Bean Casserole

Serving: 8 servings. | Prep: 20mins | Cook: 01hours30mins | Ready in:

Ingredients

- 1-1/4 pounds boneless skinless chicken breasts or pork tenderloin, cut into 3/4-inch pieces
- 4 cans (15 ounces each) great northern beans, rinsed and drained
- 12 to 16 ounces smoked sausage links, halved and cut into 1/2-inch slices
- 1 tablespoon olive oil
- 1-1/2 cups chopped onion
- 1 cup chopped sweet red pepper
- 4 to 6 garlic cloves, minced
- 1 can (14-1/2 ounces) Italian diced tomatoes, undrained
- 1 can (14-1/2 ounces) chicken broth
- 1 teaspoon dried thyme
- Pepper to taste
- 2 to 2-1/2 cups soft bread crumbs

Direction

- Add sausage and chicken to a Dutch oven, cook in oil until the chicken juices run out clear, about 10 minutes. Take the chicken and sausage out of the oven with a slotted spoon and keep warm.

- Keep the drippings in the oven, put in garlic, red pepper, and onion and sauté for 5 minutes. Whisk in the sausage, chicken, pepper, thyme, broth, tomatoes, and the beans.
- Bake without covering for 45 minutes at 350°. Top with bread crumbs. Bake until it becomes golden brown, for 45 minutes more.

Nutrition Information

- Calories: 334 calories
- Cholesterol: 66mg cholesterol
- Protein: 25g protein.
- Total Fat: 16g fat (5g saturated fat)
- Sodium: 1056mg sodium
- Fiber: 4g fiber)
- Total Carbohydrate: 23g carbohydrate (7g sugars

---

279. Mexican Chicken Bake

Serving: 6 servings | Prep: 15mins | Cook: | Ready in:

Ingredients

- 1 pkg. (6 oz.) STOVE TOP Lower Sodium Stuffing Mix for Chicken
- 1 cup frozen corn , divided
- 1-1/2 lb. boneless skinless chicken breast s, cut into bite-size pieces
- 1 tsp. chili powder
- 1 green pepper , chopped
- 1 cup TACO BELL® Thick & Chunky Salsa
- 1 cup KRAFT Mexican Style 2% Milk Finely Shredded Four Cheese

Direction

- 1. Based on the instruction on the package, prepare stuffing. Mix in half cup of corn.
- 2. Add chicken into a 13x9-inch baking dish that sprayed using cooking spray; drizzle with

chili powder. Add stuffing, cheese, salsa, leftover corn and peppers. Keep it covered.

- 3. Bake for 15 minutes. While uncovered; bake for 15 - 20 minutes or till chicken is done.

Nutrition Information

- Calories: 390
- Saturated Fat: 4.5 g
- Sodium: 840 mg
- Sugar: 4 g
- Cholesterol: 80 mg
- Total Fat: 14 g
- Fiber: 3 g
- Total Carbohydrate: 33 g
- Protein: 34 g

---

280. Mexican Chicken And Rice

Serving: 6 servings. | Prep: 10mins | Cook: 10mins | Ready in:

Ingredients

- 2 pounds boneless skinless chicken breasts, cut into 1-inch pieces
- 1 medium green pepper, chopped
- 1 small onion, chopped
- 2 tablespoons canola oil
- 1 can (8-3/4 ounces) whole kernel corn, drained
- 1 cup chicken broth
- 1 cup salsa
- 1/2 to 1 teaspoon salt
- 1/2 to 1 teaspoon chili powder, optional
- 1/4 teaspoon pepper
- 1-1/2 cups uncooked instant rice
- 1/2 to 1 cup shredded cheddar cheese

Direction

- Combine onion, and chicken green pepper in a large skillet, sauté in oil until vegetable is crisp-tender and chicken loses its pink color. Add pepper, chili powder (optional), salt, salsa, broth and corn; bring to a boil.

- Stir in the rice, remove from the heat and allow to stand, covered, for 5 minutes. Then fluff with a fork. Add cheese on top. Allow to stand, covered, for an additional 2 minutes or until cheese is fully melted.

Nutrition Information

- Calories: 381 calories
- Sodium: 782mg sodium
- Fiber: 3g fiber)
- Total Carbohydrate: 29g carbohydrate (4g sugars
- Cholesterol: 94mg cholesterol
- Protein: 36g protein.
- Total Fat: 11g fat (4g saturated fat)

281.   Nacho Chicken

Serving: 8-10 servings. | Prep: 15mins | Cook: 30mins | Ready in:

Ingredients

- 4 cups cubed cooked chicken
- 1 pound process America cheese (Velveeta), cubed
- 2 cans (10-3/4 ounces each) condensed cream of chicken soup, undiluted
- 1 can (10 ounces) diced tomatoes and green chilies, undrained
- 1 cup chopped onion
- 1/2 teaspoon garlic salt
- 1/4 teaspoon pepper
- 1 package (14-1/2 ounces) nacho cheese tortilla chips

Direction

- Mix the first seven ingredients in a large bowl until well combined. Crush chips and reserve 1 cup for topping. Add remaining chips to

chicken mixture. Drop spoonfuls of mixture onto a greased 13x9 inch baking dish, add reserve chips on top. Bake when uncover at 350° for 30 minutes or until cheese is fully melted and bubbles appear at edges.

Nutrition Information

- Calories: 496 calories
- Sodium: 1299mg sodium
- Fiber: 2g fiber)
- Total Carbohydrate: 32g carbohydrate (8g sugars
- Cholesterol: 81mg cholesterol
- Protein: 29g protein.
- Total Fat: 27g fat (11g saturated fat)

282.   Nacho Chicken Bake

Serving: 8-10 servings. | Prep: 15mins | Cook: 40mins | Ready in:

Ingredients

- 8 cups nacho tortilla chips
- 2 cans (10-3/4 ounces each) condensed cream of chicken soup, undiluted
- 1 can (10 ounces) chunk white chicken, drained
- 1 cup picante sauce
- 1 cup shredded cheddar cheese
- 1 medium onion, chopped
- 1 can (4 ounces) chopped green chilies
- Additional shredded cheddar cheese, optional
- Shredded lettuce and chopped fresh tomatoes

Direction

- Place chips in a greased 13x9 inch baking dish. Combine chilies, onion, cheese, picante sauce, chicken and soup in a large bowl; add to chips. Add additional cheese on top if desired.
- Bake for 40 to 45 minutes at 325° or until bubbles appear, remember not to cover the baking dish. Serve with tomatoes and lettuce.

Nutrition Information

- Calories: 335 calories
- Fiber: 3g fiber)
- Total Carbohydrate: 35g carbohydrate (4g sugars
- Cholesterol: 28mg cholesterol
- Protein: 12g protein.
- Total Fat: 17g fat (5g saturated fat)
- Sodium: 835mg sodium

283. Nacho Chicken Casserole

Serving: 2 servings. | Prep: 10mins | Cook: 25mins | Ready in:

Ingredients

- 1 cup cubed cooked chicken
- 3/4 cup crushed nacho tortilla chips
- 2/3 cup condensed cream of chicken soup, undiluted
- 1/2 cup sliced fresh mushrooms
- 1/4 cup sour cream
- 2 tablespoons 2% milk
- 1 tablespoon chopped green chilies
- 1/2 teaspoon finely chopped jalapeno pepper, optional
- 1/4 cup shredded part-skim mozzarella cheese
- 1/4 cup shredded cheddar cheese

Direction

- Mix the initial 8 ingredients in a big bowl. Mix the cheeses in a small-sized bowl; mix half into the chicken mixture.
- Move into one 1-qt. baking dish that coated using cooking spray. Drizzle with the rest of the cheeses. Bake, while uncovered, at 350 degrees till cheese becomes bubbly or for 25 to 30 minutes.

Nutrition Information

- Calories: 396 calories
- Total Fat: 15g fat (8g saturated fat)
- Sodium: 732mg sodium
- Fiber: 2g fiber)
- Total Carbohydrate: 31g carbohydrate (5g sugars
- Cholesterol: 97mg cholesterol
- Protein: 33g protein.

284. Old Fashioned Chicken Potpie

Serving: 6 servings. | Prep: 30mins | Cook: 30mins | Ready in:

Ingredients

- 1/3 cup butter
- 1/3 cup all-purpose flour
- 1 garlic clove, minced
- 1/2 teaspoon salt
- 1/4 teaspoon pepper
- 1-1/2 cups water
- 2/3 cup milk
- 2 teaspoons chicken bouillon granules
- 2 cups cubed cooked chicken
- 1 cup frozen mixed vegetables
- PASTRY:
- 1-2/3 cups all-purpose flour
- 2 teaspoons celery seed
- 1 package (8 ounces) cream cheese, cubed
- 1/3 cup cold butter

Direction

- Melt butter in a saucepan. Mix in pepper, salt, garlic and flour till blended. Slowly mix in bouillon, milk and water. Let mixture come to a boil; boil, stirring for 2 minutes. Take away from the heat. Mix in vegetables and chicken; set aside.
- To make pastry, in a bowl, mix celery seed and flour. Cut in butter and cream cheese till crumbly. Using your hands, work mixture till a ball of dough forms. Roll 2/3 of the dough

on a lightly floured work surface, to a 12-inch square. Move into an 8-inch square baking sheet. Transfer the filling into the crust. Roll the remaining dough into a 9-inch square; put over the filling. Trim, seal and flute the edges. Make slits in the pastry.

- Bake at 425° till the filling is bubbly and the crust turns golden brown, 30-35 minutes.

Nutrition Information

- Calories: 591 calories
- Fiber: 3g fiber)
- Total Carbohydrate: 39g carbohydrate (4g sugars
- Cholesterol: 141mg cholesterol
- Protein: 23g protein.
- Total Fat: 38g fat (22g saturated fat)
- Sodium: 860mg sodium

---

285.   Orange Chicken Supper

Serving: 4 servings. | Prep: 15mins | Cook: 15mins | Ready in:

Ingredients

- 1 package (6.9 ounces) chicken-flavored rice mix
- 2 tablespoons butter
- 1-1/2 cups hot water
- 1 cup orange juice
- 1/4 teaspoon garlic powder
- 1/4 teaspoon ground ginger
- 1/8 teaspoon cayenne pepper, optional
- 2 cups cubed cooked chicken
- 1-1/2 cups frozen sliced carrots, thawed

Direction

- Remove seasoning packet from rice mix and set aside. Put butter in a big frying pan and cook rice until golden brown on medium heat. Stir in ginger, water, cayenne if desired, garlic powder, seasoning packet, and orange juice.

Heat to a boil. Cover, decrease heat, and simmer for 10 minutes. Add carrots and chicken. Cover; simmer until liquid is absorbed and cooked through, 5-10 minutes. Use a fork to fluff.

Nutrition Information

- Calories: 399 calories
- Fiber: 3g fiber)
- Total Carbohydrate: 47g carbohydrate (10g sugars
- Cholesterol: 78mg cholesterol
- Protein: 26g protein.
- Total Fat: 12g fat (5g saturated fat)
- Sodium: 847mg sodium

---

286.   Overnight Chicken Casserole

Serving: 8-10 servings. | Prep: 20mins | Cook: 01hours15mins | Ready in:

Ingredients

- 8 slices day-old white bread
- 4 cups chopped cooked chicken
- 1 jar (4-1/2 ounces) sliced mushrooms, drained
- 1 can (8 ounces) sliced water chestnuts, drained
- 4 large eggs, lightly beaten
- 2 cups whole milk
- 1/2 cup mayonnaise
- 1/2 teaspoon salt
- 6 to 8 slices process American cheese
- 1 can (10-3/4 ounces) condensed cream of celery soup, undiluted
- 1 can (10-3/4 ounces) condensed cream of mushroom soup, undiluted
- 1 jar (2 ounces) chopped pimientos, drained
- 2 tablespoons butter, melted

Direction

- Take the crusts off the bread and set crusts aside. In a 13x9-in. greased pan, arrange the bread slices. Put on the chicken; cover with water chestnuts and mushrooms. Whisk together salt, eggs, mayonnaise, and milk in a big bowl. Dump over the chicken. Put the cheese on. Mix pimientos and soups; dump over cheese. Cover; place in refrigerator overnight. Thirty minutes before baking, remove from refrigerator. Crumble the crusts and mix with melted butter. Sprinkle mixture on top. Do not cover; bake in a 325-degree oven until a knife poked in the middle comes out clean, 1 1/4 hours. Before cutting, let it cool for 10 minutes.

Nutrition Information

- Calories: 438 calories
- Protein: 26g protein.
- Total Fat: 27g fat (9g saturated fat)
- Sodium: 1093mg sodium
- Fiber: 3g fiber)
- Total Carbohydrate: 22g carbohydrate (6g sugars
- Cholesterol: 164mg cholesterol

287.   Party Casserole

Serving: 6 servings. | Prep: 25mins | Cook: 30mins | Ready in:

Ingredients

- 6 boneless skinless chicken breast halves (4 ounces each)
- 1 cup water
- 2 cups sliced zucchini , cut 1/4 inch slices
- 1 package (14 ounces) frozen baby carrots or 3 cups fresh baby carrots
- 5 tablespoons butter, divided
- 2 tablespoons all-purpose flour
- 1-1/2 cups half-and-half cream or milk
- 2 teaspoons chicken bouillon granules

- 1/2 teaspoon prepared mustard
- 1/2 teaspoon dill weed, divided
- 1/8 teaspoon pepper
- Dash nutmeg
- 1 can (14-1/2 ounces) small whole onions, drained
- 1-1/2 cups soft bread crumbs
- 3/4 cup shredded cheddar cheese
- 1/2 cup coarsely chopped walnuts

Direction

- Boil water and chicken in a large skillet. Lower the heat; simmer without a cover for 3 minutes per side (the chicken will not be fully cook). Take the chicken out of cooking liquid; place down the center of an ungreased 13x9-inch baking sheet; set aside.
- Cook carrots and zucchini in the cooking liquid till the zucchini just starts to soften, 5 minutes; strain and put aside. Melt 2 tablespoons of butter in a large saucepan; mix in flour and cook for a minute. Mix in cream till smooth. Put in nutmeg, pepper, 1/4 teaspoon of dill, mustard and bouillon. Boil the mixture; cook while stirring till thicken, 2 minutes. Take away from the heat.
- Scoop 1/2 cup of the sauce over the chicken. Put onions, carrots and zucchini into the remaining sauce. Scoop alongside of the baking sheet. Melt the remaining butter; toss with the remaining dill, walnuts, cheese and bread crumbs.
- Spoon over the vegetables and chicken. Bake without a cover at 375° till the sauce is bubbly and the topping turns brown, 30-35 minutes.

Nutrition Information

- Calories: 517 calories
- Fiber: 5g fiber)
- Total Carbohydrate: 25g carbohydrate (10g sugars
- Cholesterol: 144mg cholesterol
- Protein: 38g protein.
- Total Fat: 29g fat (14g saturated fat)
- Sodium: 657mg sodium

288.   Phyllo Chicken Potpie

Serving: 6 servings. | Prep: 35mins | Cook: 10mins | Ready in:

Ingredients

- 6 cups water
- 2 cups fresh pearl onions
- 1-1/2 pounds boneless skinless chicken breasts, cubed
- 2 tablespoons canola oil, divided
- 2 medium red potatoes, peeled and chopped
- 1 cup sliced fresh mushrooms
- 1 can (14-1/2 ounces) reduced-sodium chicken broth
- 1/2 pound fresh asparagus, trimmed and cut into 1-inch pieces
- 3 tablespoons sherry or additional reduced-sodium chicken broth
- 3 tablespoons cornstarch
- 1/2 cup fat-free milk
- 1-1/2 teaspoons minced fresh thyme
- 1/2 teaspoon salt
- 1/4 teaspoon pepper
- 10 sheets phyllo dough (14 inches x 9 inches)
- Refrigerated butter-flavored spray

Direction

- In a Dutch oven, boil water. Put in pearl onions; boil for approximately 3 minutes. Let drain and rinse in cold water; peel and leave aside.
- In a large skillet, cook chicken in 1 tablespoon oil over medium till no longer pink; take out and keep warm. In the same pan, sauté potatoes in remaining oil for around 5 minutes. Put in mushrooms and onions; sauté for an addition of 3 minutes. Put in the asparagus, broth and sherry or additional broth. Let boil. Lower heat; simmering with cover for around 5 minutes till potatoes are soften.
- Combine milk and cornstarch until smooth; stir into skillet. Let boil; cook and stir for nearly 2 minutes till thicken. Let chicken drain; add to onion mixture. Mix in pepper, salt and thyme. Place to a baking dish of 8-inch square covered with cooking spray.
- Stack all 10 phyllo sheets. Roll up, starting at a long side; cut into strips of a half inch. In a large bowl, place strips and toss to separate. Use butter-flavored spray to spritz over. Place over chicken mixture; spritz again.
- Bake with no cover at 425° for around 10 to 15 minutes until it has golden brown color.

Nutrition Information

- Calories: 325 calories
- Total Fat: 8g fat (1g saturated fat)
- Sodium: 542mg sodium
- Fiber: 2g fiber)
- Total Carbohydrate: 33g carbohydrate (5g sugars
- Cholesterol: 63mg cholesterol
- Protein: 29g protein. Diabetic Exchanges: 3 lean meat

289.   Poppy Seed Chicken

Serving: 6 | Prep: 15mins | Cook: 45mins | Ready in:

Ingredients

- 6 skinless, boneless chicken breast halves - diced
- 1 (10.75 ounce) can condensed cream of chicken soup
- 1 (8 ounce) container sour cream
- 2 tablespoons dry sherry
- salt and pepper to taste
- 8 ounces buttery round crackers, crushed
- 1 1/2 tablespoons poppy seeds
- 1/2 cup butter, melted

Direction

- Preheat to 175°C/350°F.
- Put diced chicken breasts on bottom of a 9x13-in. baking dish sprayed with nonstick cooking spray. Mix sherry, sour cream and soup in bowl; spoon/pour mixture on top of chicken. Sprinkle pepper and salt over.
- Mix crushed crackers and poppy seeds; sprinkle mixture on top of pepper, salt and chicken. Drizzle melted margarine/butter on the poppyseed/cracker layer; bake in preheated oven, covered, for 30-45 minutes. Uncover at the final 5 minutes; before serving, allow to stand for several minutes.

Nutrition Information

- Calories: 602 calories;
- Cholesterol: 129
- Protein: 29.7
- Total Fat: 40.4
- Sodium: 893
- Total Carbohydrate: 28.6

290.   Poppy Seed Chicken Casserole

Serving: 6 | Prep: 20mins | Cook: 50mins | Ready in:

Ingredients

- 4 skinless, boneless chicken breast halves
- 1/2 cup butter, melted
- 1 sleeve buttery round crackers (such as Ritz®), crushed
- 1 teaspoon poppy seeds, or more if desired
- 1 (8 ounce) container sour cream
- 1 (10.75 ounce) can condensed cream of chicken soup
- 2 cups shredded Cheddar cheese

Direction

- Cover chicken breasts in water in a big pot; boil on high heat. Lower heat to medium then

cover; simmer for 20 minutes till chicken breasts are not pink anymore in the middle. Drain water; shred chicken.
- Preheat oven to 175°C/350°F. Mix poppy seeds, crackers and butter in bowl; put aside.
- Blend cream of chicken soup and sour cream in bowl; put 1/2 soup mixture in a 9x9-in. baking dish. Add shredded chicken; put leftover 1/2 soup mixture over. Sprinkle Cheddar cheese over; put cracker mixture on top.
- In preheated oven, bake for 25-30 minutes till sauce is bubbly and cheese melts.

Nutrition Information

- Calories: 593 calories;
- Cholesterol: 142
- Protein: 28.4
- Total Fat: 45.7
- Sodium: 900
- Total Carbohydrate: 16.9

291.   Potato Chicken Casserole

Serving: 6 servings. | Prep: 20mins | Cook: 20mins | Ready in:

Ingredients

- 1/2 pound medium fresh mushrooms, quartered
- 2 medium onions, chopped
- 5 tablespoons butter, divided
- 2 cups cubed cooked chicken
- 2 cups diced cooked peeled potatoes
- 1 jar (2 ounces) diced pimientos, drained
- 1/4 cup minced fresh parsley
- 1 cup half-and-half cream
- 1 teaspoon chicken bouillon granules
- 1 teaspoon salt
- 1/2 teaspoon dried rosemary, crushed
- 1/8 teaspoon pepper
- 1 cup soft bread crumbs

Direction

- Put 3 tablespoons butter in a big frying pan, sauté onions and mushrooms until tender. Add pimientos, pepper, bouillon, rosemary, potatoes, cream, chicken, salt, and parsley; cook through. Put mixture in a 2-qt. greased dish. Melt the rest of the butter; mix in bread crumbs and spread on top of dish. Do not cover; bake in a 350-degree oven until crumbs are toasted, 20-25 minutes.

Nutrition Information

- Calories: 325 calories
- Protein: 18g protein.
- Total Fat: 17g fat (10g saturated fat)
- Sodium: 738mg sodium
- Fiber: 3g fiber)
- Total Carbohydrate: 23g carbohydrate (6g sugars
- Cholesterol: 87mg cholesterol

292. Potluck Chicken Casserole

Serving: 8-10 servings. | Prep: 25mins | Cook: 30mins | Ready in:

Ingredients

- 1/2 cup chopped fresh mushrooms
- 3 tablespoons finely chopped onion
- 4 tablespoons butter, divided
- 2 garlic cloves, minced
- 3 tablespoons all-purpose flour
- 1-1/4 cups milk
- 3/4 cup mayonnaise
- 4 cups cubed cooked chicken
- 3 cups cooked long grain rice
- 1 cup chopped celery
- 1 cup frozen peas, thawed
- 1 jar (2 ounces) diced pimientos, drained
- 2 teaspoons lemon juice

- 1 teaspoon salt
- 1/2 teaspoon pepper
- 3/4 cup coarsely crushed cornflakes

Direction

- Sauté onion and mushrooms in 3 tablespoons of butter in a large saucepan till tender. Put in garlic; cook for 1 more minute. Mix in flour till blended. Slowly put in milk; boil the mixture. Cook while stirring till bubbly and thicken, 2 minutes. Take away from the heat; mix in mayonnaise till smooth. Put in pepper, salt, lemon juice, pimientos, peas, celery, rice and chicken.
- Transfer into an ungreased 13x9-inch baking sheet. Melt the remaining butter; toss with cornflakes. Scatter over the top. Bake without a cover at 350° till bubbly, 30-35 minutes.

Nutrition Information

- Calories: 397 calories
- Total Carbohydrate: 25g carbohydrate (3g sugars
- Cholesterol: 72mg cholesterol
- Protein: 20g protein.
- Total Fat: 23g fat (6g saturated fat)
- Sodium: 512mg sodium
- Fiber: 1g fiber)

293. Puff Pastry Chicken Potpie

Serving: 8 servings. | Prep: 45mins | Cook: 45mins | Ready in:

Ingredients

- 1 package (17.3 ounces) frozen puff pastry, thawed
- 2 pounds boneless skinless chicken breasts, cut into 1-inch pieces
- 1 teaspoon salt, divided

- 1 teaspoon pepper, divided
- 4 tablespoons butter, divided
- 1 large onion, chopped
- 2 garlic cloves, minced
- 1 teaspoon minced fresh thyme or 1/4 teaspoon dried thyme
- 1 teaspoon minced fresh sage or 1/4 teaspoon rubbed sage
- 1/2 cup all-purpose flour
- 2 cups chicken broth
- 1 cup plus 1 tablespoon half-and-half cream, divided
- 2 cups frozen mixed vegetables (about 10 ounces)
- 1 tablespoon lemon juice
- 1 large egg yolk

Direction

- Set oven to 400° to preheat. Roll each pastry sheet into a rectangle of 12x10-inch on a lightly floured work surface. Cut one sheet horizontally into 6 strips of 2-inch; cut the leftover sheet vertically into 5 strips of 2-inch. Tightly weave strips to make a lattice of 12x10-inch on a baking sheet. Keep the lattice in the freezer while preparing filling.
- Season chicken with 1/2 teaspoon pepper and 1/2 teaspoon salt; toss to coat. Heat 1 tablespoon butter over medium-high heat in a large skillet; sauté chicken in melted butter for 5 to 7 minutes until browned. Take chicken out of the pan.
- Melt the remaining butter over medium-high heat in the same skillet; sauté onion for 5 to 7 minutes until softened. Add herbs and garlic; sauté for another minute. Mix in flour until combined; sauté for 1 minute. Slowly mix in 1 cup cream and broth. Bring to a boil, stirring frequently; cook for about 2 minutes until thickened, stirring well while cooking.
- Mix in the remaining pepper and salt, chicken, lemon juice, and vegetables; bring to another boil. Pour mixture into an oiled 2-quart oblong baking dish. Place the lattice on top, cutting off the excess to fit.

- Stir together the remaining cream and egg yolk; brush egg mixture over pastry. Baking without covering for 45 to 55 minutes until filling is bubbly and top is golden brown. Allow to cool for 15 minutes before serving.

Nutrition Information

- Calories: 523 calories
- Fiber: 6g fiber)
- Total Carbohydrate: 42g carbohydrate (4g sugars
- Cholesterol: 118mg cholesterol
- Protein: 30g protein.
- Total Fat: 25g fat (10g saturated fat)
- Sodium: 829mg sodium

294. Quick Chicken Rice Casserole

Serving: 4 servings. | Prep: 20mins | Cook: 20mins | Ready in:

Ingredients

- 1 package (5.6 ounces) instant rice and chicken-flavored sauce mix
- 2 cups cubed cooked chicken
- 1 can (10-3/4 ounces) condensed cream of celery soup, undiluted
- 1/2 cup mayonnaise
- 1/2 teaspoon Worcestershire sauce
- 1/4 teaspoon pepper
- 1 cup shredded cheddar cheese

Direction

- Cook rice mix following the instruction of the package. In a large bowl, combine the soup, chicken, mayonnaise, pepper and Worcestershire sauce. Mix in rice.
- Place to a greased baking dish of 1 and a half quarts. Use cheese to sprinkle. Bake with no

cover at 350° for approximately 20 to 25 minutes till heated through.

Nutrition Information

- Calories: 643 calories
- Sodium: 1516mg sodium
- Fiber: 1g fiber)
- Total Carbohydrate: 38g carbohydrate (5g sugars
- Cholesterol: 107mg cholesterol
- Protein: 32g protein.
- Total Fat: 40g fat (12g saturated fat)

295.   Quick Creamy Chicken Enchiladas

Serving: 2 servings. | Prep: 10mins | Cook: 20mins | Ready in:

Ingredients

- 2/3 cup condensed cream of chicken soup, undiluted
- 2/3 cup sour cream
- 2 cups shredded cooked chicken breast
- 1/2 cup shredded Monterey Jack cheese, divided
- 4 flour tortillas (6 inches), warmed

Direction

- Mix sour cream and soup together in a small bowl. Smear 1/2 of sour cream mixture on the bottom of an 8-inch, cooking spray coated, square baking dish.
- Put 1 tablespoon of cheese and 1/2 cup of chicken down the middle of every tortilla, then roll it up and put in the baking dish. Put the rest of soup mixture on top and sprinkle remaining cheese over.
- Bake at 350 degrees without a cover until heated through, about 18 to 22 minutes.

Nutrition Information

- Calories: 658 calories
- Protein: 62g protein.
- Total Fat: 28g fat (10g saturated fat)
- Sodium: 1370mg sodium
- Fiber: 1g fiber)
- Total Carbohydrate: 40g carbohydrate (6g sugars
- Cholesterol: 161mg cholesterol

296.   Ranch Chicken 'n' Rice

Serving: 4 servings. | Prep: 10mins | Cook: 35mins | Ready in:

Ingredients

- 2 cups uncooked instant rice
- 1-1/2 cups 2% milk
- 1 cup water
- 1 envelope ranch salad dressing mix
- 1 pound boneless skinless chicken breasts, cut into 1/2-inch strips
- 1/4 cup butter, melted
- Paprika

Direction

- In a greased shallow baking dish of 2-quart, place the rice. In a small bowl, combine the salad dressing mix, water and milk; leave aside 1/4 cup. Pour over rice the remaining mixture. Place chicken strips on top. Sprinkle reserved milk mixture and butter over.
- Bake with cover at 350° for nearly 35 to 40 minutes till chicken is no longer pink and rice is tender. Dust with paprika.

Nutrition Information

- Calories:
- Total Carbohydrate:
- Cholesterol:
- Protein:

- Total Fat:
- Sodium:
- Fiber:

- Cholesterol: 122mg cholesterol
- Protein: 28g protein.

297.   Saucy Chicken Casserole

Serving: 6 servings. | Prep: 15mins | Cook: 60mins | Ready in:

Ingredients

- 1 can (10-3/4 ounces) condensed cream of chicken soup, undiluted
- 1 can (10-3/4 ounces) condensed cream of mushroom soup, undiluted
- 2 cups sour cream
- 3/4 cup dry white wine or chicken broth
- 1/2 medium onion, chopped
- 1 cup sliced fresh mushrooms
- 1/2 teaspoon garlic powder
- 1/2 teaspoon salt
- 1/2 teaspoon poultry seasoning
- 1/4 teaspoon pepper
- 6 boneless skinless chicken breast halves
- Cooked noodles or rice
- Minced fresh parsley

Direction

- In a baking dish of 13x9-inch, combine the sour cream, soups, onion, wine, seasoning and mushrooms. Arrange chicken over top.
- Bake with no cover at 350° for around 1 hour till chicken juices run clear. Serve over noodles or rice. Jazz up with parsley.

Nutrition Information

- Calories: 397 calories
- Total Fat: 21g fat (12g saturated fat)
- Sodium: 1035mg sodium
- Fiber: 1g fiber)
- Total Carbohydrate: 12g carbohydrate (4g sugars

298.   Saucy Chicken Squares

Serving: 6-8 servings. | Prep: 10mins | Cook: 55mins | Ready in:

Ingredients

- 2 cups soft bread crumbs
- 2 cups chicken broth
- 4 eggs, lightly beaten
- 1 celery rib, chopped
- 1 jar (4 ounces) diced pimientos, drained
- 2 tablespoons finely chopped onion
- 1/2 teaspoon salt
- 1/4 teaspoon poultry seasoning
- 3 cups cubed cooked chicken
- 1 cup cooked rice
- 1 cup sliced fresh mushrooms
- 1/3 cup butter, cubed
- 3 tablespoons all-purpose flour
- 1/2 teaspoon salt
- 1/4 teaspoon pepper
- 1-1/2 cups 2% milk

Direction

- In a big bowl, combine poultry seasoning, salt, onion, pimientos, celery, eggs, broth and bread crumbs. Blend in the rice and chicken.
- Move into a greased 8-inch square baking dish. Bake with no cover at 350° for around 55-65 minutes or till bubbly and golden brown.
- Meanwhile, in a big saucepan, sauté mushrooms in butter. Mix in the pepper, salt, and flour till blended. Slowly pour in milk. Set to a boil; cook and mix for 2 minutes or up to condensed. Chop chicken casserole into squares. Serve along with mushroom sauce.

Nutrition Information

- Calories: 310 calories
- Sodium: 771mg sodium
- Fiber: 1g fiber)
- Total Carbohydrate: 18g carbohydrate (4g sugars
- Cholesterol: 180mg cholesterol
- Protein: 23g protein.
- Total Fat: 16g fat (8g saturated fat)

299. Saucy Comforting Chicken

Serving: 4 servings. | Prep: 15mins | Cook: 55mins | Ready in:

Ingredients

- 1 pound boneless skinless chicken breasts, cut into cubes
- 1/2 cup finely chopped onion
- 1/2 cup finely chopped green pepper
- 1 tablespoon canola oil
- 1 tablespoon butter
- 1 can (10-3/4 ounces) condensed cream of mushroom soup, undiluted
- 1 cup water
- 3/4 cup uncooked long grain rice
- 1/2 teaspoon salt
- 1/2 teaspoon chili powder
- 1/4 teaspoon pepper
- 1/4 teaspoon paprika

Direction

- Cook green pepper, onion and chicken in oil and butter in a large skillet till the vegetables become tender and the chicken is not pink anymore. Mix in the remaining ingredients.
- Transfer onto a 1 1/2-quart baking sheet lightly coated with grease. Bake with a cover at 375° till bubbly and the rice turns tender, 55-60 minutes.

Nutrition Information

- Calories: 379 calories
- Sodium: 919mg sodium
- Fiber: 2g fiber)
- Total Carbohydrate: 37g carbohydrate (2g sugars
- Cholesterol: 73mg cholesterol
- Protein: 27g protein.
- Total Fat: 13g fat (4g saturated fat)

300. Saucy Garlic Chicken For Two

Serving: 2 servings. | Prep: 40mins | Cook: 35mins | Ready in:

Ingredients

- 2 whole garlic bulb
- 1 tablespoon olive oil, divided
- 4-1/2 cups fresh baby spinach
- 1/2 teaspoon salt, divided
- 1/4 teaspoon coarsely ground pepper, divided
- 2 boneless skinless chicken breast halves (6 ounces each)
- 2 tablespoons butter, cubed
- 2 tablespoons all-purpose flour
- 1-1/2 cups 2% milk
- 1-1/4 cups grated Parmesan cheese, divided
- Dash ground nutmeg
- Hot cooked pasta
- Chopped tomato and minced fresh parsley, optional

Direction

- Discard the garlic's papery outer skin but do not separate the cloves or peel. Slice off the garlic bulb tops; slather 1/2 of oil on the bulbs. Use heavy-duty foil to wrap each bulb; bake for 30-35mins in a 425 degrees oven until soft. Let bulbs cool for 10-15mins.
- In the meantime, put spinach in an oiled 11-in by 7-in baking dish; scatter 1/2 the pepper and salt. Brown each side of the chicken in a big

pan with the remaining oil; nestle on top of the spinach.

- Melt butter in a big pot. Mix in flour until the mixture is smooth; pour in milk gradually then boil. Cook and stir for 1-2mins until thick. Mix in the remaining salt, nutmeg, and a cup of cheese. Move to a blender and squeeze into blender with softened garlic. Pour the mixture all over the chicken.
- Bake for 30-35mins in a 425 degrees while covered until the sauce is bubbly and a thermometer registers 170 degrees. Remove the cover then top with the remaining cheese; bake for another 5mins. Serve with pasta. If desired, add parsley and tomato on top.

Nutrition Information

- Calories:
- Total Fat:
- Sodium:
- Fiber:
- Total Carbohydrate:
- Cholesterol:
- Protein:

---

301.   Sausage 'N' Chicken Casserole

Serving: 4 servings. | Prep: 10mins | Cook: 55mins | Ready in:

Ingredients

- 5 medium potatoes (about 3 pounds), peeled and quartered
- 1 teaspoon salt
- 1 teaspoon dried oregano
- 1 teaspoon paprika
- 1/2 teaspoon garlic salt
- 1/2 pound Johnsonville® Mild Italian Sausage Links, cooked and cut into 1-inch pieces
- 4 bone-in chicken breast halves, skin removed (7 ounces each)

- 2 tablespoons canola oil

Direction

- Arrange potatoes in a greased 13x9-in. baking dish. Combine garlic salt, paprika, oregano, and salt in a small bowl; sprinkle 1/2 over potatoes.
- Arrange over the potatoes with chicken and sausage. Spray with oil and sprinkle with the leftover seasonings.
- Cover and bake for 55-60 minutes at 400°, or until inserting a thermometer in the chicken and it states 170°.

Nutrition Information

- Calories: 397 calories
- Sodium: 1109mg sodium
- Fiber: 3g fiber)
- Total Carbohydrate: 47g carbohydrate (4g sugars
- Cholesterol: 45mg cholesterol
- Protein: 18g protein.
- Total Fat: 15g fat (4g saturated fat)

---

302.   Scalloped Chicken Supper

Serving: 4 servings. | Prep: 10mins | Cook: 45mins | Ready in:

Ingredients

- 1 package (4.9 ounces) scalloped potatoes
- 1-3/4 cups boiling water
- 1 can (10-3/4 ounces) condensed cream of chicken soup, undiluted
- 1/8 teaspoon poultry seasoning
- 2 cups cubed cooked chicken
- 1 cup shredded carrots
- 1/2 cup chopped celery
- 1/4 cup finely chopped onion

Direction

- In a large bowl, place the contents of the sauce mix; leave the potatoes aside. Whisk in the poultry seasoning, soup and water. Mix in carrots, chicken, celery, reserved potatoes and onion.
- Place to a greased baking dish of 2-quart. Bake with no cover at 400° for approximately 45 to 50 minutes till vegetables are soften.

Nutrition Information

- Calories: 343 calories
- Sodium: 1209mg sodium
- Fiber: 5g fiber)
- Total Carbohydrate: 35g carbohydrate (5g sugars
- Cholesterol: 70mg cholesterol
- Protein: 25g protein.
- Total Fat: 11g fat (3g saturated fat)

---

303.   Simple Chicken Enchiladas

Serving: 6 servings | Prep: 15mins | Cook: | Ready in:

Ingredients

- 3 cups shredded cooked chicken breast s
- 1 jar (16 oz.) TACO BELL® Thick & Chunky Mild Salsa , divided
- 1-1/2 cups KRAFT 2% Milk Shredded Mild Cheddar Cheese , divided
- 12 flour tortillas (6 inch)

Direction

- In a bowl, combine 1/2 cup cheese, 1/2 cup salsa, and chicken.
- On the bottom of 13x9-in. baking dish, spread 1/2 cup of the leftover salsa. Down middles of tortillas, spoon the chicken mixture; roll up. Put in the baking dish with the seam-sides

---

turning down. Put leftover salsa and cheese on top.
- Bake until completely heated, about 20 minutes.

Nutrition Information

- Calories: 400
- Total Fat: 12 g
- Sodium: 1170 mg
- Cholesterol: 80 mg
- Protein: 34 g
- Saturated Fat: 5 g
- Fiber: 2 g
- Sugar: 3 g
- Total Carbohydrate: 36 g

---

304.   Sombrero Bake

Serving: 6 servings. | Prep: 10mins | Cook: 45mins | Ready in:

Ingredients

- 2-1/2 cups cubed cooked chicken
- 1 can (4 ounces) chopped green chilies
- 1 cup shredded cheddar cheese
- 1 medium tomato, chopped
- 1 can (10-3/4 ounces) condensed cream of chicken soup, undiluted
- 1/2 cup 2% milk
- 1/2 teaspoon hot pepper sauce
- BISCUIT TOPPING:
- 3/4 cup biscuit/baking mix
- 1/2 cup cornmeal
- 2/3 cup 2% milk
- 1 can (2.8 ounces) french-fried onions, divided
- 1/2 cup shredded cheddar cheese

Direction

- In one greased 13x9-in. baking dish, layer with chicken, chilies, cheese and tomato. Mix hot pepper sauce, milk and soup in a small-sized bowl. Add on top of the chicken mixture. Keep it covered and baked at 375 degrees for 20 minutes.

- Mix three quarters cup of onion, milk, cornmeal and biscuit mix in a small-sized bowl. Drop into eight mounds on top of the casserole.
- Bake, while uncovered, for 20 minutes, the topping will spread out. Drizzle with cheese and the rest of the onions. Bake till cheese becomes melted or for 5 minutes more.

Nutrition Information

- Calories: 483 calories
- Protein: 28g protein.
- Total Fat: 26g fat (12g saturated fat)
- Sodium: 1011mg sodium
- Fiber: 2g fiber)
- Total Carbohydrate: 32g carbohydrate (4g sugars
- Cholesterol: 92mg cholesterol

305.   Spanish Chicken

Serving: 8 | Prep: 15mins | Cook: 6hours | Ready in:

Ingredients

- 2 pounds boneless chicken thighs
- 1 quart boiling water
- 1/2 teaspoon salt
- 5 onions, cut into 2 inch pieces
- 5 large green bell peppers, cut into 2 inch pieces
- 1 (8 ounce) jar chili sauce
- 1 (15 ounce) can tomato sauce
- 1 cup ketchup

Direction

- Add chicken into a big slow cooker. Add in enough boiling water to totally cover the chicken, and put in half tsp. of salt. Keep it

covered, and set slow cooker to HIGH. Cook till the chicken meat becomes white.

- Put in onions and peppers. Let it simmer for roughly 10 minutes or till peppers and onions become slightly soft. Mix in ketchup, chili sauce, and tomato sauce. Keep it covered, set slow cooker to LOW, and cook for roughly 6 hours.

Nutrition Information

- Calories: 342 calories;
- Protein: 23.3
- Total Fat: 17.7
- Sodium: 850
- Total Carbohydrate: 24
- Cholesterol: 95

306.   Spanish Style Paella

Serving: 6-8 servings. | Prep: 10mins | Cook: 35mins | Ready in:

Ingredients

- 1/2 pound Johnsonville® Ground Mild Italian sausage
- 1/2 pound boneless skinless chicken breasts, cubed
- 1 tablespoon olive oil
- 1 garlic clove, minced
- 1 cup uncooked long grain rice
- 1 cup chopped onion
- 1-1/2 cups chicken broth
- 1 can (14-1/2 ounces) stewed tomatoes, undrained
- 1/2 teaspoon paprika
- 1/4 teaspoon ground cayenne pepper
- 1/4 teaspoon salt
- 10 strands saffron, crushed or 1/8 teaspoon ground saffron
- 1/2 pound uncooked medium shrimp, peeled and deveined
- 1/2 cup sweet red pepper strips

- 1/2 cup green pepper strips
- 1/2 cup frozen peas

Direction

- On a heat of medium high, cook the chicken and sausage in a big saucepan with oil until the sausage gets a bit brown and the chicken isn't pink anymore or for about 5 minutes while mixing it regularly. Put garlic in and cook it for another a minute and then drain it if needed.
- Mix in the onion and rice. Cook it until the onion becomes tender and the rice is slightly browned while mixing it regularly. Put in the broth, paprika, salt, saffron, cayenne, and tomatoes. Bring it to a boil. Lower the heat to low, cover it, and cook it for about 10 minutes.
- Mix in the peas, shrimp, and pepper. Cover it again and cook it for another 10 minutes or until the rice becomes tender, the shrimp is pink, and the liquid gets absorbed.

Nutrition Information

- Calories: 237 calories
- Cholesterol: 62mg cholesterol
- Protein: 16g protein.
- Total Fat: 7g fat (2g saturated fat)
- Sodium: 543mg sodium
- Fiber: 2g fiber)
- Total Carbohydrate: 27g carbohydrate (5g sugars

307.   Spicy Chicken Enchiladas

Serving: 6 | Prep: 15mins | Cook: 25mins | Ready in:

Ingredients

- 1 (4.5 ounce) package dry rice and chicken sauce mix with broccoli
- 1 tablespoon vegetable oil
- 1 pound ground chicken

- 3 tablespoons chopped onion
- 1 tablespoon minced garlic
- 1 fresh jalapeno pepper, chopped
- 1 (10 ounce) can diced tomatoes with green chile peppers, drained
- 1 (14.5 ounce) can enchilada sauce
- 1 1/4 cups shredded mild Cheddar cheese
- 6 (10 inch) flour tortillas

Direction

- Follow the directions on package to make the chicken sauce mix with broccoli and rice. Set the oven to 375 degrees F or 190 degrees C and start preheating. Put a little grease on a medium pan.
- In a large frying pan, heat oil on medium heat. Put the chicken in the frying pan. Add jalapeno, onion, and garlic to the frying pan. While cooking, stir until the chicken browns evenly. Add in the 2/3 enchilada sauce, prepared rice mix, 3/4 cup cheddar cheese, and diced tomatoes with green chile peppers. Put the mixture evenly into the tortillas. Form enchiladas by wrapping tortillas around the mixture. Arrange prepared enchiladas in greased pan. Dump the rest of the enchilada sauce on and sprinkle the rest of the cheese on top.
- Place in heated oven until sauce and cheese are bubbling and melty, 15 minutes.

Nutrition Information

- Calories: 763 calories;
- Sodium: 1623
- Total Carbohydrate: 122.5
- Cholesterol: 32
- Protein: 24.6
- Total Fat: 21.7

308. Spinach Chicken Casserole

Serving: 6 servings. | Prep: 20mins | Cook: 20mins | Ready in:

Ingredients

- 2 cups uncooked penne pasta
- 3/4 pound boneless skinless chicken breasts, cubed
- 1 small onion, chopped
- 1/2 cup chopped green pepper
- 1 jar (26 ounces) spaghetti sauce
- 1 package (16 ounces) frozen leaf spinach, thawed and squeezed dry
- 1 jar (6 ounces) sliced mushrooms, drained
- 1 can (2-1/4 ounces) sliced ripe olives, drained
- 2 cups shredded part-skim mozzarella cheese, divided

Direction

- Following package instructions to cook pasta. At the same time, sauté chicken in a big nonstick saucepan coated with cooking spray until meat is not pink anymore; put aside.
- Sauté green pepper and onion in the same pan until crisp-tender. Put in olives, mushrooms, spinach, and spaghetti sauce; heat to a boil. Lower heat and simmer for 5 minutes without cover. Drain pasta. Place pasta and chicken into the pan. Add 1 cup cheese over the top, toss to coat.
- Move to a 13x9-inch baking dish coated with cooking spray; sprinkle the rest of cheese over top. Put on cover and bake at 350 degrees for 20-25 minutes or until cheese melts.

Nutrition Information

- Calories: 492 calories
- Sodium: 1323mg sodium
- Fiber: 5g fiber)
- Total Carbohydrate: 38g carbohydrate (12g sugars
- Cholesterol: 78mg cholesterol

- Protein: 39g protein.
- Total Fat: 20g fat (9g saturated fat)

309. Spinach Chicken Enchiladas

Serving: 8 servings. | Prep: 30mins | Cook: 45mins | Ready in:

Ingredients

- 4 boneless skinless chicken breast halves, cut into thin strips
- 1/4 cup chopped onion
- 1 package (10 ounces) frozen chopped spinach, thawed and well drained
- 1 can (10-3/4 ounces) condensed cream of mushroom soup, undiluted
- 3/4 cup fat-free milk
- 1 cup sour cream
- 1 teaspoon ground nutmeg
- 1 teaspoon garlic powder
- 1 teaspoon onion powder
- 2 cups shredded part-skim mozzarella cheese
- 8 flour tortillas (8 inches)
- Minced fresh parsley

Direction

- Spray cooking spray over a big skillet to coat; cook while mixing the onion and chicken over medium heat until the chicken juices run clear, or for 6-8 minutes. Take away from heat, mix in spinach.
- Mix seasonings, sour cream, milk, and soup together in a big bowl. Mix into the chicken mixture with 3/4 cup soup mixture. Down the middle of each tortilla, put the filling. Roll up and put in a greased 13x9-inch baking pan with the seam-side facing down. Pour over the enchiladas with the leftover soup mixture.
- Put a cover on and bake for 30 minutes at 350°. Remove the cover and sprinkle cheese over, bake until cheese is bubbly and melts, or for another 15 minutes. Use parsley to garnish.

Nutrition Information

- Calories: 295 calories
- Fiber: 0 fiber)
- Total Carbohydrate: 22g carbohydrate (0 sugars
- Cholesterol: 58mg cholesterol
- Protein: 29g protein. Diabetic Exchanges: 3 lean meat
- Total Fat: 11g fat (0 saturated fat)
- Sodium: 496mg sodium

310. Stacked Enchilada

Serving: 4 servings. | Prep: 20mins | Cook: 20mins | Ready in:

Ingredients

- 2/3 cup chopped green pepper
- 2 teaspoons canola oil
- 1 garlic clove, minced
- 1 cup shredded cooked chicken
- 1 cup canned black beans, rinsed and drained
- 1/3 cup thinly sliced green onions
- 1/2 cup enchilada sauce
- 1/2 cup picante sauce
- 4 corn tortillas (6 inches)
- 1 cup shredded cheddar cheese
- Sour cream and shredded lettuce, optional

Direction

- Sauté pepper with oil in a big skillet for 3 minutes. Add garlic and cook until the pepper is crisp-tender, or for another 2 minutes. Mix in onions, beans, and chicken; thoroughly heat. Remove into a bowl and keep warm.
- Mix together picante sauces and enchilada in the same skillet. With the sauce mixture, coat 1 tortilla on both sides; put in a 9-inch pie plate coated with grease. Put 1/4 cup the cheese and 1/3 the chicken mixture on top. Continue

layering until having 2 more layers. Put cheese, sauce, and the leftover tortilla on top.
- Put a cover on and bake at 350° until thoroughly heated, or for 18-22 minutes. Transfer onto a serving plate and slice into wedges. Enjoy with lettuce and sour cream if wished.

Nutrition Information

- Calories: 318 calories
- Fiber: 5g fiber)
- Total Carbohydrate: 28g carbohydrate (3g sugars
- Cholesterol: 61mg cholesterol
- Protein: 22g protein.
- Total Fat: 14g fat (7g saturated fat)
- Sodium: 764mg sodium

311. Summer Squash Enchiladas

Serving: 8 | Prep: 25mins | Cook: 38mins | Ready in:

Ingredients

- cooking spray
- 1 tablespoon olive oil
- 1 onion, chopped
- 2 cloves garlic, minced
- 3 cups chopped yellow summer squash
- 1 (4 ounce) can diced green chile peppers, divided
- 2 teaspoons chili powder, divided
- 1/4 teaspoon ground black pepper
- Sauce:
- 2 tablespoons butter
- 2 tablespoons all-purpose flour
- 1/4 teaspoon salt
- 1/8 teaspoon ground black pepper
- 1 cup milk
- 1 1/2 cups shredded Monterey Jack cheese, divided

- 8 (8 inch) flour tortillas
- 1 1/2 cups chopped tomatoes

Direction

- Set an oven to 200°C (400°F) and start preheating. Use cooking spray to lightly coat a 9x13-inch baking dish.
- In a large skillet, heat the olive oil on medium heat. Stir and cook garlic and onion for 3-5 minutes until they slightly become soft. Put in summer squash; stir and cook for 3-5 minutes until nearly tender. Stir in 1/4 teaspoon of pepper, a teaspoon of chili powder, and half of the green chile peppers; cook for a minute. Take away from the heat.
- In a saucepan, melt the butter on medium heat. Stir in 1/8 teaspoon of pepper, salt, flour, and the remaining 1 teaspoon of chili powder; cook for a minute. Add milk and stir for 5 minutes until the sauce becomes thick. Take away from the heat. Add a cup of Monterey Jack cheese and stir, then put in the remaining green chile peppers.
- Add 1/2 cup of the sauce into the squash mixture and stir. Fill the center of each tortilla with 1/3 cup of the squash and sauce mixture, then roll tortillas up.
- In the baking dish, place the stuffed tortillas. Use the remaining sauce to cover. Use aluminum foil to cover the baking dish.
- In the prepared oven, bake for 25 minutes until heated thoroughly. Put tomatoes and the remaining 1/2 cup of Monterey Jack cheese on top.

Nutrition Information

- Calories: 335 calories;
- Sodium: 737
- Total Carbohydrate: 36.2
- Cholesterol: 29
- Protein: 12.1
- Total Fat: 16.1

312.   Sunday Chicken

Serving: 4-6 servings. | Prep: 15mins | Cook: 02hours00mins | Ready in:

Ingredients

- 1 can (10-3/4 ounces) condensed cream of mushroom soup, undiluted
- 1 can (10-3/4 ounces) condensed cream of celery soup, undiluted
- 1 can (10-3/4 ounces) condensed cream of chicken soup, undiluted
- 1/3 cup butter, melted, divided
- 1-1/4 cups quick-cooking rice
- 1 broiler/fryer chicken (3 to 4 pounds), cut up
- Salt and pepper to taste
- Paprika

Direction

- Set oven to 350 degrees and start preheating. Combine rice, 1/4 cup butter, and soups in a big bowl. Transfer to an oiled 13x9-inch baking dish. Arrange chicken pieces on top. Drizzle the rest of butter over chicken. Sprinkle with paprika, pepper, and salt.
- Bake for 2 hours without a cover, till rice is tender and chicken juices run clear.

Nutrition Information

- Calories: 541 calories
- Protein: 31g protein.
- Total Fat: 33g fat (12g saturated fat)
- Sodium: 1156mg sodium
- Fiber: 3g fiber)
- Total Carbohydrate: 28g carbohydrate (1g sugars
- Cholesterol: 123mg cholesterol

313.   Swiss Chicken Bake

Serving: 6 | Prep: 10mins | Cook: 55mins | Ready in:

Ingredients

- 6 skinless, boneless chicken breast halves
- 5 ounces sliced fresh mushrooms
- 2 cups shredded Swiss cheese
- 1 (10.75 ounce) can condensed cream of mushroom soup
- 1/4 cup sour cream
- 1/4 cup chicken broth
- 1/4 cup Parmesan cheese

Direction

- Set the oven to 350°F (175°C) and start preheating.
- In a large baking dish, place chicken. Scatter mushrooms around, top with sprinkled Swiss cheese. Mix chicken broth, sour cream and cream of mushroom soup in a small bowl. Top over chicken with sauce mixture.
- Bake chicken breasts in the prepared oven for about 50 minutes until juices run clear and the center is no longer pink. An inserted instant-read thermometer into the center should register at least 165°F (74°C). Take out of the oven; drizzle with Parmesan cheese and transfer back to the oven. Bake for 5 more minutes.

Nutrition Information

- Calories: 350 calories;
- Total Fat: 18.9
- Sodium: 513
- Total Carbohydrate: 6.7
- Cholesterol: 107
- Protein: 37.3

314.   Texan Ranch Chicken Casserole

Serving: 8 servings. | Prep: 25mins | Cook: 30mins | Ready in:

Ingredients

- 1 large onion, finely chopped
- 2 celery ribs, finely chopped
- 1 medium green pepper, finely chopped
- 1 medium sweet red pepper, finely chopped
- 1 tablespoon canola oil
- 1 garlic clove, minced
- 3 cups cubed cooked chicken breast
- 1 can (10-3/4 ounces) reduced-fat reduced-sodium condensed cream of celery soup, undiluted
- 1 can (10-3/4 ounces) reduced-fat reduced-sodium condensed cream of chicken soup, undiluted
- 1 can (10 ounces) diced tomatoes and green chilies, undrained
- 1 tablespoon chili powder
- 12 corn tortillas (6 inches), cut into 1-inch strips
- 2 cups shredded reduced-fat cheddar cheese, divided

Direction

- In a big nonstick skillet that coated using cooking spray, sauté the peppers, celery and onion in oil till becoming tender-crisp. Put in garlic; cook for 60 seconds more. Mix in chili powder, tomatoes, soups and chicken.
- Line the bottom of a 3-qt. baking dish with 1/2 of the tortilla strips; add 1 cup of cheese and 1/2 of the chicken mixture on top. Repeat the layers. Bake, while uncovered, at 350 degrees till becoming bubbly or for 30 to 35 minutes.

Nutrition Information

- Calories: 329 calories
- Protein: 26g protein. Diabetic Exchanges: 3 lean meat
- Total Fat: 12g fat (5g saturated fat)
- Sodium: 719mg sodium
- Fiber: 3g fiber)
- Total Carbohydrate: 31g carbohydrate (4g sugars
- Cholesterol: 65mg cholesterol

315. Tomato Garlic Chicken

Serving: 4 servings. | Prep: 10mins | Cook: 01hours15mins | Ready in:

Ingredients

- 3 to 4 garlic cloves, minced
- 1 teaspoon salt
- 5 medium red potatoes, cut into 1/4-inch slices
- 5 tablespoons olive oil, divided
- 1 large onion, thinly sliced
- 1 broiler/fryer chicken (3 to 4 pounds), cut up
- 2 medium tomatoes, chopped
- 1 tablespoon minced fresh basil

Direction

- Combine salt and garlic in a big bowl; let it sit for 15-20 minutes. Add in 2 tablespoons oil and potatoes.
- Layer tomatoes, chicken, onion, and potato mixture in an oiled 13x9-inch baking dish. Arrange basil and drizzle the remaining oil over the top.
- Put on cover and bake for 1 hour at 350 degrees. Remove cover and bake for 15 to 20 more minutes until potatoes are tender and chicken juices run clear.

Nutrition Information

- Calories: 762 calories
- Total Fat: 39g fat (8g saturated fat)
- Sodium: 727mg sodium
- Fiber: 6g fiber)
- Total Carbohydrate: 55g carbohydrate (8g sugars
- Cholesterol: 131mg cholesterol
- Protein: 48g protein

316. Turkey Broccoli Hollandaise

Serving: 6 servings. | Prep: 25mins | Cook: 25mins | Ready in:

Ingredients

- 1 cup fresh broccoli florets
- 1 package (6 ounces) stuffing mix
- 1 envelope hollandaise sauce mix
- 2 cups cubed cooked turkey or chicken
- 1 can (2.8 ounces) french-fried onions

Direction

- Place broccoli and 1 inch of water in a large saucepan; bring to a boil. Lower heat. Simmer, covered until tender-crisp, about 5 to 8 minutes. Meanwhile, prepare sauce mixes and stuffing as directed on package.
- Scoop stuffing into an oiled 11x7-inch baking dish. Place turkey atop the stuffing. Strain broccoli; place over turkey. Scoop sauce over the top; top mixture with onions.
- Bake without a cover for 25 to 30 minutes at 325°, or until thoroughly heated.

Nutrition Information

- Calories:
- Sodium:
- Fiber:
- Total Carbohydrate:
- Cholesterol:
- Protein:
- Total Fat:

317. Vegetable Chicken

Serving: 4 servings. | Prep: 20mins | Cook: 01hours30mins | Ready in:

Ingredients

- 1 broiler/fryer chicken (3-1/2 to 4 pounds), cut up and skin removed
- 2 cups sliced celery
- 2 cups fresh or frozen cut green beans
- 1-1/2 cups sliced carrots
- 1 large onion, sliced
- 1 small zucchini, diced
- 1 can (14-1/2 ounces) diced tomatoes, undrained
- 3 tablespoons quick-cooking tapioca
- 1 tablespoon sugar
- 2 teaspoons salt, optional
- 1/2 teaspoon pepper

Direction

- In an ungreased baking dish of 13- x 9-inch, place the celery, chicken, green beans, onion and carrots.
- In a small bowl, combine the tomatoes, zucchini, sugar, tapioca, pepper and salt (if desired). Pour over vegetables and chicken.
- Bake with tight cover at 350° for 1 and a half hours till vegetable mixture thickens and chicken juices run clear. Stir vegetables during baking occasionally.

Nutrition Information

- Calories: 242 calories
- Sodium: 298mg sodium
- Fiber: 0 fiber)
- Total Carbohydrate: 27g carbohydrate (0 sugars
- Cholesterol: 62mg cholesterol
- Protein: 25g protein. Diabetic Exchanges: 3 lean meat
- Total Fat: 4g fat (0 saturated fat)

318.   Vegetable Chicken Casserole

Serving: 5 servings. | Prep: 10mins | Cook: 60mins | Ready in:

Ingredients

- 3 cups cubed cooked chicken
- 4 medium carrots, cut into chunks
- 3 medium red potatoes, cut into chunks
- 3 celery ribs, sliced
- 1 can (10-3/4 ounces) condensed cream of chicken soup, undiluted
- 2/3 cup water
- 1/2 teaspoon salt
- 1/4 teaspoon pepper

Direction

- In a shallow 2-quart baking dish that is greased, put the chicken. Spread the potatoes, celery and carrots evenly over the chicken. Mix the salt, soup, pepper and water together and pour the soup mixture all over the vegetables.
- Cover the baking dish and put it in the preheated 350° oven; let it bake for 60-75 minutes until the vegetables have softened.

Nutrition Information

- Calories: 288 calories
- Total Fat: 10g fat (3g saturated fat)
- Sodium: 812mg sodium
- Fiber: 4g fiber)
- Total Carbohydrate: 21g carbohydrate (5g sugars
- Cholesterol: 80mg cholesterol
- Protein: 28g protein.

319.   Wild Rice Chicken Bake

Serving: 4 servings. | Prep: 5mins | Cook: 55mins | Ready in:

Ingredients

- 4 boneless skinless chicken breast halves
- 1 package (6 ounces) long grain and wild rice mix

- 1 envelope onion soup mix
- 2-1/3 cups water
- 1 tablespoon butter

Direction

- In a greased 13 x 9-inch baking dish, set the chicken. Blend the rice mix with butter, water, soup mix, and contents of seasoning packet. Add over chicken. Bake with cover at 350° for around 55-60 minutes, or till chicken juices flow out clear.

Nutrition Information

- Calories:
- Protein:
- Total Fat:
- Sodium:
- Fiber:
- Total Carbohydrate:
- Cholesterol:

---

320. Wild Rice Chicken Casserole

Serving: 4-6 servings. | Prep: 15mins | Cook: 30mins | Ready in:

Ingredients

- 1 package (6 ounces) long grain and wild rice
- 1/3 cup chopped onion
- 3 tablespoons chopped almonds
- 2 tablespoons dried parsley flakes
- 1/4 cup butter, cubed
- 1/3 cup all-purpose flour
- 2 cups 2% milk
- 1-1/2 cups chicken broth
- 1/2 to 1 teaspoon salt
- 1/4 teaspoon pepper
- 1 can (10 ounces) chunk white chicken, drained

Direction

- Prepare the rice following the instruction of the package. In the meantime, in a small skillet, sauté the parsley, almonds and onion in butter for around 4 to 5 minutes till onion is soften and almonds are toasted lightly.
- In a large bowl, combine milk, flour, broth, pepper and salt until smooth. Mix in the vegetables, rice and chicken.
- In a greased baking dish of 13- x 9-inch, pour the mixture (mixture will be thin). Bake with no cover at 425° for nearly 30 to 35 minutes until it has a golden-brown color and bubbly.

Nutrition Information

- Calories: 313 calories
- Protein: 17g protein.
- Total Fat: 13g fat (7g saturated fat)
- Sodium: 1117mg sodium
- Fiber: 2g fiber)
- Total Carbohydrate: 32g carbohydrate (5g sugars
- Cholesterol: 54mg cholesterol

---

321. Wild Rice Harvest Casserole

Serving: 10-12 servings. | Prep: 20mins | Cook: 01hours45mins | Ready in:

Ingredients

- 4 to 5 cups diced cooked chicken
- 1 cup chopped celery
- 2 tablespoons butter
- 2 cans (10-3/4 ounces each) condensed cream of mushroom soup, undiluted
- 2 cups chicken broth
- 1 jar (4-1/2 ounces) sliced mushrooms, drained
- 1 small onion, chopped
- 1 cup uncooked wild rice, rinsed and drained

- 1/4 teaspoon poultry seasoning
- 3/4 cup cashew pieces
- Chopped fresh parsley

Direction

- Brown celery and chicken with butter in a skillet. Put together broth and soup in a big bowl till smooth. Put the chicken mixture, poultry seasoning, rice, onion and mushrooms. Put into a 13x9-inch greased baking dish. Put cover and bake at 350° for an hour. Remove cover and bake for half hour. Mix; scatter cashews over. Put back to the oven till the rice is soft for 15 minutes. Jazz it up with parsley.

Nutrition Information

- Calories: 252 calories
- Cholesterol: 48mg cholesterol
- Protein: 18g protein.
- Total Fat: 12g fat (4g saturated fat)
- Sodium: 510mg sodium
- Fiber: 2g fiber)
- Total Carbohydrate: 18g carbohydrate (2g sugars

322.   Winning Creamy Chicken Casserole

Serving: 2 servings. | Prep: 20mins | Cook: 25mins | Ready in:

Ingredients

- 2/3 cup uncooked instant rice
- 1/4 cup chopped onion
- 2 teaspoons butter
- 1/2 cup 4% cottage cheese
- 1/3 cup French onion dip
- 3 tablespoons sour cream
- 1/4 teaspoon salt
- Dash white pepper

- 1/2 cup cubed cooked chicken
- 1/2 cup shredded cheddar cheese
- 2 tablespoons chopped green chilies

Direction

- Based on the instruction on the package, cook rice. At the same time, sauté onion in butter in a small-sized skillet till becoming soft; put aside. Mix pepper, salt, sour cream, onion dip and cottage cheese in a small-sized bowl. Mix in onion and rice.
- Spread 1/2 of the rice mixture into one 3-cup baking dish that coated using cooking spray. Layer with chicken, a quarter cup of cheddar cheese and green chilies. Add the leftover rice mixture on top; drizzle with the leftover cheese.
- Bake, while uncovered, at 350 degrees till becoming bubbly or for 25 to 30 minutes.

Nutrition Information

- Calories: 454 calories
- Total Carbohydrate: 38g carbohydrate (5g sugars
- Cholesterol: 69mg cholesterol
- Protein: 29g protein.
- Total Fat: 20g fat (12g saturated fat)
- Sodium: 1085mg sodium
- Fiber: 1g fiber)

323.   Zesty Chicken Casserole

Serving: 6 servings. | Prep: 15mins | Cook: 55mins | Ready in:

Ingredients

- 2 cups uncooked instant rice
- 1 package (16 ounces) frozen broccoli cuts, thawed
- 1 medium onion, chopped
- 1 celery rib, chopped
- 2 tablespoons minced fresh parsley

- 1 teaspoon salt
- 6 boneless skinless chicken breast halves (4 ounces each)
- 1 can (10-3/4 ounces) condensed cream of celery soup, undiluted
- 1-1/4 cups water
- 3/4 cup process cheese sauce
- 1/2 cup Italian salad dressing
- 1/2 cup 2% milk
- Fresh red currants, optional

Direction

- In a greased baking dish of 13x9-inch, place rice. Have the onion, broccoli, celery, salt and parsley to top. Place chicken over vegetables.
- In a large saucepan, combine water, soup, cheese sauce, milk and salad dressing. Cook and stir till mixture is smooth and cheese sauce melts. Pour over chicken.
- Bake with cover at 375° for around 45 minutes. Uncover and bake for an addition of 10 to 15 minutes till a thermometer measure 170°. Jazz up using red currants if you want.

Nutrition Information

- Calories: 508 calories
- Total Fat: 20g fat (8g saturated fat)
- Sodium: 1739mg sodium
- Fiber: 3g fiber)
- Total Carbohydrate: 42g carbohydrate (6g sugars
- Cholesterol: 98mg cholesterol
- Protein: 37g protein.

324. Zesty Chicken And Rice

Serving: 6 servings. | Prep: 5mins | Cook: 01hours20mins | Ready in:

Ingredients

- 6 chicken breast halves (bone in)

- 1/3 cup Italian salad dressing
- 1 can (14-1/2 ounces) chicken broth
- 1 package (16 ounces) frozen broccoli, carrots and water chestnuts
- 2/3 cup uncooked long grain rice
- 1-1/4 teaspoons Italian seasoning

Direction

- Put chicken into a 13-in. x 9-in. greased baking dish. Add dressing on top of the chicken. Bake at 400°, uncovered, for 20 minutes. Combine Italian seasoning, rice, vegetables and broth; add on top of chicken.
- Bake at 350°, covered, for 30 minutes. Take off the cover; bake for another 30 minutes or until rice is tender and chicken juices run clear.

Nutrition Information

- Calories: 266 calories
- Protein: 31g protein. Diabetic Exchanges: 3 lean meat
- Total Fat: 6g fat (0 saturated fat)
- Sodium: 208mg sodium
- Fiber: 0 fiber)
- Total Carbohydrate: 21g carbohydrate (0 sugars
- Cholesterol: 73mg cholesterol

325. Zippy Chicken Noodle Casserole

Serving: 12 servings. | Prep: 20mins | Cook: 30mins | Ready in:

Ingredients

- 5 cups uncooked egg noodles
- 1/4 cup butter, cubed
- 1/2 cup all-purpose flour
- 1-1/2 cups 2% milk
- 1 cup chicken broth
- 2 cups (16 ounces) sour cream

- 1 can (4 ounces) mushroom stems and pieces, drained
- 1 jar (4 ounces) diced pimientos, drained
- 3 teaspoons dried parsley flakes
- 2 teaspoons seasoned salt
- 1/2 teaspoon salt
- 1 teaspoon paprika
- 1/4 to 1/2 teaspoon pepper
- 1/8 to 1/4 teaspoon cayenne pepper
- 4 cups diced cooked chicken
- 1/4 cup dry bread crumbs
- 2 tablespoons shredded Parmesan cheese

Direction

- Follow directions on package to cook noodles. In the meantime, melt butter in a big pot; mix in flour until smooth. Slowly add broth and milk. Heat to a boil. Stirring constantly, cook until thick, 2 minutes. Take away from heat. Mix in pimientos, sour cream, seasonings, and mushrooms. Drain water from pasta. Grease a 3-qt. dish and layer with half of each: noodles, chicken, and sauce. Repeat the layers. Mix Parmesan and bread crumbs. Sprinkle on top. Do not cover; bake in a 350-degree oven until bubbling, 30-35 minutes.

Nutrition Information

- Calories: 315 calories
- Cholesterol: 97mg cholesterol
- Protein: 20g protein.
- Total Fat: 16g fat (9g saturated fat)
- Sodium: 615mg sodium
- Fiber: 1g fiber)
- Total Carbohydrate: 21g carbohydrate (3g sugars

Chapter 4: Hamburger Casserole Recipes

***

326. Acapulco Delight

Serving: 10 servings. | Prep: 25mins | Cook: 25mins | Ready in:

Ingredients

- 2 pounds ground beef
- 1 envelope (1-1/4 ounces) taco seasoning
- 3/4 cup water
- 1 bottle (15 ounces) mild green taco sauce
- 9 flour tortillas (6 inches)
- 2 cups shredded cheddar cheese
- 1 can (16 ounces) refried beans
- 2 cups sour cream
- 4 green onions, chopped
- 1 can (2-1/4 ounces) sliced ripe olives, drained
- Chopped tomatoes, optional
- Chopped avocados, optional

Direction

- Start preheating oven to 350°F. Take a large skillet on medium heat, crumble and cook beef until it is no longer pink; drain grease. Mix in water and taco seasoning. Put in taco sauce and cook until its texture is slightly thick, 5-10 minutes.
- Take 3 tortillas and cover the bottom of a 13x9-in. pan. Tear tortillas into pieces if necessary. Place half of the meat mixture on top of the tortillas; top with half of cheese. Take another 3 tortillas and layer once again; distribute refried beans. Coat with sour cream and drizzle with olives and green onions. Take left tortillas and re-layer. Coat with left meat

mixture and cheese. For 25-30 minutes, bake. Rest a couple of minutes before serving. Partner with chopped tomatoes and avocadoes if desired.

Nutrition Information

- Calories: 468 calories
- Sodium: 1064mg sodium
- Fiber: 3g fiber)
- Total Carbohydrate: 26g carbohydrate (3g sugars
- Cholesterol: 104mg cholesterol
- Protein: 28g protein.
- Total Fat: 27g fat (14g saturated fat)

327.   Asian Rice

Serving: 8 servings. | Prep: 15mins | Cook: 01hours30mins | Ready in:

Ingredients

- 1-1/2 pounds ground beef
- 1-1/2 cups water
- 1 can (10-3/4 ounces) condensed cream of mushroom soup, undiluted
- 2 celery ribs, chopped
- 3/4 cup uncooked long grain rice
- 1 can (8 ounces) sliced water chestnuts, drained
- 1 medium onion, chopped
- 1/2 cup chopped green pepper
- 3 tablespoons soy sauce
- 1/2 teaspoon salt

Direction

- In a skillet over medium heat, cook beef until not pink anymore; drain. Put in the remaining ingredients; mix well. Place to a greased baking dish (13x9 inches). Cover and bake at 350° until heated through, about 90 minutes.

Nutrition Information

- Calories: 256 calories
- Sodium: 829mg sodium
- Fiber: 2g fiber)
- Total Carbohydrate: 23g carbohydrate (3g sugars
- Cholesterol: 43mg cholesterol
- Protein: 18g protein.
- Total Fat: 10g fat (4g saturated fat)

328.   Baked Beans Ole

Serving: 6-8 servings. | Prep: 10mins | Cook: 20mins | Ready in:

Ingredients

- 1/2 pound ground beef
- 1 cup chopped onion
- 2 garlic cloves, minced
- 2 cans (16 ounces each) pork and beans
- 1 cup picante sauce

Direction

- In a frying pan, cook ground beef with garlic and onion till the onion becomes softened and the beef becomes browned; let drain. Whisk in the remaining ingredients. Let it boil; lower heat and simmer while stirring from time to time for 10 minutes.

Nutrition Information

- Calories: 111 calories
- Total Carbohydrate: 14g carbohydrate (5g sugars
- Cholesterol: 14mg cholesterol
- Protein: 8g protein.
- Total Fat: 3g fat (1g saturated fat)
- Sodium: 333mg sodium
- Fiber: 3g fiber)

329.   Baked Beef And Brown Rice

Serving: 6 servings. | Prep: 15mins | Cook: 01hours30mins | Ready in:

Ingredients

- 1 cup uncooked brown rice
- 1 large onion, sliced
- 4 medium carrots, grated
- 1-1/2 pounds lean ground beef
- 1 medium green pepper, diced
- 2 teaspoons salt
- 2 cups tomato juice
- 2 tablespoons Worcestershire sauce
- 1/2 teaspoon dried basil
- 1-1/2 cups shredded cheddar cheese
- 1/2 cup toasted wheat germ

Direction

- Layer rice, onion, carrots, beef, and green pepper in an oiled 13x9-inch baking dish. Scatter with salt. Mix together basil, Worcestershire sauce, and tomato juice; spread atop the mixture. Sprinkle top with wheat germ and cheese. Bake, covered at 350° until rice is tender, about 1 hour and 30 minutes.

Nutrition Information

- Calories: 468 calories
- Total Fat: 19g fat (10g saturated fat)
- Sodium: 1372mg sodium
- Fiber: 4g fiber)
- Total Carbohydrate: 41g carbohydrate (8g sugars
- Cholesterol: 99mg cholesterol
- Protein: 34g protein.

330.   Baked Meal In One Casserole

Serving: 4 servings. | Prep: 15mins | Cook: 50mins | Ready in:

Ingredients

- 1 pound lean ground beef (90% lean)
- 3 medium unpeeled potatoes, thinly sliced
- 1 medium onion, sliced and separated into rings
- 1 cup frozen peas
- 1-1/2 cups sliced mushrooms
- 1-1/2 teaspoons salt, optional
- 1/4 teaspoon pepper
- 1 teaspoon sesame seeds
- 3 tablespoons butter, melted

Direction

- In a skillet, cook beef over medium heat until there is not pink anymore; and then drain. Arrange potatoes in a greased baking dish of 2-quart. Place beef and onion on top. In the center, place peas; and around the peas, arrange mushrooms. Sprinkle with the sesame seeds, pepper and salt; have butter for drizzling.
- Bake while covered at 375° for approximately 50 to 60 minutes until potatoes are soften.

Nutrition Information

- Calories: 391 calories
- Protein: 29g protein. Diabetic Exchanges: 2 starch
- Total Fat: 16g fat (0 saturated fat)
- Sodium: 231mg sodium
- Fiber: 0 fiber)
- Total Carbohydrate: 33g carbohydrate (0 sugars
- Cholesterol: 41mg cholesterol

331.   Baked Nachos

*Serving: 8 servings. | Prep: 15mins | Cook: 30mins
| Ready in:*

Ingredients

- 2 pounds ground beef
- 3 cups shredded Colby-Monterey Jack cheese, divided
- 3 cups salsa
- 1 package (10 ounces) frozen corn, thawed
- 1 cup sour cream
- 1 to 2 tablespoons chili powder
- 1 teaspoon ground cumin
- 6 cups tortilla chips

Direction

- Cook beef in a skillet over medium heat until the pink color disappears from meat; drain. Stir in cumin, chili powder, sour cream, corn, salsa and 2 cups cheese; mix properly.
- In a greased 13x9 baking dish, pour half of the mixture. Place half of the chips on top; repeat layering with remaining ingredients. Bake, uncovered, for 25 minutes at 350° or until heated through. Add remaining cheese on top. Bake for an additional 5 minutes or until cheese is fully melted.

Nutrition Information

- Calories: 537 calories
- Cholesterol: 113mg cholesterol
- Protein: 32g protein.
- Total Fat: 31g fat (18g saturated fat)
- Sodium: 843mg sodium
- Fiber: 5g fiber)
- Total Carbohydrate: 25g carbohydrate (5g sugars

332.   Baked Simple Meatball Stroganoff

*Serving: 6 servings. | Prep: 40mins | Cook: 30mins
| Ready in:*

Ingredients

- 1/3 cup chopped green onions
- 1/4 cup seasoned bread crumbs
- 3 tablespoons grated Parmesan cheese
- 1 pound ground beef
- 1 loaf (1 pound) Italian bread, cut into 1-inch slices
- 1 package (8 ounces) cream cheese, softened
- 1/2 cup mayonnaise
- 1 teaspoon Italian seasoning
- 1/4 teaspoon pepper
- 2 cups shredded part-skim mozzarella cheese
- 3-1/2 cups spaghetti sauce
- 1 cup water
- 2 garlic cloves, minced

Direction

- Combine the Parmesan cheese, breadcrumbs and onions in a big bowl. Let the beef crumbled over mixture and stir thoroughly. Form into 1-inch balls, then arrange on a greased rack in a shallow baking pan. Let bake at 400° for about 15-20 minutes until not pink anymore.
- Meanwhile, in an ungreased 13x9-inch baking dish, line bread in a single layer (all of the bread may not be used). Mix in the pepper, Italian seasoning, mayonnaise and cream cheese; pour over the bread. Top with a half cup of mozzarella.
- Whisk in the garlic, water and spaghetti sauce; put in meatballs. Spread over cheese mixture, then dust with the leftover mozzarella. Bake while uncovered at 350° for about 30 minutes until heated through.

Nutrition Information

- Calories: 641 calories

- Fiber: 3g fiber)
- Total Carbohydrate: 43g carbohydrate (9g sugars
- Cholesterol: 94mg cholesterol
- Protein: 29g protein.
- Total Fat: 39g fat (15g saturated fat)
- Sodium: 1234mg sodium

333. Barbecued Beef And Beans

Serving: 8-10 servings. | Prep: 15mins | Cook: 60mins | Ready in:

Ingredients

- 1 pound ground beef
- 1 medium onion, finely diced
- 1 garlic clove, minced
- 1/2 cup barbecue sauce
- 1/2 cup ketchup
- 1/4 cup molasses
- 1/2 cup packed brown sugar
- 1 jar (32 ounces) northern beans, rinsed and drained
- 1 can (28 ounces) baked beans
- 1 can (16 ounces) red kidney beans
- 1 can (15-3/4 ounces) lima beans, rinsed and drained
- 1 can (15 ounces) garbanzo beans or chickpeas, rinsed and drained
- 1 can (14-1/2 ounces) cut green beans, drained

Direction

- In a skillet, cook garlic, onion and beef over medium heat until beef is not pink anymore. Drain; then in a large greased casserole or roaster, place the beef. Stir in the ketchup, barbecue sauce, brown sugar and molasses. Add all beans and well mix.
- Uncovered while baking at 325° for nearly 30 minutes. Bake while covered for another 30 minutes.

Nutrition Information

- Calories: 433 calories
- Cholesterol: 28mg cholesterol
- Protein: 23g protein.
- Total Fat: 7g fat (2g saturated fat)
- Sodium: 1220mg sodium
- Fiber: 15g fiber)
- Total Carbohydrate: 72g carbohydrate (27g sugars

334. Beans And Biscuits

Serving: 4-6 servings. | Prep: 10mins | Cook: 20mins | Ready in:

Ingredients

- 1 pound ground beef
- 2 green onions, chopped
- 1 garlic clove, minced
- 1 can (28 ounces) baked beans, drained
- 1/2 cup barbecue sauce
- 1/4 cup packed brown sugar
- 1/4 cup ketchup
- 1 tablespoon prepared mustard
- 1 tube (4-1/2 ounces) refrigerated buttermilk biscuits
- 1/2 cup shredded cheddar cheese

Direction

- Over medium heat in a large skillet, cook onions and ground beef until meat is no longer pink. Put in garlic; cook for 1 more minute. Drain. Add in mustard, ketchup, brown sugar, barbecue sauce and beans. Allow to simmer until heated through, about 5 minutes.
- Place into a greased baking dish of 11x7 inches. Separate biscuits and divide in half; place over beef mixture. Bake with no cover, at 400° until biscuits are golden brown, about 18 minutes. Sprinkle cheese on top; bake until cheese is melted, about 2-3 more minutes.

Nutrition Information

- Calories: 407 calories
- Total Fat: 12g fat (6g saturated fat)
- Sodium: 1157mg sodium
- Fiber: 8g fiber)
- Total Carbohydrate: 52g carbohydrate (21g sugars
- Cholesterol: 56mg cholesterol
- Protein: 25g protein.

335.   Beef & Tater Bake

Serving: 8 servings. | Prep: 10mins | Cook: 35mins | Ready in:

Ingredients

- 4 cups frozen Tater Tots
- 1 pound ground beef
- 1/4 teaspoon garlic powder
- 1/8 teaspoon pepper
- 1 can (10-3/4 ounces) condensed cream of broccoli soup, undiluted
- 1/3 cup 2% milk
- 1 package (16 ounces) frozen chopped broccoli, thawed
- 1 can (2.8 ounces) French-fried onions, divided
- 1 cup shredded Colby-Monterey Jack cheese, divided
- 1 medium tomato, chopped

Direction

- Preheat oven to 400°. In an ungreased baking dish of 13x9-inch, spread Tater Tots evenly. Uncovered while baking for around 10 minutes.
- In the meantime, in a large skillet over medium heat, cook and crumble beef for nearly 5 to 7 minutes until there is not pink anymore; and then drain. Stir in broccoli, soup, seasonings, milk, 3/4 cup onions, tomato and 1/2 cup cheese; heat through. Then pour over potatoes.

- Covered while baking for another 20 minutes. Have cheese and the remaining onions to sprinkle. Uncovered during bake for approximately 5 to 10 minutes until cheese is melted.

Nutrition Information

- Calories: 400 calories
- Sodium: 805mg sodium
- Fiber: 4g fiber)
- Total Carbohydrate: 29g carbohydrate (3g sugars
- Cholesterol: 50mg cholesterol
- Protein: 17g protein.
- Total Fat: 24g fat (9g saturated fat)

336.   Beef 'n' Biscuit Bake

Serving: 6-8 servings. | Prep: 10mins | Cook: 20mins | Ready in:

Ingredients

- 1 pound ground beef
- 1 can (16 ounces) kidney beans, rinsed and drained
- 1 can (15-1/4 ounces) whole kernel corn, drained
- 1 can (10-3/4 ounces) condensed tomato soup, undiluted
- 1/4 cup milk
- 2 tablespoons finely chopped onion
- 1/2 teaspoon chili powder
- 1/4 teaspoon salt
- 1 cup cubed process cheese (Velveeta)
- 1 tube (12 ounces) refrigerated biscuits
- 2 to 3 tablespoons butter, melted
- 1/3 cup yellow cornmeal

Direction

- Set the oven to 375° and start preheating. Cook beef in a saucepan over medium heat until not pink anymore; drain. Put in salt, chilli powder, onion, milk, soup, corn and beans; let it come to a boil. Take it away from the heat; add in cheese and stir until melted. Scoop into a greased baking dish (2-1/2-quart). Bake with no cover for 10 minutes.

- In the meantime, brush butter onto all sides of biscuits; roll in cornmeal. Put atop bubbling meat mixture. Put back to oven and bake for 10-12 minutes or until biscuits are cooked through and lightly browned.

Nutrition Information

- Calories: 439 calories
- Protein: 21g protein.
- Total Fat: 19g fat (8g saturated fat)
- Sodium: 1180mg sodium
- Fiber: 5g fiber)
- Total Carbohydrate: 44g carbohydrate (10g sugars
- Cholesterol: 46mg cholesterol

337.   Beef 'n' Noodle Casserole

Serving: 6 servings. | Prep: 15mins | Cook: 30mins | Ready in:

Ingredients

- 1 package (8 ounces) medium noodles
- 1/3 cup sliced green onions
- 1/3 cup chopped green pepper
- 2 tablespoons butter
- 1 pound ground beef
- 1 can (6 ounces) tomato paste
- 1/2 cup sour cream
- 1 cup 4% cottage cheese
- 1 can (8 ounces) tomato sauce

Direction

- Cook noodles following the package instructions; strain.

- Sauté green pepper and onions with butter in a big skillet until soft, about 3 minutes. Add beef and cook until no pink remained. Strain the excess fat.
- Mix sour cream and tomato paste together in a medium-sized bowl, mixing in cottage cheese and noodles. In a 2-quart casserole, layer 1/2 the noodle mixture; put 1/2 the beef mixture on top. Continue doing the same.
- Evenly pour over the top of the casserole with tomato sauce. Bake at 350° until thoroughly heated, about 30-35 minutes.

Nutrition Information

- Calories: 404 calories
- Sodium: 412mg sodium
- Fiber: 3g fiber)
- Total Carbohydrate: 37g carbohydrate (7g sugars
- Cholesterol: 105mg cholesterol
- Protein: 26g protein.
- Total Fat: 16g fat (7g saturated fat)

338.   Beef 'n' Rice Bake

Serving: 4-6 servings. | Prep: 15mins | Cook: 30mins | Ready in:

Ingredients

- 1 pound ground beef
- 3 celery ribs, thinly sliced
- 1 medium onion, chopped
- 2 cups cooked rice
- 1/2 cup chopped green pepper
- 1/2 cup chopped sweet red pepper
- 1 jar (4-1/2 ounces) sliced mushrooms, drained
- 1/2 cup soy sauce
- 2 tablespoons butter
- 1 tablespoon brown sugar
- 1 can (3 ounces) chow mein noodles

Direction

- In a large skillet over the medium heat, cook onion, celery and beef till meat is no longer pink; drain. Mix in brown sugar, butter, soy sauce, mushrooms, peppers and rice; heat through.
- Place into a greased baking dish of 2 quarts. Cover up and bake at 350° for 25-30 minutes. Sprinkle chow mein noodles on top. Bake with no cover until the noodles are crisp, about 5-10 more minutes.

Nutrition Information

- Calories: 342 calories
- Sodium: 1488mg sodium
- Fiber: 3g fiber)
- Total Carbohydrate: 31g carbohydrate (5g sugars
- Cholesterol: 47mg cholesterol
- Protein: 20g protein.
- Total Fat: 15g fat (6g saturated fat)

---

339.   Beef Broccoli Supper

Serving: 4-6 servings. | Prep: 25mins | Cook: 35mins | Ready in:

Ingredients

- 3/4 cup uncooked long grain rice
- 1 pound ground beef
- 1-1/2 cups fresh broccoli florets
- 1 can (10-3/4 ounces) condensed broccoli cheese soup, undiluted
- 1/2 cup milk
- 1 teaspoon salt-free seasoning blend
- 1 teaspoon salt
- 1/2 teaspoon pepper
- 1/2 cup dry bread crumbs
- 2 tablespoons butter, melted

Direction

- Follow the package instructions to prepare the rice.
- Add beef to a big frying pan, cook over medium heat until it is not pink any longer; drain. Mix in the pepper, salt, seasoning blend, milk, soup, broccoli and rice. Take the mixture to a 2-quart baking dish coated with cooking spray.
- Mix the bread crumbs with butter and dredge on top of the meat mixture. Set oven at 350°, bake while covered for half an hour. Uncover and bake until heated through, about 5 to 10 more minutes.

Nutrition Information

- Calories: 364 calories
- Fiber: 2g fiber)
- Total Carbohydrate: 31g carbohydrate (2g sugars
- Cholesterol: 67mg cholesterol
- Protein: 20g protein.
- Total Fat: 17g fat (8g saturated fat)
- Sodium: 914mg sodium

---

340.   Beef Florentine

Serving: 6 | Prep: 20mins | Cook: 25mins | Ready in:

Ingredients

- 2 cups medium egg noodles
- 1 1/2 pounds ground beef
- 2 cloves garlic, chopped
- 1 teaspoon dried oregano
- 1/2 teaspoon salt
- 1/4 teaspoon pepper
- 2 (8 ounce) cans tomato sauce
- 1/2 cup water
- 1 (10 ounce) package frozen chopped spinach, thawed and drained
- 1 (8 ounce) container cottage cheese
- 1/4 cup chopped onion
- 2 tablespoons grated Parmesan cheese

- 8 ounces shredded mozzarella cheese

Direction

- Place a lightly salted water in a big pot and make it boil. Cook in the pasta for 8-10 minutes or until al dente; strain.
- Prepare the oven by preheating to 350°F (175°C).
- Sear ground beef in a skillet over medium heat until equally brown; remove extra fat. Add pepper, salt and oregano to taste. Mix in water and tomato sauce. Separate the skillet from heat and mix in cooked noodles.
- Mix together in a medium-sized bowl the Parmesan cheese, onion, cottage cheese and spinach. In a big casserole dish, spread half of the noodle mixture. Put a layer of all of the spinach mixture then top with the remaining noodle mixture.
- Place in the preheated oven and bake for 15 minutes. Add mozzarella on top and keep on baking for 10 more minutes or until cheese is dissolved.

Nutrition Information

- Calories: 574 calories;
- Cholesterol: 137
- Protein: 37.7
- Total Fat: 39.4
- Sodium: 1110
- Total Carbohydrate: 17.2

---

341.   Beef Pastitsio

Serving: 6-8 servings. | Prep: 30mins | Cook: 30mins | Ready in:

Ingredients

- 1 pound ground beef
- 1 cup chopped onion
- 1 can (15 ounces) tomato sauce
- 1/2 teaspoon salt
- 1/2 teaspoon dried oregano
- 1/4 teaspoon pepper
- 1 garlic clove, minced
- 2 cups uncooked elbow macaroni
- 1 cup shredded cheddar cheese
- 1 large egg, lightly beaten
- CHEESE SAUCE:
- 3 tablespoons butter, melted
- 3 tablespoons all-purpose flour
- 1-1/2 cups whole milk
- 1 cup shredded cheddar cheese
- 1/2 teaspoon salt

Direction

- Put the onion and beef in a large skillet and cook on medium heat until meat is not pink any more. Strain. Mix in the garlic, pepper, oregano, salt and tomato sauce. Cover and boil gently for 15 minutes.
- In the meantime, cook macaroni based on the package instructions. Strain and rinse.
- Using a large bowl, mix the egg, cheese and macaroni; reserve. Melt the butter in a large saucepan. Mix in flour until it turns smooth; slowly add the milk. Let it boil. Stir and cook for 2 minutes or until it becomes thick. Turn off heat and add in salt and cheese.
- In a 13x9-inch baking dish, scoop half of the macaroni mixture then spread with the meat mixture. Add the remaining macaroni mixture on top. Put cheese mixture over top.
- Place in the oven without cover, and bake for 30 minutes at 350°, or until heated through. Allow to stand for 5-10 minutes prior serving.

Nutrition Information

- Calories: 363 calories
- Sodium: 674mg sodium
- Fiber: 2g fiber)
- Total Carbohydrate: 24g carbohydrate (5g sugars
- Cholesterol: 102mg cholesterol
- Protein: 22g protein.
- Total Fat: 20g fat (12g saturated fat)

- Total Fat: 16g fat (9g saturated fat)
- Sodium: 835mg sodium

342. Beef Spinach Hot Dish

Serving: 6-8 servings. | Prep: 30mins | Cook: 20mins | Ready in:

Ingredients

- 1 pound ground beef
- 1 medium onion, chopped
- 2 garlic cloves, minced
- 1 can (4 ounces) mushroom stems and pieces, drained
- 1 teaspoon salt
- 1 teaspoon dried oregano
- 1/4 teaspoon pepper
- 2 packages (10 ounces each) frozen chopped spinach, thawed and squeezed dry
- 1 can (10-3/4 ounces) condensed cream of celery soup, undiluted
- 1 cup (8 ounces) sour cream
- 2 cups shredded part-skim mozzarella cheese, divided

Direction

- Cook onion and beef in a large skillet over medium heat until the beef is no longer pink. Put in garlic; cook for 1 more minute. Drain. Mix in pepper, oregano, salt and mushrooms. Add in sour cream, soup and spinach. Stir in 1/2 the cheese.
- Place into a greased 2-quart baking dish. Bake without covering at 350° for 15 minutes. Sprinkle remaining cheese on top; bake until cheese is melted, about 5 more minutes.

Nutrition Information

- Calories: 269 calories
- Fiber: 2g fiber)
- Total Carbohydrate: 9g carbohydrate (3g sugars
- Cholesterol: 66mg cholesterol
- Protein: 20g protein.

343. Beef And Broccoli Casserole

Serving: 6 servings. | Prep: 20mins | Cook: 15mins | Ready in:

Ingredients

- 1 pound ground beef
- 1/2 cup chopped onion
- 1 tablespoon Worcestershire sauce
- 1 teaspoon garlic salt
- 1 teaspoon Italian seasoning
- 1 cup uncooked instant rice
- 1 can (10-3/4 ounces) condensed cream of mushroom soup, undiluted
- 1/2 cup water
- 2 pounds fresh broccoli, chopped or 6 cups frozen chopped broccoli, cooked and drained
- 6 ounces sliced part-skim mozzarella cheese
- Chopped fresh parsley, optional

Direction

- In a skillet, cook onion and beef in oil until meat is no longer pink; drain. Mix in water, soup, rice, Italian seasoning, garlic salt and Worcestershire sauce.
- Arrange cooked broccoli in a baking dish of 11x7 inches; add meat mixture on top. Sprinkle mozzarella cheese on top. Bake with no cover, at 400° for 15-20 minutes. Add parsley on top for extra flavor, if desired.

Nutrition Information

- Calories: 368 calories
- Total Fat: 17g fat (7g saturated fat)
- Sodium: 928mg sodium
- Fiber: 5g fiber)

- Total Carbohydrate: 28g carbohydrate (4g sugars
- Cholesterol: 54mg cholesterol
- Protein: 28g protein.

344. Beef And Corn Casserole

Serving: 8-10 servings. | Prep: 20mins | Cook: 60mins | Ready in:

Ingredients

- 1 package (10 ounces) fine egg noodles
- 1 pound ground beef
- 1 medium onion, chopped
- 1 can (15-1/4 ounces) whole kernel corn, drained
- 1 can (10-3/4 ounces) condensed tomato soup, undiluted
- 1 cup water
- 1 cup diced process cheese (Velveeta)
- 1/2 medium green pepper, chopped
- 1 medium carrot, thinly sliced
- 1 teaspoon salt
- 1/2 teaspoon pepper

Direction

- Follow package instructions to cook noodles; drain. Cook beef and onion in a big skillet on medium heat, until meat is not pink anymore; drain. Add in the rest of ingredients and noodles.
- Move to an oiled 13x9-inch baking dish. Put on cover and bake for 30 minutes at 325 degrees. Remove cover and bake for 30-35 minutes more or until bubbly.

Nutrition Information

- Calories: 295 calories
- Sodium: 698mg sodium
- Fiber: 3g fiber)

- Total Carbohydrate: 33g carbohydrate (7g sugars
- Cholesterol: 64mg cholesterol
- Protein: 17g protein.
- Total Fat: 10g fat (4g saturated fat)

345. Beef And Noodle Bake

Serving: 5 | Prep: 30mins | Cook: 30mins | Ready in:

Ingredients

- 1 pound ground beef
- 2 cups elbow macaroni
- 4 cups spaghetti sauce
- 12 ounces processed cheese food (eg. Velveeta), sliced

Direction

- Set oven to 375 degrees F or 190 degrees C and start preheating.
- In a big frying pan, brown beef on medium-high heat; set it aside. Follow directions on package to cook macaroni, drain water and set it aside.
- In a 9x13 pan, make layers of macaroni, beef, tomato sauce, and cheese, repeat layers twice.
- Bake in a 375-degree F or 190-degree C oven until the cheese on top is bubbling, 30 minutes.

Nutrition Information

- Calories: 640 calories;
- Total Carbohydrate: 66.8
- Cholesterol: 87
- Protein: 37.4
- Total Fat: 23.8
- Sodium: 1941

346. Beef And Noodle Casserole

Serving: 4 | Prep: 30mins | Cook: 30mins | Ready in:

Ingredients

- 6 ounces egg noodles
- 1 pound ground beef
- 2 (10.75 ounce) cans condensed tomato soup
- 2 tablespoons Worcestershire sauce
- 2 cloves garlic, minced
- 1/2 pound shredded Cheddar cheese
- 1/4 cup dry sherry
- 1/4 cup grated Parmesan cheese

Direction

- Set an oven to 190°C (375°F) and start preheating.
- Following the package instructions, cook the noodles.
- In a large skillet, brown the ground beef on medium-high heat. Stir in garlic, Worcestershire sauce, and tomato soup, then boil, turn down the heat to low and allow to simmer.
- Stir the cheese and noodles into the simmering sauce once the noodles are finished, until the cheese melts. Add the sherry into the sauce and stir for a minute, arrange in a 2-quart casserole dish and dust to taste with Parmesan cheese.
- In the prepared oven, bake for half an hour.

Nutrition Information

- Calories: 745 calories;
- Total Fat: 38.1
- Sodium: 1540
- Total Carbohydrate: 55.5
- Cholesterol: 169
- Protein: 44.1

347. Beef And Potato Moussaka

Serving: 8-10 servings. | Prep: 25mins | Cook: 60mins | Ready in:

Ingredients

- 1 pound ground beef
- 1 medium onion, chopped
- 1 garlic clove, minced
- 3/4 cup water
- 1 can (6 ounces) tomato paste
- 3 tablespoons minced fresh parsley
- 1 teaspoon salt
- 1/2 teaspoon dried mint, optional
- 1/4 teaspoon ground cinnamon
- 1/4 teaspoon pepper
- PARMESAN SAUCE:
- 1/4 cup butter, cubed
- 1/4 cup all-purpose flour
- 2 cups milk
- 4 eggs, lightly beaten
- 1/2 cup grated Parmesan cheese
- 1/2 teaspoon salt
- 5 medium potatoes, peeled and thinly sliced

Direction

- Over medium heat, cook onion and beef in a large skillet until the meat is no more pink. Add garlic and continue to cook for 1 minute more. Allow to drain. Stir in the water, pepper, cinnamon, (mint if desired), salt, parsley, and tomato paste. Set aside.
- To make the sauce: Over medium heat, melt butter in a saucepan. Stir in flour until smooth; add milk gradually. Boil; cook while stirring until thickened, for 2 minutes. Remove from the heat. Next, stir a small amount of the hot mixture into the eggs; bring all back to the pan, stirring constantly. Add salt and cheese.
- In a greased shallow 3-qt. baking dish, arrange 1/2 of the potato slices. Lay all of the meat mixture and 1/2 of the cheese sauce on top. Arrange over the meat mixture with the

leftover potatoes; put the remaining cheese sauce on top.

- Bake without cover at 350° for 60 minutes, or until a thermometer registers 160°. Allow to sit for 10 minutes before serving.

Nutrition Information

- Calories: 285 calories
- Sodium: 570mg sodium
- Fiber: 3g fiber)
- Total Carbohydrate: 25g carbohydrate (7g sugars
- Cholesterol: 129mg cholesterol
- Protein: 16g protein.
- Total Fat: 14g fat (7g saturated fat)

348. Beef And Wild Rice Casserole

Serving: 6-8 servings. | Prep: 15mins | Cook: 01hours20mins | Ready in:

Ingredients

- 1-1/2 pounds ground beef
- 1 medium onion, chopped
- 1 cup uncooked wild rice, rinsed
- 1 can (10-3/4 ounces) condensed cream of mushroom soup, undiluted
- 1 can (10-3/4 ounces) condensed chicken noodle soup, undiluted
- 2 soup cans water

Direction

- In a skillet, brown ground beef with onion until the onion is soften and the beef is browned; drain. Place in a casserole of 3-quart. Add all the rest ingredients and mix well. Bake while covered at 375° for around 1 hour and 20 minutes, stirring often.

Nutrition Information

- Calories: 279 calories
- Fiber: 2g fiber)
- Total Carbohydrate: 25g carbohydrate (2g sugars
- Cholesterol: 45mg cholesterol
- Protein: 20g protein.
- Total Fat: 10g fat (4g saturated fat)
- Sodium: 612mg sodium

349. Beefy Barbecue Macaroni

Serving: 4 servings. | Prep: 15mins | Cook: 0mins | Ready in:

Ingredients

- 3/4 pound ground beef
- 1/2 cup chopped onion
- 3 garlic cloves, minced
- 3-1/2 cups cooked elbow macaroni
- 3/4 cup barbecue sauce
- 1/4 teaspoon pepper
- Dash cayenne pepper
- 1/4 cup whole milk
- 1 tablespoon butter
- 1 cup shredded sharp cheddar cheese
- Additional cheddar cheese, optional

Direction

- Cook garlic, beef, and onion on medium heat in a big frying pan until meat is not pink, 5-6 minutes. As it cooks, break the meat into crumbles; drain excess grease. Add pepper, macaroni, cayenne, and barbecue sauce. In a small pot on medium heat, cook butter and milk until the butter melts. Add the cheese and stir until it melts. Dump over macaroni mixture; carefully mix to coat. If desired, sprinkle with more cheese.

Nutrition Information

- Calories: 456 calories
- Sodium: 647mg sodium
- Fiber: 2g fiber)
- Total Carbohydrate: 39g carbohydrate (9g sugars
- Cholesterol: 81mg cholesterol
- Protein: 28g protein.
- Total Fat: 21g fat (12g saturated fat)

350. Beefy Hash Brown Bake

Serving: 4 servings. | Prep: 15mins | Cook: 25mins | Ready in:

Ingredients

- 4 cups frozen shredded hash brown potatoes
- 3 tablespoons canola oil
- 1/8 teaspoon pepper
- 1 pound ground beef
- 1 cup water
- 1 envelope brown gravy mix
- 1/2 teaspoon garlic salt
- 2 cups frozen mixed vegetables
- 1 can (2.8 ounces) french-fried onions, divided
- 1 cup shredded cheddar cheese, divided

Direction

- Mix pepper, oil and potatoes together in a large bowl. Press into a greased 8-in square baking dish. Bake with no cover at 350° until potatoes are thawed and set, about 15-20 minutes.
- In the meantime, cook the beef in a large saucepan over medium heat until not pink anymore; drain. Mix in garlic salt, gravy mix and water. Let it come to a boil; cook and stir for 2 minutes. Put in vegetables; cook and stir for 5 minutes. Stir in 1/2 of the cheese and onions.
- Spread over potatoes. Bake for 5-10 minutes. Sprinkle the remaining cheese and onions on top; bake until cheese is melted, about 5 more minutes.

Nutrition Information

- Calories: 682 calories
- Sodium: 1201mg sodium
- Fiber: 5g fiber)
- Total Carbohydrate: 39g carbohydrate (5g sugars
- Cholesterol: 105mg cholesterol
- Protein: 35g protein.
- Total Fat: 43g fat (16g saturated fat)

351. Beefy Kraut And Rice

Serving: 4-6 servings. | Prep: 15mins | Cook: 55mins | Ready in:

Ingredients

- 1 pound ground beef
- 1 can (14 ounces) sauerkraut, rinsed and drained
- 1-1/2 cups water
- 1 can (10-3/4 ounces) condensed cream of mushroom soup, undiluted
- 1 cup uncooked long grain rice
- 1 envelope beefy mushroom soup mix
- 1/2 cup shredded Swiss cheese, optional

Direction

- Cook beef over medium heat in a big skillet until no longer pink; drain. Mix soup mix together with rice, soup, water, sauerkraut and beef in a bowl.
- Shift to a 2-quart greased baking dish. Cover and bake for 50 to 60 minutes at 350°, until rice is soft. If desired, dust with Swiss cheese. Bake for another 5 minutes, until cheese is melted.

Nutrition Information

- Calories: 330 calories
- Total Fat: 12g fat (5g saturated fat)

- Sodium: 1150mg sodium
- Fiber: 3g fiber)
- Total Carbohydrate: 35g carbohydrate (2g sugars
- Cholesterol: 52mg cholesterol
- Protein: 19g protein.

352. Beefy Rice Dinner

Serving: 4-6 servings. | Prep: 20mins | Cook: 10mins | Ready in:

Ingredients

- 1 package (6.8 ounces) beef-flavored rice mix
- 1/2 pound lean ground beef (90% lean)
- 1/3 cup chopped celery
- 1/3 cup chopped green pepper
- 1/8 to 1/4 teaspoon salt
- 1/8 teaspoon pepper
- 1/3 cup shredded cheddar cheese

Direction

- Cook rice following the package instructions. In the meantime, cook green pepper, celery, and beef in a big frying pan until the vegetables are soft and the meat turns brown; strain. Add pepper, salt, and rice.
- Remove into a 2-quart baking dish coated with cooking spray. Sprinkle cheese over. Bake without a cover at 350° until fully heated and the cheese melts, about 10-15 minutes.

Nutrition Information

- Calories:
- Fiber:
- Total Carbohydrate:
- Cholesterol:
- Protein:
- Total Fat:
- Sodium:

353. Biscuits And Beans

Serving: 5 servings. | Prep: 20mins | Cook: 20mins | Ready in:

Ingredients

- 1 pound ground beef
- 1 can (15-3/4 ounces) pork and beans
- 3/4 cup barbecue sauce
- 2 tablespoons brown sugar
- 1 tablespoon dried minced onion
- 1/2 teaspoon salt
- 1 tube (12 ounces) refrigerated buttermilk biscuits
- 1/2 to 1 cup shredded cheddar cheese

Direction

- Over medium heat in a large skillet, cook beef till no longer pink; drain. Put in salt, onion, brown sugar, barbecue sauce and beans; stir well. Let it come to a boil.
- Place into a greased baking dish of 2 quarts. Separate biscuits and place over the hot beef mixture. Sprinkle cheese on top.
- Bake with no cover, at 400° until biscuits are golden brown, about 18-20 minutes.

Nutrition Information

- Calories: 472 calories
- Protein: 29g protein.
- Total Fat: 14g fat (6g saturated fat)
- Sodium: 1542mg sodium
- Fiber: 5g fiber)
- Total Carbohydrate: 59g carbohydrate (15g sugars
- Cholesterol: 56mg cholesterol

354. Bow Tie Bake

Serving: 12 servings. | Prep: 25mins | Cook: 30mins | Ready in:

Ingredients

- 1 pound ground beef
- 1 large onion, chopped
- 1 can (8 ounces) mushroom stems and pieces, drained
- 1/2 cup chopped green pepper
- 1 package (16 ounces) bow tie pasta, cooked and drained
- 1 can (10-3/4 ounces) condensed tomato soup, undiluted
- 3 cups shredded part-skim mozzarella cheese, divided
- 1 can (10-3/4 ounces) condensed cream of mushroom soup, undiluted

Direction

- Over medium heat in a large skillet, cook green pepper, mushrooms, onion and beef till meat is no longer pink; drain.
- In a greased baking dish of 3 quarts, layer 1/2 the pasta, 1/2 the meat mixture, all tomato soup and 1 cup of cheese. Place the meat mixture and remaining pasta on top. Spread with mushroom soup. Add atop the remaining cheese.
- Bake with no cover, at 350° until heated through, about 30-45 minutes.

Nutrition Information

- Calories:
- Protein:
- Total Fat:
- Sodium:
- Fiber:
- Total Carbohydrate:
- Cholesterol:

355. Bubbly & Golden Mexican Beef Cobbler

Serving: 6 servings. | Prep: 20mins | Cook: 35mins | Ready in:

Ingredients

- 1 pound ground beef
- 1 envelope reduced-sodium taco seasoning
- 3/4 cup water
- 1 jar (16 ounces) salsa
- 1 can (8-3/4 ounces) whole kernel corn, drained
- 2 cups shredded sharp cheddar cheese
- 3-1/3 cups biscuit/baking mix
- 1-1/3 cups 2% milk
- 1/8 teaspoon pepper

Direction

- Put a large skillet over medium heat setting and cook beef for about 6-8 minutes or until brown in color and starting to crumble then drain excess oil. Add in water and taco seasoning into the cooked beef. Cook the mixture bringing it to a boil until the liquid has reduced. Once done, transfer the mixture into an 11x7-inch baking dish and put corn, cheese and salsa on top.
- Put biscuit mix and milk together in a separate large bowl and mix thoroughly then put a couple tablespoonfuls of the mixture over cheese until the baking dish is fully filled. Season with pepper.
- Keep the baking dish uncovered then put into an oven at 350 degrees for about 35-45 minutes or until the topping is bubbling and golden brown in color.

Nutrition Information

- Calories: 646 calories
- Protein: 30g protein.
- Total Fat: 31g fat (14g saturated fat)
- Sodium: 1877mg sodium
- Fiber: 3g fiber)

- Total Carbohydrate: 59g carbohydrate (11g sugars
- Cholesterol: 90mg cholesterol

356. Busy Day Spaghetti Dinner

Serving: 4-6 servings. | Prep: 15mins | Cook: 15mins | Ready in:

Ingredients

- 1 pound ground beef
- 1/4 cup chopped onion
- 3/4 teaspoon salt
- 1/4 teaspoon pepper
- Dash garlic powder
- 1 can (19 ounces) ready-to-serve chunky beef vegetable soup
- 4 ounces spaghetti, cooked and drained
- 1 cup shredded cheddar cheese
- Minced fresh parsley, optional

Direction

- In a skillet over medium heat, cook onion and beef until meat is not pink anymore; and then drain. Stir in garlic powder, pepper and salt. Remove to a greased baking dish of 2-quart. Pour soup over meat mixture. Place spaghetti and cheese on top.
- Uncovered while baking at 350° for around 15 to 20 minutes until heated through. If you want, sprinkle with parsley.

Nutrition Information

- Calories: 305 calories
- Protein: 21g protein.
- Total Fat: 14g fat (7g saturated fat)
- Sodium: 779mg sodium
- Fiber: 2g fiber)
- Total Carbohydrate: 23g carbohydrate (3g sugars

- Cholesterol: 57mg cholesterol

357. Buttermilk Noodle Bake

Serving: 6 servings. | Prep: 25mins | Cook: 45mins | Ready in:

Ingredients

- 1-1/2 pounds ground beef
- 1 large onion, finely chopped
- 1/4 cup butter or margarine
- 1/4 cup all-purpose flour
- 2-1/2 teaspoons salt
- Dash pepper
- 2 cups buttermilk
- 1 can (4 ounces) mushroom stems and pieces, undrained
- 1/3 cup ketchup
- 1 tablespoon Worcestershire sauce
- 8 ounces medium egg noodles, cooked and drained

Direction

- In a skillet over medium heat, cook onion and beef until meat is no longer pink; drain. Melt butter in a large saucepan. Add in pepper, salt and flour until smooth. Slowly put in buttermilk. Stir in Worcestershire sauce, ketchup and mushrooms. Let it come to a boil; cook and stir until thickened, about 2 minutes. Add in beef mixture and noodles; stir well. Transfer to a greased 2 1/2-quart baking dish. Bake without covering at 350° for about 45 minutes until heated through.

Nutrition Information

- Calories: 469 calories
- Sodium: 1485mg sodium
- Fiber: 2g fiber)
- Total Carbohydrate: 42g carbohydrate (8g sugars
- Cholesterol: 115mg cholesterol

- Protein: 30g protein.
- Total Fat: 20g fat (10g saturated fat)

358.   Cabbage Hamburger Bake

Serving: 4 servings. | Prep: 10mins | Cook: 50mins | Ready in:

Ingredients

- 1 pound ground beef
- 1 medium onion, chopped
- 1 to 1-1/2 teaspoons salt
- 1 medium head cabbage, chopped
- 1 can (10-3/4 ounces) condensed tomato soup, undiluted

Direction

- In a big frying pan over medium heat, cook onion and beef till meat is not pink anymore; let drain. Mix in salt. In a greased 2-1/2-quart baking dish, layer half of the beef mixture, cabbage and soup. Redo the layers till the dish is full.
- Bake, covered, at 350° for about 50-60 minutes or till cabbage becomes softened. Use a slotted spoon to serve.

Nutrition Information

- Calories: 343 calories
- Sodium: 1135mg sodium
- Fiber: 7g fiber)
- Total Carbohydrate: 27g carbohydrate (14g sugars
- Cholesterol: 75mg cholesterol
- Protein: 27g protein.
- Total Fat: 15g fat (6g saturated fat)

359.   Cajun Rice Dish

Serving: 6-8 servings. | Prep: 5mins | Cook: 60mins | Ready in:

Ingredients

- 5 cups beef broth
- 2 cups uncooked long grain rice
- 1 pound ground beef
- 1 medium onion, chopped
- 1 cup sliced carrots
- 1/2 cup sliced celery
- 1/2 cup frozen corn
- 1/2 cup frozen peas
- 1/2 cup chopped sweet red pepper
- 1 teaspoon salt
- 1 teaspoon Cajun seasoning

Direction

- Place the rice and broth in a roasting pan. Combine by mixing it well. Cover. Bake in a 350 -degree oven for thirty minutes.
- In the meantime, over medium heat in a large skillet, cook the onion and beef until the meat isn't pink anymore. Drain and add to the rice. Stir in the Cajun seasoning, vegetables, and salt.
- Cover and bake it for 30 minutes more or until the rice is tender.

Nutrition Information

- Calories: 303 calories
- Protein: 16g protein.
- Total Fat: 6g fat (3g saturated fat)
- Sodium: 953mg sodium
- Fiber: 2g fiber)
- Total Carbohydrate: 45g carbohydrate (4g sugars
- Cholesterol: 28mg cholesterol

360. Campfire Casserole

Serving: 10-12 servings. | Prep: 15mins | Cook: 60mins | Ready in:

Ingredients

- 1/3 cup packed brown sugar
- 1/2 cup ketchup
- 1 teaspoon ground mustard
- 1/2 cup barbecue sauce
- 1/3 cup sugar
- 1/2 teaspoon chili powder
- 1/2 teaspoon salt
- 1/4 teaspoon pepper
- 1/2 pound ground beef, cooked and drained
- 1/2 pound bacon, cooked and crumbled
- 1/2 pound fully cooked bratwurst links, cut into 1-inch slices
- 1 can (16 ounces) kidney beans, rinsed and drained
- 1 can (16 ounces) pork and beans
- 1 can (16 ounces) chili beans, undrained
- 1 can (15-1/4 ounces) lima beans, rinsed and drained

Direction

- Mix the first eight ingredients together in a large bowl. Put in bratwurst, bacon and beef. Mix in the beans. Place into a greased baking dish of 2 quarts.
- Bake with no cover, at 350° until heated through, about 60 minutes.

Nutrition Information

- Calories: 378 calories
- Sodium: 1120mg sodium
- Fiber: 7g fiber)
- Total Carbohydrate: 40g carbohydrate (17g sugars
- Cholesterol: 37mg cholesterol
- Protein: 19g protein.
- Total Fat: 17g fat (6g saturated fat)

361. Casserole Italiano

Serving: 6 servings. | Prep: 20mins | Cook: 60mins | Ready in:

Ingredients

- 1-1/2 pounds ground beef
- 1 medium onion, chopped
- 1 jar (14 ounces) spaghetti sauce
- 1/3 cup water
- 1-1/2 teaspoons salt
- 1 teaspoon sugar
- 1 teaspoon dried basil
- 1 teaspoon pepper
- 4 medium potatoes, peeled and thinly sliced
- 1/2 cup shredded mozzarella cheese

Direction

- Over medium heat in a large skillet, cook onion and beef until the beef is no longer pink; drain. Put in seasonings, water and spaghetti sauce.
- In a greased baking dish of 13 x 9 inches, layer 1/2 the potatoes and meat mixture; repeat layers. Bake with no cover at 375° for 50 minutes. Sprinkle cheese on top. Bake until the potatoes are tender, about 10 more minutes.

Nutrition Information

- Calories: 353 calories
- Protein: 26g protein.
- Total Fat: 15g fat (6g saturated fat)
- Sodium: 1034mg sodium
- Fiber: 3g fiber)
- Total Carbohydrate: 29g carbohydrate (8g sugars
- Cholesterol: 64mg cholesterol

362. Cheeseburger Biscuit Bake

Serving: 5 servings. | Prep: 15mins | Cook: 20mins | Ready in:

Ingredients

- 1 pound ground beef
- 1/4 cup chopped onion
- 1 can (8 ounces) tomato sauce
- 1/4 cup ketchup
- Dash pepper
- 2 cups shredded cheddar cheese, divided
- 1 tube (12 ounces) refrigerated buttermilk biscuits, separated into 10 biscuits

Direction

- In a large skillet, cook onion and beef over medium heat until meat is there is not pink anymore; and then drain. Mix in the pepper, ketchup and tomato sauce. Spoon half into a greased baking dish of 8-inch square; use half of the cheese for sprinkling. Repeat layers.
- Around edges of dish, place biscuits. Uncovered while baking at 400° for around 18 to 22 minutes until biscuits are golden brown and the meat mixture is bubbly.

Nutrition Information

- Calories: 492 calories
- Total Fat: 23g fat (14g saturated fat)
- Sodium: 1264mg sodium
- Fiber: 1g fiber)
- Total Carbohydrate: 40g carbohydrate (3g sugars
- Cholesterol: 92mg cholesterol
- Protein: 32g protein.

363. Cheeseburger Casserole

Serving: 4 servings. | Prep: 25mins | Cook: 0mins | Ready in:

Ingredients

- 1 pound ground beef
- 1/2 cup chopped onion
- 2 cups water
- 2/3 cup ketchup
- 2 tablespoons prepared mustard
- 1 teaspoon salt
- 1/4 teaspoon pepper
- 2 cups uncooked instant rice
- 2 slices cheddar cheese, cut into 1-inch strips

Direction

- In a frying pan over medium heat, cook the onion and beef until browned; let drain. Put in pepper, salt, mustard, ketchup and water; stir thoroughly. Let it boil. Mix in rice. Cover and take it away from the heat; allow to rest for 5 minutes. Sprinkle with cheese; cover and allow to rest for 3-5 minutes or till cheese becomes melted.

Nutrition Information

- Calories: 469 calories
- Total Carbohydrate: 53g carbohydrate (6g sugars
- Cholesterol: 70mg cholesterol
- Protein: 28g protein.
- Total Fat: 15g fat (8g saturated fat)
- Sodium: 1315mg sodium
- Fiber: 2g fiber)

364. Cheesy Potato Beef Bake

Serving: 8 servings. | Prep: 10mins | Cook: 35mins | Ready in:

Ingredients

- 1 pound ground beef
- 2 cans (4 ounces each) mushroom stems and pieces, drained, optional
- 2 packages (5-1/4 ounces each) au gratin potatoes
- 4 cups boiling water
- 1-1/3 cups 2% milk
- 2 teaspoons butter
- 1 teaspoon salt
- 1/2 teaspoon seasoned salt
- 1/2 teaspoon pepper
- 1 cup shredded cheddar cheese

Direction

- In a big frying pan, cook beef over medium heat until no pink remains; strain. Put in a 13x9-inch baking pan coated with cooking spray. Put mushrooms on top.
- Mix potatoes with pepper, seasoned salt, salt, butter, milk, water, contents of sauce mix packets in a small bowl. Add to the mushrooms and beef. Put a cover on and bake at 400° until fully heated, about 30 minutes.
- Sprinkle cheese over. Bake without a cover to melt the cheese, about another 5 minutes. Allow to sit before eating, about 10 minutes.

Nutrition Information

- Calories: 243 calories
- Sodium: 908mg sodium
- Fiber: 1g fiber)
- Total Carbohydrate: 17g carbohydrate (3g sugars
- Cholesterol: 51mg cholesterol
- Protein: 16g protein.
- Total Fat: 12g fat (7g saturated fat)

365.   Cheesy Tortilla Bake

Serving: 8 servings. | Prep: 30mins | Cook: 30mins | Ready in:

Ingredients

- TORTILLAS:
- 1 cup all-purpose flour
- 1/2 cup yellow cornmeal
- 1/2 teaspoon salt
- 1-2/3 cups whole milk
- 1 large egg, beaten
- 2 tablespoons butter, melted
- FILLING:
- 1 pound ground beef
- 1/2 cup chopped onion
- 1 garlic clove, minced
- 1 can (10-3/4 ounces) condensed tomato soup, undiluted
- 1/2 cup taco sauce
- 1 teaspoon dried oregano
- 1 can (2-1/4 ounces) sliced ripe olives, drained
- 2 cups shredded cheddar cheese

Direction

- In a bowl, mix salt, cornmeal and flour. Put in butter, egg and milk. Whip till becoming smooth. Position a lightly greased small-sized skillet on medium heat. For each tortilla, add about 3 tbsp. of batter into skillet. Lift and tilt skillet to spread batter. Bring back to the heat source. Cook till browned lightly; flip and brown the other side. Take out to a warm platter; repeat with rest of the batter. Put aside.
- To make filling, cook garlic, onion and ground beef till onion becomes soft and meat turns browned; drain. Mix in olives, oregano, taco sauce and soups.
- At the same time, cover the bottom of a 13x9-in. baking dish with six tortillas, overlapping as necessary. Cover with 1/2 of meat mixture. Add the leftover meat mixture and leftover tortillas on top. Drizzle with cheese.
- Bake at 350 degrees till thoroughly heated or for half an hour. Allow to rest for several minutes prior to serving.

Nutrition Information

- Calories: 389 calories

- Cholesterol: 99mg cholesterol
- Protein: 22g protein.
- Total Fat: 20g fat (11g saturated fat)
- Sodium: 804mg sodium
- Fiber: 2g fiber)
- Total Carbohydrate: 31g carbohydrate (7g sugars

- Calories: 521 calories
- Total Carbohydrate: 35g carbohydrate (4g sugars
- Cholesterol: 92mg cholesterol
- Protein: 35g protein.
- Total Fat: 26g fat (9g saturated fat)
- Sodium: 1444mg sodium
- Fiber: 3g fiber)

366. Chili Beef Bake

Serving: 8 servings. | Prep: 15mins | Cook: 30mins | Ready in:

Ingredients

- 2 pounds ground beef
- 1 medium onion, chopped
- 1 garlic clove, minced
- 1 teaspoon chili powder
- 1 teaspoon salt
- 1/4 teaspoon pepper
- 12 flour tortillas (6 inches)
- 2 cans (15 ounces each) pinto beans, rinsed and drained
- 6 slices process cheese (Velveeta)
- 2 cans (10-3/4 ounces each) condensed cream of chicken soup, undiluted
- 1 can (10 ounces) diced tomatoes and green chilies, undrained

Direction

- Brown beef in a skillet, drain. Add garlic and onion; cook until softened. Remove from the heat; add pepper, salt and chili powder.
- In a greased 13x9 inch baking dish, arrange 6 tortillas slightly overlapping. Add half of the meat mixture on top. Arrange beans, remaining meat mixture, cheese and remaining tortillas in layers.
- Combine tomatoes and soup; add to tortillas (the dish will be full) and bake when uncover for 30 minutes at 350° or until heated through and bubbles appear.

367. Chili Beef Corn Bread Casserole

Serving: 6 servings. | Prep: 25mins | Cook: 25mins | Ready in:

Ingredients

- 1 pound ground beef
- 1 tablespoon cornstarch
- 1 tablespoon dried minced onion
- 1 teaspoon chili powder
- 1/2 teaspoon garlic powder
- 1 can (15 ounces) tomato sauce
- 3/4 cup all-purpose flour
- 3/4 cup yellow cornmeal
- 3 tablespoons sugar
- 2 teaspoons baking powder
- 2 large eggs
- 1/2 cup 2% milk
- 3 tablespoons canola oil
- 1 can (8-1/4 ounces) cream-style corn
- 1 cup shredded cheddar cheese
- Sour cream and salsa, optional

Direction

- Preheat oven to 375 degrees. Cook beef on medium heat in a big skillet for 6 to 8 minutes or till meat is not pink anymore, crumble; drain. Mix in garlic powder, chili powder, onion and cornstarch. Mix in tomato sauce. Cook and stir till becoming thick or 2 minutes. Take out of the heat.

- Mix baking powder, sugar, cornmeal and flour in a big bowl. Stir oil, milk, and eggs in a separate bowl till blended; mix in corn. Put to flour mixture; mix just till moistened. Mix in cheese.
- Spread 1/2 of the batter into one greased 2-qt. baking dish. Add beef mixture on top. Spread the rest of the batter on top of filling.
- Bake, while uncovered, till a toothpick inserted in corn bread portion comes out clean, 25 to 30 minutes. Allow to rest for 5 minutes prior to serving. Serve along with salsa and sour cream if you want.

Nutrition Information

- Calories: 482 calories
- Total Carbohydrate: 46g carbohydrate (10g sugars
- Cholesterol: 130mg cholesterol
- Protein: 25g protein.
- Total Fat: 22g fat (9g saturated fat)
- Sodium: 773mg sodium
- Fiber: 3g fiber)

368.   Chili Casserole

Serving: 6 | Prep: 20mins | Cook: 20mins | Ready in:

Ingredients

- 1 1/2 pounds ground beef
- 1/2 cup chopped onion
- 3 stalks celery, chopped
- 1 (15 ounce) can chili
- 1 (14.5 ounce) can peeled and diced tomatoes with juice
- 1/4 cup taco sauce
- 1 (15 ounce) can corn
- 1 (8 ounce) package egg noodles
- 1/4 cup shredded Cheddar cheese

Direction

- Preheat oven to 350°F (175° C).
- Sauté onion and beef in a big frying pan over medium high heat for about 5-10 minutes or until onion is softened and meat becomes browned; drain the fat. Put in the corn, taco sauce, tomatoes, chili and celery. Let it heat thoroughly, decrease heat to low and let simmer.
- Meanwhile, prepare the noodles as directed in the package. Pour in a 9x13-inch baking dish once cooked. Spread the meat mixture over the noodles, mixing thoroughly. Put cheese atop.
- Bake at 350°F (175°C) for about 20 minutes or until cheese becomes completely bubbly and melted.

Nutrition Information

- Calories: 671 calories;
- Total Fat: 37.7
- Sodium: 843
- Total Carbohydrate: 52.3
- Cholesterol: 145
- Protein: 31.9

369.   Chili Mac Casserole

Serving: 10 servings. | Prep: 15mins | Cook: 30mins | Ready in:

Ingredients

- 1 cup uncooked elbow macaroni
- 2 pounds lean ground beef (90% lean)
- 1 medium onion, chopped
- 2 garlic cloves, minced
- 1 can (28 ounces) diced tomatoes, undrained
- 1 can (16 ounces) kidney beans, rinsed and drained
- 1 can (6 ounces) tomato paste
- 1 can (4 ounces) chopped green chilies
- 1-1/4 teaspoons salt
- 1 teaspoon chili powder
- 1/2 teaspoon ground cumin

- 1/2 teaspoon pepper
- 2 cups shredded reduced-fat Mexican cheese blend
- Thinly sliced green onions, optional

Direction

- Based on the instruction on package, cook macaroni. At the same time, cook the garlic, onion and beef on medium heat in a big nonstick skillet till meat is not pink anymore; drain. Mix in seasonings, chilies, tomato paste, beans, and tomatoes. Drain macaroni; put to beef mixture.
- Move to one 13x9-in. baking dish that coated using cooking spray. Keep it covered and baked at 375 degrees till becoming bubbly or for 25 to 30 minutes. Uncover it; drizzle with cheese. Bake till cheese becomes melted or for 5 to 8 minutes more. Add green onion slices on top if you wish.

Nutrition Information

- Calories: 313 calories
- Protein: 30g protein. Diabetic Exchanges: 3 lean meat
- Total Fat: 13g fat (6g saturated fat)
- Sodium: 758mg sodium
- Fiber: 5g fiber)
- Total Carbohydrate: 22g carbohydrate (6g sugars
- Cholesterol: 69mg cholesterol

370.   Chili Macaroni Casserole

Serving: 12 | Prep: 15mins | Cook: 55mins | Ready in:

Ingredients

- 1 (16 ounce) package elbow macaroni
- 2 pounds lean ground beef
- 1/2 cup chopped onion
- 2 (8 ounce) cans tomato sauce

- 1 (14.5 ounce) can diced tomatoes
- 1 (14 ounce) can whole kernel corn, drained
- 1 (15 ounce) can kidney beans, rinsed and drained
- 1 (1.25 ounce) package taco seasoning mix
- 1 (1.25 ounce) package chili seasoning mix
- 1 (10.75 ounce) can condensed cheddar cheese soup
- 1 (10.75 ounce) can milk
- 1 cup shredded Cheddar cheese
- 1/2 cup sour cream
- 1 1/2 teaspoons garlic powder
- 1/2 teaspoon salt
- 1/2 teaspoon black pepper
- 1 cup shredded Cheddar cheese
- 1 cup crushed tortilla chips
- 1/2 cup sour cream (optional)

Direction

- Prepare the oven by preheating to 350°F (175°C).
- Pour lightly salted water in a large pot over high heat and allow to boil over. When the water is simmering, add the macaroni, and continue to boil. Cook the pasta for about 8 minutes, without covering, whisking occasionally, until the pasta has cooked through, yet still firm to the bite. Use a colander set in the sink to strain well.
- Stir and cook ground beef with onion in a large skillet over medium heat for about 10 minutes until the meat turns brown. Crumble the meat as it cooks; strain extra grease. Add in the chili seasoning, taco seasoning, kidney beans, corn, diced tomatoes and tomato sauce; allow to boil, lower the heat to a simmer, and cook for about 20 minutes, stirring occasionally.
- In a saucepan, mix milk and Cheddar cheese soup until it becomes smooth, and allow to boil over medium-low heat. Mix in garlic powder, 1/2 cup sour cream and 1 cup shredded Cheddar cheese; add black pepper and salt to taste.
- At the bottom of a 10x15-inch baking dish, pile the cooked macaroni, and combine with the

soup mixture. Place the ground beef chili over the macaroni, and Drizzle with 1 more cup shredded Cheddar cheese and mashed tortilla chips.

- Place in the preheated oven and bake for 20-30 minutes until the casserole is bubbling and hot and the cheese topping is dissolved. Place dollops of sour cream on top to serve.

Nutrition Information

- Calories: 539 calories;
- Total Fat: 22.8
- Sodium: 1389
- Total Carbohydrate: 53.1
- Cholesterol: 81
- Protein: 30.1

---

371.   Chili Tots

Serving: 2 casseroles (6 servings each). | Prep: 15mins | Cook: 35mins | Ready in:

Ingredients

- 1 pound ground beef
- 2 cans (15 ounces each) chili without beans
- 1 can (8 ounces) tomato sauce
- 1 can (2-1/4 ounces) sliced ripe olives, drained
- 1 can (4 ounces) chopped green chilies
- 2 cups shredded cheddar cheese
- 1 package (32 ounces) frozen Tater Tots

Direction

- Cook beef on medium heat in a big skillet till not pink anymore; drain. Mix in green chilies, olives, tomato sauce and chili. Move to 2 greased 8-in. square baking dishes. Drizzle with cheese; add Tater Tots on top. Keep it covered and frozen one casserole for maximum of 3 months.
- Keep it covered and baked the leftover casserole at 350 degrees till thoroughly heated or for 35 to 40 minutes.

- To use frozen casserole: Take out of the freezer half an hour prior to baking (do not thaw). Keep it cover and baked at 350 degrees till thoroughly heated or for 1-1/4 to 1-1/2 hours.

Nutrition Information

- Calories: 297 calories
- Protein: 15g protein.
- Total Fat: 18g fat (7g saturated fat)
- Sodium: 761mg sodium
- Fiber: 3g fiber)
- Total Carbohydrate: 24g carbohydrate (1g sugars
- Cholesterol: 44mg cholesterol

---

372.   Chuck Wagon Mac

Serving: 6-8 servings. | Prep: 20mins | Cook: 15mins | Ready in:

Ingredients

- 1 package (7-1/4 ounces) macaroni and cheese dinner mix
- 1 pound ground beef
- 1/2 cup sliced celery
- 1/4 cup chopped green pepper
- 1/4 cup chopped onion
- 1 can (15-1/4 ounces) whole kernel corn, drained
- 1 can (15 ounces) tomato sauce
- 1/2 teaspoon salt
- 1/4 teaspoon pepper
- Minced fresh parsley

Direction

- Create macaroni and cheese following the package directions; put aside. Cook onion, green pepper, celery and beef in a big skillet on medium heat until meat is not pink; strain. Mix in the leftover macaroni and cheese, pepper, salt, tomato sauce and corn.

- Place in a 13x9-inch baking dish that is greased. Place in the oven and bake for 15-20 minutes or until heated through at 350 degrees Fahrenheit. Decorate with parsley.

Nutrition Information

- Calories:
- Sodium:
- Fiber:
- Total Carbohydrate:
- Cholesterol:
- Protein:
- Total Fat:

373.   Church Supper Hot Dish

Serving: 8 servings. | Prep: 40mins | Cook: 30mins | Ready in:

Ingredients

- 1 pound ground beef
- 2 cups sliced peeled potatoes
- 2 cups finely chopped celery
- 3/4 cup finely chopped carrots
- 1/4 cup finely chopped green pepper
- 1/4 cup finely chopped onion
- 2 tablespoons butter
- 1 cup water
- 2 cans (10-3/4 ounces each) condensed cream of mushroom soup, undiluted
- 1 can (5 ounces) chow mein noodles, divided
- 1 cup shredded cheddar cheese

Direction

- Preheat oven to 350°. In a big frying pan over medium heat, cook beef till not pink anymore; let drain and set it aside.
- Sauté onion, green pepper, carrots, celery and potatoes in butter in the same pan for 5 minutes. Put in water; simmer, covered, for 10 minutes or until vegetables becomes softened.

Mix in cooked ground beef and soup until blended.
- In a greased shallow 2-quart baking dish, add half of the chow mein noodles. Spread meat mixture over noodles. Bake, covered, for 20 minutes. Top with the leftover noodles and cheese. Bake while uncovered for 10 more minutes or until heated through.

Nutrition Information

- Calories: 339 calories
- Sodium: 537mg sodium
- Fiber: 3g fiber)
- Total Carbohydrate: 25g carbohydrate (2g sugars
- Cholesterol: 53mg cholesterol
- Protein: 16g protein.
- Total Fat: 20g fat (9g saturated fat)

374.   Church Supper Spaghetti

Serving: 12 servings. | Prep: 50mins | Cook: 20mins | Ready in:

Ingredients

- 1 pound ground beef
- 1 large onion, chopped
- 1 medium green pepper, chopped
- 1 can (14-1/2 ounces) diced tomatoes, undrained
- 1 cup water
- 2 tablespoons chili powder
- 1 package (10 ounces) frozen corn, thawed
- 1 package (10 ounces) frozen peas, thawed
- 1 can (4 ounces) mushroom stems and pieces, drained
- Salt and pepper to taste
- 12 ounces spaghetti, cooked and drained
- 2 cups shredded cheddar cheese, divided

Direction

- In a large skillet over medium heat, cook green pepper, onion and beef until meat is not pink anymore. Mix in chili powder, water and tomatoes. Cover while simmering for around 30 minutes. Add the peas, corn, mushrooms, pepper and salt. Stir in spaghetti.
- In a greased baking dish of 4-quart size, layer half of the mixture. Have 1 cup cheese to sprinkle; repeat layers.
- Bake with no cover at 350° for 20 minutes until heated through.

Nutrition Information

- Calories: 290 calories
- Protein: 17g protein.
- Total Fat: 10g fat (6g saturated fat)
- Sodium: 259mg sodium
- Fiber: 4g fiber)
- Total Carbohydrate: 34g carbohydrate (5g sugars
- Cholesterol: 39mg cholesterol

375.   Company Casserole

Serving: 5 | Prep: 20mins | Cook: 30mins | Ready in:

Ingredients

- 1 (8 ounce) package egg noodles
- 1 pound lean ground beef
- 1 onion, chopped
- 2 (7 ounce) cans tomato sauce with mushrooms
- 1 teaspoon salt
- 1/4 teaspoon black pepper
- 1/4 teaspoon ground cinnamon
- 1 cup cottage cheese
- 1/2 cup chopped green onions
- 1/2 cup shredded Cheddar cheese

Direction

- Preheat oven to 350°F (175°C). In a large pot, boil lightly salted water. Add pasta and cook for around 8 to 10 minutes until al dente; drain.
- In a skillet, brown onion and the ground beef over medium heat until no pink shows; drain. Mix in salt, one of the tomato sauce cans, cinnamon and pepper. In a shallow casserole baking dish of 3-quart, pour the mixture.
- Pour in noodles in an even layer. Place cottage cheese on top; have Cheddar cheese and onions to sprinkle. Pour on remaining can of tomato sauce.
- In a preheated oven, bake for approximately 30 minutes.

Nutrition Information

- Calories: 467 calories;
- Total Fat: 20.7
- Sodium: 1182
- Total Carbohydrate: 39.1
- Cholesterol: 106
- Protein: 31

376.   Corn Chip Beef Bake

Serving: 2 servings. | Prep: 20mins | Cook: 15mins | Ready in:

Ingredients

- 1/2 pound lean ground beef (90% lean)
- 1/3 cup finely chopped onion
- 1/3 cup thinly sliced celery
- 1/3 cup finely chopped green pepper
- 1/4 teaspoon minced garlic
- 1 cup cooked brown rice
- 1 medium tomato, chopped
- 1 teaspoon lemon juice
- 1/4 teaspoon salt
- 1/4 teaspoon hot pepper sauce
- 1/4 cup mayonnaise
- 1/2 to 1 cup corn chips, crushed

Direction

- Preheat oven to 350 degrees. Cook green pepper, celery, onion and beef on medium heat in a big skillet till meat is not pink anymore. Put in garlic; cook for 60 seconds more; drain. Mix in hot pepper sauce, salt, lemon juice, tomato and rice; heat through. Mix in mayonnaise.
- Scoop into two 15-oz. baking dishes that coated using cooking spray. Drizzle with crushed corn chips. Bake, while uncovered, till thoroughly heated or for 13 to 15 minutes.

Nutrition Information

- Calories: 456 calories
- Total Carbohydrate: 46g carbohydrate (7g sugars
- Cholesterol: 59mg cholesterol
- Protein: 27g protein.
- Total Fat: 18g fat (5g saturated fat)
- Sodium: 722mg sodium
- Fiber: 5g fiber)

---

377. Cornbread Beef Bake

Serving: 4-6 servings. | Prep: 20mins | Cook: 30mins | Ready in:

Ingredients

- 1 pound ground beef
- 2 cans (16 ounces each) pork and beans
- 1/4 cup ketchup
- 2 tablespoons brown sugar
- 1/8 teaspoon pepper
- 1 package (8-1/2 ounces) cornbread/muffin mix
- 1/3 cup milk
- 1 large egg

Direction

- Over medium heat, cook beef in a skillet until no longer pink; drain. Add pepper, brown sugar, ketchup, and beans; mix well. Then transfer to a greased 11x7-in. baking dish.
- Combine egg, milk, and dry cornbread mix in a bowl, mix just until combined. Scoop over the bean mixture.
- Uncover and bake at 350° for 35 minutes or until inserting a toothpick in the cornbread and it comes out clean.

Nutrition Information

- Calories: 393 calories
- Total Carbohydrate: 50g carbohydrate (19g sugars
- Cholesterol: 83mg cholesterol
- Protein: 21g protein.
- Total Fat: 13g fat (5g saturated fat)
- Sodium: 765mg sodium
- Fiber: 4g fiber)

---

378. Cornbread With Black Eyed Peas

Serving: 8-10 servings. | Prep: 15mins | Cook: 40mins | Ready in:

Ingredients

- 1 pound ground beef, browned and drained
- 1 cup cornmeal
- 1/2 cup all-purpose flour
- 3/4 cup cream-style corn
- 1 cup cooked or canned black-eyed peas, drained
- 1 medium onion, chopped
- 1/2 cup canola oil
- 1 cup buttermilk
- 2 large eggs, beaten
- 2 cups shredded cheddar cheese
- 1/2 teaspoon baking soda

Direction

- Mix in all the ingredients in a bowl then transfer to a greased 13x9-inch baking dish. Let it bake for about 40 to 45 minutes at 350°F, or until the bread becomes golden, without the cover.

Nutrition Information

- Calories: 419 calories
- Protein: 21g protein.
- Total Fat: 23g fat (9g saturated fat)
- Sodium: 325mg sodium
- Fiber: 5g fiber)
- Total Carbohydrate: 32g carbohydrate (4g sugars
- Cholesterol: 90mg cholesterol

379.   Country Oven Omelet

Serving: 4-6 servings. | Prep: 20mins | Cook: 50mins | Ready in:

Ingredients

- 1 large onion, chopped, divided
- 3 tablespoons canola oil
- 3-1/2 cups frozen shredded hash brown potatoes
- 1-1/2 teaspoons salt, divided
- 1/2 teaspoon pepper, divided
- 1 pound ground beef
- 1/4 cup chopped green pepper
- 1/4 cup chopped sweet red pepper
- 1 tablespoon dried parsley flakes
- 1 cup shredded Swiss cheese or shredded part-skim mozzarella cheese
- 4 large eggs
- 1-1/4 cups whole milk
- 1/4 teaspoon paprika

Direction

- Sauté 1/2 cup onion in oil in a skillet. Add 1/4 teaspoon pepper, 3/4 teaspoon salt and harsh

browns. Cook for 5 minutes over medium heat until harsh browns are defrosted. Place mixture into an ungreased 10 inch pie plate and press until it forms a shell.
- Bake at 400° for 20 minutes. In the meantime, cook remaining onion, peppers and beef in a skillet over medium heat until meat loses its pink color; drain. Stir in parsley. Place mixture into the potato shell. Add cheese on top.
- Beat paprika, milk, eggs and the leftover salt and pepper in a bowl then pour over the meat mixture. Bake at 400° for 30 minutes until a knife is still clean after being inserted into the center. Allow to rest for 5 minutes before cutting.

Nutrition Information

- Calories: 376 calories
- Protein: 26g protein.
- Total Fat: 24g fat (9g saturated fat)
- Sodium: 761mg sodium
- Fiber: 1g fiber)
- Total Carbohydrate: 14g carbohydrate (6g sugars
- Cholesterol: 202mg cholesterol

380.   Cowboy Casserole

Serving: 5 | Prep: 5mins | Cook: 20mins | Ready in:

Ingredients

- 1/2 pound bacon
- 1 pound ground beef
- 1 small onion, chopped
- 2 (15 ounce) cans baked beans with pork
- 1/3 cup barbeque sauce
- 1 (7.5 ounce) package refrigerated biscuit dough

Direction

- Cook bacon in Dutch oven/big skillet on medium heat till browned evenly; drain. Cut to bite-sized pieces; put aside. Add onion and hamburger to skillet; cook till onion is tender and not pink. Drain.
- Mix barbeque sauce, baked beans and bacon into ground beef; boil. Lower heat to medium low; in 1 layer, put biscuits over mixture. Cover; simmer till biscuits are done for 10 minutes. Put 2 biscuits on every plate; put beans over.

Nutrition Information

- Calories: 601 calories;
- Sodium: 1580
- Total Carbohydrate: 62
- Cholesterol: 84
- Protein: 32.8
- Total Fat: 25.2

381. Creamy Beef Casserole

Serving: 8 servings. | Prep: 20mins | Cook: 30mins | Ready in:

Ingredients

- 2 pounds ground beef
- 1 large onion, chopped
- 6 ounces medium egg noodles, cooked and drained
- 1 can (15-1/4 ounces) whole kernel corn, drained
- 1 can (10-3/4 ounces) condensed cream of chicken soup, undiluted
- 1 can (10-3/4 ounces) condensed cream of mushroom soup, undiluted
- 1 cup (8 ounces) sour cream
- 1 can (2 ounces) diced pimientos, drained
- 3/4 teaspoon salt
- 1/4 teaspoon pepper
- 1 cup soft bread crumbs
- 1/4 cup butter, melted

Direction

- In a skillet over the medium heat, cook onion and beef till meat is no longer pink; drain. Put in pepper, salt, pimientos, sour cream, soups, corn and noodles; stir well. Place into a greased baking dish of 3 quarts. Toss butter and bread crumbs together; sprinkle on top of the casserole. Bake with no cover, at 350° until heated through, about half an hour.

Nutrition Information

- Calories: 492 calories
- Sodium: 1107mg sodium
- Fiber: 3g fiber)
- Total Carbohydrate: 32g carbohydrate (6g sugars
- Cholesterol: 115mg cholesterol
- Protein: 27g protein.
- Total Fat: 26g fat (13g saturated fat)

382. Creole Beef Casserole

Serving: 8 servings. | Prep: 25mins | Cook: 40mins | Ready in:

Ingredients

- 2 cans (10-3/4 ounces each) condensed cream of chicken soup, undiluted
- 2 cups (16 ounces) sour cream
- 1 small onion, chopped
- 1/4 teaspoon pepper
- 1 package (30 ounces) frozen shredded hash brown potatoes, thawed
- 2 cups shredded cheddar cheese
- 1-1/2 pounds ground beef
- 1 cup ketchup
- 1/4 cup packed brown sugar
- 3 teaspoons Creole seasoning
- 1 teaspoon garlic salt
- 1 teaspoon dried oregano
- 1/4 teaspoon cayenne pepper

- 3/4 cup crushed cornflakes
- 1/4 cup butter, melted

Direction

- Set oven to 350 degrees and preheat. Mix together in a big bowl onion, sour cream, pepper and soup. Add cheese and potatoes and blend, pour it to a 3-qt baking dish that is greased.
- Cook beef in a large pan on medium heat until not pink; let it drain. Add brown sugar, ketchup and seasonings. Mix well and spread it over the potatoes. Mix together butter and cornflakes then sprinkle on top. Bake for 40-45 minutes or until bubbling without cover.

Nutrition Information

- Calories: 654 calories
- Cholesterol: 133mg cholesterol
- Protein: 28g protein.
- Total Fat: 36g fat (21g saturated fat)
- Sodium: 1763mg sodium
- Fiber: 2g fiber)
- Total Carbohydrate: 51g carbohydrate (19g sugars

383.   Crescent Beef Casserole

Serving: 6 servings. | Prep: 5mins | Cook: 25mins | Ready in:

Ingredients

- 1 pound lean ground beef (90% lean)
- 1 cup diced zucchini
- 1/4 cup chopped onion
- 1/4 cup chopped green pepper
- 2 teaspoons olive oil
- 1 cup tomato puree
- 1 teaspoon dried oregano
- 1/4 teaspoon salt
- 1/8 teaspoon pepper

- 1-1/2 cups mashed potatoes
- 1 cup (4 ounces) crumbled feta cheese
- 1 tube (8 ounces) refrigerated crescent rolls

Direction

- In a large skillet over medium heat, cook beef until not pink anymore; drain and put aside. In the same skillet, sauté green pepper, onion and zucchini in oil until crisp-tender. Mix in pepper, salt, oregano, tomato puree and beef; heat through.
- In an 11x7-in. baking dish greased with cooking spray, spread mashed potatoes. Add beef mixture on top; sprinkle with feta cheese.
- Unroll the crescent dough. Cut into four rectangles; place three rectangles over casserole. Bake at 375° until the top is browned, about 12-15 minutes. Roll the remaining dough into two crescent rolls; bake for later use.

Nutrition Information

- Calories: 442 calories
- Protein: 26g protein.
- Total Fat: 22g fat (9g saturated fat)
- Sodium: 938mg sodium
- Fiber: 2g fiber)
- Total Carbohydrate: 30g carbohydrate (4g sugars
- Cholesterol: 67mg cholesterol

384.   Crescent Topped Casserole

Serving: 6-8 servings. | Prep: 15mins | Cook: 25mins | Ready in:

Ingredients

- 2 pounds ground beef
- 1/4 cup chopped onion
- 2 cans (8 ounces each) tomato sauce

- 1 envelope spaghetti sauce mix
- 3/4 cup sour cream
- 2 cups shredded part-skim mozzarella cheese
- 1 tube (8 ounces) refrigerated crescent rolls
- 2 tablespoons butter, melted
- 1/3 cup grated Parmesan cheese

Direction

- In a large skillet over the medium heat, cook onion and beef till meat is no longer pink; drain. Mix in spaghetti sauce mix and tomato sauce. Lower the heat; let it simmer with no cover, for 5 minutes. Take away from heat; mix in sour cream. Place into a greased baking dish of 13x9 inches. Sprinkle mozzarella cheese on top.
- Unroll crescent dough into a rectangle; seal seams and perforations. Add on top of the mozzarella cheese. Brush with butter and sprinkle Parmesan cheese on top.
- Bake with no cover, at 375° until golden brown, about 25-30 minutes.

Nutrition Information

- Calories:
- Fiber:
- Total Carbohydrate:
- Cholesterol:
- Protein:
- Total Fat:
- Sodium:

385. Crunchy Rice Casserole

Serving: 6-8 servings. | Prep: 15mins | Cook: 35mins | Ready in:

Ingredients

- 1 pound ground beef
- 1 large onion, chopped
- 1/2 cup chopped green pepper

- 2 tablespoons ketchup
- 1/2 teaspoon ground mustard
- 1/4 teaspoon salt
- 1-1/2 cups cooked long grain rice
- 1-1/2 cups shredded cheddar cheese
- 1 can (10-3/4 ounces) condensed cream of mushroom soup, undiluted
- 1 cup whole milk
- 1 teaspoon Worcestershire sauce
- 2 cups cornflakes, coarsely crushed
- 3 tablespoons butter, melted

Direction

- Cook green pepper, onion and beef in a frying pan over medium heat till meat is not pink anymore; drain. Put in the salt, mustard and ketchup; stir thoroughly. Pour to a greased 2-quart baking dish. Put rice on top.
- Mix the Worcestershire sauce, milk, soup and cheese together in a bowl. Pour over rice. Mix in butter and cornflakes; dust atop. Bake while uncovered at 375° for about 35 minutes or till heated through.

Nutrition Information

- Calories: 329 calories
- Protein: 18g protein.
- Total Fat: 18g fat (11g saturated fat)
- Sodium: 667mg sodium
- Fiber: 1g fiber)
- Total Carbohydrate: 23g carbohydrate (4g sugars
- Cholesterol: 67mg cholesterol

386. Dinner In A Bag

Serving: 4 servings. | Prep: 5mins | Cook: 25mins | Ready in:

Ingredients

- 1 pound ground beef

- 2 cans (14-1/2 ounces each) stewed tomatoes
- 1/4 cup dried minced onion
- 1 teaspoon salt
- 1 teaspoon chili powder
- 1/4 to 1/2 teaspoon pepper
- 1/4 teaspoon sugar
- 1 cup uncooked elbow macaroni

Direction

- Cook beef in a large skillet over medium heat until not pink; strain. Put in the sugar, seasonings and tomatoes; make it boil. Lower heat and simmer for 5 minutes.
- Mix in macaroni; cover and gently boil for 15 minutes. Take off cover; gently boil until macaroni is softened and sauce turns thick.

Nutrition Information

- Calories: 289 calories
- Sodium: 858mg sodium
- Fiber: 2g fiber)
- Total Carbohydrate: 25g carbohydrate (8g sugars
- Cholesterol: 56mg cholesterol
- Protein: 24g protein.
- Total Fat: 11g fat (5g saturated fat)

387. Double Crust Pizza Casserole

Serving: 12 servings. | Prep: 25mins | Cook: 20mins | Ready in:

Ingredients

- 2 pounds lean ground beef (90% lean)
- 2 cans (15 ounces each) pizza sauce, divided
- 2 teaspoons dried oregano
- 3 cups biscuit/baking mix
- 1-1/4 cups 2% milk
- 1 large egg, lightly beaten
- 2 cups shredded part-skim mozzarella cheese

- 1 cup sliced fresh mushrooms
- 1 medium green pepper, chopped
- 1 medium onion, chopped
- 1/4 cup grated Parmesan cheese
- 1 plum tomato, chopped

Direction

- Set oven to 400° to preheat. Sauté beef for 8 to 10 minutes over medium heat in a large skillet, or until no longer pink, crumbling into pieces while cooking; drain. Mix in oregano and 1 can pizza sauce. Bring to a boil. Lower heat; simmer without covering, stirring sometimes, until slightly thickened, about 5 to 6 minutes. Turn off the heat.
- Combine egg, milk, and biscuit mix in a large bowl, mix until just moistened. Distribute 1/2 of the batter over the bottom of an oiled 13x9-inch baking pan. Spread the remaining pizza sauce over the batter. Sprinkle with mozzarella cheese, beef mixture, onion, pepper, and mushrooms. Cover with the remaining batter by a spoon; sprinkle top with Parmesan cheese.
- Bake without covering until top turns golden brown, about 20 to 25 minutes. Add tomato on top. Allow to cool for 5 minutes before serving.

Nutrition Information

- Calories: 369 calories
- Protein: 26g protein.
- Total Fat: 16g fat (7g saturated fat)
- Sodium: 710mg sodium
- Fiber: 3g fiber)
- Total Carbohydrate: 30g carbohydrate (4g sugars
- Cholesterol: 78mg cholesterol

388. Dumpling Company Casserole

Serving: 4-6 servings. | Prep: 30mins | Cook: 20mins | Ready in:

Ingredients

- 2 pounds lean ground beef
- 1/2 cup sour cream
- 3 tablespoons onion soup mix
- 1 large egg, beaten
- 1-1/2 cups soft bread crumbs
- 1/4 cup butter
- 1 can (8 ounces) mushroom stems and pieces, drained
- 1 can (10-3/4 ounces) condensed cream of chicken soup, undiluted
- 1-2/3 cups water
- SAUCE: (optional)
- 1 can (10-3/4 ounces) condensed cream of chicken soup, undiluted
- 1/4 teaspoon poultry seasoning
- 1 teaspoon dried minced onion
- 1/2 cup sour cream
- BUTTER CRUMB DUMPLINGS:
- 2 cups all-purpose flour
- 4 teaspoons baking powder
- 1 tablespoon poppy seed
- 1 teaspoon celery salt
- 1 teaspoon poultry seasoning
- 2 teaspoons dried minced onion
- 1/4 cup vegetable oil
- 3/4 cup plus 2 tablespoons whole milk
- 1/4 cup butter, melted
- 2 cups soft bread crumbs

Direction

- Mix the first five ingredients together in a bowl. Form into 16 balls. Melt butter in a skillet, then brown the meatballs over medium-low heat. Mix in water, soup and mushrooms. Let it simmer for 20 minutes, pouring more water if necessary.
- Turn into a 3-quart baking dish. If extra sauce is desired, mix minced onion, poultry

seasoning and the cream of chicken soup together in a small saucepan. Cook until heated through. Take it away from the heat and mix in sour cream; add to meatball mixture.
- To make dumplings: In a bowl, mix onion, poultry seasoning, salt, celery, poppy seed, baking powder and flour together. Stir in milk and oil. Mix breadcrumbs and butter. Spoon heaping tablespoonful of dough into the buttered crumbs; roll to evenly coat. Cover the meatball mixture with dumplings.
- Bake with no cover at 400° until dumplings are golden, about 20-25 minutes.

Nutrition Information

- Calories: 900 calories
- Sodium: 2141mg sodium
- Fiber: 4g fiber)
- Total Carbohydrate: 59g carbohydrate (7g sugars
- Cholesterol: 209mg cholesterol
- Protein: 43g protein.
- Total Fat: 53g fat (23g saturated fat)

389. Easy Beef And Rice

Serving: | Prep: 5mins | Cook: 20mins | Ready in:

Ingredients

- 1 pound ground beef
- 1 can (10-3/4 ounces) condensed cream of celery soup, undiluted
- 1 can (10-3/4 ounces) condensed cream of chicken soup, undiluted
- 1 cup water
- 1 cup uncooked instant rice
- 3 tablespoons chopped onion
- 1/2 teaspoon salt
- 1/4 teaspoon pepper

Direction

- In an ungreased 2- quart microwavable dish, crumble the beef. Cover and microwave on high until not pink anymore, about 3 minutes; drain. Mix in the remaining ingredients. Cover and heat on high until rice is tender, about 9-10 minutes. Allow to sit for 5 minutes and serve.

Nutrition Information

- Calories: 438 calories
- Total Fat: 21g fat (8g saturated fat)
- Sodium: 1481mg sodium
- Fiber: 2g fiber)
- Total Carbohydrate: 32g carbohydrate (2g sugars
- Cholesterol: 84mg cholesterol
- Protein: 27g protein.

390.   Farmhouse Dinner

Serving: 4-6 servings. | Prep: 20mins | Cook: 30mins | Ready in:

Ingredients

- 1 pound ground beef
- 2 large eggs
- 1/4 cup milk
- 1 can (14-3/4 ounces) cream-style corn
- 1 cup soft bread crumbs
- 1/4 cup finely chopped onion
- 2 teaspoons prepared mustard
- 1 teaspoon salt
- 1/2 cup dry bread crumbs
- 2 tablespoons butter, melted
- Minced fresh parsley, optional

Direction

- Cook beef in a big frying pan over medium heat until no pink remains; strain and put aside.

- Mix milk and eggs together in a big bowl. Add beef, salt, mustard, onion, soft bread crumbs, and corn.
- Remove into a 9-inch square baking dish coated with cooking spray. Mix together butter and dry bread crumbs, sprinkle the mixture over the meat mixture. Bake without a cover at 350° until turning golden brown, about 30 minutes. Sprinkle parsley over if wanted.

Nutrition Information

- Calories: 292 calories
- Total Carbohydrate: 24g carbohydrate (4g sugars
- Cholesterol: 120mg cholesterol
- Protein: 19g protein.
- Total Fat: 14g fat (6g saturated fat)
- Sodium: 843mg sodium
- Fiber: 1g fiber)

391.   Five Vegetable Delight

Serving: 8 servings. | Prep: 20mins | Cook: 01hours30mins | Ready in:

Ingredients

- 2 cups each diced carrots, celery and onion
- 2 cups diced peeled potatoes and rutabagas
- 1 pound lean ground beef
- 1 can (10-3/4 ounces) condensed tomato soup, undiluted
- 1-1/3 cups water
- 1 teaspoon salt
- 1/4 teaspoon pepper

Direction

- Combine the vegetables together in a bowl; mix well. Crumble beef on top of the mixture and toss gently. Place into a greased baking dish (13x9 inches).

- Mix pepper, salt, water and soup together in a bowl. Spread over vegetable mixture. Bake with no cover at 350° until vegetables are tender, about 90 minutes.

Nutrition Information

- Calories: 154 calories
- Total Carbohydrate: 16g carbohydrate (5g sugars
- Cholesterol: 35mg cholesterol
- Protein: 12g protein.
- Total Fat: 5g fat (2g saturated fat)
- Sodium: 360mg sodium
- Fiber: 3g fiber)

392.   Fourth Of July Bean Casserole

Serving: 12 servings. | Prep: 20mins | Cook: 60mins | Ready in:

Ingredients

- 1/2 pound bacon strips, diced
- 1/2 pound ground beef
- 1 cup chopped onion
- 1 can (28 ounces) pork and beans
- 1 can (16 ounces) kidney beans, rinsed and drained
- 1 can (15-1/4 ounces) lima beans, rinsed and drained
- 1/2 cup barbecue sauce
- 1/2 cup ketchup
- 1/2 cup sugar
- 1/2 cup packed brown sugar
- 2 tablespoons prepared mustard
- 2 tablespoons molasses
- 1 teaspoon salt
- 1/2 teaspoon chili powder

Direction

- Cook onion, beef, and bacon over medium heat in a large skillet until meat is no longer pink; drain off grease.
- Pour mixture into an oiled 2 1/2-quart baking dish. Mix in all of the beans; stir well. Combine the remaining ingredients in a small bowl; mix into bean and beef mixture.
- Bake, covered for 45 minutes at 350°; remove cover, and bake for 15 more minutes.

Nutrition Information

- Calories: 278 calories
- Protein: 12g protein.
- Total Fat: 6g fat (2g saturated fat)
- Sodium: 933mg sodium
- Fiber: 7g fiber)
- Total Carbohydrate: 47g carbohydrate (26g sugars
- Cholesterol: 15mg cholesterol

393.   Fries 'N' Beef Bake

Serving: 6-8 servings. | Prep: 10mins | Cook: 45mins | Ready in:

Ingredients

- 1 pound ground beef
- 1 medium onion, chopped
- 1 pound frozen crinkle-cut French fries, thawed
- 2 cups frozen peas, thawed
- 1 can (10-3/4 ounces) condensed cream of mushroom or cream of chicken soup, undiluted
- 3/4 cup water
- 2 tablespoons ketchup
- 1 teaspoon dried parsley flakes
- 1 teaspoon Worcestershire sauce
- 1/2 teaspoon dried marjoram
- 1/4 teaspoon ground mustard
- Salt and pepper to taste

Direction

- In a skillet over the medium heat, cook onion and beef till the beef is no longer pink; drain. In a greased baking dish of 13 x 9 inches, layer 1/2 the French fries, peas and meat mixture. Repeat layers.
- Mix pepper, salt, mustard, marjoram, Worcestershire sauce, parsley, ketchup, water and soup in a bowl. Add the mixture on top. Bake with no cover, at 350° until heated through, about 45-50 minutes.

Nutrition Information

- Calories: 286 calories
- Sodium: 400mg sodium
- Fiber: 4g fiber)
- Total Carbohydrate: 26g carbohydrate (4g sugars
- Cholesterol: 39mg cholesterol
- Protein: 15g protein.
- Total Fat: 14g fat (4g saturated fat)

394. Green Bean Beef Bake

Serving: 4-6 servings. | Prep: 25mins | Cook: 30mins | Ready in:

Ingredients

- 1 pound ground beef
- 1 medium onion, chopped
- 3/4 teaspoon salt
- Dash pepper
- 1 can (14-1/2 ounces) cut or French-style green beans, drained
- 1 can (10-3/4 ounces) condensed tomato soup, undiluted
- 1 can (4 ounces) mushroom stems and pieces, drained
- 2 cups mashed potatoes (without added milk and butter)
- 1 egg

- 1/4 cup milk
- 1/4 cup shredded cheddar cheese

Direction

- Over medium heat, cook pepper, salt, onion and beef in a skillet until the meat is no longer pink; drain. Add mushrooms, soup, and beans; mix well. Then transfer to a greased 8-in. square baking dish.
- Combine milk, egg, and mashed potatoes in a bowl; beat until fluffy and light. Spread over the beef mixture. Dust with cheese. Uncover and bake for 30-35 minutes, at 350°, or until heated through.

Nutrition Information

- Calories: 291 calories
- Sodium: 980mg sodium
- Fiber: 5g fiber)
- Total Carbohydrate: 23g carbohydrate (7g sugars
- Cholesterol: 92mg cholesterol
- Protein: 21g protein.
- Total Fat: 12g fat (5g saturated fat)

395. Green Chili Flautas

Serving: 10 flautas. | Prep: 25mins | Cook: 5mins | Ready in:

Ingredients

- 1-1/2 pounds ground beef
- 1 cup shredded cheddar cheese
- 1 can (4 ounces) chopped green chilies, drained
- 1/2 teaspoon ground cumin
- 10 flour tortillas (6 inches)
- 1/3 cup butter, melted, divided
- Shredded lettuce, guacamole, salsa, sour cream

Direction

- Cook beef on medium heat in a big skillet till meat is not pink anymore; drain. Put in the cumin, chilies and cheese; put aside.
- Warm the tortillas; use some butter to brush both sides. Scoop roughly one third cup beef mixture down the middle of each tortilla. Roll up tightly; place seam-side facing downward in one greased 13x9-in. baking pan.
- Bake, while uncovered, at 500 degrees for 5 to 7 minutes or till turns golden brown, brushing one time with the rest of butter. Serve along with toppings that you like.

Nutrition Information

- Calories: 296 calories
- Fiber: 0 fiber)
- Total Carbohydrate: 14g carbohydrate (0 sugars
- Cholesterol: 63mg cholesterol
- Protein: 18g protein.
- Total Fat: 19g fat (9g saturated fat)
- Sodium: 450mg sodium

396.   Green Pepper Casserole

Serving: 16 servings. | Prep: 10mins | Cook: 01hours25mins | Ready in:

Ingredients

- 3 pounds ground beef
- 5 small onions, chopped
- 3 cans (10-3/4 ounces each) condensed tomato soup, undiluted
- 1 tablespoon paprika
- 3 medium green peppers, chopped
- 1 can (16 ounces) peas, drained
- 1 can (8 ounces) mushroom stems and pieces, drained
- 1 jar (4 ounces) pimientos, drained
- Salt and pepper to taste
- 1 package (16 ounces) medium pasta shells
- Grated Parmesan cheese

Direction

- Cook onions and beef over in a Dutch oven medium heat till meat is not pink anymore; drain. Put in paprika and soup. Simmer, covered, for 1 hour.
- Mix in the pepper, salt, pimientos, mushrooms, peas and green peppers. Simmer, covered, for 15 minutes or till peppers become softened.
- Meanwhile, cook macaroni as directed in the package; let drain. Put in a big serving bowl; pour meat mixture over. Top with Parmesan cheese.

Nutrition Information

- Calories: 281 calories
- Total Fat: 9g fat (4g saturated fat)
- Sodium: 300mg sodium
- Fiber: 3g fiber)
- Total Carbohydrate: 31g carbohydrate (5g sugars
- Cholesterol: 42mg cholesterol
- Protein: 21g protein.

397.   Ground Beef 'n' Biscuits

Serving: 6 servings. | Prep: 20mins | Cook: 20mins | Ready in:

Ingredients

- 1-1/2 pounds ground beef
- 1/2 cup chopped celery
- 1/2 cup chopped onion
- 2 tablespoons all-purpose flour
- 1 teaspoon salt
- 1/4 teaspoon dried oregano
- 1/8 teaspoon pepper
- 2 cans (8 ounces each) tomato sauce
- 1 package (10 ounces) frozen peas
- 1 tube (12 ounces) refrigerated buttermilk biscuits

- 1 cup shredded cheddar cheese

Direction

- In a big skillet on medium heat, cook the onion, celery and beef until the meat is not pink. Drain then stir the pepper, oregano, salt and flour in until combined. Place in the peas and tomato sauce then let it simmer for 5 minutes.
- Transfer the beef mixture into a 13x9-inch greased baking dish. Arrange the separated biscuits on beef mixture, top off with cheese. Bake without a cover at 350°F until the cheese melts and the biscuits become golden, about 20 minutes.

Nutrition Information

- Calories:
- Total Fat:
- Sodium:
- Fiber:
- Total Carbohydrate:
- Cholesterol:
- Protein:

398. Ground Beef Baked Beans

Serving: 2 casseroles (10-12 servings each). | Prep: 15mins | Cook: 45mins | Ready in:

Ingredients

- 3 pounds ground beef
- 4 cans (15-3/4 ounces each) pork and beans
- 2 cups ketchup
- 1 cup water
- 2 envelopes onion soup mix
- 1/4 cup packed brown sugar
- 1/4 cup ground mustard
- 1/4 cup molasses
- 1 tablespoon white vinegar

- 1 teaspoon garlic powder
- 1/2 teaspoon ground cloves

Direction

- Cook the beef over medium heat in a Dutch oven until it is not pink anymore; then drain. Add the remaining ingredients and stir; heat through. Place into two 2-quart baking dishes coated with cooking spray. Put on a cover and freeze a dish for maximum of 3 months.
- Put on a cover and bake the second dish for half an hour at 400 degrees. Remove the cover; then bake until bubbling, 10-15 more minutes.
- In case of using frozen casserole: Put in into refrigerator to thaw. Bake, covered, at 400 degrees for 40 minutes. Remove the cover and bake until bubbly, about 15 – 20 more minutes.

Nutrition Information

- Calories: 157 calories
- Total Fat: 6g fat (2g saturated fat)
- Sodium: 544mg sodium
- Fiber: 1g fiber)
- Total Carbohydrate: 15g carbohydrate (8g sugars
- Cholesterol: 28mg cholesterol
- Protein: 12g protein.

399. Ground Beef Noodle Casserole

Serving: 6 servings. | Prep: 25mins | Cook: 30mins | Ready in:

Ingredients

- 1 envelope brown gravy mix
- 1 cup cold water
- 1 pound ground beef
- 1 small onion, diced
- 3 garlic cloves, minced
- 1 jar (14 ounces) spaghetti sauce

- 1/2 cup half-and-half cream
- 1-1/2 teaspoons Italian seasoning
- 1/2 teaspoon dried rosemary, crushed
- Salt and pepper to taste
- 8 ounces wide egg noodles, cooked and drained
- 2/3 cup grated Parmesan cheese, divided

Direction

- Mix water and gravy mix in a small bowl until smooth; put aside. Over medium heat in a large skillet, cook onion and beef until meat is no longer pink. Put in garlic; cook for 1 more minute. Drain.
- Put in gravy, seasonings, cream and spaghetti sauce; let it come to a boil. Lower the heat; cover up and let it simmer for 15 minutes. Mix in 1/3 cup of cheese and noodles.
- Place into a greased baking dish of 3 quarts; sprinkle the remaining cheese on top. Cover up and bake at 350° until heated through, about half an hour.

Nutrition Information

- Calories: 409 calories
- Fiber: 2g fiber)
- Total Carbohydrate: 39g carbohydrate (8g sugars
- Cholesterol: 92mg cholesterol
- Protein: 26g protein.
- Total Fat: 16g fat (7g saturated fat)
- Sodium: 924mg sodium

---

400.   Ground Beef Summer Squash Casserole

Serving: 4-6 servings. | Prep: 25mins | Cook: 35mins | Ready in:

Ingredients

- 1 pound ground beef
- 4 to 6 medium yellow summer squash, chopped (about 1-1/2 pounds)
- 1 medium onion, chopped
- 3/4 cup dry bread crumbs
- 3/4 teaspoon salt
- 1/4 teaspoon pepper
- 1/4 teaspoon dried thyme
- SAUCE:
- 1/4 cup butter, divided
- 1/4 cup all-purpose flour
- 1/2 teaspoon salt
- 2 cups whole milk
- 1-1/4 cups shredded cheddar cheese
- 3/4 cup dry bread crumbs

Direction

- Cook onion, squash and beef in a skillet over medium heat until the meat is no longer pink; drain. Put in thyme, pepper, salt and breadcrumbs; stir well and put aside. Melt 1/4 cup of butter in a saucepan. Stir in salt and flour until smooth. Slowly pour in milk. Let it come to a boil; cook and stir until thickened, about 2 minutes. Lower the heat. Add in cheese and stir until melted. Layer 1/2 the meat mixture and cheese sauce in a greased 11x7-inch baking dish; repeat layers. Melt the remaining butter and toss with breadcrumbs. Sprinkle mixture atop cheese sauce. Bake with no cover at 350° until golden brown, about 35 minutes.

Nutrition Information

- Calories: 480 calories
- Total Fat: 26g fat (15g saturated fat)
- Sodium: 1037mg sodium
- Fiber: 4g fiber)
- Total Carbohydrate: 36g carbohydrate (9g sugars
- Cholesterol: 94mg cholesterol
- Protein: 27g protein.

401. Hamburger 'n' Fries Dinner

Serving: 4-6 servings. | Prep: 20mins | Cook: 30mins | Ready in:

Ingredients

- 1 pound ground beef
- 1 small onion, chopped
- 2 cups frozen french fries, thawed
- 1 can (15-1/4 ounces) whole kernel corn, drained
- 1 can (10-3/4 ounces) condensed cream of mushroom soup, undiluted
- 1/2 cup shredded process cheese (Velveeta)

Direction

- Cook onion and beef in a frying pan over medium heat till meat is not pink anymore; let drain. Line French fries on a greased 9-inch square baking dish. Top with cheese, soup, corn, and beef mixture.
- Bake while uncovered at 375° for around 30 minutes or until bubbly and hot.

Nutrition Information

- Calories:
- Protein:
- Total Fat:
- Sodium:
- Fiber:
- Total Carbohydrate:
- Cholesterol:

402. Hamburger Fry Pan Supper

Serving: 6 servings. | Prep: 10mins | Cook: 25mins | Ready in:

Ingredients

- 1 pound ground beef
- 1 medium onion, chopped
- 2 medium unpeeled red potatoes, julienned
- 2 cups shredded cabbage
- 2 cups thinly sliced celery
- 1/2 cup water
- Salt and pepper to taste

Direction

- Cook onion and beef in a large skillet over medium heat until meat is no longer pink; drain. Put in the remaining ingredients. Cover and let it simmer until vegetables are tender for about 20 minutes, stirring occasionally.

Nutrition Information

- Calories:
- Protein:
- Total Fat:
- Sodium:
- Fiber:
- Total Carbohydrate:
- Cholesterol:

403. Hamburger Hash Browns

Serving: 4 | Prep: 20mins | Cook: 30mins | Ready in:

Ingredients

- 4 cups frozen shredded hash brown potatoes, thawed
- 3 tablespoons vegetable oil
- 1/8 teaspoon ground black pepper
- 1 pound ground beef
- 1/2 teaspoon garlic powder
- 1/2 teaspoon onion powder
- 1 cup water
- 1 (.75 ounce) packet dry brown gravy mix
- 1 cup shredded Cheddar cheese, divided

Direction

- Preheat oven to 350° F (175° C). Prepare a greased 9-inch square baking dish.
- In a bowl, mix black pepper, vegetable oil, and hash brown potatoes; press into the base of the greased baking dish.
- Heat a big frying pan over medium-high heat. Cook and combine onion powder, garlic powder, and beef in the hot pan for 5 -7 minutes until beef is crumbly and browned; let drain and throw away the grease.
- Mix gravy mix, water, and the cooked beef together; allow to boil. Lessen heat, cover the pan, then simmer for about 5 minutes until water evaporates. Fold in a half cup of Cheddar cheese. Spoon beef mixture into the potato crust.
- Bake for 15 minutes in the preheated oven. Top with the leftover half cup of Cheddar cheese, then bake for 5 more minutes until cheese turns lightly browned.

Nutrition Information

- Calories: 590 calories;
- Total Fat: 47.4
- Sodium: 547
- Total Carbohydrate: 31.7
- Cholesterol: 99
- Protein: 29.6

404.   Hamburger Hot Dish

Serving: 8 servings. | Prep: 25mins | Cook: 25mins | Ready in:

Ingredients

- 2 cups uncooked elbow macaroni
- 2 pounds ground beef
- 1 can (28 ounces) diced tomatoes, undrained
- 1 can (15 ounces) tomato sauce
- 1 jar (12 ounces) beef gravy
- 1/2 cup chopped onion
- 1 teaspoon garlic powder

Direction

- Following the package instructions, cook the macaroni. In a big skillet on medium heat, cook the beef until it's not pink anymore. Drain then stir the garlic powder, onion, gravy, tomato sauce and tomatoes in. Strain the macaroni and add it to the beef mixture.
- Move the coated macaroni into a shallow greased 3-qt. baking dish and leave it uncovered. Bake at 350°F until thoroughly heated, about 25 to30 minutes.

Nutrition Information

- Calories: 346 calories
- Protein: 28g protein.
- Total Fat: 15g fat (6g saturated fat)
- Sodium: 748mg sodium
- Fiber: 2g fiber)
- Total Carbohydrate: 24g carbohydrate (5g sugars
- Cholesterol: 77mg cholesterol

405.   Hamburger Macaroni Casserole

Serving: 6-8 servings. | Prep: 15mins | Cook: 25mins | Ready in:

Ingredients

- 8 ounces uncooked elbow macaroni
- 1 pound ground beef
- 12 ounces process cheese (Velveeta), cubed
- 1-1/2 cups milk
- 1 cup sliced fresh mushrooms
- 1 cup diced seeded tomatoes
- 1/3 cup sliced green onions
- 1/8 teaspoon cayenne pepper
- 2 tablespoons grated Parmesan cheese

Direction

- Cook macaroni following the instruction of the package. In the meantime, in a skillet, cook beef over medium heat until there is not pink anymore; and then drain. In a large saucepan, combine milk and cheese together. Cook and stir over medium-low heat until mixture is smooth and cheese is melted. Add mushrooms, beef, tomatoes, cayenne and onions; take away from the heat.
- Drain macaroni and stir into beef mixture. Place to a greased baking dish of 2-quart. Bake while covered at 350° for around 20 minutes. Uncover and stir mixture; use Parmesan cheese to sprinkle. Bake for an addition of 5 to 10 minutes until bubbly.

Nutrition Information

- Calories: 396 calories
- Sodium: 621mg sodium
- Fiber: 2g fiber)
- Total Carbohydrate: 28g carbohydrate (7g sugars
- Cholesterol: 72mg cholesterol
- Protein: 26g protein.
- Total Fat: 20g fat (11g saturated fat)

---

406.   Hamburger Noodle Bake

Serving: 12 servings. | Prep: 20mins | Cook: 20mins | Ready in:

Ingredients

- 1-1/2 pounds ground beef
- 1 medium onion, chopped
- 2 teaspoons salt
- 1 teaspoon chili powder
- 1/4 teaspoon pepper
- 1 package (16 ounces) elbow macaroni, cooked and drained
- 1 package (10 ounces) frozen mixed vegetables, thawed
- 2 cans (6 ounces each) tomato paste

- 2 cups water
- 1 cup (4 ounces) process cheese (Velveeta)

Direction

- In a skillet over medium heat, cook onion and beef until meat is not pink anymore; and then drain. Add in pepper, chili powder and salt.
- In a greased baking dish of 4-quart, place macaroni; place mixed vegetables and beef mixture on top. Combine water and tomato paste; pour mixture over meat. Use cheese to sprinkle.
- Uncovered while baking at 400° for nearly 20 minutes until heated through.

Nutrition Information

- Calories: 205 calories
- Protein: 15g protein.
- Total Fat: 8g fat (4g saturated fat)
- Sodium: 565mg sodium
- Fiber: 3g fiber)
- Total Carbohydrate: 19g carbohydrate (5g sugars
- Cholesterol: 34mg cholesterol

---

407.   Hamburger Rice Hot Dish

Serving: 4-6 servings. | Prep: 10mins | Cook: 50mins | Ready in:

Ingredients

- 1 pound ground beef
- 1 can (10-3/4 ounces) condensed cream of chicken soup, undiluted
- 1 cup water
- 1 cup uncooked instant rice
- Minced fresh parsley

Direction

- Over medium heat in a large skillet, cook beef till no longer pink; drain. Mix in the remaining ingredients. Spoon into a baking dish of 1-1/2 quarts.
- Cover up and bake at 325° until rice is tender, about 50-60 minutes.

Nutrition Information

- Calories: 223 calories
- Total Fat: 10g fat (4g saturated fat)
- Sodium: 436mg sodium
- Fiber: 1g fiber)
- Total Carbohydrate: 17g carbohydrate (0 sugars
- Cholesterol: 41mg cholesterol
- Protein: 16g protein.

408.   Hamburger Spanish Rice

Serving: 4 servings. | Prep: 5mins | Cook: 30mins | Ready in:

Ingredients

- 1 pound lean ground beef (90% lean)
- 1 medium onion, chopped
- 1/2 green pepper, chopped
- 1 cup uncooked instant rice
- 1 can (15 ounces) tomato sauce
- 3/4 cup hot water
- 1 teaspoon prepared mustard
- 1 teaspoon Worcestershire sauce
- 1 teaspoon salt
- 1 teaspoon sugar

Direction

- Brown rice, green pepper, onion and beef in a big skillet. Mix in the leftover ingredients. Boil. Lower the heat; keep it cover and let simmer till the rice is soft or for 20 - 25 minutes.

Nutrition Information

- Calories: 314 calories
- Fiber: 3g fiber)
- Total Carbohydrate: 29g carbohydrate (4g sugars
- Cholesterol: 71mg cholesterol
- Protein: 26g protein.
- Total Fat: 11g fat (4g saturated fat)
- Sodium: 1169mg sodium

409.   Harvest Hamburger Casserole

Serving: 8 servings. | Prep: 20mins | Cook: 01hours15mins | Ready in:

Ingredients

- 1 pound lean ground beef
- 1 cup finely chopped onion
- 1 can (28 ounces) diced tomatoes, undrained
- 1 tablespoon Worcestershire sauce
- 1 teaspoon salt
- 2 cups sliced peeled potatoes
- 1/3 cup all-purpose flour
- 2 cups frozen corn, thawed
- 1-1/2 cups frozen lima beans, thawed
- 1 medium green pepper, julienned
- 1-1/2 cups shredded cheddar cheese

Direction

- Cook beef in a large skillet over medium heat until not pink anymore; drain. Mix in salt, Worcestershire sauce, tomatoes and onion. Place into a greased 3-quart baking dish.
- Layer with potatoes, flour, corn, lima beans and green pepper. Cover and bake at 375° for 45 minutes. Add cheese on top. Bake with no cover until bubbly, about 30 minutes.

Nutrition Information

- Calories: 314 calories

- Total Carbohydrate: 34g carbohydrate (6g sugars
- Cholesterol: 57mg cholesterol
- Protein: 21g protein.
- Total Fat: 11g fat (6g saturated fat)
- Sodium: 662mg sodium
- Fiber: 5g fiber)

410. Hearty Bean Casserole

Serving: 6-8 servings. | Prep: 20mins | Cook: 45mins | Ready in:

Ingredients

- 1-1/4 pounds ground beef
- 1 large onion, chopped
- 1 large green pepper, diced
- 1 garlic clove, minced
- 1 can (16 ounces) pork and beans, undrained
- 1 can (16 ounces) kidney beans, rinsed and drained
- 1 can (15 ounces) garbanzo beans or chickpeas, rinsed and drained
- 1 cup ketchup
- 3 tablespoons brown sugar
- 3 tablespoons cider vinegar
- 2 tablespoons prepared mustard
- 1 teaspoon salt
- 1/2 teaspoon pepper
- 3 bacon strips, cooked and crumbled

Direction

- In a Dutch oven over medium heat, cook beef till not pink anymore; drain. Put in the garlic, green pepper and onion; cook till softened. Mix in all of the beans.
- Mix pepper, salt, mustard, vinegar, brown sugar, and ketchup together; pour to bean mixture and stir thoroughly. Transfer into a greased 2-1/2-quart baking dish. Put bacon atop. Bake while uncovered at 350° for about 45 minutes or until heated through.

Nutrition Information

- Calories: 337 calories
- Cholesterol: 37mg cholesterol
- Protein: 22g protein.
- Total Fat: 9g fat (3g saturated fat)
- Sodium: 1124mg sodium
- Fiber: 9g fiber)
- Total Carbohydrate: 44g carbohydrate (15g sugars

411. Hearty Mac 'n' Cheese

Serving: 6-8 servings. | Prep: 25mins | Cook: 0mins | Ready in:

Ingredients

- 1 pound ground beef
- 1 small onion, chopped
- 2 packages (7-1/4 ounces each) macaroni and cheese dinner mix
- 1 cup shredded part-skim mozzarella cheese
- 6 bacon strips, cooked and crumbled

Direction

- In a large skillet, cook onion and beef over medium heat until the meat is not pink anymore. In the meantime, prepare cheese and macaroni following the instruction of the package.
- Drain beef mixture; stir into cheese and macaroni. Place to a greased shallow baking dish of 2 and a half quart. Use bacon and mozzarella cheese to sprinkle. Broil for around 2 to 3 minutes or until cheese is melted.

Nutrition Information

- Calories:
- Protein:
- Total Fat:
- Sodium:
- Fiber:

- Total Carbohydrate:
- Cholesterol:

- Calories: 470 calories
- Sodium: 795mg sodium
- Fiber: 1g fiber)
- Total Carbohydrate: 25g carbohydrate (7g sugars
- Cholesterol: 115mg cholesterol
- Protein: 28g protein.
- Total Fat: 29g fat (18g saturated fat)

412. Hearty Macaroni Casserole

Serving: 2 casseroles (4 servings each). | Prep: 20mins | Cook: 30mins | Ready in:

Ingredients

- 1 package (7-1/4 ounces) macaroni and cheese dinner mix
- 1 pound ground beef
- 1 cup chopped green pepper
- 1/2 cup chopped onion
- 1 can (14-1/2 ounces) Italian diced tomatoes, drained
- 2 cups shredded cheddar cheese, divided
- 1 cup French-fried onions

Direction

- Follow directions on package to prepare macaroni and cheese. In the meantime, cook onion, beef, and green pepper in a big frying pan on medium heat until beef is not pink. Drain excess grease. Mix into prepared macaroni. Stir in the tomatoes. Divide in half. Take one half and split between two 1-1/2-qt. greased dishes. Sprinkle a 1/2 cup of cheese on each. Split the second half of mixture put on both. Put the remaining cheese on top of one dish; cover and place in freezer for up to 3 months. Sprinkle French-fried onions on second dish. Do not cover; bake in a 350-degree oven until cooked through, 30 minutes. To use the frozen one: place in fridge to completely thaw. Take it out of fridge 30 minutes before baking. Follow directions for baking.

Nutrition Information

413. Hearty Pork And Beans

Serving: 4-6 servings. | Prep: 15mins | Cook: 15mins | Ready in:

Ingredients

- 1 pound ground beef
- 1 medium tart apple, peeled and diced
- 1 medium onion, chopped
- 1 can (16 ounces) pork and beans
- 4 bacon strips, cooked and diced
- 1/4 cup barbecue sauce
- 1/4 cup molasses
- 1 cup corn chips, coarsely crushed

Direction

- In an ungreased shallow 2-quart. microwave-safe dish, crumble beef; add onion and apple. Microwave, covered, on High for 2-4 minutes while stirring once; let drain. Mix in the pork and beans, molasses, barbecue sauce, and bacon. Cook, covered, on high while stirring once for around 4-6 minutes or till heated through. Allow to rest for 5 minutes. Top with chips just before serving.

Nutrition Information

- Calories:
- Sodium:
- Fiber:
- Total Carbohydrate:
- Cholesterol:

- Protein:
- Total Fat:

414. Hereford Casserole

Serving: 7 servings. | Prep: 20mins | Cook: 35mins | Ready in:

Ingredients

- 4-1/2 cups uncooked fusilli pasta
- 1-1/2 pounds ground beef
- 1 jar (14 ounces) spaghetti sauce
- 4 ounces cream cheese, softened
- 1 can (10-3/4 ounces) condensed cream of mushroom soup, undiluted
- 1 cup (8 ounces) sour cream
- 1 cup shredded cheddar cheese

Direction

- Cook pasta following package instructions. In the meantime, over medium heat in a large skillet, cook beef till no longer pink; drain. Mix in spaghetti sauce; put aside.
- Beat cream cheese in a small bowl until smooth. Put in sour cream and soup; beat until blended. Drain the pasta.
- Spoon 1/2 the beef mixture into a greased baking dish of 13x9 inches. Put the pasta, soup mixture then leftover beef mixture on top. Sprinkle with the cheddar cheese.
- Bake with no cover, at 350° until cheese is melted and heated through, about 35-40 minutes.

Nutrition Information

- Calories: 622 calories
- Sodium: 817mg sodium
- Fiber: 3g fiber)
- Total Carbohydrate: 53g carbohydrate (8g sugars
- Cholesterol: 109mg cholesterol

415. Hobo Knapsacks

Serving: 6 servings. | Prep: 15mins | Cook: 50mins | Ready in:

Ingredients

- 2 medium potatoes, peeled and thinly sliced
- 2 large tomatoes, chopped
- 1 large onion, chopped
- 1 package (10 ounces) frozen mixed vegetables, thawed
- 1 can (4 ounces) mushroom stems and pieces, drained
- 1 large egg, beaten
- 1/2 cup tomato juice
- 1/2 cup old-fashioned oats
- 1 tablespoon finely chopped onion
- 1 teaspoon salt
- 1/4 teaspoon pepper
- 1 pound lean ground beef (90% lean)
- Additional salt and pepper, optional

Direction

- Combine mushrooms, mixed vegetables, onion, tomatoes and potatoes in a large bowl; put aside.
- In another large bowl, mix pepper, salt, onion, oats, tomato juice and egg together; crumble beef over the mixture; stir well. Separate the meat mixture into six portions; crumble each portion onto a foil piece of 18x12 inches.
- Place vegetable mixture on top; add in additional pepper and salt for seasoning if desired. Gather the edges of foil together; crimp to seal, creating a packet. Arrange on baking sheets.
- Bake at 350° until a thermometer reads 160° and no more pink color, about 50-60 minutes.

Nutrition Information

- Calories: 252 calories
- Sodium: 603mg sodium
- Fiber: 5g fiber)
- Total Carbohydrate: 27g carbohydrate (7g sugars
- Cholesterol: 82mg cholesterol
- Protein: 20g protein.
- Total Fat: 8g fat (3g saturated fat)

---

416. Home Style Beef Noodle Casserole

Serving: 3 servings. | Prep: 15mins | Cook: 20mins | Ready in:

Ingredients

- 2 cups uncooked egg noodles
- 1/2 pound lean ground beef (90% lean)
- 1 can (8 ounces) tomato sauce
- 1/4 cup chopped green onions
- 1/4 cup canned chopped green chilies
- 1 small garlic clove, minced
- 1/8 teaspoon salt
- 1/2 cup sour cream
- 2 ounces cream cheese, softened
- 1/4 cup shredded part-skim mozzarella cheese

Direction

- Follow directions on package to cook noodles. In the meantime, cook beef in a big frying pan on medium heat until not pink; drain excess grease. Mix in salt, tomato sauce, garlic, onions, and chilies. Combine sour cream and cream cheese in a small bowl. Drain water from noodles.
- Put 1/2 cup of meat mixture in a greased 1-qt. dish. Layer with half of each: noodles, cream cheese mixture, and cheese. Put 1/2 cup meat mixture on cheese; repeat the layers. Put remaining meat mixture on top.

- Cover; bake in a 350-degree oven until bubbling, 20-25 minutes.

Nutrition Information

- Calories: 359 calories
- Total Carbohydrate: 27g carbohydrate (6g sugars
- Cholesterol: 90mg cholesterol
- Protein: 27g protein.
- Total Fat: 15g fat (8g saturated fat)
- Sodium: 698mg sodium
- Fiber: 2g fiber)

---

417. Hominy Beef Bake

Serving: 4-6 servings. | Prep: 15mins | Cook: 30mins | Ready in:

Ingredients

- 1 pound ground beef
- 1 small onion, chopped
- 2 garlic cloves, minced
- 1 can (15-1/2 ounces) hominy, drained
- 1 can (15 ounces) chili with beans
- 1 can (8 ounces) tomato sauce
- 1/2 cup water
- 3 teaspoons chili powder
- Salt and pepper to taste
- 1 package (10-1/2 ounces) corn chips, crushed

Direction

- Add onion and beef to a big frying pan, cook over medium heat until the meat is not pink any longer. Put in garlic, cook for 60 more seconds. Drain. Mix in the pepper, salt, chili powder, water, tomato sauce, chili and hominy.
- Take the mixture to a 13x9-inch baking dish coated with cooking spray. Dredge corn chips over top. Set oven at 350°, bake while

uncovered until heated through, about half an hour.

Nutrition Information

- Calories: 462 calories
- Total Fat: 13g fat (4g saturated fat)
- Sodium: 1217mg sodium
- Fiber: 9g fiber)
- Total Carbohydrate: 63g carbohydrate (3g sugars
- Cholesterol: 57mg cholesterol
- Protein: 25g protein.

---

418.   Hurry Up Casserole

Serving: 4 servings. | Prep: 15mins | Cook: 30mins | Ready in:

Ingredients

- 1 pound ground beef
- 1 medium onion, chopped
- 2 celery ribs, chopped
- 1 package (10 ounces) frozen pea pods
- 2 cups chow mein noodles
- 1 can (10-3/4 ounces) condensed cream of mushroom soup or cream of celery soup, undiluted

Direction

- Cook celery, onion, and beef in a skillet over medium heat till vegetables get softened and meat is not pink anymore; strain. Add soup mix, noodles, and pea pods; mix well. Prepare a greased 9-inch square baking dish then place mixture in. Allow to bake at 350 degrees, uncovered, till thoroughly heated, about 30 minutes.

Nutrition Information

- Calories: 407 calories

- Cholesterol: 59mg cholesterol
- Protein: 26g protein.
- Total Fat: 21g fat (7g saturated fat)
- Sodium: 727mg sodium
- Fiber: 5g fiber)
- Total Carbohydrate: 30g carbohydrate (6g sugars

---

419.   Inside Out Stuffed Peppers

Serving: 4-6 servings. | Prep: 15mins | Cook: 01hours05mins | Ready in:

Ingredients

- 1 pound ground beef
- 1/2 cup chopped onion
- 1 can (14-1/2 ounces) stewed tomatoes, cut up
- 1 large green pepper, chopped
- 1/2 cup uncooked long grain rice
- 1/2 cup water
- 2 teaspoons Worcestershire sauce
- 1/2 teaspoon salt
- 1/4 teaspoon pepper
- 1 cup shredded cheddar cheese

Direction

- In a big frying pan over medium heat, cook beef till not pink anymore; let drain. Put to a greased 2-quart casserole. Put in the next eight ingredients.
- Bake, covered, at 350° for 1 hour or until the rice becomes softened. Uncover and dust with cheese; cook for 5 more minutes or until cheese becomes melted.

Nutrition Information

- Calories: 276 calories
- Cholesterol: 57mg cholesterol
- Protein: 19g protein.
- Total Fat: 12g fat (7g saturated fat)

- Sodium: 516mg sodium
- Fiber: 2g fiber)
- Total Carbohydrate: 22g carbohydrate (5g sugars

420.   Italian Cabbage Casserole

Serving: 6 | Prep: 20mins | Cook: 55mins | Ready in:

Ingredients

- 3 slices bacon, diced
- 1 pound bulk mild Italian sausage
- 1 (14 ounce) can beef broth
- 2 cups diced celery
- 1 white onion, diced
- 5 ounces shredded carrots
- 2 tablespoons Italian seasoning
- 2 teaspoons ground coriander
- 1 1/2 teaspoons garlic, minced
- 1 teaspoon ground black pepper
- 1/2 teaspoon coarse sea salt
- 1 head cabbage, shredded
- 1 sweet apple, diced

Direction

- In a Dutch oven over medium heat, cook and stir bacon until browned and crisp, about 5 - 10 minutes. Place bacon to a plate lined with paper-towel and drain grease from Dutch oven.
- In the same oven, cook and stir Italian sausage until browned and crumbly, about 5 - 10 minutes. Add beef broth into Dutch oven and let it come to a boil while using a wooden spoon to scrap the browned food bits off of the pan's bottom.
- Mix sea salt, black pepper, garlic, coriander, Italian seasoning, carrot, onion and celery into beef broth mixture; bring to a simmer and cook until liquid is lessened and vegetables are tender, about 15 - 20 minutes. Mix cooked bacon, apple and cabbage into vegetable mixture; cook for 30 - 45 minutes, until desired

consistency is reached and apples and cabbage are tender.

Nutrition Information

- Calories: 302 calories;
- Total Fat: 16.9
- Sodium: 1181
- Total Carbohydrate: 23.8
- Cholesterol: 35
- Protein: 16

421.   Italian Casserole

Serving: 4 | Prep: 20mins | Cook: 3hours20mins | Ready in:

Ingredients

- 3/4 pound lean ground beef
- 1 onion, chopped
- 1 (28 ounce) can whole peeled tomatoes, chopped
- 1 (6 ounce) can tomato paste
- 1 teaspoon salt
- 1 tablespoon dried parsley
- 1/2 teaspoon garlic salt
- black pepper to taste
- 8 ounces wide egg noodles
- 1 (12 ounce) package process sharp cheddar cheese singles

Direction

- In large skillet, brown onion and ground beef. Mix in tomato paste, tomatoes, parsley, salt, pepper and garlic salt, then simmer over low heat for nearly 3 hours.
- Preheat oven to 350°F (175°C). Boil lightly salted water in a large pot. Add pasta and cook for approximately 8 to 10 minutes or until al dente; drain.
- In a casserole dish of 2-quart, combine meat mixture and noodles. Place cheese slices on

top and bake for nearly 15 to 20 minutes until cheese is melted.

Nutrition Information

- Calories: 739 calories;
- Sodium: 2572
- Total Carbohydrate: 62.1
- Cholesterol: 164
- Protein: 41.2
- Total Fat: 39

---

422.   Layered Beef Casserole

Serving: 8 servings. | Prep: 25mins | Cook: 02hours00mins | Ready in:

Ingredients

- 6 medium potatoes, peeled and thinly sliced
- 1 can (15-1/4 ounces) whole kernel corn, drained
- 1/2 cup chopped green pepper
- 1 cup chopped onion
- 2 cups sliced fresh carrots
- 1-1/2 pounds lean ground beef (90% lean)
- 1 can (8 ounces) tomato sauce
- Salt and pepper to taste
- 1 cup shredded process cheese (Velveeta)

Direction

- Combine carrots, onion, green pepper, corn, and potatoes in a 13x9-inch baking dish coated with cooking spray. Crumble the beef and add into the vegetables. Top with tomato sauce. Dust with pepper and salt.
- Put a cover on and bake at 350 degrees until the meat is not pink anymore and a thermometer registers 160 degrees, for 2 hours. Before serving, allow to stand for 10 minutes.
- Note: You can divide the Placed Beef Casserole into two 1 1/2-quart baking dishes. Bake a casserole to serve and freeze the other

for another recipe. You can freeze the casserole for a maximum of 3 months.
- To use frozen casserole: Put in the fridge overnight to thaw. Bake according to the instruction. Before serving, dust with cheese.

Nutrition Information

- Calories: 341 calories
- Protein: 23g protein.
- Total Fat: 11g fat (5g saturated fat)
- Sodium: 526mg sodium
- Fiber: 4g fiber)
- Total Carbohydrate: 35g carbohydrate (8g sugars
- Cholesterol: 64mg cholesterol

---

423.   Layered Tortilla Pie

Serving: 4-6 servings. | Prep: 20mins | Cook: 20mins | Ready in:

Ingredients

- 1 pound ground beef
- 1 medium onion, chopped
- 1 can (8 ounces) tomato sauce
- 1 garlic clove, minced
- 1 tablespoon chili powder
- 1/2 teaspoon salt
- 1/4 teaspoon pepper
- 1 can (2-1/4 ounces) sliced ripe olives, drained, optional
- 1 tablespoon butter
- 6 corn tortillas (6 inches)
- 2 cups shredded cheddar cheese
- 1/4 cup water

Direction

- Cook onion and beef in a big skillet till meat is not pink anymore; drain. Put in pepper, salt, chili powder, garlic and tomatoes sauce and, if you want, olives. Boil. Lower the heat; let simmer till becoming thick or for 5 minutes.

- Butter tortillas a bit on one side; add 1 tortilla, buttered side facing downward, in a 2-qt. round casserole. Add a third cup of cheese and roughly half cup of meat mixture on top. Repeat the layers, ending with cheese.
- Add water around the sides of casserole (but don't add on top). Keep it covered and baked at 400 degrees till becoming thoroughly heated or for 20 minutes. Allow to rest for 5 minutes prior to cutting.

Nutrition Information

- Calories: 350 calories
- Total Fat: 20g fat (12g saturated fat)
- Sodium: 722mg sodium
- Fiber: 3g fiber)
- Total Carbohydrate: 19g carbohydrate (2g sugars
- Cholesterol: 82mg cholesterol
- Protein: 24g protein.

---

424. Lighter Hamburger Noodle Casserole

Serving: 10 servings. | Prep: 30mins | Cook: 35mins | Ready in:

Ingredients

- 5 cups uncooked yolk-free noodles
- 1-1/4 pounds lean ground beef (90% lean)
- 2 garlic cloves, minced
- 3 cans (8 ounces each) tomato sauce
- 1/2 teaspoon sugar
- 1/2 teaspoon salt
- 1/8 teaspoon pepper
- 1 package (8 ounces) reduced-fat cream cheese
- 1 cup reduced-fat ricotta cheese
- 1/4 cup fat-free sour cream
- 3 green onions, thinly sliced, divided
- 2/3 cup shredded reduced-fat cheddar cheese

Direction

- Following the instructions on package, cook noodles. At the same time, in the big nonstick skillet on medium heat, cook the beef till not pink anymore. Put in the garlic; cook for 60 seconds more. Drain off. Whisk in pepper, salt, sugar, and tomato sauce; thoroughly heat. Drain off the noodles; whisk into the beef mixture.
- In the small-sized bowl, whip sour cream, ricotta cheese and cream cheese till blended. Whisk 1/2 of onions in.
- Scoop 1/2 of noodle mixture into the 13x9-inch baking dish that is coated with the cooking spray. Put the rest of the noodle mixture and cheese mixture on top.
- Put cover on and bake at 350 degrees for half an hour. Remove the cover; drizzle with the cheddar cheese. Bake till the cheese melts and thoroughly heated or for 5 to 10 more minutes. Drizzle with the rest of the onions.

Nutrition Information

- Calories: 290 calories
- Total Carbohydrate: 23g carbohydrate (5g sugars
- Cholesterol: 56mg cholesterol
- Protein: 22g protein. Diabetic Exchanges: 2 lean meat
- Total Fat: 12g fat (7g saturated fat)
- Sodium: 650mg sodium
- Fiber: 2g fiber)

---

425. Lori's Marzetti Bake

Serving: 2 casseroles (12 servings each). | Prep: 30mins | Cook: 35mins | Ready in:

Ingredients

- 2 pounds ground beef
- 1 cup sliced fresh mushrooms

- 1 medium onion, finely chopped
- 1/3 cup chopped green pepper
- 2 garlic cloves, minced
- 1 teaspoon salt
- 1/2 teaspoon pepper
- 3 cans (15 ounces each) plus 1 can (8 ounces) tomato sauce
- 1 can (15 ounces) diced tomatoes, undrained
- 2 tablespoons brown sugar
- 1 package (16 ounces) egg noodles
- 3 cups shredded cheddar cheese, divided

Direction

- Set the oven to 400° and start preheating. In a Dutch oven over medium heat, cook the first seven ingredients until vegetables are tender and beef is no longer pink for about 8-10 minutes, breaking beef into crumbles; drain. Stir in brown sugar, tomatoes and tomato sauce; let it come to a boil. Lower the heat; let it simmer while stirring occasionally until flavors are blended, about 10-15 minutes.
- In the meantime, cook noodles following package instructions. Drain; pour into the sauce. Mix in 2 cups of cheese. Place onto two greased 11x7-inch baking dishes.
- Use greased foil to cover and bake until heated through, about 30-35 minutes. Top with the remaining cheese; bake with no cover until cheese is melted, about 5 more minutes.

Nutrition Information

- Calories:
- Sodium:
- Fiber:
- Total Carbohydrate:
- Cholesterol:
- Protein:
- Total Fat:

426. Makeover Zucchini Supper

Serving: 8 servings. | Prep: 30mins | Cook: 50mins | Ready in:

Ingredients

- 1-1/2 pounds lean ground beef (90% lean)
- 1/2 pound reduced-fat bulk pork sausage
- 1 large onion, chopped
- 1 medium carrot, chopped
- 1 celery rib, chopped
- 2 cups cubed day-old whole wheat bread
- 1/2 cup fat-free milk
- 1 tablespoon all-purpose flour
- 4 cups chopped zucchini
- 3/4 pound reduced-fat process cheese (Velveeta), cubed
- 1 can (10-3/4 ounces) reduced-fat reduced-sodium condensed cream of mushroom soup, undiluted
- 3/4 cup egg substitute
- 1 teaspoon garlic powder
- 1/2 teaspoon onion powder
- 1/2 teaspoon rubbed sage
- 1/2 teaspoon dried thyme
- 1/2 teaspoon pepper

Direction

- Cook the celery, carrot, onion, sausage and beef in a Dutch oven on medium heat until the vegetables become crisp-tender and the meat is not pink anymore. In the meantime, mix together the milk and bread cubes in a small bowl, then put aside.
- Take the meat mixture away from heat, then drain. Mix in flour until combined. Stir in leftover ingredients and bread mixture, then move to a cooking spray coated 13x9-inch baking dish.
- Put cover on and bake for 40 to 45 minutes at 350 degrees until a thermometer registers 160 degrees. Take off the cover and mix. Let bake for 8 to 12 minutes more or until golden brown.

Nutrition Information

- Calories: 373 calories
- Sodium: 1119mg sodium
- Fiber: 2g fiber)
- Total Carbohydrate: 21g carbohydrate (8g sugars
- Cholesterol: 80mg cholesterol
- Protein: 34g protein.
- Total Fat: 17g fat (7g saturated fat)

427. Mashed Potato Beef Casserole

Serving: 4-6 servings. | Prep: 30mins | Cook: 25mins | Ready in:

Ingredients

- 2 bacon strips, diced
- 1 pound ground beef
- 1-3/4 cups sliced fresh mushrooms
- 1 large onion, finely chopped
- 1 large carrot, finely chopped
- 1 celery rib, finely chopped
- 2 tablespoons all-purpose flour
- 1 cup beef broth
- 1 tablespoon Worcestershire sauce
- 1 teaspoon dried tarragon
- 1/4 teaspoon pepper
- 3 cups hot mashed potatoes
- 3/4 cup shredded cheddar cheese, divided
- Paprika

Direction

- Cook bacon in a large skillet until crisp; allow to drain, saving 1 teaspoon drippings. Put the bacon aside. Over medium heat, cook beef in the drippings until no more pink; let drain.
- Toss celery, carrot, onion, and mushrooms in flour; add to the skillet with the broth, pepper, tarragon, and Worcestershire sauce. Bring to a

boil. Lower the heat; simmer without cover until the greens are soft, for 15-20 minutes.
- Put in the bacon, then transfer to a greased 2-qt. baking dish. Next, combine 1/2 cup of the cheese and potatoes; spread over the beef mixture. Dust with the remaining cheese and paprika.
- Bake without cover for 20-25 minutes at 350°, or until heated through. Then broil 4 in. from the heat until bubbly, for 5 minutes.

Nutrition Information

- Calories: 381 calories
- Protein: 23g protein.
- Total Fat: 19g fat (9g saturated fat)
- Sodium: 625mg sodium
- Fiber: 1g fiber)
- Total Carbohydrate: 28g carbohydrate (3g sugars
- Cholesterol: 73mg cholesterol

428. Meal In A Packet

Serving: 4 servings. | Prep: 20mins | Cook: 45mins | Ready in:

Ingredients

- 1 pound lean ground beef
- 8 medium carrots, julienned
- 1 medium green pepper, julienned
- 1 envelope onion gravy mix
- 2 firm fresh tomatoes, halved

Direction

- Form beef into 4 patties. Arrange each on an ungreased 14-in. square of heavy-duty foil. Place green pepper and carrots around the patties. Dust with the gravy mix. Next, put a tomato half on each patty with the cut side down. Fold the foil around the vegetables and meat; tightly seal up. Arrange them on an

ungreased baking sheet. Then bake at 350°
until the meat is no more pink, for 45 minutes.

Nutrition Information

- Calories: 262 calories
- Fiber: 5g fiber)
- Total Carbohydrate: 20g carbohydrate (9g sugars
- Cholesterol: 69mg cholesterol
- Protein: 24g protein.
- Total Fat: 10g fat (4g saturated fat)
- Sodium: 438mg sodium

---

429. Meat 'n' Pepper Cornbread

Serving: 6 servings. | Prep: 15mins | Cook: 20mins | Ready in:

Ingredients

- 1 pound ground beef
- 1 cup chopped green pepper
- 1 cup chopped onion
- 2 cans (8 ounces each) tomato sauce
- 1-1/2 teaspoons chili powder
- 1/2 teaspoon salt
- 1/4 teaspoon pepper
- 1 cup all-purpose flour
- 3/4 cup cornmeal
- 1/4 cup sugar
- 1 tablespoon baking powder
- 1/2 teaspoon salt
- 1 large egg, beaten
- 1 cup whole milk
- 1/4 cup canola oil

Direction

- Put together green pepper, onion and ground beef in an ovenproof or 10-inch cast-iron pan and cook to brown lightly. Drain and add chili

powder, salt, pepper and tomato sauce. Let it simmer for 10 to 15 minutes.
- In a bowl, combine the dry ingredients together. In a separate bowl, mix milk, oil, and egg. Beat together then stir into the dry ingredients. Blend until dry ingredients have moistened then pour over beef mixture.
- Set oven to 400 degrees. Bake mixture in the oven for 20 to 25 minutes until golden. Let it cool briefly then loosen the edges with a knife. Transfer to a serving plate by inverting. This dish can also be served straight from skillet. Cut into wedges then serve.

Nutrition Information

- Calories: 432 calories
- Total Carbohydrate: 46g carbohydrate (13g sugars
- Cholesterol: 87mg cholesterol
- Protein: 22g protein.
- Total Fat: 18g fat (5g saturated fat)
- Sodium: 839mg sodium
- Fiber: 3g fiber)

---

430. Meatball Hash Brown Bake

Serving: 8 servings. | Prep: 25mins | Cook: 60mins | Ready in:

Ingredients

- 1 can (10-3/4 ounces) condensed cream of chicken soup, undiluted
- 1 large onion, chopped
- 1 cup shredded cheddar cheese
- 1 cup (8 ounces) sour cream
- 1-1/2 teaspoons pepper, divided
- 1 teaspoon salt, divided
- 1 package (30 ounces) frozen shredded hash brown potatoes, thawed and patted dry
- 2 large eggs, lightly beaten
- 3/4 cup crushed saltines (20-25 crackers)

- 6 to 8 garlic cloves, minced
- 1 pound lean ground beef (90% lean)

Direction

- Start preheating the oven to 350°. Combine 1/2 teaspoon salt, 1 teaspoon pepper, and the first 4 ingredients; mix in potatoes. Evenly spread the mixture into a 13x9-inch baking dish coated with cooking spray.
- Mix the leftover salt and pepper, garlic, cracker crumbs, and eggs together in a big bowl. Add beef, gently stir but thoroughly. Form into balls, about 1-inch each ball.
- Brown the meatballs in a big frying pan over medium-high heat. Add to the potato mixture, gently press in.
- Put a cover on and bake for 45 minutes. Remove the cover, bake for 10-15 minutes until the potatoes are soft and the meatballs have fully cooked.

Nutrition Information

- Calories: 387 calories
- Total Carbohydrate: 32g carbohydrate (4g sugars
- Cholesterol: 106mg cholesterol
- Protein: 21g protein.
- Total Fat: 20g fat (9g saturated fat)
- Sodium: 808mg sodium
- Fiber: 3g fiber)

431. Meatball Potato Supper

Serving: 6-8 servings. | Prep: 30mins | Cook: 60mins | Ready in:

Ingredients

- 2 eggs
- 1/2 cup dry bread crumbs
- 1 envelope onion soup mix
- 1-1/2 pounds lean ground beef (90% lean)
- 2 tablespoons all-purpose flour

- 6 medium potatoes, peeled and thinly sliced
- 1 can (10-3/4 ounces) condensed cream of celery soup, undiluted
- 1 cup 2% milk
- Paprika, optional

Direction

- Mix soup mix, bread crumbs, and eggs together in a big bowl. Crumble over the mixture with beef and stir thoroughly. Form into balls, about 1-inch each ball. Working in small batches, brown the meatballs in a big frying pan over medium heat; strain. Sprinkle flour over, lightly roll to blend.
- In a 2 1/2-quart greased baking dish, put 1/2 of the potatoes. Put the leftover potatoes and the meatballs on top. Mix together milk and soup in a small bowl until combined, add to the potatoes. If wanted, sprinkle paprika over.
- Put a cover on and bake at 350° until the potatoes are soft, about 60-65 minutes.

Nutrition Information

- Calories: 361 calories
- Protein: 24g protein.
- Total Fat: 11g fat (4g saturated fat)
- Sodium: 739mg sodium
- Fiber: 3g fiber)
- Total Carbohydrate: 42g carbohydrate (5g sugars
- Cholesterol: 100mg cholesterol

432. Meatballs Sausage Dinner

Serving: 6-8 servings. | Prep: 25mins | Cook: 40mins | Ready in:

Ingredients

- 3 cups frozen broccoli florets, thawed
- 2 medium potatoes, peeled and cubed
- 3 medium carrots, sliced
- 1 medium onion, chopped

- 1 pound Johnsonville® Fully Cooked Polish Kielbasa Sausage Rope, halved and cut into 1-inch pieces
- 1/2 pound lean ground beef
- 1 can (14-1/2 ounces) beef broth
- Lemon-pepper seasoning to taste

Direction

- Set oven to 350 degrees and start preheating. Combine onion, carrots, potatoes, and broccoli. Move to an oiled 13x9-inch baking dish. Top with sausage. Form beef into 1-inch balls; place over top. Spread broth over the casserole; sprinkle lemon-pepper seasoning over the surface. Bake for 40 minutes without cover, until meatballs are not pink anymore.

Nutrition Information

- Calories:
- Total Carbohydrate:
- Cholesterol:
- Protein:
- Total Fat:
- Sodium:
- Fiber:

433.   Meaty Chili Lasagna

Serving: 12 servings. | Prep: 20mins | Cook: 45mins | Ready in:

Ingredients

- 12 uncooked lasagna noodles
- 1-1/2 pounds ground beef
- 1 medium onion, chopped
- 1 medium green pepper, chopped
- 2 to 3 jalapeno peppers, seeded and chopped
- 1 to 2 tablespoons chili powder
- 1 garlic clove, minced
- 1 can (10-3/4 ounces) condensed cream of mushroom soup, undiluted

- 1 cup frozen corn
- 1 can (8 ounces) tomato sauce
- 3 tablespoons tomato paste
- 1 can (2-1/4 ounces) sliced ripe olives, drained
- 4 cups shredded cheddar cheese

Direction

- Cook noodles, refer to package instructions. Meanwhile, mix the onion, beef, peppers and chili powder in a large skillet. Add garlic and cook a minute longer. Drain. Put the corn, soup, tomato paste, tomato sauce and olives. Simmer until heated through.
- Strain pasta. Put half cup meat sauce in a greased 13x9 in. baking pan. Layer 4 pasta, 1/2 of the remaining sauce and 1/3 cheese. Do layer again. Put the remaining pasta and cheese on top.
- Cover and bake for 350° F for 30 min. without cover. Bake for about 15 minutes more until cheese are melted. Let set for 15 min. before slicing.

Nutrition Information

- Calories: 405 calories
- Total Fat: 21g fat (12g saturated fat)
- Sodium: 597mg sodium
- Fiber: 3g fiber)
- Total Carbohydrate: 29g carbohydrate (4g sugars
- Cholesterol: 82mg cholesterol
- Protein: 25g protein.

434.   Meaty Corn Bread Casserole

Serving: 6 servings. | Prep: 20mins | Cook: 15mins | Ready in:

Ingredients

- 1/2 pound ground beef

- 1/2 pound Jones No Sugar Pork Sausage Roll sausage
- 1-3/4 cups frozen corn, thawed
- 1 cup water
- 1 envelope brown gravy mix
- 1 package (8-1/2 ounces) corn bread/muffin mix
- 1 tablespoon bacon bits
- 1-1/2 teaspoons pepper
- 1/8 teaspoon garlic powder
- 1 envelope country gravy mix

Direction

- In a big skillet on medium heat, cook sausage and beef until they are not pink anymore; drain. Mix in brown gravy mix, water, and corn. Heat to a boil. Stir and cook for about 1 minute or until thickened. Use a spoon to transfer to an oiled 8-inch square baking dish.
- Following package instructions to prepare corn bread batter. Mix in garlic powder, pepper, and bacon bits. Arrange over the meat mixture.
- Bake at 400 degrees without cover for 15-20 minutes or until you insert a toothpick into corn bread layer and it comes out clean. At the same time, follow package instructions to prepare country gravy mix; serve along with the casserole.

Nutrition Information

- Calories: 447 calories
- Protein: 17g protein.
- Total Fat: 21g fat (6g saturated fat)
- Sodium: 1345mg sodium
- Fiber: 2g fiber)
- Total Carbohydrate: 49g carbohydrate (12g sugars
- Cholesterol: 78mg cholesterol

Serving: 6 servings. | Prep: 10mins | Cook: 20mins | Ready in:

Ingredients

- 1 pound ground beef
- 1 medium onion, chopped
- 1/2 cup chopped green pepper
- 1 jar (14 ounces) spaghetti sauce
- 1-1/2 cups uncooked elbow macaroni
- 1 cup water
- Salt and pepper to taste
- 1 cup shredded part-skim mozzarella cheese

Direction

- Crumble the beef over a 2-quart microwave-safe dish. Put in green pepper and onion. Put on a cover and microwave on high heat setting, stirring once, until the meat is not pink anymore, 3-5 minutes; drain. Stir in pepper, salt, water, macaroni, and spaghetti sauce.
- Microwave, covered, on high heat setting, stirring once for 9 minutes. Dust with cheese. Before serving, allow to stand for 5 minutes.

Nutrition Information

- Calories: 338 calories
- Total Carbohydrate: 24g carbohydrate (7g sugars
- Cholesterol: 66mg cholesterol
- Protein: 23g protein.
- Total Fat: 16g fat (7g saturated fat)
- Sodium: 462mg sodium
- Fiber: 2g fiber)

Serving: 6 servings. | Prep: 10mins | Cook: 10mins | Ready in:

Ingredients

- 1 pound ground beef
- 1 medium onion, chopped
- 1 garlic clove, minced
- 1 can (10-3/4 ounces) condensed cream of mushroom soup, undiluted
- 1 can (11 ounces) Mexicorn
- 1 can (4 ounces) chopped green chilies
- 1 package (10-1/2 ounces) corn chips
- 1 can (10 ounces) enchilada sauce
- 1 to 2 cups shredded Colby-Monterey Jack cheese

Direction

- Cook garlic, onion, and beef on medium heat in a skillet till meat is not pink anymore and onion is soft; drain. Put in chilies, corn and soup; stir them well.
- In one ungreased shallow 3-qt. baking dish, layer meat mixture, chips and sauce; add cheese on top. Bake, while uncovered, at 350 degrees till thoroughly heated or for 8 to 10 minutes.

Nutrition Information

- Calories: 613 calories
- Cholesterol: 69mg cholesterol
- Protein: 26g protein.
- Total Fat: 36g fat (10g saturated fat)
- Sodium: 1168mg sodium
- Fiber: 5g fiber)
- Total Carbohydrate: 47g carbohydrate (6g sugars

437.   Mexican Tater Topped Casserole

Serving: 10 servings. | Prep: 30mins | Cook: 40mins | Ready in:

Ingredients

- 1 package (14 ounces) frozen pepper strips

- 1 can (11 ounces) Mexicorn, drained
- 1 can (11 ounces) condensed beefy mushroom soup, undiluted
- 1 can (10-3/4 ounces) condensed cream of celery soup, undiluted
- 2/3 cup 2% milk
- 2 teaspoons ground cumin
- 1/2 teaspoon dried oregano
- 4 cups reserved mixture from Cajun Beef and Beans
- 1 package (32 ounces) frozen Tater Tots
- 2 cups shredded Mexican cheese blend
- 2 green onions, thinly sliced

Direction

- Mix first seven ingredients in a big frying pan. Stir the meat mixture in. Heat to a boil. Move to a 13x9-in. greased pan. Put Tater Tots on top. Cover; bake in a 350-degree oven for 30 minutes. Sprinkle on green onions and cheese. Do not cover; bake until cheese melts and filling is bubbling, 10-15 minutes.

Nutrition Information

- Calories: 529 calories
- Protein: 24g protein.
- Total Fat: 27g fat (9g saturated fat)
- Sodium: 1533mg sodium
- Fiber: 5g fiber)
- Total Carbohydrate: 48g carbohydrate (6g sugars
- Cholesterol: 66mg cholesterol

438.   Microwave Beef Casserole

Serving: 4-6 servings. | Prep: 15mins | Cook: 15mins | Ready in:

Ingredients

- 1 pound ground beef

- 1 small onion, chopped
- 1/2 cup uncooked instant rice
- 1-1/2 cups water, divided
- 1 can (10-3/4 ounces) condensed cream of mushroom soup, undiluted
- 1 cup slivered almonds
- 5 large fresh mushrooms, chopped
- 1 package (6 ounces) seasoned stuffing mix
- 1/4 cup butter, melted

Direction

- In a microwave-safe dish of 3-quart, crumble beef; then add onion. Loosely cover during microwave on high setting for around 3 to 5 minutes until meat is not pink anymore, stirring twice; drain. Mix in 1/2 cup water and rice. Cover while cooking for approximately 2 minutes. Stir in mushrooms, almonds and soup.
- In a large bowl, combine the remaining water, butter and stuffing mix; spoon over beef mixture. Uncovered while microwave for nearly 1 to 3 minutes until heated through.

Nutrition Information

- Calories: 510 calories
- Sodium: 988mg sodium
- Fiber: 4g fiber)
- Total Carbohydrate: 36g carbohydrate (5g sugars
- Cholesterol: 73mg cholesterol
- Protein: 25g protein.
- Total Fat: 30g fat (10g saturated fat)

---

439. Microwave Pizza Casserole

Serving: 6-8 servings. | Prep: 10mins | Cook: 20mins | Ready in:

Ingredients

- 1 pound ground beef
- 1/2 cup chopped onion
- 1/2 cup chopped green pepper
- 1 can (16 ounces) pizza sauce
- 1 can (4 ounces) sliced mushrooms
- 4 ounces sliced pepperoni
- 1/2 teaspoon salt, optional
- 2 cups uncooked noodles
- 1-1/2 cups water
- 1/2 teaspoon oregano
- 1/2 teaspoon garlic powder
- 1/2 teaspoon basil leaves, crushed
- 3/4 cup shredded mozzarella cheese

Direction

- Microwave the ground beef in a 2-qt. casserole dish for 2 minutes; stir and continue to microwave until done, for 1 1/2 minutes more. Let drain thoroughly. Next, put in the leftover ingredients except for cheese; mix well. Then cook on HIGH for 10-1/2 minutes, during cooking, stir twice. Sprinkle over the casserole with cheese; keep cooking on HIGH for 30 seconds, or until the cheese is melted.

Nutrition Information

- Calories:
- Total Fat:
- Sodium:
- Fiber:
- Total Carbohydrate:
- Cholesterol:
- Protein:

---

440. Midwest Meatball Casserole

Serving: 6 servings. | Prep: 40mins | Cook: 20mins | Ready in:

Ingredients

- 2 cans (8 ounces each) tomato sauce, divided
- 1 large egg
- 1/4 cup dry bread crumbs
- 1/4 cup chopped onion
- 1 teaspoon salt
- 1 pound lean ground beef (90% lean)
- 1 package (10 ounces) frozen mixed vegetables
- 1/2 teaspoon dried thyme
- 1/8 teaspoon pepper
- 1 package (16 ounces) frozen shredded hash brown potatoes, thawed
- 1 tablespoon butter, melted
- 3 slices process American cheese, cut into 1/2-inch strips

Direction

- Combine egg, 2 tbsp. of tomato sauce, bread crumbs, salt and onion in a large bowl. Crumble beef over mixture and mix well. Form into balls of 1-inch.
- On a greased rack in a shallow baking pan, place meatballs and bake at 375° for approximately 15 to 20 minutes until meatballs are not pink anymore; drain.
- In the meantime, in a large skillet, combine the rest tomato sauce with seasonings and vegetables. Simmer while covered for around 10 to 15 minutes until heated through; mix in meatballs and leave aside.
- In a greased baking dish of 11x7-inch, place potatoes. Brush with butter and bake at 375° for nearly 15 to 20 minutes until lightly browned. Take away from the oven; put meatball mixture on top. Place cheese strips in a lattice pattern on top. Uncovered while baking for an addition of 20 to 25 minutes until cheese is melted and heated through.

Nutrition Information

- Calories: 310 calories
- Protein: 23g protein.
- Total Fat: 12g fat (6g saturated fat)
- Sodium: 884mg sodium
- Fiber: 4g fiber)

- Total Carbohydrate: 27g carbohydrate (4g sugars
- Cholesterol: 97mg cholesterol

441.   Nacho Mac 'n' Cheese

Serving: 6 servings. | Prep: 5mins | Cook: 20mins | Ready in:

Ingredients

- 3 cups uncooked gemelli or spiral pasta
- 1 pound ground beef
- 2 cups chopped sweet red peppers
- 1/4 cup butter, cubed
- 1/4 cup all-purpose flour
- 1 envelope taco seasoning
- 1/4 teaspoon pepper
- 2-1/4 cups 2% milk
- 2 cups shredded cheddar cheese
- 1 cup frozen corn, thawed
- 1 cup coarsely crushed tortilla chips

Direction

- Based on the instruction on the package, cook gemelli. At the same time, cook red peppers and beef on medium heat in a Dutch oven till meat is not pink anymore; drain.
- Mix in pepper, taco seasoning, flour, and butter till blended. Slowly mix in milk. Boil; cook and stir till becoming thick or for 2 minutes. Take out of the heat. Mix in corn and cheese till cheese is melted.
- Drain gemelli; add to beef mixture and coat by mixing. Drizzle with tortilla chips.

Nutrition Information

- Calories:
- Protein:
- Total Fat:
- Sodium:
- Fiber:

- Total Carbohydrate:
- Cholesterol:

442.   Next Day Meat Loaf Pie

Serving: 4 servings. | Prep: 15mins | Cook: 30mins | Ready in:

Ingredients

- 1-1/3 cups water
- 1/3 cup 2% milk
- 2 tablespoons butter
- 1/2 teaspoon salt
- 1-1/3 cups mashed potato flakes
- 1 can (11 ounces) whole kernel corn, drained
- 1 can (10-3/4 ounces) condensed cream of mushroom soup, undiluted
- 2 slices Old-World Pizza Meat Loaf, cubed
- 1/4 cup shredded cheddar cheese
- 2 tablespoons thinly sliced green onions

Direction

- Mix salt, butter, milk, and water together in a big saucepan; boil it. Mix in potato flakes. Lower the heat; put a cover on and let sit for 5 minutes.
- In the meantime, mix together soup and corn in a big bowl; carefully fold in a meatloaf. Remove into an 8-inch square baking dish coated with cooking spray. Mix green onions and cheese into the potatoes, spread onto the top.
- Bake without a cover at 350° until turning golden brown at the edges and thoroughly heated, about 30-35 minutes.

Nutrition Information

- Calories: 443 calories
- Protein: 18g protein.
- Total Fat: 20g fat (9g saturated fat)
- Sodium: 1597mg sodium

- Fiber: 5g fiber)
- Total Carbohydrate: 43g carbohydrate (6g sugars
- Cholesterol: 59mg cholesterol

443.   Olive Raisin Rice

Serving: 8-10 servings. | Prep: 5mins | Cook: 50mins | Ready in:

Ingredients

- 4 cups water
- 2 cups uncooked long grain rice
- 4 beef bouillon cubes
- 1 pound ground beef
- 3 medium green peppers, chopped
- 3 medium onions, chopped
- 2 garlic cloves, minced
- 1 cup water
- 3/4 cup raisins
- 3/4 cup sliced ripe olives
- 3 bay leaves
- Salt and pepper to taste

Direction

- In a large saucepan, combine the bouillon, rice and water. Allow to boil. Lower heat; cover while simmering for 15 minutes. In the meantime, in a large skillet over medium heat, cook green peppers, beef, garlic and onions until meat is not pink anymore; and then drain. Mix in raisins, water, bay leaves and olives. Simmer while covered for 30 minutes until heated through. Eliminate bay leaves. Stir in pepper, salt and rice.

Nutrition Information

- Calories: 281 calories
- Total Fat: 6g fat (2g saturated fat)
- Sodium: 469mg sodium
- Fiber: 3g fiber)

- Total Carbohydrate: 46g carbohydrate (11g sugars
- Cholesterol: 22mg cholesterol
- Protein: 12g protein.

444. One Pot Casserole

Serving: 4-6 servings. | Prep: 15mins | Cook: 60mins | Ready in:

Ingredients

- 1 pound ground beef, cooked and drained
- 2 medium potatoes, cooked and cubed
- 2 cans (8 ounces each) tomato sauce
- 1 can (15-1/2 ounces) black-eyed peas, rinsed and drained
- 1 can (15 ounces) lima beans, rinsed and drained
- 1 can (8 ounces) mixed vegetables, drained
- 1 medium onion, chopped
- 1/2 teaspoon liquid smoke, optional
- 1/8 teaspoon garlic powder
- Salt and pepper to taste

Direction

- Mix all the ingredients in a big bowl. Then, place the contents into a 13x9-inch baking dish with grease. Cover the baking dish and let it cook in the oven for about an hour at 350°F.

Nutrition Information

- Calories: 288 calories
- Sodium: 700mg sodium
- Fiber: 6g fiber)
- Total Carbohydrate: 34g carbohydrate (4g sugars
- Cholesterol: 37mg cholesterol
- Protein: 21g protein.
- Total Fat: 7g fat (3g saturated fat)

445. Onion Topped Hot Dish

Serving: 6-8 servings. | Prep: 10mins | Cook: 50mins | Ready in:

Ingredients

- 1-1/2 pounds ground beef
- 1 package (16 ounces) frozen California-blend vegetables, thawed
- 1 can (10-3/4 ounces) condensed cheddar cheese soup, undiluted
- 1 cup shredded part-skim mozzarella cheese
- 1/2 cup 2% milk
- 1/2 teaspoon salt
- 1/4 teaspoon pepper
- 1 package (32 ounces) frozen shredded hash brown potatoes, thawed
- 1/4 cup butter, melted
- 1/2 teaspoon seasoned salt
- 20 frozen large onion rings
- 1 cup shredded cheddar cheese

Direction

- In a large skillet over medium heat, cook beef until not pink anymore; drain. Mix in pepper, salt, milk, mozzarella cheese, soup and vegetables. Place into a greased 13x9-inch baking dish. Sprinkle potatoes on top, then drizzle with butter. Sprinkle with onion rings and seasoned salt.
- Cover and bake at 350° until heated through, about 45-50 minutes. Uncover; add cheddar cheese on top. Bake for 3-5 more minutes or until cheese is melted.

Nutrition Information

- Calories: 654 calories
- Sodium: 1006mg sodium
- Fiber: 5g fiber)
- Total Carbohydrate: 51g carbohydrate (3g sugars
- Cholesterol: 104mg cholesterol

- Protein: 31g protein.
- Total Fat: 37g fat (17g saturated fat)

| **446.**   **Pan Burritos** |

Serving: 8-10 servings. | Prep: 35mins | Cook: 35mins | Ready in:

Ingredients

- 2 packages (1-1/2 ounces each) enchilada sauce mix
- 3 cups water
- 1 can (12 ounces) tomato paste
- 1 garlic clove, minced
- 1/4 teaspoon pepper
- Salt to taste
- 2 pounds ground beef
- 9 large flour tortillas (9-inch)
- 4 cups shredded cheddar cheese or Mexican cheese blend
- 1 can (16 ounces) refried beans, warmed
- Taco sauce, sour cream, chili peppers, chopped onion and/or guacamole, optional

Direction

- Mix together the first six ingredients in a saucepan. Let it simmer for 15 to 20 minutes.
- Brown the beef in a skillet. Let it drain and mix in 1/3 of the sauce. On the bottom of a 13x9-in. greased baking pan, spread another 1/3 of the sauce.
- Put three tortillas on top of the sauce and tear to fit the bottom of the baking pan. Place half of the meat mixture on the tortillas and drizzle with 1 and a half cup of cheese. Put in another three tortillas. Over the tortillas, spread the refried beans. Put the rest of the meat on top. Drizzle again with 1 and a half cup of cheese. Put in the rest of the tortillas and put the rest of the sauce on top. Drizzle with the remaining cheese.
- Without cover, bake for 35 to 40 minutes at 350°. Allow to rest for 10 minutes and cut. If

you want, you can serve it with guacamole (or not), chopped onion, chili peppers, sour cream and taco sauce.

Nutrition Information

- Calories: 578 calories
- Sodium: 1421mg sodium
- Fiber: 11g fiber)
- Total Carbohydrate: 46g carbohydrate (6g sugars
- Cholesterol: 96mg cholesterol
- Protein: 35g protein.
- Total Fat: 25g fat (14g saturated fat)

| **447.**   **Pizza Rice Casserole** |

Serving: 4 servings. | Prep: 25mins | Cook: 30mins | Ready in:

Ingredients

- 3/4 pound ground beef
- 1 medium onion, chopped
- 2 cans (8 ounces each) tomato sauce
- 1 teaspoon sugar
- 1 teaspoon salt
- 1 teaspoon dried parsley flakes
- 1/4 teaspoon garlic powder
- 1/4 teaspoon oregano
- Dash pepper
- 2 cups cooked rice
- 1/2 cup 4% cottage cheese
- 1/2 cup shredded part-skim mozzarella cheese

Direction

- In a big skillet on medium heat, cook onion and beef until meat is not pink anymore; drain. Put in pepper, oregano, garlic powder, parsley, salt, sugar, and tomato sauce. Heat to a boil. Lower heat, put cover and simmer for 15 minutes.

- Mix cottage cheese and rice together; spoon half into an oiled 11x7-inch baking dish. Arrange 1/2 of meat mixture over top. Repeat layers. Top with mozzarella cheese.
- Bake at 325 degrees without cover for 30-35 minutes or until bubbly and heated through.

Nutrition Information

- Calories: 335 calories
- Sodium: 1075mg sodium
- Fiber: 2g fiber)
- Total Carbohydrate: 31g carbohydrate (6g sugars
- Cholesterol: 56mg cholesterol
- Protein: 25g protein.
- Total Fat: 11g fat (6g saturated fat)

448.   Pizza Tater Tot Casserole

Serving: 8 servings. | Prep: 10mins | Cook: 35mins | Ready in:

Ingredients

- 1-1/2 pounds ground beef
- 1 medium green pepper, chopped, optional
- 1 medium onion, chopped
- 1/2 pound sliced fresh mushrooms
- 1 can (15 ounces) pizza sauce
- 1 teaspoon dried basil
- 3 cups shredded part-skim mozzarella cheese
- 1 package (32 ounces) frozen Tater Tots
- 1 cup shredded cheddar cheese

Direction

- Cook mushrooms, beef, onion, and green pepper in a big frying pan on medium heat until beef is not pink; drain excess grease. Add basil and pizza sauce. Move to a 3-qt. greased dish. Put potatoes and mozzarella on top. Do not cover; bake in a 400-degree oven until potatoes are light brown, 30-35 minutes.

Sprinkle on cheddar cheese; bake until cheese melts, 5 minutes.

Nutrition Information

- Calories: 572 calories
- Total Carbohydrate: 41g carbohydrate (7g sugars
- Cholesterol: 96mg cholesterol
- Protein: 36g protein.
- Total Fat: 32g fat (13g saturated fat)
- Sodium: 1081mg sodium
- Fiber: 5g fiber)

449.   Pizza Tot Casserole

Serving: 6-8 servings. | Prep: 10mins | Cook: 30mins | Ready in:

Ingredients

- 1 pound ground beef
- 1 medium green pepper, chopped
- 1 medium onion, chopped
- 1 can (10-3/4 ounces) condensed tomato soup, undiluted
- 1 jar (4-1/2 ounces) sliced mushrooms, drained
- 1 teaspoon Italian seasoning
- 2 cups shredded part-skim mozzarella cheese
- 1 package (32 ounces) frozen Tater Tots

Direction

- Cook pepper, onion, and beef on medium heat in a big frying pan until beef is not pink. Drain excess grease. Add Italian seasoning, mushrooms, and soup. Move to a 13x9-in. greased pan. Top with potatoes and cheese. Do not cover; bake in a 400-degree oven until golden brown, 30-35 minutes.

Nutrition Information

- Calories: 399 calories
- Sodium: 954mg sodium
- Fiber: 4g fiber)
- Total Carbohydrate: 38g carbohydrate (5g sugars
- Cholesterol: 46mg cholesterol
- Protein: 21g protein.
- Total Fat: 21g fat (7g saturated fat)

---

450.   Poor Man's Dinner

Serving: 6 servings. | Prep: 20mins | Cook: 01hours15mins | Ready in:

Ingredients

- 1 pound ground beef
- 1/4 teaspoon pepper
- 1/4 teaspoon garlic powder
- 5 large potatoes, peeled and sliced
- 1 large onion, sliced
- 2 cans (10-3/4 ounces each) condensed cream of mushroom soup, undiluted
- 1/2 cup 2% milk
- Minced fresh parsley

Direction

- Over medium heat in a large skillet, cook beef till no longer pink; drain. Add in garlic powder and pepper for seasoning. Layer the beef, potatoes and onion slices in a shallow baking dish of 2 quarts. Mix milk and soup together; pour over all.
- Cover up and bake at 350° until potatoes are tender, about 1-1/4 hours. Sprinkle with parsley.

Nutrition Information

- Calories: 272 calories
- Cholesterol: 39mg cholesterol
- Protein: 17g protein.
- Total Fat: 9g fat (4g saturated fat)

- Sodium: 410mg sodium
- Fiber: 3g fiber)
- Total Carbohydrate: 30g carbohydrate (4g sugars

---

451.   Pork 'n' Beans Bake

Serving: 6-8 servings. | Prep: 20mins | Cook: 30mins | Ready in:

Ingredients

- 1-1/2 pounds ground beef
- 1 medium onion, chopped
- 1 medium green pepper, chopped
- 3/4 cup chopped celery
- 2 cans (15-3/4 ounces each) pork and beans
- 1 can (8 ounces) tomato sauce
- 1 tablespoon sugar
- 1 tablespoon ground mustard
- 1 tablespoon white vinegar
- 1/4 teaspoon dried thyme

Direction

- In a large skillet over medium heat, cook onion, beef, celery and green pepper until meat is not pink anymore; and then drain. Add the rest ingredients.
- Remove to a greased baking dish 3-quart. Uncovered while baking at 375° for around 30 to 35 minutes until heated through.

Nutrition Information

- Calories: 213 calories
- Sodium: 380mg sodium
- Fiber: 4g fiber)
- Total Carbohydrate: 16g carbohydrate (7g sugars
- Cholesterol: 42mg cholesterol
- Protein: 19g protein.
- Total Fat: 8g fat (3g saturated fat)

Serving: 4 servings. | Prep: 20mins | Cook: 01hours10mins | Ready in:

Ingredients

- 1 pound lean ground beef (90% lean)
- 1/2 cup chopped onion
- 1/2 cup chopped celery
- 2 tablespoons chopped celery leaves
- 1 can (10-3/4 ounces) condensed cream of mushroom soup, undiluted
- 1/2 cup milk
- 1 teaspoon Worcestershire sauce
- 1/2 teaspoon pepper
- 4 medium potatoes, peeled and thinly sliced
- 1 teaspoon salt, optional

Direction

- In the skillet, cook celery leaves, celery, onion and beef on medium heat till the veggies soften and the meat is not pink anymore; drain off. Take out of heat; whisk in the pepper, Worcestershire sauce, milk and soup. Add 1/2 potatoes into the greased 2-quart baking dish; drizzle with half tsp. of the salt if you want. Add 1/2 beef mixture on top.
- Repeat the layers. Keep covered and bake at 400 degrees till potatoes soften or for 70 minutes.

Nutrition Information

- Calories: 353 calories
- Total Carbohydrate: 32g carbohydrate (0 sugars
- Cholesterol: 48mg cholesterol
- Protein: 28g protein. Diabetic Exchanges: 3 meat
- Total Fat: 12g fat (0 saturated fat)
- Sodium: 428mg sodium
- Fiber: 3g fiber)

Serving: 8-10 servings. | Prep: 10mins | Cook: 35mins | Ready in:

Ingredients

- 2 pounds ground beef
- 2 cans (8 ounces each) tomato sauce
- 1 cup sliced fresh mushrooms, optional
- 2 garlic cloves, minced
- Salt and pepper to taste
- 4 cups hot mashed potatoes (prepared with milk and butter)
- 2 cups shredded cheddar cheese

Direction

- In a big skillet over medium heat, cook beef till not pink anymore; let drain. Mix in the pepper, salt, garlic, tomato sauce, and mushrooms if wanted.
- Put to a greased 13x9-inch baking dish. Put potatoes on top; scatter cheese over. Bake while uncovered at 350° for about 35-40 minutes or until heated through and cheese becomes melted.

Nutrition Information

- Calories: 353 calories
- Sodium: 531mg sodium
- Fiber: 2g fiber)
- Total Carbohydrate: 16g carbohydrate (1g sugars
- Cholesterol: 94mg cholesterol
- Protein: 25g protein.
- Total Fat: 21g fat (12g saturated fat)

Serving: 6-8 servings. | Prep: 10mins | Cook: 60mins | Ready in:

Ingredients

- 1 pound ground beef
- 1 medium onion, chopped
- 1 can (28 ounces) diced tomatoes, undrained
- 1 can (16 ounces) sauerkraut, rinsed and drained
- 1-1/2 cups cooked rice
- 1 medium green pepper, chopped

Direction

- In a skillet, brown onion and ground beef; drain. Put in the remaining ingredients; place to a baking dish of 2 quarts. Cover up and bake at 350° for 60 minutes.

Nutrition Information

- Calories: 170 calories
- Sodium: 594mg sodium
- Fiber: 3g fiber)
- Total Carbohydrate: 18g carbohydrate (4g sugars
- Cholesterol: 28mg cholesterol
- Protein: 12g protein.
- Total Fat: 5g fat (2g saturated fat)

---

455.   Quick Tomato Mac 'n' Beef

Serving: 4 servings. | Prep: 20mins | Cook: 10mins | Ready in:

Ingredients

- 1 pound ground beef
- 1 cup chopped onion
- Salt and pepper to taste
- 1 can (14-1/2 ounces) diced tomatoes with garlic and onion, undrained
- 1 cup water
- 1 cup uncooked elbow macaroni
- 1 cup shredded cheddar cheese

- Sliced green onions and sour cream, optional

Direction

- Cook onion and beef in a big skillet on medium heat until meat is not pink; strain. Add pepper and salt to season. Stir in water and tomatoes; boil. Mix in macaroni.
- Cover then simmer for 10 minutes or until macaroni is soft. Mix in cheese. Decorate with sour cream and onions if wished.

Nutrition Information

- Calories:
- Sodium:
- Fiber:
- Total Carbohydrate:
- Cholesterol:
- Protein:
- Total Fat:

---

456.   Red And Green Casserole

Serving: 4-6 servings. | Prep: 15mins | Cook: 30mins | Ready in:

Ingredients

- 1-1/2 pounds ground beef
- 2 medium onions, chopped
- 1 green pepper, chopped
- 1 sweet red pepper, chopped
- 2 cans (10-3/4 ounces each) condensed tomato soup, undiluted
- 1/4 cup water
- 1 teaspoon sugar
- 1/2 teaspoon chili powder
- Salt and pepper to taste
- 8 ounces wide noodles, cooked and drained
- 1 cup shredded cheddar cheese

Direction

- In a skillet, cook peppers, onions and beef until the vegetables are tender. Drain well. Mix in pepper, salt, chilli powder, sugar, water and soup. Mix in noodles. Place into a greased 13x9-inch baking dish. Sprinkle cheese on top. Bake with no cover at 350° for half an hour.

Nutrition Information

- Calories:
- Sodium:
- Fiber:
- Total Carbohydrate:
- Cholesterol:
- Protein:
- Total Fat:

Nutrition Information

- Calories:
- Total Carbohydrate:
- Cholesterol:
- Protein:
- Total Fat:
- Sodium:
- Fiber:

457. Sauerkraut Beef Bake

Serving: 6 servings. | Prep: 15mins | Cook: 60mins | Ready in:

Ingredients

- 1 pound ground beef
- 1 can (27 ounces) sauerkraut, rinsed and well drained
- 1/2 cup uncooked instant rice
- 1 can (10-3/4 ounces) condensed cream of mushroom soup, undiluted
- 1 soup can water
- 2 tablespoons onion soup mix
- 1 can (4 ounces) mushroom stems and pieces, drained, optional

Direction

- In a skillet over medium heat, cook beef until not pink anymore; drain.
- Combine soup mix, water, soup, rice, sauerkraut and beef together in a greased 2-quart baking dish. If desired, put in mushrooms. Cover and bake at 350° until heated through, about 60 minutes.

458. Sausage Hot Dish

Serving: 8 servings. | Prep: 20mins | Cook: 35mins | Ready in:

Ingredients

- 1 pound lean ground beef
- 3 medium potatoes, peeled and cut into 1/4-inch slices
- 2 medium carrots, thinly sliced
- 1 small onion, thinly sliced
- 1 teaspoon dried thyme
- 1 teaspoon salt
- 1/8 teaspoon pepper
- 1/4 cup water
- 1 pound Jones No Sugar Pork Sausage Roll sausage
- 2 cups shredded cheddar cheese

Direction

- In a 2-1/2-quart microwave-safe dish, crumble half of the beef. Layer with 1/2 potatoes, carrots and onion. Dust with pepper, salt, and half of the thyme. Redo layers. Pour water atop. Microwave, covered, at 70% power for about 16 minutes. Meanwhile, in a frying pan over medium heat, cook sausage till not pink anymore; drain. Pour over beef mixture. Microwave while uncovered on High for about 5-7 minutes. Dust with cheese. Heat for 30 more seconds. Allow to rest for 5 minutes before serving.

Nutrition Information

- Calories: 358 calories
- Protein: 22g protein.
- Total Fat: 23g fat (12g saturated fat)
- Sodium: 730mg sodium
- Fiber: 1g fiber)
- Total Carbohydrate: 15g carbohydrate (3g sugars
- Cholesterol: 85mg cholesterol

459.   Six Layer Dinner

Serving: 6-8 servings. | Prep: 5mins | Cook: 01hours20mins | Ready in:

Ingredients

- 1-1/2 pounds ground beef
- 2 medium onions, thinly sliced
- 3 medium potatoes, peeled and thinly sliced
- 1 large green pepper, chopped
- 1-1/2 teaspoons salt
- 1/2 teaspoon pepper
- 2 celery ribs, chopped
- 1 can (14-1/2 ounces) stewed tomatoes
- 1/4 teaspoon dried basil

Direction

- In a Dutch oven over medium heat, cook beef till no longer pink; drain. Layer beef with onions, potatoes and green pepper, add pepper and salt into each layer lightly to taste. Add in basil, tomatoes and celery.
- Let it come to a boil. Lower the heat; cover up and let it simmer until vegetables are tender, about 1 hour.

Nutrition Information

- Calories: 233 calories
- Total Fat: 8g fat (3g saturated fat)
- Sodium: 607mg sodium
- Fiber: 3g fiber)

- Total Carbohydrate: 23g carbohydrate (7g sugars
- Cholesterol: 42mg cholesterol
- Protein: 18g protein.

460.   Skillet Casserole

Serving: 4 servings. | Prep: 20mins | Cook: 15mins | Ready in:

Ingredients

- 1 pound ground beef
- 2 medium onions, diced
- 1medium green pepper, diced
- 4 medium potatoes, peeled, cut into 1/2-inch cubes and parboiled
- 2 medium tomatoes, seeded and chopped
- 1 can (10-3/4 ounces) condensed cream of chicken soup, undiluted
- 1/4 cup chili sauce
- 3/4 teaspoon salt
- 1/4 teaspoon pepper
- 1/4 cup grated Parmesan cheese

Direction

- In a large frying pan, cook green pepper, onions and beef over medium heat till meat is not pink anymore; drain. Remove and leave aside. In the same pan, cook ground beef until browned; let drain. Mix in the pepper, salt, chili sauce, soup, tomatoes and potatoes.
- Put to a greased 13x9-inch baking dish. Dust with Parmesan. Bake while uncovered at 350° for 15 minutes or until bubbly.

Nutrition Information

- Calories: 460 calories
- Protein: 28g protein.
- Total Fat: 16g fat (7g saturated fat)
- Sodium: 1432mg sodium
- Fiber: 6g fiber)

- Total Carbohydrate: 50g carbohydrate (13g sugars
- Cholesterol: 66mg cholesterol

Serving: 8 servings. | Prep: 15mins | Cook: 25mins | Ready in:

Ingredients

- 1-1/2 pounds ground beef
- 1 can (15-1/2 ounces) sloppy joe sauce
- 2 cups shredded cheddar cheese
- 2 cups biscuit/baking mix
- 2 large eggs, lightly beaten
- 1 cup 2% milk
- 1 tablespoon sesame seeds

Direction

- In a large skillet, cook the beef over medium heat until there is not pink anymore; and then drain. Add in sloppy joe sauce. Place to a lightly greased baking dish of 13x9-inch; have cheese for sprinkling.
- In a large bowl, combine milk, eggs and biscuit mix just until blended. Pour over cheese; use sesame seeds to sprinkle. Uncovered while baking at 400° for nearly 25 minutes until it has the color of golden brown.

Nutrition Information

- Calories: 423 calories
- Protein: 27g protein.
- Total Fat: 23g fat (12g saturated fat)
- Sodium: 961mg sodium
- Fiber: 1g fiber)
- Total Carbohydrate: 26g carbohydrate (6g sugars
- Cholesterol: 129mg cholesterol

Serving: 4 servings. | Prep: 20mins | Cook: 30mins | Ready in:

Ingredients

- 1 pound ground beef
- 1 medium onion, chopped
- 2 cans (14-1/2 ounces each) cut green beans, drained
- 1 can (8 ounces) tomato sauce
- 1 teaspoon salt
- 1/4 teaspoon pepper
- 2-1/2 cups hot mashed potatoes (prepared with milk and butter)
- 1/4 cup butter, melted
- Paprika

Direction

- In a large skillet over the medium heat, cook onion and beef until the beef is no longer pink; drain. Mix in pepper, salt, tomato sauce and beans.
- Place into a greased shallow baking dish of 2 quarts. Add eight mounds of mashed potatoes on top. Add in a drizzle of butter; sprinkle with the paprika. Bake with no cover, at 350° until potatoes are browned, about half an hour.

Nutrition Information

- Calories: 463 calories
- Protein: 25g protein.
- Total Fat: 27g fat (15g saturated fat)
- Sodium: 1760mg sodium
- Fiber: 6g fiber)
- Total Carbohydrate: 32g carbohydrate (6g sugars
- Cholesterol: 102mg cholesterol

463.   Sombrero Casserole

*Serving: 6 servings. | Prep: 25mins | Cook: 35mins
| Ready in:*

Ingredients

- 1 pound ground beef
- 1 small onion, chopped
- 1 small green pepper, chopped
- 2 packages (8-1/2 ounces each) cornbread/muffin mix
- 1 can (14-3/4 ounces) cream-style corn
- 2 large eggs
- 4 cups shredded cheddar cheese, divided
- 1 cup picante sauce

Direction

- Combine green pepper, onion and beef in a skillet, cook on medium heat until the pink color disappears from meat; drain and set aside. Combine eggs, corn and cornbread mixes in a bowl; mix properly.
- In a greased 13x9 baking dish, spread half of the corn mixture, place picante sauce, 3 cups of cheese and meat mixture on top. Top with remaining cornbread mixture; place remaining cheese on top. Bake when uncover for 35 to 40 minutes at 350° or until a knife is still clean after being inserted into the center. Allow to stand for 5 minutes and serve.

Nutrition Information

- Calories: 643 calories
- Total Carbohydrate: 49g carbohydrate (14g sugars
- Cholesterol: 197mg cholesterol
- Protein: 36g protein.
- Total Fat: 34g fat (21g saturated fat)
- Sodium: 1230mg sodium
- Fiber: 2g fiber)

464.   Southwestern Casserole

*Serving: 2 casseroles (6 servings each). | Prep: 15mins |
Cook: 40mins | Ready in:*

Ingredients

- 2 cups (8 ounces) uncooked elbow macaroni
- 2 pounds ground beef
- 1 large onion, chopped
- 2 garlic cloves, minced
- 2 cans (14-1/2 ounces each) diced tomatoes, undrained
- 1 can (16 ounces) kidney beans, rinsed and drained
- 1 can (6 ounces) tomato paste
- 1 can (4 ounces) chopped green chilies, drained
- 1-1/2 teaspoons salt
- 1 teaspoon chili powder
- 1/2 teaspoon ground cumin
- 1/2 teaspoon pepper
- 2 cups shredded Monterey Jack cheese
- 2 jalapeno peppers, seeded and chopped

Direction

- Based on the instruction on the package, cook macaroni. At the same time, cook onion and beef on medium heat in a big saucepan, crumbling beef, till meat is not pink anymore. Put in garlic; cook for 1 minute more. Drain. Mix in the following 8 ingredients. Boil. Lower the heat; let it simmer, while uncovered, for 10 minutes. Drain macaroni; mix into beef mixture.
- Preheat oven to 375 degrees. Move macaroni mixture into 2 greased 2-qt. baking dishes. Add jalapenos and cheese on top. Keep it covered and baked at 375 degrees for half an hour. Uncover it; bake till bubbly and thoroughly heated for roughly 10 minutes more. Serve one casserole. Cool the second; keep it covered and frozen for the maximum of 3 months.
- To use frozen casserole: Thaw in the fridge 8 hours. Preheat the oven to 375 degrees. Take out of the fridge half an hour prior to baking.

Keep it covered and baked, increasing time as needed to heat through and for a thermometer inserted in the middle to reach 165 degrees, 20 to 25 minutes.

Nutrition Information

- Calories: 321 calories
- Cholesterol: 64mg cholesterol
- Protein: 24g protein.
- Total Fat: 15g fat (7g saturated fat)
- Sodium: 673mg sodium
- Fiber: 4g fiber)
- Total Carbohydrate: 23g carbohydrate (5g sugars

465.　Southwestern Taco Casserole

Serving: 6-8 servings. | Prep: 20mins | Cook: 20mins | Ready in:

Ingredients

- 2-1/2 pounds ground beef
- 2 envelopes taco seasoning
- 2/3 cup water
- 1 can (16 ounces) kidney beans, rinsed and drained
- 1 cup shredded Monterey Jack or pepper jack cheese
- 2 large eggs, lightly beaten
- 1 cup 2% milk
- 1-1/2 cups biscuit/baking mix
- 1 cup (8 ounces) sour cream
- 1 cup shredded cheddar cheese
- 2 cups shredded lettuce
- 1 medium tomato, diced
- 1 can (2-1/4 ounces) sliced ripe olives, drained

Direction

- Cook ground beef in a frying pan on medium heat until not pink. Drain excess grease. Mix in

water and taco seasoning. Heat to a boil then decrease heat and keep a slow boil for 5 minutes. Mix in beans. Put the beef mixture in an 8-in. greased square pan. Spread Monterey Jack cheese on top. Mix biscuit mix, eggs, and milk in large mixing bowl. Pour the mixture on top of cheese. Do not cover; bake in a 400-degree oven until slightly brown and a knife poked into the middle comes out clean, 25 minutes. Put the sour cream on top and evenly spread. Eat topped with olives, cheddar cheese, lettuce, and tomato.

Nutrition Information

- Calories: 601 calories
- Sodium: 1544mg sodium
- Fiber: 4g fiber)
- Total Carbohydrate: 35g carbohydrate (4g sugars
- Cholesterol: 172mg cholesterol
- Protein: 40g protein.
- Total Fat: 32g fat (17g saturated fat)

466.　Spaghetti Beef Casserole

Serving: 2 casseroles (8 servings each). | Prep: 25mins | Cook: 20mins | Ready in:

Ingredients

- 1-1/2 pounds uncooked spaghetti
- 3 pounds ground beef
- 1 cup chopped onion
- 2/3 cup chopped green pepper
- 1 teaspoon minced garlic
- 2 cans (10-3/4 ounces each) condensed cream of mushroom soup, undiluted
- 2 cans (10-3/4 ounces each) condensed tomato soup, undiluted
- 1-1/3 cups water
- 1 can (8 ounces) mushroom stems and pieces, drained
- 3 cups shredded cheddar cheese, divided

Direction

- Cook spaghetti as directed in the package. Meanwhile, cook the green pepper, onion and beef in two big frying pans over medium heat until meat is not pink anymore. Put in garlic; cook for 1 more minute. Let it drain. Mix in the mushrooms, water and soups.
- Drain spaghetti. Put in 1 cup of cheese and spaghetti to beef mixture. Put to two greased 13x9-inch baking dishes. Dust with the leftover cheese. Cover and freeze one casserole for up to 3 months. Bake the remaining casserole without cover at 350° for about 20-25 minutes or until cheese becomes melted.
- To use frozen casserole: Let it thaw in the fridge overnight. Thirty minutes before baking, take it out from the refrigerator. Bake, covered, at 350° for 1 hour to 1 and a quarter hours or until heated through and cheese becomes melted.

Nutrition Information

- Calories: 434 calories
- Total Fat: 17g fat (8g saturated fat)
- Sodium: 732mg sodium
- Fiber: 3g fiber)
- Total Carbohydrate: 43g carbohydrate (6g sugars
- Cholesterol: 66mg cholesterol
- Protein: 26g protein.

---

467. Spaghetti Goulash

Serving: 12-16 servings. | Prep: 25mins | Cook: 35mins | Ready in:

Ingredients

- 1 package (16 ounces) thin spaghetti, broken in half
- 3/4 pound ground beef

- 3/4 pound Jones No Sugar Pork Sausage Roll sausage
- 1 medium green pepper, chopped
- 1 medium onion, chopped
- 2 cans (14-1/2 ounces each) diced tomatoes
- 1 bottle (12 ounces) chili sauce
- 1 can (8 ounces) mushroom stems and pieces, drained
- 1 tablespoon Worcestershire sauce
- 1 teaspoon salt
- 1/4 teaspoon pepper
- 1 cup shredded cheddar cheese, divided

Direction

- Follow directions on package to cook spaghetti. Drain off water. Cook sausage, onion, beef, and green pepper in a big frying pan on medium heat until meat is not pink. Drain excess grease. Mix in tomatoes, cover, and gently boil for 45 minutes. Take away from heat. Mix in pepper, chili sauce, salt, spaghetti, mushrooms, and Worcestershire sauce. Move to a 4-qt. greased dish or put in two 2-qt. greased dishes. Sprinkle cheese on. Cover; bake in a 350-degree oven until cooked through, 35-40 minutes.

Nutrition Information

- Calories: 240 calories
- Total Fat: 8g fat (4g saturated fat)
- Sodium: 676mg sodium
- Fiber: 2g fiber)
- Total Carbohydrate: 30g carbohydrate (7g sugars
- Cholesterol: 26mg cholesterol
- Protein: 11g protein.

---

468. Spaghetti Squash Meatball Casserole

Serving: 6 servings. | Prep: 35mins | Cook: 30mins | Ready in:

Ingredients

- 1 medium spaghetti squash (about 4 pounds)
- 1/2 teaspoon salt, divided
- 1/2 teaspoon fennel seed
- 1/4 teaspoon ground coriander
- 1/4 teaspoon dried basil
- 1/4 teaspoon dried oregano
- 1 pound lean ground beef (90% lean)
- 2 teaspoons olive oil
- 1 medium onion, chopped
- 1 garlic clove, minced
- 2 cups chopped collard greens
- 1 cup chopped fresh spinach
- 1 cup reduced-fat ricotta cheese
- 2 plum tomatoes, chopped
- 1 cup pasta sauce
- 1 cup shredded part-skim mozzarella cheese

Direction

- Halve squash lengthwise; throw seeds. On a microwave-safe plate, put the halves, cut side facing down. Allow to microwave on high without cover for 15 to 20 minutes, till soft. Let cool slightly.
- Preheat an oven to 350°. Combine quarter teaspoon salt with the rest of the seasonings; put to beef, combining slightly yet well. Form into 1-1/2-inch rounds. Brown meatballs in a big skillet over medium heat; take off from pan.
- Heat oil in same pan over medium heat; sauté the onion for 3 to 4 minutes till soft. Put the garlic; let cook and mix for a minute. Mix in the rest of the salt, ricotta cheese, spinach and collard greens; take off from heat.
- Part strands of squash spaghetti with a fork; mix into greens mixture. Put to an oiled baking dish, 13x9-inch in size. Put cheese, sauce, meatballs and tomatoes on top. Allow to bake without cover for 30 to 35 minutes, till meatballs are cooked completely.

Nutrition Information

- Calories: 362 calories

- Protein: 26g protein. Diabetic Exchanges: 3 lean meat
- Total Fat: 16g fat (6g saturated fat)
- Sodium: 618mg sodium
- Fiber: 7g fiber)
- Total Carbohydrate: 32g carbohydrate (7g sugars
- Cholesterol: 69mg cholesterol

469.   Spaghetti Style Rice

Serving: 4 servings. | Prep: 10mins | Cook: 15mins | Ready in:

Ingredients

- 1 pound ground beef, cooked and drained
- 1 jar (15-1/2 ounces) garden-style spaghetti sauce
- 1-1/2 cups shredded Monterey Jack cheese
- 1 cup uncooked instant rice
- 1 can (4 ounces) mushroom stems and pieces, drained

Direction

- In a large bowl, combine all ingredients. Place to a greased baking dish of 11x7-inch. Uncovered while baking at 375° for around 15 minutes; stir. Bake for an addition of 10 minutes until rice is tender.

Nutrition Information

- Calories: 508 calories
- Cholesterol: 98mg cholesterol
- Protein: 35g protein.
- Total Fat: 26g fat (13g saturated fat)
- Sodium: 821mg sodium
- Fiber: 3g fiber)
- Total Carbohydrate: 34g carbohydrate (9g sugars

470. Speedy Beef Hash

Serving: 4 servings. | Prep: 15mins | Cook: 15mins | Ready in:

Ingredients

- 1 pound ground beef
- 1 medium onion, chopped
- 3 cups frozen O'Brien potatoes, thawed
- 1/2 teaspoon salt
- 1/4 teaspoon pepper
- 1 cup salsa
- 1/2 cup shredded Colby-Monterey Jack cheese
- Sliced green onions and ripe olives, optional

Direction

- Cook onion and beef in a big frying pan over medium heat until the meat is not pink anymore; strain. Mix in pepper, salt, and potatoes. Stir and cook over medium-high heat until the potatoes turn light brown, about 7-9 minutes.
- Mix in salsa. Sprinkle cheese over, cook until melted. Sprinkle olives and onions over if you want.

Nutrition Information

- Calories: 373 calories
- Protein: 26g protein.
- Total Fat: 14g fat (8g saturated fat)
- Sodium: 784mg sodium
- Fiber: 6g fiber)
- Total Carbohydrate: 32g carbohydrate (4g sugars
- Cholesterol: 68mg cholesterol

471. Spice Baked Rice

Serving: 4-6 servings. | Prep: 25mins | Cook: 45mins | Ready in:

Ingredients

- 1 pound ground beef
- 1 medium green pepper, chopped
- 1 medium onion, chopped
- 3 cups cooked long grain rice
- 1 can (14-1/2 ounces) stewed tomatoes
- 1-1/2 cups tomato juice
- 1 teaspoon salt
- 1 teaspoon chili powder
- 1 teaspoon ground mustard
- 1 teaspoon dried oregano
- 1/2 teaspoon hot pepper sauce
- 1 cup shredded cheddar cheese

Direction

- Cook onion, green pepper and beef in a skillet over medium heat till meat is not pink anymore pink; drain. Put in the following 8 ingredients.
- Move into one greased 2-qt. baking dish. Keep it covered and baked at 350 degrees for 35 minutes. Uncover it and drizzle with cheese. Bake till cheese becomes melted or for 10 minutes more.

Nutrition Information

- Calories: 337 calories
- Sodium: 908mg sodium
- Fiber: 2g fiber)
- Total Carbohydrate: 35g carbohydrate (8g sugars
- Cholesterol: 57mg cholesterol
- Protein: 21g protein.
- Total Fat: 13g fat (7g saturated fat)

472. Spicy Cabbage Casserole

Serving: 8-10 servings. | Prep: 10mins | Cook: 01hours30mins | Ready in:

Ingredients

- 1 small head cabbage, finely chopped

- 1 pound ground beef
- 1 can (10-3/4 ounces) condensed French onion soup, undiluted
- 1 can (14-1/2 ounces) Mexican diced tomatoes, undrained
- 1 cup uncooked long grain rice
- 1 egg, lightly beaten
- 1 large onion, chopped
- 1 medium green pepper, chopped
- 1/2 cup vegetable oil
- 1 tablespoon garlic salt
- 1 tablespoon chili powder
- 1 tablespoon salt
- Dash cayenne pepper

Direction

- Stir all ingredients well in a big bowl. Add to a small-sized covered roasting pan. Bake at 350 degrees for 1-1/2 hours without lifting the lid.

Nutrition Information

- Calories: 321 calories
- Cholesterol: 53mg cholesterol
- Protein: 13g protein.
- Total Fat: 18g fat (4g saturated fat)
- Sodium: 1712mg sodium
- Fiber: 4g fiber)
- Total Carbohydrate: 27g carbohydrate (7g sugars

473.   Spicy Enchilada Casserole

Serving: 2 casseroles (4 servings each). | Prep: 20mins | Cook: 40mins | Ready in:

Ingredients

- 1-1/2 pounds ground beef
- 1 large onion, chopped
- 1 cup water
- 2 to 3 tablespoons chili powder

- 1-1/2 teaspoons salt
- 1/2 teaspoon pepper
- 1/4 teaspoon garlic powder
- 2 cups salsa, divided
- 10 flour tortillas (8 inches), cut into 3/4-inch strips, divided
- 1 cup (8 ounces) sour cream
- 2 cans (15-1/4 ounces each) whole kernel corn, drained
- 4 cups shredded part-skim mozzarella cheese

Direction

- Cook onion and beef on medium heat in a big skillet till meat is not pink anymore; drain. Mix in garlic powder, pepper, salt, chili powder, and water. Boil. Lower the heat; let it simmer, while uncovered, for 10 minutes.
- Add a quarter cup of salsa in each of two greased 8-in. square baking dishes. Add a quarter cup of salsa and a quarter of tortillas on top of each.
- Separate corn, sour cream and meat mixture among the two casseroles. Add cheese, salsa and the rest of the tortillas on top.
- Keep it covered and frozen one casserole for maximum of 1 month. Keep it covered and baked second casserole at 350 degrees for 35 minutes. Uncover it; bake till thoroughly heated or for 5 to 10 minutes more.
- To use frozen casserole: Thaw in fridge for 1 day. Take out of the fridge half an hour prior to baking. Bake following the directions above.

Nutrition Information

- Calories: 592 calories
- Total Carbohydrate: 45g carbohydrate (8g sugars
- Cholesterol: 94mg cholesterol
- Protein: 37g protein.
- Total Fat: 26g fat (13g saturated fat)
- Sodium: 1535mg sodium
- Fiber: 4g fiber)

474. Spicy Nacho Bake

Serving: 2 casseroles (15 servings each). | Prep: 60mins | Cook: 20mins | Ready in:

Ingredients

- 2 pounds ground beef
- 2 large onions, chopped
- 2 large green peppers, chopped
- 2 cans (28 ounces each) diced tomatoes, undrained
- 2 cans (16 ounces each) hot chili beans, undrained
- 2 cans (15 ounces each) black beans, rinsed and drained
- 2 cans (11 ounces each) whole kernel corn, drained
- 2 cans (8 ounces each) tomato sauce
- 2 envelopes taco seasoning
- 2 packages (13 ounces each) spicy nacho-flavored tortilla chips
- 4 cups shredded cheddar cheese

Direction

- Cook green peppers, onions, and beef on medium heat in a Dutch oven till meat is not pink anymore; drain. Mix in taco seasoning, tomato sauce, corn, beans, and tomatoes. Boil. Lower heat; let it simmer, while uncovered, for half an hour (mixture might be thin).
- In each of 2 greased 13x9-in. baking dishes, layer 5 cups of chips and 4-2/3 cups of meat mixture. Repeat the layers. Add 2 cups of cheese and 4 cups of chips on top of each.
- Bake, while uncovered, at 350 degrees till becoming golden brown in color or for 20 to 25 minutes.

Nutrition Information

- Calories: 314 calories
- Cholesterol: 31mg cholesterol
- Protein: 14g protein.
- Total Fat: 13g fat (6g saturated fat)
- Sodium: 845mg sodium

- Fiber: 5g fiber)
- Total Carbohydrate: 33g carbohydrate (5g sugars

475. Spinach Beef Biscuit Bake

Serving: 6 servings. | Prep: 15mins | Cook: 25mins | Ready in:

Ingredients

- 2 tubes (6 ounces each) refrigerated buttermilk biscuits
- 1-1/2 pounds ground beef
- 1/2 cup finely chopped onion
- 2 eggs
- 1 package (10 ounces) frozen chopped spinach, thawed and squeezed dry
- 1 can (4 ounces) mushroom stems and pieces, drained
- 4 ounces crumbled feta cheese
- 1/4 cup grated Parmesan cheese
- 1-1/2 teaspoons garlic powder
- Salt and pepper to taste
- 1 to 2 tablespoons butter, melted

Direction

- Flatten and pack the biscuits on the sides and bottom of an oil 11-in by 7-in baking dish; set it aside.
- On medium heat, cook onion and beef in a pan until the meat is not pink; drain.
- Whisk eggs in a bowl; stir in mushrooms and spinach thoroughly. Mix in beef mixture, cheeses, pepper, salt, and garlic powder to combine well; scoop to the prepared crust then sprinkle with butter.
- Bake for 25-30 minutes in 375 degrees oven without cover until the crust is pale brown.

Nutrition Information

- Calories: 418 calories
- Sodium: 686mg sodium
- Fiber: 3g fiber)
- Total Carbohydrate: 19g carbohydrate (1g sugars
- Cholesterol: 164mg cholesterol
- Protein: 34g protein.
- Total Fat: 22g fat (10g saturated fat)

476. Spoon Bread Tamale Bake

Serving: 8 servings. | Prep: 25mins | Cook: 30mins | Ready in:

Ingredients

- 1-1/2 pounds lean ground beef (90% lean)
- 1 large onion, chopped
- 1 small green pepper, chopped
- 1 garlic clove, minced
- 1 can (28 ounces) diced tomatoes, undrained
- 1-1/2 cups frozen corn
- 1 can (2-1/4 ounces) sliced ripe olives, drained
- 4-1/2 teaspoons chili powder
- 1/2 teaspoon salt
- 1/4 teaspoon pepper
- 1/2 cup cornmeal
- 1 cup water
- TOPPING:
- 1-1/2 cups fat-free milk, divided
- 1/2 cup cornmeal
- 1/2 teaspoon salt
- 1/2 cup shredded reduced-fat cheddar cheese
- 2 tablespoons butter
- 1/2 cup egg substitute

Direction

- Cook garlic, green pepper, onion and beef on medium heat in a Dutch oven coated with cooking spray till meat is not pink anymore; drain. Mix in pepper, salt, chili powder, olives, corn and tomatoes. Boil. Lower the heat; let simmer, while uncovered, for 5 minutes.
- Mix water and cornmeal till becoming smooth; slowly mix into the pan. Boil. Lower the heat; let simmer, while uncovered, for 10 minutes, mixing once in a while. Move to a 2-1/2-qt. baking dish that's coated using cooking spray.
- Boil 1 cup of milk in a small-sized saucepan. Mix the leftover milk, salt and cornmeal; gradually mix into boiling milk. Cook and stir till mixture is back to a boil. Lower the heat; cook and stir till becoming thick a bit or for 3 to 4 minutes.
- Take out of the heat; mix in butter and cheese till becoming melted. Mix in egg substitute. Add on top of meat mixture. Bake, while uncovered, at 375 degrees till topping becomes browned a bit or for 30 to 40 minutes.

Nutrition Information

- Calories: 331 calories
- Total Carbohydrate: 30g carbohydrate (7g sugars
- Cholesterol: 55mg cholesterol
- Protein: 25g protein. Diabetic Exchanges: 3 lean meat
- Total Fat: 12g fat (6g saturated fat)
- Sodium: 754mg sodium
- Fiber: 4g fiber)

477. Stovetop Hamburger Casserole

Serving: 6 servings. | Prep: 15mins | Cook: 10mins | Ready in:

Ingredients

- 1 package (7 ounces) small pasta shells
- 1-1/2 pounds ground beef
- 1 large onion, chopped
- 3 medium carrots, chopped
- 1 celery rib, chopped

- 3 garlic cloves, minced
- 3 cups cubed cooked red potatoes
- 1 can (15-1/4 ounces) whole kernel corn, drained
- 2 cans (8 ounces each) tomato sauce
- 1-1/2 teaspoons salt
- 1/2 teaspoon pepper
- 1 cup shredded cheddar cheese

Direction

- Cook pasta as directed in the package. Meanwhile, cook onion and beef in a frying pan over medium heat till meat is not pink anymore; let drain. Put in celery and carrots; cook and mix for 5 minutes, or until vegetables become crisp-tender. Put in garlic and cook for 1 minute more.
- Mix in the pepper, salt, tomato sauce, corn and potatoes; let heat through. Let the pasta drain and pour onto the skillet; stir to coat. Top with cheese. Cook while covered until cheese is melted.

Nutrition Information

- Calories: 508 calories
- Cholesterol: 76mg cholesterol
- Protein: 32g protein.
- Total Fat: 17g fat (9g saturated fat)
- Sodium: 1172mg sodium
- Fiber: 5g fiber)
- Total Carbohydrate: 53g carbohydrate (9g sugars

478. Taco Biscuit Bake

Serving: 8 servings. | Prep: 20mins | Cook: 25mins | Ready in:

Ingredients

- 1 pound lean ground beef (90% lean)
- 2/3 cup water

- 1 envelope taco seasoning
- 2 tubes (12 ounces each) refrigerated buttermilk biscuits
- 1 can (15 ounces) chili con carne
- 1 cup shredded reduced-fat cheddar cheese
- Salsa and sour cream, optional

Direction

- Cook beef on medium heat in a big skillet till meat is not pink anymore; drain. Mix in taco seasoning and water. Boil; cook and stir till becoming thick or for 2 minutes.
- At the same time, cut the biscuits in quarter; add into one greased 13x9-in. baking dish. Layer with beef mixture, chili and cheese.
- Bake, while uncovered, at 375 degrees for 25 to 30 minutes or till cheese becomes melted and biscuits turn golden brown in color. Serve along with salsa and sour cream if you want.

Nutrition Information

- Calories: 422 calories
- Protein: 26g protein.
- Total Fat: 14g fat (6g saturated fat)
- Sodium: 1439mg sodium
- Fiber: 1g fiber)
- Total Carbohydrate: 49g carbohydrate (1g sugars
- Cholesterol: 62mg cholesterol

479. Taco Pie

Serving: 8 | Prep: 20mins | Cook: 10mins | Ready in:

Ingredients

- 1 (8 ounce) package refrigerated crescent rolls
- 1 pound ground beef
- 1 (1 ounce) package taco seasoning mix
- 1 (16 ounce) container sour cream
- 8 ounces shredded Mexican-style cheese blend
- 1 (14 ounce) bag tortilla chips, crushed

Direction

- Preheat oven to 175 degrees C (350 degrees F).
- Lay crescent dough flat onto the bottom of a square cake pan and then following the instructions on the package, bake it.
- At the same time, in a big skillet, brown the ground beef on medium-high heat. Put in the taco seasoning and mix together well. Once dough is done, take out of the oven and add meat mixture over, then layer with sour cream and cheese, and then top off with the crushed nacho chips.
- Bring back to the oven and bake at 175 degrees C (350 degrees F) till cheese is melted or for 10 minutes.

Nutrition Information

- Calories: 687 calories;
- Total Fat: 43.4
- Sodium: 863
- Total Carbohydrate: 50.6
- Cholesterol: 100
- Protein: 24.4

---

480.   Taco Potato Shells

Serving: 6 servings. | Prep: 25mins | Cook: 01hours45mins | Ready in:

Ingredients

- 3 large baking potatoes
- 1 tablespoon butter, melted
- 1 pound ground beef
- 1 can (14-1/2 ounces) diced tomatoes, undrained
- 1 envelope taco seasoning
- 1/2 cup shredded cheddar cheese
- 1/3 cup sour cream
- 2 green onions, sliced

Direction

- Scrub and pierce potatoes. Bake for 1 hour at 375° or until softened. Allow to cool until can be handled easily, cut potatoes in half by the length. Scoop out pulp carefully, leaving a thin shell (place pulp in refrigerator for later use). Coat butter on inside and outside of potato shells and arrange on an ungreased baking sheet cut side up. Bake when uncover for 20 minutes at 375°.
- In the meantime, cook beef in a large skillet over medium heat until the pink color disappears from meat; drain. Add taco seasoning and tomatoes. Bring to a boil; lower the heat to simmer, uncovered, for 20 minutes.
- Place spoonfuls of mixture into shells; add cheese on top. Bake, uncovered, for an additional 5 to 10 minutes or until cheese is completely melted. Add onions and sour cream on top.

Nutrition Information

- Calories: 375 calories
- Fiber: 4g fiber)
- Total Carbohydrate: 42g carbohydrate (6g sugars
- Cholesterol: 61mg cholesterol
- Protein: 20g protein.
- Total Fat: 14g fat (8g saturated fat)
- Sodium: 766mg sodium

---

481.   Taco Salad Casserole

Serving: 4 servings. | Prep: 25mins | Cook: 15mins | Ready in:

Ingredients

- 1 pound ground beef
- 1/4 cup chopped onion
- 1/4 cup chopped green pepper
- 1 envelope taco seasoning
- 1/2 cup water
- 1 cup crushed tortilla chips

- 1 can (16 ounces) refried beans
- 1 cup shredded cheddar cheese
- Toppings: chopped lettuce and tomatoes, sliced ripe olives, sour cream and picante sauce

Direction

- Combine green pepper, onion and beef in a large skillet, cook over medium heat until the pink color disappears from meat; drain. Stir in water and taco seasoning. Cook for about 3 minutes until thickened, remember to stir while cooking. Set aside.
- Arrange chips in a greased 8 inches square baking dish. Stir refried beans in a small bowl and spread on top of chips. Place cheese and beef mixture on top.
- Bake, uncovered, for 15 to 20 minutes at 375° or until heated through. Add olives, tomatoes and lettuce on top. Serve with picante sauce and sour cream.

Nutrition Information

- Calories: 405 calories
- Fiber: 6g fiber)
- Total Carbohydrate: 31g carbohydrate (0 sugars
- Cholesterol: 47mg cholesterol
- Protein: 37g protein.
- Total Fat: 12g fat (0 saturated fat)
- Sodium: 1181mg sodium

482. Tahoe Casserole

Serving: 8 servings. | Prep: 40mins | Cook: 30mins | Ready in:

Ingredients

- 2 pounds ground beef
- 1 large onion, chopped
- 1/2 teaspoon salt
- 1/4 teaspoon pepper

- 2 cans (8 ounces each) tomato sauce
- 1 can (15-1/4 ounces) whole kernel corn
- 1 can (6 ounces) ripe olives, drained and chopped, divided
- 1/2 teaspoon chili powder
- 4 cups shredded cheddar cheese
- 1 package (7 ounces) corn tortillas

Direction

- Cook pepper, salt, onion, and beef on medium heat in a skillet till meat is not pink anymore; drain. Put in the chili powder, 1/2 of the olives, tomatoes, corn, and tomato sauce. Boil. Lower the heat; keep it covered and simmered for half an hour. In one greased 13x9-in. baking dish, layer 1/2 of the meat mixture, cheese and tortillas. Repeat the layers. Drizzle with the rest of olives. Keep it covered and baked at 350 degrees for half an hour. Uncover it and bake till thoroughly heated or for 15 minutes more.

Nutrition Information

- Calories: 510 calories
- Total Carbohydrate: 24g carbohydrate (4g sugars
- Cholesterol: 116mg cholesterol
- Protein: 35g protein.
- Total Fat: 30g fat (17g saturated fat)
- Sodium: 1067mg sodium
- Fiber: 3g fiber)

483. Tater Taco Casserole

Serving: 8 servings. | Prep: 20mins | Cook: 30mins | Ready in:

Ingredients

- 2 pounds ground beef
- 1/4 cup chopped onion
- 1 envelope taco seasoning
- 2/3 cup water

- 1 can (11 ounces) whole kernel corn, drained
- 1 can (11 ounces) condensed fiesta nacho cheese soup, undiluted
- 1 package (32 ounces) frozen Tater Tots

Direction

- Cook onion and beef on medium heat in a big skillet till meat is not pink anymore; drain. Mix in water and taco seasoning. Let it simmer, while uncovered, for 5 minutes. Mix in soup and corn.
- Move to a greased 13x9-inch baking dish. Arrange Tater Tots in one layer on the top. Bake, while uncovered, at 350 degrees for 30 to 35 minutes or till potatoes become crispy and golden brown in color.

Nutrition Information

- Calories: 461 calories
- Protein: 25g protein.
- Total Fat: 24g fat (8g saturated fat)
- Sodium: 1307mg sodium
- Fiber: 4g fiber)
- Total Carbohydrate: 40g carbohydrate (3g sugars
- Cholesterol: 60mg cholesterol

484.   Tater Topped Beef Casserole

Serving: 2 servings. | Prep: 10mins | Cook: 30mins | Ready in:

Ingredients

- 1/2 pound lean ground beef (90% lean)
- 1/4 cup chopped onion
- 2/3 cup condensed cream of mushroom soup, undiluted
- 1/4 cup 2% milk
- 2 cups frozen Tater Tots
- 1/3 cup shredded cheddar cheese

Direction

- Cook onion and beef in a small skillet on moderate heat until meat is not pink anymore, then drain. Stir in milk and soup.
- Turn to a shallow 1-quart baking dish coated with cooking spray, then put Tater Tots on top.
- Bake at 350 degrees without a cover until bubbly, about 25 to 30 minutes. Sprinkle cheese over and bake until cheese melts, about 5 more minutes.

Nutrition Information

- Calories: 525 calories
- Fiber: 4g fiber)
- Total Carbohydrate: 41g carbohydrate (4g sugars
- Cholesterol: 75mg cholesterol
- Protein: 31g protein.
- Total Fat: 29g fat (10g saturated fat)
- Sodium: 1292mg sodium

485.   Tater Topped Casserole

Serving: 4-6 servings. | Prep: 15mins | Cook: 45mins | Ready in:

Ingredients

- 1 pound lean ground beef (90% lean)
- 1/2 cup chopped onion
- 1/3 cup sliced celery
- 1/2 teaspoon salt
- 1/4 teaspoon pepper
- 1 can (10-3/4 ounces) condensed cream of celery soup, undiluted
- 1 package (16 ounces) frozen Tater Tots
- 1 cup shredded cheddar cheese

Direction

- Cook the celery, onion and beef in a large skillet until the vegetables become tender and the meat is not pink anymore; let drain. Stir in pepper and salt.

- Place the mixture into a 3-quart baking dish coated with cooking spray. Place with soup. Put the frozen potatoes on top. Bake at 400 degrees until bubbling, 40 minutes. Dust with cheese. Bake until the cheese melts, 5 minutes.

Nutrition Information

- Calories: 353 calories
- Protein: 21g protein.
- Total Fat: 20g fat (8g saturated fat)
- Sodium: 1040mg sodium
- Fiber: 3g fiber)
- Total Carbohydrate: 25g carbohydrate (2g sugars
- Cholesterol: 59mg cholesterol

486. The Firehouse Special

Serving: 2 casseroles (10 servings each). | Prep: 45mins | Cook: 55mins | Ready in:

Ingredients

- 2 cans (14-1/2 ounces each) chicken broth
- 3 cups uncooked instant rice
- 4 tablespoons butter, divided
- 2 pounds ground beef
- 2 packages (12 ounces each) bulk spicy pork sausage
- 1 pound sliced fresh mushrooms
- 3 garlic cloves, minced
- 2 packages (10 ounces each) frozen chopped spinach, thawed and squeezed dry
- 2 cups (16 ounces) 4% cottage cheese
- 8 eggs, lightly beaten
- 1 envelope onion soup mix
- 1 envelope leek soup mix
- 2 teaspoons garlic powder
- 1 teaspoon Creole seasoning
- 1/4 cup grated Parmesan cheese

Direction

- Preheat oven to 350°. In a large saucepan, boil the broth. Add rice to the broth; cover and take away from heat. Allow 5 minutes for resting. Stir in 2 tablespoons butter; leave aside.
- In the meantime, in a large skillet over medium heat, cook sausage and beef until there is not pink anymore; and then drain. Remove to a large bowl.
- In same skillet, sauté mushrooms in remaining butter until soften. Add garlic; cook for around 1 minute. Add to meat mixture. Stir in cottage cheese, spinach, soup mixes, eggs, garlic powder, reserved rice mixture and Creole seasoning.
- Divide equally to two greased baking dishes 13x9-inch; have cheese to sprinkle. Bake while covered for approximately 45 minutes. Then bake uncovered for an addition of 10 to 15 minutes until heated through.

Nutrition Information

- Calories: 315 calories
- Sodium: 787mg sodium
- Fiber: 2g fiber)
- Total Carbohydrate: 19g carbohydrate (3g sugars
- Cholesterol: 136mg cholesterol
- Protein: 21g protein.
- Total Fat: 17g fat (7g saturated fat)

487. Three Bean Bake

Serving: 12-14 servings. | Prep: 20mins | Cook: 01hours30mins | Ready in:

Ingredients

- 3 pounds ground beef
- 1 large onion, chopped
- 1/2 cup chopped sweet red pepper

- 2 cans (16 ounces each) pork and beans, drained
- 1 can (16 ounces) chili beans, undrained
- 1 can (15 ounces) pinto beans, rinsed and drained
- 1 cup ketchup
- 1/2 cup packed brown sugar
- 3 to 4 tablespoons chili powder
- 1 tablespoon white vinegar
- 1 teaspoon salt
- 1 teaspoon ground cumin
- 1 teaspoon cayenne pepper
- 1/2 teaspoon hot pepper sauce
- 1/8 teaspoon garlic powder
- 1/8 teaspoon pepper

Direction

- Cook red pepper, onion and beef in an ovenproof Dutch oven over medium heat until meat is no longer pink; drain. Mix in the remaining ingredients.
- Cover and bake at 350° until heated through, about 90 – 120 minutes, stirring once.

Nutrition Information

- Calories: 291 calories
- Cholesterol: 48mg cholesterol
- Protein: 22g protein.
- Total Fat: 10g fat (4g saturated fat)
- Sodium: 690mg sodium
- Fiber: 6g fiber)
- Total Carbohydrate: 31g carbohydrate (13g sugars

488.   Tomato Beef And Rice Casserole

Serving: 6 servings. | Prep: 10mins | Cook: 01hours30mins | Ready in:

Ingredients

- 1 pound lean ground beef (90% lean)
- 3 cups canned diced tomatoes, undrained
- 1 medium green pepper, chopped
- 1 cup uncooked long grain rice
- 1 large onion, chopped
- 1 teaspoon chili powder
- 1/2 teaspoon salt
- 1/4 teaspoon pepper

Direction

- Combine all ingredients in a large bowl. Arrange in a greased 2-qt. baking dish. Bake at 400°, covered, for 1-1/2 hours, stirring once or twice. During the last 15 minutes, uncover to get brown.

Nutrition Information

- Calories: 267 calories
- Protein: 18g protein.
- Total Fat: 6g fat (2g saturated fat)
- Sodium: 413mg sodium
- Fiber: 3g fiber)
- Total Carbohydrate: 34g carbohydrate (6g sugars
- Cholesterol: 37mg cholesterol

489.   Tomato Cornbread Bake

Serving: 6 servings. | Prep: 25mins | Cook: 25mins | Ready in:

Ingredients

- 1-1/2 pounds ground beef
- 3/4 cup chopped onion
- 2-1/2 cups canned diced tomatoes, drained
- 1-1/2 cups fresh or frozen corn
- 1 teaspoon salt
- 1/8 teaspoon pepper
- 1 package (8-1/2 ounces) corn bread/muffin mix
- 1 egg

- 1/3 cup milk

Direction

- Cook onion and beef in a frying pan over medium heat until the meat is not pink anymore; strain. Add pepper, salt, corn, and tomatoes; boil it. Remove into an 11x7-in. greased baking dish coated.
- Mix together milk, egg, and cornbread mix until barely moistened. Put on the meat mixture. Bake without a cover at 400° until turning golden brown, about 25-30 minutes.

Nutrition Information

- Calories: 422 calories
- Total Carbohydrate: 44g carbohydrate (16g sugars
- Cholesterol: 102mg cholesterol
- Protein: 27g protein.
- Total Fat: 16g fat (6g saturated fat)
- Sodium: 958mg sodium
- Fiber: 4g fiber)

490. Tomato Orange Beef Patties

Serving: 8 servings. | Prep: 20mins | Cook: 25mins | Ready in:

Ingredients

- 2 pounds ground beef
- 3 large onions, sliced and separated into rings
- 2 tablespoons butter
- 1 tablespoon all-purpose flour
- Salt and pepper to taste
- 1 cup orange juice
- 2 tablespoons white wine vinegar
- 4 medium tomatoes, peeled, seeded and chopped

Direction

- Form the beef into 8 oval patties. Add onions and the patties to a big frying pan, cook over medium heat until the meat is not pink any longer. Take them to a 13x9-inch baking dish coated with cooking spray.
- Add butter to a big frying pan, heat over medium heat until melted. Mix in pepper, salt and flour until smooth. Mix in the vinegar and orange juice little by little. Boil them together, stir and cook until it gets thick, about 2 minutes. Mix in tomatoes. Spread the sauce over the beef. Set oven at 350°, bake while covered until it turn bubbly and hot, about 25 to 30 minutes.

Nutrition Information

- Calories: 303 calories
- Total Fat: 17g fat (7g saturated fat)
- Sodium: 91mg sodium
- Fiber: 2g fiber)
- Total Carbohydrate: 13g carbohydrate (8g sugars
- Cholesterol: 83mg cholesterol
- Protein: 24g protein.

491. Tortilla Beef Bake

Serving: 6 servings. | Prep: 10mins | Cook: 30mins | Ready in:

Ingredients

- 1-1/2 pounds ground beef
- 1 can (10-3/4 ounces) condensed cream of chicken soup, undiluted
- 2-1/2 cups crushed tortilla chips, divided
- 1 jar (16 ounces) salsa
- 1-1/2 cups shredded cheddar cheese

Direction

- Cook beef on medium heat in a big skillet till meat is not pink anymore; drain. Mix in soup. Drizzle 1-1/2 cups tortilla chips in one greased shallow 2-1/2-qt. baking dish. Add cheese, salsa, and beef mixture.

- Bake, while uncovered, at 350 degrees for 25 to 30 minutes or till becoming bubbly. Drizzle with the rest of the chips. Bake for 3 minutes more or till chips are toasted a bit.

Nutrition Information

- Calories: 464 calories
- Total Carbohydrate: 23g carbohydrate (3g sugars
- Cholesterol: 90mg cholesterol
- Protein: 29g protein.
- Total Fat: 26g fat (12g saturated fat)
- Sodium: 1083mg sodium
- Fiber: 4g fiber)

492.   Two Meat Macaroni

Serving: 8 servings. | Prep: 15mins | Cook: 01hours30mins |Ready in:

Ingredients

- 1/2 pound ground beef
- 1/2 pound ground pork
- 2 cans (14-1/2 ounces each) diced tomatoes
- 2 cups shredded cheddar cheese
- 2 cups uncooked elbow macaroni
- 1 medium onion, finely chopped
- 1 cup frozen peas, thawed
- 2 cans (2-1/2 ounces each) sliced ripe olives, drained
- 1 jar (2 ounces) diced pimientos, drained
- 1 teaspoon salt
- 1/2 teaspoon paprika
- 1/4 teaspoon celery salt

Direction

- Cook pork and beef in a large skillet over medium heat until not pink anymore; drain. Put in the remaining ingredients.

- Place into a greased 3-quart baking dish. Bake without covering at 350° until the macaroni is tender for about 90 minutes, stirring every 30 minutes.

Nutrition Information

- Calories: 315 calories
- Total Carbohydrate: 22g carbohydrate (5g sugars
- Cholesterol: 63mg cholesterol
- Protein: 20g protein.
- Total Fat: 16g fat (9g saturated fat)
- Sodium: 710mg sodium
- Fiber: 3g fiber)

493.   Unstuffed Cabbage Casserole

Serving: 4 servings. | Prep: 20mins | Cook: 45mins |Ready in:

Ingredients

- 6 cups chopped cabbage
- 1/2 pound lean ground beef (90% lean)
- 1 small onion, chopped
- 1 cup uncooked instant rice
- 1/2 teaspoon salt, optional
- 1/4 teaspoon pepper
- 2 cans (10-3/4 ounces each) condensed tomato soup, undiluted
- 1 cup water
- 1/3 cup shredded cheddar cheese

Direction

- Add the cabbage into a greased 2-1/2-qt. baking dish. Cook onion and beef on medium heat in a big skillet till meat is not pink anymore; drain. Mix in pepper, salt if you want and rice; scoop on top of cabbage.
- Mix water and soup; add on top of beef mixture. Keep it covered and bake at 350

degrees till cabbage and rice become soft or for 40 to 50 minutes. Uncover it; drizzle along with cheese. Bake till cheese becomes melted or for 5 to 10 minutes longer.

Nutrition Information

- Calories: 342 calories
- Fiber: 5g fiber)
- Total Carbohydrate: 48g carbohydrate (0 sugars
- Cholesterol: 23mg cholesterol
- Protein: 19g protein. Diabetic Exchanges: 2-1/2 starch
- Total Fat: 8g fat (3g saturated fat)
- Sodium: 690mg sodium

494.   Unstuffed Peppers

Serving: 6 servings. | Prep: 20mins | Cook: 10mins | Ready in:

Ingredients

- 1 cup uncooked instant rice
- 1 pound ground beef
- 2 medium green peppers, cut into 1-inch pieces
- 1/2 cup chopped onion
- 1 jar (26 ounces) marinara sauce
- 1-1/2 teaspoons salt-free seasoning blend
- 1/2 cup shredded Italian cheese blend
- 1/2 cup seasoned bread crumbs
- 1 tablespoon olive oil

Direction

- Set the oven to 350°, and start preheating. Cook rice following package instructions.
- In the meantime, in a large skillet over the medium-high heat, cook onion, green peppers and beef until meat is no longer pink; drain. Mix in seasoning blend, marinara sauce and rice. Mix in cheese.

- Place to a greased baking dish of 2 quart. Toss oil and bread crumbs; sprinkle over the top. Bake until topping is golden brown and heated through, about 8-10 minutes.

Nutrition Information

- Calories: 343 calories
- Protein: 20g protein.
- Total Fat: 12g fat (5g saturated fat)
- Sodium: 469mg sodium
- Fiber: 3g fiber)
- Total Carbohydrate: 38g carbohydrate (12g sugars
- Cholesterol: 43mg cholesterol

495.   Upside Down Pizza Casserole

Serving: 12 servings. | Prep: 20mins | Cook: 25mins | Ready in:

Ingredients

- 1 pound ground beef
- 1 medium onion, chopped
- 1 jar (14 ounces) spaghetti sauce
- 2 cups shredded mozzarella cheese
- 1 cup whole milk
- 2 large eggs
- 1 teaspoon vegetable oil
- 1 cup all-purpose flour
- 1/2 teaspoon salt

Direction

- Over medium heat, cook onion and beef in a large skillet until the meat is no more pink; allow to drain. Then add spaghetti sauce. Simmer, covered, until heated through. Next, pour into a greased 13x9-in. baking dish. Dust with cheese.
- Combine the milk, salt, flour, oil, and eggs in a blender; cover and process until smooth. Then

pour the mixture over the cheese. Bake without cover for 25-30 minutes at 400°, or until golden brown.

Nutrition Information

- Calories: 225 calories
- Sodium: 373mg sodium
- Fiber: 1g fiber)
- Total Carbohydrate: 14g carbohydrate (4g sugars
- Cholesterol: 79mg cholesterol
- Protein: 15g protein.
- Total Fat: 12g fat (5g saturated fat)

---

496. Western Beef And Corn Casserole

Serving: 6-8 servings. | Prep: 20mins | Cook: 25mins | Ready in:

Ingredients

- FILLING:
- 1 pound ground beef
- 1 can (11 ounces) Mexicorn, drained
- 1 can (8 ounces) tomato sauce
- 1 cup shredded cheddar cheese
- 1/2 cup hickory-flavored sauce
- 1/2 teaspoon salt
- 1/2 teaspoon chili powder
- CRUST:
- 1 cup all-purpose flour
- 1/2 cup yellow cornmeal
- 2 tablespoons sugar
- 1 teaspoon salt
- 1 teaspoon baking powder
- 1 cup shredded cheddar cheese, divided
- 1/4 cup cold butter
- 1/2 cup whole milk
- 1 large egg, lightly beaten

Direction

- Cook beef on medium heat in a big skillet till meat is not pink anymore; drain. Mix in the rest of filling ingredients; put aside.
- To make crust, mix baking powder, salt, sugar, cornmeal and flour in a big bowl. Fold in half cup cheese. Chop in butter till mixture looks like coarse crumbs. Mix in egg and milk.
- Spread crust mixture on the bottom and up the sides of one greased 9-in. square baking dish. Add filling to the crust. Bake, while uncovered, at 400 degrees till becoming bubbly or for 20 to 25 minutes. Drizzle with the rest of cheese; bake till cheese becomes melted or for 5 minutes more.

Nutrition Information

- Calories: 434 calories
- Sodium: 1277mg sodium
- Fiber: 3g fiber)
- Total Carbohydrate: 35g carbohydrate (9g sugars
- Cholesterol: 112mg cholesterol
- Protein: 23g protein.
- Total Fat: 22g fat (13g saturated fat)

---

497. Wild Rice Hot Dish

Serving: 8-12 servings. | Prep: 15mins | Cook: 02hours30mins | Ready in:

Ingredients

- 3 cups boiling water
- 1 cup wild rice
- 1-1/2 pounds ground beef
- 1 medium onion, chopped
- 2 cans (10-3/4 ounces each) condensed cream of chicken soup, undiluted
- 2 cans (4 ounces each) sliced mushrooms, undrained
- 1 can (28 ounces) bean sprouts, drained
- 1 can (10-1/2 ounces) condensed beef broth
- 1-1/3 cups water

- 1/4 cup soy sauce
- 1 bay leaf, crushed
- 1 tablespoon dried parsley flakes
- 1/4 teaspoon each celery salt, onion salt, poultry seasoning, garlic powder, paprika and pepper
- 1/8 teaspoon dried thyme
- 1/2 cup sliced almonds

Direction

- Pour water over rice in a large bowl; allow to stand for 15 minutes. Drain and put aside. Brown onion and ground beef in a skillet. Drain; add to rice along with the remaining ingredients, except for almonds. Place into a 13x9-inch baking dish. Cover and bake at 350° for 2 hours. Add almonds on top; bake with no cover for 30 more minutes.

Nutrition Information

- Calories: 216 calories
- Total Fat: 9g fat (3g saturated fat)
- Sodium: 853mg sodium
- Fiber: 3g fiber)
- Total Carbohydrate: 18g carbohydrate (1g sugars
- Cholesterol: 30mg cholesterol
- Protein: 16g protein.

498. Winter Day Dinner

Serving: 8 servings. | Prep: 25mins | Cook: 01hours30mins | Ready in:

Ingredients

- 1-1/2 pounds ground beef
- 1 medium onion, chopped
- 2 tablespoons Worcestershire sauce
- 1 teaspoon salt
- 1/2 teaspoon pepper
- 8 medium potatoes, sliced

- 1 package (16 ounces) frozen peas, thawed
- CHEESE SAUCE:
- 1/4 cup butter, cubed
- 1/3 cup all-purpose flour
- 1/2 teaspoon salt
- 1/4 teaspoon pepper
- 2 cups milk
- 4 ounces process cheese (Velveeta), cubed

Direction

- In a large skillet over medium heat, cook the onion and beef until meat is not pink anymore; and then drain. Add in the pepper, salt and Worcestershire sauce.
- In a greased baking dish of 13 x 9-inch, place half of the potatoes; layer next with the meat mixture, peas and leftover potatoes. Leave aside.
- In a large saucepan over medium heat, melt butter. Mix in the pepper, salt and flour until smooth. Stir in milk gradually. Allow to boil; cook and stir for around 2 minutes until thickened. Mix in cheese until melted. Pour over potatoes.
- Bake while covered at 350° for 1 and a half hours until potatoes are tender.

Nutrition Information

- Calories: 529 calories
- Protein: 28g protein.
- Total Fat: 22g fat (11g saturated fat)
- Sodium: 852mg sodium
- Fiber: 7g fiber)
- Total Carbohydrate: 57g carbohydrate (12g sugars
- Cholesterol: 85mg cholesterol

499. Yummy Pizza Bake

Serving: 8 servings. | Prep: 25mins | Cook: 40mins | Ready in:

Ingredients

- 1-1/2 pounds lean ground beef (90% lean)
- 1 medium onion, chopped
- 1 medium green pepper, chopped
- 1 cup sliced fresh mushrooms
- 1 can (15 ounces) pizza sauce
- 1/4 teaspoon garlic powder
- 1/4 teaspoon dried oregano
- 1 cup shredded part-skim mozzarella cheese
- 1 cup all-purpose flour
- 2 large eggs, lightly beaten
- 1 cup fat-free milk
- 1 tablespoon canola oil
- 1/2 teaspoon salt
- 1/2 cup grated Parmesan cheese
- 10 slices pepperoni, chopped

Direction

- Cook mushrooms, green pepper, onion, and beef in a big frying pan over medium heat until the vegetables are soft and the meat is not pink anymore; strain. Mix in oregano, garlic powder, and pizza sauce. Remove into a greased 13x9-inch baking dish, sprinkle mozzarella cheese over.
- Mix salt, oil, milk, eggs, and flour together in a small bowl; add to the meat mixture. Sprinkle pepperoni and Parmesan cheese over. Bake without a cover at 350° until turning golden brown, about 40-45 minutes.

Nutrition Information

- Calories: 331 calories
- Protein: 28g protein. Diabetic Exchanges: 3 lean meat
- Total Fat: 14g fat (6g saturated fat)
- Sodium: 589mg sodium
- Fiber: 2g fiber)
- Total Carbohydrate: 21g carbohydrate (6g sugars
- Cholesterol: 110mg cholesterol

500.   Yummy Tater Topped Casserole

Serving: 6-8 servings. | Prep: 15mins | Cook: 60mins | Ready in:

Ingredients

- 1-1/2 pounds ground beef
- 1 package (16 ounces) frozen vegetables, thawed
- 1 can (2.8 ounces) french-fried onions
- 1/4 cup butter
- 1 can (10-3/4 ounces) condensed cream of celery soup, undiluted
- 1 can (10-3/4 ounces) condensed cream of chicken soup, undiluted
- 1/2 cup milk
- 1 package (16 ounces) frozen Tater Tots, thawed

Direction

- Cook beef in a large skillet over medium heat until not pink anymore; drain. Layer the beef, vegetables and onions in a greased 13x9-inch baking dish. Dot with butter.
- Mix milk and soups in a bowl; pour over vegetables. Add Tater Tots on top. Bake without covering at 350° until golden brown, about 60 minutes.

Nutrition Information

- Calories: 482 calories
- Total Fat: 31g fat (12g saturated fat)
- Sodium: 1006mg sodium
- Fiber: 4g fiber)
- Total Carbohydrate: 32g carbohydrate (3g sugars
- Cholesterol: 78mg cholesterol
- Protein: 22g protein.

501. Zesty Oven Fried Rice

Serving: 10 servings. | Prep: 35mins | Cook: 30mins | Ready in:

Ingredients

- 2 cans (14-1/2 ounces each) chicken broth
- 1-1/2 cups uncooked long grain rice
- 1-1/2 pounds ground beef
- 2 large onions, thinly sliced
- 1 large green pepper, chopped
- 4 garlic cloves, minced
- 3 eggs, lightly beaten
- 1 can (4 ounces) mushroom stems and pieces, drained
- 1/3 cup soy sauce
- 1 tablespoon hot pepper sauce

Direction

- Bring a saucepan of broth to a boil. Add in rice. Lower the heat; cover and let it simmer for 20 minutes. In the meantime, cook garlic, green pepper, onions and beef in a skillet over medium heat until vegetables are tender and meat is no longer pink. Drain and put in a large bowl.
- Cook and stir eggs in the same skillet until set but still moist. Put into meat mixture. Use a fork to fluff rice. Mix the hot pepper sauce, soy sauce, mushrooms and rice into meat mixture.
- Place into a greased 13x9-inch baking dish. Cover and bake at 350° until heated through, about 30 minutes.

Nutrition Information

- Calories: 258 calories
- Protein: 18g protein.
- Total Fat: 8g fat (3g saturated fat)
- Sodium: 770mg sodium
- Fiber: 1g fiber)
- Total Carbohydrate: 27g carbohydrate (3g sugars
- Cholesterol: 97mg cholesterol

502. Zippy Beef Bake

Serving: 4 servings. | Prep: 15mins | Cook: 20mins | Ready in:

Ingredients

- 3/4 pound ground beef
- 1 tablespoon butter
- 2 medium zucchini, thinly sliced
- 1/4 pound sliced fresh mushrooms, sliced
- 2 tablespoons sliced green onions
- 1-1/2 teaspoons chili powder
- 1 teaspoon salt
- 1/8 teaspoon garlic powder
- 1-1/2 cups cooked rice
- 1 can (4 ounces) chopped green chilies
- 1/2 cup sour cream
- 1 cup shredded Monterey Jack cheese, divided

Direction

- Cook beef in a large frying pan with heat on medium until not pink. Drain excess grease. Mix in zucchini, onions, butter, and mushrooms. Continue cooking and stir until veggies are soft. Drain any water. Mix in garlic powder, chili powder, and salt. Then put in the chilies, half the cheese, rice, and sour cream. Place in a 2-qt. greased dish. Spread the rest of the cheese on top. Do not cover; bake in a 350-degree oven until cheese is melty, 20-22 minutes.

Nutrition Information

- Calories: 462 calories
- Protein: 29g protein.
- Total Fat: 27g fat (15g saturated fat)
- Sodium: 944mg sodium
- Fiber: 2g fiber)
- Total Carbohydrate: 23g carbohydrate (3g sugars
- Cholesterol: 109mg cholesterol

503. Zippy Beef Supper

Serving: 6-8 servings. | Prep: 15mins | Cook: 35mins | Ready in:

Ingredients

- 2 pounds ground beef
- 1 medium onion, chopped
- 1 cup cubed cooked potatoes
- 1 can (11 ounces) condensed nacho cheese soup, undiluted
- 1 can (10-3/4 ounces) condensed cream of onion soup, undiluted
- 1 can (10 ounces) diced tomatoes and green chilies, undrained
- 2 to 3 teaspoons ground cumin
- 1/2 to 1 teaspoon garlic powder
- 3 cups crushed tortilla chips
- 1 cup shredded cheddar cheese

Direction

- Cook onion and beef on medium heat in a big saucepan till meat is not pink anymore; drain. Put in potatoes; cook and stir till becoming heated through. Mix in the garlic powder, cumin, tomatoes and soups.
- Move to a greased 13x9-in. baking dish. Keep it covered and bake at 350 degrees for half an hour. Uncover it; drizzle with tortilla chips and cheese. Bake, while uncovered, till cheese becomes melted or for 5 to 10 minutes longer.

Nutrition Information

- Calories: 589 calories
- Sodium: 1251mg sodium
- Fiber: 4g fiber)
- Total Carbohydrate: 40g carbohydrate (3g sugars
- Cholesterol: 106mg cholesterol
- Protein: 37g protein.
- Total Fat: 31g fat (13g saturated fat)

504. Zucchini Beef Bake

Serving: 6-8 servings. | Prep: 20mins | Cook: 25mins | Ready in:

Ingredients

- 6 cups water
- 4 cups sliced zucchini
- 1 pound ground beef
- 1 large onion, chopped
- 1 garlic clove, minced
- 2 cups cooked rice
- 1 can (8 ounces) tomato sauce
- 1 cup (8 ounces) 4% cottage cheese
- 1 large egg, lightly beaten
- 1-1/2 teaspoons minced fresh oregano or 1/2 teaspoon dried oregano
- 1 teaspoon minced fresh basil or 1/4 teaspoon dried basil
- 1/2 teaspoon salt
- 1 cup shredded cheddar cheese

Direction

- Boil water in a big saucepan. Put in zucchini. Bring back to a boil. Lower the heat; keep it covered and let simmer for 3 minutes or just till tender. Drain and instantly add zucchini into ice water. Drain and pat dry.
- Cook onion and beef on medium heat in a big skillet till meat is not pink anymore. Put in garlic; cook 60 seconds more. Drain. Mix in salt, basil, oregano, egg, cottage cheese, tomato sauce, and rice.
- Arrange 1/2 of the zucchini into one greased 13x9-in. baking dish. Layer with meat mixture and the rest of zucchini; drizzle with cheddar cheese. Bake, while uncovered, at 350 degrees for 25 to 30 minutes or till bubbly and cheese is melted.

Nutrition Information

- Calories: 274 calories

- Fiber: 1g fiber)
- Total Carbohydrate: 18g carbohydrate (4g sugars
- Cholesterol: 85mg cholesterol
- Protein: 21g protein.
- Total Fat: 13g fat (7g saturated fat)
- Sodium: 500mg sodium

505. Zucchini Beef Casserole

Serving: 4 servings. | Prep: 30mins | Cook: 0mins | Ready in:

Ingredients

- 3/4 pound lean ground beef (90% lean)
- 1 teaspoon garlic powder
- 1-1/2 cups diced zucchini
- 1 can (14-1/2 ounces) diced tomatoes, drained
- 1/2 cup instant rice
- 1/2 cup water
- 1/4 cup chopped onion
- 1/4 cup reduced-sodium soy sauce
- 3/4 teaspoon dried basil

Direction

- Crumble beef into a 1-1/2-qt. microwave-safe plate; drizzle with garlic powder. Keep it covered and microwave on high for 1-1/2 minutes; mix. Heat till meat is not pink anymore or 1 to 2 minutes more; drain.
- Mix in the rest ingredients. Keep it covered and microwave on high for 15 to 20 minutes or till veggies and rice become softened, mixing two times.

Nutrition Information

- Calories: 230 calories
- Protein: 21g protein. Diabetic Exchanges: 3 lean meat
- Total Fat: 8g fat (3g saturated fat)
- Sodium: 845mg sodium

- Fiber: 2g fiber)
- Total Carbohydrate: 17g carbohydrate (0 sugars
- Cholesterol: 31mg cholesterol

506. Zucchini Cheese Casserole

Serving: 6 servings. | Prep: 15mins | Cook: 45mins | Ready in:

Ingredients

- 4 cups shredded unpeeled zucchini (about 3 medium)
- 1/2 teaspoon salt
- 1 cup shredded part-skim mozzarella cheese, divided
- 1 cup shredded cheddar cheese, divided
- 1/2 cup grated Parmesan cheese
- 2 large eggs
- 1 pound ground beef
- 1/2 cup chopped onion
- 1 can (8 ounces) tomato sauce
- 1/4 teaspoon garlic powder
- 1/4 teaspoon dried oregano
- 1 cup chopped green pepper
- 2 cans (4 ounces each) mushroom stems and pieces, drained

Direction

- Put zucchini into a double thickness of cheesecloth; season with salt. Allow to sit for 10 minutes. Gather ends of cheesecloth and squeeze to remove as much liquid as possible.
- Mix eggs, Parmesan cheese, 1/2 cup mozzarella cheese and zucchini together in a bowl. Press into a greased 13x9-inch baking dish. Bake without a cover at 400° until crust is set, about 20 minutes.
- In the meantime, cook onion and beef in a large skillet over medium heat until not pink anymore; drain. Mix in oregano, garlic powder

and tomato sauce; let it come to a boil. Spread over crust.

- Scatter mushrooms and green pepper on top; sprinkle with the remaining cheeses. Return to the oven and bake until heated through and cheeses are melted, about 25-35 more minutes.

Nutrition Information

- Calories: 326 calories
- Protein: 29g protein.
- Total Fat: 19g fat (11g saturated fat)
- Sodium: 848mg sodium
- Fiber: 2g fiber)
- Total Carbohydrate: 9g carbohydrate (5g sugars
- Cholesterol: 144mg cholesterol

Chapter 5: Italian Casseroles Recipes

***

507.   Alfredo Chicken 'n' Biscuits

Serving: 4 servings. | Prep: 20mins | Cook: 20mins | Ready in:

Ingredients

- 2 cups chopped fresh broccoli
- 1-1/2 cups sliced fresh carrots
- 1 cup chopped onion
- 2 tablespoons olive oil
- 2 cups cubed cooked chicken
- 1 carton (10 ounces) refrigerated Alfredo sauce
- 1 cup biscuit/baking mix
- 1/3 cup 2% milk

- 1/4 teaspoon dill weed

Direction

- Set oven to 400° to preheat. Sauté onion, carrots and broccoli in oil in a large skillet until crispy but tender. Mix in Alfredo sauce and chicken; cook thoroughly. Place onto a lightly greased 8-in. square baking pan.
- Mix dill, milk and baking mix just until moistened in a small bowl. Put by heaping tablespoonfuls onto chicken mix.
- Bake for 18-22 minutes, uncovered, until biscuits are golden brown and bubbling on top.

Nutrition Information

- Calories: 578 calories
- Sodium: 1161mg sodium
- Fiber: 4g fiber)
- Total Carbohydrate: 33g carbohydrate (10g sugars
- Cholesterol: 94mg cholesterol
- Protein: 28g protein.
- Total Fat: 38g fat (12g saturated fat)

508.   Asparagus Spaghetti Pie

Serving: 6-8 servings. | Prep: 15mins | Cook: 35mins | Ready in:

Ingredients

- CRUST:
- 2 large eggs
- 1 package (7 ounces) spaghetti, cooked and drained
- 1/2 cup grated Parmesan cheese
- 2 tablespoons butter, melted
- FILLING:
- 1 cup cubed fully cooked ham
- 1 package (8 ounces) frozen asparagus spears, thawed and cut into 1-inch pieces

- 1 jar (4-1/2 ounces) sliced mushrooms, drained
- 1-1/2 cups shredded Swiss cheese
- 2 large eggs
- 1/2 cup sour cream
- 1 teaspoon dill weed
- 1 teaspoon minced chives

Direction

- Whisk eggs in a big bowl; add butter, Parmesan cheese, and spaghetti; combine well. Press up the sides and onto the bottom of an oiled 10-inch pie plate.
- Mix together mushrooms, asparagus, and ham; scoop into the crust. Sprinkle Swiss cheese over top. Whisk chives, dill, sour cream, and eggs; spread over cheese.
- Bake for 35-40 minutes at 350 degrees or till the center is slightly browned and the crust is set. Let it sit for 10 minutes then serve.

Nutrition Information

- Calories: 323 calories
- Total Carbohydrate: 23g carbohydrate (3g sugars
- Cholesterol: 156mg cholesterol
- Protein: 19g protein.
- Total Fat: 17g fat (9g saturated fat)
- Sodium: 509mg sodium
- Fiber: 2g fiber)

509. Baked Eggplant Italiano

Serving: 6 servings. | Prep: 30mins | Cook: 30mins | Ready in:

Ingredients

- 2 small eggplants, peeled and cut into 1/2-inch slices
- 3 tablespoons olive oil, divided
- 1 teaspoon garlic powder

- 1 teaspoon salt, divided
- 1/2 teaspoon pepper, divided
- 2 small tomatoes, finely chopped
- 1 small onion, finely chopped
- 1 tablespoon Italian seasoning
- 2 teaspoons minced garlic
- 1 package (6 ounces) fresh baby spinach
- 1 cup reduced-fat ricotta cheese
- 1 cup shredded part-skim mozzarella cheese, divided
- 1 large egg, lightly beaten
- 2 cups garden-style pasta sauce

Direction

- Brush 2 tablespoons oil on both sides of eggplant slices; drizzle with 1/4 teaspoon pepper, half a teaspoon of salt and garlic powder. Grill with a cover over medium heat or broil 4-6 in. from the heat for 2-3 minutes per side. Put aside.
- Sauté Italian seasoning, onion, tomatoes and the rest of pepper and salt in the remaining oil in a large skillet. Add spinach; cook for 1 more minute. Add spinach; stir until wilted. Mix egg, half a cup mozzarella and ricotta; stir into tomato mixture.
- Place eggplant in a single layer in a 13x9-in. baking dish coated with cooking spray. Place tomato mixture and pasta sauce on top. Scatter with the rest of the mozzarella.
- Bake without a cover at 350° until bubbly or for 30-35 minutes. Rest 5 minutes; serve.

Nutrition Information

- Calories: 275 calories
- Total Fat: 15g fat (4g saturated fat)
- Sodium: 885mg sodium
- Fiber: 7g fiber)
- Total Carbohydrate: 25g carbohydrate (15g sugars
- Cholesterol: 60mg cholesterol
- Protein: 13g protein. Diabetic Exchanges: 2 vegetable

510.   Baked Rice With Sausage

Serving: 12-14 servings. | Prep: 30mins | Cook: 50mins | Ready in:

Ingredients

- 2 pounds Johnsonville® Ground Mild Italian sausage
- 4 celery ribs, thinly sliced
- 1 large onion, chopped
- 1 large green pepper, chopped
- 4-1/2 cups water
- 3/4 cup dry chicken noodle soup mix
- 1 can (10-3/4 ounces) condensed cream of chicken soup, undiluted
- 1 cup uncooked long grain rice
- 1/4 cup dry bread crumbs
- 2 tablespoons butter, melted

Direction

- In a big skillet on medium heat, cook green pepper, onion, celery, and sausage until vegetables are tender and meat is not pink anymore; drain. Heat water in a big saucepan to a boil; put in dry soup mix. Lower heat and allow to simmer without cover for about 5 minutes or until noodles are tender. Mix in sausage mixture, rice, and canned soup; combine thoroughly.
- Remove to an oiled 13x9-inch baking dish. Bake with cover for 40 minutes at 350 degrees. Toss butter and bread crumbs; spread them over the rice mixture. Bake without cover until rice is tender or for about 10-15 minutes. Let it sit for 10 minutes then serve.

Nutrition Information

- Calories: 234 calories
- Sodium: 771mg sodium
- Fiber: 1g fiber)
- Total Carbohydrate: 20g carbohydrate (2g sugars

- Cholesterol: 38mg cholesterol
- Protein: 10g protein.
- Total Fat: 12g fat (5g saturated fat)

511.   Baked Spaghetti

Serving: 8 | Prep: 25mins | Cook: 1hours | Ready in:

Ingredients

- 1 (16 ounce) package spaghetti
- 1 pound ground beef
- 1 onion, chopped
- 1 (32 ounce) jar meatless spaghetti sauce
- 1/2 teaspoon seasoned salt
- 2 eggs
- 1/3 cup grated Parmesan cheese
- 5 tablespoons butter, melted
- 2 cups small curd cottage cheese, divided
- 4 cups shredded mozzarella cheese, divided

Direction

- Preheat the oven to 175°C or 350°Fahrenheit. Oil a 9-in x 13-in baking dish lightly.
- Boil a big pot of lightly salted water. Cook spaghetti for about 12mins, stirring from time to time, until cooked through yet firm to chew; drain.
- On medium heat, heat a big pan; add onion and beef. Cook and stir for about 7mins until the onions are translucent and soft and the beef is brown; drain. Mix in seasoned salt and spaghetti sauce.
- In a big bowl, beat butter, Parmesan cheese, and eggs. Toss in spaghetti until well coated. Transfer 1/2 of the spaghetti mixture in the prepared baking dish. Top with 1/2 of cottage cheese and mozzarella. Spread meat sauce on top. Repeat process with the next layers; use a sheet of aluminum foil to cover.
- Bake for 40mins in the 350°Fahrenheit or 175°C preheated oven. Take off the foil and bake for another 20-25mins until the cheese melts and lightly browned.

Nutrition Information

- Calories: 728 calories;
- Total Fat: 33.6
- Sodium: 1250
- Total Carbohydrate: 61.9
- Cholesterol: 150
- Protein: 42.5

---

512.   Baked Spaghetti Potluck Casserole

Serving: 12 servings. | Prep: 20mins | Cook: 40mins | Ready in:

Ingredients

- 1 package (16 ounces) spaghetti
- 1-1/2 pounds ground beef
- 1 medium onion, chopped
- 1/2 cup chopped green pepper
- 1 can (10-3/4 ounces) condensed cream of mushroom soup, undiluted
- 1 can (10-3/4 ounces) condensed tomato soup, undiluted
- 1 can (8 ounces) tomato sauce
- 1 cup water
- 2 tablespoons brown sugar
- 1 teaspoon salt
- 1 teaspoon dried basil
- 1 teaspoon dried oregano
- 1/2 teaspoon dried marjoram
- 1/2 teaspoon dried rosemary, crushed
- 1/8 teaspoon garlic salt
- 1 cup shredded part-skim mozzarella cheese, divided

Direction

- Break spaghetti in half; cook as directed on the package. In the meantime, cook green pepper, onion and beef until meat is no longer pink in a Dutch oven over medium heat. Stir in

seasonings, brown sugar, water, tomato sauce and soups.
- Drain spaghetti; stir into meat sauce. Add half a cup of cheese. Place into a greased 13x9-in. baking dish.
- Bake with a cover for half an hour at 350°. Uncover; drizzle with the rest of cheese. Bake for 10-15 more minutes or until cheese is melted.

Nutrition Information

- Calories: 313 calories
- Fiber: 2g fiber)
- Total Carbohydrate: 39g carbohydrate (7g sugars
- Cholesterol: 36mg cholesterol
- Protein: 18g protein.
- Total Fat: 9g fat (4g saturated fat)
- Sodium: 706mg sodium

---

513.   Baked Ziti

Serving: 2 casseroles (12 servings each). | Prep: 20mins | Cook: 60mins | Ready in:

Ingredients

- 1 pound lean ground beef (90% lean)
- 2 medium onions, chopped
- 3 garlic cloves, minced
- 1 jar (28 ounces) reduced-sodium meatless spaghetti sauce
- 1 can (28 ounces) diced tomatoes, undrained
- 1 can (12 ounces) tomato paste
- 3/4 cup water
- 2 tablespoons minced fresh parsley
- 1 tablespoon Worcestershire sauce
- 2 teaspoons dried basil
- 1-1/2 teaspoons dried oregano, divided
- 1 package (16 ounces) ziti or 16 ounces small tube pasta
- 1 carton (15 ounces) reduced-fat ricotta cheese
- 2 cups shredded part-skim mozzarella cheese

- 1/2 cup grated Parmesan cheese, divided
- 1/2 cup egg substitute
- 1/2 teaspoon salt
- 1/2 teaspoon pepper

Direction

- Cook onions and beef over medium heat in a large saucepan until meat is no longer pink. Add garlic; cook for 1 more minute. Drain. Stir in teaspoon of oregano, basil, Worcestershire sauce, parsley, water, tomato paste, tomatoes and spaghetti sauce. Simmer with a cover while stirring occasionally for 3 hours.
- Cook pasta as directed on the package; drain. Mix pepper, salt, egg substitute, 1/4 cup Parmesan cheese, mozzarella and ricotta in a large bowl.
- Spread a cup of meat sauce in 2 greased 13x9-in. baking dishes coated with cooking spray. Layer 1/4 of pasta, a cup of meat sauce and 1/4 of cheese mixture in each dish. Place another layer with the same order on top.
- Pour the rest of the sauce on top. Scatter with oregano and the rest of Parmesan cheese. Bake with a cover at 350° until heated through or for an hour.

Nutrition Information

- Calories: 324 calories
- Total Carbohydrate: 30g carbohydrate (0 sugars
- Cholesterol: 38mg cholesterol
- Protein: 26g protein. Diabetic Exchanges: 3 lean meat
- Total Fat: 11g fat (6g saturated fat)
- Sodium: 796mg sodium
- Fiber: 3g fiber)

514.   Baked Ziti And Sausage

Serving: 6 servings. | Prep: 25mins | Cook: 30mins |Ready in:

Ingredients

- 3 cups uncooked ziti or other small tube pasta
- 1/2 pound Johnsonville® Mild Italian Sausage Links
- 1/4 cup butter, cubed
- 1/4 cup all-purpose flour
- 1-1/2 teaspoons salt, divided
- 1/4 teaspoon plus 1/8 teaspoon pepper, divided
- 2 cups 2% milk
- 1/2 cup grated Parmesan cheese, divided
- 1 large egg, lightly beaten
- 2 cups 4% cottage cheese
- 1 tablespoon minced fresh parsley
- 1 cup shredded part-skim mozzarella cheese
- Paprika

Direction

- Cook pasta as directed on the package. Drain; put in a large bowl. Cook sausage over medium heat in a small skillet until no longer pink; drain, cut into 1/2-in. slices.
- Melt butter in a large saucepan. Stir in 1/4 teaspoon of pepper, 1 teaspoon of salt and flour until smooth; add milk gradually. Bring to boiling; cook while stirring until thickened or for 2 minutes. Take out of the heat; stir in 1/4 cup of Parmesan cheese. Spread over pasta; toss to coat.
- Mix salt, pepper, the remaining Parmesan cheese, parsley, cottage cheese and egg in a small bowl. Use a spoon to place 1/2 of the pasta mixture into a greased 2-1/2-qt. baking dish. Sprinkle with cottage cheese mixture. Add sausage to the remaining pasta mixture; use spoon to put on top. Top with paprika and mozzarella cheese.
- Bake without a cover at 350° until the thermometer registers 160° or for 30-35 minutes.

Nutrition Information

- Calories:
- Cholesterol:

- Protein:
- Total Fat:
- Sodium:
- Fiber:
- Total Carbohydrate:

515.   Baked Ziti With Cheese

Serving: 8 | Prep: | Cook: |Ready in:

Ingredients

- 1 (16 ounce) box Barilla® Ziti
- 5 tablespoons butter
- 4 tablespoons all-purpose flour
- 3 cups milk
- 1/2 teaspoon ground nutmeg
- 2 teaspoons kosher salt
- 2 tablespoons kosher salt (optional)
- 2 cups Barilla® Marinara Sauce
- 1 pound buffalo mozzarella cheese, cut into 1/4-inch cubes
- 1/2 cup freshly grated Parmigiano-Reggiano cheese
- 1/2 cup fresh breadcrumbs

Direction

- To make bechamel sauce: Melt butter in a medium pot. Stir in flour until smooth. Cook until golden brown on medium heat, 6-7 minutes.
- In the meantime, in a different pan heat milk until it is just about to boil.
- One cup at a time, add milk to the butter mixture, stir constantly until mixture is very smooth and boiling. Cook it 30 seconds and then take away from heat. Season with 2 teaspoons salt and nutmeg; set it aside.
- Start preheating oven to 425 degrees F.
- Boil 6 quarts of water in a large pot and, if desired, add 2 tablespoons of salt.
- Cook the ziti 30 seconds less than the package directions say.

- Add mozzarella, bechamel sauce, grated cheese, and marinara sauce to the ziti and stir well.
- Divide the mixture between six gratin individual pans. Sprinkle on bread crumbs.
- Bake until crusty and bubbly on top, 20 minutes. Enjoy immediately.

Nutrition Information

- Calories: 578 calories;
- Total Fat: 25.7
- Sodium: 2429
- Total Carbohydrate: 61.6
- Cholesterol: 75
- Protein: 24.5

516.   Beef Mushroom Spaghetti

Serving: 4 servings. | Prep: 15mins | Cook: 35mins | Ready in:

Ingredients

- 1 pound ground beef
- 1 medium onion, chopped
- 1 can (15 ounces) tomato sauce
- 1 can (10-3/4 ounces) condensed cream of mushroom soup, undiluted
- 1/4 cup water
- 1 package (7 ounces) thin spaghetti, cooked and drained

Direction

- Cook onion and beef over medium heat in a large skillet until meat is no longer pink; drain. Stir in water, soup and tomato sauce. Add spaghetti; toss to coat.
- Transfer to a greased 8-in. square baking dish. Freeze, covered, for up to 3 months.
- To use frozen casserole: Thaw in the fridge.

Bake with a cover at 350° until heated through or for 35-40 minutes.

Nutrition Information

- Calories: 464 calories
- Total Fat: 15g fat (6g saturated fat)
- Sodium: 1102mg sodium
- Fiber: 3g fiber)
- Total Carbohydrate: 52g carbohydrate (6g sugars
- Cholesterol: 59mg cholesterol
- Protein: 30g protein.

---

517.   Beef Stuffed Manicotti

Serving: 2 servings. | Prep: 30mins | Cook: 25mins | Ready in:

Ingredients

- 4 uncooked manicotti shells
- 1/2 pound ground beef
- 1 small onion, finely chopped
- 1/2 medium green pepper, finely chopped
- 1 can (15 ounces) tomato sauce
- 1 to 1-1/2 teaspoons dried oregano
- 1 teaspoon dried thyme
- 1 cup shredded mozzarella cheese, divided

Direction

- Cook manicotti as directed on the package; drain. Cook green pepper, onion and beef until meat is no longer pink in a large skillet over medium heat; drain. Mix in thyme, oregano and tomato sauce; bring to boiling. Lower the heat; simmer without a cover for 10 minutes. Add half a cup of cheese; stir until melted.
- Stuff 1/2 meat mixture into manicotti shells; place in a greased 8-in. square baking dish. Scoop the rest of the mixture over shells.
- Bake without a cover for 20 minutes at 325°. Drizzle with the rest of the cheese; bake until

heated through and cheese is melted or for 5-10 more minutes.

Nutrition Information

- Calories: 533 calories
- Fiber: 5g fiber)
- Total Carbohydrate: 42g carbohydrate (8g sugars
- Cholesterol: 99mg cholesterol
- Protein: 40g protein.
- Total Fat: 23g fat (12g saturated fat)
- Sodium: 1264mg sodium

---

518.   Beef Stuffed Manicotti With Basil Tomato Sauce

Serving: 4 servings. | Prep: 55mins | Cook: 30mins | Ready in:

Ingredients

- 1 pound ground beef
- 2 cups water
- 2 cans (6 ounces each) tomato paste
- 1 medium onion, chopped
- 6 tablespoons minced fresh parsley, divided
- 1 tablespoon dried basil
- 1 garlic clove, minced
- 2 teaspoons salt, divided
- 1/4 teaspoon pepper, divided
- 3 cups ricotta cheese
- 1-1/4 cups grated Romano or Parmesan cheese, divided
- 2 eggs, lightly beaten
- 8 large manicotti shells, cooked and drained

Direction

- Cook beef until no longer pink over medium heat in a large skillet; drain. Stir in 1/8 teaspoon pepper, garlic, basil, 2 tablespoons parsley, 1-1/2 teaspoons salt, onion, tomato paste and water. Simmer without a cover while stirring occasionally for half an hour.

- In the meantime, mix pepper, salt, the rest of parsley, eggs, 3/4 cup Romano cheese and ricotta cheese. Stuff into manicotti shells.
- Transfer 1/2 the meat sauce into a greased 11x7-in. baking dish. Place shells over sauce. Pour sauce over top; scatter with the rest of the Romano cheese. Bake without a cover at 350° until heated through or for 30-35 minutes.

Nutrition Information

- Calories: 813 calories
- Fiber: 5g fiber)
- Total Carbohydrate: 47g carbohydrate (19g sugars
- Cholesterol: 274mg cholesterol
- Protein: 66g protein.
- Total Fat: 43g fat (25g saturated fat)
- Sodium: 2075mg sodium

---

519.   Beef And Cheese Shells

Serving: 7-9 servings. | Prep: 25mins | Cook: 30mins | Ready in:

Ingredients

- 1 pound ground beef, cooked and drained
- 2 cups small-curd cottage cheese
- 2 cups shredded mozzarella cheese
- 1 large egg, beaten
- 2 tablespoons dried parsley flakes
- 1 tablespoon dried minced onion
- 1/4 teaspoon garlic powder
- 1/4 teaspoon dried oregano
- 28 jumbo pasta shells, cooked and drained
- 2 cups spaghetti sauce
- Grated Parmesan cheese

Direction

- Mix the first 8 ingredients in a large bowl. Stuff into pasta shells; place in a greased 13x9-in. baking dish. Pour spaghetti sauce on top. Bake with a cover at 350° until heated through or for half an hour. Scatter with Parmesan cheese.

Nutrition Information

- Calories: 360 calories
- Cholesterol: 80mg cholesterol
- Protein: 25g protein.
- Total Fat: 15g fat (7g saturated fat)
- Sodium: 579mg sodium
- Fiber: 2g fiber)
- Total Carbohydrate: 30g carbohydrate (7g sugars

---

520.   Beef Stuffed Shells

Serving: 6-8 servings. | Prep: 20mins | Cook: 30mins | Ready in:

Ingredients

- 20 jumbo pasta shells
- 1 jar (26 ounces) spaghetti sauce, divided
- 1 portion Ground Beef Mix, thawed
- 1-1/2 to 2 cups shredded part-skim mozzarella cheese

Direction

- Cook pasta shells as directed on the package; drain.
- Spread about a cup of spaghetti sauce in a greased 13x9-in. baking dish.
- Fill beef mix into shells; transfer into pan. Pour the rest of the spaghetti sauce on top. Bake with a cover for half an hour at 350°. Uncover; drizzle with cheese. Bake until meat is no longer pink or for 10 more minutes.

Nutrition Information

- Calories:
- Fiber:
- Total Carbohydrate:
- Cholesterol:
- Protein:
- Total Fat:
- Sodium:

---

521. Beefy Eggplant Parmigiana

Serving: 8 servings. | Prep: 01hours10mins | Cook: 35mins | Ready in:

Ingredients

- 1/3 cup chopped onion
- 1/4 cup finely chopped celery
- 1/8 teaspoon garlic powder
- 2 tablespoons canola oil
- 1 can (14-1/2 ounces) Italian stewed tomatoes
- 1/4 cup tomato paste
- 1 teaspoon dried parsley flakes
- 1/2 teaspoon dried oregano
- 1-1/4 teaspoons salt, divided
- 1/2 teaspoon pepper, divided
- 1 bay leaf
- 1 pound ground beef
- 3/4 cup all-purpose flour
- 1 cup buttermilk
- 1 medium eggplant, peeled and cut into 1/2-inch slices
- Additional canola oil
- 1/2 cup grated Parmesan cheese
- 2 cups shredded part-skim mozzarella cheese, divided
- Minced fresh parsley

Direction

- Sauté garlic powder, celery and onion in oil in a large saucepan until tender. Mix in bay leaf, 1/4 teaspoon of pepper, 1/2 teaspoon salt, oregano, parsley, tomato paste and tomatoes.

Let it come to a boil. Lower heat; cover up and allow to simmer for 1 hour. Remove the bay leaf.
- Over medium heat in a large skillet, cook beef till no longer pink; drain and put aside. Mix the remaining pepper and salt and flour in a shallow dish. In another shallow dish, pour buttermilk. Dip eggplant in buttermilk, then in flour mixture.
- In a large skillet, cook eggplant in batches in 1/2 in. of hot oil until both sides turns golden brown; drain.
- Put 1/2 eggplant in a greased baking dish of 13x9 inches. Top with 1/2 Parmesan cheese, beef and tomato mixture. Sprinkle 1 cup of mozzarella cheese on top. Top with remaining eggplant, Parmesan cheese, beef and tomato mixture.
- Bake with no cover, at 350° until heated through, about half an hour. Sprinkle the remaining mozzarella cheese on top. Bake till cheese is melted, about 5-10 more minutes. Allow to sit for 10 minutes prior to serving. Garnish with parsley then serve.

Nutrition Information

- Calories: 307 calories
- Protein: 23g protein.
- Total Fat: 15g fat (7g saturated fat)
- Sodium: 846mg sodium
- Fiber: 3g fiber)
- Total Carbohydrate: 21g carbohydrate (9g sugars
- Cholesterol: 49mg cholesterol

---

522. Biscuit Pizza Bake

Serving: 6-8 servings. | Prep: 15mins | Cook: 30mins | Ready in:

Ingredients

- 1 pound ground beef

- 2 tubes (12 ounces each) refrigerated buttermilk biscuits
- 1 package (3-1/2 ounces) sliced pepperoni
- 1 can (4 ounces) mushroom stems and pieces, drained
- 1 can (15 ounces) pizza sauce
- 1 cup chopped green pepper
- 1/2 cup chopped onion
- 1 cup shredded cheddar cheese
- 1 cup shredded part-skim mozzarella cheese

Direction

- Set oven to 350 degrees and start preheating. In a big skillet on medium heat, cook beef for 6-8 minutes or until not pink anymore, breaking into crumbles. At the same time, cut the biscuits into quarters then put in an oiled 13x9-inch baking dish. Drain beef and arrange over biscuits.
- Layer with onion, green pepper, pizza sauce, mushrooms, and pepperoni. Bake for 15 minutes without cover. Sprinkle cheese over top. Continue to bake for 15-20 minutes or until cheese melts. Let it sit for 5-10 minutes then serve.

Nutrition Information

- Calories: 369 calories
- Protein: 23g protein.
- Total Fat: 19g fat (9g saturated fat)
- Sodium: 968mg sodium
- Fiber: 2g fiber)
- Total Carbohydrate: 27g carbohydrate (3g sugars
- Cholesterol: 64mg cholesterol

523. Butternut Squash And Sausage Stuffed Shells

Serving: 10 servings. | Prep: 55mins | Cook: 30mins | Ready in:

Ingredients

- 5 cups peeled butternut squash, cut into 1-inch cubes
- 3 tablespoons extra virgin olive oil, divided
- 32 uncooked jumbo pasta shells
- 3/4 pound Johnsonville® Ground Hot Italian sausage
- 2 cups finely chopped sweet onion, divided
- 1 package (5 ounces) baby kale salad blend, chopped
- 8 ounces crumbled goat cheese, divided
- 4 garlic cloves, minced
- 1 carton (26.46 ounces) chopped tomatoes, undrained
- 2 tablespoons fresh sage
- 1 tablespoon sugar
- 1/2 cup fat-free half-and-half

Direction

- Preheat oven to 400°. Use 1 tablespoon olive oil to toss squash on a foil-lined baking sheet. Roast squash for nearly 40 minutes, stirring halfway through, until starting to caramelize and softened. Transfer to a large bowl; mash roughly. Decease heat to 350°.
- Cook pasta following the instruction of the package. Let it drain.
- In a large nonstick skillet, cook over medium-high heat with 1 cup onion and sausage, crumbling meat, until no longer pink. Add baby kale; cook for around 3 to 5 minutes until kale is soft. Mix with squash. Stir in goat cheese (about 4 ounces).
- Heat the remaining olive oil in the same skillet. Put in the rest onion; cook for around 3 to 5 minutes till softened. Add garlic; cook and stirring for an addition of 1 minute. Add sugar, sage and tomatoes; set to a boil. Lower the heat; simmer for approximately 15 minutes, stirring occasionally, till sauce is thickened. Allow 5 minutes for cooling. In a blender, pulse till combined. Put in half-and-half; pulse till smooth. In a greased baking dish of 13x9-inch, pour about half of the sauce.

- In each shell, stuff about 2 tablespoons squash mixture; place into the baking dish. Pour over shells with the rest tomato sauce; use the remaining goat cheese to top. Bake with a cover for nearly 20 minutes until beginning to bubble. Take away the cover; bake for an addition of 10 minutes. Allow 10 minutes to rest before serving.

Nutrition Information

- Calories: 379 calories
- Total Carbohydrate: 43g carbohydrate (9g sugars
- Cholesterol: 47mg cholesterol
- Protein: 15g protein.
- Total Fat: 18g fat (7g saturated fat)
- Sodium: 344mg sodium
- Fiber: 6g fiber)

---

524. Cannelloni

Serving: 8-10 servings. | Prep: 30mins | Cook: 20mins | Ready in:

Ingredients

- FILLING:
- 1 large onion, finely chopped
- 2 tablespoons olive oil
- 1 garlic clove, minced
- 1 package (10 ounces) frozen chopped spinach, thawed and squeezed dry
- 1 pound ground beef
- 1/4 cup grated Parmesan cheese
- 2 tablespoons heavy whipping cream
- 2 large eggs, lightly beaten
- 1/2 teaspoon dried oregano
- 1 teaspoon salt
- 1/4 teaspoon pepper
- 10 lasagna noodles
- 1 can (24 ounces) tomato sauce, divided
- CREAM SAUCE:
- 6 tablespoons butter

- 6 tablespoons all-purpose flour
- 1 cup whole milk
- 1 cup heavy whipping cream
- Salt and pepper to taste
- 1/2 cup grated Parmesan cheese

Direction

- In a large skillet, sauté onion in olive oil until tender. Stir in garlic; cook for approximately 1 minute. Stir in spinach. Cook for around 5 minutes until the spinach starts to stick to the pan and all the water has evaporated, stirring constantly. Place to a large bowl.
- Brown meat in the same skillet; drain and add to the spinach mixture. Mix in the cream, cheese, oregano, eggs, pepper and salt; mix well. Leave aside.
- Cook lasagna noodles following the instruction of the package; drain. Cut in half the width of each noodle; on a large piece of foil, spread noodles out side by side. At one end of noodle, place 1 heaping tablespoon of filling; roll up. With remaining noodles and filling, repeat.
- In a baking dish of 13x9-inch, pour about 1 cup of tomato sauce to the bottom. In the baking dish, place two rolls vertically with seam side down on both sides. Place the rest rolls in four rows of three rolls each; leave aside.
- For making cream sauce, in a heavy saucepan over medium heat, melt butter; mix in flour until smooth; stir in milk and cream gradually. Allow to boil, cook and stir for 1 minute until thickened. Take away from heat; taste with salt and pepper. Spread over lasagna rolls with the cream sauce. Have the rest tomato sauce to cover. Use cheese to sprinkle.
- Bake uncovered at 375° for approximately 20 to 30 minutes until bubbly and hot.

Nutrition Information

- Calories: 443 calories
- Total Carbohydrate: 30g carbohydrate (5g sugars

- Cholesterol: 128mg cholesterol
- Protein: 19g protein.
- Total Fat: 28g fat (15g saturated fat)
- Sodium: 817mg sodium
- Fiber: 3g fiber)

525.   Cheddar Chicken Spaghetti

Serving: 8 servings. | Prep: 15mins | Cook: 20mins | Ready in:

Ingredients

- 1 package (7 ounces) spaghetti, broken
- 2 cups cubed cooked chicken
- 2 cups shredded cheddar cheese, divided
- 1 can (10-3/4 ounces) condensed cream of chicken soup, undiluted
- 1 cup whole milk
- 1 tablespoon diced pimientos, optional
- 1/4 teaspoon salt
- 1/4 teaspoon pepper

Direction

- Follow the package cooking instructions to cook spaghetti. At the same time, mix pepper, salt, pimientos if desired, milk, soup, 1 cup of cheese, and chicken in a big bowl. Strain pasta; add to the chicken mixture and toss to coat.
- Pour in a 13x9-inch baking dish coated with grease. Scatter the remaining cheese on top. Bake without a cover for 20 to 25 minutes at 350 degrees until heated through.

Nutrition Information

- Calories: 311 calories
- Total Fat: 14g fat (8g saturated fat)
- Sodium: 579mg sodium
- Fiber: 1g fiber)
- Total Carbohydrate: 23g carbohydrate (3g sugars

- Cholesterol: 68mg cholesterol
- Protein: 21g protein.

526.   Cheese & Pumpkin Filled Manicotti

Serving: 7 servings. | Prep: 30mins | Cook: 25mins | Ready in:

Ingredients

- 1 package (8 ounces) manicotti shells
- 1 container (15 ounces) ricotta cheese
- 2 cups shredded part-skim mozzarella cheese, divided
- 1 cup canned pumpkin
- 1/4 cup grated Parmesan cheese
- 2 large egg yolks
- 1/4 teaspoon ground nutmeg
- 1 jar (24 ounces) garlic pasta sauce, divided

Direction

- Preheat the oven to 350 degrees F. Cook the manicotti shells following the package instructions until al dente; drain.
- Combine nutmeg, ricotta cheese, egg yolks, a cup of mozzarella cheese, Parmesan cheese, and pumpkin in a big bowl; scoop into the manicotti.
- In a greased 13-in by 9-in baking dish, spread a cup of pasta sauce. Add stuffed manicotti on top. Transfer the rest of the pasta sauce on top; scatter the rest of the mozzarella cheese. Bake for 25-30mins while covering or until the cheese melts.

Nutrition Information

- Calories: 392 calories
- Sodium: 704mg sodium
- Fiber: 4g fiber)
- Total Carbohydrate: 41g carbohydrate (13g sugars

- Cholesterol: 100mg cholesterol
- Protein: 22g protein.
- Total Fat: 16g fat (9g saturated fat)

527.   Cheese Manicotti

Serving: 20 servings, 2 manicotti each | Prep: 1hours | Cook: | Ready in:

Ingredients

- 3-1/4 cups flour, divided
- 5   eggs, divided
- 1/2 cup warm water
- 3 lb. POLLY-O Original Ricotta Cheese
- 1 pkg. (8 oz.) POLLY-O Whole Milk Mozzarella Cheese, shredded, divided
- 3/4 cup KRAFT Grated Parmesan Cheese, divided
- 1/4 cup chopped fresh parsley
- 4 cups OLIVO by CLASSICO Traditional Pasta Sauce

Direction

- In a medium-sized bowl, put 3 cups flour, form a well in the middle. Add water and 2 eggs to the well, use a fork to mix until the mixture makes a stiff dough. On a surface lightly scattered with flour, put the dough and knead until the dough is not sticky anymore and becomes smooth, add the leftover 1/4 cup flour if needed. Put a cover on and let sit for 15 minutes.
- Turn the oven to 375°F. Separate the dough into 8 even portions. With a pasta roller, roll each portion out into thin strip, about 20x5-in. each strip. Slice each strip crosswise into 5 even pieces. Working in batches, put the strips in a big pan full of boiling water. Cook until soft, about 5 minutes. Strain thoroughly. Use paper towels to tap dry.
- Mix together parsley, the leftover eggs, 1/2 cup Parmesan, 1/2 the mozzarella, and ricotta. Onto the bottom of each of two 13x9-in. baking

dishes, spread 1/2 cup pasta sauce. Spread onto each pasta piece with 2 tablespoons ricotta cheese, roll up. In each baking dish, put 20 manicotti with the seam sides facing down. In each dish, pour over the manicotti with 1/2 the leftover pasta sauce, put 1/2 the leftover Parmesan and mozzarella on top each.
- Bake until fully heated, about 25-30 minutes.

Nutrition Information

- Calories: 480
- Sugar: 9 g
- Protein: 26 g
- Sodium: 750 mg
- Fiber: 2 g
- Total Carbohydrate: 36 g
- Cholesterol: 155 mg
- Total Fat: 25 g
- Saturated Fat: 14 g

528.   Cheese Spinach Manicotti

Serving: 7 servings. | Prep: 55mins | Cook: 55mins | Ready in:

Ingredients

- 1 large onion, chopped
- 2 garlic cloves, minced
- 1 tablespoon olive oil
- 3 cans (8 ounces each) no-salt-added tomato sauce
- 2 cans (6 ounces each) tomato paste
- 1-1/2 cups water
- 1/2 cup dry red wine or vegetable broth
- 2 tablespoons Italian seasoning
- 2 teaspoons sugar
- 2 teaspoons dried oregano
- FILLING:
- 1 package (8 ounces) fat-free cream cheese
- 1-1/4 cups (10 ounces) 2% cottage cheese
- 1 package (10 ounces) frozen chopped spinach, thawed and squeezed dry

- 1/4 cup grated Parmesan cheese
- 2 large eggs, lightly beaten
- 1/2 teaspoon salt
- 1 package (8 ounces) manicotti shells
- 1 cup shredded part-skim mozzarella cheese

Direction

- Sauté onion and garlic in oil until tender in a large saucepan. Stir in oregano, sugar, Italian seasoning, wine, water, tomato paste and tomato sauce. Bring to boiling. Lower the heat; simmer without a cover while stirring occasionally for 15-20 minutes.
- In the meantime, to prepare filling: Whisk cream cheese until smooth in a large bowl. Stir in salt, eggs, Parmesan cheese, spinach and cottage cheese.
- Stuff cream cheese mixture into uncooked manicotti shells. Pour 1 cup sauce into a 13x9-in. baking dish coated with cooking spray; spread evenly. Place manicotti on top of the sauce. Top with the rest of the sauce.
- Bake with a cover at 350° until pasta becomes tender or for 50-55 minutes. Uncover then drizzle with mozzarella cheese. Bake until cheese is melted or for 5-10 more minutes.

Nutrition Information

- Calories: 389 calories
- Fiber: 5g fiber)
- Total Carbohydrate: 50g carbohydrate (15g sugars
- Cholesterol: 80mg cholesterol
- Protein: 25g protein.
- Total Fat: 9g fat (4g saturated fat)
- Sodium: 722mg sodium

529.   Cheese Stuffed Shells

Serving: 12 servings. | Prep: 35mins | Cook: 50mins | Ready in:

Ingredients

- 1 pound Johnsonville® Ground Mild Italian sausage
- 1 large onion, chopped
- 1 package (10 ounces) frozen chopped spinach, thawed and squeezed dry
- 1 package (8 ounces) cream cheese, cubed
- 1 large egg, lightly beaten
- 2 cups shredded part-skim mozzarella cheese, divided
- 2 cups shredded cheddar cheese
- 1 cup 4% cottage cheese
- 1 cup grated Parmesan cheese
- 1/4 teaspoon salt
- 1/4 teaspoon pepper
- 1/8 teaspoon ground cinnamon, optional
- 24 jumbo pasta shells, cooked and drained
- SAUCE:
- 1 can (29 ounces) tomato sauce
- 1 tablespoon dried minced onion
- 1-1/2 teaspoons dried basil
- 1-1/2 teaspoons dried parsley flakes
- 2 garlic cloves, minced
- 1 teaspoon sugar
- 1 teaspoon dried oregano
- 1/2 teaspoon salt
- 1/4 teaspoon pepper

Direction

- Set a large skillet over medium heat, add the sausage and onion and cook until the sausage's meat is no longer pink; let it drain and place in a big bowl. Add in the cream cheese, spinach and egg; stir. Add a cup of mozzarella cheese, cottage cheese, cheddar cheese, Parmesan cheese, pepper, salt, and cinnamon if preferred.
- Fill the pasta shells with sausage mixture, stuffing it evenly. Assemble in two 11x7-in. baking dishes coated using a cooking spray. Mix together the sauce ingredients and pour over shells.
- Cover and let it bake inside the oven at 350° for 45 minutes. Remove the cover and top it off with the rest of the mozzarella. Allow to bake

for additional 5-10 minutes or until bubbly and cheese has melt. Let it sit for 5 minutes before you serve it in.

Nutrition Information

- Calories: 397 calories
- Protein: 24g protein.
- Total Fat: 23g fat (14g saturated fat)
- Sodium: 1097mg sodium
- Fiber: 2g fiber)
- Total Carbohydrate: 24g carbohydrate (5g sugars
- Cholesterol: 94mg cholesterol

---

530. Cheesy Chicken Manicotti

Serving: 4 servings. | Prep: 30mins | Cook: 40mins | Ready in:

Ingredients

- 8 manicotti shells
- 1 can (10-3/4 ounces) condensed tomato soup, undiluted
- 1/2 cup half-and-half cream
- 1/2 cup sour cream
- 1/2 cup water
- 2 tablespoons mayonnaise
- 1 to 2 tablespoons grated Parmesan cheese
- FILLING:
- 1 large egg
- 3 cups shredded mozzarella cheese, divided
- 2 cups cubed cooked chicken
- 1/2 cup 4% cottage cheese
- 1 to 2 tablespoons grated Parmesan cheese
- 1/8 teaspoon pepper
- 1 tablespoon minced chives, optional

Direction

- Follow the package cooking instructions to cook manicotti. At the same time, mix

Parmesan cheese, mayonnaise, water, sour cream, cream, and soup in a bowl. Scatter about 3/4 cup in an 11x7-inch baking dish coated with oil. Mix pepper, Parmesan cheese, cottage cheese, chicken, 1 cup of mozzarella cheese, and egg in a different bowl.
- Drain the manicotti shells; fill each with about 1/3 cup of the chicken mixture. Put over sauce. Drizzle the remainder of sauce over the shells. Arrange the remainder of mozzarella cheese on top. Scatter with chives if you wish.
- Bake without a cover at 350 degrees until bubbly and heated through, 40 to 45 minutes.

Nutrition Information

- Calories: 748 calories
- Protein: 50g protein.
- Total Fat: 41g fat (21g saturated fat)
- Sodium: 1054mg sodium
- Fiber: 2g fiber)
- Total Carbohydrate: 41g carbohydrate (11g sugars
- Cholesterol: 227mg cholesterol

---

531. Cheesy Chicken Spaghetti

Serving: 2 casseroles (5 servings each). | Prep: 35mins | Cook: 50mins | Ready in:

Ingredients

- 4 cups cubed cooked chicken
- 2 cans (10-3/4 ounces each) condensed cream of mushroom soup, undiluted
- 2-1/2 cups chicken broth
- 1 medium green pepper, chopped
- 1 medium onion, chopped
- 2 celery ribs, chopped
- 2 tablespoons dried parsley flakes
- 1/2 teaspoon salt
- 1/2 teaspoon pepper
- 1 pound process cheese (Velveeta), cubed

- 1 package (12 ounces) spaghetti, cooked and drained
- 1 can (2-1/4 ounces) sliced ripe olives, optional

Direction

- Mix the first nine ingredients together in a Dutch oven or a soup kettle. Bring to a boil. Lower heat; cover and let it simmer for 15-20 minutes. Mix in cheese until melted. Add in olives and spaghetti if desired.
- Move to two greased 11x7-inch baking dishes. Cover and freeze 1 casserole for up to 3 months. Cover and bake the second casserole in the oven at 325° for 40 minutes. Remove the cover and bake for 10 more minutes.
- How to use the frozen casserole: Thaw in the fridge for a day. Bake as instructed above.

Nutrition Information

- Calories: 421 calories
- Sodium: 1163mg sodium
- Fiber: 2g fiber)
- Total Carbohydrate: 34g carbohydrate (6g sugars
- Cholesterol: 80mg cholesterol
- Protein: 31g protein.
- Total Fat: 17g fat (9g saturated fat)

532.   Cheesy Clam Manicotti

Serving: 4 servings. | Prep: 30mins | Cook: 25mins | Ready in:

Ingredients

- 1 jar (24 ounces) meatless spaghetti sauce
- 1/4 teaspoon hot pepper sauce
- 2 cans (6-1/2 ounces each) minced clams
- 1 carton (8 ounces) ricotta cheese
- 4 ounces cream cheese, softened
- 1/4 cup spreadable chive and onion cream cheese

- 2 cups shredded part-skim mozzarella cheese
- 1/3 cup grated Parmesan cheese
- 1 teaspoon minced garlic
- 1/2 teaspoon pepper
- 1/4 teaspoon dried oregano
- 8 manicotti shells, cooked and drained

Direction

- Mix hot pepper sauce and spaghetti sauce in a large saucepan. Drain a can of clams; add clams to sauce. Stir in juice and clams from another can. Bring to boiling. Lower the heat; simmer without a cover for 20 minutes.
- In the meantime, whisk cream cheeses and ricotta until smooth in a large bowl. Stir in oregano, pepper, garlic and cheeses. Stuff into manicotti shells.
- In a greased 11x7-in. baking dish, spread 3/4 cup of clam sauce. Place manicotti over sauce; pour the rest of the sauce over manicotti.
- Bake without a cover at 350° until bubbly or for 25-30 minutes. Rest for 5 minutes; then serve.

Nutrition Information

- Calories: 640 calories
- Protein: 33g protein.
- Total Fat: 35g fat (22g saturated fat)
- Sodium: 1559mg sodium
- Fiber: 4g fiber)
- Total Carbohydrate: 49g carbohydrate (18g sugars
- Cholesterol: 126mg cholesterol

533.   Cheesy Pizza Casserole

Serving: 8-10 servings. | Prep: 25mins | Cook: 0mins | Ready in:

Ingredients

- 1 pound ground beef

- 1 package (3-1/2 ounces) sliced pepperoni
- 1 medium onion, chopped
- 1 medium green pepper, chopped
- 1 jar (4-1/2 ounces) sliced mushrooms, drained
- 7 ounces vermicelli, cooked and drained
- 1/3 cup butter, melted
- 1 can (15 ounces) tomato sauce, divided
- 1 cup shredded Swiss cheese
- 4 cups shredded part-skim mozzarella cheese
- 1/2 teaspoon dried oregano
- 1/2 teaspoon dried basil

Direction

- Sauté green pepper, onion, pepperoni, and beef over medium heat in a large skillet until meat is no longer pink; drain. Mix in mushrooms; put to one side.
- Toss vermicelli with butter in an oiled 13x9-inch baking dish, coat by tossing. Add 1 cup of tomato sauce to pasta mixture; spread half of meat mixture over. Combine mozzarella cheese and Swiss cheese; scatter half of cheese mixture over top. Sprinkle with basil and oregano. Arrange the rest of meat and cheese mixture over top. Cover top with the rest of tomato sauce.
- Bake without covering for 25 to 30 minutes at 350°, or until bubbly.

Nutrition Information

- Calories: 422 calories
- Total Carbohydrate: 21g carbohydrate (4g sugars
- Cholesterol: 83mg cholesterol
- Protein: 28g protein.
- Total Fat: 25g fat (14g saturated fat)
- Sodium: 764mg sodium
- Fiber: 2g fiber)

534.   Cheesy Sausage Spaghetti Pie

Serving: 3 pies, 18 servings, 6 per pie. | Prep: 25mins | Cook: 35mins | Ready in:

Ingredients

- 1 package (1 pound) spaghetti
- 4 large eggs, lightly beaten
- 2/3 cup grated Parmesan cheese
- 1 cup chopped onion
- 1/4 cup butter, cubed
- 2 cups sour cream
- 2 teaspoons Italian seasoning
- 2 pounds Jones No Sugar Pork Sausage Roll sausage
- 2 cups water
- 1 can (12 ounces) tomato paste
- 1 cup shredded part-skim mozzarella cheese
- 1/2 cup shredded cheddar cheese

Direction

- Follow package instructions to cook spaghetti; drain and put in a big bowl. Add Parmesan cheese and eggs. Remove to three of 9-inch pie plate then press the mixture up the sides and onto the bottom of the plates to make a crust. Put aside.
- In a big saucepan with butter, sauté onion until tender. Take away from the heat; mix in Italian seasoning and sour cream. Using a spoon to transfer into crusts.
- Cook sausage on medium heat in a big skillet until not pink anymore; drain. Mix in tomato paste and water. Allow to simmer 5 to 10 minutes without a cover or until thickened. Place over the sour cream mixture using a spoon. Sprinkle with cheddar and mozzarella cheeses.
- Cover and keep 2 pies frozen for up to a month. Put on cover and bake the third pie 35-40 minutes at 350 degrees or until heated through.
- To cook frozen pies: Fully thaw in the fridge.

Take out of the fridge 30 minutes prior to baking. Bake as instructions.

Nutrition Information

- Calories: 348 calories
- Protein: 13g protein.
- Total Fat: 21g fat (10g saturated fat)
- Sodium: 373mg sodium
- Fiber: 2g fiber)
- Total Carbohydrate: 26g carbohydrate (6g sugars
- Cholesterol: 100mg cholesterol

---

535.   Chicken Alfredo Stuffed Shells

Serving: 10 servings. | Prep: 45mins | Cook: 40mins | Ready in:

Ingredients

- 1 package (12 ounces) jumbo pasta shells
- 1-1/2 pounds boneless skinless chicken breasts, cut into 1/2-inch cubes
- 2 tablespoons olive oil, divided
- 1/2 pound sliced baby portobello mushrooms
- 1 large egg, lightly beaten
- 1 carton (15 ounces) ricotta cheese
- 3-1/4 cups grated Parmesan cheese, divided
- 1 cup shredded part-skim mozzarella cheese
- 1 teaspoon dried parsley flakes
- 3/4 teaspoon salt
- 1/2 teaspoon pepper
- 1/2 cup butter, cubed
- 2 garlic cloves, minced
- 2 cups heavy whipping cream

Direction

- Cook pasta as directed on the package.
- In the meantime, brown chicken in 1 tablespoon oil in a large skillet. Take out and put aside. In the same pan, sauté the

mushrooms until tender in remaining oil; put aside. In a small bowl, combine the seasonings, 1-1/2 cups Parmesan, mozzarella, ricotta, and egg.

- Drain pasta and rinse using cold water; stuff around 1 tablespoon of cheese mixture into each shell. Put into a 13x9-in. greased baking dish. Add mushrooms and chicken on top.
- In a large saucepan, melt butter over medium heat. Add the garlic; cook and stir for 1 minute. Add the cream; cook for 5 more minutes. Put in 1-1/2 cups Parmesan cheese; cook and stir until it thickens.
- Add the sauce atop the casserole. Sprinkle the remaining Parmesan cheese on top. Bake at 350°, covered, for 30 minutes. Take off the cover; bake until bubbly, or for another 10-15 minutes.
- You can cover the unbaked shells and freeze them for up to 1 month.
- Using the frozen shells: Place in refrigerator to thaw. Let it sit for 30 minutes at room temperature. Bake as instructed.

Nutrition Information

- Calories: 684 calories
- Protein: 38g protein.
- Total Fat: 45g fat (26g saturated fat)
- Sodium: 805mg sodium
- Fiber: 2g fiber)
- Total Carbohydrate: 32g carbohydrate (5g sugars
- Cholesterol: 195mg cholesterol

---

536.   Chicken Broccoli Manicotti

Serving: 6 servings. | Prep: 45mins | Cook: 40mins | Ready in:

Ingredients

- 12 uncooked manicotti shells

- 1 small onion, chopped
- 3 tablespoons butter
- 3 tablespoons all-purpose flour
- 1/4 teaspoon salt
- 1 cup half-and-half cream
- 1 cup chicken broth
- 1-1/2 cups shredded Monterey Jack cheese
- 1/4 cup shredded Parmesan cheese
- FILLING:
- 2 large eggs, lightly beaten
- 3/4 cup soft bread crumbs
- 1/4 cup minced fresh parsley
- 1/4 teaspoon crushed red pepper flakes
- 1/4 teaspoon salt
- 1/8 teaspoon ground nutmeg
- 4 cups cubed cooked chicken breasts
- 6 cups frozen chopped broccoli, thawed

Direction

- Cook manicotti, following package instructions. To make sauce, sauté onion in butter in a saucepan. Mix in salt and flour until combined. Slowly whisk in broth and cream; let it come to a boil. Cook and stir until thick and bubbly, or about 1-2 minutes. Stir in cheeses until just melted.
- Mix nutmeg, salt, pepper flakes, parsley, bread crumbs and eggs together in a bowl. Stir in broccoli and chicken; add in 1 cup of sauce. Drain manicotti; fill with chicken mixture.
- Add about 1/2 cup of cheese sauce in two greased 11x7-inch baking dishes. Place the manicotti on top; pour the remaining sauce on top. Cover and bake at 350° for 35-40 minutes. Remove the cover and bake until golden brown, or about 5 more minutes.

Nutrition Information

- Calories: 558 calories
- Cholesterol: 206mg cholesterol
- Protein: 46g protein.
- Total Fat: 25g fat (14g saturated fat)
- Sodium: 762mg sodium
- Fiber: 3g fiber)

- Total Carbohydrate: 36g carbohydrate (5g sugars

537. Chicken Broccoli Spaghetti

Serving: 2 casseroles (6 servings each). | Prep: 25mins | Cook: 30mins | Ready in:

Ingredients

- 1-1/2 pounds boneless skinless chicken breasts
- 1 package (1 pound) spaghetti
- 2 cups fresh broccoli florets
- 1 can (10-3/4 ounces) condensed cream of chicken soup, undiluted
- 1 can (10-3/4 ounces) condensed cream of mushroom soup, undiluted
- 1-1/4 cups water
- 1 package (16 ounces) process cheese (Velveeta), cubed
- 1/4 teaspoon pepper

Direction

- In a large saucepan, place chicken and pour in water to cover. Let mixture come to a boil. Lower the heat; cover and let it simmer until no longer pink, or about 12-14 minutes. In the meantime, cook spaghetti, following package instructions; drain. Drain chicken and cube; put aside.
- Bring 1 inch of water in a Dutch oven to a boil. Put in broccoli; cover and cook until crisp-tender, or about 3-5 minutes. Drain and put aside. Mix water and soups in the same pan. Mix in cheese; cook and stir until cheese is melted. Mix in spaghetti, pepper, broccoli and chicken.
- Remove to two greased 11x7-inch baking dishes. Cover and freeze the first casserole for up to 3 months. Bake the second casserole without covering at 350° until lightly browned and edges are bubbly, or about 30-40 minutes.

- For baking frozen casserole: Thaw thoroughly in the fridge. Cover and bake at 350° until heated through, or about 45-50 minutes.

Nutrition Information

- Calories:
- Sodium:
- Fiber:
- Total Carbohydrate:
- Cholesterol:
- Protein:
- Total Fat:

---

538.   Chicken Mexican Manicotti

Serving: 2 servings. | Prep: 25mins | Cook: 25mins | Ready in:

Ingredients

- 4 uncooked manicotti shells
- 1 cup cubed cooked chicken breast
- 1 cup salsa, divided
- 1/2 cup reduced-fat ricotta cheese
- 2 tablespoons sliced ripe olives
- 4 teaspoons minced fresh parsley
- 1 tablespoon diced pimientos
- 1 green onion, thinly sliced
- 1 small garlic clove, minced
- 1/4 to 1/2 teaspoon hot pepper sauce
- 1/3 cup shredded reduced-fat Monterey Jack cheese or reduced-fat Mexican cheese blend

Direction

- Follow the package cooking instructions to cook manicotti. Mix pepper sauce, garlic, green onion, pimientos, parsley, olives, ricotta cheese, 1/4 cup of salsa, and chicken in a small bowl. Drain the manicotti; fill with the chicken mixture.

- Drizzle 1/4 cup of salsa in a cooking spray-greased 8-inch square baking dish. Arrange the remaining salsa, and manicotti shells to the top.
- Bake with a cover for 20 minutes at 400 degrees. Uncover; scatter with Monterey Jack cheese and bake until filling is heated through and cheese melts, 5 to 10 minutes more.

Nutrition Information

- Calories: 390 calories
- Total Carbohydrate: 38g carbohydrate (9g sugars
- Cholesterol: 81mg cholesterol
- Protein: 35g protein. Diabetic Exchanges: 4 lean meat
- Total Fat: 10g fat (4g saturated fat)
- Sodium: 783mg sodium
- Fiber: 2g fiber)

---

539.   Chicken Spaghetti Bake

Serving: 8 | Prep: 10mins | Cook: 45mins | Ready in:

Ingredients

- 1 (16 ounce) package spaghetti
- 3 (12.5 fl oz) cans chicken chunks, drained
- 1 (10.75 ounce) can condensed cream of mushroom soup
- 1 (10.75 ounce) can condensed cream of chicken soup
- 4 cups shredded Cheddar cheese

Direction

- Set oven to 350°F (175°C) and start preheating.
- Boil a big pot of lightly salted water. Cook spaghetti in the bubbling water, stirring occasionally, for about 12 minutes or until cooked through but still firm to the bite. Drain and Pour pasta onto a big bowl.

- Combine cream of chicken soup, cream of mushroom soup, and chicken into spaghetti. Pour the mixture onto a 9x13-in. baking dish and sprinkle Cheddar cheese on top.
- Bake in prepared oven for about 30 minutes or until the sauce is bubbly and the cheese melts.

Nutrition Information

- Calories: 719 calories;
- Sodium: 1510
- Total Carbohydrate: 47.8
- Cholesterol: 144
- Protein: 51.5
- Total Fat: 34.4

---

540. Chicken Spaghetti With Bacon

Serving: 8-10 servings. | Prep: 20mins | Cook: 30mins | Ready in:

Ingredients

- 8 ounces spaghetti
- 1 medium onion, chopped
- 1/2 cup chopped green pepper
- 2 celery ribs, chopped
- 4 tablespoons butter, divided
- 2 cans (10-3/4 ounces each) condensed cream of mushroom soup, undiluted
- 1 can (4 ounces) mushroom stems and pieces, drained
- 2-1/2 cups cubed cooked chicken
- 2 cups shredded cheddar cheese
- 1/2 cup dry bread crumbs
- 5 bacon strips, cooked and crumbled

Direction

- Cook spaghetti following the package instructions, then drain. Sauté the celery, green pepper and onion in 2 tablespoons butter in a small skillet, until tender. Place into a large

bowl. Put in cheese, chicken, spaghetti, mushrooms and soup; toss to coat.
- Place into an oiled 13x9-in. baking dish. Sprinkle with bacon and breadcrumbs; dot with the remaining butter. Bake, uncovered, at 350° until heated through or 30 to 35 mins.

Nutrition Information

- Calories: 347 calories
- Protein: 21g protein.
- Total Fat: 17g fat (10g saturated fat)
- Sodium: 574mg sodium
- Fiber: 2g fiber)
- Total Carbohydrate: 27g carbohydrate (2g sugars
- Cholesterol: 71mg cholesterol

---

541. Chicken Spinach Manicotti

Serving: 3 servings. | Prep: 25mins | Cook: 50mins | Ready in:

Ingredients

- 1 package (10 ounces) frozen chopped spinach, thawed, divided
- 6 ounces frozen diced cooked chicken breast, thawed
- 3 tablespoons butter
- 3 tablespoons all-purpose flour
- 1 cup chicken broth
- 1/2 cup whole milk
- 3 cans (8 ounces each) tomato sauce
- 1 teaspoon dried basil
- 1 teaspoon dried oregano
- 3/4 teaspoon garlic powder
- 3/4 teaspoon brown sugar
- 6 uncooked manicotti shells
- 1 cup shredded Monterey Jack cheese

Direction

- Split spinach in half and refrigerate a portion for another use. Drain the remaining spinach in a colander or sieve, squeezing to get rid of the excess liquid. Pat dry; put in the small bowl. Add chicken and put aside.
- Melt butter in a large saucepan. Stir in the flour until smooth; gradually add milk and broth. Bring to a boil; cook while stirring until thickened or 2 mins. Mix in brown sugar, garlic powder, oregano, basil and tomato sauce. Cook for 3 to 4 mins over medium heat or until heated through.
- In the meantime, stuff a quarter cup of chicken mixture into each uncooked manicotti shell. Spread 1/2 cup sauce into an oiled 11x7-in. baking dish. Place manicotti on top of sauce; add the remaining sauce on top.
- Bake, covered, at 350° until the manicotti shells are tender or 40 to 45 mins. Uncover and top with a sprinkle of cheese. Bake until the cheese is melted or 8 to 10 mins longer. Allow to stand for 5 mins, then serve.

Nutrition Information

- Calories: 554 calories
- Cholesterol: 104mg cholesterol
- Protein: 34g protein.
- Total Fat: 27g fat (16g saturated fat)
- Sodium: 1862mg sodium
- Fiber: 5g fiber)
- Total Carbohydrate: 48g carbohydrate (9g sugars

542. Chicken Stuffed Pasta Shells

Serving: 6 servings. | Prep: 15mins | Cook: 30mins | Ready in:

Ingredients

- 1-1/2 cups cooked stuffing
- 2 cups diced cooked chicken or turkey

- 1/2 cup frozen peas, thawed
- 1/2 cup mayonnaise
- 18 jumbo pasta shells, cooked and drained
- 1 can (10-3/4 ounces) condensed cream of chicken soup, undiluted
- 2/3 cup water
- Paprika
- Minced fresh parsley

Direction

- Mix mayonnaise, peas, chicken, and stuffing in a big bowl; spoon into the pasta shells. Put in a 13x9-inch baking dish coated with oil. Mix water and soup in a small bowl; drizzle over shells. Scatter with paprika.
- Bake with a cover at 350 degrees until heated through, about half an hour. Scatter with parsley.

Nutrition Information

- Calories: 467 calories
- Sodium: 811mg sodium
- Fiber: 3g fiber)
- Total Carbohydrate: 37g carbohydrate (3g sugars
- Cholesterol: 52mg cholesterol
- Protein: 21g protein.
- Total Fat: 26g fat (5g saturated fat)

543. Chicken Ricotta Stuffed Shells

Serving: 2 servings. | Prep: 25mins | Cook: 30mins | Ready in:

Ingredients

- 6 uncooked jumbo pasta shells
- 2/3 cup ricotta cheese
- 2 ounces cream cheese, softened
- 1/8 teaspoon chicken bouillon granules
- 2/3 cup shredded cooked chicken breast

- 2 tablespoons shredded Parmesan cheese
- SAUCE:
- 1/3 cup heavy whipping cream or half-and-half cream
- 1 tablespoon butter
- 5 tablespoons shredded Parmesan cheese, divided
- 1/2 teaspoon dried parsley flakes

Direction

- Cook pasta following the package instructions. In the meantime, beat the bouillon, cream cheese and ricotta in a small bowl until blended. Mix in Parmesan cheese and chicken. Drain the shells; fill with the chicken mixture. Transfer to a shallow 3-cup baking dish coated with cooking spray.
- Bring butter and cream to a boil in a small saucepan. Whisk in the parsley and 3 tablespoons cheese. Mix until the cheese is melted. Pour over the shells.
- Bake, covered, for 25 mins at 350°. Uncover and sprinkle the remaining cheese on top. Bake until the filling is heated through and cheese is melted or 5 to 10 mins longer.

Nutrition Information

- Calories: 499 calories
- Sodium: 618mg sodium
- Fiber: 1g fiber)
- Total Carbohydrate: 28g carbohydrate (8g sugars
- Cholesterol: 124mg cholesterol
- Protein: 35g protein.
- Total Fat: 26g fat (16g saturated fat)

544. Chickpea Stuffed Shells

Serving: 6 servings. | Prep: 15mins | Cook: 30mins | Ready in:

Ingredients

- 18 uncooked jumbo pasta shells
- 1 can (15 ounces) garbanzo beans or chickpeas, rinsed and drained
- 2 large egg whites
- 1 carton (15 ounces) reduced-fat ricotta cheese
- 1/2 cup minced fresh parsley
- 1/3 cup grated Parmesan cheese
- 1 small onion, quartered
- 1 garlic clove, minced
- 1 jar (28 ounces) meatless spaghetti sauce, divided
- 1-1/2 cups shredded part-skim mozzarella cheese

Direction

- Cook pasta shells following the package instructions. Meanwhile, put egg whites and chickpeas in the food processor. Process, covered, until smooth. Put in garlic, onion, Parmesan, parsley and the ricotta. Continue processing, covered, until they are well blended. Add 1-1/4 cups spaghetti sauce to an unoiled 13x9-in. baking dish and put aside.
- Drain the pasta shells; fill with the chickpea mixture. Transfer over the sauce. Drizzle with the remaining sauce. Bake, uncovered, for half an hour at 350°. Top with the mozzarella cheese. Bake until the sauce is bubbly and the cheese is melted, about 5 to 10 mins more.

Nutrition Information

- Calories: 508 calories
- Sodium: 1066mg sodium
- Fiber: 8g fiber)
- Total Carbohydrate: 58g carbohydrate (0 sugars
- Cholesterol: 42mg cholesterol
- Protein: 27g protein.
- Total Fat: 19g fat (9g saturated fat)

545. Chili Manicotti

Serving: 5 servings. | Prep: 15mins | Cook: 40mins | Ready in:

Ingredients

- 10 uncooked manicotti shells
- 2 cups shredded part-skim mozzarella cheese, divided
- 1 carton (15 ounces) ricotta cheese
- 1/4 cup shredded Parmesan cheese
- 1 large egg, lightly beaten
- 3 cups Four-Bean Taco Chili
- 1 jar (14 ounces) meatless spaghetti sauce
- Minced fresh parsley, optional

Direction

- Cook manicotti following the package instructions. In the meantime, combine egg, a cup of Parmesan cheese, ricotta cheese and mozzarella cheese in a large bowl. Put aside. Mix spaghetti sauce and the chili; transfer 1/2 into an oiled 13x9-in. baking dish.
- Rinse and wet the manicotti shells; fill with the cheese mixture. Put over the sauce. Add the remaining sauce on top; top with the remaining cheese.
- Bake, uncovered, at 350° until heated through, or about 40 to 45 minutes. If desired, top with parsley

Nutrition Information

- Calories:
- Protein:
- Total Fat:
- Sodium:
- Fiber:
- Total Carbohydrate:
- Cholesterol:

546. Confetti Spaghetti

Serving: 12 servings. | Prep: 20mins | Cook: 35mins | Ready in:

Ingredients

- 1 package (16 ounces) spaghetti
- 1-1/2 pounds ground beef
- 1 medium green pepper, chopped
- 1 medium onion, chopped
- 1 can (14-1/2 ounces) diced tomatoes, undrained
- 1 can (8 ounces) tomato sauce
- 1 tablespoon brown sugar
- 1 teaspoon salt
- 1 teaspoon chili powder
- 1/2 teaspoon pepper
- 1/4 teaspoon garlic powder
- 1/8 teaspoon cayenne pepper
- 3/4 cup shredded cheddar cheese

Direction

- Preheat the oven to 350 degrees. Cook the spaghetti following the instructions on package. At the same time, in the big skillet, cook the onion, green pepper and beef on medium heat till the meat is not pink anymore; drain off. Whisk in the following eight ingredients. Drain the spaghetti; put into the beef mixture.
- Move into a greased 13x9-inch baking dish. Put cover on and bake for half an hour. Remove the cover; drizzle with the cheese. Bake for approximately 5 minutes more or till the cheese melts.

Nutrition Information

- Calories: 259 calories
- Total Carbohydrate: 27g carbohydrate (4g sugars
- Cholesterol: 42mg cholesterol
- Protein: 16g protein.
- Total Fat: 10g fat (4g saturated fat)
- Sodium: 424mg sodium

- Fiber: 2g fiber)

---

the edge of the pan to loosen; remove sides. Cut into wedges.

Nutrition Information

- Calories: 255 calories
- Sodium: 342mg sodium
- Fiber: 3g fiber)
- Total Carbohydrate: 27g carbohydrate (5g sugars
- Cholesterol: 123mg cholesterol
- Protein: 12g protein.
- Total Fat: 11g fat (5g saturated fat)

---

547. Confetti Spaghetti Pie

Serving: 6-8 servings. | Prep: 25mins | Cook: 30mins | Ready in:

Ingredients

- 1 package (7 ounces) spaghetti
- 1 medium onion, chopped
- 2 garlic cloves, minced
- 2 tablespoons canola oil
- 2 medium tomatoes, chopped
- 3 tablespoons tomato paste
- 1/4 cup minced fresh parsley
- 1/2 teaspoon dried oregano
- 1/2 to 1 teaspoon salt
- 1/4 teaspoon pepper
- 4 large eggs, lightly beaten
- 1/2 cup frozen peas, thawed
- 1/2 cup frozen cut green beans, thawed
- 1/2 cup chopped fresh broccoli
- 1 cup shredded cheddar cheese, divided
- 1/4 cup grated Parmesan cheese

Direction

- Break spaghetti in half; cook as directed on the package. Drain; rinse in cold water; put aside. Sauté garlic and onion in oil until tender in a skillet. Stir in pepper, salt, oregano, parsley, tomato paste and tomatoes. Cook for about 5 minutes until heated through.
- Toss eggs and spaghetti in a large bowl. Stir in Parmesan cheese, 1/4 cup cheddar cheese, tomato mixture, broccoli, beans and peas. Place into a greased 9-in. spring form pan. Transfer pan onto a baking sheet.
- Bake without a cover for 25 minutes at 350°. Scatter with the rest of the cheddar cheese. Bake until an inserted knife in the center is clean when coming out or for 5-10 more minutes. Rest 10 minutes. Run a knife around

---

548. Crab Stuffed Manicotti

Serving: 2 servings. | Prep: 25mins | Cook: 25mins | Ready in:

Ingredients

- 4 uncooked manicotti shells
- 1 tablespoon butter
- 4 teaspoons all-purpose flour
- 1 cup fat-free milk
- 1 tablespoon grated Parmesan cheese
- 1 cup lump crabmeat, drained
- 1/3 cup reduced-fat ricotta cheese
- 1/4 cup shredded part-skim mozzarella cheese
- 1/4 teaspoon lemon-pepper seasoning
- 1/4 teaspoon pepper
- 1/8 teaspoon garlic powder
- Minced fresh parsley

Direction

- Cook manicotti following the directions on the package. Melt butter in a small saucepan. Add flour and stir until smooth; pour in milk gradually. Boil, cook and stir until the mixture is thickened, 2 minutes. Take the saucepan away from the heat; blend in Parmesan cheese.
- Mix garlic powder, pepper, lemon pepper, mozzarella cheese, ricotta cheese and the crab

in a small bowl. Drain the manicotti; stuff it with crab mixture. In an 8-inch square baking dish greased with cooking spray, spread 1/4 cup of sauce. Put stuffed manicotti on top of the sauce. Top with remaining sauce.

- Bake at 350° with a cover for 25-30 minutes or until thoroughly heated. Top with parsley just before serving.

Nutrition Information

- Calories: 359 calories
- Total Fat: 12g fat (7g saturated fat)
- Sodium: 793mg sodium
- Fiber: 1g fiber)
- Total Carbohydrate: 38g carbohydrate (11g sugars
- Cholesterol: 98mg cholesterol
- Protein: 26g protein. Diabetic Exchanges: 2 starch

549. Crowd Pleasing Baked Ziti

Serving: 12 servings. | Prep: 01hours45mins | Cook: 40mins | Ready in:

Ingredients

- 1/2 pound ground beef
- 1/2 pound Johnsonville® Ground Mild Italian sausage
- 1 medium onion, chopped
- 2 garlic cloves, minced
- 1 can (28 ounces) crushed tomatoes
- 1 can (15 ounces) tomato sauce
- 1 bay leaf
- 1 tablespoon Italian seasoning
- 1 teaspoon dried basil
- 1/2 teaspoon sugar
- 1/2 teaspoon salt
- 1/2 teaspoon crushed red pepper flakes
- 1/2 teaspoon pepper
- 1 package (16 ounces) ziti or small tube pasta

- 2 cups shredded part-skim mozzarella cheese
- 1/2 cup grated Romano cheese
- 1/2 cup grated Parmesan cheese
- 1 cup ricotta cheese

Direction

- Cook the garlic, onion, sausage and beef in a big saucepan over medium heat until meat is not pink anymore; drain. Stir in pepper, pepper flakes, salt, sugar, basil, Italian seasoning, bay leaf, tomato sauce and tomatoes.
- Boil. Reduce heat; simmer with a cover for 1 hour, stir occasionally. Simmer without a cover for another 15-30 minutes or until desired thickness for the sauce is reached. Remove bay leaf. Cool.
- Meanwhile, cook pasta following the directions on packaging; drain. Mix pasta, 1/4 cup Parmesan cheese, 1/4 cup Romano cheese, 1 cup mozzarella cheese and 1 cup sauce mixture in a big bowl.
- Spread 1-1/2 cups sauce mixture into a greased 13x9-inch baking dish. Dot using the remaining ricotta cheese. Put pasta mixture on top. Pour the remaining sauce mixture over. Dot using the remaining ricotta cheese. Top with Parmesan cheeses, Romano and remaining mozzarella.
- Bake at 350° with a cover for 20 minutes. Then bake without a cover for another 20-25 minutes or until bubbly.

Nutrition Information

- Calories:
- Protein:
- Total Fat:
- Sodium:
- Fiber:
- Total Carbohydrate:
- Cholesterol:

550. Easy To Stuff Manicotti

Serving: 6-8 servings. | Prep: 20mins | Cook: 30mins | Ready in:

Ingredients

- 1 package (8 ounces) manicotti shells
- 1 pound ground beef
- 1/2 cup chopped onion
- 1 jar (24 ounces) spaghetti sauce
- 14 pieces string cheese
- 1-1/2 cups shredded part-skim mozzarella cheese

Direction

- Following the instructions on package, cook the manicotti. At the same time, in the big skillet, cook the onion and beef on medium heat till the meat is not pink anymore; drain off. Whisk in the spaghetti sauce. Spread 1/2 meat sauce into the greased 13x9-inch baking dish.
- Drain the manicotti; stuff each shell with one piece of the string cheese. Put on top of the meat sauce; pour the rest of the sauce over. Put cover on and bake at 350 degrees till thoroughly heated or for 25 to 30 minutes.
- Drizzle with the mozzarella cheese. Bake till cheese melts or for 5 to 10 more minutes.

Nutrition Information

- Calories: 468 calories
- Sodium: 999mg sodium
- Fiber: 3g fiber)
- Total Carbohydrate: 31g carbohydrate (8g sugars
- Cholesterol: 82mg cholesterol
- Protein: 32g protein.
- Total Fat: 24g fat (13g saturated fat)

551. Eggplant & Zucchini Rollatini

Serving: 8 servings. | Prep: 60mins | Cook: 30mins | Ready in:

Ingredients

- 1 large eggplant
- 1/2 teaspoon salt
- SAUCE:
- 1/3 cup chopped onion
- 3 garlic cloves, minced
- 1 tablespoon olive oil
- 2 cans (28 ounces each) crushed tomatoes
- 1/4 cup dry red wine or vegetable broth
- 1 tablespoon sugar
- 2 teaspoons each dried oregano and dried basil
- 1 teaspoon salt
- 1/4 teaspoon pepper
- ROLLATINI:
- 4 cups shredded part-skim mozzarella cheese
- 1 package (8 ounces) cream cheese, softened and cubed
- 1 large zucchini, thinly sliced
- 2 tablespoons plus 1/2 cup olive oil, divided
- 2 large eggs, lightly beaten
- 1 cup dry bread crumbs
- 1/2 cup grated Parmesan cheese

Direction

- Peel the eggplant then cut into 16 of 1/8-inch thick portion lengthwise. Put the eggplant slices and scatter with salt in a colander set on top of a plate then mix. Let it sit for half an hour; rinse then drain.
- Sauté garlic and onion in a big saucepan with oil until tender; put in the rest of the sauce ingredients then boil. Lower the heat; let it simmer for 20-25 mins without a cover while mixing from time to time to let the flavors blend.
- Preheat the oven to 350 degrees F. Mix cream cheese and mozzarella well in a big bowl. Sauté zucchini in a big skillet with 2 tbsp. oil

until tender; remove the zucchini then set aside.

- In separate shallow bowls, put bread crumbs and eggs. Submerge the eggplant in eggs then dredge in breadcrumbs. Fry in batches for 2-3 mins per side in the remaining oil or until golden brown. Place on paper towels to drain.
- In an ungreased 13-in by 9-in baking dish, scoop a cup of sauce then arrange eggplant slices and zucchini in a layer. Put 3 tbsp. cheese mixture on top of each. Roll up then arrange on the baking dish with the seam-side down. Add the remaining sauce on top; cover. Bake for 30-35 mins until bubbly. Scatter with Parmesan cheese.

Nutrition Information

- Calories: 601 calories
- Sodium: 1244mg sodium
- Fiber: 7g fiber)
- Total Carbohydrate: 36g carbohydrate (8g sugars
- Cholesterol: 116mg cholesterol
- Protein: 26g protein.
- Total Fat: 41g fat (16g saturated fat)

552.   Enchilada Stuffed Shells

Serving: 5 servings. | Prep: 20mins | Cook: 30mins | Ready in:

Ingredients

- 15 uncooked jumbo pasta shells
- 1 pound lean ground turkey
- 1 can (10 ounces) enchilada sauce
- 1/2 teaspoon dried minced onion
- 1/4 teaspoon dried basil
- 1/4 teaspoon dried oregano
- 1/4 teaspoon ground cumin
- 1/2 cup fat-free refried beans
- 1 cup shredded reduced-fat cheddar cheese

Direction

- Cook pasta as directed on the package; strain and wash with cold water. Cook turkey in a nonstick skillet over medium heat until no longer pink; drain well. Mix in seasonings and enchilada sauce; put to one side.
- Put a rounded teaspoonful of refried beans into each pasta shell, stuff with turkey mixture. Arrange in an 11x7-inch baking dish greased with cooking spray.
- Bake, covered, for 25 minutes at 350°. Remove the cover; scatter top with cheese. Bake until cheese is melted, for 5 more minutes.

Nutrition Information

- Calories: 345 calories
- Sodium: 622mg sodium
- Fiber: 3g fiber)
- Total Carbohydrate: 30g carbohydrate (2g sugars
- Cholesterol: 79mg cholesterol
- Protein: 31g protein. Diabetic Exchanges: 2 starch
- Total Fat: 13g fat (5g saturated fat)

553.   Fire Island Ziti

Serving: 5 servings. | Prep: 30mins | Cook: 20mins | Ready in:

Ingredients

- 2 pounds plum tomatoes, halved lengthwise
- 3 tablespoons olive oil, divided
- 2 garlic cloves, minced
- 1 teaspoon salt
- 8 ounces ziti or small tube pasta
- 2 cups fresh broccoli florets
- 1 pound Johnsonville® Mild Italian Sausage Links, cut into 1/2-inch slices
- 1/2 teaspoon crushed red pepper flakes
- 1/3 cup grated Romano cheese

Direction

- Mix in salt, 2 tablespoons oil, and garlic, toss tomatoes. Putting the cut side down, place in a 15x10x1-in. pan. Bake in a 450-degree oven until tender, 20-25 minutes. When it is cool enough to handle, chop. Follow directions on package to cook ziti. Add the broccoli for last 4 minutes. In the meantime, put remaining oil in a big frying pan, cook sausage on medium heat until not pink. Add the pepper flakes and cook for 1 more minute. Mix in tomatoes and cook through. Drain water from broccoli and ziti mixture; mix with sausage mixture. Sprinkle on cheese.

Nutrition Information

- Calories: 477 calories
- Protein: 23g protein.
- Total Fat: 25g fat (8g saturated fat)
- Sodium: 1122mg sodium
- Fiber: 5g fiber)
- Total Carbohydrate: 44g carbohydrate (8g sugars
- Cholesterol: 48mg cholesterol

554.   Five Cheese Jumbo Shells

Serving: 8 servings. | Prep: 45mins | Cook: 50mins | Ready in:

Ingredients

- 24 uncooked jumbo pasta shells
- 1 tablespoon olive oil
- 1 medium zucchini, shredded and squeezed dry
- 1/2 pound baby portobello mushrooms, chopped
- 1 medium onion, finely chopped
- 2 cups reduced-fat ricotta cheese
- 1/2 cup shredded part-skim mozzarella cheese
- 1/2 cup shredded provolone cheese
- 1/2 cup grated Romano cheese
- 1 large egg, lightly beaten
- 1 teaspoon Italian seasoning
- 1/2 teaspoon crushed red pepper flakes
- 1 jar (24 ounces) meatless spaghetti sauce
- 1/4 cup grated Parmesan cheese

Direction

- Set the oven to 350° and start preheating. Cook shells as directed on the package for al dente; drain; rinse in cold water.
- Heat oil over medium high heat in a large skillet. Add vegetables; cook while stirring until tender. Take out of the heat. Mix Romano, provolone, mozzarella and ricotta cheeses in a bowl; stir in vegetables, seasonings and egg.
- Spread a cup sauce into a 13x9-in. baking dish coated with cooking spray. Fill cheese mixture into pasta shells; transfer into baking dish. Pour the rest of the sauce on top. Scatter with Parmesan cheese.
- Bake with a cover for 40 minutes. Bake without a cover until cheese is melted or for 10 more minutes. Rest 10 minutes; serve. Freeze option: Cool unbaked casserole; freeze with a cover. When using, thaw partially in the fridge for 1 night. Take out of the fridge half an hour before baking. Set the oven to 350° and start preheating. Use foil to cover casserole; bake for 50 minutes. Bake without a cover until heated through and thermometer inserted in center registers 165° or for 15-20 more minutes.

Nutrition Information

- Calories: 298 calories
- Protein: 18g protein. Diabetic Exchanges: 2 starch
- Total Fat: 9g fat (5g saturated fat)
- Sodium: 642mg sodium
- Fiber: 3g fiber)
- Total Carbohydrate: 36g carbohydrate (12g sugars
- Cholesterol: 55mg cholesterol

555.   Grilled Vegetable And Goat Cheese Napoleons

Serving: 4 servings. | Prep: 50mins | Cook: 10mins | Ready in:

Ingredients

- 2 plum tomatoes, halved lengthwise
- 1/4 cup olive oil, divided
- 1/8 teaspoon dried oregano
- 1/8 teaspoon dried basil
- 3/4 teaspoon salt, divided
- 1/2 teaspoon pepper, divided
- 1 large zucchini, cut into 1/2-inch slices
- 1 large yellow summer squash, cut into 1/2-inch slices
- 4 large portobello mushrooms
- 4 slices eggplant (1/2 inch thick)
- 1 package (5.3 ounces) fresh goat cheese
- 1 teaspoon minced fresh parsley
- 1 teaspoon minced garlic, divided
- 4 ounces fresh mozzarella cheese, cut into 4 slices
- 1 package (10 ounces) fresh spinach
- 1/4 cup balsamic vinaigrette

Direction

- Brush 2 teaspoons oil over tomatoes; sprinkle 1/4 teaspoon pepper, 1/4 teaspoon salt, basil, and oregano over. Remove into a non-oiled 15x10x1-inch baking pan. Bake at 350° until soft, or about 20-25 minutes.
- Brush 2 tablespoons oil over yellow squash and zucchini; sprinkle 1/4 teaspoon salt over. In a grill basket or wok, put the vegetables. Grill without covering on medium heat until soft, or about 8-10 minutes, tossing sometimes.
- Take out and get rid of the gills and stems from mushrooms. Brush 1 tablespoon oil over eggplant and mushrooms; sprinkle the leftover salt over. Close the lid and grill the mushrooms over medium heat until soft, or

about 12-15 minutes. Close the lid and grill the eggplant over medium heat until soft, about 4-5 minutes per side.

- Mix the leftover pepper, 1/2 teaspoon garlic, parsley, and goat cheese together in a small bowl.
- On a baking sheet coated with oil, put the mushrooms; spread 2 teaspoons the cheese mixture over each mushroom. Place on zucchini, squash, 2 teaspoons of cheese mixture, eggplant and the leftover cheese mixture. Put tomato and mozzarella cheese on top. Bake at 350° until the cheese melts, or about 8-10 minutes.
- Sauté the leftover garlic with the leftover oil in a big frying pan for 1 minute. Add spinach; cook until wilted, or about 4-5 minutes. Distribute among 4 dishes; put a mushroom stack on top of each. Drizzle vinaigrette over.

Nutrition Information

- Calories: 377 calories
- Fiber: 6g fiber)
- Total Carbohydrate: 20g carbohydrate (9g sugars
- Cholesterol: 47mg cholesterol
- Protein: 16g protein.
- Total Fat: 27g fat (9g saturated fat)
- Sodium: 833mg sodium

556.   Ground Turkey Spaghetti Pie

Serving: 2 servings. | Prep: 25mins | Cook: 15mins | Ready in:

Ingredients

- 2 ounces uncooked spaghetti, broken in half
- 1 egg, lightly beaten
- 2 tablespoons grated Parmesan cheese
- 3 tablespoons sour cream
- 1/2 pound ground turkey

- 1/4 cup chopped green pepper
- 2 tablespoons chopped onion
- 1 teaspoon butter
- 1/3 cup tomato sauce
- 1/4 teaspoon garlic salt
- 1/4 teaspoon dried oregano
- Salt and pepper to taste
- 1/3 cup shredded part-skim mozzarella cheese

Direction

- Following the package instructions, cook the spaghetti; drain the spaghetti. Mix spaghetti, Parmesan cheese, and egg in a small bowl. Press the spaghetti mixture up the sides and onto the bottom of a 7-inch pie plate or a shallow 2-cup baking dish coated with cooking spray. Spread with sour cream.
- Crumble the turkey and add to a skillet; put in butter, onion, and pepper. Cook over medium heat until the meat is not pink anymore; then drain. Stir in pepper, salt, oregano, garlic salt, and tomato sauce. Fill into the spaghetti crust. Dust with mozzarella cheese. Use foil to loosely cover the edges.
- Bake at 350 degrees until heated through and the cheese melts, 15-20 minutes. Then serve right away.

Nutrition Information

- Calories: 527 calories
- Sodium: 757mg sodium
- Fiber: 2g fiber)
- Total Carbohydrate: 28g carbohydrate (4g sugars
- Cholesterol: 222mg cholesterol
- Protein: 32g protein.
- Total Fat: 31g fat (13g saturated fat)

557. Ham Stuffed Jumbo Shells

Serving: 8 servings. | Prep: 20mins | Cook: 30mins | Ready in:

Ingredients

- 24 jumbo pasta shells
- 3 tablespoons all-purpose flour
- 2 cups 1% milk
- 1/2 pound fresh mushrooms, halved and sliced
- 1/2 cup chopped onion
- 1/2 cup chopped green pepper
- 1 tablespoon canola oil
- 3 cups cubed fully cooked lean ham
- 1 cup shredded reduced-fat Swiss cheese, divided
- 3 tablespoons grated Parmesan cheese
- 2 tablespoons minced fresh parsley
- 1/4 teaspoon paprika

Direction

- Cook pasta following the package instructions. In the meantime, mix together milk and flour in a small saucepan until smooth. Boil it, cook while stirring until thickened, about 2 minutes. Take away from heat, put aside.
- Sauté green pepper, onion, and mushrooms with oil in a big nonstick frying pan until soft. Lower the heat; add Parmesan cheese, 1/2 cup Swiss cheese, and ham. Cook while stirring until the cheese melts. Take away from heat. Mix in 1/2 cup of the saved sauce.
- Strain the pasta; stuff approximately 3 tablespoons of the filling into each shell. Put in a greased 13x9-inch baking dish. Put the leftover sauce on top. Put a cover on and bake at 350° until fully heated, about 30 minutes. Sprinkle the leftover Swiss cheese, paprika, and parsley over.

Nutrition Information

- Calories: 274 calories

332

- Total Fat: 7g fat (2g saturated fat)
- Sodium: 703mg sodium
- Fiber: 2g fiber)
- Total Carbohydrate: 30g carbohydrate (0 sugars
- Cholesterol: 26mg cholesterol
- Protein: 23g protein. Diabetic Exchanges: 2 starch

558. Italian Baked Ziti

Serving: 6 servings. | Prep: 20mins | Cook: 60mins | Ready in:

Ingredients

- 1/2 pound lean ground beef (90% lean)
- 1 medium onion, chopped
- 2 garlic cloves, minced
- 1-3/4 cups spaghetti sauce
- 1 can (14-1/2 ounces) diced tomatoes, undrained
- 1 can (6 ounces) tomato paste
- 6 tablespoons water
- 1 tablespoon minced fresh parsley
- 1-1/2 teaspoons Worcestershire sauce
- 1 teaspoon dried basil
- 3/4 teaspoon dried oregano, divided
- 8 ounces ziti or small tube pasta
- 1 cup part-skim ricotta cheese
- 1 cup shredded part-skim mozzarella cheese
- 1/4 cup grated Parmesan cheese, divided
- 1 large egg, lightly beaten
- 1/4 teaspoon salt
- 1/4 teaspoon pepper

Direction

- Cook onion and beef over medium heat in a large saucepan until meat is no longer pink. Add garlic; cook for 1 more minute. Drain.
- Stir in parsley, water, tomato paste, tomatoes, spaghetti sauce, Worcestershire sauce, half a teaspoon oregano and basil. Simmer with a cover while stirring occasionally for 3 hours.

- Cook pasta as directed on the package; drain. Mix pepper, salt, egg, 2 tablespoons Parmesan, mozzarella and ricotta in a large bowl.
- Spread a cup of meat sauce into a greased 13x9-in. baking dish. Layer with 1/2 the pasta, 1/3 of meat sauce and 1/2 cheese mixture. Place other similar layers on top. Pour the remaining sauce on top. Scatter with the rest of the Parmesan and oregano.
- Bake with a cover until heated through or for an hour at 350 degrees.

Nutrition Information

- Calories: 431 calories
- Protein: 27g protein.
- Total Fat: 14g fat (7g saturated fat)
- Sodium: 818mg sodium
- Fiber: 6g fiber)
- Total Carbohydrate: 50g carbohydrate (15g sugars
- Cholesterol: 81mg cholesterol

559. Italian Cheese Stuffed Shells

Serving: 7 servings. | Prep: 60mins | Cook: 50mins | Ready in:

Ingredients

- 1 medium onion, chopped
- 1/2 cup chopped green pepper
- 1/2 cup chopped sweet red pepper
- 1/2 pound sliced fresh mushrooms
- 2 garlic cloves, minced
- 1-1/2 cups water
- 1 can (14-1/2 ounces) Italian stewed tomatoes
- 1 can (6 ounces) tomato paste
- 1-1/2 teaspoons Italian seasoning
- 2 large eggs, lightly beaten
- 1 carton (15 ounces) reduced-fat ricotta cheese
- 2 cups shredded part-skim mozzarella cheese, divided

- 1/2 cup grated Parmesan cheese
- 21 jumbo pasta shells, cooked and drained

Direction

- Cook peppers and onion in a large nonstick frying pan coated with cooking spray, for 2 mins over medium heat. Put in the mushrooms; cook until tender, about 4 to 5 mins. Put in garlic; cook one more minute. Mix in Italian seasoning, tomato paste, tomatoes and water. Bring to a boil. Lower the heat; simmer, covered, for half an hour.
- In a meantime, start preheating oven to 350°. Combine Parmesan cheeses, half cup of mozzarella, ricotta and eggs in a small bowl. Fill into the shells. Spread one cup of the vegetable sauce in a 13x9-in. baking dish coated with cooking spray. Place shells over the sauce. Add the remaining sauce on top.
- Bake, covered, for 45 mins. Uncover and top with the remaining mozzarella. Bake until the cheese is melted and the mixture is bubbly, about 5 to 10 mins more. Allow to stand 5 mins. Serve.

Nutrition Information

- Calories: 351 calories
- Cholesterol: 99mg cholesterol
- Protein: 23g protein. Diabetic Exchanges: 2 medium-fat meat
- Total Fat: 11g fat (6g saturated fat)
- Sodium: 457mg sodium
- Fiber: 4g fiber)
- Total Carbohydrate: 39g carbohydrate (14g sugars

560.   Italian Chicken And Rice

Serving: Makes 4 servings. | Prep: 5mins | Cook: |Ready in:

Ingredients

- 1 Tbsp. oil
- 1 lb. boneless skinless chicken breasts, cut into strips
- 3 cups cut-up mixed fresh vegetables (broccoli, carrots and red peppers)
- 1 can (14-1/2 oz.) fat-free reduced-sodium chicken broth
- 2 cups instant white rice, uncooked
- 1/4 cup KRAFT Zesty Italian Dressing
- 1/4 cup KRAFT Parmesan Cheese

Direction

- In a large skillet, heat oil over medium heat. Sauté chicken in heated oil until lightly browned, stirring sometimes.
- Stir in vegetables until tender but crisp, or about 3 to 5 minutes. Mix in broth. Bring to a boil.
- Mix in cheese, dressing, and rice. Turn heat to low. Cook, covered until chicken is thoroughly cooked and liquid is absorbed, or about 5 minutes.

Nutrition Information

- Calories: 410
- Fiber: 4 g
- Cholesterol: 65 mg
- Total Fat: 11 g
- Saturated Fat: 2.5 g
- Protein: 24 g
- Sodium: 530 mg
- Sugar: 5 g
- Total Carbohydrate: 52 g

561.   Italian Heritage Casserole

Serving: 6 servings. | Prep: 15mins | Cook: 60mins |Ready in:

Ingredients

- 6 potatoes, peeled and quartered

- 1 red pepper, cut in lengthwise strips
- 1 green pepper, cut in lengthwise strips
- 1 teaspoon oregano
- 1 teaspoon paprika
- 1/2 teaspoon garlic powder
- 1/2 teaspoon salt
- 1/2 teaspoon black pepper
- 1 frying chicken (3 pounds), skinned and cut in pieces or 6 chicken breast halves, cut in chunks
- 1 pound Johnsonville® Mild Italian Sausage Links, cut in 1-inch to 2-inch chunks

Direction

- Use vegetable cooking oil to spray a 13x9-in. baking dish. In the dish, place peppers and potatoes. Mix together the seasoning; use 1/3 of the seasoning mixture to sprinkle over the vegetables.
- Use sausage and chicken pieces to layer in reverse order over the vegetables; use the remaining seasoning mixture to season on top. Put into the oven to bake at 425 degrees with a cover for 30 minutes. Lower the heat to 375 degrees; bake for another 30-40 minutes.

Nutrition Information

- Calories: 419 calories
- Total Fat: 16g fat (5g saturated fat)
- Sodium: 619mg sodium
- Fiber: 3g fiber)
- Total Carbohydrate: 33g carbohydrate (4g sugars
- Cholesterol: 103mg cholesterol
- Protein: 35g protein.

562. Italian Spaghetti Bake

Serving: 2 casseroles (8 servings each). | Prep: 20mins | Cook: 20mins | Ready in:

Ingredients

- 2 packages (one 16 ounces, one 8 ounces) spaghetti
- 1-1/2 pounds ground beef
- 1 large green pepper, chopped
- 1 medium onion, chopped
- 2 cans (15 ounces each) tomato sauce
- 1 package (8 ounces) sliced pepperoni
- 1 can (8 ounces) mushroom stems and pieces, drained
- 1 can (3.8 ounces) sliced ripe olives, drained
- 1/2 teaspoon dried basil
- 1/2 teaspoon dried oregano
- 1/4 teaspoon garlic salt
- 1/4 teaspoon pepper
- 4 cups shredded part-skim mozzarella cheese
- 1/2 cup grated Parmesan cheese

Direction

- Cook spaghetti as directed on the package. In the meantime, cook onion, green pepper and beef over medium heat in a Dutch oven until meat is longer pink; drain. Stir in seasonings, olives, mushrooms, pepperoni and tomato sauce. Drain spaghetti.
- Scoop a cup of meat mixture into each of 2 greased 13x9-in. baking dishes. Place layer of spaghetti on top, then pour over the spaghetti with the rest of the meat mixture. Scatter with cheeses.
- Freeze one casserole with a cover for up to 3 months. Bake the other casserole without a cover at 350° until heated through or for 20-25 minutes.
- To use frozen casserole: Thaw in the fridge for one night. Take out of the fridge half an hour before baking. Bake with a cover for 40 minutes at 350°. Bake without a cover until cheese is melted or for 5-10 more minutes.

Nutrition Information

- Calories: 415 calories
- Sodium: 841mg sodium
- Fiber: 3g fiber)

- Total Carbohydrate: 38g carbohydrate (4g sugars
- Cholesterol: 57mg cholesterol
- Protein: 25g protein.
- Total Fat: 18g fat (8g saturated fat)

563. Italian Zucchini Bake

Serving: 6 servings. | Prep: 15mins | Cook: 40mins | Ready in:

Ingredients

- 3-1/2 cups shredded zucchini
- 1/2 teaspoon salt
- 3/4 cup egg substitute
- 1/2 cup dry bread crumbs
- 1/4 cup all-purpose flour
- 2 teaspoons Italian seasoning
- 1/2 pound fresh mushrooms, sliced
- 2 teaspoons olive oil
- 1 can (15 ounces) pizza sauce, divided
- 3/4 cup chopped green pepper
- 1/4 cup sliced ripe olives, drained
- 1-1/2 cups shredded part-skim mozzarella cheese, divided

Direction

- Put zucchini in a colander above a dish, dredge salt over zucchini and mix. Let rest for 15 minutes. Rinse then drain carefully.
- Mix the Italian seasoning, flour, bread crumbs, egg substitute and zucchini together in a big bowl. Add the mixture to an 11x7-inch baking dish greased with cooking spray and spread out. Set oven at 350°, bake while uncovered for 25 minutes.
- Sauté mushrooms in oil in a nonstick frying pan until they are crisp-tender. Distribute half of the pizza sauce on top of zucchini mixture, dredge with 1/2 of the cheese, olives, green pepper and mushrooms. Add the rest of cheese and pizza sauce on top. Bake for 15 more minutes until it gets hot and bubbly.

Nutrition Information

- Calories: 226 calories
- Protein: 16g protein. Diabetic Exchanges: 2 vegetable
- Total Fat: 8g fat (4g saturated fat)
- Sodium: 818mg sodium
- Fiber: 3g fiber)
- Total Carbohydrate: 24g carbohydrate (0 sugars
- Cholesterol: 17mg cholesterol

564. Kids Love It Casserole

Serving: 10-12 servings. | Prep: 35mins | Cook: 30mins | Ready in:

Ingredients

- 1-1/2 pounds ground beef
- 1 cup chopped onion
- 1 garlic clove, minced
- 1 jar (14 ounces) spaghetti sauce
- 1 can (8 ounces) tomato sauce
- 1 can (6 ounces) tomato paste
- 3/4 cup water
- 1 teaspoon Italian seasoning
- 1/2 teaspoon salt
- Dash pepper
- 1 package (7 ounces) small pasta shells, cooked and drained
- 1 package (10 ounces) frozen chopped spinach, thawed and squeezed dry
- 2 large eggs, lightly beaten
- 1 cup shredded sharp cheddar cheese
- 1/2 cup soft bread crumbs
- 1/4 cup grated Parmesan cheese

Direction

- In a large saucepan over medium heat, cook garlic, onion and beef till beef is no longer pink; drain. Put in the next seven ingredients;

let it come to a boil. Lower the heat; cover up and allow to simmer for 10 minutes. Mix in bread crumbs, cheese, eggs, spinach and macaroni.

- Place into a greased baking dish of 13x9 inches. Sprinkle Parmesan cheese on top. Cover up and bake at 350° until bubbly, about 30-35 minutes. Allow to sit for 10 minutes before serving.

Nutrition Information

- Calories: 275 calories
- Protein: 19g protein.
- Total Fat: 12g fat (5g saturated fat)
- Sodium: 517mg sodium
- Fiber: 3g fiber)
- Total Carbohydrate: 24g carbohydrate (6g sugars
- Cholesterol: 84mg cholesterol

---

565.   Lactose Free Veggie Stuffed Shells

Serving: 12 servings. | Prep: 30mins | Cook: 35mins | Ready in:

Ingredients

- 1 package (12 ounces) jumbo pasta shells
- 1/2 pound sliced fresh mushrooms
- 1 medium onion, chopped
- 1 tablespoon olive oil
- 4 garlic cloves, minced
- 1 package (12.3 ounces) silken extra-firm tofu
- 3 tablespoons lemon juice
- 1 package (10 ounces) frozen chopped spinach, thawed and squeezed dry
- 1 can (3.8 ounces) sliced ripe olives, drained
- 3 tablespoons minced fresh basil
- 1/2 teaspoon salt
- 1/8 teaspoon pepper
- 1 jar (24 ounces) meatless spaghetti sauce
- 1/4 cup pine nuts

Direction

- Cook pasta following the package instructions, then drain. In the meantime, sauté the onion and mushrooms in oil in a large skillet until tender. Put in garlic and cook for one more minute.
- Mash the tofu with the lemon juice in a large bowl. Mix in pepper, salt, basil, olives and the spinach. Transfer into the mushroom mixture and heat through. Spoon the mixture into shells.
- Spread one cup of the spaghetti sauce in a 13-in. x 9-in. baking dish coated with cooking spray. Place the shells over the sauce; add the remaining sauce on top. Top with pine nuts.
- Bake, covered, for half an hour at 375°. Uncover and bake until bubbly, or about 5 to 10 minutes more.

Nutrition Information

- Calories: 198 calories
- Cholesterol: 0 cholesterol
- Protein: 9g protein. Diabetic Exchanges: 1-1/2 starch
- Total Fat: 5g fat (1g saturated fat)
- Sodium: 485mg sodium
- Fiber: 4g fiber)
- Total Carbohydrate: 32g carbohydrate (7g sugars

---

566.   Makeover Cheese Stuffed Shells

Serving: 12 servings. | Prep: 35mins | Cook: 50mins | Ready in:

Ingredients

- 3/4 pound lean ground beef (90% lean)
- 1 Italian turkey sausage link (4 ounces), casing removed
- 1 large onion, chopped

- 1 package (10 ounces) frozen chopped spinach, thawed and squeezed dry
- 1 cup ricotta cheese
- 1 large egg, lightly beaten
- 1-1/2 cups shredded part-skim mozzarella cheese, divided
- 1-1/2 cups 4% cottage cheese
- 1 cup grated Parmesan cheese
- 1 cup shredded sharp cheddar cheese
- 1 teaspoon Italian seasoning
- 1/4 teaspoon pepper
- 1/8 teaspoon ground cinnamon, optional
- 24 jumbo pasta shells, cooked and drained
- SAUCE:
- 3 cans (8 ounces each) no-salt-added tomato sauce
- 1 tablespoon dried minced onion
- 1-1/2 teaspoons dried basil
- 1-1/2 teaspoons dried parsley flakes
- 2 garlic cloves, minced
- 1 teaspoon sugar
- 1 teaspoon dried oregano
- 1/4 teaspoon pepper

Direction

- Crumble the sausage and beef into a big nonstick frying pan, then add onion. Let it cook and stir on medium heat until the meat has no visible pink color, then drain.
- Move to a big bowl. Stir in egg, ricotta and spinach, then add cinnamon if preferred, pepper, Italian seasoning, cheddar cheese, Parmesan cheese, cottage cheese and 1cup mozzarella cheese, then stir well.
- Stuff meat mixture on the pasta shells. Lay out in two cooking spray coated 11x7-inch baking dishes. Mix together the sauce ingredients, then scoop it over the shells.
- Put cover and let it bake for 45 minutes at 350 degrees. Take off the cover, then sprinkle it with leftover mozzarella cheese. Let it bake for an additional 5 to 10 minutes or until the cheese melts and becomes bubbly. Allow it to stand for 5 minutes prior to serving.

Nutrition Information

- Calories: 318 calories
- Sodium: 714mg sodium
- Fiber: 2g fiber)
- Total Carbohydrate: 23g carbohydrate (5g sugars
- Cholesterol: 79mg cholesterol
- Protein: 25g protein.
- Total Fat: 14g fat (8g saturated fat)

567.   Manicotti

Serving: 4 | Prep: 30mins | Cook: 45mins | Ready in:

Ingredients

- 1 pint part-skim ricotta cheese
- 8 ounces shredded mozzarella cheese
- 3/4 cup grated Parmesan cheese
- 2 eggs
- 1 teaspoon dried parsley
- salt to taste
- ground black pepper to taste
- 1 (16 ounce) jar spaghetti sauce
- 5 1/2 ounces manicotti pasta

Direction

- Cook manicotti in boiling water until done. Drain; rinse with cold water.
- Set the oven to 350°F (175°C) and start preheating.
- Mix pepper, salt, parsley, eggs, half a cup Parmesan, mozzarella and ricotta in a large bowl. Combine well.
- Transfer half a cup of sauce to an 11x17 inch baking dish. Fill 3 tablespoon of cheese mixture into each manicotti shell; place over sauce. Top with the rest of the sauce; scatter with the rest of Parmesan cheese.
- Bake until bubbly or for 45 minutes.

Nutrition Information

- Calories: 676 calories;
- Total Fat: 30.9
- Sodium: 1255
- Total Carbohydrate: 53.2
- Cholesterol: 189
- Protein: 46

568. Manicotti With Spicy Sausage

Serving: 8-10 servings. | Prep: 30mins | Cook: 60mins | Ready in:

Ingredients

- 1 pound Johnsonville® Ground Hot Italian sausage
- 1 can (28 ounces) crushed tomatoes
- 1 jar (26 ounces) marinara sauce
- 2 eggs, lightly beaten
- 3 cups ricotta cheese
- 3/4 cup grated Parmesan cheese
- 1 can (4 ounces) chopped green chilies
- 3 tablespoons minced fresh parsley
- 1 teaspoon Italian seasoning
- 1/2 teaspoon salt
- 1/2 teaspoon garlic powder
- 1/2 teaspoon pepper
- 18 uncooked manicotti shells
- 1/2 cup shredded part-skim mozzarella cheese

Direction

- Cook sausage until no longer pink over medium heat in a large skillet; drain and put aside. Bring marinara sauce and tomatoes to boiling in the same skillet. Lower the heat; simmer with a cover for 10 minutes.
- Mix pepper, garlic powder, salt, Italian seasoning, parsley, chilies, Parmesan cheese, ricotta and eggs in a large bowl.
- Distribute 2 cups of sauce into 2 greased 13-in. x 9-in. baking dishes. Stuff cheese mixture into uncooked manicotti shells. Transfer into

prepped pans. Scatter over with sausage; pour the rest of the sauce on top.
- Bake with a cover for 50 minutes at 375°. Uncover; drizzle with mozzarella cheese. Bake until cheese is melted and manicotti becomes tender or for 10 minutes. Rest 5 minutes; serve.

Nutrition Information

- Calories: 418 calories
- Sodium: 846mg sodium
- Fiber: 4g fiber)
- Total Carbohydrate: 42g carbohydrate (11g sugars
- Cholesterol: 100mg cholesterol
- Protein: 24g protein.
- Total Fat: 18g fat (9g saturated fat)

569. Meat Lover's Pizza Bake

Serving: 6 servings. | Prep: 20mins | Cook: 25mins | Ready in:

Ingredients

- 1 pound ground beef
- 1/2 cup chopped green pepper
- 1 can (15 ounces) pizza sauce
- 1 package (3-1/2 ounces) sliced pepperoni, chopped
- 1 can (2-1/4 ounces) sliced ripe olives, drained
- 2 cups shredded part-skim mozzarella cheese
- 3/4 cup biscuit/baking mix
- 2 large eggs
- 3/4 cup whole milk

Direction

- In a big skillet on medium heat, cook green pepper and beef until meat is not pink anymore; drain. Mix in olives, pepperoni, and pizza sauce. Move to an oiled 11x7-inch baking dish. Sprinkle cheese over top.

- Combine milk, eggs, and biscuit mix in a small bowl until mixed. Evenly spread over cheese. Bake at 400 degrees without cover for 25-30 minutes or until golden brown. Let it sit for 10 minutes then serve.

Nutrition Information

- Calories: 411 calories
- Sodium: 1025mg sodium
- Fiber: 2g fiber)
- Total Carbohydrate: 18g carbohydrate (6g sugars
- Cholesterol: 77mg cholesterol
- Protein: 29g protein.
- Total Fat: 25g fat (11g saturated fat)

570.   Meatball Sub Casserole

Serving: 8 | Prep: 10mins | Cook: 50mins | Ready in:

Ingredients

- 1 (16 ounce) package frozen garlic bread
- 2 (24 ounce) jars spaghetti sauce
- 40 Italian-style frozen meatballs
- 2 cups shredded mozzarella cheese
- 1/4 cup grated Parmesan cheese

Direction

- Set the oven to 220°C or 425°F.
- In the preheated oven, heat garlic bread on a baking sheet, spread side up, for 10-12 minutes, until warm and turn golden brown. Set aside to let it cool.
- Lower the heat of the oven to 175°C or 350°F.
- In a big pot, bring spaghetti sauce to a boil, put into sauce frozen meatballs. Lower heat to low and simmer for 20 minutes, until meatballs are heated through.
- Separate garlic bread into bite-size pieces and scatter into the bottom of a 9"x13" baking dish. Pour over garlic bread with meatballs and

spaghetti sauce, distributing meatballs evenly and coating bread well with sauce. Spread over top with mozzarella cheese, in one layer, followed by a layer of Parmesan cheese.
- Bake casserole for 20-25 minutes, until cheese is melted.

Nutrition Information

- Calories: 733 calories;
- Protein: 39.1
- Total Fat: 37.2
- Sodium: 1386
- Total Carbohydrate: 58
- Cholesterol: 140

571.   Meatball Submarine Casserole

Serving: 4 servings. | Prep: 15mins | Cook: 15mins | Ready in:

Ingredients

- 1 package (12 ounces) frozen fully cooked Italian meatballs
- 4 slices sourdough bread
- 1-1/2 teaspoons olive oil
- 1 garlic clove, halved
- 1-1/2 cups pasta sauce with mushrooms
- 1/2 cup shredded part-skim mozzarella cheese, divided
- 1/2 cup grated Parmesan cheese, divided

Direction

- Start heating the broiler. Set microwave on high and cook meatballs, covered, for 4-6 minutes or until heated. In the meantime, put bread on a cookie sheet that is not greased. Use a brush to put oil on one side of bread. Place pan 4-6 in. from heat and broil 1-2 minutes or until golden brown. Rub garlic on the cut side of the bread; throw out the garlic.

Break bread into small pieces. Place bread pieces in an 11x7-in. greased dish. Reduce oven to 350 degrees. Add 1/4 cup Parmesan, pasta sauce, and 1/4 cup mozzarella to the meatballs. Mix to combine. Pour meatball mixture over the bread and sprinkle the rest of the cheeses on top. Do not cover; bake 15-18 minutes until cheeses melt.

Nutrition Information

- Calories: 417 calories
- Total Fat: 28g fat (13g saturated fat)
- Sodium: 1243mg sodium
- Fiber: 3g fiber)
- Total Carbohydrate: 22g carbohydrate (8g sugars
- Cholesterol: 59mg cholesterol
- Protein: 23g protein.

---
572.   Meatless Spaghetti Pie

Serving: 6 servings. | Prep: 20mins | Cook: 25mins | Ready in:

Ingredients

- 6 ounces uncooked spaghetti
- 1/2 cup egg substitute
- 1/2 cup grated parmesan cheese, divided
- 3 ounces reduced-fat cream cheese
- 1/2 cup reduced-fat sour cream
- 1/2 cup chopped green pepper
- 1/2 pound fresh mushrooms, sliced
- 4 garlic cloves, minced
- 2 tablespoons butter
- 2 cups meatless spaghetti sauce
- 1/2 cup shredded part-skim mozzarella cheese

Direction

- Cook spaghetti following the package directions; drain. Add 1/4 cup Parmesan cheese and the egg substitute. Press up the

sides and onto the bottom of a 9-in. deep-dish pie plate greased with cooking spray. Beat the remaining Parmesan cheese, green pepper, sour cream, and cream cheese in a bowl. Spread over the spaghetti crust.

- Sauté garlic and mushrooms in butter in a nonstick skillet until softened. Scoop over the cheese mixture and spread with the spaghetti sauce. Uncover and bake for 20 minutes at 350°. Sprinkle with mozzarella cheese; continue to bake until the cheese is melted, for another 5 minutes. Allow to sit for 10-15 minutes before cutting.

Nutrition Information

- Calories: 326 calories
- Sodium: 707mg sodium
- Fiber: 3g fiber)
- Total Carbohydrate: 36g carbohydrate (0 sugars
- Cholesterol: 37mg cholesterol
- Protein: 17g protein. Diabetic Exchanges: 2 starch
- Total Fat: 13g fat (8g saturated fat)

---
573.   Mexican Style Chicken Manicotti

Serving: 2 servings. | Prep: 25mins | Cook: 25mins | Ready in:

Ingredients

- 4 uncooked manicotti shells
- 1 cup cubed cooked chicken breast
- 1 cup salsa, divided
- 1/2 cup ricotta cheese
- 2 tablespoons sliced ripe olives
- 4 teaspoons minced fresh parsley
- 1 tablespoon diced pimientos
- 1 green onion, thinly sliced
- 1 small garlic clove, minced
- 1/4 to 1/2 teaspoon hot pepper sauce

- 1/3 cup shredded Monterey Jack cheese

Direction

- Follow the package cooking instructions to cook manicotti. Mix pepper sauce, garlic, green onion, pimientos, parsley, olives, ricotta cheese, 1/4 cup of salsa, and chicken in a small bowl. Drain the manicotti; fill with the chicken mixture.
- Drizzle a cooking spray-greased 8-inch square baking dish with 1/4 cup of salsa. Pour the remaining salsa and manicotti shells on top.
- Bake with a cover for 20 minutes at 400 degrees. Uncover; scatter Monterey Jack cheese over and bake until the filling is heated through and cheese melts, 5 to 10 minutes more.

Nutrition Information

- Calories: 395 calories
- Cholesterol: 82mg cholesterol
- Protein: 35g protein.
- Total Fat: 10g fat (4g saturated fat)
- Sodium: 795mg sodium
- Fiber: 2g fiber)
- Total Carbohydrate: 38g carbohydrate (9g sugars

574.   Mushroom Penne Bake

Serving: 8 servings. | Prep: 25mins | Cook: 25mins | Ready in:

Ingredients

- 1 package (12 ounces) whole wheat penne pasta
- 1 tablespoon olive oil
- 1 pound sliced baby portobello mushrooms
- 2 garlic cloves, minced
- 1 jar (24 ounces) marinara sauce
- 1 teaspoon Italian seasoning
- 1/2 teaspoon salt

- 2 cups reduced-fat ricotta cheese
- 1 cup shredded part-skim mozzarella cheese, divided
- 1/2 cup grated Parmesan cheese

Direction

- Set the oven to 350° and start preheating. Cook pasta as directed on the package in a 6-qt. stockpot. Drain; transfer back to pot; cool slightly.
- Heat oil over medium-high heat in a large skillet; sauté mushroom for 4-6 minutes until tender. Add garlic; cook for a minute. Stir in seasonings and marinara sauce. Spread 1/2 of the mixture into a 13x9-in. baking dish coated with cooking spray.
- Stir half cup of mozzarella cheese and ricotta cheese into pasta; scoop over mushroom mixture. Spread with the rest of the mushroom mixture.
- Top with the rest of Parmesan cheese and mozzarella cheese. Bake without a cover for 25-30 minutes until bubbly.

Nutrition Information

- Calories: 353 calories
- Sodium: 748mg sodium
- Fiber: 7g fiber)
- Total Carbohydrate: 44g carbohydrate (10g sugars
- Cholesterol: 30mg cholesterol
- Protein: 20g protein. Diabetic Exchanges: 3 starch
- Total Fat: 11g fat (4g saturated fat)

575.   Mushroom Pizza Casserole

Serving: 6 servings. | Prep: 15mins | Cook: 25mins | Ready in:

Ingredients

- 8 ounces uncooked wagon wheels or pasta of your choice
- 1 pound ground beef
- 1 small onion, chopped
- 1 jar (14 ounces) pizza sauce
- 1 can (4 ounces) mushroom stems and pieces, drained
- 1 can (2-1/4 ounces) sliced ripe olives, drained
- 1/2 teaspoon Italian seasoning
- Salt to taste
- 1/2 to 1 cup shredded mozzarella cheese

Direction

- Cook pasta following the package instructions. In the meantime, cook onion and beef in a big frying pan over medium heat until the meat is not pink anymore; strain. Mix in salt, Italian seasoning, olives, mushrooms, and pizza sauce. Strain the pasta, mix into the beef mixture.
- Remove into a shallow 2-quart baking dish coated with cooking spray, sprinkle cheese over. Bake without a cover at 350° until the cheese melts and fully heated, about 25 minutes.

Nutrition Information

- Calories: 335 calories
- Protein: 22g protein.
- Total Fat: 12g fat (5g saturated fat)
- Sodium: 522mg sodium
- Fiber: 3g fiber)
- Total Carbohydrate: 35g carbohydrate (6g sugars
- Cholesterol: 44mg cholesterol

---

576.   Oregano Turkey Casserole

Serving: 6-8 servings. | Prep: 10mins | Cook: 20mins | Ready in:

Ingredients

- 4 ounces uncooked spaghetti
- 2 cups sliced fresh mushrooms
- 1/2 cup julienned green pepper
- 1/4 cup butter, cubed
- 2 tablespoons all-purpose flour
- 2 tablespoons minced fresh oregano or 2 teaspoons dried oregano
- 1/2 teaspoon salt
- 1/4 teaspoon pepper
- 1 teaspoon chicken bouillon granules
- 1/4 cup boiling water
- 1-1/3 cups evaporated milk
- 2-1/2 cups cubed cooked turkey
- 2 tablespoons chopped pimientos
- 2 tablespoons grated Parmesan cheese

Direction

- Cook spaghetti following the package instructions. In the meantime, sauté green pepper and mushrooms with butter in a big frying pan until soft. Mix in pepper, salt, oregano, and flour. Put bouillon in water to dissolve; slowly add to the frying pan. Mix in milk. Boil it, stir and cook until thickened, about 2 minutes. Add pimientos and turkey.
- Strain the spaghetti, mix with the turkey mixture. Add to an 11x7-inch baking dish coated with cooking spray. Sprinkle Parmesan cheese over. Bake without a cover at 350° until fully heated, about 18-22 minutes.

Nutrition Information

- Calories: 252 calories
- Sodium: 407mg sodium
- Fiber: 1g fiber)
- Total Carbohydrate: 18g carbohydrate (5g sugars
- Cholesterol: 63mg cholesterol
- Protein: 19g protein.
- Total Fat: 11g fat (7g saturated fat)

577. Oven Spaghetti

Serving: 4 servings. | Prep: 30mins | Cook: 30mins | Ready in:

Ingredients

- 1/2 pound ground beef
- 1/4 cup chopped onion
- 1/3 cup nonfat dry milk powder
- 3 tablespoons all-purpose flour, divided
- 1 envelope onion soup mix, divided
- 1/2 teaspoon salt
- Dash pepper
- 1 cup water
- 1/2 cup sour cream
- 4 ounces spaghetti, cooked and drained
- 1/2 cup dry bread crumbs
- 1 tablespoon butter, melted

Direction

- Cook onion and beef in a large skillet until no longer pink, over medium heat; drain. Stir in pepper, salt, 1/2 soup mix, 2 tablespoons flour and milk powder; combine well.
- Add water gradually. Bring to boiling. Cook while stirring until thickened or for 2 minutes; put aside. Mix the rest of the flour and soup mix with sour cream in a bowl; stir until blended. Add spaghetti.
- Press onto the bottom and up the sides of a greased 1-qt. baking dish. Scoop beef mixture into shell. Toss butter and bread crumbs; scatter on top of beef mixture. Bake without a cover at 350° until heated through or for half an hour.

Nutrition Information

- Calories:
- Total Carbohydrate:
- Cholesterol:
- Protein:
- Total Fat:
- Sodium:
- Fiber:

578. Over The Top Baked Ziti

Serving: 8 servings. | Prep: 20mins | Cook: 20mins | Ready in:

Ingredients

- 2 cans (29 ounces each) tomato puree
- 1 can (12 ounces) tomato paste
- 1 medium onion, chopped
- 1/4 cup minced fresh parsley
- 2 tablespoons dried oregano
- 4 teaspoons sugar
- 3 garlic cloves, minced
- 1 tablespoon dried basil
- 1 teaspoon salt
- 1/2 teaspoon pepper
- ZITI:
- 1 package (16 ounces) ziti
- 1 large egg, beaten
- 1 carton (15 ounces) reduced-fat ricotta cheese
- 2 cups shredded part-skim mozzarella cheese, divided
- 3/4 cup grated Parmesan cheese
- 1/4 cup minced fresh parsley
- 1/2 teaspoon salt
- 1/4 teaspoon pepper

Direction

- Mix the first ten ingredients together in a 3- or 4-qt. slow cooker. Cook with a cover for 4 hours on low.
- Following the package directions, cook ziti. In a large bowl, mix together 5 cups of sauce, pepper, salt, parsley, Parmesan, 1 cup of mozzarella, ricotta cheese and egg. Strain the ziti; mix into the cheese mixture.
- Place on a 13x9-in. baking sheet coated with cooking spray. Top with the remaining sauce; sprinkle the remaining mozzarella cheese over. Bake at 350° till bubbly, for 20-25 minutes.

Nutrition Information

- Calories: 499 calories
- Total Carbohydrate: 72g carbohydrate (16g sugars
- Cholesterol: 62mg cholesterol
- Protein: 29g protein.
- Total Fat: 10g fat (6g saturated fat)
- Sodium: 826mg sodium
- Fiber: 6g fiber)

579. Overnight Spinach Manicotti

Serving: 7 servings. | Prep: 10mins | Cook: 40mins | Ready in:

Ingredients

- 1 carton (15 ounces) reduced-fat ricotta cheese
- 1 package (10 ounces) frozen chopped spinach, thawed and squeezed dry
- 1-1/2 cups shredded part-skim mozzarella cheese, divided
- 1/2 cup grated Parmesan cheese, divided
- 2 large egg whites
- 2 teaspoons minced fresh parsley
- 1/2 teaspoon salt
- 1/2 teaspoon onion powder
- 1/2 teaspoon pepper
- 1/4 teaspoon garlic powder
- 4-1/2 cups meatless spaghetti sauce
- 3/4 cup water
- 1 package (8 ounces) manicotti shells

Direction

- Mix 1 cup mozzarella, spinach, 1/4 cup Parmesan, garlic powder, egg whites, pepper, ricotta, onion powder, salt, and parsley in a big bowl. Mix water and spaghetti sauce in a different bowl. Put 1 cup on the bottom of a 13x9-in. ungreased pan. Stuff the ricotta mixture into the uncooked manicotti shells. Place on top of the tomato sauce. Top with the

rest of the sauce. Cover; place in refrigerator overnight. Thirty minutes before baking, take it out the refrigerator. Sprinkle with Parmesan and remaining mozzarella cheeses. Do not cover; bake in a 350-degree oven until heated, 40-45 minutes.

Nutrition Information

- Calories: 423 calories
- Cholesterol: 37mg cholesterol
- Protein: 24g protein. Diabetic Exchanges: 2-1/2 starch
- Total Fat: 13g fat (7g saturated fat)
- Sodium: 1128mg sodium
- Fiber: 6g fiber)
- Total Carbohydrate: 51g carbohydrate (0 sugars

580. Parmesan Penne

Serving: 12 servings. | Prep: 30mins | Cook: 40mins | Ready in:

Ingredients

- 1 pound ground beef
- 1 medium onion, chopped
- 1 can (28 ounces) tomato sauce
- 1 cup grated Parmesan cheese, divided
- 1/2 teaspoon ground allspice
- Salt and pepper to taste
- 1 package (16 ounces) penne pasta
- 1/2 cup butter, cubed, divided
- 1/4 cup all-purpose flour
- 2 cups whole milk
- 2 large eggs, lightly beaten

Direction

- In a large skillet over medium heat, cook and stir onion and beef until meat is no longer pink; drain. Mix in pepper, salt, allspice, 1/3 cup of cheese and tomato sauce. Let it come to a boil. Lower the heat; let it simmer without covering for 15 minutes.

- In the meantime, cook pasta following package instructions. Melt 1/4 cup butter in a large saucepan. Add in flour and stir until smooth. Slowly pour in milk. Let it come to a boil; cook and stir until thickened, about 2 minutes. Take it away from the heat; add in 1/3 cup of Parmesan cheese. Slowly whisk in eggs until well combined.
- Drain pasta. Toss with the remaining butter and cheese to coat.
- Arrange 1/3 amount of meat mixture in a greased 13x9-inch baking dish. Layer with 1/2 the pasta, 1/3 meat mixture and 1/2 white sauce. Repeat layers.
- Bake without covering at 350° until bubbly, about 40-45 minutes.

Nutrition Information

- Calories: 360 calories
- Sodium: 563mg sodium
- Fiber: 2g fiber)
- Total Carbohydrate: 36g carbohydrate (5g sugars
- Cholesterol: 85mg cholesterol
- Protein: 18g protein.
- Total Fat: 16g fat (9g saturated fat)

---

581.   Pepperoni Pizza Bake

Serving: 8 servings. | Prep: 15mins | Cook: 15mins | Ready in:

Ingredients

- 1 package (16 ounces) wide egg noodles
- 2-1/4 cups pizza sauce, divided
- 1 cup sliced fresh mushrooms
- 1 can (2-1/4 ounces) sliced ripe olives, drained
- 1 package (3-1/2 ounces) sliced pepperoni
- 2 cups shredded part-skim mozzarella cheese

Direction

- Cook noodles following the package directions; allow to drain. Mix noodles and 3/4 cup pizza sauce in a large bowl. Transfer to a greased 13x9-in. baking dish. Put the remaining pizza sauce on top.
- Layer with pepperoni, olives, and mushrooms. Then sprinkle with cheese. Bake without cover for 15-18 minutes at 375°, or until heated through and the cheese is melted.

Nutrition Information

- Calories: 392 calories
- Sodium: 735mg sodium
- Fiber: 3g fiber)
- Total Carbohydrate: 47g carbohydrate (6g sugars
- Cholesterol: 81mg cholesterol
- Protein: 19g protein.
- Total Fat: 14g fat (6g saturated fat)

---

582.   Pepperoni Pizza Casserole

Serving: 8 | Prep: 15mins | Cook: 45mins | Ready in:

Ingredients

- 1 pound ground beef
- 1 (8 ounce) package uncooked egg noodles
- 1 (16 ounce) jar spaghetti sauce, or as needed
- 1 (2.25 ounce) can sliced black olives, drained
- 1 (2.5 ounce) can sliced mushrooms, drained
- 1 (8 ounce) package sliced pepperoni, coarsely chopped
- 20 ounces shredded mozzarella cheese, divided

Direction

- Set oven temperature to 375* F or 190* C.

- In a frying pan, place ground beef and cook on medium heat until not pink. While the beef is cooking, break it into small pieces like crumbles. Should be done in 10 minutes.
- Place water and a little salt in a large saucepan and bring to a boil. Add the egg noodles and cook for 5 minutes. The noodles should be a little firm but cooked through. Drain the water from the noodles.
- In a large bowl, mix together noodles, pepperoni, spaghetti sauce, mushrooms, half the mozzarella cheese, and black olives. Transfer noodle mixture to a 9x13-inch pan and place rest of cheese on top. Use foil to cover.
- Place pan in heated oven for 30-45 minutes or until the mixture is bubbly.

Nutrition Information

- Calories: 586 calories;
- Protein: 38.2
- Total Fat: 33.9
- Sodium: 1276
- Total Carbohydrate: 30.6
- Cholesterol: 134

583.   Pepperoni Potatoes

Serving: 12-15 servings. | Prep: 20mins | Cook: 25mins | Ready in:

Ingredients

- 3 tablespoons butter
- 2 tablespoons all-purpose flour
- 2 cups whole milk
- 1 teaspoon salt
- 1/2 teaspoon dried thyme
- 1/2 teaspoon dried parsley flakes
- 1/4 teaspoon dried basil
- 1/8 teaspoon pepper
- 1 package (28 ounces) frozen O'Brien potatoes, thawed

- 1/4 cup chopped sweet red pepper
- 1 cup frozen corn, thawed
- 1 cup shredded part-skim mozzarella cheese
- 1-1/2 ounces sliced pepperoni (about 25 slices), quartered

Direction

- Over medium heat, melt butter in a small saucepan. Add flour and stir until smooth. Stir in milk gradually. Boil; cook while stirring until thickened, for 2 minutes. Remove from the heat; then mix in the seasonings.
- Layer potatoes and red pepper then the corn in a greased 13x9-in. baking dish. Top with the sauce, followed by the cheese, then pepperoni. Bake without cover at 375° until heated through, for 25-30 minutes.

Nutrition Information

- Calories: 127 calories
- Protein: 5g protein.
- Total Fat: 6g fat (3g saturated fat)
- Sodium: 304mg sodium
- Fiber: 2g fiber)
- Total Carbohydrate: 13g carbohydrate (3g sugars
- Cholesterol: 17mg cholesterol

584.   Pepperoni Ziti Casserole

Serving: 10 servings. | Prep: 20mins | Cook: 30mins | Ready in:

Ingredients

- 1 package (1 pound) uncooked ziti or small tube pasta
- 1/2 pound lean ground turkey
- 2 cans (one 29 ounces, one 8 ounces) tomato sauce, divided
- 1-1/2 cups shredded part-skim mozzarella cheese, divided

- 1 can (8 ounces) mushroom stems and pieces, drained
- 5 ounces frozen chopped spinach, thawed and squeezed dry
- 1/2 cup reduced-fat ricotta cheese
- 4 teaspoons Italian seasoning
- 2 garlic cloves, minced
- 1/2 teaspoon garlic powder
- 1/2 teaspoon crushed red pepper flakes
- 1/4 teaspoon pepper
- 1/2 cup water
- 1 tablespoon grated Parmesan cheese
- 1-1/2 ounces sliced turkey pepperoni

Direction

- Cook pasta based on the package directions.
- In the meantime, cook turkey in a large nonstick skillet over medium heat until not pink anymore; drain. Place to a large bowl. Include in pepper, pepper flakes, garlic powder, garlic, Italian seasoning, ricotta cheese, spinach, mushrooms, 1 cup of mozzarella cheese, and 29-ounce can of tomato sauce. Drain the pasta; fold into the turkey mixture.
- Place to a 13x9-inch baking dish greased with cooking spray. Whisk the tomato sauce left and water; transfer over the pasta mixture. Scatter with mozzarella cheese left and Parmesan cheese. Arrange pepperoni on top.
- Bake, covered, at 350° about 25 to 30 minutes, or until bubbling. Remove the cover; bake for an extra 5 minutes, or until cheese melts.

Nutrition Information

- Calories: 306 calories
- Cholesterol: 37mg cholesterol
- Protein: 20g protein. Diabetic Exchanges: 2-1/2 starch
- Total Fat: 7g fat (3g saturated fat)
- Sodium: 795mg sodium
- Fiber: 4g fiber)
- Total Carbohydrate: 42g carbohydrate (0 sugars

585.   Peppy Potato Casserole

Serving: 4 servings. | Prep: 15mins | Cook: 35mins | Ready in:

Ingredients

- 2 cans (8 ounces each) tomato sauce
- 1-1/2 cups water
- 1-1/2 teaspoons Italian seasoning
- 1 package (4.9 ounces) scalloped potatoes
- 1/2 pound ground beef
- 24 pepperoni slices
- 4 ounces sliced provolone cheese
- 1/2 cup shredded part-skim mozzarella cheese
- 1 tablespoon grated Parmesan cheese

Direction

- Mix Italian seasoning, water, and tomato sauce together in a big saucepan; boil it. Add contents of sauce mix and potatoes. Remove into a non-oiled 2-quart baking dish.
- In the meantime, cook beef in a big frying pan over medium heat until no pink remains; strain. Add to the potatoes, put pepperoni on top.
- Bake without a cover for 20 minutes at 400°. Put cheeses on top. Bake until the potatoes are soft, about another 15-20 minutes.

Nutrition Information

- Calories: 455 calories
- Sodium: 1392mg sodium
- Fiber: 4g fiber)
- Total Carbohydrate: 30g carbohydrate (3g sugars
- Cholesterol: 81mg cholesterol
- Protein: 28g protein.
- Total Fat: 25g fat (12g saturated fat)

586. Pesto Chicken Mostaccioli

Serving: 2 casseroles (5 servings each). | Prep: 25mins | Cook: 25mins | Ready in:

Ingredients

- 1 package (16 ounces) mostaccioli
- 1 package (16 ounces) frozen breaded chicken tenders
- 4 cups shredded cheddar cheese
- 1 container (16 ounces) sour cream
- 1 carton (15 ounces) ricotta cheese
- 3/4 cup prepared pesto
- 2/3 cup heavy whipping cream
- 1/2 cup grated Parmesan cheese
- 1/2 cup dry bread crumbs
- 1/4 cup butter, melted

Direction

- Cook mostaccioli and chicken as directed on the package. In the meantime, mix Parmesan cheese, cream, pesto, ricotta, sour cream and cheddar cheese in a large bowl.
- Chop chicken tenders; drain mostaccioli; add to cheese mixture. Toss to coat. Place in 2 greased 11x7-in. baking dishes (dishes should be full). Mix butter and bread crumbs; scatter over.
- Bake without a cover at 350° until golden brown or for 25-30 minutes.

Nutrition Information

- Calories: 921 calories
- Sodium: 963mg sodium
- Fiber: 3g fiber)
- Total Carbohydrate: 57g carbohydrate (7g sugars
- Cholesterol: 177mg cholesterol
- Protein: 38g protein.
- Total Fat: 59g fat (32g saturated fat)

587. Potato Pepperoni Dish

Serving: 6 servings. | Prep: 10mins | Cook: 30mins | Ready in:

Ingredients

- 2 to 4 tablespoons butter, cubed
- 5 large unpeeled potatoes, cut into 1/8-inch slices
- 1 small onion, chopped
- 1/2 teaspoon salt
- 1/8 teaspoon pepper
- 2 cups shredded mozzarella cheese
- 1 can (8 ounces) tomato sauce
- 1 package (3-1/2 ounces) sliced pepperoni
- 2 large tomatoes, diced

Direction

- Melt butter in a nonstick 12 in. frying pan; take off heat. Place potatoes up the sides and in the bottom of the pan; season with pepper, onion, and salt. Cover; cook on low heat for 20 minutes or until potatoes are tender. Sprinkle on cheese; layer on half the tomato sauce, all the tomatoes and pepperoni, and the rest of the tomato sauce. Cover; cook over low heat until tomatoes are cooked through and cheese melts.

Nutrition Information

- Calories: 487 calories
- Cholesterol: 53mg cholesterol
- Protein: 18g protein.
- Total Fat: 20g fat (10g saturated fat)
- Sodium: 877mg sodium
- Fiber: 6g fiber)
- Total Carbohydrate: 62g carbohydrate (8g sugars

588.   Potato Pizza Hot Dish

Serving: 8 servings. | Prep: 15mins | Cook: 01hours25mins | Ready in:

Ingredients

- 3 to 4 cups sliced peeled potatoes
- 1 can (11 ounces) condensed cheddar cheese soup, undiluted
- 1/2 cup milk
- 1-1/2 pounds ground beef
- 1 medium onion, chopped
- 1 jar (14 ounces) pizza sauce
- 2 cups shredded part-skim mozzarella cheese

Direction

- In a 13x9-inch baking dish coated with cooking spray, put potatoes. Mix together milk and soup, add to the potatoes.
- Cook onion and beef in a big frying pan over medium heat until the meat is not pink anymore; strain. Spread onto the soup mixture. Put pizza sauce on the top.
- Put a cover on and bake at 350° until the potatoes are soft, about 80-90 minutes. Sprinkle cheese over, bake until the cheese melts, about another 5 minutes.

Nutrition Information

- Calories: 324 calories
- Total Fat: 16g fat (8g saturated fat)
- Sodium: 702mg sodium
- Fiber: 3g fiber)
- Total Carbohydrate: 21g carbohydrate (6g sugars
- Cholesterol: 65mg cholesterol
- Protein: 26g protein.

589.   Potluck Baked Spaghetti

Serving: 12 servings. | Prep: 25mins | Cook: 25mins | Ready in:

Ingredients

- 2 pounds ground beef
- 2 medium onions, chopped
- 2 cans (one 15 ounces, one 8 ounces) tomato sauce
- 1 can (8 ounces) sliced mushrooms, drained
- 1 teaspoon garlic powder
- 1 teaspoon dried oregano
- 2 packages (7 ounces each) uncooked spaghetti
- 1 package (8 ounces) cream cheese, softened
- 2 cups (16 ounces) 4% cottage cheese
- 1/2 cup sour cream
- 2 tablespoons minced chives
- 1/4 cup dry bread crumbs
- 1-1/2 teaspoons butter, melted

Direction

- Cook onions and beef over medium heat in a large skillet until no longer pink; drain. Add oregano, garlic powder, mushrooms and tomato sauce. Bring to boiling. Lower the heat; simmer without a cover while stirring occasionally for 15 minutes.
- In the meantime, cook the spaghetti as directed on the package; drain. Mix chives, sour cream, cottage cheese and cream cheese in a small bowl; whisk well. Transfer 1/2 of the spaghetti sauce in a greased 4-qt. baking dish. Scoop cream cheese mixture over the top evenly. Layer the rest of the spaghetti over and top with all beef mixture.
- Toss butter and bread crumbs; scatter over the beef mixture. Bake with a cover for 20 minutes at 350°. Bake without a cover until heated through or for 5-10 more minutes.

Nutrition Information

- Calories: 378 calories

- Total Carbohydrate: 23g carbohydrate (5g sugars
- Cholesterol: 87mg cholesterol
- Protein: 25g protein.
- Total Fat: 20g fat (10g saturated fat)
- Sodium: 586mg sodium
- Fiber: 2g fiber)

590. Puffed Pizza Casserole

Serving: 2 servings. | Prep: 25mins | Cook: 20mins | Ready in:

Ingredients

- 1/3 pound lean ground beef (90% lean)
- 1/4 cup chopped onion
- 1/2 cup tomato sauce
- 3 tablespoons water
- 3 teaspoons spaghetti sauce mix
- 1/3 cup all-purpose flour
- 1/3 cup 2% milk
- 2 tablespoons beaten egg
- 1 teaspoon canola oil
- 1/2 cup shredded part-skim mozzarella cheese
- 2 tablespoons grated Parmesan cheese

Direction

- Cook onion and beef in a big frying pan medium heat until the meat is not pink anymore; strain. Add spaghetti sauce mix, water, and tomato sauce. Boil it. Lower the heat; simmer without a cover for 5 minutes. In the meantime, in a small bowl, put flour. Mix together oil, egg, and milk; stir into the flour until barely combined.
- Add the meat mixture to a greased 3-cup baking dish. Sprinkle mozzarella cheese over. Add the flour mixture to the top. Sprinkle Parmesan cheese over.
- Bake without a cover at 400° until set in the middle and turning golden brown, about 20-25 minutes.

Nutrition Information

- Calories: 382 calories
- Fiber: 2g fiber)
- Total Carbohydrate: 27g carbohydrate (6g sugars
- Cholesterol: 125mg cholesterol
- Protein: 30g protein. Diabetic Exchanges: 4 lean meat
- Total Fat: 16g fat (7g saturated fat)
- Sodium: 995mg sodium

591. Ratatouille With Polenta

Serving: 4 servings. | Prep: 20mins | Cook: 15mins | Ready in:

Ingredients

- 1/2 pound small fresh mushrooms, halved
- 1 medium sweet red pepper, chopped
- 1 small onion, chopped
- 4 teaspoons olive oil, divided
- 4 cups cubed peeled eggplant
- 1 small zucchini, chopped
- 1 cup cherry tomatoes
- 2 garlic cloves, minced
- 1-1/2 teaspoons Italian seasoning
- 1/2 teaspoon salt
- 1 tube (1 pound) polenta, cut into 1/2-inch slices
- Grated Parmesan cheese, optional

Direction

- In a large skillet, sauté onion, pepper and mushrooms in 2 teaspoons of oil till almost tender. Include in salt, Italian seasoning, garlic, tomatoes, zucchini and eggplant. Sauté till the vegetables become tender, for 8-10 minutes.
- Place another skillet on medium-high heat; cook polenta slices in the remaining oil till slightly browned, 3-4 minutes per side. Serve

with ratatouille; if desired, sprinkle with cheese.

Nutrition Information

- Calories: 195 calories
- Protein: 6g protein. Diabetic Exchanges: 2 starch
- Total Fat: 5g fat (1g saturated fat)
- Sodium: 689mg sodium
- Fiber: 6g fiber)
- Total Carbohydrate: 34g carbohydrate (8g sugars
- Cholesterol: 0 cholesterol

592.   Rich Baked Spaghetti

Serving: 6 servings. | Prep: 20mins | Cook: 30mins | Ready in:

Ingredients

- 8 ounces uncooked spaghetti, broken into thirds
- 1 large egg
- 1/2 cup fat-free milk
- 1/2 pound lean ground beef (90% lean)
- 1/2 pound Italian turkey sausage links, casings removed
- 1 small onion, chopped
- 1/4 cup chopped green pepper
- 1 jar (14 ounces) meatless spaghetti sauce
- 1 can (8 ounces) no-salt-added tomato sauce
- 1/2 cup shredded part-skim mozzarella cheese

Direction

- Following package directions, cook spaghetti; drain. Beat milk with egg in a large bowl. Put in spaghetti; toss to coat. Move to a 13x9-in. baking sheet coated with cooking spray.
- In a large skillet over medium heat, cook green pepper, onion, sausage and beef till the meat is not pink anymore; drain. Mix in tomato sauce

and spaghetti sauce. Distribute over the spaghetti mixture with a spoon.
- Bake without a cover for 20 minutes at 350°. Sprinkle cheese over top. Bake till the cheese is melted, 10 more minutes. Allow to sit for 10 minutes before cutting.

Nutrition Information

- Calories: 343 calories
- Protein: 23g protein. Diabetic Exchanges: 2 starch
- Total Fat: 10g fat (3g saturated fat)
- Sodium: 616mg sodium
- Fiber: 3g fiber)
- Total Carbohydrate: 39g carbohydrate (9g sugars
- Cholesterol: 87mg cholesterol

593.   Roasted Vegetable Ziti Bake

Serving: 12 servings. | Prep: 40mins | Cook: 40mins | Ready in:

Ingredients

- 1 pound eggplant, peeled and cut into 1-inch cubes
- 1 large red onion, cut into 1-inch pieces
- 2 medium sweet yellow peppers, cut into 1-inch pieces
- 1 tablespoon olive oil
- 1/2 teaspoon salt
- SAUCE:
- 1-1/2 cups chopped onions
- 2 teaspoons olive oil
- 6 garlic cloves, minced
- 1/2 teaspoon crushed red pepper flakes
- 1/2 teaspoon fennel seed, crushed
- 1 can (28 ounces) crushed tomatoes
- 1 can (14-1/2 ounces) diced tomatoes, undrained
- 1/4 cup minced fresh parsley

- 1-1/4 teaspoons salt
- 1/2 teaspoon pepper
- 1/4 teaspoon sugar
- 1/8 teaspoon dried thyme
- 1 package (16 ounces) ziti or other small tube pasta
- 4 cups chopped fresh spinach
- 1 cup shredded part-skim mozzarella cheese

Direction

- Mix yellow peppers, red onion and eggplant in a 15x10x1-in. baking pan coated with cooking spray. Drizzle with oil, scatter with salt. Bake without a cover at 400° until edges of peppers start browning or for 35-45 minutes; after every 10 minutes, stir.
- In the meantime, sauté onion in oil until tender in a saucepan. Add fennel, red pepper flakes and garlic; cook while stirring for a minute. Add thyme, sugar, pepper, salt, parsley and tomatoes. Bring to boiling. Lower the heat; simmer without a cover for 15 minutes. Cook pasta as directed on the package.
- Pour half cup of sauce into each of 2 greased 2-qt. baking dishes. Layer 1/4 pasta, 1/4 roasted vegetables and half cup sauce in each dish. Place 2 cups of spinach and half a cup of sauce on top. Place the rest of roasted vegetables, pasta and sauce on top.
- Bake with a cover for half an hour at 350°. Uncover; drizzle with cheese. Bake until heated through and cheese is melted or for 10-15 more minutes.

Nutrition Information

- Calories: 230 calories
- Protein: 10g protein. Diabetic Exchanges: 2 starch
- Total Fat: 5g fat (1g saturated fat)
- Sodium: 497mg sodium
- Fiber: 4g fiber)
- Total Carbohydrate: 40g carbohydrate (0 sugars
- Cholesterol: 5mg cholesterol

594.   Saucy Stuffed Zucchini

Serving: 3-4 servings. | Prep: 30mins | Cook: 25mins | Ready in:

Ingredients

- 3 to 4 medium zucchini (1-3/4 to 2 pounds)
- 12 ounces Johnsonville® Ground Mild Italian sausage, cooked and drained
- 1/2 cup chopped sweet red pepper
- 1/2 cup chopped green pepper
- 2 tablespoons chopped onion
- 1-1/2 teaspoons Italian seasoning
- 1 can (8 ounces) tomato sauce
- 2 tablespoons butter
- 2 tablespoons all-purpose flour
- 1/4 teaspoon salt
- 1-1/4 cups milk
- 1/2 cup grated Parmesan cheese, divided
- 1 teaspoon Dijon mustard

Direction

- Halve the zucchini lengthwise; scoop the pulp out and set it aside, keep a quarter-inch shell. In salted water, cook shells for 2mins; remove the shells then drain. Set the shells aside.
- Chop the pulp then put it in a pot; boil with tomato sauce, sausage, Italian seasoning, onion, and peppers. Lower heat; let it simmer for 5mins while covered. Put the shells in a greased 13x9-in baking dish; put the filling in the shells.
- Melt butter in a pot; stir in salt and flour until smooth. Pour in milk gradually then boil; cook and mix for 2mins until bubbly and thick. Take off heat. Put in mustard and quarter cup Parmesan cheese.
- Pour the mixture on top of the zucchini then top with the remaining Parmesan. Bake for 25-30mins in a 350 degrees oven without cover until completely heated.

Nutrition Information

- Calories: 346 calories
- Sodium: 1126mg sodium
- Fiber: 3g fiber)
- Total Carbohydrate: 18g carbohydrate (9g sugars
- Cholesterol: 67mg cholesterol
- Protein: 19g protein.
- Total Fat: 23g fat (11g saturated fat)

---

595. Sausage Broccoli Manicotti

Serving: 6-8 servings. | Prep: 25mins | Cook: 40mins | Ready in:

Ingredients

- 1 package (8 ounces) manicotti shells
- 2 cups 4% cottage cheese
- 3 cups frozen chopped broccoli, thawed and well drained
- 1-1/2 cups shredded part-skim mozzarella cheese, divided
- 3/4 cup shredded Parmesan cheese, divided
- 1 large egg
- 2 teaspoons minced fresh parsley
- 1/2 teaspoon onion powder
- 1/2 teaspoon pepper
- 1/8 teaspoon garlic powder
- 1 pound Johnsonville® Ground Mild Italian sausage
- 4 cups meatless spaghetti sauce
- 2 garlic cloves, minced

Direction

- Cook manicotti as directed on the package. In the meantime, mix garlic powder, pepper, onion powder, parsley, egg, 1/4 cup Parmesan cheese, a cup of mozzarella cheese, broccoli and cottage cheese in a large bowl; put aside.
- Cook sausage until no longer pink in a large skillet over medium heat; drain. Add garlic

and spaghetti sauce. Spread a cup of meat sauce in a greased 13x9-in. baking dish.
- Rinse and drain shells; stuff broccoli mixture into shells. Place on sauce. Pour the rest of the sauce on top. Scatter with the rest of the Parmesan and mozzarella cheeses. Bake without a cover at 350° until heated through or for 40-50 minutes.

Nutrition Information

- Calories: 417 calories
- Fiber: 4g fiber)
- Total Carbohydrate: 38g carbohydrate (13g sugars
- Cholesterol: 83mg cholesterol
- Protein: 27g protein.
- Total Fat: 18g fat (9g saturated fat)
- Sodium: 1244mg sodium

---

596. Sausage Cheese Manicotti

Serving: 5 servings. | Prep: 25mins | Cook: 45mins | Ready in:

Ingredients

- 10 uncooked manicotti shells
- 8 ounces turkey Italian sausage links, casings removed
- 1 cup finely chopped sweet red pepper
- 1/4 cup chopped onion
- 2 large egg whites
- 3 cups fat-free cottage cheese
- 1 cup shredded part-skim mozzarella cheese
- 1/2 cup shredded Parmesan cheese, divided
- 3 tablespoons minced fresh parsley
- 1/2 teaspoon dried basil
- 1/2 teaspoon fennel seed
- 1/4 teaspoon white pepper
- 2 cups meatless spaghetti sauce
- 1/2 cup water

Direction

- Cook manicotti as directed on the package. In the meantime, break sausage into crumbles into a nonstick skillet; add onion and red pepper. Over medium heat, cook until vegetables become tender and meat is no longer pink; drain. Drain manicotti; put aside.
- Mix pepper, fennel, basil, parsley, 1/4 cup Parmesan cheese, mozzarella cheese, cottage cheese, egg whites and sausage mixture in bowl. Stuff the mixture into manicotti shells. Mix water and spaghetti sauce; spread half a cup in an ungreased 13x9-in. baking dish. Place shells over sauce; pour the rest of the sauce on top.
- Bake with a cover for 35-40 minutes at 350°. Uncover and drizzle with the rest of the Parmesan cheese. Bake until cheese is melted or for 10-15 more minutes. Rest 10 minutes; serve.

Nutrition Information

- Calories: 462 calories
- Total Carbohydrate: 48g carbohydrate (0 sugars
- Cholesterol: 51mg cholesterol
- Protein: 39g protein. Diabetic Exchanges: 4 lean meat
- Total Fat: 13g fat (5g saturated fat)
- Sodium: 1418mg sodium
- Fiber: 4g fiber)

597.   Sausage Fettuccine Bake

Serving: 2 casseroles (6 servings each). | Prep: 25mins | Cook: 25mins | Ready in:

Ingredients

- 1-1/2 pounds uncooked fettuccine
- 2 pounds Johnsonville® Ground Mild Italian sausage
- 2 large onions, chopped
- 1 medium green pepper, chopped
- 2 cans (28 ounces each) diced tomatoes, undrained
- 2 jars (4-1/2 ounces each) sliced mushrooms, drained
- 4 teaspoons Italian seasoning
- 4 cups (1 pound) shredded part-skim mozzarella cheese, divided
- 2 cans (10-3/4 ounces each) condensed cream of mushroom soup, undiluted
- 1/2 cup beef broth
- 1 cup grated Parmesan cheese

Direction

- Cook fettucine as directed on the package. In the meantime, cook the green pepper, onions and sausage in a Dutch oven over medium heat until the meat is no longer pink. Drain. Add Italian seasoning, mushrooms and tomatoes. Bring to boiling. Lower the heat; simmer without a cover for 5 minutes.
- Drain fettuccine; stir into meat mixture. Place 1/2 of the sausage mixture in 2 greased 13x9-in. baking dishes. Scatter over each with a cup of mozzarella cheese; pour the rest of the sausage mixture on top.
- Beat broth and soup in a small bowl; spread over casseroles. Scatter on top with the rest of the mozzarella and Parmesan cheese.
- Freeze one casserole, covered, for up to 3 months. Bake the other casserole with a cover for 20 minutes at 350°. Bake 5-10 more minutes without a cover or until bubbly and cheese is melted. Rest for 10 minutes; serve.
- To use frozen casserole: Take out of the freezer half an hour before baking (do not thaw). Bake with a cover for 70 minutes at 350°. Bake without a cover until heated through or for 5-10 minutes. Rest for 10 minutes; serve.

Nutrition Information

- Calories: 531 calories
- Protein: 30g protein.
- Total Fat: 22g fat (9g saturated fat)

- Sodium: 1311mg sodium
- Fiber: 6g fiber)
- Total Carbohydrate: 55g carbohydrate (10g sugars
- Cholesterol: 60mg cholesterol

---

598.   Sausage Green Bean Bake

Serving: 6 servings. | Prep: 5mins | Cook: 40mins | Ready in:

Ingredients

- 3-1/2 cups spaghetti sauce
- 1-1/2 pounds Johnsonville® Mild Italian Sausage Links, cooked and cut into 1/2-inch pieces
- 1 package (16 ounces) frozen cut green beans
- 2 jars (4-1/2 ounces each) sliced mushrooms, drained
- 2 cups shredded part-skim mozzarella cheese

Direction

- Mix mushrooms, beans, sausage, and spaghetti sauce together in a large bowl until well combined. Pour mixture into an oiled 13x9-inch baking dish; sprinkle mozzarella cheese over the top of sausage mixture.
- Bake without covering for 40 to 45 minutes at 350° or until cheese is completely melted.

Nutrition Information

- Calories: 426 calories
- Sodium: 1511mg sodium
- Fiber: 4g fiber)
- Total Carbohydrate: 20g carbohydrate (11g sugars
- Cholesterol: 77mg cholesterol
- Protein: 23g protein.
- Total Fat: 28g fat (11g saturated fat)

---

599.   Sausage Lasagna

Serving: 12 servings. | Prep: 45mins | Cook: 35mins | Ready in:

Ingredients

- 1 pound Johnsonville® Ground Mild Italian sausage
- 1 medium onion, chopped
- 2 garlic cloves, minced
- 1 can (6 ounces) tomato paste
- 1 can (28 ounces) crushed tomatoes
- 1 can (8 ounces) tomato sauce
- 3 teaspoons dried basil
- 3/4 teaspoon pepper, divided
- 1/4 teaspoon salt
- 1 large egg, lightly beaten
- 1 carton (15 ounces) whole-milk ricotta cheese
- 1-1/2 cups grated Parmesan cheese, divided
- 12 no-cook lasagna noodles
- 4 cups shredded part-skim mozzarella cheese

Direction

- Turn the oven to 400°. Cook sausage, crumbling it with onion on moderate heat until meat is not pink in a big skillet, 5 to 7 minutes; drain grease. Put in tomato paste and garlic; stir and cook for one minute.
- Add in tomato sauce, tomatoes, half teaspoon pepper, salt and basil; let it boil. Lower the heat and let simmer, without cover, until a little thick, 10 to 15 minutes.
- Combine ricotta cheese, 1 1/4 cups Parmesan, remaining pepper and egg in a bowl. Grease a 13x 9-inch baking tray and pour 1 1/2 cups meat sauce in bottom. Layer on top 4 pastas, 1 1/2 cups of ricotta cheese mixture, 1 1/2 cups of mozzarella cheese and 1 1/2 cups of sauce. Make the layers again. Finish with remaining pasta, meat sauce, Parmesan and mozzarella cheeses.
- Use greased foil to cover and bake half an hour. Discard the foil; bake until slightly

brown and heated completely, 5 to 10 minutes.
Let it sit 15 minutes. Serve.

Nutrition Information

- Calories: 416 calories
- Total Carbohydrate: 29g carbohydrate (8g sugars
- Cholesterol: 83mg cholesterol
- Protein: 25g protein.
- Total Fat: 23g fat (11g saturated fat)
- Sodium: 978mg sodium
- Fiber: 3g fiber)

---

600. Sausage Mushroom Manicotti

Serving: 7 servings. | Prep: 20mins | Cook: 30mins | Ready in:

Ingredients

- 1 package (8 ounces) manicotti shells
- 1 pound Johnsonville® Ground Mild Italian sausage
- 1/2 cup thinly sliced green onions
- 1 garlic clove, minced
- 2 tablespoons butter
- 1 jar (4-1/2 ounces) sliced mushrooms, drained
- 1 can (10-3/4 ounces) condensed cream of mushroom soup, undiluted
- 1/2 cup sour cream
- 1/4 teaspoon pepper
- SAUCE:
- 1 can (5 ounces) evaporated milk
- 1 jar (4-1/2 ounces) sliced mushrooms, drained
- 1 tablespoon minced fresh parsley
- 2 cups shredded part-skim mozzarella cheese, divided

Direction

- Follow package directions to cook manicotti shells. Meanwhile, cook sausage till no pink anymore in a skillet over medium heat. Drain; put aside. Sauté garlic and onions in butter till tender in the same skillet. Add mushrooms and heat through. Drain shells; put aside.
- Put mushroom mixture into a bowl; mix in pepper, sour cream, soup and sausage. Stuff into the manicotti shells; put into a 13x9-in. greased baking dish.
- Sauce: Heat parsley, mushrooms and milk in a saucepan. Take off heat. Add 1 1/2 cups of cheese; mix till melted. Put on top of the stuffed shells.
- Cover; bake for 25 minutes at 350°. Uncover; sprinkle with leftover cheese. Bake till cheese melts or for 5-10 minutes more.

Nutrition Information

- Calories: 449 calories
- Total Carbohydrate: 33g carbohydrate (5g sugars
- Cholesterol: 79mg cholesterol
- Protein: 21g protein.
- Total Fat: 26g fat (13g saturated fat)
- Sodium: 949mg sodium
- Fiber: 3g fiber)

---

601. Sausage Pizza Casserole

Serving: 6-8 servings. | Prep: 25mins | Cook: 25mins | Ready in:

Ingredients

- 3/4 cup chopped onion
- 1 medium sweet yellow pepper, diced
- 1 medium sweet red pepper, diced
- 1 tablespoon olive oil
- 1 medium zucchini, halved lengthwise and sliced
- 1 teaspoon minced garlic

- 2 cans (14-1/2 ounces each) diced tomatoes, drained
- 3/4 pound Johnsonville® Fully Cooked Smoked Sausage Rope, sliced
- 1 can (6 ounces) tomato paste
- 1 teaspoon salt
- 1 teaspoon Italian seasoning
- 1/2 teaspoon pepper
- 1/4 cup grated Parmesan cheese, divided
- 2 cups shredded part-skim mozzarella cheese
- 1 tube (11 ounces) refrigerated breadsticks

Direction

- Sauté peppers and onion with oil in a big frying pan until crisp-tender, about 2-3 minutes. Add zucchini, sauté until the vegetables are soft, about another 4-6 minutes. Add garlic; cook for another 1 minute.
- Mix in 2 tablespoons Parmesan cheese, pepper, Italian seasoning, salt, tomato paste, sausage, and tomatoes. Boil it. Lower the heat; simmer without a cover until fully heated, about 8-10 minutes.
- In a 13x9-inch baking dish coated with cooking spray, spread 1/2 the sausage mixture. Sprinkle mozzarella cheese over; put the rest of the sausage mixture on top. Split the breadsticks, arrange over the top with a lattice pattern. Sprinkle the rest of the Parmesan cheese over.
- Bake without a cover at 375° until the filling is bubbling and the topping turns golden brown, about 25-30 minutes. Let sit before serving, about 10 minutes.

Nutrition Information

- Calories: 389 calories
- Fiber: 4g fiber)
- Total Carbohydrate: 32g carbohydrate (11g sugars
- Cholesterol: 47mg cholesterol
- Protein: 19g protein.
- Total Fat: 21g fat (8g saturated fat)
- Sodium: 1327mg sodium

602.   Sausage Spaghetti Pie

Serving: 4 servings. | Prep: 20mins | Cook: 25mins | Ready in:

Ingredients

- 4 ounces uncooked spaghetti
- 1/2 pound smoked turkey kielbasa, diced
- 1 cup garden-style spaghetti sauce
- 1 cup reduced-fat ricotta cheese
- 3 egg whites
- 1/3 cup grated Parmesan cheese
- 1/4 cup shredded part-skim mozzarella cheese

Direction

- Cook spaghetti as directed on the package. In the meantime, sauté sausage in a small nonstick skillet until browned or for 3-4 minutes; stirring in spaghetti sauce.
- Mix one egg white and ricotta cheese in a small bowl; put aside. Drain spaghetti. Add the rest of egg whites and Parmesan cheese. Press onto the bottom and up the sides of a 9-in. deep-dish pie plate coated with cooking spray. Scoop ricotta mixture into crust. Place sausage mixture on top.
- Bake without a cover for 20 minutes at 350°. Scatter with mozzarella cheese. Bake until filling is heated through and cheese is melted or for 5 more minutes. Allow to rest for 5 minutes; then slice.

Nutrition Information

- Calories: 341 calories
- Cholesterol: 47mg cholesterol
- Protein: 24g protein. Diabetic Exchanges: 3 lean meat
- Total Fat: 9g fat (4g saturated fat)
- Sodium: 980mg sodium
- Fiber: 2g fiber)
- Total Carbohydrate: 38g carbohydrate (12g sugars

- Cholesterol: 77mg cholesterol
- Protein: 27g protein.
- Total Fat: 24g fat (12g saturated fat)

603. Sausage Spinach Casserole

Serving: 4 servings. | Prep: 15mins | Cook: 30mins | Ready in:

Ingredients

- 2 packages (10 ounces each) frozen chopped spinach, thawed and drained
- 1 can (15 ounces) great northern beans, rinsed and drained
- 2 cooked Italian sausage links, sliced
- 1 can (12 ounces) evaporated milk
- 3/4 cup chopped onion
- 1/2 cup grated Parmesan cheese, divided
- 1 tablespoon lemon juice
- 1 teaspoon grated lemon zest
- 1/4 teaspoon ground nutmeg
- 1/8 teaspoon pepper
- 2 garlic cloves, minced
- 4 teaspoons butter
- 1/3 cup dry bread crumbs

Direction

- Mix the first 5 ingredients in a bowl. Stir in pepper, nutmeg, lemon zest and juice and 1/4 cup of cheese. Place into a greased 2-qt. baking dish.
- Sauté garlic until tender in butter in a skillet. Take out of the heat; stir in the rest of cheese and bread crumbs. Drizzle over spinach mixture. Bake without a cover for half an hour or until heat through at 375°.

Nutrition Information

- Calories: 474 calories
- Sodium: 1066mg sodium
- Fiber: 8g fiber)
- Total Carbohydrate: 37g carbohydrate (11g sugars

604. Sausage Stuffed Shells

Serving: 2 servings. | Prep: 25mins | Cook: 20mins | Ready in:

Ingredients

- 1/3 pound Johnsonville® Ground Mild Italian sausage
- 1 can (8 ounces) tomato sauce
- 1/4 cup tomato paste
- 2 tablespoons water
- 1 teaspoon brown sugar
- 1/2 teaspoon Italian seasoning
- 1/3 cup 4% cottage cheese
- 3/4 cup shredded part-skim mozzarella cheese, divided
- 2 tablespoons beaten egg
- 1/2 teaspoon minced fresh parsley
- 6 jumbo pasta shells, cooked and drained
- Grated Parmesan cheese, optional

Direction

- Cook sausage in a small saucepan over medium heat until the sausage is not pink anymore; strain. Put 1/2 of the sausage aside to use for filling. Add Italian seasoning, brown sugar, water, tomato paste, and tomato sauce to the pan with the sausage. Boil it. Lower the heat, simmer without a cover, whisking sometimes, about 15 minutes.
- Mix the saved sausage, parsley, egg, 1/2 cup mozzarella cheese, and cottage cheese together in a small bowl. Stuff the mixture into the shells. In a non-oiled 1-quart shallow baking dish, spread 1/4 cup meat sauce. In the dish, put the stuffed shells, drizzle the leftover meat sauce over.
- If you want, sprinkle the leftover Parmesan cheese and mozzarella cheese over. Bake

without a cover at 350° until the filling reaches 160°, about 20-25 minutes.

Nutrition Information

- Calories: 437 calories
- Protein: 36g protein.
- Total Fat: 14g fat (7g saturated fat)
- Sodium: 1371mg sodium
- Fiber: 4g fiber)
- Total Carbohydrate: 40g carbohydrate (13g sugars
- Cholesterol: 67mg cholesterol

605.   Seafood In Tomato Sauce

Serving: 4 servings. | Prep: 20mins | Cook: 45mins | Ready in:

Ingredients

- 1-3/4 cups sliced fresh mushrooms
- 1 garlic clove, minced
- 3 tablespoons canola oil, divided
- 1 can (14-1/2 ounces) diced tomatoes, drained
- 1-1/2 teaspoons dried oregano
- 1 teaspoon sugar
- 1 teaspoon dried thyme
- Salt and pepper to taste
- 1/2 pound lump crabmeat or imitation crabmeat
- 1/2 pound bay scallops
- 1/2 pound uncooked small shrimp, peeled and deveined
- 1 cup cooked long grain rice
- 3/4 cup shredded Parmesan cheese

Direction

- Sauté garlic and mushrooms for 3-4 minutes in a tablespoon of oil in a large saucepan. Add pepper, salt, thyme, sugar, oregano and tomatoes.

- Bring to boiling. Lower the heat; cook and simmer for half an hour. Cook without a cover for 10 more minutes. Take out of the heat; stir in crab.
- In the meantime, cook shrimp and scallops in the remaining oil in a large skillet until scallops are opaque and shrimps turn pink.
- Distribute rice into 4 individual baking sheets. Place scallops and shrimps on top. Scoop tomato mixture over rice; drizzle with Parmesan cheese. Bake until heated through and cheese is melted or for 10 minutes at 350°.

Nutrition Information

- Calories: 399 calories
- Protein: 39g protein.
- Total Fat: 17g fat (4g saturated fat)
- Sodium: 834mg sodium
- Fiber: 2g fiber)
- Total Carbohydrate: 21g carbohydrate (5g sugars
- Cholesterol: 171mg cholesterol

606.   Simple Manicotti

Serving: 7 servings. | Prep: 35mins | Cook: 10mins | Ready in:

Ingredients

- 1-1/2 pounds ground beef
- 2 cups spaghetti sauce, divided
- 1 tablespoon onion powder
- 1 teaspoon salt
- 1/2 teaspoon pepper
- 1 cup shredded part-skim mozzarella cheese
- 14 large manicotti shells, cooked and drained

Direction

- Cook the beef on medium heat in a large skillet until it is not pink anymore; then drain. Take out if the heat. Stir in pepper, salt, onion powder, and a cup of the spaghetti sauce.

Allow to cool for 5 minutes. Put aside 1/2 cup. Add the cheese onto the remaining meat mixture

- Fill in manicotti shells; place in a 13x9-inch baking dish coated with cooking spray. Mix the saved meat mixture and the remaining spaghetti sauce; spread on the shells.
- Remove the cover and bake at 350 degrees until heated through, or for 10 minutes.

Nutrition Information

- Calories: 415 calories
- Protein: 29g protein.
- Total Fat: 19g fat (8g saturated fat)
- Sodium: 800mg sodium
- Fiber: 2g fiber)
- Total Carbohydrate: 32g carbohydrate (6g sugars
- Cholesterol: 79mg cholesterol

607.   Skinny Eggplant Parmesan

Serving: 4 servings. | Prep: 45mins | Cook: 30mins | Ready in:

Ingredients

- 1/2 cup fat-free milk
- 1 cup dry bread crumbs
- 2 teaspoons Italian seasoning, divided
- 1 large eggplant, peeled and cut into 1/2-inch slices
- 1/2 pound sliced fresh mushrooms
- 1 cup chopped sweet onion
- 2 teaspoons olive oil
- 2 garlic cloves, minced
- 8 fresh basil leaves, thinly sliced
- 1 jar (24 ounces) marinara sauce
- 1/4 cup dry red wine or vegetable broth
- 3/4 cup shredded part-skim mozzarella cheese
- 3/4 cup part-skim ricotta cheese
- 1/4 cup shredded Parmesan cheese

Direction

- Pour milk into a shallow bowl. Mix a teaspoon of Italian seasoning and bread crumbs in another shallow bowl. Dip eggplant in milk, then in the bread crumb mixture. Transfer onto a baking sheet coated with cooking spray. Bake until tender or for 30-40 minutes at 350°.
- In the meantime, sauté onion and mushrooms in oil until tender in a large skillet. Add garlic; cook for 1 more minute. Take out of the heat. Stir in the rest of the Italian seasoning and basil.
- Spread half a cup of marinara sauce into a 2-qt. baking dish coated with cooking spray. Mix the rest of the marinara sauce and wine in a small bowl. Layer with 1/2 of eggplant, mushroom mixture, mozzarella cheese, ricotta cheese and 3/4 cup of sauce mixture. Place other similar layers on top. Pour the rest of the sauce on top; scatter with Parmesan cheese.
- Bake without a cover at 350° until heated through and cheese is melted or for 30-35 minutes. Rest 10 minutes; cut.

Nutrition Information

- Calories: 342 calories
- Total Carbohydrate: 42g carbohydrate (21g sugars
- Cholesterol: 31mg cholesterol
- Protein: 20g protein. Diabetic Exchanges: 2 lean meat
- Total Fat: 11g fat (6g saturated fat)
- Sodium: 560mg sodium
- Fiber: 10g fiber)

608.   Slow Cooker Stuffed Shells

Serving: 10 servings. | Prep: 30mins | Cook: 04hours00mins | Ready in:

Ingredients

- 1 carton (15 ounces) part-skim ricotta cheese
- 1 package (10 ounces) frozen chopped spinach, thawed and squeezed dry
- 2-1/2 cups shredded Italian cheese blend
- 1/2 cup diced red onion
- 1/2 teaspoon garlic powder
- 2 teaspoons dried basil
- 1/2 teaspoon dried oregano
- 1/2 teaspoon dried thyme
- 2 jars (24 ounces each) roasted garlic Parmesan pasta sauce
- 2 cups water
- 1 package (12 ounces) jumbo pasta shells
- Additional shredded Italian cheese blend and sliced fresh basil, optional

Direction

- Combine together the first eight ingredients. (The mixture should be stiff.) Combine water with one jar pasta sauce in a greased 6-qt. slow cooker. Fill ricotta mixture into the shells; layer in the slow cooker. Transfer the remaining jar of pasta sauce on top.
- Cook with a cover on low for 4-5 hours, or till the pasta is tender. Serve with fresh basil and more cheese if desired.

Nutrition Information

- Calories: 303 calories
- Total Fat: 10g fat (6g saturated fat)
- Sodium: 377mg sodium
- Fiber: 3g fiber)
- Total Carbohydrate: 34g carbohydrate (4g sugars
- Cholesterol: 34mg cholesterol
- Protein: 17g protein. Diabetic Exchanges: 2 starch

609. Slow Cooker Two Meat Manicotti

Serving: 7 servings. | Prep: 45mins | Cook: 04hours00mins | Ready in:

Ingredients

- 1/2 pound medium fresh mushrooms, chopped
- 2 small green peppers, chopped
- 1 medium onion, chopped
- 1-1/2 teaspoons canola oil
- 4 garlic cloves, minced
- 3/4 pound ground sirloin
- 3/4 pound Johnsonville® Ground Mild Italian sausage
- 2 jars (23-1/2 ounces each) Italian sausage and garlic spaghetti sauce
- 1 carton (15 ounces) ricotta cheese
- 1 cup minced fresh parsley
- 1/2 cup shredded part-skim mozzarella cheese, divided
- 1/2 cup grated Parmesan cheese, divided
- 2 large eggs, lightly beaten
- 1/2 teaspoon salt
- 1/4 teaspoon pepper
- 1/8 teaspoon ground nutmeg
- 1 package (8 ounces) manicotti shells

Direction

- In the big skillet on medium high heat, sauté onion, peppers and mushrooms in the oil till becoming soft. Put in the garlic; cook for 60 seconds longer. Take out of the pan.
- In that skillet, cook the sausage and beef on medium heat till not pink anymore; drain off. Whisk in the spaghetti sauce and mushroom mixture; put aside.
- In the small-sized bowl, mix seasonings, eggs, a quarter cup of the parmesan cheese, a quarter cup of the mozzarella cheese, parsley, and ricotta cheese. Stuff into the uncooked manicotti shells.
- Spread 2.25 cups of the sauce onto bottom of the 6-quart slow cooker. Arrange five stuffed

manicotti shells on top of the sauce; repeat twice, using four shells on top layer. Pour the rest of the sauce on top. Drizzle with the rest of the cheeses. Keep covered and cook over low heat till the pasta softens or for 4 to 5 hours.

Nutrition Information

- Calories: 657 calories
- Protein: 39g protein.
- Total Fat: 33g fat (14g saturated fat)
- Sodium: 1609mg sodium
- Fiber: 7g fiber)
- Total Carbohydrate: 55g carbohydrate (22g sugars
- Cholesterol: 155mg cholesterol

610.　　Spaghetti Hot Dish

Serving: 4 servings. | Prep: 20mins | Cook: 30mins | Ready in:

Ingredients

- 1 pound lean ground beef (90% lean)
- 2 medium onions, diced
- 3 celery ribs with leaves, diced
- 1/4 cup butter, cubed
- 5 tablespoons all-purpose flour
- Salt and pepper to taste
- 3-1/2 cups milk
- 2 tablespoons chopped pimientos
- 1 to 2 teaspoons soy sauce
- 1-1/4 cups broken spaghetti, cooked and drained
- 1 cup finely crushed butter-flavored crackers (about 25 crackers)

Direction

- Cook celery, onions and beef over medium heat in butter in a large skillet until no longer pink; drain. Stir in pepper, salt and flour until

blended. Add pimientos, soy sauce and milk gradually. Bring to boiling; cook while stirring until thickened or for 2 minutes. Stir in spaghetti.
- Place into a greased 11x7-in. baking dish. Scatter with cracker crumbs. Bake without a cover at 350° until heated through or for 30-35 minutes.

Nutrition Information

- Calories: 653 calories
- Protein: 35g protein.
- Total Fat: 33g fat (16g saturated fat)
- Sodium: 587mg sodium
- Fiber: 4g fiber)
- Total Carbohydrate: 54g carbohydrate (17g sugars
- Cholesterol: 115mg cholesterol

611.　　Spaghetti Pie Casserole

Serving: 8 servings. | Prep: 30mins | Cook: 30mins | Ready in:

Ingredients

- 1 package (8 ounces) spaghetti
- 1 pound ground beef
- 1 small onion, chopped
- 2 garlic cloves, minced
- 1 jar (14 ounces) spaghetti sauce
- 1/2 teaspoon salt
- 1/4 teaspoon pepper
- 3 ounces reduced-fat cream cheese
- 1 cup (8 ounces) reduced-fat sour cream
- 3 green onions, chopped
- 1-1/2 cups shredded cheddar-Monterey Jack cheese

Direction

- Cook spaghetti following the package instructions; strain. In the meantime, cook garlic, onion, and beef in a big skillet over medium heat until the beef is not pink anymore, about 6-8 minutes; crumble the beef into small portions then strain. Mix in pepper, salt, and spaghetti sauce. Boil it. Lower the heat; simmer without a cover, tossing sometimes, about 20 minutes.

- Combine sour cream and cream cheese in a small bowl until combined; mix in green onions. Layer the meat mixture, the cream cheese mixture, and the spaghetti in an 11x7-inch baking dish coated with cooking spray. Put shredded cheese on top.
- Put a cover on and bake for 25 minutes at 350°. Remove the cover. Bake until the cheese is bubbling, about another 5-10 minutes.

Nutrition Information

- Calories: 396 calories
- Fiber: 2g fiber)
- Total Carbohydrate: 31g carbohydrate (7g sugars
- Cholesterol: 73mg cholesterol
- Protein: 23g protein.
- Total Fat: 20g fat (11g saturated fat)
- Sodium: 622mg sodium

612. Spaghetti Turkey Pie

Serving: 6 servings. | Prep: 30mins | Cook: 30mins | Ready in:

Ingredients

- 1 pound ground turkey breast
- 1 cup chopped green pepper
- 1/2 cup chopped onion
- 1/2 cup tomato sauce
- 1/2 teaspoon dried basil
- 1/2 teaspoon fennel seed, crushed
- 1/8 teaspoon pepper
- 6 ounces spaghetti
- 1/4 cup egg substitute

- 1 tablespoon reduced-fat stick margarine, melted
- 1 tablespoon grated Parmesan cheese
- 1 teaspoon dried parsley flakes
- 1/2 cup shredded part-skim mozzarella cheese, divided

Direction

- In a large skillet over medium heat, cook onion, green pepper, and turkey till the meat is not pink anymore; drain. Mix in pepper, fennel seed, basil and tomato sauce. Boil. Lower the heat; simmer without a cover for 20-30 minutes.
- Meanwhile, following package instructions, cook spaghetti; drain. Combine parsley flakes, Parmesan cheese, margarine, egg substitute and the spaghetti in a bowl. Make a crust in a greased 9-in. pie plate.
- Mix 1/4 cup of mozzarella cheese into the prepared turkey mixture; using a spoon, transfer to the spaghetti crust. Bake with a cover for 30 minutes at 350°. Uncover; sprinkle the remaining mozzarella cheese over top. Bake till the cheese is melted, 15 more minutes. Allow to sit for 10 minutes before cutting into wedges.

Nutrition Information

- Calories: 213 calories
- Sodium: 296mg sodium
- Fiber: 2g fiber)
- Total Carbohydrate: 13g carbohydrate (0 sugars
- Cholesterol: 66mg cholesterol
- Protein: 19g protein. Diabetic Exchanges: 2 lean meat
- Total Fat: 9g fat (3g saturated fat)

613. Spaghetti With Bacon

Serving: 8 | Prep: 10mins | Cook: 15mins | Ready in:

Ingredients

- 1 (16 ounce) package spaghetti
- 1/4 cup olive oil
- 8 slices bacon, cut into 1/4 inch pieces
- 4 cloves garlic, minced
- 1/2 cup chopped fresh flat-leaf parsley

Direction

- Boil a large pot with slightly salted water over high heat. Bring to a rolling boil. Once it boils, add in the spaghetti then return to a boil. Cook the pasta without cover, stirring from time to time, until the pasta is has cooked through but is still firm to the bite, for about 12 minutes. Strain well in a colander set in the sink.
- Meanwhile, heat the olive oil in a large frypan over medium heat. Add in the bacon, cook until it has begun to shrink, for about 3 minutes. Stir in garlic, stir and cook until the garlic tenders and the bacon is crispy, for about 5 minutes. Add the drained pasta with the oil, bacon and parsley to serve.

Nutrition Information

- Calories: 399 calories;
- Total Carbohydrate: 42.7
- Cholesterol: 19
- Protein: 10.8
- Total Fat: 20.2
- Sodium: 239

614. Spicy Bratwurst Supper

Serving: 4 servings. | Prep: 15mins | Cook: 10mins | Ready in:

Ingredients

- 6 bacon strips, diced
- 1/3 cup chopped onion
- 5 fully cooked bratwurst links, cut into 1/2-inch slices

- 1/2 pound sliced fresh mushrooms
- 1 tablespoon diced jalapeno pepper
- 2 cups meatless spaghetti sauce
- 2 ounces Gouda cheese, shredded
- Hot cooked rice

Direction

- Cook onion and bacon over medium heat until bacon becomes almost crisp in a large skillet. Transfer to paper towels; drain.
- Sauté jalapeno, mushrooms and bratwurst in the same skillet until mushrooms become tender or for 3-4 minutes. Stir in bacon mixture and spaghetti sauce.
- Cook with a cover until heated through or for 4-6 minutes. Scatter with cheese. Serve with rice.

Nutrition Information

- Calories: 630 calories
- Sodium: 1525mg sodium
- Fiber: 3g fiber)
- Total Carbohydrate: 17g carbohydrate (12g sugars
- Cholesterol: 103mg cholesterol
- Protein: 25g protein.
- Total Fat: 51g fat (20g saturated fat)

615. Spinach Cheese Manicotti

Serving: 6 | Prep: 20mins | Cook: 45mins | Ready in:

Ingredients

- 1 (15 ounce) container ricotta cheese
- 1 (10 ounce) package frozen chopped spinach, thawed and squeezed dry
- 1/2 cup minced onion
- 1 egg
- 2 teaspoons minced fresh parsley
- 1/2 teaspoon pepper
- 1/4 teaspoon garlic powder

- 1 1/2 cups shredded mozzarella cheese, divided
- 1/2 cup grated Parmesan cheese, divided
- 2 (26 ounce) jars spaghetti sauce
- 1 1/2 cups water
- 1 (8 ounce) package manicotti shells

Direction

- Set the oven to 350°F (175°C) and start preheating.
- Mix egg, onion, spinach and ricotta in a large bowl. Season with garlic powder, pepper and parsley. Mix in 1/4 cup Parmesan and 1 cup mozzarella. Stir water and spaghetti sauce together in another bowl.
- Spread a cup of sauce in the bottom of a 9x13 inch baking dish. Stuff ricotta mixture into uncooked manicotti shells; place in a single layer in the dish. Pour the rest of the sauce to cover the top. Scatter with the rest of Parmesan and mozzarella.
- Bake in the prepared oven until noodles become soft or for 45-55 minutes.

Nutrition Information

- Calories: 576 calories;
- Protein: 29.8
- Total Fat: 20.5
- Sodium: 1410
- Total Carbohydrate: 69
- Cholesterol: 82

616.   Spinach Chicken Manicotti

Serving: 6 servings. | Prep: 60mins | Cook: 35mins | Ready in:

Ingredients

- 1 large onion, chopped
- 1 teaspoon olive oil
- 1 garlic clove, minced
- 2-1/2 cups diced cooked chicken breast
- 1 package (10 ounces) frozen chopped spinach, thawed and squeezed dry
- 3/4 cup diced fully cooked lean ham
- 1/4 cup grated Parmesan cheese
- 2 egg whites
- 1/2 teaspoon dried basil
- 1/8 teaspoon pepper
- Dash ground nutmeg
- 12 uncooked manicotti shells
- SAUCE:
- 3/4 cup all-purpose flour
- 3 cups reduced-sodium chicken broth
- 1 cup fat-free milk
- 1/4 teaspoon salt
- 1/8 teaspoon ground nutmeg
- 1/8 teaspoon pepper
- Dash cayenne pepper
- 1/4 cup grated Parmesan cheese

Direction

- Cook onion in oil in a small skillet until tender. Put in garlic and cook for 1 more minute. Mix the nutmeg, pepper, basil, egg whites, cheese, ham, spinach, chicken and the onion mixture in a large bowl; put aside.
- Prepare manicotti shells following package directions. In the meantime, stir broth and flour until smooth in a big saucepan to make the sauce; mix in the cayenne, pepper, nutmeg, salt and milk gradually. Boil on medium heat; cook and mix until thickened for 2 minutes. Scoop a cup into chicken mix. Put cheese to the remaining sauce.
- Put a cup of sauce into a 13x9-inch baking pan sprayed with cooking spray. Strain shells; fill with chicken mixture. Put over the sauce. Pour remaining sauce on top. Bake, covered, for 35-40 minutes at 375° or until bubbly and thoroughly heated.

Nutrition Information

- Calories: 372 calories

- Protein: 35g protein. Diabetic Exchanges: 4 lean meat
- Total Fat: 7g fat (2g saturated fat)
- Sodium: 866mg sodium
- Fiber: 3g fiber)
- Total Carbohydrate: 43g carbohydrate (6g sugars
- Cholesterol: 58mg cholesterol

617. Spinach Manicotti

Serving: 7 | Prep: 15mins | Cook: 1hours10mins | Ready in:

Ingredients

- 1 (15 ounce) container nonfat ricotta cheese
- 2 cups shredded part-skim mozzarella cheese, divided
- 1 (10 ounce) package frozen chopped spinach, thawed and squeezed dry
- 1/2 cup reduced-fat sour cream
- 1/4 cup dry bread crumbs
- 1 tablespoon Italian seasoning
- 1 teaspoon garlic powder
- 1 teaspoon onion powder
- 2 cups tomato juice
- 1 cup chunky salsa
- 1 (15 ounce) can crushed tomatoes
- 14 uncooked manicotti shells

Direction

- Mix onion powder, garlic powder, Italian seasoning, bread crumbs, sour cream, spinach, 1-1/2 cup mozzarella cheese and ricotta in a large bowl. Mix crushed tomatoes, salsa and tomato juice; spread a cup sauce into an ungreased 13-in. x 9-in. x 2-in. baking dish. Stuff spinach mixture into uncooked manicotti; place over sauce. Top over manicotti with the rest of sauce.
- Bake with a cover for 55 minutes at 350°F. Uncover and drizzle with the rest of

mozzarella cheese. Bake until noodles become tender or for another 15 minutes.

Nutrition Information

618. Spinach Beef Spaghetti Pie

Serving: 8 servings. | Prep: 20mins | Cook: 20mins | Ready in:

Ingredients

- 6 ounces uncooked angel hair pasta
- 2 large eggs, lightly beaten
- 1/3 cup grated Parmesan cheese
- 1 pound ground beef
- 1/2 cup chopped onion
- 1/4 cup chopped green pepper
- 1 jar (14 ounces) meatless pasta sauce
- 1 teaspoon Creole seasoning
- 3/4 teaspoon garlic powder
- 1/2 teaspoon dried basil
- 1/2 teaspoon dried oregano
- 1 package (8 ounces) cream cheese, softened
- 1 package (10 ounces) frozen chopped spinach, thawed and squeezed dry
- 1/2 cup shredded part-skim mozzarella cheese

Direction

- Following the package instructions, cook the pasta; then drain. Put in Parmesan cheese and eggs. Press up the sides and onto the bottom of a 9-inch deep-dish pie plate coated with cooking spray. Bake for 10 minutes at 350 degrees.
- At the same time, cook green pepper, onion, beef over medium heat until the meat is not pink anymore; then drain. Stir in the seasonings and pasta sauce. Boil. Turn down the heat; put on a cover and simmer for 10 minutes.

- Roll out the cream cheese to form into a 7-inch circle between 2 pieces of waxed paper. Fill into the crust. Put the meat sauce and spinach on top. Dust with mozzarella cheese. Bake at 350 degrees until set, 20-30 minutes.

Nutrition Information

- Calories: 377 calories
- Cholesterol: 130mg cholesterol
- Protein: 22g protein.
- Total Fat: 21g fat (11g saturated fat)
- Sodium: 544mg sodium
- Fiber: 3g fiber)
- Total Carbohydrate: 24g carbohydrate (5g sugars

619.   Stuffed Artichokes

Serving: 6 | Prep: 25mins | Cook: 1hours | Ready in:

Ingredients

- 6 whole artichokes
- 3 slices Italian bread, cubed
- 1 clove garlic, minced
- 1/8 cup chopped fresh parsley
- 1/4 cup grated Romano cheese
- 1/2 teaspoon dried oregano
- 5 tablespoons vegetable oil, divided
- salt and pepper to taste

Direction

- Cut the stems and pointed tips of the artichoke leaves; rinse and drain. Hold the base of the artichoke firmly. Bash the top on any hard surface to open.
- Add pepper, salt, bread cubes, 2 tbsp. vegetable oil, garlic, Romano cheese, and parsley in a medium bowl; stir well.
- Stuff half cup of the mixture in every artichoke. Place the stuffed artichokes in a Dutch oven or big saucepan. Pour water until

half of the artichokes are covered, add 3 tbsp. oil.
- Boil on high heat. Lower heat and let it simmer for an hour with a cover until the leaves can be easily removed.

Nutrition Information

- Calories: 175 calories;
- Sodium: 149
- Total Carbohydrate: 11.6
- Cholesterol: 5
- Protein: 4
- Total Fat: 13.2

620.   Stuffed Manicotti

Serving: 7 servings. | Prep: 01hours15mins | Cook: 25mins | Ready in:

Ingredients

- SPAGHETTI SAUCE:
- 1 medium onion, chopped
- 1/2 green pepper, chopped
- 3 tablespoons olive oil
- 2 garlic cloves, minced
- 1 can (29 ounces) tomato sauce
- 3/4 cup water
- 3/4 cup dry red wine or water
- 1 teaspoon dried oregano
- 1/2 teaspoon dried basil
- 1/2 teaspoon salt
- 1/4 teaspoon pepper
- MANICOTTI:
- 1-1/2 pound ground beef
- 1/2 medium onion, finely chopped
- 2 garlic cloves, minced
- 1 package (10 ounces) frozen chopped spinach, thawed
- 3/4 cup grated Parmesan cheese, divided
- 3 large eggs, lightly beaten
- 1 teaspoon dried oregano
- 1/2 teaspoon salt

- 1/4 teaspoon pepper
- 1 package (8 ounces) manicotti, cooked and drained
- 3/4 cup shredded part-skim mozzarella cheese

Direction

- Sauté green pepper and onion in a large saucepan in olive oil until they become tender. Put in garlic and cook for 1 more minute. Put in the remaining sauce ingredients and stir; then boil. Turn down the heat; put a cover on and simmer, stirring from time to time, for an hour. Remove the cover and simmer until thick, 10-15 more minutes.
- At the same time, for manicotti: in a skillet, cook onion and beef until the meat is not pink anymore. Put in garlic and cook for 1 more minute. Then drain and allow to slightly cool.
- Squeeze thoroughly the spinach to get rid of the excess water; put into the skillet with pepper, salt, oregano, eggs, and a half cup of Parmesan cheese. Combine properly. Chill 1 1/2 cups of the sauce in the fridge for another use from 4 cups sauce made.
- Place a cup of the remaining sauce into a 13x9-inch baking dish. Fill the meat mixture in the manicotti and spread over the sauce. Top with another 1 1/2 cups of the sauce. Dust with the remaining Parmesan cheese and mozzarella.
- Bake at 350 degrees without a cover, until a thermometer registers 160 degrees, for 25-30 minutes.

Nutrition Information

- Calories: 505 calories
- Total Carbohydrate: 34g carbohydrate (5g sugars
- Cholesterol: 172mg cholesterol
- Protein: 35g protein.
- Total Fat: 24g fat (9g saturated fat)
- Sodium: 976mg sodium
- Fiber: 4g fiber)

621.   Stuffed Portobellos

Serving: 4 servings. | Prep: 15mins | Cook: 20mins | Ready in:

Ingredients

- 4 large portobello mushrooms (about 5 inches)
- 3/4 cup shredded part-skim mozzarella cheese, divided
- 1/3 cup dry bread crumbs
- 1/3 cup chopped walnuts
- 1/3 cup finely chopped onion
- 1/3 cup golden raisins, optional
- 3 tablespoons grated Parmesan cheese
- 1/4 teaspoon salt
- 1/4 teaspoon pepper
- 1large egg, lightly beaten
- 2 tablespoons vegetable broth

Direction

- Take the mushrooms and remove stems; save for a different dish or discard. Put the caps aside. Mix walnuts, Parmesan, raisins if desired, 1/4 cup mozzarella, pepper, bread crumbs, salt, and onion in a small bowl. Stir in broth and egg until combined. Separate into mushroom caps; sprinkle on the rest of the mozzarella. Put them into a 15x10x1-in. greased pan. Do not cover; bake in a 350-degree oven until mushroom caps are tender, 20-25 minutes.

Nutrition Information

- Calories: 221 calories
- Fiber: 2g fiber)
- Total Carbohydrate: 14g carbohydrate (3g sugars
- Cholesterol: 68mg cholesterol
- Protein: 14g protein. Diabetic Exchanges: 2 fat
- Total Fat: 12g fat (4g saturated fat)
- Sodium: 435mg sodium

622. Stuffed Shells With Arrabbiata Sauce

Serving: 12 servings. | Prep: 30mins | Cook: 20mins | Ready in:

Ingredients

- 1 package (12 ounces) jumbo pasta shells
- 1 pound ground beef or turkey
- 1/2 pound fresh chorizo or bulk spicy pork sausage
- 1/2 large onion, chopped (about 1 cup)
- 3 garlic cloves, minced
- 1 package (10 ounces) frozen chopped spinach, thawed and squeezed dry
- 3/4 teaspoon salt, divided
- 1/2 teaspoon pepper, divided
- 1 carton (15 ounces) part-skim ricotta cheese
- 3/4 cup grated Parmesan cheese
- 2 large eggs, lightly beaten
- 1/4 cup chopped fresh basil
- 2 tablespoons chopped fresh parsley
- ARRABBIATA SAUCE:
- 2 tablespoons olive oil
- 6 ounces sliced pancetta, coarsely chopped
- 2 teaspoons crushed red pepper flakes
- 2 garlic cloves, minced
- 2 jars (24 ounces each) marinara sauce
- 1-1/2 cups shredded part-skim mozzarella cheese

Direction

- Set the oven to 400° to preheat. Cook pasta following the package instructions for al dente. Drain and rinse with cold water.
- Cook for 6-8 minutes while crumbling chorizo and beef with garlic and onion in a large skillet over medium heat until vegetables are softened, and the meat is no longer pink; drain. Stir in spinach, 1/4 teaspoon pepper and 1/2 teaspoon salt. Transfer to a bowl; allow to cool.
- Stir ricotta and Parmesan cheeses, basil, eggs, parsley and the leftover salt and pepper into the meat mixture. To make sauce, heat oil in a

saucepan over medium heat. Add in pancetta; cook for 6 to 8 minutes while stirring until golden brown. Add garlic and pepper flakes; cook for 1 minute while stirring. Add in marinara sauce; and bring to a simmer.

- Spread 1 cup of sauce into a 13x9-in. baking dish coated with grease. Put meat mixture into pasta shells to fill; arrange in baking dish, lightly overlapping their ends. Put the rest of sauce on top. Sprinkle top with mozzarella cheese. Bake for 20 to 25 minutes until heated through and cheese melts.

Nutrition Information

- Calories:
- Total Fat:
- Sodium:
- Fiber:
- Total Carbohydrate:
- Cholesterol:
- Protein:

623. Tasty Mexican Manicotti

Serving: 6 servings. | Prep: 20mins | Cook: 45mins | Ready in:

Ingredients

- 1-1/2 pounds Jones No Sugar Pork Sausage Roll sausage
- 1/2 cup chopped onion
- 1 can (16 ounces) refried beans
- 1/2 teaspoon chili powder
- 1/2 teaspoon ground cumin
- 1 package (8 ounces) manicotti, cooked and drained
- 1 can (15 ounces) tomato sauce
- 1 can (4 ounces) chopped green chilies, optional
- 2 cups shredded cheddar cheese

Direction

- Cook onion and sausage in a big frying pan until the sausage is not pink anymore; strain. Mix in cumin, chili powder, and beans. Stuff the mixture into manicotti shells.
- Put in a 13x9-inch baking dish coated with cooking spray. If you want, mix together chilies and tomato sauce, add to the manicotti. Sprinkle cheese over. Bake without a cover at 350° until fully heated, about 45 minutes.

Nutrition Information

- Calories: 593 calories
- Total Carbohydrate: 47g carbohydrate (6g sugars
- Cholesterol: 87mg cholesterol
- Protein: 27g protein.
- Total Fat: 34g fat (16g saturated fat)
- Sodium: 1248mg sodium
- Fiber: 6g fiber)

---

624. The Best Eggplant Parmesan

Serving: 2 casseroles (8 servings each). | Prep: 01hours15mins | Cook: 35mins |Ready in:

Ingredients

- 3 garlic cloves, minced
- 1/3 cup olive oil
- 2 cans (28 ounces each) crushed tomatoes
- 1 cup pitted ripe olives, chopped
- 1/4 cup thinly sliced fresh basil leaves or 1 tablespoon dried basil
- 3 tablespoons capers, drained
- 1 teaspoon crushed red pepper flakes
- 1/4 teaspoon pepper
- EGGPLANT:
- 1 cup all-purpose flour
- 4 large eggs, beaten
- 3 cups dry bread crumbs
- 1 tablespoon garlic powder

- 1 tablespoon minced fresh oregano or 1 teaspoon dried oregano
- 4 small eggplants (about 1 pound each), peeled and cut lengthwise into 1/2-inch slices
- 1 cup olive oil
- CHEESE:
- 2 large eggs, beaten
- 2 cartons (15 ounces each) ricotta cheese
- 1-1/4 cups shredded Parmesan cheese, divided
- 1/2 cup thinly sliced fresh basil leaves or 2 tablespoons dried basil
- 1/2 teaspoon pepper
- 8 cups shredded part-skim mozzarella cheese

Direction

- In a Dutch oven, cook the garlic in oil over medium heat for a minute. Mix in pepper, pepper flakes, capers, basil, olives and tomatoes. Bring to a boil. Lower the heat; simmer, uncovered, until thickened, or about 45-60 minutes.
- For the eggplant: In the meantime, put eggs and flour in separate shallow bowls. Combine oregano, garlic powder and bread crumbs in another bowl. Dip the eggplant in the flour, then in eggs and last in the bread crumb mixture.
- Pour oil in a large skillet, cook eggplant in batches until tender, or about 5 minutes on each side. Drain on the paper towels. Combine pepper, basil, half cup of Parmesan cheese, ricotta and eggs in a large bowl.
- Start preheating oven to 350°. In each of 2 oiled 13x9-in. baking dishes, layer one to half cups of the tomato sauce, 4 eggplant slices, one cup of the ricotta mixture and two cups of the mozzarella cheese. Repeat the layers. Top each with the remaining Parmesan cheese. Bake, uncovered, until bubbly, or about 35 to 40 minutes. Allow to stand for 10 minutes. Cut and enjoy!

Nutrition Information

- Calories: 562 calories

- Cholesterol: 138mg cholesterol
- Protein: 29g protein.
- Total Fat: 38g fat (14g saturated fat)
- Sodium: 778mg sodium
- Fiber: 7g fiber)
- Total Carbohydrate: 31g carbohydrate (8g sugars

---

625.   Tuna Spaghetti Pie

Serving: 6 servings. | Prep: 30mins | Cook: 35mins | Ready in:

Ingredients

- 4 ounces uncooked spaghetti, broken into 2-inch pieces
- 1/4 cup grated Parmesan cheese
- 1 egg, lightly beaten
- 1 teaspoon butter
- 1 garlic clove, minced
- 1/4 teaspoon salt
- 1/8 teaspoon pepper
- FILLING:
- 1 tablespoon finely chopped onion
- 1 teaspoon butter, melted
- 1 tablespoon all-purpose flour
- 1/2 teaspoon salt
- 1/4 teaspoon celery salt
- 1/4 teaspoon garlic and herb seasoning
- 1/8 teaspoon pepper
- 1/4 cup milk
- 1/4 cup sour cream
- 1 egg, lightly beaten
- 1 can (6 ounces) tuna, drained and flaked
- 1/4 cup grated Parmesan cheese, divided
- 1 small tomato, thinly sliced
- Minced fresh parsley

Direction

- Follow package instructions to cook spaghetti. Wash in cold water; drain. Combine pepper, salt, garlic, butter, egg, Parmesan cheese, and spaghetti in a big bowl. Press up the sides and

onto the bottom of an oiled 9-inch pie plate; put aside.
- In a big skillet, in butter, sauté onion until tender. Take away from heat. Mix in seasonings and flour until combined. Whisk egg, sour cream, and milk together in a small bowl. Blend into onion mixture until mixed.
- Fold in tuna; use a spoon to transfer into crust. Sprinkle pie with 1/2 of the Parmesan. Place tomato slices atop cheese; sprinkle the remaining Parmesan over the surface.
- Bake at 350 degrees for 35-40 minutes or until filling is puffy and the crust is golden. Top with parsley. Let it sit for 5-10 minutes then slice.

Nutrition Information

- Calories: 216 calories
- Sodium: 636mg sodium
- Fiber: 1g fiber)
- Total Carbohydrate: 17g carbohydrate (2g sugars
- Cholesterol: 99mg cholesterol
- Protein: 16g protein.
- Total Fat: 9g fat (5g saturated fat)

---

626.   Turkey Alfredo Tetrazzini

Serving: 4 servings. | Prep: 20mins | Cook: 30mins | Ready in:

Ingredients

- 4 ounces thin spaghetti
- 1 jar (15 ounces) Alfredo sauce
- 2 cups frozen peas
- 1-1/2 cups cubed cooked turkey or chicken
- 1 can (4 ounces) mushroom stems and pieces, drained
- 1/4 cup shredded Swiss cheese
- 1/4 cup shredded Parmesan cheese
- 2 tablespoons white wine or chicken broth
- 1/2 teaspoon onion powder

- 1/2 cup french-fried onions
- 1/2 teaspoon paprika

Direction

- Follow directions on package to cook spaghetti. In the meantime, mix onion powder, mushrooms, Alfredo sauce, wine, peas, cheeses, and turkey in a big bowl. Drain water from spaghetti. Add to the sauce mixture and mix to coat. Move to an 8-in. greased pan. Sprinkle on paprika and onions. Cover; bake in a 350-degree oven for 30-35 minutes or until cooked through.

Nutrition Information

- Calories: 504 calories
- Sodium: 808mg sodium
- Fiber: 6g fiber)
- Total Carbohydrate: 44g carbohydrate (5g sugars
- Cholesterol: 79mg cholesterol
- Protein: 32g protein.
- Total Fat: 21g fat (12g saturated fat)

---

627. Turkey Potato Tetrazzini

Serving: 12-15 servings. | Prep: 20mins | Cook: 01hours05mins | Ready in:

Ingredients

- 1 jar (16 ounces) Alfredo sauce
- 1 cup 2% milk
- 7 medium potatoes, peeled and thinly sliced
- 4 tablespoons grated Parmesan cheese, divided
- 1-1/2 cups diced cooked turkey or chicken
- 2 cups shredded Swiss cheese, divided
- 3 cups frozen chopped broccoli, thawed

Direction

- In a large bowl, blend milk and Alfredo sauce; pour 1/4 cup into an oiled 13x9-inch baking dish and spared out. Arrange 1/3 of the potatoes on top; dust with 1 tablespoon of Parmesan cheese.
- In a separate bowl, mix broccoli, 1 1/2 cups of Swiss cheese, and turkey; scoop about 2 cups over the potatoes. Spread with 2/3 cup of sauce mixture on top. Repeat layers twice.
- Bake, covered, for 45 minutes at 400°. Spread with cheeses left (dish will be full) on the top. Bake, without covering, until potatoes soften, or for an extra 20 to 25 minutes. Allow to stand for 5 minutes before enjoying.

Nutrition Information

- Calories: 221 calories
- Cholesterol: 36mg cholesterol
- Protein: 13g protein.
- Total Fat: 9g fat (6g saturated fat)
- Sodium: 211mg sodium
- Fiber: 2g fiber)
- Total Carbohydrate: 22g carbohydrate (4g sugars

---

628. Turkey Spaghetti Pie

Serving: 6 servings. | Prep: 30mins | Cook: 25mins | Ready in:

Ingredients

- 6 ounces uncooked spaghetti
- 5 tablespoons grated Parmesan cheese
- 1/2 cup egg substitute
- 3/4 pound lean ground turkey breast
- 1 medium onion, chopped
- 1/2 medium green pepper, chopped
- 1-1/2 cups meatless spaghetti sauce
- 1 cup (8 ounces) fat-free cottage cheese
- 1/2 cup shredded part-skim mozzarella cheese

Direction

- Cook spaghetti as directed on the package. Drain well; cool to room temperature. Mix egg substitute, Parmesan cheese and spaghetti in a bowl. Remove to a 9-in. pie plate coated with cooking spray and shape into a crust; put aside.
- Cook green pepper, onion and turkey in a nonstick skillet over medium heat until turkey is no longer pink; drain. Add spaghetti sauce; heat through. Spread cottage cheese over crust; place turkey mixture on top.
- Bake without a cover for 20 minutes at 350°. Scatter on top with mozzarella cheese. Bake until cheese is melted or for 5 more minutes. Rest for 5 minutes; then cut.

Nutrition Information

- Calories: 274 calories
- Protein: 25g protein. Diabetic Exchanges: 3 lean meat
- Total Fat: 11g fat (4g saturated fat)
- Sodium: 710mg sodium
- Fiber: 2g fiber)
- Total Carbohydrate: 19g carbohydrate (0 sugars
- Cholesterol: 57mg cholesterol

629.   Upside Down Pizza

Serving: 8 | Prep: 10mins | Cook: 30mins |Ready in:

Ingredients

- 1 pound ground beef
- 2 Italian sausage links, casings removed
- 1 (28 ounce) jar spaghetti sauce with meat
- 1/2 cup pizza sauce
- 4 ounces sliced pepperoni
- 1 (16 ounce) package shredded pizza cheese blend
- 1 (13.8 ounce) can refrigerated pizza crust

Direction

- Set oven to 450 degrees F or 230 degrees C and start preheating.
- Place Italian sausage and ground beef in a big frying pan and heat on medium-high. Cook until evenly browned, and no longer pink; break the meat into crumbles while cooking. Drain excess grease. Mix in the pizza sauce, pepperoni, and spaghetti sauce. Heat mixture until bubbling. Place it in an 11x13-in. dish.
- Evenly spread with shredded pizza cheese. Put dough on top.
- Bake in hot oven for 20 minutes or until crust is light brown.

Nutrition Information

- Calories: 651 calories;
- Cholesterol: 109
- Protein: 36.3
- Total Fat: 39.8
- Sodium: 1757
- Total Carbohydrate: 35.1

630.   Upside Down Pizza Bake

Serving: 4 servings. | Prep: 20mins | Cook: 25mins | Ready in:

Ingredients

- 1/2 pound Johnsonville® Mild Italian Sausage Links, cut into 1/4-inch slices
- 1 cup spaghetti sauce
- 1/2 cup sliced fresh mushrooms
- 1/2 cup julienned green pepper
- 1 cup shredded part-skim mozzarella cheese, divided
- 1 cup biscuit/baking mix
- 1 large egg
- 1/2 cup 2% milk

Direction

- Over medium heat, cook sausage in a large skillet until it is no more pink; allow to drain.
- Next, pour spaghetti sauce into an oiled 8-in. square baking dish. Layer with mushrooms, the green pepper, then the sausage, finally half cup cheese.
- Combine milk, egg, and biscuit mix in a small bowl until blended. Pour over the top of the layer. Dust with the leftover cheese.
- Bake without cover for 25-30 minutes at 400°, or until golden brown.

Nutrition Information

- Calories: 378 calories
- Total Carbohydrate: 28g carbohydrate (8g sugars
- Cholesterol: 96mg cholesterol
- Protein: 19g protein.
- Total Fat: 21g fat (8g saturated fat)
- Sodium: 1117mg sodium
- Fiber: 2g fiber)

631.   Vegetable Spaghetti Bake

Serving: 9 servings. | Prep: 20mins | Cook: 40mins | Ready in:

Ingredients

- 8 ounces uncooked spaghetti
- 1 jar (28 ounces) meatless spaghetti sauce, divided
- 1-1/2 cups cut zucchini (1/2-inch pieces)
- 1 cup sliced celery
- 1 cup thinly sliced carrots
- 1 cup sliced fresh mushrooms
- 1 medium onion, chopped
- 1 tablespoon olive oil
- 2 cups (16 ounces) fat-free cottage cheese
- 2 cups shredded part-skim mozzarella cheese
- 2 tablespoons grated Parmesan cheese

Direction

- Cook spaghetti following the package instructions; strain and put in a big bowl. Add 1 1/2 cups spaghetti sauce, put aside. Sauté onion, mushrooms, carrots, celery, and zucchini with oil until soft in a big nonstick skillet.
- Spread into a greased 13x9-inch baking dish with 1/2 cup spaghetti sauce. Layer with half each of mozzarella cheese, vegetables, cottage cheese, and spaghetti mixture. Repeat layers. Add the leftover sauce to cover, sprinkle Parmesan cheese over. Put a cover on and bake for 30 minutes at 350°. Remove the cover, bake until bubbly, about another 10-15 minutes. Let sit before serving, about 10 minutes.

Nutrition Information

- Calories: 290 calories
- Sodium: 645mg sodium
- Fiber: 4g fiber)
- Total Carbohydrate: 36g carbohydrate (0 sugars
- Cholesterol: 20mg cholesterol
- Protein: 18g protein. Diabetic Exchanges: 2-1/2 starch
- Total Fat: 7g fat (3g saturated fat)

632.   Vegetarian Stuffed Peppers

Serving: 6 | Prep: 10mins | Cook: 1hours10mins | Ready in:

Ingredients

- 1 1/2 cups brown rice
- 6 large green bell peppers
- 3 tablespoons soy sauce
- 3 tablespoons cooking sherry
- 1 teaspoon vegetarian Worcestershire sauce
- 1 1/2 cups extra firm tofu
- 1/2 cup sweetened dried cranberries

- 1/4 cup chopped pecans
- 1/2 cup grated Parmesan cheese
- salt and pepper to taste
- 2 cups tomato sauce
- 2 tablespoons brown sugar

Direction

- Preheat the oven to 350°F (175°C). Fill a saucepan with 3 cups of water and let it boil. Add in the rice and give it a mix. Lower the heat setting then cover the pan and allow the mixture to simmer for 40 minutes.
- While waiting for the rice to cook, remove the seeds and the core of the green peppers without damaging the bottom of each green pepper. Fill the bottom of a microwavable dish with about 1/2 inch of water then put in the prepared green peppers. Put it inside the microwave and microwave it on high setting for 6 minutes.
- Put the wine, Worcestershire sauce and soy sauce in a small frying pan and let it simmer. Put in the tofu and let it simmer until the tofu has absorbed the cooking liquid. Mix the cranberries, pepper, cooked rice that has already cooled down, salt, nuts, cooked tofu and cheese together, then securely stuff it inside the microwaved green peppers. Put the stuffed green peppers back into the same microwavable dish that you used to microwave the green peppers, then put it in the preheated oven and let it bake for 25-30 minutes until the top turns light brown in color.
- While the stuffed green peppers are baking, mix the brown sugar and tomato sauce together in small saucepan and let it heat up over low heat setting until the entire mixture is hot. Scoop sauce on top of every serving.

Nutrition Information

- Calories: 375 calories;
- Sodium: 1055
- Total Carbohydrate: 59.6
- Cholesterol: 6

- Protein: 14.9
- Total Fat: 10.2

633.   Ziti Casserole

Serving: 2 servings. | Prep: 20mins | Cook: 10mins | Ready in:

Ingredients

- 1-1/2 cups uncooked ziti or small tube pasta
- 1 Johnsonville® Mild Italian Sausage Links link (about 1/4 pound), casing removed
- 1 small onion
- 1 garlic clove, minced
- 1-1/2 cups spaghetti sauce
- 2 tablespoons dry red wine or beef broth, optional
- 1/2 teaspoon Italian seasoning
- Salt and pepper to taste
- 1/2 cup shredded mozzarella cheese

Direction

- Cook pasta as directed on the package; drain. Break the sausage to crumbles into a skillet; add garlic and onion. Cook until the meat is no longer pink over medium heat, and drain. Mix spaghetti sauce, pasta, sausage mixture, broth or wine if preferred and seasonings.
- Place on a greased 1-quart baking dish; put cheese over. Bake without a cover at 350° until heated through and cheese melts or for 10 to 15 minutes.

Nutrition Information

- Calories: 550 calories
- Fiber: 6g fiber)
- Total Carbohydrate: 64g carbohydrate (17g sugars
- Cholesterol: 49mg cholesterol
- Protein: 24g protein.
- Total Fat: 22g fat (8g saturated fat)

- Sodium: 1306mg sodium

Serving: 3 servings. | Prep: 15mins | Cook: 20mins | Ready in:

Ingredients

- 2 cups uncooked ziti or small tube pasta
- 1/2 pound lean ground beef
- 1/4 cup chopped onion
- 1/4 cup chopped green pepper
- 1 can (8 ounces) tomato sauce
- 1/2 teaspoon Italian seasoning
- 1/4 teaspoon garlic powder
- Dash pepper
- 3/4 cup ricotta cheese
- 1 cup shredded part-skim mozzarella cheese

Direction

- Cook ziti following package instructions. Stir the onion, green pepper and beef in a pan on medium heat until meat is not pink; drain the excess grease. Add in the Italian seasoning, tomato sauce, pepper and garlic powder. Stir and cook until cooked completely, 3 minutes.
- Drain the pasta. Pour 1/2 of meat sauce in a 1-quart pan sprayed with cooking spray. Layer with half each of ziti, ricotta cheese, and mozzarella. Make the layers again. Bake without cover at 350° until baked thoroughly, 20 to 25 minutes. Let it sit 5 minutes then serve.

Nutrition Information

- Calories: 437 calories
- Sodium: 613mg sodium
- Fiber: 2g fiber)
- Total Carbohydrate: 38g carbohydrate (8g sugars
- Cholesterol: 83mg cholesterol

- Protein: 35g protein.
- Total Fat: 15g fat (8g saturated fat)

Serving: 4 servings. | Prep: 25mins | Cook: 30mins | Ready in:

Ingredients

- 4 cups thinly sliced zucchini
- Water
- 1 pound ground beef
- 1 garlic clove, minced
- 1/2 cup chopped onion
- 1 cup cooked rice
- 1 can (8 ounces) tomato sauce
- 1/2 teaspoon dried oregano
- 1/2 teaspoon salt
- 1/4 teaspoon pepper
- 1 large egg, lightly beaten
- 1/2 cup 4% cottage cheese
- 1/2 cup shredded cheddar cheese

Direction

- In the boiling water, cook zucchini until it nearly becomes tender, 2-3 minutes. Then drain thoroughly and put aside.
- Cook onion, garlic, and beef in a large skillet on medium heat until the meat is not pink anymore; then drain. Stir in pepper, salt, oregano, tomato sauce, and rice. Boil. Reduce the heat; bring to a simmer without a cover for 10 minutes.
- Blend cottage cheese and egg in a small bowl. In an 8-inch square baking dish coated with cooking spray, place half of the zucchini slices, slices can overlap each other if necessary. Place the meat mixture over the zucchini; add the cottage cheese mixture on the meat. Put the remaining zucchini slices on top.
- Bake at 350 degrees without a cover until cooked thoroughly, 25 minutes. Dust around

the edges with Cheddar cheese; bake until the cheese melts, for 2-3 more minutes.

Nutrition Information

- Calories: 366 calories
- Sodium: 836mg sodium
- Fiber: 2g fiber)
- Total Carbohydrate: 21g carbohydrate (5g sugars
- Cholesterol: 130mg cholesterol
- Protein: 31g protein.
- Total Fat: 17g fat (9g saturated fat)

Chapter 6: Mexican Casserole Recipes

***

636.   4 H Corn Special

Serving: 6-8 servings. | Prep: 15mins | Cook: 30mins | Ready in:

Ingredients

- 1 pound ground beef
- 1 small onion, finely chopped
- 1-1/2 cups cooked rice
- 2 cups seeded chopped fresh tomatoes or 1 can (14-1/2 ounces) diced tomatoes, undrained
- 2 cups fresh, frozen or canned sweet corn
- Salt and pepper to taste
- 1 tablespoon Worcestershire sauce
- 1 teaspoon hot pepper sauce
- 1 cup crushed saltines
- 1/4 cup butter, melted

Direction

- Brown onion and beef in a big skillet; drain. Mix in hot pepper sauce, Worcestershire sauce, pepper, salt, corn, tomatoes and rice.
- Add to a greased 13x9-inch baking dish. Mix butter and cracker crumbs; drizzle over top. Bake at 350 degrees for half an hour.

Nutrition Information

- Calories: 256 calories
- Cholesterol: 43mg cholesterol
- Protein: 13g protein.
- Total Fat: 12g fat (6g saturated fat)
- Sodium: 227mg sodium
- Fiber: 2g fiber)
- Total Carbohydrate: 24g carbohydrate (4g sugars

637.   Au Gratin Taco Bake

Serving: 4-6 servings. | Prep: 15mins | Cook: 01hours10mins | Ready in:

Ingredients

- 1 pound ground beef
- 1 package (4.9 ounces) au gratin potatoes
- 1 can (15-1/4 ounces) whole kernel corn, undrained
- 1 can (14-1/2 ounces) no-salt-added stewed tomatoes, undrained
- 3/4 cup 2% milk
- 1/2 cup water
- 2 tablespoons taco seasoning
- 1 cup shredded cheddar cheese

Direction

- Cook beef on medium heat in a big skillet till meat is not pink anymore; drain. Mix in taco seasoning, water, milk, tomatoes, corn, contents of sauce mix and potatoes. Move into one greased 2-qt. baking dish.

- Keep it covered and baked at 350 degrees for 65 to 70 minutes or till potatoes become soft. Drizzle with cheese. Bake, while uncovered, till cheese becomes melted or 5 minutes more.

Nutrition Information

- Calories: 373 calories
- Cholesterol: 61mg cholesterol
- Protein: 22g protein.
- Total Fat: 15g fat (8g saturated fat)
- Sodium: 1113mg sodium
- Fiber: 3g fiber)
- Total Carbohydrate: 34g carbohydrate (8g sugars

638.   Baked Beef Tacos

Serving: 12 servings. | Prep: 15mins | Cook: 20mins | Ready in:

Ingredients

- 1-1/2 pounds ground beef
- 1 envelope taco seasoning
- 2 cans (10 ounces each) diced tomatoes and green chilies, divided
- 1 can (16 ounces) refried beans
- 2 cups shredded Mexican cheese blend, divided
- 1/4 cup chopped fresh cilantro
- 1 teaspoon hot pepper sauce, optional
- 12 taco shells
- Chopped green onions

Direction

- Preheat oven to 425 degrees. Cook beef on medium heat in a big skillet till meat is not pink anymore or for 6 to 8 minutes, crumble the beef; drain. Mix in 1 can of undrained tomatoes and taco seasoning; heat through.
- At the same time, whisk the rest can of undrained tomatoes, cilantro, half cup of

cheese, and beans, if you want, pepper sauce, in a bowl. Spread onto bottom of one greased 13x9-in. baking dish.
- Stand taco shells upright on top of bean mixture. Fill each with 1 tbsp. of cheese and roughly a third cup beef mixture. Bake, while covered, 15 minutes.
- Uncover it; drizzle with the rest of cheese. Bake, while uncovered, 5 to 7 minutes or till cheese become melted and shells turn browned a bit. Drizzle with green onions.

Nutrition Information

- Calories: 277 calories
- Cholesterol: 52mg cholesterol
- Protein: 17g protein.
- Total Fat: 15g fat (7g saturated fat)
- Sodium: 836mg sodium
- Fiber: 3g fiber)
- Total Carbohydrate: 17g carbohydrate (0 sugars

639.   Baked Beefy Spanish Rice

Serving: 8 servings. | Prep: 20mins | Cook: 55mins | Ready in:

Ingredients

- 1 cup uncooked brown rice
- 1 pound ground beef
- 1 medium onion, chopped
- 1 can (28 ounces) stewed tomatoes
- 1 teaspoon celery salt
- 1 teaspoon salt
- 1 teaspoon honey
- 1/2 teaspoon garlic salt
- 1/2 teaspoon pepper
- 1 cup shredded cheddar cheese

Direction

- Based on the instruction on the package, cook rice. At the same time, cook onion and beef and onion on medium heat in a skillet till meat is not pink anymore; drain. Mix in rice, seasonings, and tomatoes.
- Move to one greased 2-qt. baking dish. Keep it covered and baked at 350 degrees for 50 to 55 minutes. Drizzle with cheese. Bake, while uncovered, till cheese becomes melted or for 5 to 10 minutes more.

Nutrition Information

- Calories: 264 calories
- Sodium: 897mg sodium
- Fiber: 2g fiber)
- Total Carbohydrate: 28g carbohydrate (7g sugars
- Cholesterol: 43mg cholesterol
- Protein: 16g protein.
- Total Fat: 10g fat (5g saturated fat)

640. Baked Black Eyed Peas

Serving: 6 servings. | Prep: 25mins | Cook: 35mins | Ready in:

Ingredients

- 1-1/2 pounds ground beef
- 1 medium onion, chopped
- 2 garlic cloves, minced
- 1 can (15-1/2 ounces) black-eyed peas, rinsed and drained
- 1 can (10-3/4 ounces) condensed cream of mushroom soup, undiluted
- 1 can (10 ounces) enchilada sauce
- 1 cup tortilla chips, crushed
- 3 cups shredded cheddar cheese

Direction

- Cook garlic, beef, and onion in a frying pan on medium heat until beef is not pink. Drain excess grease. Add enchilada sauce, peas, and

soup; stir well. Sprinkle the tortilla chips in an 11x7-in. greased pan. Layer half of meat mixture and cheese. Repeat the layers. Do not cover; bake in a 350-degree oven until cooked through, 35 minutes.

Nutrition Information

- Calories: 524 calories
- Sodium: 1049mg sodium
- Fiber: 4g fiber)
- Total Carbohydrate: 24g carbohydrate (4g sugars
- Cholesterol: 118mg cholesterol
- Protein: 38g protein.
- Total Fat: 31g fat (17g saturated fat)

641. Baked Mexican Casserole

Serving: 8 servings. | Prep: 30mins | Cook: 45mins | Ready in:

Ingredients

- 1 pound ground turkey
- 1 medium onion, chopped
- 1 can (14-1/2 ounces) diced tomatoes, undrained
- 1 envelope taco seasoning
- 7 flour tortillas (10 inches)
- 2 large eggs
- 1-1/3 cups 4% cottage cheese
- 1-1/2 cups shredded cheddar cheese, divided
- Chopped fresh tomatoes, shredded lettuce and sour cream, optional

Direction

- Cook onion and turkey on medium heat in a big skillet till meat is not pink anymore; drain. Put in taco seasoning and tomatoes; cook and stir for about 5 minutes till becoming thick.
- Layer 4 tortillas, overlapping a bit, on the bottom and up the sides of a greased 13x9-in. baking dish. Add leftover tortillas and meat

mixture on top. Mix three quarters cup of Cheddar cheese, cottage cheese and eggs; add on top of tortillas.

- Keep it covered and bake at 350 degrees for 45 to 55 minutes or till a knife inserted in the middle comes out clean. Drizzle with the rest of cheese. Serve along with lettuce, tomatoes and sour cream if you want.

Nutrition Information

- Calories: 466 calories
- Total Fat: 21g fat (9g saturated fat)
- Sodium: 1146mg sodium
- Fiber: 6g fiber)
- Total Carbohydrate: 38g carbohydrate (4g sugars
- Cholesterol: 123mg cholesterol
- Protein: 25g protein.

642.   Barbecued Pork With Beans

Serving: 4 servings. | Prep: 10mins | Cook: 50mins |Ready in:

Ingredients

- 4 bone-in pork loin chops (3/4 inch thick)
- 1 tablespoon vegetable oil
- 2 cans (11 ounces each) pork and beans
- 3 tablespoons Worcestershire sauce, divided
- 1/4 cup ketchup
- 1/4 to 1/2 teaspoon chili powder

Direction

- Place pork chops and some oil in a large frying pan and brown chops on all sides. Mix 2 tablespoons Worcestershire sauce, beans, and pork. Put mixture in an 11x7-in. greased dish. Place pork chops on top. In a separate bowl, mix rest of the Worcestershire sauce, ketchup, and chili powder. Use a spoon to pour over

pork chops. Do not cover; bake in a 350-degree oven until chops are tender, 50-55 minutes.

Nutrition Information

- Calories:
- Total Fat:
- Sodium:
- Fiber:
- Total Carbohydrate:
- Cholesterol:
- Protein:

643.   Beef Tortilla Casserole

Serving: 6-8 servings. | Prep: 30mins | Cook: 0mins |Ready in:

Ingredients

- 2 pounds ground beef
- 1 medium onion, chopped
- 1 bottle (8 ounces) taco sauce
- 6 corn tortillas (6 inches), halved and cut into 1-inch strips
- 2 cups sour cream
- 1 cup shredded cheddar cheese
- 1 cup shredded part-skim mozzarella cheese

Direction

- Crumble beef into a big microwave-safe plate. Mix in onion. Microwave, while uncovered, on high till meat is not pink anymore or for 6 to 7 minutes, mixing and draining every 2 minutes. Mix in tortillas and taco sauce.
- In one greased 2-1/2-qt. microwave-safe plate, layer 1/2 of the beef mixture, sour cream and cheeses. Repeat the layers. Keep it covered and cook at 70% power till thoroughly heated or for 7 to 9 minutes. Allow to rest for 2 to 4 minutes prior to serving.

Nutrition Information

- Calories: 439 calories
- Fiber: 2g fiber)
- Total Carbohydrate: 16g carbohydrate (5g sugars
- Cholesterol: 117mg cholesterol
- Protein: 30g protein.
- Total Fat: 27g fat (16g saturated fat)
- Sodium: 441mg sodium

- Total Carbohydrate:
- Cholesterol:
- Protein:
- Total Fat:
- Sodium:

644. Beef And Cheese Casserole

Serving: 6-8 servings. | Prep: 10mins | Cook: 30mins | Ready in:

Ingredients

- 1-1/2 pounds ground beef
- 1 envelope taco seasoning
- 2 cups water
- 2 cups uncooked instant rice
- 1 can (10-3/4 ounces) condensed cream of chicken soup, undiluted
- 1 can (10-3/4 ounces) condensed cream of mushroom soup, undiluted
- 1 can (4 ounces) chopped green chilies, undrained
- 2 cups shredded Mexican cheese blend

Direction

- Cook beef on medium heat in a big skillet till not pink anymore; drain. Mix in chilies, soups, rice, water and taco seasoning. Move into one greased 13x9-in. baking dish.
- Keep it covered and baked at 350 degrees for 25 minutes. Uncover it; drizzle with cheese. Bake till cheese becomes melted or thoroughly heated or for 5 more minutes.

Nutrition Information

- Calories:
- Fiber:

645. Beef And Potato Nacho Casserole

Serving: 8 servings. | Prep: 20mins | Cook: 01hours15mins | Ready in:

Ingredients

- 2 pounds lean ground beef (90% lean)
- 3/4 cup chopped onion, divided
- 1 envelope taco seasoning
- 1 can (8 ounces) tomato sauce
- 3/4 cup water
- 1 can (4 ounces) chopped green chilies, drained
- 1 can (16 ounces) kidney beans, rinsed and drained
- 1 package (24 ounces) frozen O'Brien potatoes, thawed
- 1 can (10-3/4 ounces) condensed nacho cheese soup, undiluted
- 1/2 cup milk
- 1/4 cup chopped green pepper
- 1 teaspoon Worcestershire sauce
- 1/4 teaspoon sugar
- Paprika

Direction

- Cook 1/2 cup of onion and beef until beef is not pink in a big frying pan with heat on medium. Drain excess grease. Add and stir water, tomato sauce, and taco seasoning. Heat to boiling. Decrease heat and gently boil for 1 minute. Grease a 13x9-in. pan and spread beef mixture in bottom. Put potatoes, green chilies, and beans on top. Mix sugar, remaining onion, milk, Worcestershire sauce, soup, and green pepper in a big bowl. Pour mixture over potatoes. Sprinkle paprika on top. Cover; bake in a 350-degree oven for 1 hour. Remove the cover and bake until light brown, 15 minutes. Let it cool for 10 minutes before serving.

Nutrition Information

- Calories: 365 calories
- Sodium: 1042mg sodium
- Fiber: 6g fiber)
- Total Carbohydrate: 34g carbohydrate (5g sugars
- Cholesterol: 62mg cholesterol
- Protein: 29g protein.
- Total Fat: 11g fat (5g saturated fat)

646.   Beef, Rice And Chili Casserole

Serving: 6-8 servings. | Prep: 20mins | Cook: 40mins | Ready in:

Ingredients

- 1/2 pound ground beef
- 1 cup chopped celery
- 1/2 cup chopped onion
- 1 small green pepper, chopped
- 1 garlic clove, minced
- 2 cups cooked rice
- 1 can (15-ounce) chili con carne with beans
- 2/3 cup mayonnaise
- Few drops hot pepper sauce
- 1/2 teaspoon salt
- 1 can (14-1/2-ounce) Mexican-style stewed tomatoes
- 1 to 2 cups shredded cheddar cheese
- 4 cups corn chips

Direction

- Cook garlic, green pepper, onion, celery and ground beef in a skillet till meat turns browned and vegetables become softened;

drain. Mix in tomatoes, salt, hot pepper sauce, mayonnaise, chili, and rice. Add mixture to one 2-1/2-qt. casserole. Bake at 350 degrees till thoroughly heated or for 35 to 45 minutes. Add corn chips and cheese. Bring back to the oven for 3 - 4 minutes or till cheese is melted. Allow to rest several minutes prior to serving.

Nutrition Information

- Calories:
- Fiber:
- Total Carbohydrate:
- Cholesterol:
- Protein:
- Total Fat:
- Sodium:

647.   Beefy Beans 'N' Rice

Serving: 4 servings. | Prep: 25mins | Cook: 0mins | Ready in:

Ingredients

- 1 pound ground beef
- 1 medium onion, chopped
- 2 cups cooked rice
- 1 can (16 ounces) Ranch Style beans (pinto beans in seasoned tomato sauce)
- 6 ounces process cheese (Velveeta), cubed
- 3 tablespoons water

Direction

- Cook onion and beef on medium heat in a big skillet till meat is not pink anymore; drain. Mix in water, cheese, beans and rice. Cook and stir on medium-low heat till cheese becomes melted.

Nutrition Information

- Calories: 540 calories

- Cholesterol: 83mg cholesterol
- Protein: 36g protein.
- Total Fat: 23g fat (12g saturated fat)
- Sodium: 1061mg sodium
- Fiber: 6g fiber)
- Total Carbohydrate: 45g carbohydrate (7g sugars

648. Beefy Corn Bread Casserole

Serving: 8-12 servings. | Prep: 20mins | Cook: 40mins | Ready in:

Ingredients

- 1 pound ground beef
- 1 small onion, chopped
- 2 to 3 jalapeno peppers, seeded and chopped
- 2 packages (8-1/2 ounces) corn bread/muffin mix
- 3/4 teaspoon salt
- 1/2 teaspoon baking soda
- 1 can (14-3/4 ounces) cream-style corn
- 1 cup whole milk
- 1/2 cup canola oil
- 2 large eggs, beaten
- 3 cups shredded cheddar cheese, divided

Direction

- Cook peppers, onion and beef on medium heat in a big skillet till meat is not pink anymore; drain and put aside. Mix eggs, oil, milk, corn, baking soda, salt, and corn bread mix in a small-sized bowl.
- Add 1/2 into one greased 13x9-in. baking dish. Layer with 1/2 of the cheese and all of the beef mixture. Add leftover cheese on top. Gently spread the rest of batter on top.
- Bake, while uncovered, at 350 degrees till a toothpick inserted in the middle comes out clean or for 40 to 45 minutes.

Nutrition Information

- Calories: 388 calories
- Sodium: 674mg sodium
- Fiber: 1g fiber)
- Total Carbohydrate: 23g carbohydrate (7g sugars
- Cholesterol: 98mg cholesterol
- Protein: 17g protein.
- Total Fat: 25g fat (10g saturated fat)

649. Beefy Rice Squares

Serving: 4 servings. | Prep: 10mins | Cook: 35mins | Ready in:

Ingredients

- 1 pound lean ground beef (90% lean)
- 1 medium onion, chopped
- 3 cups Italian tomato sauce, divided
- 1/2 cup seasoned bread crumbs
- 1/4 teaspoon salt
- 1/8 teaspoon pepper
- 1-1/3 cups uncooked instant rice
- 1 cup shredded cheddar cheese

Direction

- Mix pepper, salt, breadcrumbs, half cup of tomato sauce, onion and beef in a big bowl. Push into a greased 8-in. square baking dish.
- Mix the rest of tomato sauce, cheese and rice in a separate big bowl. Add on top of meat mixture. Keep it covered and bake at 350 degrees for 25 minutes. Uncover it; bake till rice becomes soft or for 10 to 15 minutes longer. Allow to rest for 5 minutes prior to cutting.

Nutrition Information

- Calories: 516 calories
- Total Fat: 19g fat (10g saturated fat)
- Sodium: 1560mg sodium

- Fiber: 5g fiber)
- Total Carbohydrate: 53g carbohydrate (6g sugars
- Cholesterol: 102mg cholesterol
- Protein: 36g protein.

650.   Biscuit Topped Taco Casserole

Serving: 6 servings. | Prep: 15mins | Cook: 20mins | Ready in:

Ingredients

- 3 cups leftover taco-seasoned ground beef
- 1 can (16 ounces) kidney beans, rinsed and drained
- 1 cup shredded Monterey Jack cheese
- 2 large eggs, lightly beaten
- 1 cup whole milk
- 1-1/2 cups biscuit/baking mix
- 1 cup (8 ounces) sour cream
- 2 cups shredded lettuce
- 1 medium tomato, diced
- 1 can (2-1/4 ounces) sliced ripe olives, drained

Direction

- Mix beans and taco meat in a big bowl; scoop into a greased 8-in. square baking dish. Drizzle with cheese.
- Mix biscuit mix, milk and eggs in a separate bowl till becoming moistened. Add on top of cheese.
- Bake, while uncovered, at 400 degrees for 20 to 25 minutes or till lightly browned and a knife inserted in the middle comes out clean. Spread along with sour cream. Add olives, tomato, and lettuce on top.

Nutrition Information

- Calories: 611 calories

- Total Carbohydrate: 44g carbohydrate (7g sugars
- Cholesterol: 174mg cholesterol
- Protein: 37g protein.
- Total Fat: 31g fat (15g saturated fat)
- Sodium: 1657mg sodium
- Fiber: 5g fiber)

651.   Black Bean Cakes

Serving: 12 | Prep: 10mins | Cook: 15mins | Ready in:

Ingredients

- 3 cups dry black beans
- 1 tablespoon ground cumin
- 1/2 teaspoon chili powder
- 1/2 teaspoon salt
- 1/3 cup chopped fresh cilantro
- 2 tablespoons vegetable oil
- 1/2 cup plain yogurt
- 1 tablespoon milk
- 1 pinch cayenne pepper

Direction

- Add black beans into a big pot with enough water to cover. Boil, lower the heat, and let simmer till softened or 60 minutes.
- Puree black beans in a food processor or an electric blender till becoming smooth. Mix in cilantro, salt, chili powder and cumin; blend. Roll the mixture into balls, allowing 3 tbsp. of mixture for each ball.
- Position balls between sheets of wax paper and push down onto the wax paper to form 1/8 in. in thickness rounds.
- Heat oil in a big non-stick skillet. Fry the cakes 2 or 3 minutes on each side.
- Mix cayenne pepper (to taste), milk and yogurt in a bowl. Serve the sauce on top of the hot black bean cakes.

Nutrition Information

- Calories: 175 calories;
- Total Fat: 3
- Sodium: 110
- Total Carbohydrate: 28.3
- Cholesterol: < 1
- Protein: 9.8

652.   Black Bean Cakes With Mole Salsa

Serving: 6 servings (1-1/4 cups salsa). | Prep: 20mins | Cook: 10mins |Ready in:

Ingredients

- 1 can (15 ounces) black beans, rinsed and drained
- 1 egg, beaten
- 1 cup shredded zucchini
- 1/2 cup dry bread crumbs
- 1/4 cup shredded Mexican cheese blend
- 2 tablespoons chili powder
- 1/4 teaspoon salt
- 1/4 teaspoon baking powder
- 1/4 teaspoon ground cumin
- 2 tablespoons olive oil
- SALSA:
- 2 medium tomatoes, chopped
- 1 small green pepper, chopped
- 3 tablespoons grated chocolate
- 1 green onion, thinly sliced
- 2 tablespoons minced fresh cilantro
- 1 tablespoon lime juice
- 1 to 2 teaspoons minced chipotle pepper in adobo sauce
- 1 teaspoon honey

Direction

- Mash beans in a small bowl. Add cumin, baking powder, salt, chili powder, cheese, breadcrumbs, zucchini and egg; mix properly.
- Form mixture into six patties; coat both sides with oil and arrange on a baking sheet.

- Place baking sheet 3 to 4 inches from the heat source and broil for 3 to 4 minutes per side or until a thermometer shows 160°.
- In the meantime, combine salsa ingredients in a small bowl. Serve with black bean cakes.

Nutrition Information

- Calories: 206 calories
- Total Carbohydrate: 23g carbohydrate (4g sugars
- Cholesterol: 39mg cholesterol
- Protein: 8g protein. Diabetic Exchanges: 2 fat
- Total Fat: 10g fat (3g saturated fat)
- Sodium: 397mg sodium
- Fiber: 6g fiber)

653.   Black Bean Cornmeal Pie

Serving: 6 servings. | Prep: 30mins | Cook: 20mins |Ready in:

Ingredients

- 1 large onion, chopped
- 1 large green pepper, chopped
- 1 teaspoon canola oil
- 1-1/2 teaspoons chili powder
- 1 garlic clove, minced
- 3/4 teaspoon ground cumin
- 1/4 teaspoon pepper
- 1 can (14-1/2 ounces) diced tomatoes, undrained
- 2 cans (15 ounces each) black beans, rinsed and drained
- 1 cup frozen corn
- TOPPING:
- 3/4 cup whole wheat pastry flour
- 3/4 cup yellow cornmeal
- 2 teaspoons sugar
- 2 teaspoons baking powder
- 2 teaspoons chopped seeded jalapeno pepper
- 1/4 teaspoon salt
- 1 egg

- 3/4 cup fat-free milk
- 1 tablespoon canola oil
- Salsa and reduced-fat sour cream, optional

Direction

- Sauté green pepper and onion in oil in a big skillet till becoming soft. Put in pepper, cumin, garlic and chili powder; sauté 60 seconds more. Put in tomatoes and boil. Lower the heat; keep it covered and let simmer 5 minutes.
- Mix in corn and beans; heat through. Move into one 11x7-in. baking dish that coated using cooking spray.
- Preheat oven to 375 degrees.
- To make topping, mix salt, jalapeno, baking powder, sugar, cornmeal and flour in a small-sized bowl. Mix oil, milk and egg; mix into dry ingredients just till moistened. Scoop on top of filling; lightly spread to cover the top.
- Bake for 20 to 25 minutes or till filling is bubbly and a toothpick inserted into topping comes out clean. Serve along with sour cream and salsa as you wish.

Nutrition Information

- Calories: 329 calories
- Sodium: 621mg sodium
- Fiber: 11g fiber)
- Total Carbohydrate: 58g carbohydrate (9g sugars
- Cholesterol: 36mg cholesterol
- Protein: 14g protein.
- Total Fat: 5g fat (1g saturated fat)

654. Black Bean Lasagna

Serving: 8 | Prep: 30mins | Cook: 35mins | Ready in:

Ingredients

- 1 tablespoon vegetable oil
- 2 onions, chopped
- 4 cloves garlic, chopped
- 1/2 green bell pepper, diced
- 1/2 red bell pepper, diced
- 1 (14.5 ounce) can chopped tomatoes
- 1 cup salsa
- 2 (15 ounce) cans black beans, drained and rinsed
- salt and black pepper to taste
- 2 avocados - peeled, pitted, and mashed
- 1 tablespoon fresh lemon juice
- 12 (6 inch) corn tortillas, quartered
- 2 cups shredded Cheddar cheese

Direction

- Preheat the oven to 400°F (200°C). Prepare and grease your 9x13-inch baking pan lightly.
- Heat the oil over a medium heat using a large skillet. Cook in onions, green bell pepper, 3 cloves of chopped garlic and red bell peppers. Wait for the onions to become translucent and tender before adding in the salsa, black beans and tomatoes with juice. Sprinkle some pepper and salt for the seasoning and let it simmer for about 3 minutes.
- Crush the avocados in a clean bowl together with lemon juice and a chopped clove of garlic.
- On the bottom of the baking pan, layer the tortillas and spread 1/3 of the bean and tomato mixture on top. Pour in half of the guacamole and drizzle a third of cheese. Make another layer of tortillas and spread on top the remaining mixture of beans and tomato. Spread over the remaining guacamole. Drizzle it with half of the cheese. Replicate the steps using the remaining ingredients.
- Let it bake in the preheated oven for 35 minutes until the sauce starts to form bubbles.

Nutrition Information

- Calories: 331 calories;
- Total Fat: 19.7
- Sodium: 472

- Total Carbohydrate: 29.8
- Cholesterol: 30
- Protein: 11.7

┌─────────────────────────────────────┐
│ **655.   Black Bean Rice Bake** │
└─────────────────────────────────────┘

Serving: 6-8 servings. | Prep: 15mins | Cook: 30mins | Ready in:

Ingredients

- 1 package (6 ounces) long grain and wild rice mix
- 1-1/2 cups sliced fresh mushrooms
- 1/2 cup chopped onion
- 1/2 cup chopped green pepper
- 1/2 cup chopped sweet red pepper
- 1 tablespoon canola oil
- 2-1/2 cups cubed cooked chicken
- 1 can (15 ounces) black beans, rinsed and drained
- 1-1/2 cups sour cream
- 1-3/4 cups shredded cheddar cheese, divided
- 1/2 cup frozen corn
- 1/2 cup frozen peas
- 2 teaspoons Italian seasoning
- Salt and pepper to taste

Direction

- Based on the instruction on the package, cook rice. At the same time, sauté onion, mushrooms and peppers in oil in a big skillet till tender-crisp. Put in pepper, salt, Italian seasoning, peas, corn, 1 cup cheese, sour cream, beans and chicken. Mix in rice.
- Move to a 3-qt. baking dish. Drizzle with leftover cheese. Bake, while uncovered, at 350 degrees till thoroughly heated or for 30 to 35 minutes.

Nutrition Information

- Calories: 418 calories

- Fiber: 4g fiber)
- Total Carbohydrate: 31g carbohydrate (4g sugars
- Cholesterol: 95mg cholesterol
- Protein: 26g protein.
- Total Fat: 20g fat (12g saturated fat)
- Sodium: 606mg sodium

┌─────────────────────────────────────┐
│ **656.   Black Bean Stuffed** │
│ **Peppers** │
└─────────────────────────────────────┘

Serving: 6 | Prep: 20mins | Cook: 35mins | Ready in:

Ingredients

- 1 1/4 cups water
- 1 (3 ounce) package reduced-fat cream cheese, softened
- 2 cups cooked brown rice
- 2 cups chopped fresh spinach
- 1 (10 ounce) can diced tomatoes with green chile peppers
- 1 (15 ounce) can no-salt-added black beans, drained and rinsed
- 2 tablespoons dried minced onion
- 1 teaspoon ground cumin
- 1 teaspoon dried oregano
- 3 large bell peppers
- 1/2 cup shredded Cheddar cheese

Direction

- Set the oven to 350°F (175°C) and start preheating. Fill a 9x13 baking dish with water. In a bowl, stir cream cheese until smooth. Fold oregano, cumin, minced onion, black beans, green chiles, diced tomatoes, spinach and brown rice into the cream cheese until evenly combined.
- Cut bell peppers in half by their length. Remove and throw away membranes, seeds and stem.
- Stuff about 3/4 cup of rice mixture into the center of each pepper half, place into baking

dish. Evenly distribute cheese on top of stuffed pepper halves.

- Bake for 35 to 45 minutes in preheated oven until pepper are softened.

Nutrition Information

- Calories: 230 calories;
- Total Carbohydrate: 33.4
- Cholesterol: 18
- Protein: 10.7
- Total Fat: 6.5
- Sodium: 309

---

657. Black Bean Tortilla Casserole

Serving: 9 servings. | Prep: 20mins | Cook: 30mins | Ready in:

Ingredients

- 2 large onions, chopped
- 1-1/2 cups chopped green peppers
- 1 can (14-1/2 ounces) diced tomatoes, drained
- 3/4 cup picante sauce
- 2 garlic cloves, minced
- 2 teaspoons ground cumin
- 2 cans (15 ounces each) black beans, rinsed and drained
- 8 corn tortillas (6 inches)
- 2 cups shredded reduced-fat Mexican cheese blend
- TOPPINGS:
- 1-1/2 cups shredded lettuce
- 1 cup chopped fresh tomatoes
- 1/2 cup thinly sliced green onions
- 1/2 cup sliced ripe olives

Direction

- Mix cumin, garlic, picante sauce, tomatoes, peppers, and onions in a big saucepan. Boil.

Lower the heat; let simmer, while uncovered, for 10 minutes. Mix in the beans.

- Spread 1/3 of the mixture in a 13x9-in. baking dish that's coated using cooking spray. Layer with 4 tortillas and two thirds cup of cheese. Repeat the layers; add the rest of beans on top.
- Keep it covered and bake at 350 degrees till thoroughly heated or for 30 to 35 minutes. Drizzle with the rest of cheese. Allow to rest for 5 minutes or till cheese is melted. Serve along with toppings.

Nutrition Information

- Calories: 251 calories
- Sodium: 609mg sodium
- Fiber: 8g fiber)
- Total Carbohydrate: 36g carbohydrate (7g sugars
- Cholesterol: 18mg cholesterol
- Protein: 14g protein. Diabetic Exchanges: 2 lean meat
- Total Fat: 7g fat (3g saturated fat)

---

658. Black Beans With Bell Peppers & Rice

Serving: 6 servings. | Prep: 15mins | Cook: 15mins | Ready in:

Ingredients

- 1 tablespoon olive oil
- 1 each medium sweet yellow, orange and red pepper, chopped
- 1 large onion, chopped
- 2 garlic cloves, minced
- 2 cans (15 ounces each) black beans, rinsed and drained
- 1 package (8.8 ounces) ready-to-serve brown rice
- 1-1/2 teaspoons ground cumin
- 1/2 teaspoon dried oregano

- 1-1/2 cups shredded Mexican cheese blend, divided
- 3 tablespoons minced fresh cilantro

Direction

- Heat oil on medium high heat in a big skillet. Put in garlic, onion and peppers; cook and stir till becoming soft or for 6 to 8 minutes. Put in oregano, cumin, rice and beans; thoroughly heat.
- Mix in 1 cup cheese; drizzle with the rest of cheese. Take out of the heat. Allow to rest, while covered, till cheese becomes melted or for 5 minutes. Drizzle along with cilantro.

Nutrition Information

- Calories: 347 calories
- Sodium: 477mg sodium
- Fiber: 8g fiber)
- Total Carbohydrate: 40g carbohydrate (4g sugars
- Cholesterol: 25mg cholesterol
- Protein: 15g protein. Diabetic Exchanges: 2-1/2 starch
- Total Fat: 12g fat (6g saturated fat)

659.   Burrito Bake

Serving: 8 servings | Prep: 15mins | Cook: | Ready in:

Ingredients

- 1 lb. lean ground beef
- 1 pkg. (1-1/4 oz.) TACO BELL® Taco Seasoning Mix
- 12   flour tortilla s (6 inch)
- 1 can (16 oz.) TACO BELL® Refried Beans
- 1 cup KRAFT Mexican Style Finely Shredded Cheddar Jack Cheese

Direction

- Cook meat with the seasoning mix according to the package instructions.
- On the base of a 9in pie plate sprayed with cooking spray, put 4 tortillas and overlap them to fully cover the base of the pie plate. Layer with cheese, meat mixture, and layers of half of each beans on top. Repeat the layering and cover it with the rest of the tortillas.
- Bake until cheese melts and meat mixture is heated through, about 30 minutes. Slice into wedges before serving.

Nutrition Information

- Calories: 440
- Sodium: 1270 mg
- Fiber: 5 g
- Sugar: 2 g
- Total Carbohydrate: 44 g
- Cholesterol: 65 mg
- Protein: 28 g
- Saturated Fat: 7 g
- Total Fat: 16 g

660.   Cheese Topped Peppers

Serving: 4 servings. | Prep: 25mins | Cook: 30mins | Ready in:

Ingredients

- 4 medium green peppers
- 1 pound ground beef
- 1 medium onion, chopped
- 1 cup cooked rice
- 1 can (10-3/4 ounces) condensed tomato soup, undiluted, divided
- 2 teaspoons Worcestershire sauce
- 1/2 teaspoon salt
- Dash pepper
- 2 slices process American cheese, cut into strips

Direction

- Trim the tops off peppers and remove seeds. Cook peppers in boiling water in a big kettle for 3 minutes. Drain and wash under cold water; invert on paper towels. Cook onion and beef on medium heat in a skillet till meat is not pink anymore; drain. Put in pepper, salt, Worcestershire sauce, 1 cup of soup and rice; stir them well. Scoop into peppers. Add into one greased 9-in. square baking dish. Bake, while uncovered, at 375 degrees for 25 minutes. Add cheese and the rest of the soup on top. Bake for 5 minutes more or till cheese is melted.

Nutrition Information

- Calories: 358 calories
- Total Fat: 13g fat (6g saturated fat)
- Sodium: 977mg sodium
- Fiber: 4g fiber)
- Total Carbohydrate: 35g carbohydrate (12g sugars
- Cholesterol: 62mg cholesterol
- Protein: 26g protein.

661.   Cheesy Chili Casserole

Serving: 8 servings. | Prep: 10mins | Cook: 40mins | Ready in:

Ingredients

- 2 cups shredded Monterey Jack cheese
- 2 cups shredded cheddar cheese
- 1 can (7 ounces) whole green chilies, rinsed and seeded
- 2 large eggs
- 2 tablespoons all-purpose flour
- 1 can (12 ounces) evaporated milk
- 1 can (8 ounces) tomato sauce or 1 cup fresh salsa, drained, divided

Direction

- Combine cheeses in a large bowl. Arrange chilies and cheese in layers in a greased 2 quart baking dish. Whisk together milk, flour and eggs; add to cheese mixture.
- Bake at 350° for 30 minutes. Place half of the salsa or tomato sauce on top; bake for another 10 minutes or until heated through. Allow to stand for 5 minutes before serving. Serve with leftover sauce.

Nutrition Information

- Calories: 304 calories
- Fiber: 0 fiber)
- Total Carbohydrate: 9g carbohydrate (5g sugars
- Cholesterol: 125mg cholesterol
- Protein: 18g protein.
- Total Fat: 21g fat (14g saturated fat)
- Sodium: 538mg sodium

662.   Cheesy Chili Tots

Serving: 2 casseroles (6 servings each). | Prep: 15mins | Cook: 35mins | Ready in:

Ingredients

- 1 pound ground beef
- 2 cans (15 ounces each) chili with beans
- 1 can (8 ounces) tomato sauce
- 1 can (2-1/4 ounces) sliced ripe olives, drained
- 1 can (4 ounces) chopped green chilies
- 2 cups shredded cheddar cheese, divided
- 1 package (32 ounces) frozen Tater Tots

Direction

- Cook beef in a large skillet over medium heat until the pink color disappears from meat; drain. Stir in chilies, olives, tomato sauce and chili, Move mixture to 2 greased 8 inch square baking dishes. Sprinkle 1 cup of cheese over the mixture and place Tater Tots on top. Place one casserole in the freezer, covered, up to 3 month.

- Bake the other casserole, covered, for 30 to 35 minutes at 350° or until heated through. Add 1/2 cup cheese on top. Bake for an additional 5 minutes until cheese is completely melted.
- To use frozen casserole: Remove casserole from the freezer 30 minutes before baking (do not defrost)
- Bake, covered, for 1-1/4 to 1-1/2 hours at 350° or until heated through. Add 1/2 cup cheese on top. Bake for an additional 5 minutes or until cheese is completely melted.

Nutrition Information

- Calories:
- Cholesterol:
- Protein:
- Total Fat:
- Sodium:
- Fiber:
- Total Carbohydrate:

---

663. Chicken Chile Relleno Casserole

Serving: 8 servings. | Prep: 20mins | Cook: 35mins | Ready in:

Ingredients

- 2 tablespoons butter
- 2 poblano peppers, seeded and coarsely chopped
- 1 small onion, finely chopped
- 2 tablespoons all-purpose flour
- 1 teaspoon ground cumin
- 1 teaspoon smoked paprika
- 1/4 teaspoon salt
- 2/3 cup 2% milk
- 1 package (8 ounces) cream cheese, cubed
- 2 cups shredded pepper jack cheese
- 2 cups coarsely shredded rotisserie chicken

- 1 can (4 ounces) chopped green chilies
- 2 packages (8-1/2 ounces each) cornbread/muffin mix

Direction

- Preheat the oven at 350°. Heat butter over medium-high heat in a big skillet. Add onion and peppers. Stir and cook for 4-6 minutes or until peppers are tender.
- Mix seasonings and flour in until blended. Mix milk in gradually. Let it boil and stir constantly. Stir and cook for 1 minute or until thickened. Mix cream cheese in until blended. Add green chilies, chicken, and pepper jack. Let heat through, stir until combined. Put into an 11x7-in. greased baking dish.
- Following package directions, prep cornbread batter. Spread onto the chicken mixture. Bake for 35-40 minutes, uncovered, till golden brown and an inserted toothpick in topping exits cleanly. Before serving, let it stand for 10 minutes.

Nutrition Information

- Calories: 610 calories
- Total Fat: 34g fat (16g saturated fat)
- Sodium: 987mg sodium
- Fiber: 5g fiber)
- Total Carbohydrate: 51g carbohydrate (16g sugars
- Cholesterol: 151mg cholesterol
- Protein: 27g protein.

---

664. Chicken Mole Casserole

Serving: 6 servings. | Prep: 25mins | Cook: 20mins | Ready in:

Ingredients

- 1 pound boneless skinless chicken breasts, cut into 1/2-inch cubes
- 1 medium green pepper, cut into strips

- 1 small onion, chopped
- 1 tablespoon butter
- 2 tablespoons baking cocoa
- 2 teaspoons brown sugar
- 1 teaspoon chili powder
- 1/2 teaspoon ground cumin
- 1/4 teaspoon salt
- 1/4 teaspoon ground coriander
- 1/4 teaspoon cayenne pepper
- 2-1/2 cups frozen corn, thawed
- 1 jar (16 ounces) chunky salsa
- 1 tube (10.2 ounces) large refrigerated flaky biscuits
- 2 teaspoons butter, melted
- 3/4 teaspoon cornmeal

Direction

- Preheat oven to 375 degrees. Sauté onion, green pepper, and chicken in butter in a big skillet till chicken juices run clear and veggies become softened.
- Put in seasonings, brown sugar and cocoa; cook and stir on medium heat for 60 seconds. Mix in salsa and corn; thoroughly heat. Move into one greased 11x7-in. baking dish.
- Halve each biscuit. Arrange biscuit pieces on top of chicken mixture with cut sides facing the outer edge of dish, overlapping a bit. Use melted butter to brush; drizzle along with cornmeal.
- Bake, while uncovered, till biscuits become golden brown in color or for 20 to 25 minutes.

Nutrition Information

- Calories: 347 calories
- Fiber: 4g fiber)
- Total Carbohydrate: 48g carbohydrate (9g sugars
- Cholesterol: 50mg cholesterol
- Protein: 22g protein.
- Total Fat: 8g fat (4g saturated fat)
- Sodium: 811mg sodium

665.   Chicken Tamale Bake

Serving: 8 servings. | Prep: 10mins | Cook: 25mins | Ready in:

Ingredients

- 1 large egg, lightly beaten
- 1 can (14-3/4 ounces) cream-style corn
- 1 package (8-1/2 ounces) cornbread/muffin mix
- 1 can (4 ounces) chopped green chilies
- 1/3 cup 2% milk
- 1/4 cup shredded Mexican cheese blend
- TOPPING:
- 2 cups coarsely shredded cooked chicken
- 1 can (10 ounces) enchilada sauce
- 1 teaspoon ground cumin
- 1/2 teaspoon onion powder
- 1-3/4 cups shredded Mexican cheese blend
- Chopped green onions, tomatoes and avocado, optional

Direction

- Preheat oven to 400 degrees. Mix the initial 6 ingredients in a big bowl; mix just till dry ingredients are moistened. Move into one greased 13x9-in. baking dish. Bake till turns light golden brown in color and a toothpick inserted in the middle comes out clean, 15 to 18 minutes.
- Mix onion powder, cumin, enchilada sauce, and chicken in a big skillet; boil, mixing from time to time. Lower the heat; let it simmer, while uncovered, for 5 minutes. Spread on top of cornbread layer; drizzle with cheese.
- Bake for 10 to 12 minutes more or till cheese is melted. Allow to rest for 10 minutes prior to serving. Add avocado, tomatoes and green onions if you want.

Nutrition Information

- Calories: 364 calories

- Total Fat: 17g fat (7g saturated fat)
- Sodium: 851mg sodium
- Fiber: 4g fiber)
- Total Carbohydrate: 35g carbohydrate (9g sugars
- Cholesterol: 81mg cholesterol
- Protein: 21g protein.

- Calories: 365 calories;
- Cholesterol: 66
- Protein: 21.8
- Total Fat: 20.2
- Sodium: 1083
- Total Carbohydrate: 25

666. Chicken Tortilla Casserole

Serving: 8 | Prep: | Cook: |Ready in:

Ingredients

- 2 cups cooked, boneless and skinless chicken, cut into bite-sized pieces
- 4 tablespoons chicken stock
- 9 (6 inch) corn tortillas, cut into strips
- 1 (10.75 ounce) can condensed cream of chicken soup
- 1 (10.75 ounce) can condensed cream of mushroom soup
- 1 cup milk
- 1 (16 ounce) jar salsa
- 1 onion, shredded
- 8 ounces shredded Cheddar cheese

Direction

- Combine onion, salsa, milk and soups in a bowl.
- Add 3 - 4 tbsp. of chicken stock into one 9 x 13 inch baking dish. Add a layer of tortilla strips, and then a layer of chicken. Add soup mixture on top of chicken and tortillas. Keep layering follow this order till dish is filled up. Add cheese on top. Keep it covered and chilled in the refrigerator for 24 hours.
- Bake at 150 degrees C (300 degrees F) for 1 to 1 1/2 hours.

Nutrition Information

667. Chicken And Cheddar Tortilla Bake

Serving: 6 servings. | Prep: 25mins | Cook: 25mins | Ready in:

Ingredients

- 1 pound boneless skinless chicken breasts, cut into 1-inch cubes
- 1/2 teaspoon ground cumin
- 1/4 teaspoon salt
- 1 tablespoon plus 1 teaspoon olive oil, divided
- 1 can (16 ounces) refried beans
- 1 can (14-1/2 ounces) diced tomatoes with mild green chilies, drained
- 8 flour tortillas (8 inches), cut into 1-inch strips
- 1 can (11 ounces) Mexicorn, drained
- 2 cups shredded cheddar cheese

Direction

- Combine salt, cumin and chicken in a large skillet, sauté in 1 tablespoon oil until chicken looses its pink color.
- Combine tomatoes and refried beans; arrange 1 cup of mixture into a greased 11x7 inch baking dish. Place 24 tortilla strips on top; place half of the corn, bean mixture, chicken and cheese in layers, repeat layering with remaining ingredients.
- Make a lattice crust on top of filling with remaining tortilla strips, brush remaining oil on top. Bake, uncovered, for 25 to 30 minutes at 350° or until heated through and cheese is fully melted.
- Serve right away or put casserole in the freezer up to 3 months, covered before baking.

- To use frozen casserole: defrost overnight in refrigerator. Remove from the fridge 30 minutes before baking. Bake casserole following directions.

Nutrition Information

- Calories: 570 calories
- Sodium: 1467mg sodium
- Fiber: 6g fiber)
- Total Carbohydrate: 61g carbohydrate (8g sugars
- Cholesterol: 88mg cholesterol
- Protein: 35g protein.
- Total Fat: 20g fat (10g saturated fat)

668. Chicken And Olive Mole Casserole

Serving: 8 servings. | Prep: 50mins | Cook: 40mins | Ready in:

Ingredients

- 2 large onions, finely chopped, divided
- 3 tablespoons olive oil
- 3 garlic cloves, minced
- 1 teaspoon salt
- 1 teaspoon dried oregano
- 1 teaspoon ground cumin
- 1/4 teaspoon ground cinnamon
- 5 tablespoons chili powder
- 3 tablespoons all-purpose flour
- 4-1/2 cups reduced-sodium chicken broth
- 1/2 ounce semisweet chocolate, coarsely chopped
- 6 cups shredded cooked chicken
- 12 corn tortillas (6 inches), warmed
- 1 cup sliced pimiento-stuffed olives
- 4 cups shredded Monterey Jack cheese

Direction

- Sauté one cup of onion in oil in a big saucepan till becoming softened. Lower the heat to low. Put in cinnamon, cumin, oregano, salt and garlic; keep it covered and cook for 10 minutes. Mix in flour and chili powder till becoming blended. Slowly mix in broth. Boil. Cook for about 35 minutes till mixture is decreased to 3 cups. Take out of the heat; mix in chocolate.
- Mix half cup of sauce and chicken in a big bowl. Spread half cup of sauce into a greased 13x9-in. baking dish. Layer with 1/2 of the tortillas, chicken mixture, rest of the onion and olives; add 2 cups of cheese and 1 cup sauce on top. Repeat the layers.
- Keep it covered and bake at 375 degrees for half an hour. Uncover it; bake till cheese becomes melted or for 10 to 15 minutes longer. Allow to rest for 10 minutes prior to serving.

Nutrition Information

- Calories: 640 calories
- Sodium: 1483mg sodium
- Fiber: 5g fiber)
- Total Carbohydrate: 32g carbohydrate (4g sugars
- Cholesterol: 144mg cholesterol
- Protein: 50g protein.
- Total Fat: 36g fat (14g saturated fat)

669. Chile Relleno Casserole

Serving: 5 | Prep: 15mins | Cook: 50mins | Ready in:

Ingredients

- 1 pound lean ground beef
- 1 onion, chopped
- 2 (4 ounce) cans whole green chile peppers, drained
- 1 1/2 cups shredded Cheddar cheese, divided
- 4 eggs
- 1/4 cup all-purpose flour

- 1 1/2 cups milk
- salt and pepper to taste

Direction

- Preheat oven to 175 degrees C (350 degrees F).
- In a big skillet, mix onions and ground beef on medium high heat and sauté till becoming browned or for 5 - 10 minutes; drain excess fat.
- Arrange 1 can of the chile peppers on the bottom of one 7x11 in. baking dish. Drizzle with 1/2 of the cheese and add the meat mixture on top. Drizzle the meat mixture along with leftover cheese, followed by the next can of chile peppers.
- Mix milk, flour and eggs in a medium-sized bowl, stirring till becoming smooth. Add this mixture into the baking dish on top of the chile peppers. Use pepper and salt to taste.
- Bake at 175 degrees C (350 degrees F) for 45 - 50 minutes. Allow to cool down for roughly 5 minutes prior to cutting.

Nutrition Information

- Calories: 511 calories;
- Sodium: 886
- Total Carbohydrate: 13.3
- Cholesterol: 258
- Protein: 33.2
- Total Fat: 35.5

670.   Chiles Relleno Casserole

Serving: 6-8 servings. | Prep: 25mins | Cook: 45mins | Ready in:

Ingredients

- 1 pound ground beef
- 1 green pepper, chopped
- 1/2 teaspoon salt
- 1/4 teaspoon pepper
- 1/4 teaspoon dried oregano

- 1/8 teaspoon garlic powder
- 2 cups shredded cheddar cheese
- 2 cups shredded Monterey Jack cheese
- 2 cans (4 ounces each) chopped green chilies
- 4 large eggs, beaten
- 1 cup half-and-half cream
- 1 tablespoon all-purpose flour
- 1 can (8 ounces) tomato sauce
- Additional shredded cheddar cheese, optional

Direction

- Cook beef in a skillet over medium heat until the pink color disappears from meat; drain. Add garlic powder, oregano, pepper, salt and green pepper. Cook until green pepper is softened. Combine Monterey Jack cheese and cheddar cheese; set aside.
- Arrange half each of meat mixture, chilies and cheese in layers in a 2-1/2 quart baking dish; repeat with remaining meat mixture then chilies and cheese.
- In the meantime, combine flour, cream and egg in a bowl; add to cheese layer.
- Bake for 35 minutes at 350°. Remove from oven and pour in tomato sauce until fully covered. Add more cheese on top if desired. Bake for an additional 10 to 15 minutes or until set.

Nutrition Information

- Calories:
- Sodium:
- Fiber:
- Total Carbohydrate:
- Cholesterol:
- Protein:
- Total Fat:

671. Chili Cheese Dog Casserole

Serving: 6 servings. | Prep: 20mins | Cook: 30mins | Ready in:

Ingredients

- 1 package (8-1/2 ounces) cornbread/muffin mix
- 1 cup chopped green pepper
- 1/2 cup chopped onion
- 1/2 cup chopped celery
- 1 tablespoon olive oil
- 1 package (1 pound) hot dogs, halved lengthwise and cut into bite-sized pieces
- 1 can (15 ounces) chili with beans
- 2 tablespoons brown sugar
- 1/2 teaspoon garlic powder
- 1/2 teaspoon chili powder
- 1 cup shredded cheddar cheese, divided

Direction

- Following the package directions, to prepare the cornbread batter. Take an 8-in square baking dish grease it and evenly distribute half the batter in it. Set it aside.
- Sauté onion, green pepper, and celery in oil until crispy and tender in a large skillet. Sauté and add in the hot dogs until lightly browned, 3-4 minutes. Heat and add in the chili, brown sugar, garlic powder and chili powder. Add in 3/4 cup cheese.
- Spread over cornbread batter and top along with the left cornbread batter. Scatter left cheese on top.
- For 28-32 minutes, set the oven at 350°F and bake without cover. If an inserted toothpick comes out clean when poked in its center, it is done. Rest for 5 minutes prior to serving.

Nutrition Information

- Calories: 615 calories
- Sodium: 1585mg sodium
- Fiber: 4g fiber)
- Total Carbohydrate: 49g carbohydrate (18g sugars
- Cholesterol: 115mg cholesterol
- Protein: 22g protein.
- Total Fat: 37g fat (16g saturated fat)

672. Chili Rellenos

Serving: 10-12 servings. | Prep: 15mins | Cook: 40mins | Ready in:

Ingredients

- 2 cans (4 ounces each) chopped green chilies
- 1 pound ground beef, cooked and drained
- 4 cups shredded cheddar cheese
- 1/2 cup all-purpose flour
- 1 teaspoon salt
- 2 large eggs
- 2 cups whole milk

Direction

- Drizzle green chilies in a greased 13x9-in. baking dish. Add beef on top. Mix salt, flour, cheese in a big bowl.
- Mix milk and eggs in a small-sized bowl; mix into cheese mixture till blended. Add on top of the beef. Bake, while uncovered, at 350 degrees for 40 minutes or till a knife inserted in middle comes out clean.

Nutrition Information

- Calories: 263 calories
- Sodium: 537mg sodium
- Fiber: 0 fiber)
- Total Carbohydrate: 8g carbohydrate (2g sugars
- Cholesterol: 103mg cholesterol
- Protein: 18g protein.
- Total Fat: 17g fat (11g saturated fat)

673. Chili Tamale Pie

Serving: 12 servings. | Prep: 45mins | Cook: 50mins | Ready in:

Ingredients

- 1 can (15-1/4 ounces) whole kernel corn, drained
- 2 cups masa harina
- 1 can (14-1/2 ounces) chicken broth
- 2 tablespoons butter, melted
- 1 large egg, lightly beaten
- 2-1/2 pounds boneless pork loin roast, cut into 1/2-inch pieces
- 1 medium onion, chopped
- 1 can (16 ounces) refried beans
- 2 dried Anaheim chilies, chopped
- 2 dried Ancho chilies, chopped
- 3 ounces Mexican or semisweet chocolate, grated
- 1/3 cup orange juice
- 2 tablespoons lime juice
- 1 tablespoon garlic powder
- 3 teaspoons cumin seeds, toasted and crushed
- 3/4 cup minced fresh cilantro, optional
- 1 jalapeno pepper, seeded and chopped, optional
- 2 cups shredded cheddar cheese

Direction

- Drain corn, saving the liquid; put corn aside. Add masa harina into a big bowl. Mix the reserved corn liquid, egg, butter and broth in a small-sized bowl; mix into masa harina just till moistened. Put aside.
- In a large skillet that coated using cooking spray, cook onion and pork on medium heat till pork is not pink anymore. Put in cilantro, reserved corn, cumin, garlic powder, lime juice, orange juice, chocolate, chilies and beans and jalapeno if you want. Boil. Lower the heat; simmer, while uncovered, for 15 minutes.

- Move to one greased 13x9-in. baking dish; drizzle with cheese. Spread masa harina mixture on top of cheese.
- Bake, while uncovered, at 325 degrees till becoming golden brown in color or for 50 to 60 minutes. Allow to rest for 10 minutes prior to serving.

Nutrition Information

- Calories:
- Total Fat:
- Sodium:
- Fiber:
- Total Carbohydrate:
- Cholesterol:
- Protein:

674. Chili Cheese Spoon Bread

Serving: 9 servings. | Prep: 10mins | Cook: 35mins | Ready in:

Ingredients

- 1/2 cup egg substitute
- 1 large egg
- 1 can (8-3/4 ounces) whole kernel corn, drained
- 1 can (8-1/4 ounces) cream-style corn
- 1 cup (8 ounces) reduced-fat sour cream
- 1 cup shredded reduced-fat cheddar cheese
- 1 cup shredded reduced-fat Mexican cheese blend or part-skim mozzarella cheese
- 1 can (4 ounces) chopped green chilies, drained
- 1/2 cup cornmeal
- 2 tablespoons butter, melted
- 1/2 teaspoon salt
- 1/2 teaspoon Worcestershire sauce
- 1/8 teaspoon cayenne pepper

Direction

- Whip egg and egg substitute in a big bowl. Put in the rest ingredients; stir them well. Add to one 9-in. square baking dish that coated using cooking spray. Bake at 350 degrees for 35 to 40 minutes or till a knife inserted in the middle comes out clean. Serve when warm.

Nutrition Information

- Calories: 213 calories
- Protein: 13g protein. Diabetic Exchanges: 1-1/2 lean meat
- Total Fat: 10g fat (6g saturated fat)
- Sodium: 525mg sodium
- Fiber: 2g fiber)
- Total Carbohydrate: 19g carbohydrate (0 sugars
- Cholesterol: 53mg cholesterol

---

675. Chilies Rellenos Casserole

Serving: 6 servings. | Prep: 15mins | Cook: 45mins | Ready in:

Ingredients

- 1 can (7 ounces) whole green chilies
- 1-1/2 cups shredded Colby-Monterey Jack cheese
- 3/4 pound ground beef
- 1/4 cup chopped onion
- 1 cup whole milk
- 4 large eggs
- 1/4 cup all-purpose flour
- 1/4 teaspoon salt
- 1/8 teaspoon pepper

Direction

- Chop chilies and remove seeds; dry over paper towels. Arrange chilies onto the bottom of a greased 2-qt. baking dish. Add cheese on top. Cook onion and beef on medium heat in a

skillet till meat is not pink anymore; drain. Scoop on top of the cheese.
- Whip pepper, salt, flour, eggs and milk in a bowl till becoming smooth; add on top of beef mixture. Bake, while uncovered, at 350 degrees for 45 to 50 minutes or until a knife inserted in the middle comes out clean. Allow to rest for 5 minutes prior to serving.

Nutrition Information

- Calories: 321 calories
- Cholesterol: 212mg cholesterol
- Protein: 24g protein.
- Total Fat: 20g fat (11g saturated fat)
- Sodium: 406mg sodium
- Fiber: 0 fiber)
- Total Carbohydrate: 9g carbohydrate (3g sugars

---

676. Chipotle Turkey Chilaquiles

Serving: 8 servings. | Prep: 30mins | Cook: 25mins | Ready in:

Ingredients

- 15 corn tortillas (6 inches), torn into 1-1/2-inch pieces
- 3 cups shredded cooked turkey or chicken
- 1 large onion, chopped
- 4 garlic cloves, minced
- 1/3 cup lime juice
- 2 chipotle peppers in adobo sauce
- 2 cans (15 ounces each) black beans, rinsed and drained
- 3 cups crumbled queso fresco or shredded part-skim mozzarella cheese
- 3 cups turkey or chicken broth
- Chopped fresh cilantro
- Hot cooked rice, optional
- Sour cream, optional

Direction

- Start preheating oven to 400 degrees. Doing several batches, put the tortilla pieces on an ungreased cookie sheet in a single layer and bake until crisp, 6-8 minutes. Mix garlic and onion with turkey in a big bowl. In a blender put in the peppers and lime juice; cover, blend until combined. Put half the tortilla pieces in the bottom of a 13x9-in. greased pan. Layer with turkey mixture, the beans, 1 1/2 cups cheese and the chipotle mixture. Put the rest of the tortilla pieces and cheese on top. Pour the broth on top. Do not cover; bake until cheese melts, 25-30 minutes. Sprinkle on cilantro. Eat with sour cream and rice, if desired.

Nutrition Information

- Calories: 364 calories
- Sodium: 766mg sodium
- Fiber: 7g fiber)
- Total Carbohydrate: 44g carbohydrate (3g sugars
- Cholesterol: 56mg cholesterol
- Protein: 29g protein.
- Total Fat: 8g fat (3g saturated fat)

677. Chorizo Scalloped Potato Casserole

Serving: 8 servings. | Prep: 40mins | Cook: 01hours05mins | Ready in:

Ingredients

- 1 pound uncooked chorizo or bulk spicy pork sausage
- 2-1/2 pounds medium potatoes, peeled and thinly sliced
- 1 small onion, chopped
- 1 cup chicken broth
- 4 ounces cream cheese, cubed
- 1/2 cup heavy whipping cream
- 1/2 teaspoon salt
- 2 cups shredded Mexican cheese blend, divided

Direction

- Cook chorizo on medium heat in a big skillet till meat is totally cooked; drain. Add chorizo onto several layers of paper towel; blot with extra paper towels.
- In one greased 2-1/2-qt. baking dish, layer 1/2 of the potatoes, onion and chorizo. Repeat the layers.
- Mix salt, cream, cream cheese and broth in a small-sized saucepan. Cook and stir till mixture comes to a boil. Lower the heat; let it simmer till liquid is decreased to about 1-1/2 cups. Take out of the heat; mix in 1 cup of Mexican cheese blend till melted. Add on top of chorizo.
- Keep it covered and baked at 350 degrees till potatoes become soft or for 60 to 70 minutes. Drizzle with leftover Mexican cheese blend. Bake, while uncovered, till cheese becomes melted or for 5 to 10 minutes more.

Nutrition Information

- Calories: 508 calories
- Total Fat: 37g fat (19g saturated fat)
- Sodium: 1211mg sodium
- Fiber: 1g fiber)
- Total Carbohydrate: 22g carbohydrate (2g sugars
- Cholesterol: 112mg cholesterol
- Protein: 21g protein.

678. Corn Tortilla Casserole

Serving: 6 servings. | Prep: 30mins | Cook: 30mins | Ready in:

Ingredients

- 1 pound ground beef

- 1 medium onion, chopped
- 3 celery rib, chopped
- 1 can (16 ounces) kidney beans, rinsed and drained
- 1 can (14-3/4 ounces) cream-style corn
- 1 can (8 ounces) tomato sauce
- 4-1/2 teaspoons Worcestershire sauce
- 1 teaspoon chili powder
- 1 garlic clove, minced
- 6 corn tortillas (6 inches)
- 1/2 cup shredded cheddar cheese

Direction

- Cook celery, onion, beef on medium heat in a big skillet till meat is not pink and vegetables become soft; drain. Mix in garlic, chili powder, Worcestershire sauce, tomato sauce, corn and beans; cook for 3 minutes.
- Add 1 tortilla into one greased round 2-qt. baking dish; add 1 cup of meat mixture on top. Repeat the layers five times. Drizzle with cheese. Bake, while uncovered, at 350 degrees till becoming bubbly or for 25 to 30 minutes.

Nutrition Information

- Calories: 351 calories
- Fiber: 7g fiber)
- Total Carbohydrate: 43g carbohydrate (6g sugars
- Cholesterol: 47mg cholesterol
- Protein: 24g protein.
- Total Fat: 11g fat (5g saturated fat)
- Sodium: 706mg sodium

679.   Cornbread Taco Bake

Serving: 6 servings. | Prep: 20mins | Cook: 25mins | Ready in:

Ingredients

- 1-1/2 pounds ground beef

- 1 can (15-1/4 ounces) whole kernel corn, drained
- 1 can (8 ounces) tomato sauce
- 1/2 cup water
- 1/2 cup chopped green pepper
- 1 envelope taco seasoning
- 1 package (8-1/2 ounces) cornbread/muffin mix
- 1 can (2.8 ounces) french-fried onions, divided
- 1/3 cup shredded cheddar cheese

Direction

- Cook beef on medium heat in a big skillet till meat is not pink anymore; drain. Mix in taco seasoning, green pepper, water, tomato sauce, and corn. Scoop into one greased 2-qt. baking dish.
- Based on the instruction on package for corn bread, prepare the cornbread. Mix in 1/2 of the onions. Spread on top of beef mixture. Bake, while uncovered, at 400 degrees for 20 minutes.
- Drizzle with leftover onions and cheese. Bake 3 to 5 minutes more or till cheese is melted and a toothpick inserted into corn bread layer comes out clean.

Nutrition Information

- Calories: 0
- Total Carbohydrate: 50 g carbohydrate
- Cholesterol: 91 mg cholesterol
- Protein: 29 g protein.
- Total Fat: 27 g fat (10 g saturated fat)
- Sodium: 1,443 mg sodium
- Fiber: 2 g fiber

680.   Corny Bread Bake

Serving: 4-6 servings. | Prep: 20mins | Cook: 40mins | Ready in:

Ingredients

- 2 cups cubed cooked chicken
- 1-1/2 cups shredded Monterey Jack cheese
- 1 can (11 ounces) Mexican-style corn, drained
- 1 can (4 ounces) chopped green chilies, drained
- 1 cup buttermilk baking mix
- 3 large eggs, separated
- 1 cup whole milk
- 1/2 teaspoon salt

Direction

- Mix chilies, corn, cheese and chicken; add into a greased shallow 2-1/2-qt. baking dish.
- Whip salt, milk, egg yolks, and baking mix in a bowl till becoming smooth. Whip egg whites in a separate bowl till forming stiff peaks; fold into yolk mixture. Add on top of chicken mixture.
- Bake, while uncovered, at 350 degrees for 40 to 45 minutes or till becoming browned and a knife inserted in the middle comes out clean.

Nutrition Information

- Calories: 382 calories
- Total Fat: 19g fat (9g saturated fat)
- Sodium: 1054mg sodium
- Fiber: 2g fiber)
- Total Carbohydrate: 25g carbohydrate (5g sugars
- Cholesterol: 179mg cholesterol
- Protein: 28g protein.

681. Creamy Layered Casserole

Serving: 6 servings. | Prep: 20mins | Cook: 40mins | Ready in:

Ingredients

- 1 pound ground beef
- 1 tablespoon finely chopped onion

- 2 cans (8 ounces each) tomato sauce
- 1 can (2-1/4 ounces) sliced ripe olives, drained
- 1/2 teaspoon garlic salt
- 1 cup 4% cottage cheese
- 1 cup sour cream
- 1 can (4 ounces) chopped green chilies
- 4 cups crushed tortilla chips
- 2 cups shredded Monterey Jack cheese
- Additional tortilla chips

Direction

- Cook onion and beef on medium heat in a skillet till meat is not pink anymore; drain. Put in garlic salt, olives and tomato sauce; put aside. Mix chilies, sour cream, and cottage cheese in a bowl; stir them well. In one greased 11x7-in. baking dish, layer 1/2 of the tortilla chips, meat mixture, cottage cheese mixture and Monterey Jack cheese. Repeat the layers. Add extra tortilla chips on top. Bake, while uncovered, at 350 degrees till thoroughly heated or for 40 minutes.

Nutrition Information

- Calories: 591 calories
- Sodium: 1057mg sodium
- Fiber: 2g fiber)
- Total Carbohydrate: 34g carbohydrate (4g sugars
- Cholesterol: 106mg cholesterol
- Protein: 32g protein.
- Total Fat: 36g fat (17g saturated fat)

682. Crowd Chicken Casserole

Serving: 2 casseroles (12 servings each). | Prep: 20mins | Cook: 20mins | Ready in:

Ingredients

- 10 cups diced cooked chicken
- 10 cups chopped celery

- 2 cups slivered almonds
- 2 bunches green onions with tops, sliced
- 2 cans (4 ounces each) chopped green chilies
- 2 cans (2-1/4 ounces each) sliced ripe olives, drained
- 5 cups shredded cheddar cheese, divided
- 2 cups mayonnaise
- 2 cups sour cream
- 5 cups crushed potato chips

Direction

- Preheat oven to 350 degrees. Mix the initial 6 ingredients in a very big bowl; put in two cups cheese. Mix sour cream and mayonnaise in a small-sized bowl; put to chicken mixture and coat by tossing.
- Move to 2 greased 3-qt. baking dishes. Drizzle with the rest of the cheese and chips. Bake, while uncovered, till thoroughly heated or for 20 to 25 minutes.

Nutrition Information

- Calories: 497 calories
- Sodium: 458mg sodium
- Fiber: 3g fiber)
- Total Carbohydrate: 12g carbohydrate (2g sugars
- Cholesterol: 97mg cholesterol
- Protein: 26g protein.
- Total Fat: 38g fat (12g saturated fat)

683.   Crowd Pleasing Tamale Casserole

Serving: 3 casseroles (8-10 servings each). | Prep: 35mins | Cook: 55mins | Ready in:

Ingredients

- 7 pounds ground beef
- 6 medium onions, chopped
- 2 celery ribs, chopped

- 3 garlic cloves, minced
- 2 cans (14-1/2 ounces each) diced tomatoes, undrained
- 2 cans (12 ounces each) tomato paste
- 2 cans (15-1/4 ounces each) whole kernel corn, drained
- 2 cans (4-1/2 ounces each) mushroom stems and pieces, drained
- 3 cans (2-1/4 ounces each) sliced ripe olives, drained
- 2-1/4 to 2-3/4 cups water
- 2 to 3 tablespoons chili powder
- 1 tablespoon seasoned salt
- 1/2 to 1 teaspoon crushed red pepper flakes
- 1 teaspoon pepper
- 3 jars (13-1/2 ounces each) tamales, papers removed and halved
- 2 cups shredded cheddar cheese

Direction

- Cook celery, onions and beef in several Dutch ovens till meat is not pink anymore. Put in garlic; cook 60 seconds more. Drain. Mix in tomatoes paste and tomato. Put in olives, mushrooms and corn. Mix in seasonings and water. Boil; take out of the heat.
- Scoop into three greased 13x9-in. baking dishes. Add tamales on top. Keep it covered and baked at 350 degrees for 50 to 60 minutes. Drizzle with cheese. Bake till cheese becomes melted or for 5 to 10 more minutes.

Nutrition Information

- Calories: 250 calories
- Total Fat: 13g fat (6g saturated fat)
- Sodium: 436mg sodium
- Fiber: 2g fiber)
- Total Carbohydrate: 10g carbohydrate (5g sugars
- Cholesterol: 62mg cholesterol
- Protein: 22g protein.

684.   Easy Cheesy Loaded Grits

Serving: 8 servings. | Prep: 35mins | Cook: 50mins | Ready in:

Ingredients

- 1 pound mild or spicy Jones No Sugar Pork Sausage Roll sausage
- 1 small onion, chopped
- 4 cups water
- 1/2 teaspoon salt
- 1 cup quick-cooking grits
- 3 cans (4 ounces each) chopped green chilies
- 1-1/2 cups shredded sharp cheddar cheese, divided
- 1-1/2 cups shredded Monterey Jack cheese, divided
- 2 tablespoons butter
- 1/4 teaspoon hot pepper sauce
- 2 large eggs, lightly beaten
- 1/4 teaspoon paprika
- Chopped fresh cilantro

Direction

- Preheat oven to 325 degrees. Cook onion and sausage on medium heat in a big skillet for 6 to 8 minutes or till meat is not pink anymore, crumble the sausage; drain.
- Boil salt and water in a big saucepan. Gradually mix in grits. Lower the heat to medium low; cook, while covered, till becoming thick or about 5 minutes, mixing once in a while. Take out of the heat.
- Put in pepper sauce, butter, three quarters cup of Jack cheese, three quarters cup of cheddar cheese and green chilies; mix till cheese is melted. Mix in eggs, then sausage mixture.
- Move into one greased 13x9-in. baking dish. Add the rest of cheese on top; drizzle with paprika. Bake, while uncovered, till becoming golden brown and set, 50 to 60 minutes. Allow to rest 10 minutes prior to serving. Drizzle with cilantro.

Nutrition Information

- Calories: 399 calories
- Cholesterol: 116mg cholesterol
- Protein: 18g protein.
- Total Fat: 28g fat (15g saturated fat)
- Sodium: 839mg sodium
- Fiber: 2g fiber)
- Total Carbohydrate: 19g carbohydrate (2g sugars

685.   Easy Taco Casserole

Serving: 6 | Prep: 15mins | Cook: 35mins | Ready in:

Ingredients

- 1 pound ground beef
- 1 cup salsa
- 1/2 cup chopped onion
- 1/2 cup mayonnaise
- 2 tablespoons chili powder
- 1 teaspoon ground cumin
- 2 cups crushed tortilla chips, divided
- 4 ounces shredded Cheddar cheese, divided
- 4 ounces shredded Monterey Jack cheese, divided

Direction

- Preheat oven to 175 degrees C (350 degrees F).
- Cook and stir ground beef on medium high heat in a big skillet for 5-7 minutes till becomes crumbly, equally browned and not pink anymore. Drain and throw away any excess grease. Mix cumin, chili powder, mayonnaise, onion and salsa into the beef. Take out of the heat.
- Spread about 1/2 of the ground beef mixture into the bottom of one 2-quart casserole dish. Spread about 1/2 the tortilla chips in one layer on top of the beef mixture. Layer about 1/2 of each of the Cheddar and Monterey Jack cheeses on top of the tortilla chip layer. Repeat the layers with the rest of the ingredients,

- ending with Monterey Jack cheese. Use aluminum foil to cover the dish.
- Bake in preheated oven for about half an hour or till the cheese becomes melted in the center.

Nutrition Information

- Calories: 481 calories;
- Sodium: 690
- Total Carbohydrate: 12.2
- Cholesterol: 90
- Protein: 24
- Total Fat: 38

---

686. Enchilada Beef

Serving: 4 servings. | Prep: 10mins | Cook: 10mins | Ready in:

Ingredients

- 1/2 cup chopped onion
- 1 pound lean ground beef (90% lean)
- 1 cup tomato juice
- 1 can (6 ounces) tomato paste
- 1 can (4 ounces) chopped green chilies, drained
- 2 tablespoons plus 2 teaspoons enchilada sauce mix
- 2 cups shredded Monterey Jack cheese, divided
- 1/2 cup coarsely crushed corn chips
- Additional corn chips, optional

Direction

- In a bowl that's microwave safe, put onions, cover it, and microwave it for 2-3 minutes on high or until the onions are tender. Crumble up the beef on the onions and mix them well. Cover it up again and cook it for 4-6 minutes on high or until the beef isn't pink anymore and stir it once. Drain it.
- Mix in tomato paste, tomato juice, sauce mix, and green chilies. Spread about half of the beef

mix in a microwave-safe dish that's 2 quarts with a cup of cheese on top. Top it off with the rest of the beef mix. Cover it up and microwave it until heated completely through or for 2-3 minutes.
- Sprinkle it with the rest of the cheese and some corn chips that are crushed. Microwave it for another minute or until the cheese melts. Eat this with some extra corn chips if you want.

Nutrition Information

- Calories: 483 calories
- Sodium: 1245mg sodium
- Fiber: 5g fiber)
- Total Carbohydrate: 20g carbohydrate (10g sugars
- Cholesterol: 106mg cholesterol
- Protein: 38g protein.
- Total Fat: 27g fat (14g saturated fat)

---

687. Enchilada Casserole

Serving: 8 | Prep: 15mins | Cook: 45mins | Ready in:

Ingredients

- 1 (15 ounce) can black beans, rinsed and drained
- 2 cloves garlic, minced
- 1 onion, chopped
- 1 (4 ounce) can diced green chile peppers
- 1 jalapeno pepper, seeded and minced
- 1 (8 ounce) package tempeh, crumbled
- 6 (6 inch) corn tortillas
- 1 (19 ounce) can enchilada sauce
- 1 (6 ounce) can sliced black olives
- 8 ounces shredded Cheddar cheese

Direction

- Preheat oven to 175 degrees C (350 degrees F). Oil one 9x13 inch baking dish a bit.

- Mix tempeh, jalapeno pepper, chile peppers, onion, garlic and beans in a medium-sized bowl. Add enchilada sauce into a shallow bowl.
- Dip 3 tortillas in the enchilada sauce, and add them into the prepped baking dish. Make sure you cover the bottom of the dish as entirely as you can. Add half of the bean mixture over the tortillas, and repeat. Sprinkle the rest of sauce on top of the casserole, and drizzle with shredded cheese and olives.
- Keep it covered, and bake for half an hour. Uncover it, and keep baking for an extra 15 minutes, or till the casserole is bubbling and the cheese is melted.

Nutrition Information

- Calories: 375 calories;
- Cholesterol: 54
- Protein: 17.4
- Total Fat: 24
- Sodium: 709
- Total Carbohydrate: 24.9

---

688.   Enchilada Casserole With Chicken

Serving: 10 servings. | Prep: 15mins | Cook: 30mins | Ready in:

Ingredients

- 1 can cream of chicken soup
- 1 can cream of mushroom soup
- 16 ounces sour cream
- 1 bunch green onions, chopped
- 1 can (4 ounces) chopped green chilies
- 8 flour tortillas (8 inches)
- 3 cups shredded cooked chicken breast
- 1 cup shredded cheddar cheese
- 1 cup shredded pepper jack cheese
- Chopped tomatoes, sliced black olives, green onions and sour cream, optional

Direction

- Preheat oven to 350 degrees.
- In a bowl, mix green chilies, green onions, sour cream and soups. Spray one 13x9-in. pan using cooking spray, and then spread a quarter of the soup mixture into the pan.
- Position four tortillas on top, tearing to overlap. Spread with 1/2 the chicken, 1/2 the rest of soup mixture, and half cup each of shredded cheddar and pepper jack cheese. Repeat the layers.
- Bake, white uncovered for half an hour or till casserole becomes bubbly and cheese becomes melted. Add toppings as your choice.

Nutrition Information

- Calories:
- Sodium:
- Fiber:
- Total Carbohydrate:
- Cholesterol:
- Protein:
- Total Fat:

---

689.   Fiesta Bean Casserole

Serving: 2 servings. | Prep: 20mins | Cook: 20mins | Ready in:

Ingredients

- 3/4 cup kidney beans, rinsed and drained
- 1/4 cup chopped onion
- 1/4 cup chopped green chilies, drained
- 1/4 teaspoon ground cumin
- 16 Triscuits or other crackers
- 3/4 cup shredded cheddar cheese
- 1/2 cup 2% milk
- 1/3 cup mayonnaise
- 2 tablespoons beaten egg
- Sour cream and sliced ripe olives, optional

Direction

- Combine cumin, green chilies, onion and beans together in a small bowl. Coat an 8x4 inch loaf pan with cooking spray and put 8 crackers in. Add half of the bean mixture on top; arrange remaining crackers and bean mixture in layer in the loaf pan. Place cheese on top.
- Combine egg, mayonnaise and milk together in a small bowl, pour over cheese. Bake when uncover for 20 to 25 minutes at 350° or until a thermometer inserted in reads 160°. Serve with olives and sour cream if desired.

Nutrition Information

- Calories: 561 calories
- Fiber: 9g fiber)
- Total Carbohydrate: 51g carbohydrate (9g sugars
- Cholesterol: 113mg cholesterol
- Protein: 25g protein.
- Total Fat: 31g fat (10g saturated fat)
- Sodium: 1103mg sodium

---

690. Firecracker Casserole

Serving: 10 | Prep: 15mins | Cook: 40mins | Ready in:

Ingredients

- 2 pounds ground beef
- 1 onion, chopped
- 1 (15 ounce) can black beans, drained and rinsed
- 2 tablespoons chili powder
- 1 tablespoon ground cumin
- 1/2 teaspoon salt
- 4 (7 inch) flour tortillas
- 1 (14.5 ounce) can diced tomatoes with green chile peppers
- 1 (10.5 ounce) can cream of mushroom soup
- 1 cup shredded Cheddar cheese

Direction

- Preheat an oven to 175 degrees C (350 degrees F). Grease one 9x13-inch baking dish.
- Heat a large skillet on medium high heat. Cook and stir the ground beef along with the onion in the hot skillet for 7-10 minutes or till browned totally; drain any excess fat. Mix salt, cumin, chili powder and black beans into the beef mixture; cook and stir for roughly 5 minutes or till becoming hot. Add the mixture into the prepped baking dish. Arrange the tortillas on top of the beef mixture.
- In a bowl, stir together cream of mushroom soup, green chile peppers with tomatoes; spread on top of the tortillas. Add the Cheddar cheese on top.
- Bake in the preheated oven for 25-30 minutes or till thoroughly cooked and the cheese becomes melted totally.

Nutrition Information

- Calories: 293 calories;
- Sodium: 701
- Total Carbohydrate: 13
- Cholesterol: 67
- Protein: 20.3
- Total Fat: 17.7

---

691. Fold Over Tortilla Bake

Serving: 6 servings. | Prep: 20mins | Cook: 20mins | Ready in:

Ingredients

- 1 pound ground beef
- 1 cup chopped onion
- 2 cans (14-1/2 ounces each) stewed tomatoes
- 1 cup enchilada sauce
- 1 to 2 teaspoons ground cumin
- 1/2 teaspoon salt
- 1/4 teaspoon pepper

- 12 flour or corn tortillas (6 inches)
- 6 ounces cream cheese, softened
- 1 can (4 ounces) chopped green chilies, drained
- 1 cup shredded Monterey Jack cheese
- minced fresh cilantro, optional

Direction

- Cook onion and ground beef in a big skillet till beef is not pink anymore; drain. Mix in seasonings, enchilada sauce and tomatoes. Boil. Lower the heat and simmer, while covered, for 5 minutes. Add 1/2 of the meat sauce into one 13x9-in. baking dish. Put aside.
- Wrap the stack of tortillas in the foil; keep warmed at 350 degrees for 8 to 10 minutes. Spread warm tortillas with cream cheese and add chilies on top. Fold tortillas in half. Arrange folded tortillas on top meat sauce; add leftover sauce on top.
- Keep it covered and baked at 350 degrees for 15 minutes. Drizzle with cheese; bake till cheese becomes melted for 5 minutes more. Add cilantro on top if you want.

Nutrition Information

- Calories: 473 calories
- Total Carbohydrate: 38g carbohydrate (7g sugars
- Cholesterol: 69mg cholesterol
- Protein: 27g protein.
- Total Fat: 25g fat (10g saturated fat)
- Sodium: 1138mg sodium
- Fiber: 2g fiber)

692. Frito Pie

Serving: 6 servings. | Prep: 15mins | Cook: 15mins | Ready in:

Ingredients

- 1 pound ground beef

- 1 medium onion, chopped
- 2 cans (15 ounces each) Ranch Style beans (pinto beans in seasoned tomato sauce)
- 1 package (9-3/4 ounces) Fritos corn chips
- 2 cans (10 ounces each) enchilada sauce
- 2 cups shredded cheddar cheese
- Thinly sliced green onions, optional

Direction

- Preheat oven to 350 degrees. Cook onion and beef on medium heat in a big skillet till onion becomes soft and beef is not pink anymore or for 6 to 8 minutes, crumble the beef; drain. Mix in beans; heat through.
- Reserve 1 cup of corn chips for topping. Add the rest of the corn chips into one greased 13x9-in. baking dish. Layer with meat mixture, enchilada sauce and cheese; add reserved chips on top.
- Bake, while uncovered, for 15 to 20 minutes or till cheese becomes melted. Drizzle using green onions if you want.

Nutrition Information

- Calories: 731 calories
- Cholesterol: 84mg cholesterol
- Protein: 34g protein.
- Total Fat: 41g fat (14g saturated fat)
- Sodium: 1733mg sodium
- Fiber: 8g fiber)
- Total Carbohydrate: 54g carbohydrate (6g sugars

693. Gaucho Casserole

Serving: 8 servings. | Prep: 5mins | Cook: 25mins | Ready in:

Ingredients

- 1 pound lean ground beef (90% lean)
- 1 medium onion, chopped

- 1 small green pepper, chopped
- 1 can (16 ounces) kidney beans, rinsed and drained
- 1 can (14-1/2 ounces) diced tomatoes, undrained
- 1 can (8 ounces) tomato sauce
- 1/4 cup water
- 1 envelope reduced-sodium taco seasoning
- 1 teaspoon chili powder
- 1-1/3 cups uncooked instant rice
- 1 cup shredded reduced-fat Mexican cheese blend

Direction

- Crumble the beef into one ungreased 2-1/2-qt. microwave-safe plate. Put in green pepper and onion. Keep it covered and microwave on high till meat is not pink anymore or for 4-1/2 minutes, mixing every 2 minutes; drain.
- Mix in chili powder, taco seasoning, water, tomato sauce, tomatoes and beans. Keep it covered and microwave on high till becoming bubbly or for 3-1/2 to 4-1/2 minutes, mixing every 2 minutes. Mix in rice.
- Move to one shallow 2-1/2-qt. microwave-safe plate that coated using cooking spray. Keep it covered and allow to rest for 6 to 8 minutes or till liquid is absorbed. Drizzle with cheese. Keep it covered and microwave on high for 1 more minute or till cheese is melted.

Nutrition Information

- Calories: 304 calories
- Total Fat: 9g fat (4g saturated fat)
- Sodium: 670mg sodium
- Fiber: 7g fiber)
- Total Carbohydrate: 49g carbohydrate (0 sugars
- Cholesterol: 31mg cholesterol
- Protein: 22g protein. Diabetic Exchanges: 2 starch

694.   Grandma's Rice Dish

Serving: 4 servings. | Prep: 20mins | Cook: 15mins | Ready in:

Ingredients

- 1 pound ground beef
- 1/3 cup chopped onion
- 1/2 cup chopped green pepper
- 2 cups cooked long grain rice
- 1 can (14-1/2 ounces) diced tomatoes, undrained
- 1 can (11 ounces) whole kernel corn, drained
- 1 can (2-1/4 ounces) sliced ripe olives, drained
- 6 bacon strips, cooked and crumbled
- 2 teaspoons chili powder
- 1 teaspoon garlic powder
- 1/2 teaspoon salt
- 1-1/2 cups shredded cheddar cheese, divided
- 1/2 cup dry bread crumbs
- 1 tablespoon butter, melted

Direction

- Preheat oven to 350 degrees. Cook green pepper, onion and beef on medium heat in a big skillet till meat is not pink anymore; drain.
- Mix in seasonings, bacon, olives, corn, tomatoes and rice; heat through. Mix in one cup of cheese till melted.
- Move to a greased 11x7-in. baking dish. Drizzle with the rest of cheese. Toss bread crumbs with butter; drizzle on top.
- Bake, while uncovered, till cheese becomes melted or for 15 to 20 minutes.

Nutrition Information

- Calories: 719 calories
- Total Carbohydrate: 52g carbohydrate (9g sugars
- Cholesterol: 136mg cholesterol
- Protein: 41g protein.
- Total Fat: 37g fat (18g saturated fat)
- Sodium: 1397mg sodium
- Fiber: 5g fiber)

Serving: 6-8 servings. | Prep: 10mins | Cook: 30mins | Ready in:

Ingredients

- 3 cups cooked long grain rice
- 1-1/2 cups shredded cheddar cheese
- 1-1/2 cups (12 ounces) 4% cottage cheese
- 1 cans (4 ounces) chopped green chilies, drained
- 1/3 cup whole milk
- 1/3 cup chopped roasted red peppers
- 1 can (8-3/4 ounces) whole kernel corn, drained
- 1/4 cup grated Parmesan cheese

Direction

- In one greased 2-qt. baking dish, mix the initial 7 ingredients. Drizzle with Parmesan cheese. Keep it covered and baked at 350 degrees till thoroughly heated or for 30 to 35 minutes.

Nutrition Information

- Calories: 243 calories
- Protein: 13g protein.
- Total Fat: 9g fat (6g saturated fat)
- Sodium: 507mg sodium
- Fiber: 1g fiber)
- Total Carbohydrate: 24g carbohydrate (4g sugars
- Cholesterol: 35mg cholesterol

Serving: 6 servings. | Prep: 30mins | Cook: 55mins | Ready in:

Ingredients

- 1/2 pound lean ground turkey
- 1 large onion, chopped
- 1 can (16 ounces) fat-free refried beans
- 1-3/4 teaspoons ground cumin
- 1-1/2 teaspoons dried oregano
- 1/2 teaspoon garlic powder
- 1/2 teaspoon salt, divided
- 1/4 teaspoon pepper
- 2 cans (4 ounces each) chopped green chilies
- 1 cup shredded reduced-fat Mexican cheese blend
- 1 cup frozen corn, thawed
- 1/3 cup all-purpose flour
- 2 large eggs, lightly beaten
- 2 large egg whites
- 1-1/3 cups fat-free milk
- 1/8 teaspoon hot pepper sauce
- 1/4 cup thinly sliced red onion
- 3 tablespoons fresh cilantro leaves

Direction

- In a big nonstick skillet that coated using cooking spray, cook onion and turkey on medium heat till meat is not pink anymore; drain. Mix in pepper, a quarter tsp. of salt, garlic powder, oregano, cumin and beans.
- Drizzle 1/2 of the chilies and cheese into a 2-qt. baking dish that coated using cooking spray. Layer with bean mixture, corn and the rest of chilies and cheese.
- Mix leftover salt and flour in a small-sized bowl. Mix pepper sauce, milk, egg whites, and eggs in a separate small-sized bowl; slowly mix into flour mixture till becoming smooth. Add on the top.
- Bake, while uncovered, at 350 degrees till set or for 55 to 65 minutes. Drizzle with cilantro and red onion.

Nutrition Information

- Calories: 312 calories
- Protein: 25g protein. Diabetic Exchanges: 3 lean meat
- Total Fat: 9g fat (3g saturated fat)
- Sodium: 884mg sodium
- Fiber: 7g fiber)
- Total Carbohydrate: 34g carbohydrate (6g sugars
- Cholesterol: 115mg cholesterol

---

697. Ground Beef Enchilada Casserole

Serving: 6-8 servings. | Prep: 35mins | Cook: 35mins | Ready in:

Ingredients

- 1 pound ground beef
- 1 large onion, chopped
- 1/4 cup chopped green pepper
- 1 can (14-1/2 ounces) diced tomatoes, drained
- 1 can (10 ounces) enchilada sauce
- 1 can (2-1/4 ounces) sliced ripe olives, drained
- 1 teaspoon salt
- 2 cups shredded cheddar cheese, divided
- 1 cup (8 ounces) 4% cottage cheese
- 1 large egg, beaten
- 1 package (10 ounces) corn tortillas (6 inches), torn into pieces

Direction

- Cook green pepper, onion and beef on medium heat in a skillet till meat is not pink anymore; drain. Mix in salt, olives, enchilada sauce, and tomatoes. Keep it covered and let simmer roughly 20 minutes.
- At the same time, mix egg, cottage cheese, and 1 cup of cheddar cheese. Put aside. Spread 1/3 of the meat mixture into one greased 13x9-in.

baking dish. Cover with 1/2 of the tortillas; spread with 1/2 of the cheese mixture. Repeat the layers with the rest ingredients, ending with the meat mixture.
- Bake at 350 degrees for half an hour. Drizzle with the rest of cheddar cheese. Bake till cheese becomes melted or for 3 to 5 minutes. Allow to rest for 5 to 10 minutes prior to serving.

Nutrition Information

- Calories: 352 calories
- Cholesterol: 91mg cholesterol
- Protein: 23g protein.
- Total Fat: 18g fat (9g saturated fat)
- Sodium: 918mg sodium
- Fiber: 4g fiber)
- Total Carbohydrate: 26g carbohydrate (5g sugars

---

698. Hamburger Chilaquiles

Serving: 8 servings. | Prep: 30mins | Cook: 30mins | Ready in:

Ingredients

- 1 pound ground beef
- 1 medium onion, chopped
- 1envelope taco seasoning
- 1 can (4 ounces) chopped green chilies
- 1 can (28 ounces) diced tomatoes, undrained
- 6 ounces tortilla chips
- 4 cups shredded Monterey Jack cheese
- 1/2 cup sour cream
- 1 cup shredded cheddar cheese

Direction

- Cook onion and ground beef in a skillet till onion becomes soft and meat turns browned; drain. Mix in tomatoes, chilies, and taco seasoning. Let it simmer, while uncovered, for 15 minutes.

- Add 1/2 the tortilla chips in a 13x9-in. baking dish. Layer 1/2 of the meat mixture and 1/2 of the Monterey Jack cheese on top of the tortilla chips. Repeat the layers.
- Bake at 350 degrees for 20 minutes. Take out of the oven. Add sour cream dollops on top. Drizzle with cheddar cheese and bake till thoroughly heated or for another 10 minutes.

Nutrition Information

- Calories:
- Protein:
- Total Fat:
- Sodium:
- Fiber:
- Total Carbohydrate:
- Cholesterol:

---

699. Hamburger Corn Bread Casserole

Serving: 6 servings. | Prep: 25mins | Cook: 15mins | Ready in:

Ingredients

- 1 pound lean ground beef (90% lean)
- 1 small onion, chopped
- 1 can (15 ounces) Ranch Style beans (pinto beans in seasoned tomato sauce)
- 1 can (14-1/2 ounces) diced tomatoes, undrained
- 1 teaspoon chili powder
- 1 teaspoon Worcestershire sauce
- TOPPING:
- 1/2 cup all-purpose flour
- 1/2 cup cornmeal
- 2 tablespoons sugar
- 2 teaspoons baking powder
- 1/4 teaspoon salt
- 1 egg, beaten
- 1/2 cup fat-free milk
- 1 tablespoon canola oil

Direction

- Set the oven to 425° and start preheating. Cook onion and beef in a large skillet over medium heat until the pink color disappears from meat; drain. Add Worcestershire sauce, chili powder, tomatoes and beans; boil. Lower the heat and simmer, uncovered, for 5 minutes.
- Move to an 11x7 inch baking dish sprayed with cooking spray. To make topping, combine salt, baking powder, sugar, cornmeal and flour in a small bowl. Combine oil, milk and egg; stir into dry ingredients until just moistened. Drop spoonfuls of mixture on top of filling then gently spread to distribute and cover the top.
- Bake, uncovered, for 14 to 18 minutes or until filling is bubbling and a toothpick is still clean after being inserted into the topping. Allow to stand for 5 minutes, cut and serve.

Nutrition Information

- Calories: 339 calories
- Total Carbohydrate: 38g carbohydrate (9g sugars
- Cholesterol: 73mg cholesterol
- Protein: 22g protein. Diabetic Exchanges: 3 lean meat
- Total Fat: 10g fat (3g saturated fat)
- Sodium: 722mg sodium
- Fiber: 6g fiber)

---

700. Hearty Tortilla Casserole

Serving: 2-4 servings. | Prep: 35mins | Cook: 30mins | Ready in:

Ingredients

- 1/2 pound ground beef
- 2 tablespoons taco seasoning
- 1/3 cup water
- 1 small onion, finely chopped

- 1 to 2 Anaheim or Poblano chilies, roasted, peeled and finely chopped or 1 can (4 ounces) chopped green chilies
- 1 jalapeno pepper, seeded and finely chopped
- 1 garlic clove, minced
- 1 tablespoon canola oil
- 1/4 cup heavy whipping cream
- 1/8 teaspoon salt
- 4 flour tortillas (8 inches)
- 1 can (16 ounces) refried beans
- 1 cup shredded Monterey Jack cheese, divided
- 1 cup shredded cheddar cheese, divided
- Sour cream and salsa, optional

Direction

- Cook beef on medium heat in a skillet till meat is not pink anymore. Strain. Pour in water and taco seasoning. Let it simmer, while uncovered, for 5 minutes; take out of the heat and put aside.
- Sauté garlic, jalapeno, and onion in oil in a saucepan roughly 8 minutes or till becoming softened.
- Mix in salt and cream. Keep it covered and let simmer for 5 minutes.
- Spread three tbsp. of sauce in one ungreased 8-in. round or square baking dish. Spread roughly 2 tsp. of sauce over each tortilla; layer with beans, beef mixture and 2 tbsp. of each kind of cheese. Roll up and place seam-side facing downward in baking dish. Add the rest of sauce on top.
- Bake, while uncovered, at 350 degrees for 25 minutes. Drizzle with the rest of cheeses; bake 5 minutes more. Serve along with sour cream and salsa if you want.

Nutrition Information

- Calories: 657 calories
- Total Carbohydrate: 51g carbohydrate (4g sugars
- Cholesterol: 112mg cholesterol
- Protein: 34g protein.
- Total Fat: 35g fat (18g saturated fat)

- Sodium: 1442mg sodium
- Fiber: 7g fiber)

701. Hearty Turkey Enchilada Casserole

Serving: 8 servings. | Prep: 25mins | Cook: 25mins | Ready in:

Ingredients

- 1 pound ground turkey
- 1-1/2 cups chopped onions
- 2 garlic cloves, minced
- 1 tablespoon plus 1/3 cup vegetable oil, divided
- 1/3 cup all-purpose flour
- 2 tablespoons chili powder
- 3/4 teaspoon seasoned salt
- 1/8 teaspoon pepper
- 4 cups water
- 12 corn tortillas (6 inches)
- 1-1/2 cups shredded cheddar cheese
- 1-1/2 cups salsa

Direction

- Put 1 tablespoon oil in a big frying pan on medium heat, cook garlic, turkey, and onions until not pink; drain excess grease. Sprinkle on pepper, chili powder, flour, and seasoned salt. Add the water and heat to boiling. Do not cover, decrease heat, and simmer until reduced, 8-10 minutes. In a different pan place remaining oil, fry tortillas for 15 seconds, turn once. Drain tortillas well. Cut in half nine tortillas. Put the cut side of one tortilla up against each of the short sides of an 11x7-in. greased pan. Put two tortillas in the pan with their cut sides against the long sides of the pan, overlap to fit. In the center, put a whole tortilla. Put 2 cups of the meat mixture over the tortillas; sprinkle on 1/2 cup cheese. Repeat the layers. Put the rest of the tortillas and meat mixture on top. Do not cover; bake in a 375-degree oven for 20 minutes. Sprinkle on remaining cheese. Bake until cheese melts, 5-10 minutes. Eat with salsa.

Nutrition Information

- Calories: 430 calories
- Protein: 17g protein.
- Total Fat: 27g fat (9g saturated fat)
- Sodium: 634mg sodium
- Fiber: 5g fiber)
- Total Carbohydrate: 29g carbohydrate (4g sugars
- Cholesterol: 63mg cholesterol

702. Hominy Beef Polenta

Serving: 6 servings. | Prep: 5mins | Cook: 25mins | Ready in:

Ingredients

- 2 tubes (1 pound each) polenta, cut into 1/2-inch slices
- 1 pound ground beef
- 1 cup chopped sweet red pepper
- 1 jar (16 ounces) picante sauce
- 1 can (16 ounces) hot chili beans, undrained
- 1 can (15-1/2 ounces) hominy, rinsed and drained
- 1/3 cup minced fresh cilantro
- 3 teaspoons ground cumin
- 2 teaspoons chili powder
- 2 cups shredded Colby-Monterey Jack cheese

Direction

- Line a greased 13x9-in. baking dish with one layer of polenta slices. Bake, while uncovered, at 350 degrees till thoroughly heated or for 15 to 20 minutes.
- At the same time, cook red pepper and beef on medium heat in a big skillet till meat is not pink anymore; drain. Mix in chili powder,

cumin, cilantro, hominy, beans and picante sauce; heat through.
- Drizzle half of the cheese on top of polenta. Add leftover cheese and meat sauce on top. Bake till cheese becomes melted or for 8 minutes.

Nutrition Information

- Calories: 503 calories
- Fiber: 8g fiber)
- Total Carbohydrate: 52g carbohydrate (6g sugars
- Cholesterol: 72mg cholesterol
- Protein: 28g protein.
- Total Fat: 18g fat (11g saturated fat)
- Sodium: 1865mg sodium

703. Hominy Sausage Bake

Serving: 8 servings. | Prep: 40mins | Cook: 35mins | Ready in:

Ingredients

- 1 pound Johnsonville® Fully Cooked Smoked Sausage Rope, cut into 1/4-inch slices
- 1 teaspoon olive oil
- 2 cups cubed fully cooked ham
- 2 packages (8 ounces each) red beans and rice mix
- 6 cups water
- 2 tablespoons butter
- 1/4 teaspoon cayenne pepper
- 1 can (29 ounces) hominy, rinsed and drained
- 1 jar (12 ounces) pickled jalapeno peppers, drained and chopped
- 1 can (15-1/4 ounces) whole kernel corn, drained
- 1 cup shredded cheddar cheese
- 1 cup corn chips, crushed

Direction

- Put some oil in a Dutch oven, brown the sausage; drain grease and set sausage aside. Add ham cubes to the Dutch oven and brown. Mix in water, cayenne, red beans and rice mix, and butter. Heat to boiling. Cover, decrease heat, and simmer until rice and beans are tender, 25 minutes. Stir sporadically. Move to a 3-qt. greased dish. Layer on hominy and the sausage, then put peppers and corn on top. Do not cover; bake in a 350-degree oven until cooked through, 30-35 minutes. Sprinkle on cheese. Bake until cheese melts, 5 minutes. Top with corn chips.

Nutrition Information

- Calories: 640 calories
- Protein: 26g protein.
- Total Fat: 29g fat (13g saturated fat)
- Sodium: 3052mg sodium
- Fiber: 8g fiber)
- Total Carbohydrate: 68g carbohydrate (10g sugars
- Cholesterol: 79mg cholesterol

704.   Hot Tamale Casserole

Serving: 6 servings. | Prep: 35mins | Cook: 30mins | Ready in:

Ingredients

- 2 cups water
- 1/4 teaspoon salt
- 1/8 teaspoon cayenne pepper
- 1/2 cup cornmeal
- 1-1/2 pounds lean ground beef (90% lean)
- 1 large onion, chopped
- 1 medium green pepper, chopped
- 2 garlic cloves, minced
- 1 can (16 ounces) kidney beans, rinsed and drained
- 1 can (10 ounces) enchilada sauce
- 1 can (4 ounces) chopped green chilies

- 1 can (2-1/4 ounces) sliced ripe olives, drained
- 2 teaspoons chili powder
- 2 teaspoons minced fresh cilantro
- 3/4 cup shredded cheddar cheese

Direction

- Heat cayenne, water, and salt to a boil in a small heavy pot. Decrease heat to a gentle boil; gradually stir in cornmeal. Stir constantly with a wooden spoon; cook until polenta cleanly pulls away from the sides of the pot and is thick, 15-20 minutes.
- In the meantime, cook garlic, onion, beef, and green pepper in a big frying pan on medium heat until beef is not pink. Mix in the chili powder, chilies, beans, cilantro, enchilada sauce, and olives; cook through.
- Spread the polenta in the bottom of a square 8-in. greased pan. Put meat mixture on top. Cover; bake in a 350-degree oven for 25 minutes. Sprinkle on cheese. Do not cover; bake until cheese melts and filling is bubbling, 2-5 minutes.

Nutrition Information

- Calories: 369 calories
- Total Carbohydrate: 30g carbohydrate (4g sugars
- Cholesterol: 86mg cholesterol
- Protein: 32g protein.
- Total Fat: 15g fat (7g saturated fat)
- Sodium: 837mg sodium
- Fiber: 7g fiber)

705.   Jumble Lala

Serving: 8-10 servings. | Prep: 15mins | Cook: 01hours20mins | Ready in:

Ingredients

- 1-1/2 pounds ground beef, browned and drained

- 1 medium onion, chopped
- 1 quart tomato juice
- 1 can (10-3/4 ounces) condensed tomato soup, undiluted
- 1 cup uncooked long grain rice
- 1 tablespoon brown sugar
- 1/4 teaspoon dried thyme
- 2 bay leaves
- 1/4 to 1/2 teaspoon curry powder
- 1 teaspoon salt
- 1/2 teaspoon pepper

Direction

- In a big bowl, mix all ingredients. Add to one greased 2-qt. baking dish. Keep it covered and baked at 350 degrees for 80 to 90 minutes or till becomes hot and bubbly.

Nutrition Information

- Calories: 222 calories
- Sodium: 813mg sodium
- Fiber: 1g fiber)
- Total Carbohydrate: 26g carbohydrate (8g sugars
- Cholesterol: 33mg cholesterol
- Protein: 15g protein.
- Total Fat: 6g fat (3g saturated fat)

706.   Kidney Bean Taco Bake

Serving: 4 servings. | Prep: 10mins | Cook: 35mins | Ready in:

Ingredients

- 1-1/2 pounds ground beef
- 2 cans (16 ounces each) kidney beans, rinsed and drained
- 2 cans (8 ounces each) tomato sauce
- 1 envelope taco seasoning
- 1 can (2-1/4 ounces) sliced ripe olives, drained
- 1 cup crumbled tortilla chips

- 1/2 cup shredded cheddar cheese

Direction

- Cook beef in a large skillet over medium heat until the pink color disappears from meat; drain. Add taco seasoning, tomato sauce and beans; bring to a boil. Move mixture to a greased shallow 2-1/2 quart baking dish.
- Bake when uncover for 30 to 35 minutes at 350°, add cheese, tortilla chips and olives on top. Bake for another 5 minutes or until cheese is fully melted.

Nutrition Information

- Calories: 616 calories
- Fiber: 12g fiber)
- Total Carbohydrate: 54g carbohydrate (5g sugars
- Cholesterol: 98mg cholesterol
- Protein: 50g protein.
- Total Fat: 22g fat (10g saturated fat)
- Sodium: 2046mg sodium

707.   Light Mexican Casserole

Serving: 6 servings. | Prep: 30mins | Cook: 25mins | Ready in:

Ingredients

- 1 pound extra-lean ground beef (95% lean)
- 1 medium onion, chopped
- 1 medium green pepper, chopped
- 3/4 cup water
- 1 tablespoon all-purpose flour
- 1 tablespoon hot chili powder
- 1 teaspoon garlic powder
- 1/2 teaspoon ground cumin
- 1/2 teaspoon ground coriander
- 1/4 teaspoon salt
- 1 can (16 ounces) refried beans
- 1/2 cup salsa

- 4 whole wheat tortillas (8 inches)
- 1 cup frozen corn
- 3/4 cup shredded sharp cheddar cheese
- Shredded lettuce and chopped tomatoes, optional

Direction

- Combine green pepper, onion and beef together in a large nonstick skillet. Cook over medium heat until the pink color disappears from meat. Stir in salt, coriander, cumin, garlic powder, chili powder, flour and water. Bring to a boil. Lover the heat to simmer when uncover for 5 to 6 minutes or until mixture is thickened.
- Combine salsa and beans in a small bowl. Coat a round 1-1/2 qt baking dish with cooking spray. Arrange 2 tortillas into prepared dish. Spread half of beef mixture, bean mixture and corn in layers on top of tortillas, repeat layering with remaining ingredients. Add cheese on top.
- Bake when uncover at 350° for 25 to 30 minutes or until heated through. Allow to stand for 5 minutes, cut and serve with tomatoes and lettuce if desired.

Nutrition Information

- Calories: 367 calories
- Fiber: 8g fiber)
- Total Carbohydrate: 39g carbohydrate (4g sugars
- Cholesterol: 64mg cholesterol
- Protein: 26g protein. Diabetic Exchanges: 3 lean meat
- Total Fat: 11g fat (5g saturated fat)
- Sodium: 657mg sodium

708. Loaded Chili

Serving: 6 servings. | Prep: 10mins | Cook: 30mins | Ready in:

Ingredients

- 1 can (40 ounces) chili with beans
- 1 can (4 ounces) chopped green chilies
- 1 can (2-1/4 ounces) sliced ripe olives, drained
- 2 cups shredded cheddar cheese
- 2 cups ranch-flavored tortilla chips, crushed

Direction

- Mix all ingredients in a bowl. Move to one greased 2-1/2-qt. baking dish. Bake, while uncovered, at 350 degrees till becoming bubbly or for 30 to 35 minutes.

Nutrition Information

- Calories:
- Total Fat:
- Sodium:
- Fiber:
- Total Carbohydrate:
- Cholesterol:
- Protein:

709. Macaroni Taco Bake

Serving: 8 servings. | Prep: 30mins | Cook: 15mins | Ready in:

Ingredients

- 2 packages (7-1/4 ounces each) macaroni and cheese dinner mix
- 1 pound ground beef
- 1 cup chunky salsa
- 2 cups crushed tortilla chips
- 1 can (2-1/4 ounces) sliced ripe olives, drained
- 2 cups shredded Mexican cheese blend
- Sour cream, optional

Direction

- Follow package instructions in cooking the mac 'n cheese. While waiting for the mac 'n cheese to cook, cook beef in a large skillet until brown then drain excess oil. Add in the salsa then put aside.

- Put macaroni evenly into a greased 13x9-inch baking dish. Put olives, beef mixture and chips on top of the macaroni then top off with cheese.
- Put the baking dish uncovered in an oven at 350 degrees and bake for 15 to 20 minutes until heated through. You may put sour cream before serving if you like.

Nutrition Information

- Calories: 597 calories
- Total Carbohydrate: 48g carbohydrate (7g sugars
- Cholesterol: 105mg cholesterol
- Protein: 28g protein.
- Total Fat: 33g fat (17g saturated fat)
- Sodium: 991mg sodium
- Fiber: 1g fiber)

710.   Meatless Chili Bake

Serving: 4-6 servings. | Prep: 20mins | Cook: 25mins | Ready in:

Ingredients

- 2-1/2 cups uncooked spiral pasta
- 1 can (15 ounces) vegetarian chili with beans
- 1 jar (12 ounces) chunky salsa
- 1 can (11 ounces) whole kernel corn, drained
- 1/2 cup shredded cheddar cheese

Direction

- Based on the instruction on the package, cook pasta; drain. Mix corn, salsa and chili in a big bowl. Put in pasta; coat by tossing.
- Move into one greased shallow 2-qt. baking dish; drizzle along with cheese. Bake, while uncovered, at 400 degrees till becoming bubbly or for 25 to 30 minutes.

Nutrition Information

- Calories: 290 calories
- Protein: 11g protein.
- Total Fat: 4g fat (2g saturated fat)
- Sodium: 560mg sodium
- Fiber: 8g fiber)
- Total Carbohydrate: 43g carbohydrate (8g sugars
- Cholesterol: 10mg cholesterol

711.   Mexicali Casserole

Serving: 6 servings. | Prep: 15mins | Cook: 55mins | Ready in:

Ingredients

- 1 pound lean ground turkey
- 2 medium onions, chopped
- 1 small green pepper, chopped
- 1 garlic clove, minced
- 1 can (16 ounces) kidney beans, rinsed and drained
- 1 can (14-1/2 ounces) diced tomatoes, undrained
- 1 cup water
- 2/3 cup uncooked long grain rice
- 1/3 cup sliced ripe olives
- 1 teaspoon chili powder
- 1/2 teaspoon salt
- 1/2 cup shredded reduced-fat cheddar cheese

Direction

- Preheat oven to 375 degrees. Cook pepper, onions and turkey on medium heat in a big skillet that coated using cooking spray, till veggies become soft and meat is not pink anymore or for 6 to 8 minutes, crumble turkey into smaller pieces. Put in garlic; cook for 60 seconds more. Drain. Mix in salt, chili powder, olives, rice, water, tomatoes and beans.

- Move to one 11x7-inch baking dish that coated using cooking spray. Bake, while covered, till rice becomes soft or for 50 to 55 minutes. Drizzle with cheese. Bake, while uncovered, till cheese becomes melted or for 5 minutes more.

Nutrition Information

- Calories: 348 calories
- Sodium: 508mg sodium
- Fiber: 9g fiber)
- Total Carbohydrate: 41g carbohydrate (0 sugars
- Cholesterol: 66mg cholesterol
- Protein: 24g protein. Diabetic Exchanges: 3 lean meat
- Total Fat: 10g fat (3g saturated fat)

712.   Mexican Beef Cobbler

Serving: 6 servings. | Prep: 20mins | Cook: 35mins | Ready in:

Ingredients

- 1-1/2 pounds ground beef
- 1 envelope taco seasoning
- 1 jar (16 ounces) salsa
- 1 can (8-3/4 ounces) whole kernel corn, drained
- 2 cups shredded sharp cheddar cheese
- 1-1/2 cups biscuit/baking mix
- 1/2 cup 2% milk
- 1/8 teaspoon freshly ground pepper

Direction

- Cook beef on medium heat in a big skillet till not pink anymore or for 8 to 10 minutes, crumble; drain. Mix in corn, salsa and taco seasoning; heat through. Move to an 11x7-in. baking dish; drizzle along with cheese.

- Whisk milk and biscuit mix in a small-sized bowl just till blended; drop by tablespoonfuls on top of cheese. Drizzle along with pepper.
- Bake, while uncovered, at 350 degrees for 35 to 45 minutes or till becoming bubbly and topping turns golden brown.

Nutrition Information

- Calories:
- Total Carbohydrate:
- Cholesterol:
- Protein:
- Total Fat:
- Sodium:
- Fiber:

713.   Mexican Casserole

Serving: 4 | Prep: 10mins | Cook: 20mins |Ready in:

Ingredients

- 1 (16 ounce) can refried beans
- 3/4 onion, diced
- 5 (10 inch) flour tortillas
- 1 cup salsa
- 2 cups shredded Cheddar or Colby Jack cheese

Direction

- Preheat oven to 190 degrees C (375 degrees F). Spray a 9-inch pie pan using non-stick cooking spray.
- Cook onions and refried beans (to make them tender) in a saucepan over medium high heat for roughly 5 minutes.
- Add one tortilla into the bottom of the greased pan. Spread roughly a third cup of the bean mixture on top of it. Layer several tbsp. of salsa on top of this. Then, add another tortilla on top of the salsa, and add more of the bean mixture. Follow the beans with a large handful of cheese, spreading equally. Repeat the

layers, spreading the ingredients equally on top of the tortillas. On the top layer, ensure you use a lot of cheese and salsa!

- Bake for roughly 15-20 minutes or till the cheese becomes melted.

Nutrition Information

- Calories: 651 calories;
- Total Fat: 20.3
- Sodium: 1505
- Total Carbohydrate: 74
- Cholesterol: 68
- Protein: 29.3

---

714.   Mexican Skillet Supper

Serving: 6-8 servings. | Prep: 10mins | Cook: 30mins | Ready in:

Ingredients

- 1 pound ground beef
- 2 celery ribs, chopped
- 1 small green pepper, chopped
- 1/4 cup chopped onion
- 1 package (8.6 ounces) beef taco pasta dinner mix
- 1 teaspoon chili powder
- 3-2/3 cups hot water
- 2 cups shredded cheddar cheese
- 1 can (14-1/2 ounces) stewed tomatoes, cut up
- 1 can (2-1/4 ounces) sliced ripe olives, drained
- Sour cream, optional

Direction

- In a large skillet, cook green pepper, onion, celery, and beef over medium heat until vegetables are soften and meat is not pink anymore; and then drain.
- Leave topping packet from the dinner mix aside for another use. Add into beef mixture with water, chili powder and the contents of

dinner mix seasoning packet. Allow to boil. Mix in noodles from dinner mix. Lessen heat; simmer while covered for nearly 12 to 15 minutes until noodles are tender.

- Stir in the olives, tomatoes and cheese; heat through. Use sour cream for serving if you want.

Nutrition Information

- Calories: 253 calories
- Sodium: 464mg sodium
- Fiber: 1g fiber)
- Total Carbohydrate: 10g carbohydrate (3g sugars
- Cholesterol: 68mg cholesterol
- Protein: 20g protein.
- Total Fat: 15g fat (9g saturated fat)

---

715.   Mexican Spoon Bread Casserole

Serving: 2 servings. | Prep: 25mins | Cook: 25mins | Ready in:

Ingredients

- 1/2 pound ground beef
- 1 small onion, chopped
- 2 tablespoons chopped green pepper
- 1 garlic clove, minced
- 2/3 cup tomato sauce
- 1/2 cup frozen corn, thawed
- 2 tablespoons sliced ripe olives
- 3/4 teaspoon chili powder
- 1/2 teaspoon salt
- Dash pepper
- TOPPING:
- 3 tablespoons cornmeal
- 1/2 cup whole milk
- 1/8 teaspoon salt
- 1/4 cup shredded cheddar cheese
- 1 large egg, lightly beaten

Direction

- Combine garlic, green pepper, onion and beef in a large skillet, cook over medium heat until the pink color disappears from meat; drain. Add pepper, salt, chili powder, olives, corn and tomato sauce; bring to a boil. Lower the heat and simmer when uncover for 10 minutes.
- In the meantime, combine salt, milk and cornmeal in a large saucepan; bring to a boil, remember to stir often while boiling. Remove from the heat. Stir in egg and cheese.
- Drop spoonfuls of mixture into an ungreased 1-qt baking dish. Add topping on top of mixture. Bake when uncovered at 375° for 22 to 26 minutes or until a knife is still clean after being inserted in the center.

Nutrition Information

- Calories: 436 calories
- Total Fat: 20g fat (10g saturated fat)
- Sodium: 1418mg sodium
- Fiber: 4g fiber)
- Total Carbohydrate: 31g carbohydrate (8g sugars
- Cholesterol: 185mg cholesterol
- Protein: 33g protein.

---

716. Mexican Turkey Hash Brown Bake

Serving: 6 servings. | Prep: 20mins | Cook: 35mins | Ready in:

Ingredients

- 1 pound lean ground turkey
- 1/4 cup chopped onion
- 3 garlic cloves, minced
- 1 package (32 ounces) frozen cubed hash brown potatoes, thawed
- 1 can (10 ounces) enchilada sauce

- 1 can (8 ounces) tomato sauce
- 1 can (4 ounces) chopped green chilies
- 1 tablespoon reduced-sodium taco seasoning
- 1 cup shredded cheddar cheese
- Reduced-fat sour cream, optional

Direction

- Cook garlic, onion and turkey on medium heat in a big skillet till meat is not pink anymore. Put in taco seasoning, chilies, tomato sauce, enchilada sauce and the hash browns; thoroughly heat.
- Move into one 13x9-inch baking dish that coated using cooking spray.
- Keep it covered and baked at 375 degrees for half an hour. Drizzle with cheese; bake, while uncovered, till cheese becomes melted or for 5 to 10 minutes more. Serve along with sour cream if you want.

Nutrition Information

- Calories: 330 calories
- Total Fat: 12g fat (6g saturated fat)
- Sodium: 799mg sodium
- Fiber: 4g fiber)
- Total Carbohydrate: 35g carbohydrate (3g sugars
- Cholesterol: 80mg cholesterol
- Protein: 23g protein. Diabetic Exchanges: 3 lean meat

---

717. Mexican Style Pork Chops

Serving: 6 servings. | Prep: 15mins | Cook: 20mins | Ready in:

Ingredients

- 6 bone-in pork loin chops (1/2 inch thick and 8 ounces each)
- 2 tablespoons canola oil

- 1 medium onion, chopped
- 1 can (16 ounces) kidney beans, rinsed and drained
- 1 can (15-1/4 ounces) whole kernel corn, drained
- 1 can (10-3/4 ounces) condensed tomato soup, undiluted
- 1-1/4 cups water
- 1 cup uncooked instant rice
- 1/2 cup sliced ripe olives
- 2 to 3 teaspoons chili powder
- 1/2 teaspoon dried oregano
- 1/2 teaspoon salt
- 1/8 teaspoon pepper

Direction

- Brown pork chops in oil on each side in the ovenproof skillet; take out and keep warm. Sauté onion in the same skillet till becoming tender. Mix in the rest of the ingredients; boil.
- Add chops on top of the onion mixture. Bake, while uncovered, at 350 degrees till thermometer reads 160 degrees or for 20 to 25 minutes.

Nutrition Information

- Calories: 330 calories
- Protein: 15g protein.
- Total Fat: 10g fat (2g saturated fat)
- Sodium: 934mg sodium
- Fiber: 7g fiber)
- Total Carbohydrate: 44g carbohydrate (10g sugars
- Cholesterol: 19mg cholesterol

718.   Ole Polenta Casserole

Serving: 6 servings. | Prep: 60mins | Cook: 45mins | Ready in:

Ingredients

- 1 cup yellow cornmeal
- 1 teaspoon salt
- 4 cups water, divided
- 1 pound ground beef
- 1 cup chopped onion
- 1/2 cup chopped green pepper
- 2 garlic cloves, minced
- 1 can (14-1/2 ounces) diced tomatoes, undrained
- 1 can (8 ounces) tomato sauce
- 1/2 pound sliced fresh mushrooms
- 1 teaspoon each dried basil, oregano and dill weed
- Dash hot pepper sauce
- 1-1/2 cups shredded part-skim mozzarella cheese
- 1/4 cup grated Parmesan cheese

Direction

- To make polenta, whisk together 1 cup of water, salt and cornmeal in a small bowl until smooth. Bring remaining water to a boil in a large saucepan. Add cornmeal mixture, stirring continuously. Bring to a boil and cook, stirring frequently, for 3 minutes or until mixture is thickened.
- Lower the heat to low and cook, covered, for 15 minutes. Evenly distribute mixture into 2 greased 8 inches square baking dishes. Keep in refrigerator, covered, for about 90 minutes until firm.
- Combine garlic, green pepper, onion and beef in a large skillet and cook over medium heat until the pink color disappears from meat; drain. Stir in hot pepper sauce, herbs, mushrooms, tomato sauce and tomatoes; bring to a boil. Remove cover and lower the heat to simmer for 20 minutes or until thickened.
- Loosen one polenta from dish's bottom and sides. Carefully transfer polenta onto a waxed paper-covered baking sheet; set aside. Drop spoonfuls of half of the meat mixture over remaining polenta. Place half of parmesan cheese and half of mozzarella cheese on top. Arrange saved polenta and remaining meat mixture on top.

- Bake, covered, for 40 minutes at 350° or until heated through. Remove the cover and add remaining cheese on top. Bake for an additional 5 minutes or until cheese is completely melted. Allow to stand for 10 minutes before cutting.

Nutrition Information

- Calories: 345 calories
- Cholesterol: 62mg cholesterol
- Protein: 25g protein.
- Total Fat: 14g fat (7g saturated fat)
- Sodium: 874mg sodium
- Fiber: 4g fiber)
- Total Carbohydrate: 29g carbohydrate (6g sugars

719.   Oven Jambalya

Serving: 8-10 servings. | Prep: 10mins | Cook: 60mins | Ready in:

Ingredients

- 2-1/4 cups water
- 1-1/2 cups uncooked long grain rice
- 1 can (10-3/4 ounces) condensed cream of celery soup, undiluted
- 1 can (10-3/4 ounces) condensed cream of onion soup, undiluted
- 1 can (10 ounces) diced tomatoes and green chilies, undrained
- 1 pound Johnsonville® Fully Cooked Smoked Sausage Rope, cut into 1/2-inch slices
- 1 pound cooked medium shrimp, peeled and deveined

Direction

- Combine the first five ingredients in a big bowl; then transfer it to a 13x9-in greased baking dish.
- Cover the dish and bake for 40 minutes at 350°. Stir in the shrimp and sausage. Cover again

and bake for another 20-30 minutes or until the rice becomes tender.

Nutrition Information

- Calories: 344 calories
- Fiber: 1g fiber)
- Total Carbohydrate: 30g carbohydrate (2g sugars
- Cholesterol: 104mg cholesterol
- Protein: 19g protein.
- Total Fat: 16g fat (6g saturated fat)
- Sodium: 1148mg sodium

720.   Peppy Bean Bake

Serving: 6 servings. | Prep: 10mins | Cook: 45mins | Ready in:

Ingredients

- 1 can (16 ounces) vegetarian baked beans
- 1 can (16 ounces) kidney beans, rinsed and drained
- 1 can (15-1/4 ounces) whole kernel corn, drained
- 1 can (15 ounces) vegetarian chili with beans
- 1 to 2 jalapeno peppers, seeded and chopped
- 1 cup shredded cheddar cheese
- 1 cup crushed nacho tortilla chips

Direction

- Mix jalapenos, chili, corn, kidney beans and baked beans in a bowl. Move into one greased 8-in. square baking dish.
- Keep it covered and baked at 350 degrees for 40 minutes. Uncover it; drizzle with cheese and chips. Bake till becoming bubbly and cheese becomes melted or for 5 to 10 more minutes.

Nutrition Information

- Calories: 373 calories
- Protein: 18g protein.
- Total Fat: 9g fat (5g saturated fat)
- Sodium: 882mg sodium
- Fiber: 13g fiber)
- Total Carbohydrate: 51g carbohydrate (11g sugars
- Cholesterol: 20mg cholesterol

721. Picante Biscuit Bake

Serving: 6 servings. | Prep: 5mins | Cook: 30mins | Ready in:

Ingredients

- 2 tubes (12 ounces each) refrigerated buttermilk biscuits
- 1 jar (16 ounces) picante sauce or salsa
- 1 medium green pepper, chopped
- 1 medium onion, chopped
- 1 can (2-1/4 ounces) sliced ripe olives, drained
- 2 cups shredded Monterey Jack cheese

Direction

- Chop the biscuits into quarters; put into one greased 13x9-in. baking dish. Add olives, onion, green pepper and picante sauce on top.
- Bake, while uncovered, at 350 degrees for 20 minutes. Drizzle with cheese. Bake till cheese becomes melted or for 10 minutes more.

Nutrition Information

- Calories: 330 calories
- Protein: 14g protein.
- Total Fat: 14g fat (8g saturated fat)
- Sodium: 1108mg sodium
- Fiber: 1g fiber)
- Total Carbohydrate: 37g carbohydrate (5g sugars
- Cholesterol: 34mg cholesterol

722. Pinto Bean Casserole

Serving: 6-8 servings. | Prep: 10mins | Cook: 20mins | Ready in:

Ingredients

- 1 package (9 ounces) tortilla chips
- 2 cans (15 ounces each) pinto beans, rinsed and drained
- 1 can (15 ounces) whole kernel corn, drained
- 1 can (14-1/2 ounces) diced tomatoes
- 1 can (8 ounces) tomato sauce
- 1 envelope taco seasoning
- 2 cups shredded cheddar cheese
- Shredded lettuce, sour cream and salsa, optional

Direction

- Take tortilla chips crush and sprinkle into the bottom of a 13x9-in. pan. Mix taco seasoning, beans, tomato sauce, corn, and tomatoes in a large bowl. Pour mixture over chips. Spread the cheese on top. Do not cover; bake in a 350-degree oven until heated, 18-25 minutes. If desired, add sour cream, salsa, and lettuce.

Nutrition Information

- Calories: 374 calories
- Protein: 13g protein.
- Total Fat: 15g fat (7g saturated fat)
- Sodium: 1117mg sodium
- Fiber: 5g fiber)
- Total Carbohydrate: 44g carbohydrate (5g sugars
- Cholesterol: 30mg cholesterol

723. Polenta Chili Casserole

Serving: 8 servings. | Prep: 20mins | Cook: 35mins | Ready in:

Ingredients

- 4 cups water
- 1/2 teaspoon salt
- 1-1/4 cups yellow cornmeal
- 2 cups shredded cheddar cheese, divided
- 3 cans (15 ounces each) vegetarian chili with beans
- 1 package (16 ounces) frozen mixed vegetables, thawed and well drained

Direction

- Heat the oven to 350 degrees. Boil salt and water in a large heavy pot. Decrease heat to a simmer and gradually stir in cornmeal. For 15-20 minutes, use a wooden spoon to stir the polenta until thick and loosens from the sides of pot. Take away from heat. Mix in 1/4 cup of cheddar cheese and stir until melted. Spread in a greased 13x9-in. pan. Do not cover; bake for 20 minutes. In the meantime, follow the directions on the package to heat the chili. Layer the polenta with veggies and then chili. Top with the rest of the cheese. Put back in the oven for 12-15 more minutes until the cheese melts. Let it cool for 10 minutes before eating.

Nutrition Information

- Calories: 297 calories
- Total Carbohydrate: 43g carbohydrate (7g sugars
- Cholesterol: 20mg cholesterol
- Protein: 19g protein.
- Total Fat: 7g fat (4g saturated fat)
- Sodium: 556mg sodium
- Fiber: 12g fiber)

---

724. Popular Potluck Casserole

Serving: 10-12 servings. | Prep: 25mins | Cook: 25mins | Ready in:

Ingredients

- 1 package (7 ounces) ring macaroni
- 2 pounds ground beef
- 1 medium onion, chopped
- 1/4 cup chopped green pepper
- 1/4 cup thinly sliced celery
- 1 can (10-3/4 ounces) condensed cream of mushroom soup, undiluted
- 1 can (10 ounces) diced tomatoes with green chilies
- 1 can (8 ounces) tomato sauce
- 1 to 2 tablespoons chili powder
- 1 can (15-1/4 ounces) whole kernel corn, drained
- 2 cups shredded cheddar cheese, divided

Direction

- Based on the instruction on the package, cook macaroni. At the same time, cook celery, green pepper, onion and beef till meat is not pink anymore and vegetables become soft; drain. Mix chili powder, tomato sauce, tomatoes and soup till combined.
- Drain the macaroni; mix into beef mixture. Put in the corn and 1-1/2 cups of cheese.
- Move into one greased 13x9-in. baking dish. Drizzle with the rest of cheese. Bake, while uncovered, at 350 degrees till thoroughly heated or for 25 to 30 minutes.

Nutrition Information

- Calories: 312 calories
- Sodium: 626mg sodium
- Fiber: 2g fiber)
- Total Carbohydrate: 23g carbohydrate (5g sugars
- Cholesterol: 58mg cholesterol
- Protein: 21g protein.
- Total Fat: 14g fat (8g saturated fat)

725. Puffy Chile Rellenos Casserole

Serving: 12 servings. | Prep: 20mins | Cook: 40mins | Ready in:

Ingredients

- 4 cans (7 ounces each) whole green chilies, drained
- 8 flour tortillas (6 inches), cut into 1-inch strips
- 2 cups shredded part-skim mozzarella cheese
- 2 cups shredded reduced-fat cheddar cheese
- 3 cups egg substitute
- 3/4 cup fat-free milk
- 1/2 teaspoon garlic powder
- 1/2 teaspoon ground cumin
- 1/2 teaspoon pepper
- 1/4 teaspoon salt
- 1 teaspoon paprika
- 1 cup salsa

Direction

- Slice each chili on one side only so they can lie flat. Grease a 13x9-in. pan. Layer in this order half the chilies, the tortilla strips, the mozzarella and cheddar cheeses in the 13x9-in. pan. Repeat the layers once more. In a separate bowl, mix milk, salt, cumin, egg substitute, pepper, and garlic powder. Pour mixture over the cheeses. Sprinkle paprika on top. Do not cover; place in a 350-degree oven and bake until knife poked 2 in. from the edge comes out clean and its puffy, 40-45 minutes. Let cool for 10 minutes. Cut and eat with salsa.

Nutrition Information

- Calories: 213 calories
- Protein: 18g protein. Diabetic Exchanges: 2 lean meat
- Total Fat: 9g fat (5g saturated fat)
- Sodium: 690mg sodium
- Fiber: 1g fiber)
- Total Carbohydrate: 14g carbohydrate (4g sugars

- Cholesterol: 25mg cholesterol

726. Quick Tamale Casserole

Serving: 4 servings. | Prep: 20mins | Cook: 30mins | Ready in:

Ingredients

- 1 pound ground beef
- 1 can (15 ounces) chili with beans
- 1 jar (13-1/2 ounces) tamales
- 1 can (15-1/4 ounces) whole kernel corn, drained
- 4 slices process American cheese

Direction

- Cook beef on medium heat in a big skillet till meat is not pink anymore; drain. Scoop into a greased 9-in. square baking dish; add chili on top.
- Take the papers out of tamales; chop each into six slices. Arrange on top of chili. Drizzle with corn and add cheese on top. Bake, while uncovered, at 350 degrees till thoroughly heated or for half an hour.

Nutrition Information

- Calories: 592 calories
- Sodium: 1556mg sodium
- Fiber: 7g fiber)
- Total Carbohydrate: 37g carbohydrate (8g sugars
- Cholesterol: 115mg cholesterol
- Protein: 38g protein.
- Total Fat: 31g fat (13g saturated fat)

727. Salsa Spaghetti Squash

Serving: 4 servings. | Prep: 10mins | Cook: 20mins | Ready in:

Ingredients

- 1 medium spaghetti squash
- 1 medium onion, chopped
- 2 cups salsa
- 1 can (15 ounces) black beans, rinsed and drained
- 3 tablespoons minced fresh cilantro
- 1 medium ripe avocado, peeled and cubed

Direction

- Lengthwise, cut squash in half; throw seeds. Put squash, cut side down, on microwave-safe plate. Microwave on high, uncovered, till tender for 15-18 minutes.
- Meanwhile, mix and cook onion in nonstick skillet coated in cooking spray on medium heat till tender. Mix cilantro, beans and salsa in; heat through. Mix avocado in gently; cook for a minute more.
- Use fork to separate strands when squash is cool to touch. Top squash with salsa mixture; serve.

Nutrition Information

- Calories: 308 calories
- Protein: 8g protein.
- Total Fat: 9g fat (2g saturated fat)
- Sodium: 822mg sodium
- Fiber: 16g fiber)
- Total Carbohydrate: 46g carbohydrate (6g sugars
- Cholesterol: 0 cholesterol

728. Salsa Verde Chicken Casserole

Serving: 6 servings. | Prep: 10mins | Cook: 20mins | Ready in:

Ingredients

- 2 cups shredded rotisserie chicken
- 1 cup (8 ounces) sour cream
- 1-1/2 cups salsa verde, divided
- 8 corn tortillas (6 inches)
- 2 cups chopped tomatoes
- 1/4 cup minced fresh cilantro
- 2 cups shredded Monterey Jack cheese
- Optional toppings: avocado slices, thinly sliced green onions or fresh cilantro leaves

Direction

- In a small bowl, mix 3/4 cup salsa, sour cream and chicken. On the bottom of an 8-in. greased square baking dish, spread 1/4 cup salsa.
- Layer 1/2 chicken mixture and tortillas. Sprinkle half of the cheese, minced cilantro, and half of the tomatoes. Repeat the layers with leftover cheese, tomatoes, chicken mixture and tortillas.
- Bake for 20-25 minutes till bubbly at 400°, uncovered. Serve with leftover salsa. If you want, put optional toppings.

Nutrition Information

- Calories: 400 calories
- Total Carbohydrate: 22g carbohydrate (5g sugars
- Cholesterol: 102mg cholesterol
- Protein: 26g protein.
- Total Fat: 23g fat (13g saturated fat)
- Sodium: 637mg sodium
- Fiber: 3g fiber)

729. San Jose Tortilla Pie

Serving: 10-12 servings. | Prep: 25mins | Cook: 25mins | Ready in:

Ingredients

- 6 corn tortillas (6 inches)
- Oil for deep-fat frying
- Salt
- 1 pound ground beef
- 1 large onion, chopped
- 1 medium green pepper, chopped
- 1 garlic clove, minced
- 1 tablespoon chili powder
- 1 teaspoon dried oregano
- 1 teaspoon ground cumin
- 2 cups shredded cheddar cheese
- 1 to 2 cans (4 ounces each) chopped green chilies
- 6 large eggs
- 1-1/2 cups whole milk
- 1/2 teaspoon salt
- Sliced ripe olives, optional

Direction

- Cut each tortilla into 8 wedges, sauté in hot oil, few at a time, until crisp. Pat with paper towels to remove excess fat and sprinkle with salt.
- Combine garlic, green pepper, onion and beef in a large skillet, cook over medium heat until vegetables are softened and meat loses its pink color; drain. Stir in cumin, oregano and chili powder.
- Arrange half of tortilla wedges, meat mixture and cheese in layers in a greased 13x9 inch baking dish, evenly place chili on top. Place remaining meat and cheese on top. Arrange remaining tortilla around edge of dish point side up.
- Beat salt, milk and eggs in a small bowl. Evenly distribute on top. Bake when uncover at 375° for 25 to 30 minutes. Place olives on top to garnish if desired.

Nutrition Information

- Calories:
- Total Carbohydrate:
- Cholesterol:
- Protein:
- Total Fat:
- Sodium:
- Fiber:

730. Slow Cooked Stuffed Peppers

Serving: 4 servings. | Prep: 15mins | Cook: 03hours00mins | Ready in:

Ingredients

- 4 medium sweet red peppers
- 1 can (15 ounces) black beans, rinsed and drained
- 1 cup shredded pepper jack cheese
- 3/4 cup salsa
- 1 small onion, chopped
- 1/2 cup frozen corn
- 1/3 cup uncooked converted long grain rice
- 1-1/4 teaspoons chili powder
- 1/2 teaspoon ground cumin
- Reduced-fat sour cream, optional

Direction

- Chop and get rid tops of peppers; squeeze out seeds. Whisk cumin, chili powder, rice, corn, onion, salsa, cheese and beans; scoop into peppers. Add into one 5-qt. slow cooker that coated using cooking spray.
- Cook, while covered, on low till filling becomes thoroughly heated and peppers become soft or for 3 to 4 hours. If you want, serve alongside sour cream.

Nutrition Information

- Calories: 317 calories

- Cholesterol: 30mg cholesterol
- Protein: 15g protein. Diabetic Exchanges: 2 starch
- Total Fat: 10g fat (5g saturated fat)
- Sodium: 565mg sodium
- Fiber: 8g fiber)
- Total Carbohydrate: 43g carbohydrate (6g sugars

731.   Sour Cream Beef 'N' Beans

Serving: 4-6 servings. | Prep: 15mins | Cook: 0mins | Ready in:

Ingredients

- 1 pound ground beef
- 1 can (15 ounces) pinto beans, rinsed and drained
- 1 can (15 ounces) enchilada sauce
- 1-1/2 cups shredded cheddar cheese, divided
- 1 can (4 ounces) chopped green chilies, undrained
- 1-1/2 cups crushed corn chips
- 1 tablespoon dried minced onion
- 1 cup (8 ounces) sour cream
- Additional corn chips

Direction

- Crumble beef into an ungreased 2-qt. microwave-safe dish; use waxed paper to cover up. Cook on high till meat is not pink anymore or for 3 to 4 minutes, mixing two times; drain. Mix in onion, crushed corn chips, chilies, one cup cheese, enchilada sauce and beans. Keep it covered and microwave on high till thoroughly heated or for 2 to 2-1/2 min., mixing one time.
- Add the rest of the cheese and sour cream on top. Heat, while uncovered, at 70% power till cheese becomes melted or for 1 to 2 minutes. Serve along with corn chips.

Nutrition Information

- Calories: 523 calories
- Fiber: 6g fiber)
- Total Carbohydrate: 41g carbohydrate (5g sugars
- Cholesterol: 105mg cholesterol
- Protein: 29g protein.
- Total Fat: 27g fat (14g saturated fat)
- Sodium: 745mg sodium

732.   Sour Cream Chili Bake

Serving: 8-10 servings. | Prep: 15mins | Cook: 35mins | Ready in:

Ingredients

- 1 can (15 ounces) pinto beans, rinsed and drained
- 1 pound ground beef
- 1 can (16 ounces) hot chili beans, undrained
- 1 can (10 ounces) enchilada sauce
- 1 can (8 ounces) tomato sauce
- 1 teaspoon chili powder
- 1-1/2 cups shredded cheddar cheese
- 1 tablespoon dried minced onion
- 2 cups corn chips, crushed, divided
- 1 cup sour cream

Direction

- Brown ground beef in a skillet; drain. Mix in 1 cup of corn chips, onion, and 1 cup of cheese, chili powder, tomato sauce, enchilada sauce and beans. Add to one 2-qt. casserole dish. Keep it covered and baked at 375 degrees for half an hour. Take out of the oven and scoop sour cream on top of casserole. Drizzle with one cup of corn chips and the leftover half of cup cheese. Bring back to the oven and bake, while uncovered, till cheese becomes melted or for 2 - 3 minutes.

Nutrition Information

- Calories:
- Total Carbohydrate:
- Cholesterol:
- Protein:
- Total Fat:
- Sodium:
- Fiber:

| 733. | **Southwest Casserole** |

Serving: 8 servings. | Prep: 25mins | Cook: 45mins | Ready in:

Ingredients

- 1 cup uncooked brown rice
- 1/3 cup uncooked wild rice
- 2-3/4 cups vegetable broth
- 4 cans (14-1/2 ounces each) diced tomatoes, drained
- 1 can (15 ounces) black beans, rinsed and drained
- 1-1/2 cups frozen corn, thawed
- 1 medium sweet red pepper, finely chopped
- 1 medium onion, finely chopped
- 6 green onions, chopped
- 1 jalapeno pepper, seeded and chopped
- 2 garlic cloves, minced
- 2 teaspoons ground cumin
- 1/4 teaspoon cayenne pepper
- 1/4 teaspoon pepper
- 1/2 cup shredded reduced-fat Mexican cheese blend

Direction

- Boil broth, wild rice and brown rice in a big saucepan. Lower the heat; keep it covered and simmered for 50 to 60 minutes or till liquid is absorbed and rice becomes softened.
- Mix pepper, cayenne, cumin, garlic, jalapeno, green onions, onion, red pepper, corn, beans and tomatoes. Mix in rice.

- Move into one 13 x 9-in. baking dish that coated using cooking spray. Keep it covered and baked at 325 degrees for 40 minutes. Uncover it; drizzle with cheese. Bake for 5 to 10 minutes more or till thoroughly heated and cheese becomes melted.

Nutrition Information

- Calories: 268 calories
- Total Carbohydrate: 53g carbohydrate (10g sugars
- Cholesterol: 5mg cholesterol
- Protein: 11g protein.
- Total Fat: 3g fat (1g saturated fat)
- Sodium: 741mg sodium
- Fiber: 8g fiber)

| 734. | **Southwest Chicken And Rice** |

Serving: 4 servings. | Prep: 5mins | Cook: 5mins | Ready in:

Ingredients

- 2 packages (8-1/2 ounces each) ready-to-serve Santa Fe whole grain rice medley
- 2 packages (6 ounces each) ready-to-use Southwestern chicken strips, cut into chunks
- 1 can (10 ounces) diced tomatoes and green chilies, drained
- 1/2 cup shredded Monterey Jack cheese

Direction

- Heat rice following package directions. Combine tomatoes and chicken in a 2 qt microwave-safe dish. Add in rice. Microwave, covered, for 2 to 3 minutes on high. Add cheese and cook for another 1 minute or until cheese is fully melted.

Nutrition Information

- Calories: 340 calories
- Total Fat: 10g fat (4g saturated fat)
- Sodium: 1292mg sodium
- Fiber: 4g fiber)
- Total Carbohydrate: 35g carbohydrate (1g sugars
- Cholesterol: 68mg cholesterol
- Protein: 28g protein.

- Calories: 315 calories
- Sodium: 775mg sodium
- Fiber: 9g fiber)
- Total Carbohydrate: 62g carbohydrate (13g sugars
- Cholesterol: 1mg cholesterol
- Protein: 11g protein.
- Total Fat: 4g fat (1g saturated fat)

735. Southwest Corn Bread Bake

Serving: 4 servings. | Prep: 10mins | Cook: 20mins | Ready in:

Ingredients

- 1 can (16 ounces) chili beans, undrained
- 1 can (8-3/4 ounces) whole kernel corn, drained
- 2 tablespoons chopped onion
- 1/2 teaspoon ground cumin
- 1/2 cup all-purpose flour
- 1/2 cup cornmeal
- 2 tablespoons sugar
- 1-1/4 teaspoons baking powder
- 1/4 teaspoon salt
- 1/2 cup plus 1 tablespoon milk
- 1-1/2 teaspoons canola oil

Direction

- Mix cumin, onion, corn and chili beans in a big bowl. Move into one 8-in. square baking dish that coated using cooking spray.
- In a separate bowl, mix dry ingredients. Whisk oil and milk; mix into dry ingredients just till moistened.
- Drop by tablespoonfuls on top of chili mixture; gently spread on the top. Bake, while uncovered, at 350 degrees till becoming golden brown in color or for 20 to 25 minutes.

Nutrition Information

736. Southwest Enchilada Bake

Serving: 2 casseroles (8 servings each). | Prep: 30mins | Cook: 20mins | Ready in:

Ingredients

- 30 corn tortillas (6 inches)
- 3 pounds lean ground beef (90% lean)
- 2 large onions, chopped
- 1 jalapeno pepper, seeded and chopped
- 4 garlic cloves, minced
- 2 cans (15 ounces each) black-eyed peas, rinsed and drained
- 2 cans (10-3/4 ounces each) condensed cream of chicken soup, undiluted
- 2 cans (10-3/4 ounces each) condensed cream of mushroom soup, undiluted
- 2 cans (10 ounces each) diced tomatoes and green chilies, undrained
- 2 cans (10 ounces each) enchilada sauce
- 1/2 teaspoon hot pepper sauce
- 4 cups shredded sharp cheddar cheese

Direction

- Slice each tortilla into eight pieces; set aside. Cook jalapeno, onions and beef in a Dutch oven over medium heat until the pink color disappears from meat. Add garlic and cook for another 1 minute. Drain. Stir in pepper sauce, enchilada sauce, tomatoes, soups and black-eyed- peas; heat through.
- Coat 2 13x9 inch baking dishes with grease, in each baking dish, spread 2-2/3 cup meat

mixture. Top with 2 cups cut tortillas and repeat layering with remaining ingredients. Place remaining meat mixture on top; add cheese dusting.

- Freeze one casserole, covered, for up to 3 months. Bake the other casserole, covered, at 350° for 20 to 25 minutes or until cheese is completely melted and bubble appears. Allow to stand for 10 minutes prior to cutting.
- How to use frozen casserole: Defrost overnight in the refrigerator. 30 minutes before baking, remove from refrigerator. Bake, covered, 350° for 55 minutes. Uncover and bake for an additional 10-15 minutes or until cheese is completely melted. Allow to stand for 10 minutes. Cut and serve.

Nutrition Information

- Calories: 468 calories
- Sodium: 1284mg sodium
- Fiber: 6g fiber)
- Total Carbohydrate: 42g carbohydrate (3g sugars
- Cholesterol: 88mg cholesterol
- Protein: 30g protein.
- Total Fat: 21g fat (10g saturated fat)

```
737.      Southwest Turkey
                Casserole
```

Serving: 2 servings. | Prep: 20mins | Cook: 20mins | Ready in:

Ingredients

- 1/2 cup uncooked elbow macaroni
- 1/4 cup chopped onion
- 1/4 cup chopped sweet red pepper
- 4-1/2 teaspoons butter
- 1 tablespoon canola oil
- 1 tablespoon all-purpose flour
- 1/2 teaspoon salt
- 1/2 teaspoon ground cumin

- Dash pepper
- 1 cup 2% milk
- 1 cup shredded cheddar cheese
- 1 cup cubed cooked turkey
- 2/3 cup canned diced tomatoes and green chilies
- 1/3 cup frozen corn
- 1/3 cup frozen peas

Direction

- Based on the instruction on the package, cook the macaroni. At the same time, sauté red pepper and onion in oil and butter in a big skillet till becoming softened. Mix in pepper, cumin, salt and flour till becoming blended; slowly pour in milk. Boil; cook and stir till becoming thick or for 1 to 2 minutes. Mix in cheese till melted.
- Drain macaroni; move to cheese mixture. Mix in peas, corn, tomatoes, and turkey. Move to a 1-qt. baking dish that coated using cooking spray. Bake, while uncovered, at 350 degrees till becoming bubbly or for 20 to 25 minutes.

Nutrition Information

- Calories: 611 calories
- Sodium: 1489mg sodium
- Fiber: 5g fiber)
- Total Carbohydrate: 43g carbohydrate (17g sugars
- Cholesterol: 131mg cholesterol
- Protein: 52g protein.
- Total Fat: 28g fat (13g saturated fat)

```
738.      Southwestern Rice Bake
```

Serving: 4 servings. | Prep: 15mins | Cook: 20mins | Ready in:

Ingredients

- 3 cups cooked brown or white rice
- 1/2 pound ground beef, cooked and drained

- 1-1/4 cups sour cream
- 1 cup shredded Monterey Jack cheese, divided
- 1 cup shredded cheddar cheese, divided
- 1 can (4 ounces) chopped green chilies
- 1/2 teaspoon salt
- 1/4 teaspoon pepper
- Sliced ripe olives, chopped tomatoes and green onions, optional

Direction

- Mix pepper, salt, chilies, three quarters cup of cheddar cheese, three quarters cup of Monterey Jack cheese, sour cream, beef and rice in a big bowl.
- Scoop into one greased 1-1/2-qt. baking dish. Drizzle with the rest of the cheeses. Bake, while uncovered, at 350 degrees till thoroughly heated or for 20 to 25 minutes. If you want, serve along with onions, tomatoes and olives.

Nutrition Information

- Calories: 612 calories
- Sodium: 811mg sodium
- Fiber: 3g fiber)
- Total Carbohydrate: 39g carbohydrate (3g sugars
- Cholesterol: 133mg cholesterol
- Protein: 29g protein.
- Total Fat: 36g fat (23g saturated fat)

---

739. Southwestern Rice Casserole

Serving: 8 servings. | Prep: 25mins | Cook: 30mins | Ready in:

Ingredients

- 1-2/3 cups uncooked long grain rice
- 3-1/3 cups water
- 1 large onion, chopped

- 1 small green pepper, chopped
- 1 teaspoon olive oil
- 3 garlic cloves, minced
- 1 can (15 ounces) garbanzo beans or chickpeas, rinsed and drained
- 1 can (2-1/4 ounces) sliced ripe olives, drained
- 2 cups shredded reduced-fat cheddar cheese, divided
- 1 cup reduced-fat ricotta cheese
- 1/4 cup reduced-fat sour cream
- 1-1/2 teaspoons chili powder
- 1 cup salsa

Direction

- Boil water and rice in a big saucepan. Lower the heat; keep it covered and simmers for 15 to 18 minutes or till water is absorbed and rice is softened.
- Sauté green pepper and onion in oil in a big nonstick saucepan till becoming soft. Put in garlic; cook 60 seconds more. Take out of the heat; mix in rice, olives, and beans. Mix chili powder, sour cream, ricotta cheese, and one and a half cups of cheddar cheese in a small-sized bowl.
- Scoop 1/2 of the rice mixture into one 13x9-in. baking dish that coated using cooking spray; layer with 1/2 of the cheese mixture and salsa. Repeat the layers.
- Bake, while uncovered, at 350 degrees for 25 minutes. Drizzle with the rest of cheddar cheese. Bake till thoroughly heated and cheese becomes melted or for 3 to 5 more minutes.

Nutrition Information

- Calories: 348 calories
- Sodium: 506mg sodium
- Fiber: 5g fiber)
- Total Carbohydrate: 46g carbohydrate (7g sugars
- Cholesterol: 30mg cholesterol
- Protein: 15g protein.
- Total Fat: 11g fat (6g saturated fat)

740. Southwestern Turkey Bake

Serving: 12 servings. | Prep: 20mins | Cook: 25mins | Ready in:

Ingredients

- 2 large onions, chopped
- 2 jalapeno peppers, seeded and chopped
- 2 tablespoons butter
- 6 cups cubed cooked turkey
- 2 cans (10-3/4 ounces each) condensed cream of chicken soup, undiluted
- 2 cups (16 ounces) sour cream
- 1 package (10 ounces) frozen chopped spinach, thawed and squeezed dry
- 2 cups shredded Monterey Jack cheese
- 1 package (12-1/2 ounces) nacho tortilla chips, crushed
- 4 green onions, sliced

Direction

- Preheat oven to 350 degrees. Sauté jalapenos and onions in a Dutch oven till becoming soft. Mix in spinach, sour cream, soup and turkey. In one greased 13x9-in. baking dish, layer 1/2 of the turkey mixture, cheese and tortilla chips. Repeat the layers.
- Bake, while uncovered, till becoming bubbly or for 25 to 30 minutes. Allow to rest for 5 minutes prior to serving. Drizzle with green onions.

Nutrition Information

- Calories: 500 calories
- Total Carbohydrate: 28g carbohydrate (5g sugars
- Cholesterol: 106mg cholesterol
- Protein: 31g protein.
- Total Fat: 28g fat (13g saturated fat)
- Sodium: 756mg sodium
- Fiber: 3g fiber)

741. Southwestern Turkey Casserole

Serving: 8 | Prep: | Cook: |Ready in:

Ingredients

- 1 (10.75 ounce) can condensed cream of chicken soup
- 1 (10.75 ounce) can condensed cream of mushroom soup
- 1 (7 ounce) can diced green chile peppers, drained
- 1 cup sour cream
- 16 (6 inch) corn tortillas, cut into strips
- 10 ounces cooked turkey, diced
- 8 ounces shredded Cheddar cheese

Direction

- Set the oven to 350°F (175°C) and start preheating.
- Combine sour cream, chile peppers, mushroom soup and chicken soup in a mixing bowl.
- Line corn tortillas on the bottom of a 9x13 inch baking pan. Then arrange turkey in layer. Add soup mixture to turkey and dust 1/2 of the cheese. Continue layering with remaining ingredients and finish with cheddar cheese on top. Bake in preheated oven for 30 to 45 minutes or until cheese is brown in color and bubbly.

Nutrition Information

- Calories: 434 calories;
- Total Carbohydrate: 31.3
- Cholesterol: 74
- Protein: 22.5
- Total Fat: 24.8
- Sodium: 1022

742. Southwestern Veggie Bake

Serving: 8 servings. | Prep: 20mins | Cook: 20mins | Ready in:

Ingredients

- 3 medium carrots, sliced
- 2 celery ribs, chopped
- 1 small onion, chopped
- 2 to 3 teaspoons chili powder
- 1 teaspoon ground cumin
- 1/4 teaspoon cayenne pepper
- 2 tablespoons butter
- 3 tablespoons all-purpose flour
- 1/2 cup milk
- 1 can (16 ounces) kidney beans, rinsed and drained
- 1 can (15 ounces) black beans, rinsed and drained
- 1 can (15-1/4 ounces) whole kernel corn, drained
- 1 can (14-1/2 ounces) diced tomatoes, undrained
- 1 can (4 ounces) chopped green chilies
- 1 tube (11-1/2 ounces) refrigerated cornbread twists

Direction

- Preheat oven to 350 degrees. Sauté seasonings, onion, celery and carrots in butter in a big skillet till veggies become tender-crisp. Mix in flour till blended. Slowly pour in milk. Boil; cook and stir till becoming thick and bubbly or for 2 minutes.
- Take out of the heat; put in chilies, tomatoes, corn and beans. Scoop into one ungreased 13x9-in. baking dish. Divide cornbread twists; weave a lattice crust on top of filling.
- Bake, while uncovered, 20 to 25 minutes or till corn bread becomes golden brown.

Nutrition Information

- Calories: 345 calories
- Cholesterol: 10mg cholesterol
- Protein: 12g protein.
- Total Fat: 10g fat (4g saturated fat)
- Sodium: 849mg sodium
- Fiber: 8g fiber)
- Total Carbohydrate: 50g carbohydrate (12g sugars

743. Spanish Corn With Fish Sticks

Serving: 8-10 servings. | Prep: 20mins | Cook: 40mins | Ready in:

Ingredients

- 1/4 cup chopped onion
- 1/4 cup chopped green pepper
- 1/4 cup butter, cubed
- 1/4 cup all-purpose flour
- 1-1/2 teaspoons salt
- 1/4 teaspoon pepper
- 2 teaspoons sugar
- 2 cans (14-1/2 ounces each) stewed tomatoes
- 2 packages (10 ounces each) frozen corn, partially thawed
- 2 packages (12 ounces each) frozen fish sticks

Direction

- Heat butter in a large skillet, add green pepper and onion and sauté until softened. Stir in sugar, pepper, salt and flour until well combined. Add tomatoes and bring to a boil. Cook for 2 minutes or until mixture is thickened, remember to stir while cooking. Lower the heat to simmer, uncovered, for 3 to 5 minutes or until heated through, remember to stir occasionally while cooking. Stir in corn.
- Move mixture to 2 greased 11x7 inch baking dishes. Bake, covered, for 25 minutes at 350°. Uncover, place fish sticks on top. Bake for another 15 minutes or until fish sticks are heated through.

Nutrition Information

- Calories: 176 calories
- Protein: 5g protein.
- Total Fat: 9g fat (4g saturated fat)
- Sodium: 620mg sodium
- Fiber: 2g fiber)
- Total Carbohydrate: 20g carbohydrate (5g sugars
- Cholesterol: 20mg cholesterol

744.   Spanish Rice Turkey Casserole

Serving: 8 servings. | Prep: 30mins | Cook: 20mins | Ready in:

Ingredients

- 2 packages (6.8 ounces each) Spanish rice and pasta mix
- 1/4 cup butter, cubed
- 4 cups water
- 1 can (14-1/2 ounces) diced tomatoes, undrained
- 1 can (10 ounces) diced tomatoes and green chilies, undrained
- 3 cups cubed cooked turkey or chicken
- 1 can (11 ounces) whole kernel corn, drained
- 1/2 cup sour cream
- 1 cup shredded Mexican cheese blend, divided

Direction

- Put butter in a big frying pan, sauté vermicelli and rice until golden brown. Slowly mix in rice seasoning packets, tomatoes, and water. Heat to a boil. Cover, decrease heat, and simmer until rice is tender, 15-20 minutes.
- In the meantime, mix 1/2 cup cheese, corn, turkey, and sour cream in a big bowl. Mix in rice mixture.

- Move to a 3-qt. greased dish. Sprinkle on rest of cheese; the dish should be full. Do not cover; bake in a 375-degree oven until cooked through, 20-25 minutes.

Nutrition Information

- Calories: 348 calories
- Cholesterol: 78mg cholesterol
- Protein: 22g protein.
- Total Fat: 16g fat (9g saturated fat)
- Sodium: 937mg sodium
- Fiber: 3g fiber)
- Total Carbohydrate: 26g carbohydrate (5g sugars

745.   Spanish Rice And Chicken

Serving: 4-6 servings. | Prep: 20mins | Cook: 01hours05mins | Ready in:

Ingredients

- 1 broiler/fryer chicken (3 pounds), cut up
- 1 teaspoon garlic salt
- 1 teaspoon celery salt
- 1 teaspoon paprika
- 1 cup uncooked rice
- 3/4 cup chopped onion
- 3/4 cup chopped green pepper
- 1/4 cup minced fresh parsley
- 1-1/2 cups chicken broth
- 1 cup chopped tomatoes
- 1-1/2 teaspoons chili powder
- 1 teaspoon salt

Direction

- Add chicken into one greased 13x 9-in. baking pan. Mix paprika, celery salt and garlic salt; drizzle on top of chicken. Bake, while uncovered, at 425 degrees for 20 minutes.

- Take the chicken out of the pan. Mix parsley, green pepper, onion and rice; scoop into the pan. Boil salt, chili powder, tomatoes and broth in a saucepan. Add on top of the rice mixture; stir them well. Add chicken pieces over top. Keep it covered and baked for 45 minutes or till chicken and rice becomes tender.

Nutrition Information

- Calories:
- Cholesterol:
- Protein:
- Total Fat:
- Sodium:
- Fiber:
- Total Carbohydrate:

---

746.   Speedy Taco Feast

Serving: 8 servings. | Prep: 15mins | Cook: 40mins | Ready in:

Ingredients

- 2 pounds ground beef
- 2 envelopes taco seasoning
- 1-1/2 cups water
- 1 jar (16 ounces) salsa
- 1 can (8-3/4 ounces) whole kernel corn, drained
- 2 cups shredded Mexican cheese blend
- 2 packages (8-1/2 ounces each) cornbread/muffin mix
- Sour cream, optional

Direction

- Cook beef on medium heat in a big skillet till not pink anymore; drain. Put in corn, salsa, water and taco seasoning; cook and stir for roughly 15 minutes or till heated through. Move to one greased 13x9-in. baking dish. Drizzle with cheese.

- Based on the instruction on package, prepare cornbread mix. Scoop batter equally on top of cheese.
- Bake, while uncovered, at 350 degrees till a toothpick inserted in the middle of corn bread comes out clean or for 40 to 45 minutes. Serve alongside sour cream if you want.

Nutrition Information

- Calories:
- Sodium:
- Fiber:
- Total Carbohydrate:
- Cholesterol:
- Protein:
- Total Fat:

---

747.   Sweet Potato Chili Bake

Serving: 7 servings. | Prep: 30mins | Cook: 20mins | Ready in:

Ingredients

- 2 cups cubed peeled sweet potato
- 1 medium sweet red pepper, chopped
- 1 tablespoon olive oil
- 1 garlic clove, minced
- 1 can (28 ounces) diced tomatoes, undrained
- 2 cups vegetable broth
- 1 can (15 ounces) black beans, rinsed and drained
- 4-1/2 teaspoons brown sugar
- 3 teaspoons chili powder
- 1 teaspoon salt
- 1/2 teaspoon pepper
- 1 package (6-1/2 ounces) corn bread/muffin mix
- 1/2 cup shredded cheddar cheese
- Optional toppings: sour cream, shredded cheddar cheese and chopped seeded jalapeno pepper

Direction

- Sauté red pepper and sweet potato in oil in a Dutch oven till tender-crisp. Put in garlic; cook for 1 minute longer. Put in pepper, salt, chili powder, brown sugar, beans, broth and tomatoes. Boil. Lower the heat; let it simmer, while uncovered, till potatoes become soft or for 15 to 20 minutes.
- At the same time, preheat oven to 400 degrees. Prepare corn bread batter based on instructions on package; mix in cheese. Drop by tablespoonfuls on top of chili.
- Keep it covered and bake for 18 to 20 minutes or till a toothpick inserted in the middle comes out clean. Serve along with toppings that you like.

Nutrition Information

- Calories: 324 calories
- Cholesterol: 54mg cholesterol
- Protein: 10g protein.
- Total Fat: 11g fat (5g saturated fat)
- Sodium: 1204mg sodium
- Fiber: 6g fiber)
- Total Carbohydrate: 47g carbohydrate (16g sugars

748. Sweet Potato Enchilada Stack

Serving: 6 servings. | Prep: 20mins | Cook: 20mins | Ready in:

Ingredients

- 1 large sweet potato, peeled and cut into 1/2-inch cubes
- 1 tablespoon water
- 1 pound ground beef
- 1 medium onion, chopped
- 1 can (15 ounces) black beans, rinsed and drained

- 1 can (10 ounces) enchilada sauce
- 2 teaspoons chili powder
- 1/2 teaspoon dried oregano
- 1/2 teaspoon ground cumin
- 3 flour tortillas (8 inches)
- 2 cups shredded cheddar cheese

Direction

- Mix water and sweet potato in a big microwave-safe bowl. Keep it covered and microwave on high for 4 to 5 minutes or till potato becomes nearly softened.
- At the same time, cook onion and beef on medium heat in a big skillet till meat is not pink anymore; drain. Mix in sweet potato, cumin, oregano, chili powder, enchilada sauce and beans; heat through.
- Put a flour tortilla into one greased 9-in. deep-dish pie dish; layer with 1/3 of the beef mixture and cheese. Repeat the layers two times. Bake at 400 degrees till becoming bubbly or for 20 to 25 minutes.

Nutrition Information

- Calories: 457 calories
- Protein: 29g protein.
- Total Fat: 22g fat (12g saturated fat)
- Sodium: 804mg sodium
- Fiber: 6g fiber)
- Total Carbohydrate: 39g carbohydrate (6g sugars
- Cholesterol: 87mg cholesterol

749. Taco Casserole

Serving: 10 | Prep: 25mins | Cook: 35mins | Ready in:

Ingredients

- 1 pound lean ground beef
- 8 ounces macaroni
- 1/2 cup chopped onion

- 1 (10.75 ounce) can condensed tomato soup
- 1 (14.5 ounce) can diced tomatoes
- 1 (1.25 ounce) package taco seasoning mix
- 2 ounces shredded Cheddar cheese
- 2 ounces shredded Monterey Jack cheese
- 1 cup crushed tortilla chips
- 1/2 cup sour cream (optional)
- 1/4 cup chopped green onions

Direction

- Prepare the oven by preheating to 350°F (175°C).
- Add the pasta in a large pot of boiling water and cook until al dente. Strain. Stir and cook chopped onion and ground beef in a large skillet over medium heat until it turns brown in color. Add in taco seasoning mix, diced tomatoes and tomato soup. Mix in pasta.
- Into a 9x13-inch baking dish, put the beef mixture. Then top with shredded cheese and crumbled taco chips.
- Place in the preheated oven and bake for 30-35 minutes until the cheese is dissolved. Put sour cream and chopped green onions to serve, if wished.

Nutrition Information

- Calories: 334 calories;
- Cholesterol: 50
- Protein: 15.6
- Total Fat: 17
- Sodium: 635
- Total Carbohydrate: 28.2

750. Taco Casseroles

Serving: 3 casseroles (8 servings each). | Prep: 25mins | Cook: 30mins | Ready in:

Ingredients

- 3 pounds ground beef

- 3 cans (16 ounces each) chili beans, undrained
- 3 cans (8 ounces each) tomato sauce
- 1/3 cup taco sauce
- 2 tablespoons chili powder
- 1 tablespoon garlic powder
- 6 cups coarsely crushed tortilla chips
- 3 cups (24 ounces) sour cream
- 3 tablespoons all-purpose flour
- 3 cups shredded cheddar cheese
- 3 medium tomatoes, chopped
- 12 green onions, sliced
- Shredded lettuce and additional taco sauce, optional

Direction

- Cook beef in a Dutch oven over medium heat until the pink color disappears from meat; drain. Stir in garlic powder, chili powder, taco sauce, tomato sauce and beans.
- Distribute chips among 3 ungreased 2 qt baking dishes; arrange beef mixture on top. Combine flour and sour cream and spread over beef mixture. Sprinkle with onions, tomatoes and cheese.
- Bake for 30 to 40 minutes at 350° until heated through, remember not to cover the dishes. Serve with additional taco sauce and shredded lettuce if desired.

Nutrition Information

- Calories: 371 calories
- Protein: 21g protein.
- Total Fat: 20g fat (10g saturated fat)
- Sodium: 555mg sodium
- Fiber: 4g fiber)
- Total Carbohydrate: 24g carbohydrate (2g sugars
- Cholesterol: 78mg cholesterol

751.   Taco Cornbread Casserole

Serving: 8 servings. | Prep: 15mins | Cook: 60mins | Ready in:

Ingredients

- 2 pounds ground beef
- 2 envelopes taco seasoning
- 2 cans (14-1/2 ounces each) diced tomatoes, drained
- 1 cup water
- 1 cup cooked rice
- 1 can (4 ounces) chopped green chilies
- 2 packages (8-1/2 ounces each) cornbread/muffin mix
- 1 can (8-3/4 ounces) whole kernel corn, drained
- 1 cup (8 ounces) sour cream
- 2 cups corn chips
- 2 cups shredded Mexican or cheddar cheese, divided
- 1 can (2-1/4 ounces) sliced ripe olives, drained
- Shredded lettuce and chopped tomatoes, optional

Direction

- Preheat oven to 400 degrees. Cook beef in a Dutch oven on medium heat till not pink anymore or for 8 to 10 minutes, crumble into small pieces; drain. Mix in taco seasoning. Put in green chilies, rice, water and tomatoes; heat the mixture through, mixing from time to time.
- At the same time, based on the instructions on the package, prepare the cornbread mix; mix in corn. Add 1/2 of the batter into one greased 13x9-inch baking dish. Layer with 1/2 of the meat mixture, all of the sour cream, 1/2 of the corn chips and one cup of cheese. Add leftover corn chips, olives, leftover meat mixture, and leftover batter.
- Bake, while uncovered, till cornbread becomes thoroughly cooked or for 55 to 60 minutes. Drizzle with leftover cheese; bake till the cheese becomes melted or for 3 to 5 minutes more. Serve alongside chopped tomatoes and lettuce if you want.

Nutrition Information

- Calories: 817 calories
- Total Fat: 40g fat (17g saturated fat)
- Sodium: 1982mg sodium
- Fiber: 4g fiber)
- Total Carbohydrate: 74g carbohydrate (20g sugars
- Cholesterol: 183mg cholesterol
- Protein: 36g protein.

752.   Taco Crescent Bake

Serving: 8 servings. | Prep: 25mins | Cook: 25mins | Ready in:

Ingredients

- 1 tube (8 ounces) refrigerated crescent rolls
- 2 cups crushed corn chips, divided
- 1-1/2 pounds ground beef
- 1 can (15 ounces) tomato sauce
- 1 envelope taco seasoning
- 1 cup (8 ounces) sour cream
- 1 cup shredded cheddar cheese

Direction

- Unroll crescent dough into a rectangle; push onto the bottom and one inch up the sides of a greased 13x9-in. baking dish. Seal seams and perforations. Drizzle using 1 cup chips; put aside.
- Cook beef on medium heat in a big skillet till meat is not pink anymore; drain. Mix in taco seasoning and tomato sauce; boil. Lower the heat; let it simmer, while uncovered, for 5 minutes. Scoop on top of chips. Add leftover chips, cheese and sour cream on top.
- Bake, while uncovered, at 350 degrees till crust turns browned a bit or for 25 to 30 minutes.

Nutrition Information

- Calories:
- Total Carbohydrate:
- Cholesterol:
- Protein:
- Total Fat:
- Sodium:
- Fiber:

---

753.   Taco Noodle Bake

Serving: 8 servings. | Prep: 20mins | Cook: 10mins | Ready in:

Ingredients

- 2 cups uncooked wide egg noodles
- 2 pounds ground beef
- 1 can (8 ounces) tomato sauce
- 1/2 cup water
- 1 can (4 ounces) chopped green chilies
- 1 envelope taco seasoning
- 1 teaspoon onion powder
- 1 teaspoon chili powder
- 1/2 teaspoon garlic powder
- 1 cup shredded cheddar cheese
- 2 cups shredded lettuce
- 1 cup diced fresh tomatoes
- 1/3 cup sliced ripe olives, drained
- 1/2 cup taco sauce
- 1/2 cup sour cream

Direction

- Preheat oven to 350 degrees. Cook noodles based on the package directions.
- At the same time, cook beef on medium heat in a big skillet till not pink anymore; drain. Mix in garlic powder, chili powder, onion powder, taco seasoning, green chilies, and water and tomato sauce. Boil. Lower the heat; let simmer, while uncovered, for 5 minutes.

- Drain noodles; add into one greased 11x7-inch baking dish. Spread with beef mixture; drizzle with cheese. Bake, while uncovered, till cheese becomes melted or for 10 to 15 minutes. Allow to rest for 10 minutes.
- Add taco sauce, olives, tomatoes and lettuce on top. Use sour cream to decorate.

Nutrition Information

- Calories: 402 calories
- Protein: 30g protein.
- Total Fat: 23g fat (11g saturated fat)
- Sodium: 906mg sodium
- Fiber: 2g fiber)
- Total Carbohydrate: 17g carbohydrate (3g sugars
- Cholesterol: 119mg cholesterol

---

754.   Taco Noodle Dish

Serving: 6 servings. | Prep: 20mins | Cook: 10mins | Ready in:

Ingredients

- 3 cups uncooked wide egg noodles
- 2 pounds lean ground turkey
- 1 envelope reduced-sodium taco seasoning
- 1 teaspoon onion powder
- 1 teaspoon chili powder
- 1/2 teaspoon garlic powder
- 1 can (8 ounces) tomato sauce
- 1 can (4 ounces) chopped green chilies
- 1/2 cup water
- 1 cup shredded cheddar cheese
- TOPPINGS:
- 2 cups shredded lettuce
- 2 medium tomatoes, chopped
- 1/3 cup sliced ripe olives
- 1/2 cup taco sauce
- 1/2 cup fat-free sour cream

Direction

- Preheat oven to 350 degrees. Based on the instruction on the package, cook noodles for al dente; drain.
- At the same time, cook and crumble turkey on medium high heat in a big nonstick skillet till meat is not pink anymore, 6 to 8 minutes; drain. Mix in water, chilies, tomato sauce and seasonings; boil. Lower the heat; let it simmer, while uncovered, for 5 minutes.
- Spread noodles in one 11x7-in. baking dish that coated using cooking spray. Add turkey mixture on top; drizzle with cheese. Bake, while uncovered, for 10 to 15 minutes or till cheese becomes melted.
- Add taco sauce, olives, tomatoes and lettuce over casserole. Serve along with sour cream.

Nutrition Information

- Calories: 455 calories
- Sodium: 954mg sodium
- Fiber: 3g fiber)
- Total Carbohydrate: 27g carbohydrate (7g sugars
- Cholesterol: 140mg cholesterol
- Protein: 40g protein.
- Total Fat: 20g fat (7g saturated fat)

755.   Taco Ramekins

Serving: 2 servings. | Prep: 15mins | Cook: 20mins | Ready in:

Ingredients

- 1/4 pound lean ground beef (90% lean)
- 1/4 teaspoon chili powder
- 1/8 teaspoon salt
- 1/8 teaspoon pepper
- 3/4 cup biscuit/baking mix
- 3 tablespoons cold water
- 1 medium tomato, sliced
- 1/4 cup chopped green pepper
- 2 tablespoons sour cream

- 2 tablespoons mayonnaise
- 2 tablespoons shredded cheddar cheese
- 1 tablespoon chopped onion

Direction

- Cook beef on medium heat in a skillet till meat is not pink anymore; drain. Mix in pepper, salt, and chili powder. Take out of the heat and put aside.
- Mix water and biscuit mix to form soft dough. Push onto the bottom and up the sides of two 10-oz. ramekins or custard cups that coated using cooking spray. Fill with meat mixture; add green pepper, and tomato on top. Mix onion, cheese, mayonnaise and sour cream; spread equally on the tops.
- Bake, while uncovered, at 375 degrees till thoroughly heated or for 20 to 25 minutes.

Nutrition Information

- Calories: 369 calories
- Fiber: 2g fiber)
- Total Carbohydrate: 40g carbohydrate (7g sugars
- Cholesterol: 43mg cholesterol
- Protein: 18g protein.
- Total Fat: 15g fat (5g saturated fat)
- Sodium: 892mg sodium

756.   Taco Twist Bake

Serving: 4 servings. | Prep: 10mins | Cook: 30mins | Ready in:

Ingredients

- 2-1/2 cups cooked Taco-Seasoned Meat
- 2 cans (8 ounces each) tomato sauce
- 1/4 cup chopped green pepper
- 1 package (8 ounces) spiral pasta, cooked and drained
- 1 cup sour cream

- 1 cup shredded cheddar cheese, divided

Direction

- Mix green pepper, tomato sauce, and taco meat in a big saucepan; boil. At the same time, mix sour cream and pasta; add into one greased 8-in. square baking dish. Drizzle with half cup of cheese. Add meat mixture on top.
- Bake, while uncovered, at 325 degrees for 25 minutes. Drizzle with leftover cheese. Bake till cheese becomes melted for 5 to 10 minutes more.

Nutrition Information

- Calories: 721 calories
- Protein: 38g protein.
- Total Fat: 35g fat (17g saturated fat)
- Sodium: 1652mg sodium
- Fiber: 5g fiber)
- Total Carbohydrate: 66g carbohydrate (8g sugars
- Cholesterol: 98mg cholesterol

757. Tamale Bake

Serving: 8 servings. | Prep: 10mins | Cook: 40mins | Ready in:

Ingredients

- 1 pound lean ground beef (90% lean)
- 1 jalapeno pepper, seeded and diced
- 2 cups frozen corn, thawed
- 1 can (28 ounces) diced tomatoes, undrained
- 1-1/2 cups fat-free milk
- 1 cup cornmeal
- 1 can (4 ounces) chopped green chilies, drained
- 1 can (2-1/2 ounces) sliced ripe olives, drained
- 2 large egg whites, lightly beaten
- 1 envelope reduced-sodium taco seasoning
- 1 cup shredded reduced-fat cheddar cheese

- 1 cup salsa

Direction

- In a big non-stick skillet over medium heat, cook jalapeno and beef until the meat is not pink anymore then drain. Stir the taco seasoning, egg whites, olives, chillies, cornmeal, milk, tomatoes and corn in until well blended. Coat a 13-inch by 9-inch baking dish with cooking spray then transfer the mixture into it. Bake it without the cover on at 350°F for 40 minutes. Scatter cheese over it and continue baking until the cheese melts, about 5 minutes more. Allow it to stand for 10 minutes. Cut and serve with salsa.

Nutrition Information

- Calories: 298 calories
- Protein: 20g protein. Diabetic Exchanges: 2 starch
- Total Fat: 9g fat (4g saturated fat)
- Sodium: 806mg sodium
- Fiber: 5g fiber)
- Total Carbohydrate: 35g carbohydrate (9g sugars
- Cholesterol: 39mg cholesterol

758. Tamale Casserole

Serving: 6 | Prep: 15mins | Cook: 45mins | Ready in:

Ingredients

- 2 (15 ounce) cans beef tamales
- 2 bunches green onions, chopped
- 8 ounces shredded Cheddar cheese
- 3 cups crushed tortilla chips
- 2 (16 ounce) cans chili without beans
- 1 tablespoon water

Direction

- Preheat oven to 175 degrees C (350 degrees F).

- Unwrap tamales and chop into thick chunks. Add a part of the chopped tamales in the bottom of a 2 quart casserole dish. Then layer the onions, cheese, tortilla chips and chili without beans.
- Repeat the layers till all ingredients are used, topping off with chips and cheese. Then drizzle with the water.
- Bake, while uncovered, at 175 degrees C (350 degrees F) for 40 - 45 minutes.

Nutrition Information

- Calories: 679 calories;
- Sodium: 1544
- Total Carbohydrate: 47.8
- Cholesterol: 93
- Protein: 30.1
- Total Fat: 42.2

---

759.   Tasty Taco Bake

Serving: 4 servings. | Prep: 15mins | Cook: 10mins | Ready in:

Ingredients

- 1-1/2 cups crushed nacho tortilla chips, divided
- 1 can (15 ounces) chili with beans
- 1 can (4 ounces) chopped green chilies
- 1 can (3.8 ounces) sliced ripe olives, drained, divided
- 1/2 cup sour cream
- 1/2 cup shredded cheddar cheese
- 1/2 cup shredded Monterey Jack cheese
- 1 jar (4-1/2 ounces) sliced mushrooms, drained
- 4 green onions, thinly sliced
- 1 cup shredded lettuce

Direction

- In an ungreased 8 inches square baking dish, spread 1 cup tortilla chips. Combine 1/2 cup olives, green chilies and chili in a small bowl; spoon over chips. Add sour cream on top and spread out. Sprinkle with remaining olives and chips, onions, mushrooms and cheeses.
- Bake, uncovered, for 10 to 15 minutes at 375° or until heated through and cheese is fully melted. Arrange lettuce on top.

Nutrition Information

- Calories:
- Total Carbohydrate:
- Cholesterol:
- Protein:
- Total Fat:
- Sodium:
- Fiber:

---

760.   Tex Mex Casserole

Serving: Makes 6 servings. | Prep: 20mins | Cook: | Ready in:

Ingredients

- 1/2 lb. lean ground beef
- 1 can (15 oz.) black beans, rinsed
- 1 Tbsp. chili powder
- 1 tsp. garlic powder
- 3   tomatoes, chopped
- 2 cups water
- 1/2 cup creamy wheat (enriched farina) hot cereal (1-min., 2-1/2-min. or 10-min. cook time), uncooked
- 1/2 cup KRAFT 2% Milk Shredded Cheddar Cheese
- 1 can (4 oz.) chopped green chiles, undrained
- 1   egg
- 1/2 cup coarsely broken baked tortilla chips

Direction

- 1. In a big skillet, brown the meat; drain. Mix in seasonings and beans; spread on the bottom of an 8-in. square baking dish. Add tomatoes on top.
- 2. In a medium-sized saucepan, boil water. Slowly mix in cereal; cook till becoming thick or for 1 - 3 minutes, mixing continuously. Cool for 5 minutes. Mix in egg, chiles, and cheese; spread on top of meat mixture. Add chips on top.
- 3. Bake till thoroughly heated or for 20 - 25 minutes. Decorate as you want.

Nutrition Information

- Calories: 250
- Total Fat: 7 g
- Sodium: 230 mg
- Sugar: 2 g
- Total Carbohydrate: 30 g
- Protein: 18 g
- Saturated Fat: 2.5 g
- Fiber: 7 g
- Cholesterol: 65 mg

761.   Texas Tamale Pie

Serving: 6 servings. | Prep: 10mins | Cook: 15mins | Ready in:

Ingredients

- 1 package (6.8 ounces) Spanish rice and pasta mix
- 1 can (15 ounces) chili with beans
- 1 can (15 ounces) beef tamales, drained and cut into 1-inch pieces
- 1 cup shredded cheddar cheese

Direction

- Based on the instruction on the package to prep rice mix. At the same time, scoop chili into one greased 8-in. square baking dish. Add tamales on top.

- Bake, while uncovered, at 350 degrees for 10 minutes. Add cooked rice on top; drizzle with cheese. Bake till cheese becomes melted or for 5 minutes more.

Nutrition Information

- Calories:
- Protein:
- Total Fat:
- Sodium:
- Fiber:
- Total Carbohydrate:
- Cholesterol:

762.   The Best Derned Southwestern Casserole

Serving: 12 servings. | Prep: 35mins | Cook: 45mins | Ready in:

Ingredients

- 1-1/2 pounds uncooked chorizo or bulk spicy pork sausage
- 1 small onion, chopped
- 1 can (15 ounces) black beans, rinsed and drained
- 1 can (15 ounces) tomato sauce
- 1 can (11 ounces) Mexicorn, drained
- 2 cans (4 ounces each) chopped green chilies
- 1 cup salsa
- 1/4 cup minced fresh cilantro
- 3 teaspoons each ground cumin, chili powder and paprika
- 2 teaspoons garlic powder
- 12 corn tortillas (6 inches)
- 2 large tomatoes, sliced
- 2 cups shredded Monterey Jack or cheddar-Monterey Jack cheese

Direction

- Set the oven to 375° and start preheating. Crumble chorizo into a large skillet; add onion and cook over medium heat until meat is completely cooked; drain. Add seasonings, cilantro, salsa, chilies, corn, tomato sauce and beans; heat through.
- In a greased 13x9 inch baking dish, arrange 6 tortillas in the bottom. Place 3-1/2 cups meat mixture, tomatoes and 1 cup cheese in layers over tortillas. Place remaining tortillas, meat mixture, and cheese on top.
- Bake in preheated oven, covered, for 40 minutes. Uncover and bake for an additional 5 to 10 minutes or until heated through. Allow to stand for 10 minutes before cutting.

Nutrition Information

- Calories: 420 calories
- Protein: 22g protein.
- Total Fat: 24g fat (10g saturated fat)
- Sodium: 1370mg sodium
- Fiber: 5g fiber)
- Total Carbohydrate: 29g carbohydrate (4g sugars
- Cholesterol: 67mg cholesterol

763. Three Bean Chili With Polenta Crust

Serving: 6 servings. | Prep: 30mins | Cook: 30mins | Ready in:

Ingredients

- 1 large onion, chopped
- 1 medium green pepper, chopped
- 2 tablespoons olive oil
- 3 garlic cloves, chopped
- 1 envelope chili seasoning
- 1 tablespoon brown sugar
- 1/4 teaspoon ground allspice
- 1 can (15 ounces) pinto beans, rinsed and drained

- 1 can (15 ounces) black beans, rinsed and drained
- 1 can (15 ounces) cannellini beans, rinsed and drained
- 1 can (14-1/2 ounces) reduced-sodium chicken broth
- 1 can (10 ounces) diced tomatoes and green chilies, undrained
- 1 tube (1 pound) polenta, cut into thin slices
- 1 cup shredded pepper Jack cheese

Direction

- Sauté pepper and onion in oil in a big skillet till becoming soft. Put in allspice, brown sugar, chili seasoning and garlic; cook for 60 seconds longer. Mix in tomatoes, broth and beans. Boil. Lower the heat; let it simmer, while uncovered, for 15 minutes.
- Move to an ungreased 11x7-in. baking dish (dish should be filled up). Position the dish onto a baking sheet. Arrange polenta slices on top; drizzle with cheese.
- Bake, while uncovered, at 375 degrees till becoming bubbly or for 30 to 35 minutes.

Nutrition Information

- Calories: 393 calories
- Protein: 18g protein.
- Total Fat: 12g fat (4g saturated fat)
- Sodium: 1495mg sodium
- Fiber: 11g fiber)
- Total Carbohydrate: 55g carbohydrate (8g sugars
- Cholesterol: 20mg cholesterol

764. Tortilla Bean Pie

Serving: 4 servings. | Prep: 25mins | Cook: 25mins | Ready in:

Ingredients

- 1 medium onion, chopped

- 2 tablespoons canola oil
- 1 garlic clove, minced
- 1 can (15 ounces) pinto beans, rinsed and drained
- 1/4 teaspoon ground cumin
- 1/4 teaspoon chili powder
- 2 tablespoons chili sauce
- 4 flour tortillas (8 inches)
- 1/4 cup salsa
- 1 can (4 ounces) chopped green chilies, drained
- 3/4 cup shredded Monterey Jack cheese
- Shredded lettuce, chopped tomatoes, sour cream and/or additional salsa, optional

Direction

- Cook onion in oil on medium heat in a big skillet till the onion becomes soft. Put in garlic; cook for 60 seconds more. Put in chili powder, cumin and beans. Lower the heat; let it simmer, while uncovered, for 5 minutes, mashing the beans using a wooden spoon. Mix in chili sauce; put aside.
- Wrap tortillas in foil; bake at 350 degrees for 10 minutes. Unwrap; add 1 tortilla into one greased 9-in. deep-dish pie dish. Layer with 1/3 of the bean mixture. Mix chilies and salsa; scoop 1/3 on top of the bean mixture. Drizzle with a quarter cup cheese. Repeat layers two times. Add the leftover tortilla on top.
- Keep it covered and baked at 350 degrees till thoroughly heated or for 15 to 20 minutes. Chop into wedges. Serve alongside sour cream, tomatoes and lettuce and salsa if you want.

Nutrition Information

- Calories: 414 calories
- Total Fat: 17g fat (5g saturated fat)
- Sodium: 805mg sodium
- Fiber: 6g fiber)
- Total Carbohydrate: 50g carbohydrate (6g sugars
- Cholesterol: 19mg cholesterol

- Protein: 15g protein.

765. Tortilla Beef Casserole

Serving: 8-10 servings. | Prep: 30mins | Cook: 25mins | Ready in:

Ingredients

- 2 pounds ground beef
- 1 can (26 ounces) condensed chicken with rice soup, undiluted
- 1 jar (16 ounces) picante sauce
- 6 flour tortillas (8 inches)
- 2 cups shredded Colby/Monterey Jack cheese
- 2 cups shredded Mexican cheese blend
- Sour cream, tomatoes, chopped lettuce, ripe olives, onions and/or additional picante sauce, optional

Direction

- Cook beef on medium heat in a Dutch oven till meat is not pink anymore; drain. Drain broth from soup, saving rice mixture (throw away broth or refrigerate for another use). Mix picante sauce and rice mixture into the beef. Boil. Lower the heat; let it simmer, while uncovered, for 5 minutes.
- Add 4 tortillas on the bottom and up the sides of one greased 13x9-in. baking dish. Spread with 1/2 of the beef mixture. Mix the cheeses; drizzle half on the beef. Add cheese, beef mixture and the rest of the tortillas on top.
- Bake, while uncovered, at 350 degrees for 25 to 30 minutes or till thoroughly heated and cheese becomes melted. Allow to rest for 10 minutes prior to serving. Serve along with picante sauce and/or onions, olives, lettuce, tomatoes and sour cream if desired.

Nutrition Information

- Calories: 453 calories
- Sodium: 1252mg sodium

- Fiber: 0 fiber)
- Total Carbohydrate: 25g carbohydrate (2g sugars
- Cholesterol: 87mg cholesterol
- Protein: 30g protein.
- Total Fat: 25g fat (14g saturated fat)

- Calories: 277 calories;
- Cholesterol: 117
- Protein: 15.5
- Total Fat: 16.7
- Sodium: 691
- Total Carbohydrate: 17.6

766. Tortilla Casserole

Serving: 12 | Prep: 20mins | Cook: 1hours | Ready in:

Ingredients

- 12 (6 inch) corn tortillas
- 2/3 cup chopped green onions
- 1 (4 ounce) can sliced black olives, drained
- 2 (4 ounce) cans diced green chile peppers, drained
- 1 (4 ounce) jar diced pimento peppers, drained
- 8 ounces Monterey Jack cheese, shredded
- 8 ounces Cheddar cheese, shredded
- 5 eggs
- 2 cups milk
- 1 (8 ounce) jar salsa

Direction

- Grease a 9-inch by 13-inch baking dish lightly. Place four tortillas at the bottom of dish. Add a third each of the chile peppers, green onions, pimento peppers, olives, Cheddar cheese, and Monterey Jack cheese. Repeat for another two layers using the leftover ingredients.
- Whisk salsa, milk, and eggs together in a big bowl; pour on top of the layers. Use a sheet of plastic wrap to cover the dish; place in the refrigerator overnight.
- Take the dish out of the refrigerator then discard the plastic wrap. Preheat the oven to 175°C or 350°Fahrenheit.
- Bake in the oven for 45-60 mins.

Nutrition Information

767. Turkey Rice Casserole

Serving: 6-8 servings. | Prep: 20mins | Cook: 15mins | Ready in:

Ingredients

- 1 medium onion, chopped
- 1 celery rib, chopped
- 2 tablespoons butter
- 2 cups whole milk
- 1-1/4 cups uncooked instant rice
- 2 cups diced cooked turkey
- 1 can (10-3/4 ounces) condensed cream of mushroom soup, undiluted
- 1 cup seasoned stuffing cubes
- 1 can (4 ounces) chopped green chilies, drained
- 1 cup shredded cheddar cheese, divided

Direction

- In a 2-qt. microwave-safe dish, mix butter, celery and onion. Keep it covered and microwave on high for 1-1/2 to 3 minutes or till butter is melted. Mix in milk. Keep it covered and cook on high till milk is steaming (but not boiling) or for 3 to 5 minutes. Mix in rice. Keep it covered and allow to rest for 2 minutes.
- Put in half cup of cheese, chilies, stuffing cubes, soup and turkey. Keep it covered and microwave on high till thoroughly heated or for 3 to 6 minutes, mixing one time. Drizzle with the rest of the cheese. Keep it covered and allow resting for 5 minutes.

Nutrition Information

- Calories: 294 calories
- Fiber: 2g fiber)
- Total Carbohydrate: 26g carbohydrate (5g sugars
- Cholesterol: 59mg cholesterol
- Protein: 18g protein.
- Total Fat: 13g fat (7g saturated fat)
- Sodium: 586mg sodium

Nutrition Information

- Calories: 662 calories
- Fiber: 12g fiber)
- Total Carbohydrate: 65g carbohydrate (5g sugars
- Cholesterol: 113mg cholesterol
- Protein: 44g protein.
- Total Fat: 24g fat (12g saturated fat)
- Sodium: 1396mg sodium

---

768. Turkey Taco Bake

Serving: 4 servings. | Prep: 15mins | Cook: 20mins | Ready in:

Ingredients

- 2 cups coarsely crushed corn chips
- 1 can (16 ounces) refried beans
- 2 cups shredded Monterey Jack cheese, divided
- 1 cup salsa
- 2 cups shredded cooked turkey
- 1 teaspoon taco seasoning
- 1 green onion, sliced
- 1 medium tomato, chopped

Direction

- Grease a shallow 2-1/2 quart. baking dish and insert the corn chips. In a small saucepan over medium heat, cook and stir the refried beans until thoroughly heated. Move the pan away from the heat then stir salsa and 1 cup of cheese in. Spread the mixture over chips.
- Combine taco seasoning and turkey together in a big bowl then scatter over bean mixture. Place the remainder of the cheese on top and sprinkle with onion.
- Bake without the cover on at 400°F until the cheese is melted, about 20-25 minutes. Finish off by sprinkling with tomato.

---

769. Vegetarian Potato Au Gratin

Serving: 6 servings. | Prep: 15mins | Cook: 50mins | Ready in:

Ingredients

- 3 medium carrots, thinly sliced
- 1 medium green pepper, chopped
- 4 tablespoons butter, divided
- 3 tablespoons all-purpose flour
- 1 teaspoon dried oregano
- 1/2 teaspoon salt
- 2-1/2 cups 2% milk
- 1 can (15 ounces) black beans, rinsed and drained
- 3 cups shredded Swiss cheese, divided
- 4 medium Yukon Gold potatoes, thinly sliced
- 1/2 cup seasoned bread crumbs

Direction

- Preheat oven to 400 degrees. Sauté pepper and carrots in 3 tbsp. of butter in a big saucepan till becoming tender. Mix in salt, oregano, and flour till becoming blended; slowly pour in milk. Boil; cook and stir till becoming thick or for 2 minutes. Mix in 2 cups of cheese and beans till cheese is melted.
- Layer 1/2 of the potatoes and sauce in one greased 13x9-in. baking dish; repeat the layers. Drizzle with leftover cheese. Melt the leftover

butter in the microwave. Mix in bread crumbs. Drizzle on top.

- Keep it covered and baked for 50 to 55 minutes. Allow to rest for 10 minutes prior to serving.

Nutrition Information

- Calories: 557 calories
- Protein: 27g protein.
- Total Fat: 25g fat (16g saturated fat)
- Sodium: 749mg sodium
- Fiber: 7g fiber)
- Total Carbohydrate: 56g carbohydrate (12g sugars
- Cholesterol: 77mg cholesterol

---

770. Vegetarian Tex Mex Peppers

Serving: 4 servings. | Prep: 20mins | Cook: 45mins | Ready in:

Ingredients

- 4 large green peppers
- 2 eggs, beaten
- 2 cups cooked brown rice
- 1 cup frozen vegetarian meat crumbles
- 1 cup canned black beans, rinsed and drained
- 1/2 teaspoon pepper
- 1/4 teaspoon hot pepper sauce
- 1/4 teaspoon ground cardamom, optional
- 1 can (14-1/2 ounces) diced tomatoes, drained
- 1 can (10 ounces) diced tomatoes and green chilies
- 1 can (8 ounces) no-salt-added tomato sauce
- 1/2 cup shredded Colby cheese

Direction

- Preheat oven to 350 degrees. Halve peppers lengthwise and remove seeds. Throw away stems. Cook peppers in boiling water in a

Dutch oven for 3 to 5 minutes. Drain and wash under cold water; put aside.

- Mix pepper sauce, pepper, beans, meat crumbles, rice and eggs, and if you want, cardamom, in a big bowl. Scoop into peppers. Add into one 13x9-in. baking dish that coated using cooking spray.
- Mix tomato sauce, green chilies, tomatoes and diced tomatoes in a small-sized bowl. Scoop on top of peppers. Keep it covered and baked for 40 to 45 minutes or till a thermometer reaches 160 degrees. Drizzle with cheese; bake till cheese becomes melted or for 5 more minutes.

Nutrition Information

- Calories: 364 calories
- Total Fat: 9g fat (4g saturated fat)
- Sodium: 769mg sodium
- Fiber: 11g fiber)
- Total Carbohydrate: 53g carbohydrate (12g sugars
- Cholesterol: 119mg cholesterol
- Protein: 19g protein.

---

771. Western Chili Casserole

Serving: 4 servings. | Prep: 15mins | Cook: 10mins | Ready in:

Ingredients

- 1 pound ground beef
- 1 cup chopped onion
- 1/2 cup chopped celery
- 1 can (15 ounces) chili with beans
- 1-1/2 cups coarsely crushed corn chips, divided
- 3/4 cup shredded cheddar cheese

Direction

- Combine celery, onion and beef in a large skillet, cook over medium heat until the pink color disappears from meat and vegetables are softened; drain. Stir in 1/2 cup corn chips and chilli.

- Move mixture to a greased1-1/2-qt baking dish. Add remaining chips around edge of dish; stuff the center with cheese. Bake when uncover at 350° for 10 minutes until heated through.

Nutrition Information

- Calories:
- Protein:
- Total Fat:
- Sodium:
- Fiber:
- Total Carbohydrate:
- Cholesterol:

772.   Zesty Corn Cakes

Serving: 4 servings. | Prep: 20mins | Cook: 25mins | Ready in:

Ingredients

- 1 pound ground beef
- 1 medium onion, chopped
- 1 small green pepper, chopped
- 1 celery rib, chopped
- 1 can (6 ounces) tomato paste
- 1/3 cup water
- 2 garlic cloves, minced
- 1 teaspoon chili powder
- 1 teaspoon salt
- 1/4 teaspoon pepper
- Cheese Sauce:
- 8 ounces process cheese (Velveeta), cubed
- 2/3 cup evaporated milk
- 1/2 teaspoon chili powder
- Corn Cakes:
- 1 package (8-1/2 ounces) corn bread/muffin mix
- 1/2 cup evaporated milk

- 1/4 cup water
- 1 egg, beaten
- 2 tablespoons butter, melted

Direction

- Cook beef in a skillet on medium heat till not pink anymore; drain. Put in the following 9 ingredients; stir well. Boil. Lower the heat; let simmer, while uncovered till becoming thick or for 2 minutes.
- Mix sauce ingredients in a saucepan. Cook and stir on low heat till cheese is melted.
- Mix corn cake ingredients in a bowl just till moistened. Add a quarter cupfuls of batter onto a hot greased griddle. Flip when bubbles form on the cake top. Cook till the second side turns golden brown.
- Add a corn cake onto four serving dishes. Add a quarter cup of filling on top of each. Repeat layers one time. Serve along with the cheese sauce.

Nutrition Information

- Calories: 834 calories
- Sodium: 2035mg sodium
- Fiber: 5g fiber)
- Total Carbohydrate: 70g carbohydrate (34g sugars
- Cholesterol: 197mg cholesterol
- Protein: 44g protein.
- Total Fat: 42g fat (22g saturated fat)

773.   Zippy Beef Fiesta

Serving: 8 servings. | Prep: 25mins | Cook: 35mins | Ready in:

Ingredients

- 1-1/2 pounds ground beef
- 1 large onion, chopped
- 2 tablespoons all-purpose flour
- 2 tablespoons chili powder

- 1 teaspoon salt
- 1/4 teaspoon ground cumin
- 2 cups water
- 2 cans (8 ounces each) tomato sauce
- 2 tablespoons vinegar
- 12 corn tortillas (6 inches)
- 2 cups shredded process cheese (Velveeta)
- 1 can (2-1/4 ounces) sliced ripe olives, drained

Direction

- Cook onion and beef on medium heat in a skillet till meat is not pink anymore; drain. Mix in seasonings and flour till becoming blended. Pour in vinegar, tomato sauce, and water; cook till thoroughly heated or for 10 minutes. Chop each tortilla into six wedges.
- In a greased 13x9-in. baking dish, layer 1/2 of the tortillas, meat mixture, cheese and olives; repeat the layers. Bake, while uncovered, at 350 degrees till thoroughly heated or for 35 minutes.

Nutrition Information

- Calories: 349 calories
- Sodium: 970mg sodium
- Fiber: 4g fiber)
- Total Carbohydrate: 26g carbohydrate (4g sugars
- Cholesterol: 60mg cholesterol
- Protein: 24g protein.
- Total Fat: 17g fat (8g saturated fat)

774.   Zippy Turkey Tortilla Bake

Serving: 8 | Prep: 10mins | Cook: 25mins | Ready in:

Ingredients

- 1 small onion, finely chopped
- 1/2 teaspoon garlic powder
- 1 teaspoon vegetable oil

- 1 pound lean ground turkey
- 1 tablespoon vinegar
- 2 teaspoons chili powder
- 1 1/2 teaspoons dried oregano
- 1/2 teaspoon ground cumin
- 1/4 teaspoon cayenne pepper
- 1 (15 ounce) can black beans, rinsed and drained
- 1 (16 ounce) jar salsa
- 3/4 cup reduced-sodium chicken broth
- 8 (8 inch) fat-free tortillas
- 1/2 cup shredded reduced-fat Monterey Jack cheese
- 1/3 cup reduced-fat sour cream

Direction

- Sauté garlic powder and onion in oil in a skillet until onion is softened. Add cayenne, cumin, oregano, chili powder, vinegar and turkey; cook over medium heat until pink color no longer remains, remember to stir while cooking. Stir in beans. Remove from the heat. Coat a 2-1/2qt baking dish with nonstick cooking spray. Combine broth and salsa and pour in the prepared baking dish to create a thin layer. Slice tortillas into 1 inch strips then into thirds; place half of them on top of salsa mixture. Arrange half of the turkey mixture and half of remaining salsa mixture on top. Repeat layering with remaining ingredients. Add cheese on top. Bake at 350°F, covered, for 25 minutes or until bubbles appear on top. Serve with sour cream on top.

Nutrition Information

775.   Zucchini Enchiladas

Serving: 4 | Prep: 35mins | Cook: | Ready in:

Ingredients

- 2 tablespoons extra-virgin olive oil

- 1 medium onion, chopped
- 1 poblano pepper, seeded and chopped
- ¼ teaspoon salt
- 12 ounces cooked chicken breast, shredded (about 3 cups)
- 1 cup shredded Mexican-blend cheese, divided
- 1 (15 ounce) can enchilada sauce (1½ cups), divided
- 3 medium zucchini (about 1 pound), trimmed
- ⅓ cup sour cream
- 3 tablespoons reduced-fat milk
- 1 cup shredded romaine lettuce
- ½ cup chopped fresh cilantro

Direction

- Preheat oven to 425 degrees F. IN a big skillet, heat oil on medium high heat. Put in salt, poblano and onion. Cook, mixing often, till the veggies have softened and are starting to brown, roughly 6 minutes. Lower the heat to medium if veggies begin to burn. Move into a big bowl. Put in half cup of enchilada sauce, half cup of cheese and chicken. Combine by mixing; put aside.
- Slice the zucchini in lengthwise into thinner strips (Tip) with a mandolin slicer or vegetable peeler. Throw away any uneven and broken pieces. You should have 48 slices at the end.
- Spread a quarter cup of enchilada sauce on the bottom of a 9x13-in. baking dish. Lay 3 strips of zucchini onto a clean working surface, overlapping the edges by a quarter of an inch or so. Add 2 generous tbsp. of the chicken filling across the center of the zucchini strips. Lightly roll the zucchini strips around the filling and position the seam-side facing downward in the prepped dish. Repeat with the rest of zucchini strips and filling. You should have 16 enchiladas. Add half cup of cheese and the rest three quarters cup of enchilada sauce on top of zucchini rolls.
- Bake for 20-25 minutes or till the sauce becomes bubbly and the cheese becomes melted.
- At the same time, in a small-sized bowl, mix milk and sour cream. Once the enchiladas

have finished baking, add cilantro and lettuce on top. Sprinkle the sour cream mixture on the top.

Nutrition Information

- Calories: 443 calories;
- Fiber: 2
- Cholesterol: 118
- Sugar: 5
- Saturated Fat: 14
- Sodium: 316
- Total Carbohydrate: 12
- Protein: 27
- Total Fat: 32

Chapter 7: Pork Casserole Recipes

***

776.   Apple Ham Bake

Serving: 8 servings. | Prep: 20mins | Cook: 35mins | Ready in:

Ingredients

- 3 medium tart apples, peeled and sliced
- 2 medium sweet potatoes, peeled and thinly sliced
- 3 cups cubed fully cooked ham
- 3 tablespoons brown sugar
- 1/2 teaspoon salt
- 1/4 teaspoon pepper
- 1/4 teaspoon curry powder
- 2 tablespoons cornstarch
- 1/3 cup apple juice
- 1 cup pancake mix

- 1 cup milk
- 2 tablespoons butter, melted
- 1/2 teaspoon ground mustard

Direction

- In a large skillet, mix together curry, pepper, salt, brown sugar, ham, sweet potatoes and apples. Over medium heat, cook until the apples are crisp-tender; drain. Mix apple juice and cornstarch together until smooth; mix into the apple mixture. Bring it to a boil; cook and stir until thickened, about 1-2 minutes.
- Remove to a greased baking dish of 2 quarts. Cover and bake at 375° until the sweet potatoes are tender, about 10 minutes. In the meantime, whisk mustard, butter, milk and pancake mix together in a large bowl; spread over ham mixture.
- Bake without a cover until puffed and golden brown, about 25-30 minutes.

Nutrition Information

- Calories: 264 calories
- Total Carbohydrate: 34g carbohydrate (18g sugars
- Cholesterol: 40mg cholesterol
- Protein: 13g protein.
- Total Fat: 9g fat (4g saturated fat)
- Sodium: 1051mg sodium
- Fiber: 2g fiber)

777. Asparagus Ham Bundles

Serving: 4 servings. | Prep: 20mins | Cook: 25mins | Ready in:

Ingredients

- 3 tablespoons butter
- 3 tablespoons all-purpose flour
- 3/4 teaspoon salt
- 2 cups whole milk
- 1 cup shredded Swiss cheese

- 2 cups cooked rice
- 8 slices fully cooked ham (about 1/8 inch thick)
- 24 fresh asparagus spears, cooked and drained
- 1/4 cup grated Parmesan cheese

Direction

- Heat butter in a saucepan; mix in salt and flour until smooth. Slowly pour in milk, boil it. Cook while stirring until bubbly and thickened. Mix in Swiss cheese until melted.
- Mix together rice and 1 cup of the cheese mixture. Spread approximately 1/4 cup of the mixture on bottom third of each ham slice. Put 3 asparagus spears on top, roll up. Put in an 11x7-inch baking dish coated with cook spray, the seam side facing down. Add the leftover cheese mixture onto the bundles. Sprinkle Parmesan cheese over.
- Bake without a cover at 350° until fully heated, about 25-30 minutes.

Nutrition Information

- Calories: 480 calories
- Cholesterol: 88mg cholesterol
- Protein: 29g protein.
- Total Fat: 24g fat (15g saturated fat)
- Sodium: 1243mg sodium
- Fiber: 2g fiber)
- Total Carbohydrate: 39g carbohydrate (8g sugars

778. Asparagus And Ham Casserole

Serving: 6-8 servings. | Prep: 15mins | Cook: 35mins | Ready in:

Ingredients

- 1 pound fresh asparagus, trimmed, cut into 1-inch pieces

- 2 cups cubed fully cooked ham
- 3 cups cooked rice
- 1 cup finely chopped celery
- 1-1/2 teaspoons lemon-pepper seasoning
- 1 can (10-3/4 ounces) condensed cream of chicken soup, undiluted
- 1 cup chicken broth
- 1 cup shredded cheddar cheese
- 1/2 cup dry bread crumbs
- 1 tablespoon butter, melted

Direction

- In a big saucepan, boil half an inch of the water. Put in the asparagus; keep covered and let it boil till tender-crisp or for 3 minutes; drain well.
- In a greased 2.5-quart baking dish, put in pepper-lemon, celery, rice, ham and asparagus; put aside. In a big saucepan, mix the broth and soup; put in the cheese. Cook and whisk on medium heat till the cheese melts. Add on top of the ham mixture.
- Mix the butter and crumbs; drizzle on the top. Bake, while uncovering, at 350 degrees till thoroughly heated or for 35 minutes.

Nutrition Information

- Calories: 268 calories
- Total Carbohydrate: 27g carbohydrate (1g sugars
- Cholesterol: 40mg cholesterol
- Protein: 14g protein.
- Total Fat: 11g fat (6g saturated fat)
- Sodium: 1113mg sodium
- Fiber: 1g fiber)

779. Au Gratin Potatoes And Ham

Serving: 8 casseroles (10 servings each). | Prep: 45mins | Cook: 45mins | Ready in:

Ingredients

- 20 pounds red potatoes
- 8 pounds fully cooked ham, cubed
- 4 cans (10-3/4 ounces each) condensed cream of celery soup, undiluted
- 1/2 cup all-purpose flour
- 8 cups milk
- 6 pounds process cheese (Velveeta), cubed
- 2 teaspoons pepper
- 2 teaspoons paprika

Direction

- In a few stockpots, put potatoes and add water to cover. Boil it. Lower the heat, put a cover on and cook until soft, about 15-20 minutes. Strain.
- Peel the skin, if desired; then dice into cubes. In each of eight 13x9-inch baking dishes coated with cooking spray, put 6 cups of potatoes. Add approximately 3 1/2 cups of cubed ham to each dish.
- Mix milk, flour, and soup together in the same kettles until smooth. Boil it, cook while stirring until thickened, about 2 minutes. Add paprika, pepper, and cheese. Lower the heat and cook until the cheese melts.
- Pour into each pan with approximately 2 1/4 cups of sauce. Put a cover on and bake for 40 minutes at 350°. Remove the cover and bake until bubbling, about 5-10 minutes.

Nutrition Information

- Calories:
- Sodium:
- Fiber:
- Total Carbohydrate:
- Cholesterol:
- Protein:
- Total Fat:

780. Au Gratin Spinach 'n' Pork

Serving: 4-6 servings. | Prep: 20mins | Cook: 25mins | Ready in:

Ingredients

- 2 large onions, sliced
- 1 tablespoon vegetable oil
- 1 tablespoon butter
- 2 bacon strips, diced
- 1 pound pork chop suey meat
- 1 package (10 ounces) fresh spinach, torn
- 2 garlic cloves, minced
- 2 teaspoons grated lemon zest
- 1 teaspoon fennel seed, crushed
- 1/2 teaspoon salt
- 1/2 teaspoon pepper
- 1 cup shredded Swiss cheese, divided
- 2 tablespoons grated Parmesan cheese

Direction

- Sauté onions in butter and oil in a big skillet till golden brown. Transfer onto paper towels; drain. Cook bacon in the same skillet on medium heat till crisp. Transfer to paper towels; drain.
- Cook pork in drippings on medium heat till not pink anymore. Add garlic and spinach; mix and cook till heated through for 6 minutes. Thoroughly drain. Mix in bacon, 1/3 cup of Swiss cheese, pepper, salt, fennel seed and lemon zest.
- Put 1/2 onions into 1-qt. greased baking dish; put leftover onions and pork mixture over (dish will get full). Sprinkle leftover Swiss cheese and parmesan cheese over; bake at 350°, with no cover, till cheese melts and pork softens for 25-30 minutes.

Nutrition Information

- Calories: 292 calories
- Protein: 24g protein.
- Total Fat: 19g fat (8g saturated fat)

- Sodium: 421mg sodium
- Fiber: 2g fiber)
- Total Carbohydrate: 7g carbohydrate (4g sugars
- Cholesterol: 72mg cholesterol

781. Bacon Tomato Casserole

Serving: 4-6 servings. | Prep: 30mins | Cook: 10mins | Ready in:

Ingredients

- 6 ounces uncooked egg noodles
- 1 pound sliced bacon, diced
- 1/3 cup chopped green pepper
- 1/3 cup chopped onion
- 1 teaspoon salt
- 1/2 teaspoon dried marjoram
- 1/2 teaspoon dried thyme
- 1/8 teaspoon pepper
- 1 can (28 ounces) stewed tomatoes
- 1 cup shredded cheddar cheese

Direction

- Cook the noodles as per the direction of the package; drain. Cook bacon in a big skillet over medium heat until crisp. Transfer to paper towels to drain, retaining 2 tablespoons drippings.
- Sauté pepper, thyme, marjoram, salt, onion and green pepper in the drippings for 5 minutes. Mix in the tomatoes. Set to a boil. Lower heat; simmer, uncovered, for 10 minutes. Mix in the noodles. Put in half of the bacon.
- Move to a greased baking dish of 2 quarts. Top with leftover bacon and cheese. Bake, uncovered, for 10 to 15 minutes at 350°, until cheese is melted.

Nutrition Information

- Calories: 363 calories

- Sodium: 1150mg sodium
- Fiber: 2g fiber)
- Total Carbohydrate: 32g carbohydrate (8g sugars
- Cholesterol: 68mg cholesterol
- Protein: 17g protein.
- Total Fat: 19g fat (9g saturated fat)

782. Bavarian Casserole

Serving: 6 servings. | Prep: 40mins | Cook: 40mins | Ready in:

Ingredients

- 4 medium red potatoes
- 6 bacon strips, diced
- 6 bone-in pork loin chops (3/4 inch thick and 7 ounces each)
- 1 large onion, chopped
- 1 jar (32 ounces) sauerkraut, rinsed and well drained
- 1 can (28 ounces) stewed tomatoes, drained
- 1 teaspoon caraway seeds
- 1/2 teaspoon salt
- 1/4 teaspoon pepper

Direction

- In a big saucepan, put the potatoes and cover with water. Set to a boil. Lower heat; cover and cook until almost softened, about 15 to 20 minutes. Drain; cut into slices of 1/4-inch if cool enough to manage.
- Cook bacon over medium heat in a big skillet until crisp. Transfer to paper towels with a slotted spoon. Brown pork chops on both sides in the drippings. Take out chops; drain, reserve 1 tablespoon drippings. Sauté onion with the reserved drippings until softened. Mix in bacon and sauerkraut; cook for about 3 to 4 minutes.
- Spoon sauerkraut blend into a greased baking dish of 13x9 inches square. Layer with pork chops, potatoes slices and tomatoes. Dust with

pepper, salt and caraway seeds. Cover and bake for 40 to 45 minutes at 350°, until a thermometer shows 160°.

Nutrition Information

- Calories: 462 calories
- Total Fat: 22g fat (8g saturated fat)
- Sodium: 1668mg sodium
- Fiber: 7g fiber)
- Total Carbohydrate: 31g carbohydrate (10g sugars
- Cholesterol: 101mg cholesterol
- Protein: 36g protein.

783. Broccoli Ham Bake

Serving: 4 servings. | Prep: 20mins | Cook: 25mins | Ready in:

Ingredients

- 3 cups frozen chopped broccoli
- 1/4 cup chopped onion
- 4 tablespoons butter, divided
- 2 tablespoons all-purpose flour
- 2-1/4 cups milk
- 1/2 cup shredded cheddar cheese
- 2 cups cubed fully cooked ham
- 1-1/2 cups seasoned stuffing cubes, divided

Direction

- Follow package directions to cook the broccoli. While cooking, place 3 tablespoons butter in large pot and sauté onion until soft. Mix flour until blended then slowly whisk in milk. Heat to boiling. Stirring constantly until thickened, about 2 minutes. Decrease heat and add cheese stirring until melted. Drain the water from the broccoli. Mix in 1 cup of stuffing mix, ham, and broccoli. Place in a 2-qt. greased dish. After melting the rest of the butter and mix with the rest of the stuffing mix. Put the butter/stuffing mixture around the edge of baking dish. Do not cover; bake at 350-degrees until brown, 25-30 minutes.

Nutrition Information

- Calories: 454 calories
- Total Carbohydrate: 30g carbohydrate (9g sugars
- Cholesterol: 101mg cholesterol
- Protein: 25g protein.
- Total Fat: 27g fat (15g saturated fat)
- Sodium: 1445mg sodium
- Fiber: 3g fiber)

784. Broccoli Scalloped Potatoes

Serving: 8 servings. | Prep: 25mins | Cook: 60mins | Ready in:

Ingredients

- 1/4 cup butter, cubed
- 2 tablespoons chopped onion
- 4 garlic cloves, minced
- 5 tablespoons all-purpose flour
- 1/4 teaspoon white pepper
- 1/8 teaspoon salt
- 2-1/2 cups whole milk
- 2 cups shredded Swiss cheese, divided
- 2 pounds potatoes, peeled and thinly sliced (about 4 cups)
- 2 cups julienned fully cooked ham
- 2 cups frozen broccoli florets, thawed and patted dry

Direction

- Start preheating the oven to 350°. Melt butter in a Dutch oven over medium-high heat. Add garlic and onion, stir and cook for 2-3 minutes until soft. Mix in salt, white pepper, and flour until combined; slowly stir in milk. Boil it,

whisking continually, stir and cook until thickened, about 2 minutes.

- Mix in 1 cup cheese. Lower the heat, cook until the cheese melts, about 1-2 minutes (the sauce should be thick). Take away from the heat.
- Add broccoli, ham, and potatoes to the sauce; lightly mix to blend. Remove into eight 8-oz. ramekins coated with cooking spray.
- Put a cover on and bake for 40 minutes. Sprinkle the leftover cheese over. Bake without a cover until the cheese melts and the potatoes are soft, about another 20-25 minutes.

Nutrition Information

- Calories: 309 calories
- Protein: 17g protein.
- Total Fat: 17g fat (10g saturated fat)
- Sodium: 626mg sodium
- Fiber: 2g fiber)
- Total Carbohydrate: 23g carbohydrate (3g sugars
- Cholesterol: 61mg cholesterol

785. Broccoli Ham Hot Dish

Serving: 8 servings. | Prep: 20mins | Cook: 30mins | Ready in:

Ingredients

- 2 packages (10 ounces each) frozen cut broccoli
- 2 cups cooked rice
- 6 tablespoons butter, cubed
- 2 cups fresh bread crumbs (about 2-1/2 slices)
- 1 medium onion, chopped
- 3 tablespoons all-purpose flour
- 1 teaspoon salt
- 1/4 teaspoon pepper
- 3 cups milk
- 1-1/2 pounds fully cooked ham, cubed
- Shredded cheddar or Swiss cheese

Direction

- Preheat an oven to 350°. Follow package directions to cook broccoli; drain. Put rice into a 13x9-in. baking pan using a spoon; put broccoli on rice.
- Melt butter in a big skillet. Sprinkle 2 tsp. of melted butter over breadcrumbs; put aside. Sauté onion till soft in reserved butter. Add pepper, salt and flour; constantly mix till blended. Mix in milk; boil. Mix and cook till thickened for 2 minutes; add ham.
- Spread over broccoli and rice; sprinkle with crumbs. Bake till heated through for 30 minutes; sprinkle with cheese. Stand for 5 minutes; serve.

Nutrition Information

- Calories: 379 calories
- Total Fat: 19g fat (10g saturated fat)
- Sodium: 1583mg sodium
- Fiber: 2g fiber)
- Total Carbohydrate: 29g carbohydrate (6g sugars
- Cholesterol: 81mg cholesterol
- Protein: 22g protein.

786. Busy Day Ham Bake

Serving: 4 servings. | Prep: 15mins | Cook: 30mins | Ready in:

Ingredients

- 1 can (10-3/4 ounces) condensed cheddar cheese soup, undiluted
- 3 cups frozen chopped broccoli, thawed
- 1 cup cooked rice
- 1 cup cubed fully cooked ham
- 1/4 cup sour cream
- 1/4 cup mayonnaise
- 1/4 cup dry bread crumbs
- 1 tablespoon butter

Direction

- Mix the first six ingredients in a large mixing bowl. Spray a 1-1/2-qt. baking pan with cooking spray and place mixture in bottom. Mix the butter and bread crumbs and evenly spread on top. Do not cover; bake in a 350-degree oven until entirely heated, 30 minutes.

Nutrition Information

- Calories: 364 calories
- Total Fat: 25g fat (8g saturated fat)
- Sodium: 1218mg sodium
- Fiber: 3g fiber)
- Total Carbohydrate: 27g carbohydrate (3g sugars
- Cholesterol: 50mg cholesterol
- Protein: 13g protein.

787. Cauliflower Ham Casserole

Serving: 6 servings. | Prep: 20mins | Cook: 40mins | Ready in:

Ingredients

- 4 cups chopped fresh cauliflower
- 1/4 cup butter, cubed
- 1/3 cup all-purpose flour
- 2 cups 2% milk
- 1 cup shredded cheddar cheese
- 1/2 cup sour cream
- 2 cups cubed fully cooked ham
- 1 jar (4-1/2 ounces) sliced mushrooms, drained
- TOPPING:
- 1 cup soft bread crumbs
- 1 tablespoon butter, melted

Direction

- Cover cauliflower with 1-in. water in a big saucepan; boil. Lower heat; cover. Simmer till tender for 5-10 minutes.

- Meanwhile, melt butter in another big saucepan. Mix in flour till smooth; add milk slowly. Boil; mix and cook till thick for 2 minutes. Take off heat; mix in sour cream and cheese till melted.
- Drain cauliflower. Mix mushrooms, ham and cauliflower in a big bowl. Add cheese sauce; toss till coated. Put into 2-qt. greased baking dish.
- Mix topping ingredients; sprinkle on casserole. Bake till heated through for 40-45 minutes at 350°, uncovered.

Nutrition Information

- Calories: 383 calories
- Total Carbohydrate: 20g carbohydrate (7g sugars
- Cholesterol: 95mg cholesterol
- Protein: 19g protein.
- Total Fat: 25g fat (15g saturated fat)
- Sodium: 1007mg sodium
- Fiber: 3g fiber)

---

788.   Cauliflower And Ham Casserole

Serving: 6 servings. | Prep: 20mins | Cook: 25mins | Ready in:

Ingredients

- 1 tablespoon chopped onion
- 3 tablespoons butter, divided
- 2 tablespoons all-purpose flour
- 1/2 teaspoon salt
- Pepper to taste
- 1 cup milk
- 1/2 cup shredded cheddar cheese
- 1 medium head cauliflower, cut into florets, cooked and drained
- 2 cups cubed fully cooked ham
- 1 jar (4-1/2 ounces) sliced mushrooms, drained

- 1 jar (2 ounces) diced pimientos, drained
- 6 saltines, crumbled

Direction

- In a saucepan with 2 tablespoons of butter, sauté chopped onion over medium heat until soft. Stir in flour, pepper, and salt until smooth. Add milk gradually; cook and stir until bubbly and thick, or for around 2 minutes.
- Next, remove from the heat, put in the cheese and stir until melted. Fold in pimientos, mushrooms, ham, and cauliflower. Pour into a coated 2-qt. casserole with cooking spray.
- Brown the cracker crumbs in the leftover butter in a small saucepan; scatter over the casserole. Bake, covered, for 20 minutes at 350°. Then uncover and continue to bake for 5-10 more minutes, or until heated through.

Nutrition Information

- Calories: 209 calories
- Fiber: 0 fiber)
- Total Carbohydrate: 11g carbohydrate (0 sugars
- Cholesterol: 33mg cholesterol
- Protein: 15g protein. Diabetic Exchanges: 2 meat
- Total Fat: 12g fat (0 saturated fat)
- Sodium: 942mg sodium

---

789.   Cheesy Company Casserole

Serving: 2 casseroles (8-10 servings each). | Prep: 20mins | Cook: 35mins | Ready in:

Ingredients

- 8 ounces process cheese (Velveeta), cubed
- 1/4 cup milk

- 2 cans (14-1/2 ounces each) diced tomatoes, undrained
- 3/4 cup mayonnaise
- 1 tablespoon Worcestershire sauce
- 4 cups cubed fully cooked ham
- 4 cups cooked elbow macaroni
- 3 cups frozen chopped broccoli, thawed and drained
- 1 package (10 ounces) frozen peas, thawed
- 1 small green pepper, chopped
- 1 small onion, chopped
- 1/2 cup crushed stuffing mix
- 1 can (2.8 ounces) french-fried onions, chopped, optional
- 1 cup soft bread crumbs
- 1/4 cup butter, melted

Direction

- Over low heat, cook and stir milk and cheese in a large saucepan until the cheese is melted. Next, add tomatoes and stir until combined. Remove from the heat; stir in the Worcestershire sauce and mayonnaise until blended. Stir in stuffing mix, green pepper, peas, broccoli, macaroni, ham, and onions if desired.
- Transfer to 2 greased 2-1/2-qt. baking dishes. Toss butter and bread crumbs; dust over the top. Bake while uncovered for 35-40 minutes at 350°, or until bubbly.

Nutrition Information

- Calories: 230 calories
- Total Fat: 15g fat (5g saturated fat)
- Sodium: 649mg sodium
- Fiber: 2g fiber)
- Total Carbohydrate: 15g carbohydrate (3g sugars
- Cholesterol: 32mg cholesterol
- Protein: 10g protein.

790. Cheesy Green Bean Casserole

Serving: 8 | Prep: | Cook: | Ready in:

Ingredients

- 2 (10.75 ounce) cans condensed cream of mushroom soup
- 3/4 cup milk
- 1 (2.8 ounce) can French fried onions
- 2 cups shredded Cheddar cheese
- 2 (16 ounce) packages frozen French cut green beans
- 1/2 pound processed cheese food (eg. Velveeta), sliced

Direction

- Preheat oven to 325° F (165° C). Oil a 2-quart casserole dish.
- In a mixing bowl, combine half of the onions, cheddar cheese, milk, and mushroom soup. Stir together.
- Layer half of the green beans on the bottom of a 2-quart casserole dish. Add half of the soup mixture on top of beans, then put in half of the processed cheese. Redo the layering, then top with the rest onions.
- Bake for around 30 - 40 minutes.

Nutrition Information

- Calories: 351 calories;
- Total Fat: 22.5
- Sodium: 1217
- Total Carbohydrate: 22
- Cholesterol: 43
- Protein: 16.4

791. Cheesy Potatoes And Ham

Serving: 4-6 servings. | Prep: 10mins | Cook: 30mins | Ready in:

Ingredients

- 1 can (10-3/4 ounces) condensed cream of mushroom soup, undiluted
- 1 cup cubed process cheese (Velveeta)
- 2 tablespoons butter, cubed
- 2 cups cubed fully cooked ham
- 1/4 cup chopped onion
- 1-1/2 teaspoons Worcestershire sauce
- 6 cups mashed potatoes (with added milk and butter)

Direction

- Mix together butter, cheese and the soup in a large saucepan. Cook while stirring over medium heat until cheese is melted. Mix in Worcestershire sauce, onion and the ham.
- Pour the mixture into a 2-qt. baking dish coated with grease. Add mashed potatoes on top. Bake without a cover at 350° for 30-35 minutes, until heated through.

Nutrition Information

- Calories: 438 calories
- Fiber: 5g fiber)
- Total Carbohydrate: 42g carbohydrate (5g sugars
- Cholesterol: 74mg cholesterol
- Protein: 17g protein.
- Total Fat: 24g fat (13g saturated fat)
- Sodium: 1849mg sodium

792. Chicken And Broccoli Company Casserole

Serving: 6 servings. | Prep: 35mins | Cook: 40mins | Ready in:

Ingredients

- 1 package (6 ounces) long grain and wild rice mix
- 4 cups frozen broccoli florets, thawed and drained
- 1-1/2 cups cubed cooked chicken breast
- 1 cup cubed fully cooked lean ham
- 1/2 cup shredded reduced-fat cheddar cheese
- 1 cup sliced fresh mushrooms
- 1 can (10-3/4 ounces) reduced-fat reduced-sodium condensed cream of mushroom soup, undiluted
- 2/3 cup reduced-fat plain yogurt
- 1/3 cup reduced-fat mayonnaise
- 1 teaspoon prepared mustard
- 1/4 teaspoon curry powder
- 2 tablespoons grated Parmesan cheese

Direction

- Cook rice following the package instructions, minus the butter. Layer the mushrooms, cheddar cheese, ham, chicken, broccoli, and rice in a greased 13x9-inch baking dish.
- Mix curry powder, mustard, mayonnaise, yogurt, and soup together in a small bowl. Evenly spread the mixture over the casserole top, sprinkle Parmesan cheese over.
- Bake without a cover at 350° until fully heated, about 40-45 minutes.

Nutrition Information

- Calories: 318 calories
- Cholesterol: 54mg cholesterol
- Protein: 24g protein.
- Total Fat: 11g fat (4g saturated fat)
- Sodium: 1129mg sodium
- Fiber: 2g fiber)

- Total Carbohydrate: 31g carbohydrate (5g sugars

- Sodium: 691mg sodium
- Fiber: 3g fiber)
- Total Carbohydrate: 21g carbohydrate (16g sugars
- Cholesterol: 86mg cholesterol

793.   Chops 'n' Kraut

Serving: 6 servings. | Prep: 25mins | Cook: 20mins | Ready in:

Ingredients

- 6 bone-in pork loin chops (7 ounces each)
- 1/4 teaspoon salt
- 1/4 teaspoon pepper
- 3 teaspoons canola oil, divided
- 1 medium onion, thinly sliced
- 2 garlic cloves, minced
- 1 can (14-1/2 ounces) petite diced tomatoes, undrained
- 1 can (14 ounces) sauerkraut, rinsed and well drained
- 1/3 cup packed brown sugar
- 1-1/2 teaspoons caraway seeds

Direction

- Sprinkle pepper and salt on both sides of the pork chops. Cook 3 chops in 1 tsp. oil in a big nonstick skillet coated in cooking spray till brown for 2-3 minutes per side; drain. Repeat using leftover 1 tsp. oil and chops.
- Put pork chops into 13x9-in. baking dish that's coated in cooking spray; put aside. Cook onion in leftover oil in same skillet till tender. Add the garlic; cook for 1 minute. Mix in caraway seeds, brown sugar, sauerkraut and tomatoes; mix and cook till it boils.
- Put on chops carefully; cover. Bake for 20-25 minutes at 350° till thermometer reads 160°.

Nutrition Information

- Calories: 311 calories
- Protein: 32g protein. Diabetic Exchanges: 4 lean meat
- Total Fat: 11g fat (3g saturated fat)

794.   Chops With Sauerkraut

Serving: 6 servings. | Prep: 15mins | Cook: 20mins | Ready in:

Ingredients

- 6 bone-in pork loin chops (1/2 inch thick, about 2-1/4 pounds)
- 1 tablespoon vegetable oil
- 1 cup applesauce
- 1 jar (16 ounces) sauerkraut, rinsed and drained
- 1/4 cup white wine or apple juice
- 4 bacon strips, cooked and crumbled
- 1/2 teaspoon brown sugar
- 1/4 teaspoon ground mustard
- Pepper to taste

Direction

- In a skillet, in oil, brown both sides of pork chops. Move to an oiled 13x9-inch baking pan. Mix the rest of ingredients together; arrange over chops. Bake at 350 degrees without cover for 20-25 minutes or until meat juices run clear.

Nutrition Information

- Calories: 324 calories
- Sodium: 626mg sodium
- Fiber: 2g fiber)
- Total Carbohydrate: 8g carbohydrate (5g sugars
- Cholesterol: 87mg cholesterol
- Protein: 29g protein.
- Total Fat: 18g fat (6g saturated fat)

- Cholesterol: 76mg cholesterol
- Protein: 33g protein. Diabetic Exchanges: 3 lean meat
- Total Fat: 13g fat (7g saturated fat)

795.　　Corn Bread Pork Casserole

Serving: 2 servings. | Prep: 15mins | Cook: 35mins | Ready in:

Ingredients

- 2 boneless pork loin chops (4 ounces each)
- 1/2 pound sliced fresh mushrooms
- 2 tablespoons all-purpose flour
- 1/2 cup reduced-sodium chicken broth
- 1/2 cup reduced-fat sour cream
- 1 tablespoon shredded Parmesan cheese
- 2 garlic cloves, minced
- Pepper to taste
- 1/2 cup crushed corn bread stuffing

Direction

- Coat a big skillet using cooking spray then cook pork chops on both sides. Remove the chops then sauté the mushrooms using the same skillet until it is tender. Apply cooking spray onto a 1-1/2-qt baking dish then place the mushrooms in.
- Mix together the flour and broth in a separate bowl until it becomes smooth. Then, add in the cheese, sour cream, pepper and garlic then pour the mushrooms. Top the mixture on the pork chops.
- Let it bake in the oven at 350°F for about 25 minutes. Drizzle the stuffing on top then bake in the oven for another ten minutes or until the meat thermometer says 160°F.

Nutrition Information

- Calories: 363 calories
- Sodium: 434mg sodium
- Fiber: 2g fiber)
- Total Carbohydrate: 27g carbohydrate (7g sugars

796.　　Creamy Ham 'n' Egg Casserole

Serving: 6 servings. | Prep: 15mins | Cook: 20mins | Ready in:

Ingredients

- 2 medium cooked potatoes, peeled and sliced
- 4 hard-boiled large eggs, chopped
- 1 cup diced fully cooked ham
- 1/2 teaspoon salt
- 1/4 teaspoon pepper
- 1 egg
- 1-1/2 cups (12 ounces) sour cream
- 1/4 cup dry bread crumbs
- 1 tablespoon butter, melted

Direction

- Mix salt, eggs, pepper, ham, and potatoes in a big bowl. In a separate bowl, whisk sour cream and egg. Pour the egg mixture into the big bowl with the potato mixture; carefully coat. Place in an 11x7-in. greased pan. In another bowl, mix butter and bread crumbs; evenly spread on top. Don't cover; bake in a 350-degree oven until thermometer reads 160 degrees, 20 minutes.

Nutrition Information

- Calories: 297 calories
- Total Fat: 19g fat (10g saturated fat)
- Sodium: 616mg sodium
- Fiber: 1g fiber)
- Total Carbohydrate: 16g carbohydrate (3g sugars
- Cholesterol: 234mg cholesterol

- Protein: 13g protein.

797. Creamy Ham Rolls

Serving: 12 servings. | Prep: 15mins | Cook: 25mins | Ready in:

Ingredients

- 1 medium onion, chopped
- 1/2 cup butter
- 1/2 cup all-purpose flour
- 1 teaspoon dill weed
- 1/2 teaspoon garlic salt
- 1/2 teaspoon pepper
- 1 can (14-1/2 ounces) chicken broth
- 1-1/2 cups half-and-half cream
- 1 tablespoon Dijon mustard
- 3 cups cooked wild rice
- 1 can (8 ounces) mushroom stems and pieces, drained
- 12 thin slices fully cooked ham (about 3/4 pound)
- 1/2 cup shredded cheddar cheese
- Minced fresh parsley

Direction

- Sauté onion in butter in a big saucepan until tender. Mix in pepper, garlic salt, dill, and flour until bubbly and smooth. Slowly pour in broth, mustard, and cream; cook until thickened.
- Transfer 1 cup to an unoiled 13x9-inch baking pan; save another cup for topping. Put mushrooms and rice into the remaining sauce; use a spoon to transfer 1/3 cup onto each slice of ham. Roll up and lay over sauce in pan, seam side down. Spread the reserved sauce atop.
- Bake at 350 degrees without cover until heated through, about 25-30 minutes. Sprinkle with parsley and cheese; serve right away.

Nutrition Information

- Calories:
- Sodium:
- Fiber:
- Total Carbohydrate:
- Cholesterol:
- Protein:
- Total Fat:

798. Creamy Pork Chop Casserole

Serving: 2 servings. | Prep: 15mins | Cook: 55mins | Ready in:

Ingredients

- 1/4 cup reduced-sodium teriyaki sauce
- 2 bone-in pork loin chops (8 ounces each and 1/2 inch thick)
- 1 can (10-3/4 ounces) condensed cream of mushroom soup, undiluted
- 1 cup frozen peas and carrots
- 3/4 cup water
- 1/2 small sweet red pepper, chopped
- 1/3 cup uncooked long grain rice
- 1 teaspoon dried minced onion
- 1/8 teaspoon pepper
- 1/4 cup shredded Mexican cheese blend

Direction

- In a large resealable plastic bag, put teriyaki sauce and add pork chops. Then seal the bag and flip to coat; chill for at least 60 minutes.
- Set the oven at 350° to preheat. Combine pepper, onion, rice, red pepper, water, peas and carrots and soup in a large bowl. Transfer to an 11x7-in. baking dish greased with cooking spray.
- Drain and discard the marinade. Put over the rice mixture with the pork chops. Bake, covered, for 40 minutes. Uncover and dust with cheese. Continue to bake until a

thermometer states 145° and the cheese is melted, for 10-20 minutes more. Allow to stand for 5 minutes before serving.

Nutrition Information

- Calories: 648 calories
- Total Carbohydrate: 47g carbohydrate (7g sugars
- Cholesterol: 127mg cholesterol
- Protein: 47g protein.
- Total Fat: 31g fat (10g saturated fat)
- Sodium: 1479mg sodium
- Fiber: 5g fiber)

r – – – – – – – – – – – – – – – – – – ⌐
799. Creamy Spaghetti Casserole
L – – – – – – – – – – – – – – – – – – ⌐

Serving: 8-10 servings. | Prep: 15mins | Cook: 30mins | Ready in:

Ingredients

- 1/2 cup sliced green onions
- 1/2 cup sliced celery
- 1 can (4 ounces) mushroom stems and pieces, drained
- 2 tablespoons butter
- 8 ounces spaghetti, cooked and drained
- 3 cups cubed fully cooked ham
- 2 cups shredded Monterey Jack cheese, divided
- 1 cup sour cream
- 1 cup 4% cottage cheese
- 1 cup frozen cut green beans, thawed
- 1 jar (2 ounces) diced pimientos, drained
- 1/4 teaspoon garlic salt
- 1/8 teaspoon pepper

Direction

- In a big Dutch oven or saucepan with butter, sauté mushrooms, celery, and onion until tender. put in pepper, garlic salt, pimientos,

beans, cottage cheese, sour cream, 1-1/2 cups Monterey Jack cheese, ham, and spaghetti; combine nicely.

- Remove to an oiled shallow 2-quart baking dish. Bake for 20 minutes at 350 degrees without cover; sprinkle the rest of Monterey Jack cheese over top. Bake for 10 minutes or until bubbly and the cheese melts.

Nutrition Information

- Calories: 339 calories
- Cholesterol: 70mg cholesterol
- Protein: 20g protein.
- Total Fat: 18g fat (10g saturated fat)
- Sodium: 883mg sodium
- Fiber: 1g fiber)
- Total Carbohydrate: 22g carbohydrate (3g sugars

r – – – – – – – – – – – – – – – – – – ⌐
800. Crunch Top Ham And Potato Casserole
L – – – – – – – – – – – – – – – – – – ⌐

Serving: 10 servings. | Prep: 10mins | Cook: 60mins | Ready in:

Ingredients

- 1 package (32 ounces) frozen cubed hash brown potatoes, thawed
- 2 cups cubed cooked ham
- 2 cups sour cream
- 1-1/2 cups shredded cheddar cheese
- 1 can (10-3/4 ounces) condensed cream of chicken soup, undiluted
- 1/2 cup butter, melted
- 1/3 cup chopped green onions
- 1/2 teaspoon pepper
- TOPPING:
- 2 cups crushed cornflakes
- 1/4 cup butter, melted

Direction

- Combine the first 8 ingredients in a large bowl. Transfer to a greased 13x9-in. baking dish. Mix the topping ingredients and dust over top. Uncover and bake at 350° for 60 minutes, or until heated through.

Nutrition Information

- Calories: 487 calories
- Sodium: 1008mg sodium
- Fiber: 2g fiber)
- Total Carbohydrate: 37g carbohydrate (4g sugars
- Cholesterol: 104mg cholesterol
- Protein: 15g protein.
- Total Fat: 31g fat (19g saturated fat)

801.   Crunchy Curried Chicken

Serving: 6-8 servings. | Prep: 15mins | Cook: 35mins | Ready in:

Ingredients

- 4-1/2 cups cooked long grain rice
- 1 cup cubed cooked chicken
- 1 cup cubed fully cooked ham
- 1 can (8 ounces) water chestnuts, drained and chopped
- 1 can (10-3/4 ounces) condensed cream of chicken soup, undiluted
- 1-1/4 cup milk
- 1/2 cup mayonnaise
- 1/4 cup minced fresh parsley
- 3/4 teaspoon salt
- 1/8 to 1/4 teaspoon curry powder
- 1/3 cup sliced almonds

Direction

- In a greased 13-in. x 9-in. baking dish, place the rice. Sprinkle with water chestnuts, ham, and chicken. Mix the next 6 ingredients, then pour over the chicken mixture.

- Bake at 350°, uncovered, until bubbly for 30-35 minutes. Sprinkle with almonds and continue to bake for 5 minutes more.

Nutrition Information

- Calories: 372 calories
- Sodium: 847mg sodium
- Fiber: 2g fiber)
- Total Carbohydrate: 34g carbohydrate (3g sugars
- Cholesterol: 38mg cholesterol
- Protein: 14g protein.
- Total Fat: 19g fat (4g saturated fat)

802.   Deluxe Potato Ham Bake

Serving: 10-12 servings. | Prep: 10mins | Cook: 60mins | Ready in:

Ingredients

- 2 cans (10-3/4 ounces each) condensed cream of chicken soup, undiluted
- 1/4 cup butter, melted
- 1 cup sour cream
- 1-1/2 cups shredded cheddar cheese
- 1 medium onion, chopped
- 2 cups cubed fully cooked ham
- 1 package (32 ounces) frozen cubed hash brown potatoes, thawed
- TOPPING:
- 1/4 cup butter, melted
- 3/4 cup crushed cornflakes

Direction

- Combine the first 5 ingredients in a large bowl. Mix in potatoes and ham. Distribute mixture over the bottom of an oiled 13x9-inch baking dish. Toss cornflakes with butter until crumbly to make topping. Scatter topping over the top of ham mixture. Bake without covering for 60 minutes at 350°, or until potatoes are soft.

Nutrition Information

- Calories: 305 calories
- Sodium: 732mg sodium
- Fiber: 2g fiber)
- Total Carbohydrate: 24g carbohydrate (3g sugars
- Cholesterol: 64mg cholesterol
- Protein: 11g protein.
- Total Fat: 18g fat (11g saturated fat)

803. Easy Cordon Bleu Casserole

Serving: 8-10 servings. | Prep: 10mins | Cook: 50mins | Ready in:

Ingredients

- 6 slices whole wheat bread
- 6 boneless skinless chicken breast halves, cooked and sliced
- 1 package (8 ounces) cream cheese, thinly sliced
- 1/2 pound sliced fully cooked ham
- 1-1/2 cups shredded Swiss cheese, divided
- 2 packages (10 ounces each) frozen broccoli spears, thawed and drained
- 2 cans (10-3/4 ounces each) condensed cream of chicken soup, undiluted
- 1/4 teaspoon pepper

Direction

- In a greased 13x9-in. baking dish, put the bread. Layer with the chicken and cream cheese slices then the ham. Next, dust with 1 cup of Swiss cheese. Put broccoli on top.
- Mix soup and pepper and scoop over the broccoli. Dust with the leftover Swiss cheese. Bake without cover for 50-55 minutes at 350°, or until bubbly.

Nutrition Information

- Calories: 355 calories
- Fiber: 4g fiber)
- Total Carbohydrate: 16g carbohydrate (3g sugars
- Cholesterol: 93mg cholesterol
- Protein: 29g protein.
- Total Fat: 19g fat (10g saturated fat)
- Sodium: 888mg sodium

804. Fancy Mac 'N' Cheese

Serving: 8 servings. | Prep: 25mins | Cook: 5mins | Ready in:

Ingredients

- 2 packages (7-1/4 ounces each) macaroni and white cheddar or cheddar cheese dinner mix
- 6 cups water
- 2 cups fresh broccoli florets
- 1/2 cup chopped onion
- 2 garlic cloves, minced
- 1/2 cup plus 1 tablespoon butter, divided
- 1/2 cup milk
- 2 cups cubed fully cooked ham
- 1 tablespoon Dijon mustard
- Salt and pepper to taste
- 1 cup soft bread crumbs
- 1/4 cup grated Parmesan cheese

Direction

- Put cheese sauce packet from the dinner mix aside. Heat water to a boil. Put in macaroni and cook for 4 minutes. Add garlic, onion, and broccoli. Cook for 3-6 minutes or until the macaroni is tender; drain.
- Melt 1/2 cup butter in a big saucepan. Mix in milk and cheese sauce mix. Add pepper, salt, mustard, and ham. Blend in the macaroni mixture.
- Move to an oiled broiler-proof 2-1/2-quart baking dish. Melt the rest of butter; toss with

cheese and bread crumbs. Arrange over top. Broil 4-6 inches from the heat for 4-5 minutes or until the top is golden brown.

Nutrition Information

- Calories: 312 calories
- Total Fat: 19g fat (10g saturated fat)
- Sodium: 932mg sodium
- Fiber: 1g fiber)
- Total Carbohydrate: 24g carbohydrate (5g sugars
- Cholesterol: 61mg cholesterol
- Protein: 14g protein.

805.   German Schnitzel And Potatoes With Gorgonzola Cream

Serving: 4 servings. | Prep: 20mins | Cook: 04hours00mins |Ready in:

Ingredients

- 1 pork tenderloin (1 pound)
- 1 cup dry bread crumbs
- 2 pounds medium Yukon Gold potatoes, peeled and cut into 1/4-inch slices
- 2 cups heavy whipping cream
- 2/3 cup crumbled Gorgonzola cheese
- 1 teaspoon salt
- 1/4 cup minced fresh Italian parsley
- Lemon wedges

Direction

- Slice the tenderloin into 12 slices. Use a meat mallet to pound to 1/4 -inch thickness. Put 4 slices in a 3- or 4-quart slow cooker. Layer with 1/3 of the potatoes and 1/4 cup of bread crumbs. Make layers twice; place over the top with the leftover bread crumbs.
- In a small bowl, combine salt, Gorgonzola and cream. Transfer over the pork mixture; cover

and cook on low, for 4 to 6 hours until meat and potatoes are softened. Sprinkle with parsley; enjoy with lemon wedges.

Nutrition Information

- Calories: 926 calories
- Sodium: 1132mg sodium
- Fiber: 5g fiber)
- Total Carbohydrate: 73g carbohydrate (9g sugars
- Cholesterol: 216mg cholesterol
- Protein: 38g protein.
- Total Fat: 54g fat (33g saturated fat)

806.   Greek Feta Casserole

Serving: 2 servings. | Prep: 20mins | Cook: 35mins |Ready in:

Ingredients

- 1/2 cup uncooked elbow macaroni
- 1 egg, lightly beaten
- 2 tablespoons milk
- 1/2 cup crumbled feta cheese or shredded part-skim mozzarella cheese, divided
- 1/2 pound ground pork
- 2 tablespoons chopped onion
- 1/2 cup tomato sauce
- 1/8 to 1/4 teaspoon ground cinnamon

Direction

- Follow package instructions to cook macaroni; drain.
- Combine 1/4 cup cheese, milk, and egg in a bowl. Mix in macaroni. Move to an oiled 3-cup baking dish. Cook onion and pork in a skillet on medium heat, until the meat is not pink anymore; drain. Mix in cinnamon and tomatoes sauce.
- Spread over the macaroni mixture. Sprinkle the rest of cheese over top. Put on cover and bake for 20 minutes at 375 degrees. Remove

cover and bake for 12-16 minutes more or until heated through and bubbly.

Nutrition Information

- Calories: 442 calories
- Total Fat: 25g fat (10g saturated fat)
- Sodium: 649mg sodium
- Fiber: 2g fiber)
- Total Carbohydrate: 20g carbohydrate (3g sugars
- Cholesterol: 199mg cholesterol
- Protein: 33g protein.

807. Ham & Veggie Casserole

Serving: 4 servings. | Prep: 20mins | Cook: 10mins | Ready in:

Ingredients

- 1 package (16 ounces) frozen broccoli florets
- 1 package (16 ounces) frozen cauliflower
- 2 teaspoons plus 2 tablespoons butter, divided
- 1/4 cup seasoned bread crumbs
- 2 tablespoons all-purpose flour
- 1-1/2 cups 2% milk
- 3/4 cup shredded sharp cheddar cheese
- 1/2 cup grated Parmesan cheese
- 1-1/2 cups cubed fully cooked ham (about 8 ounces)
- 1/4 teaspoon pepper

Direction

- Preheat an oven to 425°. Follow package directions to cook cauliflower and broccoli; drain.
- Meanwhile, melt 2 tsp. butter in a small skillet. Add bread crumbs; mix and cook on medium heat till lightly toasted for 2-3 minutes. Take off heat.
- Melt leftover butter in a big saucepan on medium heat. Mix in flour till smooth; whisk

in milk slowly. Boil, constantly mixing; mix and cook till thick for 1-2 minutes. Take off heat; mix in cheeses till blended. Mix in veggies, pepper and ham.
- Put into 8-in. square greased baking dish; sprinkle toasted crumbs. Bake for 10-15 minutes till heated through, uncovered.

Nutrition Information

- Calories: 420 calories
- Sodium: 1233mg sodium
- Fiber: 6g fiber)
- Total Carbohydrate: 25g carbohydrate (10g sugars
- Cholesterol: 89mg cholesterol
- Protein: 28g protein.
- Total Fat: 23g fat (13g saturated fat)

808. Ham 'n' Potato Au Gratin

Serving: 8 servings. | Prep: 20mins | Cook: 30mins | Ready in:

Ingredients

- 1/4 cup chopped green onions
- 1/4 cup chopped green pepper
- 2 tablespoons butter, divided
- 3 cups diced peeled potatoes, cooked
- 1 pound fully cooked ham, cubed
- 1/4 cup mayonnaise
- 1 tablespoon all-purpose flour
- 1/8 teaspoon pepper
- 3/4 cup whole milk
- 1 cup shredded cheddar cheese

Direction

- Sauté green pepper and onions with 1 tablespoon butter in a frying pan until soft. Mix potatoes with pepper and onions, mayonnaise and ham; add a non-oiled 11x7-inch baking dish.

470

- Heat the leftover butter in a saucepan. Mix in pepper and flour until smooth. Slowly pour in milk, boil it. Cook while stirring for 1 minute. Mix in cheese until barely melted. Add to the potato mixture. Put a cover on and bake at 350° until bubbly, about 30 minutes.

Nutrition Information

- Calories: 287 calories
- Cholesterol: 58mg cholesterol
- Protein: 15g protein.
- Total Fat: 18g fat (8g saturated fat)
- Sodium: 891mg sodium
- Fiber: 1g fiber)
- Total Carbohydrate: 16g carbohydrate (2g sugars

809. Ham 'n' Potato Bake

Serving: 10 servings. | Prep: 15mins | Cook: 30mins | Ready in:

Ingredients

- 2 pounds red potatoes, peeled and cubed
- 1 cup chopped onion
- 1/2 cup chopped green pepper
- 1/2 cup chopped sweet red pepper
- 1 tablespoon canola oil
- 1/3 cup all-purpose flour
- 1/4 teaspoon each pepper and dried thyme
- 2-1/4 cups milk
- 1 cup plus 2 tablespoons shredded sharp cheddar cheese, divided
- 2 tablespoons Dijon mustard
- 1-1/2 pounds fully cooked ham slices, cut into strips
- 1 package (16 ounces) frozen sliced carrots, cooked and drained
- 1/4 cup minced fresh parsley

Direction

- In a big saucepan, put potatoes and add water to cover. Boil it. Lower the heat, put a cover on and cook until soft, about 10-15 minutes. Strain.
- Sauté peppers and onion with oil in a big frying pan until soft. Mix in thyme, pepper, and flour until combined. Slowly pour in the milk. Boil it, stir and cook until thickened, about 2 minutes. Lower the heat, mix in mustard and 1 cup cheese until the cheese melts. Fold in parsley, carrots, ham, and potatoes.
- Remove into a 3-quart baking dish coated with cooking spray. Put a cover on and bake for 20 minutes at 400°. Remove the cover, bake for another 10 minutes. Sprinkle the leftover cheese over.

Nutrition Information

- Calories: 380 calories
- Total Fat: 18g fat (8g saturated fat)
- Sodium: 854mg sodium
- Fiber: 4g fiber)
- Total Carbohydrate: 32g carbohydrate (0 sugars
- Cholesterol: 63mg cholesterol
- Protein: 22g protein.

810. Ham Broccoli Bake

Serving: 4 servings. | Prep: 15mins | Cook: 20mins | Ready in:

Ingredients

- 1-1/4 cups uncooked elbow macaroni
- 1-1/2 cups chopped fresh broccoli
- 1 can (10-3/4 ounces) condensed cream of mushroom soup, undiluted
- 1 cup cubed fully cooked ham
- 1 cup shredded cheddar cheese
- 1/2 cup shredded part-skim mozzarella cheese
- 1/2 cup 2% milk

- 1 tablespoon dried minced onion
- 1/4 teaspoon pepper
- 1 cup crushed potato chips

Direction

- Cook macaroni following the package instructions. In the meantime, mix pepper, onion, milk, cheeses, ham, soup, and broccoli together in a big bowl. Strain the macaroni, add to the ham mixture.
- Remove into an 8-inch square baking dish coated with cooking spray; sprinkle potato chips over. Bake without a cover at 350° until bubbly, about 20-25 minutes.

Nutrition Information

- Calories: 442 calories
- Protein: 23g protein.
- Total Fat: 23g fat (12g saturated fat)
- Sodium: 1324mg sodium
- Fiber: 3g fiber)
- Total Carbohydrate: 36g carbohydrate (4g sugars
- Cholesterol: 64mg cholesterol

811.   Ham Casserole

Serving: 8 | Prep: 20mins | Cook: 50mins | Ready in:

Ingredients

- 2 cups peeled and cubed potatoes
- 2 stalks celery, chopped
- 1 large carrot, sliced
- 3 cups water
- 3 tablespoons butter
- 2 cups cubed fully cooked ham
- 2 tablespoons chopped green bell pepper
- 2 teaspoons chopped onion
- 1/4 cup butter
- 3 tablespoons all-purpose flour
- 1 cup milk, or more as needed

- 1/8 teaspoon salt
- 1/8 teaspoon ground black pepper
- 1 cup shredded Cheddar cheese
- 1/2 cup dry bread crumbs

Direction

- Preheat the oven to 175 degrees C (350 degrees F).
- Add the carrot, celery and potatoes into the big pot and cover with the water; boil. Lower the heat to medium-low and let simmer for roughly 20 minutes or till softened. Drain off and move into the 2-qt. baking dish.
- Melt 3 tbsp. of the butter on medium heat in the big skillet; cook and whisk the onion, green bell pepper and ham for roughly 5 minutes or till the vegetables soften. Move the ham mixture into the baking plate and mix with the potatoes.
- Melt the leftover a quarter cup of the butter in the clean skillet; cook and whisk the flour in the melted butter for roughly 3 minutes or till smooth. Slowly whisk in the milk and use the black pepper and salt to season. Boil, whisk continuously, for roughly 2 minutes or till thick. Put in the Cheddar cheese; whisk till melted. Add the cheese mixture on top of the potatoes and ham. Drizzle with the breadcrumbs.
- Bake in the preheated oven for 25-30 minutes or till bubbling. Let the casserole stand for 5 - 10 minutes prior to serving.

Nutrition Information

- Calories: 304 calories;
- Total Fat: 21.1
- Sodium: 641
- Total Carbohydrate: 16.9
- Cholesterol: 60
- Protein: 12

812. Ham Corn Au Gratin

Serving: 2 servings. | Prep: 10mins | Cook: 20mins | Ready in:

Ingredients

- 2 teaspoons butter
- 5 teaspoons all-purpose flour
- 1/4 teaspoon ground mustard
- 1/8 teaspoon pepper
- 1 cup milk
- 1 cup diced fully cooked ham
- 1-1/4 cups frozen corn, thawed
- 2 tablespoons finely chopped green pepper
- 1 tablespoon finely chopped onion
- TOPPING:
- 1/4 cup shredded cheddar cheese
- 1/4 cup crushed butter-flavored crackers (about 7 crackers)
- 2 teaspoons butter, melted
- Paprika

Direction

- Melt butter in a saucepan. Stir in the pepper, mustard and flour until smooth; add the milk gradually. Boil; cook and stir until thickened, for 2 minutes.
- Layer the ham, corn, green pepper and onion in a greased 1-qt. baking dish. Pour over the top with the sauce. Combine butter, crumbs, and cheese in a bowl; dust over the top. Then sprinkle with paprika.
- Uncover and bake for 10-15 minutes, at 375°, or until heated through and the top is golden brown.

Nutrition Information

- Calories: 552 calories
- Cholesterol: 110mg cholesterol
- Protein: 25g protein.
- Total Fat: 33g fat (17g saturated fat)
- Sodium: 1290mg sodium
- Fiber: 3g fiber)

- Total Carbohydrate: 43g carbohydrate (9g sugars

813. Ham Fettuccine Bake

Serving: 5 servings. | Prep: 15mins | Cook: 25mins | Ready in:

Ingredients

- 1/4 cup dry bread crumbs
- 1/4 teaspoon dried parsley flakes
- 3 tablespoons butter, divided
- 2 tablespoons all-purpose flour
- 2 cups milk
- 1-1/2 cups (6 ounces) sharp white cheddar cheese, shredded
- 2 cups cubed fully cooked ham
- 1-1/2 cups cooked fettuccine
- 1 cup frozen peas

Direction

- Put 1 tablespoon of butter in a small frying pan and on medium heat cook parsley and bread crumbs until golden brown, 4-5 minutes. Remove mixture from pan and set it aside. Melt the rest of the butter in a large frying pan. Whisk in flour until smooth; slowly add milk. Heat to a boil. Stirring constantly, cook until thick, 2 minutes. Mix in cheese and cook until melted, 2-3 minutes. Mix in peas, fettuccine, and ham. Put in an 11x7-in. greased dish and sprinkle bread crumb mixture on top. Cover; bake in a 350-degree oven for 20 minutes. Remove cover; bake until bubbling, 5-10 minutes.

Nutrition Information

- Calories: 483 calories
- Fiber: 2g fiber)
- Total Carbohydrate: 28g carbohydrate (7g sugars
- Cholesterol: 99mg cholesterol

- Protein: 28g protein.
- Total Fat: 29g fat (16g saturated fat)
- Sodium: 1121mg sodium

814. Ham Hot Dish

Serving: 6-8 servings. | Prep: 20mins | Cook: 20mins | Ready in:

Ingredients

- 1/4 cup chopped onion
- 1/4 cup butter
- 3 tablespoons all-purpose flour
- 1/2 teaspoon salt
- Dash ground nutmeg
- Dash pepper
- 2-3/4 cups milk
- 1/4 cup chopped green pepper
- 1 can (4 ounces) mushrooms stems and pieces, drained
- 1 jar (4 ounces) diced pimientos, drained
- 1 package (7 ounces) macaroni, cooked and drained
- 1-1/2 cups cubed fully cooked ham
- 1/2 cup plus 2 tablespoons grated Parmesan cheese, divided

Direction

- Stir-fry onion in butter in a saucepan for 3 minutes or until tender. Mix in pepper, nutmeg, salt and flour. Slowly stir in milk, whisking constantly. Mix in the pimientos, mushrooms and green pepper. Let it boil then stir and boil for 2 minutes. Separate the pan from heat then stir in the macaroni and combine well.
- Scoop half of the macaroni mixture into a 13x9-inch baking pan that is greased. Top with 1/2 cup Parmesan cheese and ham. Place the remaining macaroni mixture on top. Top off with the remaining cheese. Place in the oven and bake for 20-30 minutes at 375°F or until bubbly.

Nutrition Information

- Calories: 228 calories
- Total Fat: 13g fat (7g saturated fat)
- Sodium: 753mg sodium
- Fiber: 1g fiber)
- Total Carbohydrate: 16g carbohydrate (5g sugars
- Cholesterol: 46mg cholesterol
- Protein: 12g protein.

815. Ham N Cheese Potato Bake

Serving: 10-12 servings. | Prep: 10mins | Cook: 60mins | Ready in:

Ingredients

- 1 package (24 ounces) frozen O'Brien potatoes
- 2 cups cubed fully cooked ham
- 3/4 cup shredded cheddar cheese, divided
- 1 small onion, chopped
- 2 cups sour cream
- 1 can (10-3/4 ounces) condensed cheddar cheese soup, undiluted
- 1 can (10-3/4 ounces) condensed cream of potato soup, undiluted
- 1/4 teaspoon pepper

Direction

- Combine onion, 1/2 cup cheese, ham and potatoes in a big bowl. Combine pepper, soups, and sour cream in another bowl; place into the potato mixture; combine thoroughly.
- Move to an oiled 3-quart baking dish. Sprinkle the rest of cheese over top. Bake for 60-65 minutes at 350 degrees without cover or until potatoes are tender and the mixture is bubbly. Let it sit for 10 minutes; serve.

Nutrition Information

- Calories: 227 calories
- Protein: 9g protein.
- Total Fat: 13g fat (8g saturated fat)
- Sodium: 769mg sodium
- Fiber: 2g fiber)
- Total Carbohydrate: 18g carbohydrate (2g sugars
- Cholesterol: 52mg cholesterol

816.   Ham Rolls Continental

Serving: 6 servings. | Prep: 20mins | Cook: 25mins | Ready in:

Ingredients

- 6 thin slices fully cooked ham (about 5-inch square)
- 6 thin slices Swiss cheese (about 4-inch square)
- 6 thin slices cheddar cheese (about 4-inch square)
- 12 frozen broccoli spears, thawed
- 1 small onion, thinly sliced into rings
- 2 tablespoons butter
- 2 tablespoons all-purpose flour
- 1/2 teaspoon salt
- Dash white pepper
- 1-1/4 cups milk

Direction

- Put a slice of Cheddar, a slice of Swiss cheese, and 2 broccoli spears (floret ends out) on top of each ham slice; roll up as jelly-roll style. Place in an ungreased 11x7-in. baking dish with the seam side down. Spread on top with the onion rings.
- Melt butter in a small saucepan. Stir in flour, pepper, and salt until smooth. Stir in milk gradually. Bring to a boil. Boil and stir for around 2 minutes. Then pour over the center of the ham rolls.

- Bake while uncovered for 25-30 minutes at 350°, or until the broccoli is soft.

Nutrition Information

- Calories: 239 calories
- Sodium: 690mg sodium
- Fiber: 2g fiber)
- Total Carbohydrate: 10g carbohydrate (5g sugars
- Cholesterol: 57mg cholesterol
- Protein: 16g protein.
- Total Fat: 16g fat (10g saturated fat)

817.   Ham Souffle

Serving: 6 servings. | Prep: 10mins | Cook: 60mins | Ready in:

Ingredients

- 1 package (1 pound) frozen Tater Tots, divided
- 1-1/4 cups frozen peas
- 1-1/2 cups diced fully cooked ham
- 1 cup shredded Swiss cheese, divided
- 1/3 cup sliced green onions
- 1-1/4 cups whole milk
- 3 large eggs
- 3/4 teaspoon salt
- 1/2 to 3/4 teaspoon dried tarragon
- 1/2 teaspoon pepper

Direction

- In an 11x7-inch baking dish coated with cook spray, put 1/2 of the potatoes. Place peas, the ham, three-fourth cup of cheese, onions, then the leftover potatoes in layers.
- Combine seasonings, eggs, and milk in a bowl; add to the potatoes. Sprinkle the leftover cheese over. Bake without a cover for 60 minutes at 350°.

Nutrition Information

- Calories: 349 calories
- Sodium: 1186mg sodium
- Fiber: 3g fiber)
- Total Carbohydrate: 28g carbohydrate (6g sugars
- Cholesterol: 148mg cholesterol
- Protein: 20g protein.
- Total Fat: 19g fat (7g saturated fat)

818. Ham And Asparagus Casserole

Serving: 6 | Prep: 15mins | Cook: 30mins | Ready in:

Ingredients

- 1 pound fresh asparagus
- 5 hard cooked eggs, chopped
- 2 cups diced ham
- 1/4 cup chopped onion
- 1/4 cup chopped green bell pepper
- 1/3 cup shredded Cheddar cheese
- 2 tablespoons tapioca
- 2 tablespoons chopped fresh parsley
- 1 tablespoon lemon juice
- 1 (10.75 ounce) can condensed cream of mushroom soup
- 1/2 cup evaporated milk

Direction

- Set the oven for preheating to 375°F (190°C).
- Cut the asparagus and slice into 3/4-inch pieces; place inside the microwave and blanch for 2 to 3 minutes and drain.
- Arrange the ham, asparagus and eggs in a 9x13 inch baking dish that's lightly greased. Mix together the milk, soup, lemon juice, parsley, tapioca, cheese, bell pepper and onion in a big bowl; combine well. Pour the mixture in the baking dish and stir together with ham, asparagus and eggs.
- Let it bake inside the oven at 375°F (190°C) for 25 to 35 minutes or until completely cooked.

Put aside to stand for 5 minutes before serving.

Nutrition Information

- Calories: 254 calories;
- Total Fat: 14.8
- Sodium: 953
- Total Carbohydrate: 13.9
- Cholesterol: 190
- Protein: 17.1

819. Ham And Asparagus Spaghetti Casserole

Serving: 2 casseroles (8 servings each). | Prep: 30mins | Cook: 45mins | Ready in:

Ingredients

- 1 package (16 ounces) spaghetti, broken into thirds
- 2 pounds fresh asparagus, trimmed and cut into 1-1/2 inch pieces
- 2 eggs, lightly beaten
- 1/2 cup grated Parmesan cheese, divided
- 1/4 cup butter, cubed
- 1/4 cup all-purpose flour
- 1 can (12 ounces) evaporated milk
- 1 cup milk
- 1/2 cup chicken broth
- 1/2 cup mayonnaise
- 2 tablespoons lemon juice
- 2 teaspoons grated onion
- 2 teaspoons prepared mustard
- 2 teaspoons minced fresh parsley
- 1/4 teaspoon dried rosemary, crushed
- 1/2 cup shredded cheddar cheese
- 3 cups cubed fully cooked ham

Direction

- Cook spaghetti following the package instructions. Rinse using cold water; drain. In the meantime, bring 2 cups of water to a boil in a large saucepan. Put in asparagus. Cook with a cover for 3-5 minutes or until tender-crisp; drain.

- Toss spaghetti together with 1/4 cup Parmesan cheese and eggs in a large bowl. Transfer into two 2-qt. baking dishes coated with cooking spray.
- Melt butter in a large saucepan. Stir in flour until it gets smooth. Slowly add in the broth, milk and evaporated milk. Boil; cook while stirring for 1-2 minutes, until thickened.
- Take away from the heat. Whisk in the rosemary, parsley, mustard, onion, lemon juice and mayonnaise. Stir in the rest of Parmesan and cheddar cheese until combined.
- Sprinkle asparagus and ham over spaghetti crust. Top with cheese sauce. Bake with a cover for 40 minutes at 350°. Take off cover; bake for 5-10 minutes more, until edges are filled with bubbles.

Nutrition Information

- Calories: 307 calories
- Cholesterol: 65mg cholesterol
- Protein: 14g protein.
- Total Fat: 15g fat (6g saturated fat)
- Sodium: 530mg sodium
- Fiber: 1g fiber)
- Total Carbohydrate: 28g carbohydrate (4g sugars

---

820. Ham And Chicken Casserole

Serving: 2 | Prep: 20mins | Cook: 35mins | Ready in:

Ingredients

- 1/2 cup uncooked egg noodles
- 2 tablespoons butter
- 2 tablespoons all-purpose flour
- 1 cup milk

- 1/2 cup cooked, cubed chicken breast meat
- 1/2 cup cooked, diced ham
- 1/4 cup chopped celery
- 1/4 teaspoon salt
- 1/4 teaspoon ground black pepper
- 3 ounces shredded Cheddar cheese
- 1 teaspoon paprika

Direction

- Preheat an oven to 200°C/400°F; grease a medium baking dish lightly.
- Boil a saucepan with lightly salted water; in boiling water, cook egg noodles till al dente for 6-8 minutes. Drain.
- Melt butter in a saucepan on medium low heat; mix flour in, heating till bubbly. Whisk milk in slowly; cook till smooth and thick for 5 minutes, constantly mixing. Take the saucepan off the heat; mix pepper, salt, celery, ham, chicken and noodles in. Put mixture into the prepped baking dish.
- In the preheated oven, bake for 15 minutes; sprinkle with paprika and cheese. Bake for 5 minutes more; serve hot.

Nutrition Information

- Calories: 514 calories;
- Total Carbohydrate: 20.7
- Cholesterol: 141
- Protein: 33.4
- Total Fat: 32.9
- Sodium: 1166

---

821. Ham And Creamy Potato Scallops

Serving: 12 servings. | Prep: 25mins | Cook: 50mins | Ready in:

Ingredients

- 5 pounds medium potatoes

- 3 tablespoons butter
- 1/4 cup all-purpose flour
- 1 can (14-1/2 ounces) chicken broth
- 1 pound diced fully cooked ham
- 1 cup process cheese sauce
- 1/2 cup sliced celery
- 1/4 cup chopped onion
- 1/4 cup mayonnaise
- Salt and pepper to taste

Direction

- Put potatoes in a Dutch oven and pour in water to cover. Bring to a boil. Lower the heat; cover and cook until partially cooked, about 20-25 minutes. Drain and cool the potatoes. Peel potatoes and slice into 1/4-in. slices. Spread in 3-qt. baking dish coated with grease.
- Set an oven to 350° and preheat. Melt butter in large saucepan. Mix in flour until smooth; pour in broth. Bring to a boil. Cook while stirring until thickened and bubbly, about 1-2 minutes. Take away from heat. Mix in the rest of ingredients. Pour over potatoes and mix gently to coat.
- Bake without a cover until potatoes are tender, about 50-60 minutes.

Nutrition Information

- Calories: 483 calories
- Protein: 22g protein.
- Total Fat: 20g fat (9g saturated fat)
- Sodium: 1424mg sodium
- Fiber: 5g fiber)
- Total Carbohydrate: 56g carbohydrate (5g sugars
- Cholesterol: 68mg cholesterol

822. Ham And Noodle Bake

Serving: 3 servings. | Prep: 25mins | Cook: 30mins | Ready in:

Ingredients

- 2 cups uncooked egg noodles
- 1 cup cubed deli ham
- 1/2 cup shredded cheddar cheese
- 1/2 cup condensed cream of celery soup, undiluted
- 1/3 cup 2% milk
- 1 teaspoon finely chopped onion
- 2 teaspoons butter, melted, divided
- 1/4 teaspoon poppy seeds
- 1/4 teaspoon dried oregano
- 1/8 teaspoon salt
- 1/8 teaspoon dried basil
- 3 tablespoons dry bread crumbs

Direction

- Follow the instruction on package to cook the noodles. At the same time, in a small-sized bowl, mix seasonings, poppy seeds, 1 teaspoon of butter, onion, milk, soup, cheese and ham. Drain the noodles; put into the ham mixture.
- Move into a 1.5-quart baking dish which is coated using the cooking spray. Mix the leftover butter and breadcrumbs; scatter on top of the casserole. Bake, with no cover, at 325 degrees till completely heated or for 30 to 35 minutes.

Nutrition Information

- Calories: 299 calories
- Sodium: 1093mg sodium
- Fiber: 2g fiber)
- Total Carbohydrate: 32g carbohydrate (3g sugars
- Cholesterol: 66mg cholesterol
- Protein: 19g protein.
- Total Fat: 11g fat (5g saturated fat)

823. Ham And Potato Bake

Serving: 8 servings | Prep: 10mins | Cook: | Ready in:

Ingredients

- 1 pkg. (24 oz.) ORE-IDA STEAM N' MASH Cut Russet Potatoes
- 2 cups frozen broccoli florets , thawed
- 1-1/2 cups chopped OSCAR MAYER Baked Cooked Ham
- 1-1/2 cups KRAFT Shredded Sharp Cheddar Cheese , divided
- 1 jar (12 oz.) HEINZ HomeStyle Pork Gravy

Direction

- Microwave potatoes and mash them following package instructions; blend with 1 cup cheese, ham, and broccoli.
- With a spoon, transfer the mixture to an 11x8-in. baking dish coated with cooking spray; arrange the remaining cheese over top.
- Bake for 15 minutes or until heated through. After approximately 10 minutes, cook gravy for 3-5 minutes or until heated through while mixing from time to time.
- Place gravy on top of potato casserole; serve.

Nutrition Information

- Calories: 190
- Total Carbohydrate: 18 g
- Cholesterol: 35 mg
- Protein: 12 g
- Total Fat: 8 g
- Sodium: 920 mg
- Fiber: 2 g
- Saturated Fat: 4.5 g
- Sugar: 0 g

824.   Ham And Potatoes Au Gratin

Serving: 2 servings. | Prep: 15mins | Cook: 35mins | Ready in:

Ingredients

- 2 cups sliced peeled potatoes, cooked
- 1 cup diced cooked ham
- 1 tablespoon finely chopped onion
- 1/3 cup butter, cubed
- 3 tablespoons all-purpose flour
- 1-1/2 cups milk
- 1 cup shredded cheddar cheese
- 3/4 teaspoon salt
- Dash white pepper
- Minced fresh parsley

Direction

- Mix onion, ham and potatoes in a greased 1-qt. baking dish; put aside.
- Melt butter over medium heat in a saucepan; stir in flour until smooth. Add milk gradually. Bring to a boil; cook while stirring until the mixture becomes bubbly and thickened or for 2 minutes. Add pepper, salt and cheese; stir until the cheese is melted. Pour over the potato mixture and gently stir to mix.
- Bake without a cover at 350° until bubbly or for 35-40 minutes. Finish with parsley as garnish.

Nutrition Information

- Calories: 872 calories
- Total Fat: 59g fat (37g saturated fat)
- Sodium: 2526mg sodium
- Fiber: 3g fiber)
- Total Carbohydrate: 53g carbohydrate (11g sugars
- Cholesterol: 204mg cholesterol
- Protein: 35g protein.

825.   Ham And Swiss Casserole

Serving: 4 | Prep: 15mins | Cook: 30mins | Ready in:

Ingredients

- 2 cups egg noodles
- 2 tablespoons vegetable oil
- 1 cup chopped onions
- 1 (6 ounce) can mushrooms, drained
- 1 cup diced cooked ham
- 1 cup diced Swiss cheese
- 1 teaspoon salt
- 1/2 teaspoon ground black pepper
- 2 eggs
- 1/4 cup milk
- 1/4 cup grated Parmesan cheese

Direction

- Boil a big pot of lightly salted water. Add egg noodles; cook till al dente for 8-10 minutes. Drain.
- Preheat oven to 400 degrees F (200 degrees C).Toss 2 tsp. oil and drained noodles. Heat leftover oil in the skillet; sauté onion till soft on medium heat. Mix pepper, salt, Swiss cheese, ham, mushrooms, onion and noodles; put in a 3-qt. greased casserole dish. Mix milk and egg in a bowl; put on noodle mixture. Sprinkle with parmesan cheese.
- In the preheated oven, bake for 30 minutes.

Nutrition Information

- Calories: 432 calories;
- Cholesterol: 163
- Protein: 24.7
- Total Fat: 28
- Sodium: 1491
- Total Carbohydrate: 21

826. Ham And Vegetable Roll Ups

Serving: 4-6 servings. | Prep: 20mins | Cook: 25mins | Ready in:

Ingredients

- 2 cups seasoned croutons
- 1/4 cup butter, melted
- 1 can (10-3/4 ounces) condensed cream of chicken soup, undiluted
- 1 cup mayonnaise
- 2 tablespoons lemon juice
- 1 package (10 ounces) frozen chopped spinach, drained
- 1/3 cup plain yogurt or sour cream
- 1 teaspoon dried minced onion
- 1 teaspoon Worcestershire sauce
- 8 slices boiled ham, sliced thin
- 8 spears fresh asparagus
- 1/2 pound sliced fresh mushrooms
- 2 tablespoons cold butter

Direction

- Mix 1/4 cup butter and croutons; spread in square 9-in. baking dish. Mix lemon juice, mayonnaise and soup. Scoop 1/2 mixture on croutons; put leftover aside.
- Mix Worcestershire sauce, onion, yogurt and spinach in a bowl; spread on the ham slices. Put an asparagus spear on top of each; roll up. Put rolls in baking dish, seam side down; scoop leftover sauce over. Sauté mushrooms in 2 tbsp. butter; sprinkle over. Bake for 25 minutes at 350° till bubbly.

Nutrition Information

- Calories:
- Protein:
- Total Fat:
- Sodium:
- Fiber:
- Total Carbohydrate:
- Cholesterol:

827. Ham Potato Phyllo Bake

Serving: 12-15 servings. | Prep: 30mins | Cook: 20mins | Ready in:

Ingredients

- 3 pounds red potatoes, peeled and thinly sliced
- 1 medium onion, chopped
- 8 tablespoons butter, divided
- 20 sheets phyllo dough (14x9 inches)
- 2 cups (16 ounces) sour cream
- 2 cups cubed fully cooked ham
- 2 cups shredded cheddar cheese
- 7 teaspoons fresh dill weed, divided
- 2 teaspoons garlic powder
- 1 teaspoon salt
- 1/2 teaspoon pepper
- 1 large egg, lightly beaten
- 2 tablespoons half-and-half cream

Direction

- In a Dutch oven, place potatoes; pour in water to cover. Heat to a boil then lower the heat. Put on cover and cook until tender or for 10-15 minutes. Drain. In a small skillet, in 1 tablespoon butter, sauté onion until tender; put aside.
- Melt the rest of butter. Brush some of butter on a 13x9-inch baking dish. Spread out phyllo sheets, cut to fit in the dish. (Cover dough with a damp cloth and plastic wrap while assembling). Arrange 1 phyllo sheet in prepared dish; brush butter on the surface. Repeat 2 times.
- Top with cheese, ham, onion, potatoes, and half of the sour cream. Combine pepper, salt, garlic powder, and 6 teaspoons dill; spread half over the cheese. Make a layer of 3 phyllo sheets, brush butter on each. Top with seasoning mixture, ham, onion, potatoes, the remaining sour cream, and cheese.
- Layer with the rest of phyllo dough, brushing butter on each sheet. Mix cream and egg together; brush over the surface. Sprinkle remaining dill over the top.
- Bake at 350 degrees without cover until heated through or for 20-25 minutes. Let it sit for 5 minutes. Slice into squares.

Nutrition Information

- Calories: 321 calories
- Protein: 12g protein.
- Total Fat: 18g fat (11g saturated fat)
- Sodium: 636mg sodium
- Fiber: 2g fiber)
- Total Carbohydrate: 26g carbohydrate (3g sugars
- Cholesterol: 79mg cholesterol

---

828.   Hash Brown Pork Bake

Serving: 8 servings. | Prep: 15mins | Cook: 60mins | Ready in:

Ingredients

- 2 cups (16 ounces) sour cream
- 1 can (10-3/4 ounces) condensed cream of chicken soup, undiluted
- 1 package (32 ounces) frozen cubed hash brown potatoes, thawed
- 2 cups cubed cooked pork
- 1 pound process cheese (Velveeta), cubed
- 1/4 cup chopped onion
- 2 cups crushed cornflakes
- 1/2 cup butter, melted
- 1 cup shredded part-skim mozzarella cheese

Direction

- Mix soup and sour cream together in a big bowl then stir in the onion, process cheese, pork and hash browns. Pour it into a 3-qt. greased baking dish. Toss butter with cornflake crumbs then spread this mixture on the top, leaving it uncovered. Bake at 350°F for 50 minutes then scatter mozzarella cheese over it. Bake until it turns bubbly for another 10 minutes.

Nutrition Information

- Calories: 721 calories

- Total Carbohydrate: 47g carbohydrate (10g sugars
- Cholesterol: 150mg cholesterol
- Protein: 33g protein.
- Total Fat: 43g fat (26g saturated fat)
- Sodium: 1371mg sodium
- Fiber: 2g fiber)

- Calories: 533 calories
- Cholesterol: 56mg cholesterol
- Protein: 22g protein.
- Total Fat: 10g fat (3g saturated fat)
- Sodium: 1859mg sodium
- Fiber: 3g fiber)
- Total Carbohydrate: 93g carbohydrate (78g sugars

829.   Hawaiian Ham Bake

Serving: 4-6 servings. | Prep: 15mins | Cook: 30mins | Ready in:

Ingredients

- 3 cups cubed fully cooked ham
- 1 medium onion, thinly sliced
- 1 small green pepper, cut into rings
- 2/3 cup raisins
- 3/4 cup pineapple tidbits, drained
- 3/4 cup packed brown sugar
- 3 tablespoons cornstarch
- 3 teaspoons ground mustard
- 1/4 teaspoon salt
- 1-1/2 cups pineapple juice
- 1/2 cup cider vinegar
- 4-1/2 teaspoons reduced-sodium soy sauce
- Hot cooked rice

Direction

- Set the oven at 350° and start preheating. Layer pineapple, raisins, green pepper, onion and ham in a greased 2-qt. baking dish.
- Combine salt, mustard, cornstarch and brown sugar in a large saucepan. Mix in vinegar and pineapple juice till smooth. Allow to boil; cook while stirring till thickened, or for 2 minutes.
- Take away from the heat; mix in soy sauce. Transfer over the pineapple. Bake with a cover till heated through, or for 30-35 minutes. Serve with rice.

Nutrition Information

830.   Hearty Ham Casserole

Serving: 5 | Prep: 45mins | Cook: 35mins | Ready in:

Ingredients

- 2 cups potatoes, cubed
- 2 cups cooked ham, cubed
- 1 (15.25 ounce) can whole kernel corn, drained
- 1/4 cup finely minced fresh parsley
- 1/4 cup butter
- 1 tablespoon chopped onions
- 1/3 cup all-purpose flour
- 1 3/4 cups milk
- 1/8 teaspoon ground black pepper
- 4 ounces processed cheese food, shredded

Direction

- Preheat an oven to 175°C/350°F.
- Boil a big pot with salted water. Add potatoes; cook for 15 minutes till tender but still firm. Drain; cool.
- Mix parsley, corn, ham and potatoes; put aside. Sauté onion in butter in a saucepan for 2 minutes; mix in flour till well blended. Add pepper and milk gradually; boil. Cook while stirring for 2 minutes. Take off heat. Pour over ham mixture; mix to combine well.
- Pour into 11x7-in. greased baking dish; cover. Bake for 25 minutes then uncover; sprinkle with cheese. Bake till cheese melts for 5-10 minutes more.

Nutrition Information

- Calories: 452 calories;
- Total Fat: 27.4
- Sodium: 1271
- Total Carbohydrate: 33
- Cholesterol: 76
- Protein: 21

831. Hot Pork Salad Supreme

Serving: 4-6 servings. | Prep: 10mins | Cook: 30mins | Ready in:

Ingredients

- 2 cups diced cooked pork
- 2 cups cooked rice
- 1 can (10-3/4 ounces) condensed cream of chicken soup, undiluted
- 1 cup diced celery
- 1/2 cup mayonnaise
- 1 can (4 ounces) mushroom stems and pieces, drained
- 1 tablespoon lemon juice
- 1 tablespoon finely chopped onion
- 1/4 teaspoon salt
- 1 cup cornflake crumbs
- 1/2 cup sliced almonds
- 2 tablespoons butter, melted

Direction

- Mix well the first 9 ingredients. Scoop into an ungreased 11x7-in. baking dish. Then combine butter, almonds, and crumbs; sprinkle on top.
- Uncover and bake for 30-40 minutes, at 350°, or until lightly browned.

Nutrition Information

- Calories: 484 calories
- Total Carbohydrate: 33g carbohydrate (3g sugars
- Cholesterol: 63mg cholesterol
- Protein: 20g protein.

- Total Fat: 30g fat (7g saturated fat)
- Sodium: 845mg sodium
- Fiber: 2g fiber)

832. Hungarian Cabbage With Noodles

Serving: 10 servings. | Prep: 15mins | Cook: 50mins | Ready in:

Ingredients

- 5 slices bacon, diced
- 2 teaspoons sugar
- 1 teaspoon salt
- 6 cups chopped cabbage (1-inch squares)
- 3 cups cooked noodles (4 ounces uncooked)
- 1 cup (8 ounces) sour cream
- Paprika

Direction

- Sauté the bacon till crispy in a big frying pan. Take the bacon out; put aside. Whisk the salt and sugar to the bacon drippings. Put in the cabbage, whisk till the cabbage coats with the bacon drippings. Cook with a cover for 7 - 10 minutes. Put in the bacon and cooked noodles, whisk till blend. Adjust the seasoning to taste.
- Scoop into 2-quart baking casserole; cover securely and bake at 325 degrees for 45 minutes. Spread the sour cream on top of the casserole; dust with the paprika and bring back to the oven for 5 minutes longer.

Nutrition Information

- Calories:
- Sodium:
- Fiber:
- Total Carbohydrate:
- Cholesterol:
- Protein:
- Total Fat:

833. Makeover Ham 'n' Potato Bake

Serving: 10 servings. | Prep: 20mins | Cook: 30mins | Ready in:

Ingredients

- 2 pounds red potatoes, peeled and cubed
- 1 cup chopped onion
- 1/2 cup chopped green pepper
- 1/2 cup chopped sweet red pepper
- 1 tablespoon canola oil
- 1/3 cup all-purpose flour
- 1/4 teaspoon dried thyme
- 1/4 teaspoon pepper
- 2 cans (12 ounces each) fat-free evaporated milk
- 1 cup plus 2 tablespoons shredded reduced-fat cheddar cheese, divided
- 2 tablespoons Dijon mustard
- 1-1/2 pounds fully cooked lean ham slices, cut into strips
- 1 package (16 ounces) frozen sliced carrots, cooked and drained
- 1/4 cup minced fresh parsley

Direction

- In a big saucepan, put the potatoes and pour water to cover, then boil. Lower the heat, put a cover and let it cook for 10 to 15 minutes or until it becomes tender, then drain.
- In the meantime, sauté the peppers and onion in oil in a big nonstick frying pan until it becomes tender. Mix in the thyme, pepper and flour until combined. Slowly add the milk, then boil. Let it cook and stir for 2 minutes or until it becomes thick. Lower the heat, then add mustard and 1 cup of cheese. Let it cook and stir until the cheese melts.
- Fold in the parsley, carrots, ham and potatoes. Move to a cooking spray coated 3-quart baking dish. Put a cover and let it bake for 20 minutes at 400 degrees. Take off the cover and bake for 10 minutes more. Sprinkle the leftover cheese on top.

Nutrition Information

- Calories: 316 calories
- Sodium: 1046mg sodium
- Fiber: 4g fiber)
- Total Carbohydrate: 38g carbohydrate (0 sugars
- Cholesterol: 26mg cholesterol
- Protein: 27g protein. Diabetic Exchanges: 2-1/2 lean meat
- Total Fat: 6g fat (2g saturated fat)

834. Meaty Noodle Casserole

Serving: 8 servings. | Prep: 20mins | Cook: 30mins | Ready in:

Ingredients

- 1 package (12 ounces) wide egg noodles
- 1 pound ground beef
- 1/2 pound Jones No Sugar Pork Sausage Roll sausage
- 3 tablespoons chopped onion
- 1/4 teaspoon garlic powder
- 1 can (14-3/4 ounces) cream-style corn
- 1 can (14-1/2 ounces) stewed tomatoes, cut up
- 1 can (10-3/4 ounces) condensed cream of chicken soup, undiluted
- 1 cup chopped pimiento-stuffed olives
- 2 tablespoons minced fresh parsley
- 1-1/2 cups (6 ounces) shredded cheddar cheese

Direction

- Cook pasta following package instructions. In the meantime, in a Dutch oven over medium heat, cook garlic powder, onion, pork sausage and beef until meat is no longer pink; drain.

Put in parsley, olives, soup, tomatoes and corn; heat through.

- Drain pasta; mix into meat mixture. Place to a greased baking dish 13x9 inches. Sprinkle cheese on top. Cover up and bake at 350° for 25 minutes. Remove the cover; bake till cheese is melted, about 5-10 more minutes.

Nutrition Information

- Calories: 509 calories
- Sodium: 1164mg sodium
- Fiber: 3g fiber)
- Total Carbohydrate: 50g carbohydrate (6g sugars
- Cholesterol: 99mg cholesterol
- Protein: 25g protein.
- Total Fat: 24g fat (10g saturated fat)

835. Microwave Cornbread Casserole

Serving: 6 servings. | Prep: 5mins | Cook: 20mins | Ready in:

Ingredients

- 2 cups frozen mixed vegetables
- 1-1/2 cups cubed fully cooked ham
- 1 package (6 ounces) cornbread stuffing mix
- 3 large eggs
- 2 cups whole milk
- 1/4 teaspoon salt
- 1/4 teaspoon pepper
- 1 cup shredded cheddar cheese

Direction

- Combine stuffing mix, ham, and vegetables in an oiled 11x7-inch microwave-safe dish; stir well. Mix pepper, salt, milk, and eggs together in a bowl. Put into cornbread mixture. Chill, covered for at least 5 hours or overnight in the fridge.

- Take out of the fridge half an hour before cooking. Cook, covered, in the microwave for 14 to 18 minutes or until a knife comes out clean from the center. Scatter top with cheese. Allow to stand, covered, for 5 minutes before enjoying.

Nutrition Information

- Calories: 358 calories
- Sodium: 1170mg sodium
- Fiber: 4g fiber)
- Total Carbohydrate: 35g carbohydrate (9g sugars
- Cholesterol: 156mg cholesterol
- Protein: 21g protein.
- Total Fat: 15g fat (7g saturated fat)

836. One Pot Pork And Rice

Serving: 6 servings. | Prep: 20mins | Cook: 60mins | Ready in:

Ingredients

- 6 boneless pork loin chops (5 ounces each)
- 2 teaspoons canola oil
- 1 cup uncooked long grain rice
- 1 large onion, sliced
- 1 large green pepper, sliced
- 1 envelope pork gravy mix
- 1 can (28 ounces) diced tomatoes, undrained
- 1-1/2 cups water

Direction

- Brown both sides of the pork chops in oil in a Dutch oven; drain. Next, take the chops out of the pan and keep warm. In the Dutch oven, layer rice, green pepper, and onion; put pork chops on top.
- Combine water, tomatoes, and gravy mix; pour over the chops. Bake at 350°, covered, until a thermometer reads 160°, or for 1 hour.

485

Nutrition Information

- Calories: 391 calories
- Sodium: 545mg sodium
- Fiber: 3g fiber)
- Total Carbohydrate: 40g carbohydrate (0 sugars
- Cholesterol: 83mg cholesterol
- Protein: 33g protein. Diabetic Exchanges: 3-1/2 lean meat
- Total Fat: 10g fat (3g saturated fat)

837.   Pantry Pork Dish

Serving: 4 servings. | Prep: 10mins | Cook: 01hours15mins | Ready in:

Ingredients

- 1 pound ground pork
- 1 small onion, chopped, divided
- 1/2 teaspoon ground allspice
- 1/2 teaspoon dried oregano
- 1/2 teaspoon salt, divided
- 1/2 teaspoon pepper, divided
- 3 medium potatoes, peeled and sliced 1/4 inch thick
- 2 tablespoons all-purpose flour
- 2-1/2 cups julienned peeled butternut squash
- 1/4 teaspoon ground nutmeg
- 1-1/2 cups frozen green beans
- 1/4 cup sliced almonds, toasted

Direction

- Mix 1/4 teaspoon pepper, allspice, pork, 1/4 teaspoon salt, oregano, and half the onion. Press mixture in a 9-in. square greased pan. Put remaining onion and potatoes on top. Mix remaining salt and flour and spread over potatoes. Cover; bake in a 350-degree oven for 40 minutes. Drain excess liquid. On top of the potatoes, layer squash, nutmeg, the rest of the pepper, and beans. Cover; bake until veggies

are tender, 30 minutes. Sprinkle on almonds; bake until bubbling, 5 minutes.

Nutrition Information

- Calories: 505 calories
- Protein: 28g protein.
- Total Fat: 20g fat (7g saturated fat)
- Sodium: 424mg sodium
- Fiber: 10g fiber)
- Total Carbohydrate: 55g carbohydrate (9g sugars
- Cholesterol: 76mg cholesterol

838.   Parsnips & Ham Au Gratin

Serving: 6 servings. | Prep: 20mins | Cook: 60mins | Ready in:

Ingredients

- 1 pound parsnips, peeled and sliced
- 1 pound Yukon Gold potatoes, peeled and sliced
- 2 cups cubed fully cooked ham
- 1 can (10-3/4 ounces) condensed cream of mushroom with roasted garlic soup, undiluted
- 2/3 cup 2% milk
- 1/2 cup grated Parmesan cheese, divided
- 1/2 teaspoon dried thyme
- 1/4 teaspoon pepper
- 1/4 cup dry bread crumbs
- 2 tablespoons butter, melted

Direction

- In a 13x9-in. greased baking dish, put ham, potatoes and parsnips. Mix pepper, thyme, 1/4 cup cheese, milk and soup; put on parsnip mixture.
- Mix leftover cheese, butter and breadcrumbs in a small bowl; sprinkle on top.

- Cover; bake for 40 minutes at 375°. Uncover; bake till potatoes are tender for 20-25 minutes.

Nutrition Information

- Calories: 296 calories
- Fiber: 5g fiber)
- Total Carbohydrate: 33g carbohydrate (6g sugars
- Cholesterol: 45mg cholesterol
- Protein: 15g protein.
- Total Fat: 12g fat (6g saturated fat)
- Sodium: 1082mg sodium

839.   Pork Chop Bake

Serving: 2 servings. | Prep: 20mins | Cook: 45mins | Ready in:

Ingredients

- 2 boneless pork loin chops (5 ounces each)
- 2 teaspoons butter
- 2 medium apples, peeled and sliced
- 3/4 cup whole-berry cranberry sauce
- 1 small sweet onion, halved and thinly sliced
- 2 tablespoons brown sugar
- 1/4 teaspoon ground cinnamon

Direction

- Set oven to 325 degrees and start preheating. In a small nonstick skillet, in butter, brown pork chops.
- At the same time, combine onion, cranberry sauce, and apple in a small bowl. Place it over an 8-inch square baking dish coated with cooking spray. Mix together cinnamon and brown sugar; arrange over the apple mixture. Put pork chops on top.
- Put on cover and bake for 45-50 minutes or until apples are tender and pork reaches 145 degrees.

Nutrition Information

- Calories: 499 calories
- Cholesterol: 75mg cholesterol
- Protein: 29g protein.
- Total Fat: 11g fat (4g saturated fat)
- Sodium: 93mg sodium
- Fiber: 5g fiber)
- Total Carbohydrate: 75g carbohydrate (57g sugars

840.   Pork Chop Casserole

Serving: 6 | Prep: | Cook: 1hours20mins | Ready in:

Ingredients

- 6 center-cut pork chops
- 6 Yukon Gold potatoes, peeled and quartered
- 2 onions, quartered
- 1 pound baby carrots
- 1 (1 ounce) package dry onion soup mix
- salt and ground black pepper to taste
- 1 (14 ounce) can beef broth

Direction

- Preheat an oven to 175°C/350°F.
- Put pork chops in a roasting pan; put carrots, onions and potatoes around the chops. Sprinkle onion soup mix on veggies and chops; season with black pepper and salt. Put beef broth over the whole mixture.
- Cover the roasting pan; in the preheated oven, bake for 1 hour till pork chops aren't pink in the middle. An inserted instant-read thermometer in the middle should read at least 63°C/145°F.

Nutrition Information

- Calories: 333 calories;
- Total Fat: 7.5
- Sodium: 731
- Total Carbohydrate: 38.1

- Cholesterol: 59
- Protein: 28.4

841. Pork Chop Potato Bake

Serving: 6 servings. | Prep: 15mins | Cook: 01hours15mins | Ready in:

Ingredients

- 6 pork chops (5 ounces each), trimmed
- 1 can (10-3/4 ounces) condensed cream of mushroom soup, undiluted
- 1 can (4 ounces) slice mushrooms, drained
- 1/4 cup chicken broth
- 1/2 teaspoon garlic salt
- 1/2 teaspoon Worcestershire sauce
- 1/4 teaspoon dried thyme
- 1 can (16 ounces) whole potatoes, drained
- 1 package (10 ounces) frozen peas, thawed
- 1 tablespoon diced pimientos

Direction

- Cook the chops until brown on each side in a cooking spray-coated big frying pan. Put the chops in an ungreased 13x9-inch baking pan. Mix together the succeeding 6 ingredients, then stir well and pour it on top of the pork. Put cover and let it bake for 1 hour at 350 degrees. Add pimientos, peas and potatoes. Put cover and let it bake for another 15 minutes or until the vegetables are heated through and the pork becomes tender.

Nutrition Information

- Calories: 232 calories
- Sodium: 787mg sodium
- Fiber: 0 fiber)
- Total Carbohydrate: 18g carbohydrate (0 sugars
- Cholesterol: 63mg cholesterol

- Protein: 25g protein. Diabetic Exchanges: 2-1/2 lean meat
- Total Fat: 6g fat (0 saturated fat)

842. Pork Chop Potato Casserole

Serving: 8 | Prep: 15mins | Cook: 50mins | Ready in:

Ingredients

- 1 tablespoon vegetable oil
- 8 pork chops
- 1 teaspoon seasoned salt
- 1 (10.75 ounce) can condensed cream of celery soup
- 2/3 cup milk
- 1/2 cup sour cream
- 1/2 teaspoon salt
- 1/4 teaspoon ground black pepper
- 1 (16 ounce) package frozen hash brown potatoes, thawed
- 3/4 cup shredded Cheddar cheese
- 1/2 (6 ounce) can French-fried onions
- 1/4 cup shredded Cheddar cheese
- 1/2 (6 ounce) can French-fried onions

Direction

- Preheat an oven to 175°C/350°F.
- Heat vegetable oil in a big skillet on medium heat. Use seasoned salt to season the pork chops. In hot oil, cook pork chops for 2-3 minutes per side till fully browned. Put pork chops on a paper towel-lined plate; drain.
- Mix pepper, salt, sour cream, milk and celery soup in a bowl. Fold 1/2 French-fried onions, 3/4 cup cheddar cheese and hash brown potatoes into the soup mixture; put into a 13x9-in. baking dish. Put pork chops over the mixture; use aluminum foil to cover the dish.
- In the preheated oven, bake for 40 minutes then remove the foil. Top pork chops with 1/4 cup Cheddar cheese and remaining half-can French-fried onions. Bake for 5 minutes till

cheese melts; an inserted instant-read thermometer in the middle of the pork chops should read 63°C/145°F.

Nutrition Information

- Calories: 422 calories;
- Cholesterol: 61
- Protein: 16.7
- Total Fat: 31.7
- Sodium: 871
- Total Carbohydrate: 23.5

---

843.   Pork Chop Skillet Meal

Serving: 4 servings. | Prep: 10mins | Cook: 25mins | Ready in:

Ingredients

- 4 pork chops (1/2 inch thick)
- 2 tablespoons vegetable oil
- 1-1/4 cup water
- 2/3 cup uncooked long grain rice
- 1/2 cup chopped onion
- 1 teaspoon salt, divided
- 1 can (11 ounces) whole kernel corn, drained
- 1 can (14-1/2 ounces) diced tomatoes, undrained
- 1/4 teaspoon pepper

Direction

- In a big skillet, in oil, brown chops; drain. Take out chops. In the skillet, mix together 1/2 teaspoon salt, onion, rice, and water. Arrange pork chops over the rice mixture; place tomatoes and corn on top. Sprinkle with the rest of salt and pepper. Heat to a boil. Lower the heat; put on cover and let simmer for 20-25 minutes or until rice and pork are tender. Let it sit for 5 minutes then serve.

Nutrition Information

- Calories: 407 calories
- Sodium: 966mg sodium
- Fiber: 4g fiber)
- Total Carbohydrate: 40g carbohydrate (8g sugars
- Cholesterol: 54mg cholesterol
- Protein: 26g protein.
- Total Fat: 14g fat (3g saturated fat)

---

844.   Pork Chop Supper Casserole

Serving: 2 servings. | Prep: 20mins | Cook: 25mins | Ready in:

Ingredients

- 1 medium tart apple, cored
- 2 bone-in pork loin chops (about 3/4 inch thick and 8 ounces each)
- 3/4 teaspoon salt, divided
- 1/4 teaspoon pepper
- 2 teaspoons canola oil
- 1/3 cup uncooked long grain rice
- 2 tablespoons chopped onion
- 3/4 cup water
- 1 teaspoon chicken bouillon granules
- 2 teaspoons butter, melted
- 2 teaspoons brown sugar
- 1/8 teaspoon ground cinnamon

Direction

- Cut the apple in 2 parts widthwise. Peel and chop 1/2 of the apple; put aside. Divide the leftover half into 3 rings; put aside.
- Sprinkle with pepper and 1/2 teaspoon salt on the chops. Brown the chops in oil in a large skillet for 3-4 minutes per side. Move to a greased 11x7-in. baking dish and keep warm.
- Cook, stir onion and rice in drippings in the same skillet until the rice is lightly browned. Stir in bouillon, water, and the remaining salt. Stir in the chopped apple. Bring to a boil.

- Lower the heat; simmer, covered, for 10 minutes.
- Scoop around the pork chops with the rice mixture. Combine cinnamon, brown sugar, and butter in a small bowl; brush over the apple slices. Then place on top of chops with the apple slices.
- Bake at 350°, covered, until the rice is tender and the juices of the meat run clear, for 25-30 minutes.

Nutrition Information

- Calories: 411 calories
- Cholesterol: 66mg cholesterol
- Protein: 21g protein.
- Total Fat: 18g fat (6g saturated fat)
- Sodium: 1385mg sodium
- Fiber: 3g fiber)
- Total Carbohydrate: 41g carbohydrate (14g sugars

---

845. Pork Chop And Chilies Casserole

Serving: 4 servings. | Prep: 15mins | Cook: 40mins | Ready in:

Ingredients

- 4 pork rib chops (3/4 to 1 inch thick)
- 1 tablespoon canola oil
- 1 medium onion, chopped
- 1 can (4 ounces) chopped green chilies
- 1/2 cup chopped celery
- 1-1/2 cups uncooked instant rice
- 1 can (10-3/4 ounces) condensed cream of mushroom soup, undiluted
- 1-1/3 cups water
- 3 tablespoons reduced-sodium soy sauce

Direction

- Set an oven at 350° to preheat. Over medium heat, cook chops in oil in a large skillet until lightly browned for 2-3 minutes per side; let drain. Then, remove and put aside.
- Sauté celery, chilies, and onion in the same skillet until the onion is soft. Add rice, sauté until lightly browned. Put in the remaining ingredients.
- Next, place in a greased 2-qt. baking dish. Lay pork chops on top. Bake until the meat is soft for 30-40 minutes.

Nutrition Information

- Calories: 415 calories
- Protein: 28g protein.
- Total Fat: 14g fat (5g saturated fat)
- Sodium: 1385mg sodium
- Fiber: 3g fiber)
- Total Carbohydrate: 41g carbohydrate (3g sugars
- Cholesterol: 57mg cholesterol

---

846. Pork Chop And Potato Casserole

Serving: 5 | Prep: 20mins | Cook: 1hours | Ready in:

Ingredients

- 1 tablespoon vegetable oil
- 6 boneless pork chops
- 1 (10.75 ounce) can condensed cream of mushroom soup
- 1 cup milk
- 4 potatoes, thinly sliced
- 1/2 cup chopped onion
- 1 cup shredded Cheddar cheese

Direction

- Preheat an oven to 200°C/400°F.
- Heat oil in a big skillet on medium high heat. Put pork chops in oil; sear.

- Mix milk and soup in a medium bowl. Put onions and potatoes in a 9x13-in. baking dish. Put browned chops over onions and potato; put soup mixture over everything.
- In the preheated oven, bake for 30 minutes. Put cheese on top; bake for 30 more minutes.

Nutrition Information

- Calories: 705 calories;
- Total Fat: 46.8
- Sodium: 636
- Total Carbohydrate: 37.9
- Cholesterol: 123
- Protein: 32.7

847.   Pork Hash Brown Bake

Serving: 6 servings. | Prep: 15mins | Cook: 30mins | Ready in:

Ingredients

- 1/4 cup all-purpose flour
- 2 teaspoons chicken bouillon granules
- 1/2 teaspoon salt
- 1 cup water
- 1/2 cup milk
- 1/4 cup sour cream
- 3 cups frozen O'Brien potatoes, thawed
- 2 cups cubed cooked pork
- 1 package (10 ounces) frozen mixed vegetables, thawed
- 1 can (4 ounces) mushroom stems and pieces, drained
- 1/2 cup crushed cornflakes
- 2 tablespoons butter, melted

Direction

- Mix together milk, water, salt, bouillon, and flour in a saucepan until smooth. Heat to a boil; stir and cook for 2 minutes or until

thickened. Take away from heat; mix in sour cream.
- Combine mushrooms, pork vegetables, and potatoes in a big bowl. Add in sour cream mixture; mix to coat nicely.
- Move to an oiled shallow 2-quart baking dish. Toss butter and cornflakes together; arrange over the top. Bake at 375 degrees without cover for 30-35 minutes or until heated through.

Nutrition Information

- Calories: 315 calories
- Protein: 19g protein.
- Total Fat: 11g fat (5g saturated fat)
- Sodium: 730mg sodium
- Fiber: 4g fiber)
- Total Carbohydrate: 35g carbohydrate (4g sugars
- Cholesterol: 62mg cholesterol

848.   Pork Noodle Casserole

Serving: 6 servings. | Prep: 10mins | Cook: 60mins | Ready in:

Ingredients

- 3 cups cubed cooked pork
- 1 can (14-3/4 ounces) cream-style corn
- 1 cup chicken broth
- 4 ounces process cheese (Velveeta), diced
- 2/3 cup chopped green pepper
- 2/3 cup chopped onion
- 1 jar (4-1/2 ounces) whole mushrooms, drained
- 2 tablespoons diced pimientos
- 1/2 teaspoon salt
- 1/4 teaspoon pepper
- 8 ounces uncooked egg noodles

Direction

- In a big bowl, mix initial 10 ingredients. Put in the noodles; coat by tossing lightly. Move into a greased 2.5-quart baking plate.
- Put a cover on and bake at 325 degrees till the noodles soften, about 60 minutes, whisking every 20 minutes.

Nutrition Information

- Calories: 418 calories
- Total Fat: 13g fat (6g saturated fat)
- Sodium: 897mg sodium
- Fiber: 3g fiber)
- Total Carbohydrate: 45g carbohydrate (6g sugars
- Cholesterol: 111mg cholesterol
- Protein: 31g protein.

849.   Pork Sauerkraut Casserole

Serving: 6 servings. | Prep: 10mins | Cook: 01hours30mins | Ready in:

Ingredients

- 1 can (27 ounces) sauerkraut, drained
- 4 cups frozen cubed hash brown potatoes, thawed
- 6 pork chops (1 inch thick)
- 1 can (10-3/4 ounces) condensed tomato soup, undiluted
- 1 medium onion, chopped
- 1/2 cup water
- 1/4 cup packed brown sugar
- 2 tablespoons cider vinegar

Direction

- Mix hash browns and sauerkraut together in a non-oiled 13x9-inch baking dish. Put pork chops on top. Mix together vinegar, sugar, water, onion, and soup; add to all. Bake without a cover for 1 1/2 hours at 350°.

Nutrition Information

- Calories: 251 calories
- Protein: 24g protein.
- Total Fat: 7g fat (2g saturated fat)
- Sodium: 1178mg sodium
- Fiber: 5g fiber)
- Total Carbohydrate: 24g carbohydrate (16g sugars
- Cholesterol: 54mg cholesterol

850.   Pork Skillet

Serving: 2 servings. | Prep: 10mins | Cook: 45mins | Ready in:

Ingredients

- 2 bone-in pork loin chops (7 ounces each)
- 1-1/2 teaspoons canola oil
- 1/8 teaspoon salt
- 1/8 teaspoon pepper
- 1-1/4 cups soft bread crumbs
- 1-1/2 cups sliced fresh or frozen rhubarb (1-inch pieces)
- 1/4 cup packed brown sugar
- 2 tablespoons all-purpose flour
- 1/2 teaspoon ground cinnamon

Direction

- Cook chops with oil in a big skillet on moderate heat until chops are browned slightly, about 2 to 3 minutes per side, sprinkle pepper and salt over cooked chops. Take out and keep warm. Combine bread crumbs with pan drippings. Save 1/4 cup and sprinkle the rest of crumbs into an 8-inch square baking dish.
- Mix together cinnamon, flour, brown sugar and rhubarb, scoop half over the bread crumbs. Place pork chops on top, scoop the leftover rhubarb mixture over chops. Bake

with a cover at 325 degrees, about 30 to 35 minutes.

- Uncover and sprinkle over with reserved bread crumbs, bake more 10 to 15 minutes, until pork is softened.

Nutrition Information

- Calories: 464 calories
- Fiber: 3g fiber)
- Total Carbohydrate: 52g carbohydrate (29g sugars
- Cholesterol: 86mg cholesterol
- Protein: 34g protein.
- Total Fat: 13g fat (4g saturated fat)
- Sodium: 417mg sodium

851.   Pork And Corn Casserole

Serving: 6-8 servings. | Prep: 15mins | Cook: 30mins | Ready in:

Ingredients

- 7 cups uncooked egg noodles
- 1 pound ground pork
- 1 small green pepper, chopped
- 1 can (14-3/4 ounces) cream-style corn
- 1 can (11-1/2 ounces) condensed chicken with rice soup, undiluted
- 1 jar (2 ounces) diced pimientos, drained
- 8 ounces process cheese (Velveeta), cubed
- 1/2 cup dry bread crumbs
- 2 tablespoons butter, melted

Direction

- Cook noodles as directed on package; strain. In the meantime, cook green pepper and pork over medium heat in a large skillet until meat is no longer pink; drain.
- Combine pork mixture, cheese, pimientos, soup, corn, and drained noodles in a large bowl. Pour noodle mixture into an oiled

shallow 2 1/2-quart baking dish. Stir bread crumbs with butter; scatter over the noodle mixture. Bake without covering for 30 to 35 minutes at 350°, or until mixture is bubbly and top turns golden brown.

Nutrition Information

- Calories: 455 calories
- Fiber: 2g fiber)
- Total Carbohydrate: 44g carbohydrate (5g sugars
- Cholesterol: 97mg cholesterol
- Protein: 23g protein.
- Total Fat: 21g fat (10g saturated fat)
- Sodium: 915mg sodium

852.   Potato Ham Bake

Serving: 6 servings. | Prep: 10mins | Cook: 01hours25mins | Ready in:

Ingredients

- 3 medium potatoes, peeled and thinly sliced
- 2 cups cubed fully cooked ham
- 1 medium onion, sliced and separated into rings
- 8 slices process American cheese
- 1 can (10-3/4 ounces) condensed cream of mushroom soup, undiluted
- 1/2 cup frozen peas, thawed

Direction

- Place 1/2 potatoes, and ham and onion, and cheese then soup in a 3-quart baking dish coated with cooking spray. Repeat layering. Put a cover on and bake at 350° until the potatoes are nearly soft, about 1 1/4 hours.
- Sprinkle peas over. Bake without a cover until fully heated, about 10 minutes.

Nutrition Information

- Calories: 282 calories
- Protein: 16g protein.
- Total Fat: 13g fat (6g saturated fat)
- Sodium: 1307mg sodium
- Fiber: 2g fiber)
- Total Carbohydrate: 26g carbohydrate (5g sugars
- Cholesterol: 45mg cholesterol

853.   Potato Pork Pie

Serving: 6 servings. | Prep: 50mins | Cook: 35mins | Ready in:

Ingredients

- 2 pounds potatoes, peeled and cubed
- 1/3 cup heavy whipping cream
- 4 tablespoons butter, divided
- 3/4 teaspoon salt
- 1/8 teaspoon pepper
- 1 medium onion, chopped
- 1 garlic clove, minced
- 1/4 cup all-purpose flour
- 1 can (14-1/2 ounces) beef broth
- 1 tablespoon Dijon mustard
- 1 teaspoon dried thyme
- 3 tablespoons minced fresh parsley, divided
- 2-1/2 cups cubed cooked pork

Direction

- In a big saucepan, place potatoes. Pour in water to cover; heat to a boil. Put on cover and cook for 15-20 minutes or until tender. Drain nicely. Mash the potatoes with pepper, salt, 2 tablespoons butter, and cream. Arrange 1-1/2 cups of mashed potatoes on an oiled shallow 1-1/2-quart baking dish.
- In a big skillet, in the remaining butter, sauté onion until tender. Put in garlic and cook for 1 more minute. Blend in flour until mixed. Slowly mix in 2 tablespoons parsley, thyme, mustard, and broth. Heat to a boil; stir and cook for 2 minutes or until thickened. Mix in

pork and heat through. Spread over potato crust.
- Spoon or pipe the rest of mashed potatoes over top. Bake at 375 degrees without cover for 35-40 minutes or when potatoes are slightly browned. Sprinkle remaining parsley over top.

Nutrition Information

- Calories: 391 calories
- Cholesterol: 91mg cholesterol
- Protein: 22g protein.
- Total Fat: 19g fat (10g saturated fat)
- Sodium: 736mg sodium
- Fiber: 3g fiber)
- Total Carbohydrate: 35g carbohydrate (5g sugars

854.   Potluck Casserole

Serving: 4 servings. | Prep: 10mins | Cook: 45mins | Ready in:

Ingredients

- 1/2 pound boneless pork, cut into 3/4-inch cubes
- 1 cup sliced celery
- 1/4 cup chopped onion
- 2 tablespoons water
- 2 cups cooked noodles
- 1 can (10-3/4 ounces) condensed cream of mushroom soup, undiluted
- 1 cup frozen peas
- 1/4 teaspoon salt, optional
- 1/8 teaspoon pepper
- 3 tablespoons seasoned or plain dry bread crumbs

Direction

- Brown pork in a big frying pan coated with cooking spray over medium-high heat until turning light brown, about 2-3 minutes on all sides. Add water, onion, and celery; put a cover on and simmer until the vegetables are soft, about 20-25 minutes.

- In the meantime, start preheating the oven to 350°. Take the frying pan away from heat; add pepper, salt (if wanted), peas, soup, and noodles.
- Remove into a non-oiled 11x7-inch baking dish, sprinkle with bread crumbs over. Bake without a cover until the meat is soft, about 20-25 minutes.

Nutrition Information

- Calories: 244 calories
- Protein: 22g protein. Diabetic Exchanges: 2 lean meat
- Total Fat: 5g fat (0 saturated fat)
- Sodium: 440mg sodium
- Fiber: 0 fiber)
- Total Carbohydrate: 26g carbohydrate (0 sugars
- Cholesterol: 51mg cholesterol

---

855. Potluck Cordon Bleu Casserole

Serving: 10 servings. | Prep: 25mins | Cook: 30mins | Ready in:

Ingredients

- 4 cups cubed cooked turkey
- 3 cups cubed fully cooked ham
- 1 cup shredded cheddar cheese
- 1 cup chopped onion
- 1/4 cup butter, cubed
- 1/3 cup all-purpose flour
- 2 cups half-and-half cream
- 1 teaspoon dill weed
- 1/8 teaspoon ground mustard
- 1/8 teaspoon ground nutmeg
- TOPPING:

- 1 cup dry bread crumbs
- 2 tablespoons butter, melted
- 1/4 teaspoon dill weed
- 1/4 cup shredded cheddar cheese
- 1/4 cup chopped walnuts

Direction

- Combine the turkey, cheese, and ham in a large bowl; put aside. Sauté onion in butter in a large saucepan until softened. Add flour; stir until combined. Add cream gradually, stirring continuously. Bring to a boil; then cook while stirring until thickened, for 1-2 minutes. Stir in nutmeg, mustard, and dill. Next, remove from the heat and pour over the meat mixture.
- Scoop into a greased 13x9-in. baking dish. Combine the dill, butter, and bread crumbs in a small bowl. Stir in walnuts and cheese. Sprinkle over the casserole.
- Bake without cover for 30 minutes at 350°, or until heated through.

Nutrition Information

- Calories: 421 calories
- Sodium: 848mg sodium
- Fiber: 1g fiber)
- Total Carbohydrate: 16g carbohydrate (3g sugars
- Cholesterol: 122mg cholesterol
- Protein: 32g protein.
- Total Fat: 24g fat (13g saturated fat)

---

856. Rhubarb Pork Chop Casserole

Serving: 4 servings. | Prep: 20mins | Cook: 40mins | Ready in:

Ingredients

- 4 boneless pork loin chops (3/4 inches thick and 4 ounces each)

- 1 tablespoon canola oil
- Salt and pepper to taste
- 2 tablespoons butter
- 3 cups soft bread crumbs
- 3 cups sliced fresh or frozen rhubarb (1-inch pieces)
- 1/2 cup packed brown sugar
- 1/4 cup all-purpose flour
- 1 teaspoon ground cinnamon

Direction

- Sauté pork chops in oil in a large skillet until browned. Scatter with pepper and salt. Take pork chops out and keep warm. Add butter to melt in the grease; add bread crumbs and mix well. Turn off the heat.
- Combine cinnamon, flour, sugar, and rhubarb in a large bowl. Scoop into an oiled 11x7-inch baking dish. Sprinkle top with crumbs mixture.
- Bake, covered with foil for 25 to 30 minutes at 350°. Uncover the dish. Place pork chops over the top. Bake without covering for 10 to 15 minutes, or until thoroughly heated.

Nutrition Information

- Calories: 477 calories
- Protein: 26g protein.
- Total Fat: 17g fat (7g saturated fat)
- Sodium: 254mg sodium
- Fiber: 3g fiber)
- Total Carbohydrate: 54g carbohydrate (30g sugars
- Cholesterol: 70mg cholesterol

857.   Saucy Ham And Rice

Serving: 4-6 servings. | Prep: 10mins | Cook: 10mins | Ready in:

Ingredients

- 1-1/2 pounds fully cooked ham, julienned
- 1 tablespoon butter
- 1 cup chopped celery
- 1 cup julienned green pepper
- 1 small onion, cut into thin wedges
- 1 can (10-3/4 ounces) condensed cream of mushroom soup, undiluted
- 2 tablespoons prepared mustard
- 3/4 teaspoon dill weed
- 1/8 teaspoon celery salt
- 1 cup sour cream
- Hot cooked rice

Direction

- Sauté ham in butter in a large skillet for 2 minutes. Add the onion, green pepper, and celery; sauté until softened.
- Stir in celery salt, dill, mustard, and soup; stir until smooth. Then stir in sour cream; heat through (but not boil). Enjoy with rice.

Nutrition Information

- Calories: 269 calories
- Total Carbohydrate: 9g carbohydrate (3g sugars
- Cholesterol: 90mg cholesterol
- Protein: 24g protein.
- Total Fat: 15g fat (8g saturated fat)
- Sodium: 1676mg sodium
- Fiber: 1g fiber)

858.   Sauerkraut Beef Supper

Serving: 6 servings. | Prep: 10mins | Cook: 01hours05mins | Ready in:

Ingredients

- 2/3 cup finely chopped fully cooked ham
- 2 cups cooked long grain rice
- 1-1/4 cups finely chopped onions, divided
- 1-1/4 teaspoons salt, divided

- 1/4 teaspoon pepper, divided
- 1 pound lean ground beef (90% lean)
- 1 can (14 ounces) sauerkraut, rinsed and drained
- 1/2 teaspoon sugar
- 1 bacon strip, diced

Direction

- Combine 1/8 teaspoon of the pepper, 1 teaspoon salt, 3/4 cup onions, rice and ham in a large bowl; crumble beef over mixture and stir gently.
- In a greased baking dish of 2-1/2-qt., arrange 1/2 the sauerkraut; sprinkle with 1/2 the remaining onions. Add the meat mixture, leftover onions and sauerkraut on top. Sprinkle with sugar and remaining pepper and salt. Place bacon on top.
- Cover up and bake at 375° until hot and bubbly, about 65-70 minutes.

Nutrition Information

- Calories: 256 calories
- Sodium: 1190mg sodium
- Fiber: 2g fiber)
- Total Carbohydrate: 21g carbohydrate (3g sugars
- Cholesterol: 57mg cholesterol
- Protein: 20g protein.
- Total Fat: 10g fat (4g saturated fat)

859. Savory Stuffed Peppers

Serving: 6 servings. | Prep: 20mins | Cook: 60mins | Ready in:

Ingredients

- 6 medium green peppers
- 1 pound ground beef, cooked and drained
- 1/2 pound ground pork, cooked and drained
- 1 cup quick-cooking oats

- 1 medium onion, chopped
- 1/2 cup sliced fresh mushrooms
- 1 egg, beaten
- 1 tablespoon salsa
- 1 tablespoon hot pepper sauce
- 2 garlic clove, minced
- 1 teaspoon each dried basil, oregano, thyme, Italian seasoning and parsley flakes
- 1/2 teaspoon pepper
- 2/3 cup tomato sauce

Direction

- Cut tops off peppers and eliminate seeds. Cook peppers in boiling water for approximately 3 minutes in a large kettle. Drain peppers rinse under cold water, then invert on paper towels.
- Combine oats, meat, mushrooms, onion, egg, seasonings and salsa in a bowl. Spoon into peppers. Arrange in a greased baking dish of 13 x 9-inch. Spoon over peppers with the tomato sauce. Uncovered while baking at 350° for around 1 hour until heated through.

Nutrition Information

- Calories: 317 calories
- Protein: 26g protein.
- Total Fat: 14g fat (6g saturated fat)
- Sodium: 236mg sodium
- Fiber: 5g fiber)
- Total Carbohydrate: 21g carbohydrate (5g sugars
- Cholesterol: 98mg cholesterol

860. Scalloped Pork Chops

Serving: 4 servings. | Prep: 15mins | Cook: 50mins | Ready in:

Ingredients

- 4 bone-in pork loin chops (1/2 inch thick and 8 ounces each)
- 1 tablespoon vegetable oil
- 1/4 cup chopped onion
- 1 can (10-3/4 ounces) condensed cream of mushroom soup, undiluted
- 1/2 cup milk
- 3 cups thinly sliced peeled potatoes (about 1/2 pound)
- 6 cups shredded cabbage (about 1 pound)
- 1/4 teaspoon salt
- 1/4 teaspoon pepper

Direction

- Over medium heat, cook pork chops in oil in a large skillet until no more pink; remove from the pan and keep warm. Allow to drain and reserve 1 teaspoon drippings. Sauté onion in drippings in the same pan until softened. Stir in milk and soup.
- Layer 1/2 of the potatoes, cabbage, pepper, and salt in a greased 2-1/2-qt. casserole. Spread on top with 3/4 cup soup mixture. Repeat the layers. Put pork chops on top.
- Pour over chops with the leftover soup mixture. Cover and bake for 50-60 minutes at 350°, or until the pork and vegetables are soft.

Nutrition Information

- Calories: 321 calories
- Sodium: 740mg sodium
- Fiber: 5g fiber)
- Total Carbohydrate: 38g carbohydrate (7g sugars
- Cholesterol: 35mg cholesterol
- Protein: 15g protein.
- Total Fat: 13g fat (4g saturated fat)

861. Scalloped Potatoes 'n' Ham Casserole

Serving: 6 servings. | Prep: 25mins | Cook: 60mins | Ready in:

Ingredients

- 3/4 cup powdered nondairy creamer
- 1-3/4 cups water
- 3 tablespoons butter
- 3 tablespoons all-purpose flour
- 2 tablespoons dried minced onion
- 1 teaspoon salt
- 3/4 teaspoon paprika
- 6 large potatoes, peeled and thinly sliced
- 2 cups diced fully cooked ham
- 1 cup shredded cheddar cheese

Direction

- Preheat the oven to 350°F. Combine water and creamer in a small bowl until smooth. Heat butter in a small saucepan over medium heat then stir the paprika, salt, onion and flour in until smooth, adding the creamer mixture in gradually. Bring it to a boil. Cook and stir until it thickens, about 1-2 minutes.
- Layer potatoes and ham in a greased 13x9-inch baking dish then pour the sauce over it. Bake it with the cover on for 15 minutes. Remove the cover and continue baking until the potatoes turn tender, about 40-50 minutes more. Sprinkle with cheese. Bake once more until the cheese melts and the edges turn bubbly, about 5-10 minutes.

Nutrition Information

- Calories: 563 calories
- Cholesterol: 60mg cholesterol
- Protein: 21g protein.
- Total Fat: 18g fat (12g saturated fat)
- Sodium: 1166mg sodium
- Fiber: 6g fiber)
- Total Carbohydrate: 78g carbohydrate (6g sugars

862. Scalloped Potatoes And Ham

Serving: 6 | Prep: 40mins | Cook: | Ready in:

Ingredients

- ½ cup onion, chopped
- 1½ cups fat-free milk
- 3 tablespoons all-purpose flour
- ⅛ teaspoon ground black pepper
- 1 teaspoon snipped fresh rosemary or ½ teaspoon dried rosemary, crushed
- 1 medium round red potato, cut into ¼-inch-thick slices
- 1 medium sweet potato, peeled and cut into ¼-inch-thick slices
- 1 medium turnip, peeled and cut into ¼-inch-thick slices
- ¼ cup water
- 8 ounces low-fat, reduced-sodium cooked boneless ham, cut into thin strips
- Paprika

Direction

- Turn oven to 350° to preheat. To make sauce, cook onion in a small amount of boiling water for 3 to 5 minutes over medium heat in a medium saucepan until tender. Drain onion; put back into the pan. Combine pepper, flour, and milk in a screw-top jar; shake, covered until well combined. Pour milk mixture into the saucepan. Cook over medium until bubbly and thickened, stirring well. Mix in rosemary.
- In the meantime, combine 1/4 cup water, turnip, and potatoes in a 2-quart microwave-safe baking dish. Tent with vented plastic wrap. Cook, covered for 8 minutes on high (100% power) or just until vegetables are tender. Transfer vegetable mixture to a colander to drain carefully.
- Layer 1/2 of the ham, 1/2 of the potato mixture, and 1/2 of the sauce in the same 2-

quart baking dish. Repeat layering until all ingredients are used up. Scatter top with paprika. Bake without covering until thoroughly heated, about half an hour. Allow to cool for 10 minutes before enjoying.

Nutrition Information

- Calories: 120 calories;
- Cholesterol: 17
- Protein: 10
- Total Fat: 2
- Saturated Fat: 1
- Sodium: 466
- Fiber: 2
- Total Carbohydrate: 17

863. Scalloped Potatoes With Ham & Cheese

Serving: 10 servings. | Prep: 20mins | Cook: 01hours05mins | Ready in:

Ingredients

- 1 can (10-3/4 ounces) condensed cream of mushroom soup, undiluted
- 1 cup milk
- 2/3 cup condensed cream of potato soup, undiluted
- 1/2 cup chopped onion
- 1/4 cup butter, melted
- 1/2 teaspoon minced garlic
- 1/2 teaspoon pepper
- 1/4 teaspoon seasoned salt
- 8 medium red potatoes, peeled and thinly sliced
- 3 cups cubed fully cooked ham
- 1-1/2 cups shredded part-skim mozzarella cheese

Direction

- Set the oven at 350° to preheat. Combine the first 8 ingredients in a large bowl. Add cheese, ham, and potatoes; toss to coat. Then transfer to a greased 13x9-in. baking dish.
- Uncover and bake until bubbly and the potatoes are softened, for 65-70 minutes. Allow to sit for 10 minutes before serving.

Nutrition Information

- Calories: 273 calories
- Sodium: 1037mg sodium
- Fiber: 2g fiber)
- Total Carbohydrate: 22g carbohydrate (3g sugars
- Cholesterol: 49mg cholesterol
- Protein: 15g protein.
- Total Fat: 14g fat (7g saturated fat)

---

864.   Scalloped Potatoes With Ham For 2

Serving: 2 servings. | Prep: 25mins | Cook: 55mins | Ready in:

Ingredients

- 2 teaspoons butter
- 2 teaspoons all-purpose flour
- 1/8 teaspoon salt
- 1/8 teaspoon pepper
- Dash Cajun seasoning
- 1/2 cup 2% milk
- 1-1/2 teaspoons sherry or chicken broth
- 1 teaspoon Worcestershire sauce
- 1/2 cup shredded cheddar cheese, divided
- 1 medium potato, peeled and thinly sliced
- 1 cup cubed fully cooked ham
- 1/4 cup thinly sliced onion

Direction

- Melt butter in a small saucepan. Add in flour, pepper, salt, and Cajun seasoning until

smooth. Slowly add in milk, Worcestershire sauce and sherry. Put to boil and stir for another minute or it becomes thick. Lower the heat; put 1/4 cup cheese. Take away from the heat and set aside.
- Spray a 1 qt. baking dish with cooking spray. Arrange half of the potato slices and layer with onion, ham and half of white sauce. Repeat the layers.
- Cover and let bake for 50 minutes to an hour or until potatoes are soft. Bake at 350 degrees F. Remove the cover and drizzle with remaining cheese. Return to oven for another 5-10 minutes or until the cheese has melted.

Nutrition Information

- Calories: 485 calories
- Fiber: 3g fiber)
- Total Carbohydrate: 40g carbohydrate (0 sugars
- Cholesterol: 108mg cholesterol
- Protein: 33g protein.
- Total Fat: 21g fat (11g saturated fat)
- Sodium: 487mg sodium

---

865.   Shipwreck

Serving: 6-8 servings. | Prep: 20mins | Cook: 60mins | Ready in:

Ingredients

- 1/2 pound sliced bacon
- 1 pound ground beef
- 1 large onion, chopped
- 1 cup ketchup
- 1/2 cup packed brown sugar
- 1 can (32 ounces) pork and beans

Direction

- In a frying pan, cook bacon until crisp. Transfer on paper towels to drain; crumble and leave it aside. Drain drippings from the pan. Cook the beef until browned; let drain. Put in onion and cook for around 5 minutes until softened. Blend brown sugar and ketchup; mix into beef mixture. Mix in beans and pork and all except for 2 tablespoons of the bacon. Put to an 8-inch square baking dish. Put leftover bacon on top. Bake while uncovered at 350° for 1 hour.

Nutrition Information

- Calories: 328 calories
- Sodium: 915mg sodium
- Fiber: 6g fiber)
- Total Carbohydrate: 43g carbohydrate (24g sugars
- Cholesterol: 36mg cholesterol
- Protein: 19g protein.
- Total Fat: 11g fat (4g saturated fat)

866. Smoked Pork Chop Casserole

Serving: 6 servings. | Prep: 25mins | Cook: 60mins | Ready in:

Ingredients

- 8 medium potatoes, peeled and cut into 1/4-inch slices
- 1 large tart apple, peeled and sliced 1/4 inch thick
- 1 tablespoon chopped onion
- 1 cup shredded Swiss cheese
- 6 smoked pork chops (6 ounces each)
- SAUCE:
- 2 tablespoons butter
- 2 tablespoons all-purpose flour
- 1 cup 2% milk
- 4 teaspoons Dijon mustard
- Salt and pepper to taste

Direction

- Put potatoes in a Dutch oven then cover with water. Boil. Lower the heat; cover then cook until soft, or for 10 to 15 minutes. Drain. Mix in onion and apple.
- Remove to a greased baking dish of 13x9 inch in size. Scatter with cheese; put pork chops on top. Cover and bake for 30 minutes at 350°.
- Melt butter over medium heat in a small saucepan. Mix in the flour until smooth; put in milk gradually. Boil; cook and mix until thickened, or for 1 to 2 minutes. Mix in the pepper, salt and mustard.
- Pour over the pork chops. Bake while uncovering until heated through, or for 30 minutes.

Nutrition Information

- Calories: 608 calories
- Total Carbohydrate: 48g carbohydrate (9g sugars
- Cholesterol: 112mg cholesterol
- Protein: 53g protein.
- Total Fat: 22g fat (10g saturated fat)
- Sodium: 2269mg sodium
- Fiber: 3g fiber)

867. Smoked Pork Chops With Sweet Potatoes

Serving: 6 servings. | Prep: 15mins | Cook: 45mins | Ready in:

Ingredients

- 6 smoked boneless pork chops (7 ounces each)
- 1 tablespoon canola oil
- 4 large sweet potatoes, cooked, peeled and cut lengthwise into thirds
- 1/2 cup packed brown sugar
- 1/8 teaspoon pepper
- 2 large tart apples, peeled and thinly sliced
- 1/4 cup apple juice or water

Direction

- Set the oven to 325 degrees and start preheating. In a big skillet, in oil, cook chops on medium heat, about 2-3 minutes per side until slightly browned; drain.
- Move to an oiled 13x9-inch baking dish. Place sweet potatoes on top. Combine pepper and brown sugar; arrange over sweet potatoes. Place apples on top; drizzle apple juice over the surface.
- Put on cover and bake for 30 minutes. Remove cover and bake for 10-15 minutes or until the meat is tender.

Nutrition Information

- Calories: 584 calories
- Total Fat: 16g fat (5g saturated fat)
- Sodium: 2462mg sodium
- Fiber: 4g fiber)
- Total Carbohydrate: 56g carbohydrate (37g sugars
- Cholesterol: 95mg cholesterol
- Protein: 52g protein.

868.   Spinach Rice Ham Bake

Serving: 3 servings. | Prep: 10mins | Cook: 25mins | Ready in:

Ingredients

- 8 ounces process cheese (Velveeta), cubed
- 1/2 cup 2% milk
- 3 cups cooked rice
- 2 cups cubed fully cooked ham
- 1 package (10 ounces) frozen chopped spinach, thawed and squeezed dry

Direction

- Mix milk and cheese together in a microwave-safe bowl. Microwave without a cover on high until the cheese melts, about 1 1/2 minutes;

whisk until smooth. Mix in spinach, ham, and rice.
- Remove into a 1 1/2-quart baking dish coated with cook spray. Put a cover on and bake at 350° until fully heated, about 25-30 minutes.

Nutrition Information

- Calories: 652 calories
- Fiber: 3g fiber)
- Total Carbohydrate: 58g carbohydrate (8g sugars
- Cholesterol: 103mg cholesterol
- Protein: 40g protein.
- Total Fat: 29g fat (15g saturated fat)
- Sodium: 2183mg sodium

869.   Sweet Potato Ham Bake

Serving: 2-3 servings. | Prep: 10mins | Cook: 30mins | Ready in:

Ingredients

- 1 can (15 ounces) cut sweet potatoes, drained and quartered lengthwise
- 2 cups cubed fully cooked ham
- 1 cup shredded cheddar cheese

Direction

- Layer 1/2 of each of the sweet potatoes, ham, and cheese in an oiled 1-quart baking dish. Repeat layers. Put on cover and bake for 20 minutes at 350 degrees. Remove cover and bake for 8-10 minutes or until cheese melts.

Nutrition Information

- Calories: 411 calories
- Sodium: 1482mg sodium
- Fiber: 4g fiber)
- Total Carbohydrate: 33g carbohydrate (19g sugars

- Cholesterol: 89mg cholesterol
- Protein: 26g protein.
- Total Fat: 19g fat (11g saturated fat)

870. Sweet Potato Ham Casserole

Serving: 2 servings. | Prep: 20mins | Cook: 15mins | Ready in:

Ingredients

- 1 large sweet potato, about (10 ounces)
- 1/4 cup water
- 1 boneless fully cooked ham steaks (1/2 pound and 3/4 inch thick)
- 1 tablespoon butter
- 1/3 cup unsweetened pineapple juice
- 2 tablespoons packed brown sugar
- 1 can (8 ounces) pineapple chunks, drained
- 1/3 cup miniature marshmallows

Direction

- Rind sweet potato and cut it into chunks, put into a microwave-safe dish and add water. Cover and microwave on high setting until softened, about 7 to 9 minutes, drain and set aside.
- Divide ham into 2 pieces. Brown both sides of ham with butter in a skillet. Mix brown sugar and pineapple juice in a bowl, stir until sugar has dissolved. Pour over ham then bring to a boil. Lower heat and simmer without a cover until thickened a bit, about 5 to 7 minutes.
- Transfer the ham to a greased shallow 1-quart baking dish. Put around the edge of dish with pineapple and sweet potato, pour over top with brown sugar mixture. Bake at 400 degrees without a cover until heated through, about 12 to 15 minutes. Sprinkle around the edge with marshmallows, bake until marshmallows turn golden brown, about 3 to 5 minutes more.

Nutrition Information

- Calories: 439 calories
- Protein: 23g protein.
- Total Fat: 13g fat (5g saturated fat)
- Sodium: 1520mg sodium
- Fiber: 3g fiber)
- Total Carbohydrate: 60g carbohydrate (41g sugars
- Cholesterol: 68mg cholesterol

871. Tater Tot Casseroles

Serving: 2 casseroles (6 servings each). | Prep: 25mins | Cook: 45mins | Ready in:

Ingredients

- 3/4 pound Johnsonville® Ground Hot Italian sausage
- 3/4 pound lean ground beef (90% lean)
- 1 small onion, chopped
- 2 cans (10-3/4 ounces each) condensed cream of celery soup, undiluted
- 2 cups frozen cut green beans, thawed
- 1 can (15-1/4 ounces) whole kernel corn, drained
- 2 cups shredded Colby-Monterey Jack cheese, divided
- 1/2 cup 2% milk
- 1 teaspoon garlic powder
- 1/4 teaspoon seasoned salt
- 1/4 to 1/2 teaspoon cayenne pepper
- 1 package (32 ounces) frozen Tater Tots

Direction

- In the Dutch oven, cook onion, beef and sausage on medium heat till the meat is not pink anymore; drain off. Put in the cayenne, seasoned salt, garlic powder, milk, 1 cup of the cheese, corn, beans and soup. Move into two greased 11x7-inch baking dishes. Add the Tater Tots on top; drizzle with the rest of the cheese.

- Put cover on and freeze 1 casserole for no more than 3 months. Bake rest of the casserole, with cover, at 350 degrees for 40 minutes. Remove the cover and bake till bubbling or for 5 to 10 minutes more.
- To use the frozen casserole: Thaw it in fridge overnight. Take out of the fridge half an hour prior to baking.
- Put cover on and bake at 350 degrees for 50 minutes. Remove the cover and bake till becoming bubbling or for 5 to 10 minutes more.

Nutrition Information

- Calories: 370 calories
- Protein: 16g protein.
- Total Fat: 22g fat (8g saturated fat)
- Sodium: 1085mg sodium
- Fiber: 3g fiber)
- Total Carbohydrate: 30g carbohydrate (4g sugars
- Cholesterol: 48mg cholesterol

872.   Turkey Cordon Bleu Casserole

Serving: 8 servings. | Prep: 20mins | Cook: 25mins | Ready in:

Ingredients

- 2 cups uncooked elbow macaroni
- 2 cans (10-3/4 ounces each) condensed cream of chicken soup, undiluted
- 3/4 cup 2% milk
- 1/4 cup grated Parmesan cheese
- 1 teaspoon prepared mustard
- 1 teaspoon paprika
- 1/2 teaspoon dried rosemary, crushed
- 1/4 teaspoon garlic powder
- 1/8 teaspoon rubbed sage
- 2 cups cubed cooked turkey
- 2 cups cubed fully cooked ham

- 2 cups shredded part-skim mozzarella cheese
- 1/4 cup crushed Ritz crackers

Direction

- Start preheating the oven to 350°. Cook macaroni following the package instructions.
- In the meantime, combine seasonings, mustard, Parmesan cheese, milk, and soup. Mix in mozzarella cheese, ham, and turkey.
- Strain the macaroni, put on the soup mixture and mix to blend. Remove into eight 8-oz. ramekins or a 13x9-inch baking dish coated with cooking spray. Sprinkle crushed crackers over. Bake without a cover for 25-30 minutes until bubbling. To freeze: Put a cover on and freeze unbaked ramekins or dish. When using, slightly thaw overnight in the fridge. Take out of the fridge before baking, about 30 minutes. Start preheating the oven to 350°. Bake following the instructions, raising the time as needed to fully heat and a thermometer displays 165° when you insert it into the middle.

Nutrition Information

- Calories:
- Fiber:
- Total Carbohydrate:
- Cholesterol:
- Protein:
- Total Fat:
- Sodium:

873.   White Cheddar Scalloped Potatoes

Serving: 10 servings. | Prep: 40mins | Cook: 01hours10mins | Ready in:

Ingredients

- 1/4 cup butter

- 1 medium onion, finely chopped
- 1/4 cup all-purpose flour
- 1 teaspoon salt
- 1 teaspoon dried parsley flakes
- 1/2 teaspoon dried thyme
- 1/2 teaspoon pepper
- 3 cups 2% milk
- 1 can (10-3/4 ounces) condensed cream of mushroom soup, undiluted
- 1 cup (8 ounces) sour cream
- 8 cups thinly sliced peeled potatoes
- 3-1/2 cups cubed fully cooked ham
- 2 cups shredded sharp white cheddar cheese

Direction

- Set the oven to 375 degrees and preheat. Heat butter in a big saucepan on moderate-high heat. Put in onion, then cook and stir until soft. Stir in seasonings and flour until combined, then whisk in milk gradually. Bring the mixture to a boil while stirring frequently, then cook and stir until thickened, about 2 minutes. Mix in soup. Take away from the heat and stir in sour cream.
- Layer in a 13"x9" baking dish coated with grease with half of each of following ingredients: potatoes, ham, cheese and sauce, then repeat layers.
- Bake with a cover for half an hour, and then bake more for 40 to 50 minutes without a cover, until potatoes are soft.

Nutrition Information

- Calories: 417 calories
- Fiber: 3g fiber)
- Total Carbohydrate: 37g carbohydrate (7g sugars
- Cholesterol: 88mg cholesterol
- Protein: 22g protein.
- Total Fat: 20g fat (12g saturated fat)
- Sodium: 1267mg sodium

874. Wild Rice And Ham Casserole

Serving: 6 servings. | Prep: 15mins | Cook: 45mins | Ready in:

Ingredients

- 1 package (6-1/4 ounces) quick-cooking long grain and wild rice mix
- 1 package (10 ounces) frozen cut broccoli, thawed and drained
- 2 cups cubed fully cooked ham
- 1 can (10-3/4 ounces) condensed cream of mushroom soup, undiluted
- 1 cup mayonnaise
- 2 teaspoons prepared mustard
- 1 cup shredded cheddar cheese

Direction

- Follow package instructions to prepare rice. Spoon into an unoiled 2 1/2-quart baking dish. Arrange broccoli and ham atop. Mix together mustard, mayonnaise, and soup; arrange over rice mixture; mix lightly.
- Cover and bake 45 for minutes at 350 degrees until bubbly. Sprinkle cheese over top. Allow to sit for 5 minutes then serve.

Nutrition Information

- Calories: 564 calories
- Cholesterol: 60mg cholesterol
- Protein: 18g protein.
- Total Fat: 41g fat (10g saturated fat)
- Sodium: 1692mg sodium
- Fiber: 2g fiber)
- Total Carbohydrate: 30g carbohydrate (1g sugars

Serving: 6 servings. | Prep: 10mins | Cook: 60mins | Ready in:

Ingredients

- 1 package (14 ounces) seasoned cubed stuffing mix, divided
- 1/4 cup butter, melted
- 2 pounds zucchini, cut into 1/2-inch pieces
- 1/2 cup grated carrots
- 1 can (10-3/4 ounces) condensed cream of celery soup, undiluted
- 1/2 cup milk
- 1 cup sour cream
- 1 tablespoon chopped fresh parsley or 1 teaspoon dried parsley flakes
- 1/2 teaspoon pepper
- 6 pork loin chops (1 inch thick and 8 ounces each)
- Water or additional milk

Direction

- Mix butter and 2/3 of the stuffing mix in a large bowl. Put half in the bottom of a 9x13-in. greased pan. In a separate bowl, mix soup, zucchini, pepper, carrots, milk, parsley, and sour cream. Pour over stuffing. On top, sprinkle the rest of the stuffing with butter. Take the rest of the stuffing mix crush and put in a short-sided bowl. In a separate short-sided bowl, put the milk or water. Dip the pork chops in the milk or water then in the bowl with the stuffing mix. Make sure each one gets the mix all over. Place the chops in the pan on the stuffing mixture. Do not cover; bake in a 350-degree oven until pork is tender, 1 hour.

Nutrition Information

- Calories: 559 calories
- Sodium: 1583mg sodium
- Fiber: 4g fiber)

- Total Carbohydrate: 57g carbohydrate (13g sugars
- Cholesterol: 70mg cholesterol
- Protein: 18g protein.
- Total Fat: 27g fat (12g saturated fat)

Chapter 8: Potato Casserole Recipes

***

Serving: 2 casseroles (4 servings each). | Prep: 10mins | Cook: 50mins | Ready in:

Ingredients

- 2 pounds ground beef
- 1 can (10-3/4 ounces) condensed cream of mushroom soup, undiluted
- 1 can (10-3/4 ounces) condensed cream of celery soup, undiluted
- 1-1/4 teaspoons dried parsley flakes
- 1 teaspoon dried minced onion
- 1/4 teaspoon pepper
- 1 package (32 ounces) frozen cubed hash brown potatoes, thawed
- 4 cups shredded cheddar cheese, divided
- 1 can (8 ounces) mushroom stems and pieces, drained

Direction

- In large skillet over medium heat, cook beef till no longer pink; drain. In the meantime, mix pepper, onion, parsley and soups together in a large bowl. Put in mushrooms, 2 cups of cheese and potatoes. Mix in beef.
- Place into two greased baking dishes of 8-in. square. Sprinkle 1 cup cheese on top of each

dish. Cover up and freeze one casserole for up to 3 months. Cover up and bake the other casserole at 375° until potatoes are tender, about 45-50 minutes. Remove the cover and bake until cheese is melted, about 5-10 minutes.

- Using frozen casserole: Allow to thaw in the fridge overnight. Take it out of the fridge half an hour prior to baking. Bake as instructed.

Nutrition Information

- Calories: 538 calories
- Sodium: 1074mg sodium
- Fiber: 3g fiber)
- Total Carbohydrate: 29g carbohydrate (2g sugars
- Cholesterol: 119mg cholesterol
- Protein: 36g protein.
- Total Fat: 30g fat (17g saturated fat)

877. Beef Potato Casserole

Serving: 4-6 servings. | Prep: 15mins | Cook: 01hours15mins | Ready in:

Ingredients

- 4 medium potatoes, peeled and sliced
- 1 pound ground beef, cooked and drained
- 1 can (10-3/4 ounces) condensed cream of chicken soup, undiluted
- 1 can (10-3/4 ounces) condensed vegetable beef soup, undiluted
- 1/2 teaspoon salt

Direction

- Mix all of the ingredients together in a big bowl. Remove into a 2-quart greased baking dish. Put a cover on and bake at 350° until the potatoes are soft, about 1 1/4-1 1/2 hours.

Nutrition Information

- Calories: 277 calories
- Sodium: 947mg sodium
- Fiber: 3g fiber)
- Total Carbohydrate: 27g carbohydrate (2g sugars
- Cholesterol: 43mg cholesterol
- Protein: 18g protein.
- Total Fat: 11g fat (4g saturated fat)

878. Beef Potato Supper

Serving: 6-8 servings. | Prep: 25mins | Cook: 35mins | Ready in:

Ingredients

- 1-1/2 pounds ground beef
- 1 large onion, chopped
- 4 cups sliced peeled potatoes
- 1 can (14-1/2 ounces) cut green beans, drained
- 1 can (10-3/4 ounces) condensed cream of mushroom soup, undiluted
- 2/3 cup whole milk
- 2/3 cup water
- 1 can (2.8 ounces) french-fried onions
- 1 cup shredded cheddar cheese

Direction

- In a large skillet, cook onion and beef over medium heat until meat is not pink anymore; and then drain. In the meantime, in a saucepan, place the potatoes and add water to cover; allow to boil. Cook for around 7 minutes; drain.
- In a greased baking dish of 13x9-inch, layer the potatoes, beans and beef mixture.
- In a large bowl, combine the water, milk and soup; pour over potatoes. Have cheese and onions to sprinkle. Uncovered during bake at 350° for nearly 35 minutes until browned.

Nutrition Information

- Calories: 372 calories
- Cholesterol: 61mg cholesterol
- Protein: 21g protein.
- Total Fat: 19g fat (9g saturated fat)
- Sodium: 674mg sodium
- Fiber: 3g fiber)
- Total Carbohydrate: 28g carbohydrate (4g sugars

879. Beef And Mashed Potato Casserole

Serving: 4 servings. | Prep: 25mins | Cook: 20mins | Ready in:

Ingredients

- 1 pound ground beef
- 1 medium onion, chopped
- 2 green onions, sliced
- 1 can (15-1/4 ounces) whole kernel corn, drained
- 1 can (11 ounces) condensed cream of tomato bisque soup, undiluted
- 2 teaspoons minced garlic
- 1/2 teaspoon ground mustard
- 3/4 teaspoon salt
- 1/2 teaspoon pepper
- 1/4 teaspoon dried basil
- 1/4 cup grated Parmesan cheese
- 2-1/2 cups hot mashed potatoes
- 6 slices process cheese

Direction

- In a big skillet over medium heat, cook onion and beef till meat is not pink anymore; let drain. Mix in the basil, pepper, salt, mustard, garlic, soup and corn. Allow to boil. Lessen heat; simmer, covered, for 10-15 minutes. Mix in the Parmesan cheese.
- Spoon the mixture into a greased 13x9-inch baking dish. Cover with cheese slices and mashed potatoes. Bake while uncovered at 350° for around 20-30 minutes or until bubbly.

Nutrition Information

- Calories: 531 calories
- Fiber: 4g fiber)
- Total Carbohydrate: 58g carbohydrate (17g sugars
- Cholesterol: 70mg cholesterol
- Protein: 31g protein.
- Total Fat: 18g fat (8g saturated fat)
- Sodium: 2002mg sodium

880. Beef And Potato Casserole

Serving: 6 servings. | Prep: 15mins | Cook: 25mins | Ready in:

Ingredients

- 4 cups frozen potato rounds
- 1 pound ground beef
- 3 cups frozen chopped broccoli, thawed
- 1 can (10-3/4 ounces) condensed cream of celery soup, undiluted
- 1/3 cup whole milk
- 1 cup shredded cheddar cheese
- 1/4 teaspoon garlic powder
- 1/8 teaspoon pepper

Direction

- Up the sides and on the bottom of a 13x9-inch baking dish, put potato rounds. Bake for 10 minutes at 400°.
- In the meantime, cook beef over medium heat until no pink remains; strain. Put over the potatoes with broccoli and beef. Mix together pepper, garlic powder, 1/2 cup cheddar cheese, milk, and celery soup. Add to the beef mixture.
- Put a cover on and bake for 20 minutes at 400°. Put the leftover cheese on top. Put back into the oven to melt the cheese, about 2-3 minutes.

Nutrition Information

- Calories: 386 calories
- Total Fat: 23g fat (10g saturated fat)
- Sodium: 884mg sodium
- Fiber: 4g fiber)
- Total Carbohydrate: 28g carbohydrate (2g sugars
- Cholesterol: 61mg cholesterol
- Protein: 22g protein.

881.   Bratwurst Potato Skillet

Serving: 3-4 servings. | Prep: 15mins | Cook: 40mins | Ready in:

Ingredients

- 3 medium red potatoes
- 1 pound fully cooked bratwurst links or Polish sausage, cut into 1/2-inch slices
- 2 teaspoons thinly sliced green onion
- 1-1/2 teaspoons canola oil
- 1-1/2 cups white wine or chicken broth
- 1 teaspoon dried thyme
- 1 teaspoon dried marjoram
- 1 tablespoon sugar
- 1 tablespoon Dijon mustard
- 3 teaspoons minced fresh parsley, divided
- 3 teaspoons minced chives, divided
- 1 to 2 teaspoons cider vinegar
- 1/2 teaspoon salt
- 1/4 teaspoon pepper
- 2 egg yolks, lightly beaten

Direction

- In a big saucepan, put potatoes and add water to cover. Put a cover on and boil on medium-high heat. Cook until soft, about 15-20 minutes; strain. Cool briefly, dice into cubes and keep warm.

- Sauté onion and sausage with oil in a big frying pan until turning light brown; strain. Mix in marjoram, thyme, and wine. Boil it. Lower the heat; simmer without a cover for 10 minutes. Take the sausage out and keep warm.
- Mix in pepper, salt, vinegar, 1 1/2 teaspoons chives, 1 1/2 teaspoons parsley, mustard, and sugar into the pan juices; thoroughly heat.
- Stir a little amount of the hot liquid into egg yolks, put all back into the pan. Stir and cook until bubbly and thickened. Mix in potatoes and sausage, thoroughly heat. Sprinkle the leftover chives and parsley over.

Nutrition Information

- Calories: 527 calories
- Protein: 19g protein.
- Total Fat: 34g fat (12g saturated fat)
- Sodium: 1035mg sodium
- Fiber: 2g fiber)
- Total Carbohydrate: 21g carbohydrate (6g sugars
- Cholesterol: 174mg cholesterol

882.   Cheesy Franks And Potatoes

Serving: 6 servings. | Prep: 20mins | Cook: 30mins | Ready in:

Ingredients

- 6 jumbo hot dogs, halved lengthwise and cut into 1/2-inch pieces
- 1 tablespoon canola oil
- 1 medium onion, chopped
- 1/2 cup chopped green pepper
- 1 can (10-3/4 ounces) condensed cheddar cheese soup, undiluted
- 2/3 cup half-and-half cream
- 2 medium potatoes, cooked, peeled and cubed
- 1/4 teaspoon salt

Direction

- Cook hotdogs in a large pan over medium heat until they become browned, for 2-3 minutes. Take the hotdogs using a slotted spoon. Set aside. Sauté green pepper and onion in the same pan, until softened.
- Mix soup, the onion mixture, and cream in a bowl. Put potatoes in an 11x7-inch baking tray that's been greased. Top them with salt. Put the hotdogs on top. Spread the soup mix over everything. Pop it in the oven without a lid. Bake at 350°F until heated through, for 30-35 minutes.

Nutrition Information

- Calories: 313 calories
- Total Carbohydrate: 23g carbohydrate (5g sugars
- Cholesterol: 43mg cholesterol
- Protein: 9g protein.
- Total Fat: 21g fat (9g saturated fat)
- Sodium: 974mg sodium
- Fiber: 2g fiber)

---

883.   Chicken Potato Casserole

Serving: 2 casseroles (6 servings each). | Prep: 20mins | Cook: 45mins | Ready in:

Ingredients

- 6 large baking potatoes, peeled and cubed
- 1-1/2 cups water
- 2 pounds boneless skinless chicken breasts, cut into 1-inch cubes
- 2 cups (16 ounces) sour cream
- 3/4 cup shredded cheddar cheese
- 1/2 cup butter, softened
- 1/4 cup shredded Parmesan cheese
- 1 envelope onion soup mix
- 1/4 cup finely chopped fresh spinach
- 1/4 cup shredded carrot

- 1/4 teaspoon salt
- 1/4 teaspoon garlic powder
- 1/4 teaspoon pepper
- 1/4 cup dry bread crumbs

Direction

- In a microwave-safe, 3-quart dish, place water and potatoes. Microwave with cover on high setting for around 12 to 15 minutes, or until soften. In the meantime, divide chicken between two 8-inch square, greased baking dishes.
- Drain potatoes and place in a large bowl. Put in cheddar cheese, sour cream, Parmesan cheese, butter, spinach, soup mix, salt, carrot, pepper and garlic powder; mash till smooth. Spoon over chicken; scatter bread crumbs over.
- Bake 1 casserole with no cover at 350° for nearly 45 to 50 minutes till chicken is no longer pink. Freeze the remaining casserole with cover for up to 3 months.
- With the frozen casserole: Thaw in the refrigerator overnight. Take out of refrigerator for around 30 minutes before baking. Bake as directed.

Nutrition Information

- Calories: 422 calories
- Sodium: 491mg sodium
- Fiber: 3g fiber)
- Total Carbohydrate: 38g carbohydrate (4g sugars
- Cholesterol: 98mg cholesterol
- Protein: 23g protein.
- Total Fat: 19g fat (12g saturated fat)

---

884.   Ham & Swiss Potato Casserole

Serving: 8 servings. | Prep: 25mins | Cook: 20mins | Ready in:

Ingredients

- 5 large potatoes (about 4 pounds), peeled and cut into 3/4-inch pieces
- 1/4 cup butter, cubed
- 1 medium onion, chopped
- 1 garlic clove, minced
- 1/3 cup all-purpose flour
- 2 cups 2% milk
- 1-1/3 cups roasted red pepper Alfredo sauce
- 1 teaspoon dried basil
- 1/4 teaspoon salt
- 1/4 teaspoon dill weed
- 1/4 teaspoon pepper
- 2 cups cubed fully cooked ham
- 2 cups shredded Swiss cheese
- 1/4 cup seasoned bread crumbs
- 1 tablespoon butter, melted

Direction

- Set an oven to 375 degrees and start preheating. In a large saucepan, arrange the potatoes and cover with water. Boil. Turn down the heat; put on a cover and simmer until tender-crisp, about 8-10 minutes. In the meantime, heat the butter over medium-high heat in a large skillet. Put in onion; stir and cook until tender, 6-8 minutes. Put in garlic; stir and cook for a minute. Mix in flour until combined; whisk in milk gradually. Boil and stir continuously; stir and cook until thickened, 1-2 minutes. Stir in the seasonings and Alfredo sauce; heat through.
- Then drain the potatoes; place into a 13x9-inch baking dish coated with cooking spray. Place ham, cheese, and sauce in layers on top. Mix butter and breadcrumbs in a small bowl. Dust onto the top. Without the cover, bake until the cheese melts and topping turns golden brown, about 18-22 minutes. Before serving, allow to stand for 5 minutes. To prepare in advance: You can make 1 day ahead. According to the instructions, prepare the recipe, placing the ham, cheese, and sauce in layers in baking dish. Put on a cover and place into a fridge overnight. Half an hour before baking, take out of the fridge. Prepare the crumb topping; dust onto the top. Bake according to the instruction.

Nutrition Information

- Calories: 456 calories
- Protein: 22g protein.
- Total Fat: 22g fat (13g saturated fat)
- Sodium: 897mg sodium
- Fiber: 3g fiber)
- Total Carbohydrate: 45g carbohydrate (7g sugars
- Cholesterol: 93mg cholesterol

---

885.   Hamburger And Potato Casserole

Serving: 10 servings. | Prep: 10mins | Cook: 45mins | Ready in:

Ingredients

- 2 pounds uncooked extra lean ground beef or ground round (90% lean)
- 4 pounds potatoes, peeled and sliced 1/4 inch thick
- 1 large onion, sliced
- 1/2 teaspoon pepper
- 1 low-sodium beef bouillon cube
- 1 cup hot water
- 1 can (28 ounces) diced tomatoes, undrained
- Chopped fresh parsley, optional

Direction

- Layer 1/2 of the meat, potatoes and onion in a Dutch oven. Top with pepper and 1/2 of the salt. Redo layers. Let bouillon dissolve in water, then spread over all. Put tomatoes atop.
- Cook while covered over medium heat for about 45-50 minutes or until potatoes become softened. If wanted, garnish with parsley.

Nutrition Information

- Calories: 314 calories
- Sodium: 189mg sodium
- Fiber: 0 fiber)
- Total Carbohydrate: 33g carbohydrate (0 sugars
- Cholesterol: 74mg cholesterol
- Protein: 28g protein. Diabetic Exchanges: 3 lean meat
- Total Fat: 8g fat (0 saturated fat)

---

886. Italian Meat And Potatoes

Serving: 10-12 servings. | Prep: 25mins | Cook: 01hours30mins | Ready in:

Ingredients

- 1 pound ground beef
- 1 pound Jones No Sugar Pork Sausage Roll sausage
- 1/2 cup chopped onion
- 1/4 teaspoon pepper
- 1/8 teaspoon salt
- 1 can (10-3/4 ounces) condensed cheddar cheese soup, undiluted
- 1-1/4 cups whole milk
- 1 can (8 ounces) tomato sauce
- 1 teaspoon garlic powder
- 1 teaspoon dried oregano
- 1/2 teaspoon sugar
- 6 medium potatoes, peeled and thinly sliced
- 2 cups shredded part-skim mozzarella cheese

Direction

- Over medium heat in a large skillet, cook salt, pepper, onion, sausage and beef until meat is no longer pink. In the meantime, mix sugar, oregano, garlic powder, tomato sauce, milk and soup in a small saucepan. Let it come to a boil. Lower heat; let it simmer without a cover, until heated through, about 5 minutes.

- Drain the meat mixture; spoon 1/2 the mixture into a greased baking dish of 13x9 inches. Layer 1/2 the potatoes. Repeat layers. Pour the soup mixture over top.
- Cover up and bake at 350° until potatoes are tender, about 1-1/4 hours. Remove the cover; sprinkle cheese on top. Bake until cheese is melted, about 15 more minutes.

Nutrition Information

- Calories:
- Cholesterol:
- Protein:
- Total Fat:
- Sodium:
- Fiber:
- Total Carbohydrate:

---

887. Layered Potato Beef Casserole

Serving: 6 servings. | Prep: 25mins | Cook: 50mins | Ready in:

Ingredients

- 3 tablespoons butter, divided
- 2 tablespoons all-purpose flour
- 3/4 teaspoon dried rosemary, crushed
- 1/4 teaspoon pepper
- 1/8 teaspoon salt
- 2 cups 2% milk
- 2 cups shredded sharp cheddar cheese
- 4 cups leftover beef stew
- 4 medium Yukon potatoes, thinly sliced
- 1/3 cup crushed butter-flavored crackers (about 8 crackers)
- 1 tablespoon dried parsley flakes
- 1/4 teaspoon garlic powder

Direction

- In a large pot, melt 2 tablespoons of butter. Mix in salt, rosemary, pepper, and flour until combined. Slowly add the milk. Heat to a boil. Stirring constantly, cook until thick, 2 minutes. Take it off the heat and mix in cheese until it melts. Put 2 cups of stew in a 2-1/2 qt. greased dish. Layer half the potatoes and then sauce mixture. Layer the rest of the stew, potatoes, and sauce. Cover; bake in a 400-degree oven until potatoes are tender, 45-50 minutes. Melt remaining butter in microwave. Stir in garlic powder, crackers, and parsley. Sprinkle on top of dish. Do not cover; bake until topping turns golden brown and bubbling, 5-10 minutes. Let it cool for 10 minutes before enjoying.

Nutrition Information

- Calories: 541 calories
- Sodium: 872mg sodium
- Fiber: 5g fiber)
- Total Carbohydrate: 48g carbohydrate (8g sugars
- Cholesterol: 88mg cholesterol
- Protein: 26g protein.
- Total Fat: 28g fat (14g saturated fat)

888. Makeover Sausage & Potato Bake

Serving: 8 servings. | Prep: 30mins | Cook: 01hours05mins | Ready in:

Ingredients

- 1 pound lean ground turkey
- 1 small onion, chopped
- 1 teaspoon fennel seed
- 1/4 teaspoon salt
- 1/4 teaspoon pepper
- 1/4 teaspoon cayenne pepper
- 1/8 teaspoon ground nutmeg
- 1 garlic clove, minced

- 1 can (10-3/4 ounces) condensed cream of potato soup, undiluted
- 3/4 cup 2% milk
- 2 pounds potatoes, peeled and thinly sliced
- 1 cup shredded sharp cheddar cheese
- 1 cup shredded part-skim mozzarella cheese

Direction

- Cook the nutmeg, cayenne, pepper, salt, fennel seed, onion and turkey in a big nonstick frying pan on medium heat, until the turkey has no visible pink color. Add the garlic and let it cook for an additional 1 minute, then drain. Mix together the milk and soup in a small bowl.
- Layer 1/2 of the potatoes, soup mixture, sausage mixture and cheeses in a 2-quart baking dish coated with cooking spray, then put sausage mixture, soup mixture and leftover potatoes on top.
- Put cover and let it bake for 60 to 70 minutes at 350 degrees until it becomes bubbly and the potatoes become tender. Sprinkle the leftover cheeses on top. Let it bake for 5 to 10 minutes more without cover or until the cheese melts.

Nutrition Information

- Calories: 281 calories
- Fiber: 2g fiber)
- Total Carbohydrate: 23g carbohydrate (3g sugars
- Cholesterol: 71mg cholesterol
- Protein: 19g protein.
- Total Fat: 12g fat (6g saturated fat)
- Sodium: 483mg sodium

889. Mashed Potato Hot Dish

Serving: 4 servings. | Prep: 15mins | Cook: 20mins | Ready in:

Ingredients

- 1 pound ground beef
- 1 can (10-3/4 ounces) condensed cream of chicken soup, undiluted
- 2 cups frozen French-style green beans
- 2 cups hot mashed potatoes (prepared with milk and butter)
- 1/2 cup shredded cheddar cheese

Direction

- Cook beef in a big frying pan over medium heat till not pink anymore; let drain. Blend in beans and soup.
- Put to a greased 2-quart baking dish. Put mashed potatoes on top; dust with cheese. Bake while uncovered at 350° for around 20-25 minutes or until bubbly and cheese becomes melted.

Nutrition Information

- Calories: 431 calories
- Total Fat: 23g fat (12g saturated fat)
- Sodium: 1050mg sodium
- Fiber: 5g fiber)
- Total Carbohydrate: 29g carbohydrate (4g sugars
- Cholesterol: 89mg cholesterol
- Protein: 28g protein.

890. Mashed Potato Sausage Bake

Serving: 7 servings. | Prep: 35mins | Cook: 10mins | Ready in:

Ingredients

- 5 medium potatoes, peeled and quartered
- 1/2 cup reduced-fat sour cream
- 1/4 cup reduced-sodium chicken broth
- 1 package (14 ounces) smoked turkey kielbasa, sliced
- 1/2 pound sliced fresh mushrooms

- 1 cup chopped onion
- 1 garlic clove, minced
- 1/4 cup shredded reduced-fat cheddar cheese
- 1 teaspoon dried parsley flakes
- 1 teaspoon dried oregano

Direction

- In a large saucepan, place potatoes and fill water to cover. Bring to a boil. Lower the heat; simmer, covered, until very soft, for around 20-25 minutes; drain.
- Transfer to a large bowl. Place in the broth and sour cream; on low speed, beat until smooth and put aside. In a large skillet, cook onion, mushrooms, and sausage until the vegetables are softened. Add garlic, continue to cook for another 1 minute.
- Coat a 9x5-in. loaf pan with cooking spray, spread 1/2 of the potato mixture into it. Lay the sausage mixture and the leftover potatoes on top. Dust with cheese, oregano and parsley.
- Uncover and bake at 350° until the cheese is melted, for 10-15 minutes.

Nutrition Information

- Calories: 255 calories
- Total Carbohydrate: 34g carbohydrate (6g sugars
- Cholesterol: 49mg cholesterol
- Protein: 17g protein. Diabetic Exchanges: 2 starch
- Total Fat: 6g fat (3g saturated fat)
- Sodium: 706mg sodium
- Fiber: 3g fiber)

891. Meat And Potato Casserole

Serving: 6 servings. | Prep: 10mins | Cook: 50mins | Ready in:

Ingredients

- 4 cups thinly sliced peeled potatoes
- 2 tablespoons butter, melted
- 1/2 teaspoon salt
- 1 pound ground beef
- 1 package (10 ounces) frozen corn
- 1 can (10-3/4 ounces) condensed cream of celery soup, undiluted
- 1/3 cup whole milk
- 1/4 teaspoon garlic powder
- 1/8 teaspoon pepper
- 1 tablespoon chopped onion
- 1 cup shredded cheddar cheese, divided
- Minced fresh parsley, optional

Direction

- With salt and butter, toss potatoes; place in a 13x9-in. greased pan, arranging up the sides and on the bottom. Do not cover; bake in a 400-degree oven until potatoes are just about tender, 25-30 minutes. In the meantime, cook beef in a big frying pan on medium heat until not pink; drain excess grease. Sprinkle corn and beef on top the potatoes. Mix pepper, 1/2 cup cheese, soup, garlic powder, onion, and milk; dump on top of meat mixture. Do not cover; bake in a 400-degree oven until veggies are tender, 20 minutes. Sprinkle on remaining cheese. Bake until cheese melts, 2-3 minutes. If desired, sprinkle on parsley.

Nutrition Information

- Calories: 374 calories
- Fiber: 3g fiber)
- Total Carbohydrate: 31g carbohydrate (3g sugars
- Cholesterol: 71mg cholesterol
- Protein: 22g protein.
- Total Fat: 19g fat (11g saturated fat)
- Sodium: 778mg sodium

892.　　　Meat And Potato Squares

Serving: 6 servings. | Prep: 15mins | Cook: 30mins | Ready in:

Ingredients

- 1 pound ground beef
- 1 large egg
- 1/4 cup whole milk
- 1 teaspoon salt
- 1 teaspoon prepared mustard
- 1/4 teaspoon pepper
- 1 cup dry bread crumbs
- 1/2 cup chopped onion
- 1 package (16 ounces) frozen shoestring potatoes
- Ketchup, optional

Direction

- In a mixing bowl, combine the first 8 ingredients until well mixed. Put to one side. Arrange 1/2 of the potatoes in a greased 8x8-inch baking dish's bottom. Evenly distribute meat all over the potato layer. Place the rest of potatoes firmly over the top. Bake without covering for 30 minutes at 400°, or until potatoes are lightly browned and meat is cooked through. Slice into squares. Serve right away with ketchup, if desired.

Nutrition Information

- Calories: 327 calories
- Protein: 19g protein.
- Total Fat: 13g fat (5g saturated fat)
- Sodium: 642mg sodium
- Fiber: 3g fiber)
- Total Carbohydrate: 35g carbohydrate (2g sugars
- Cholesterol: 74mg cholesterol

893. Orange Flavored Beef And Potatoes

Serving: 6 servings. | Prep: 15mins | Cook: 02hours00mins | Ready in:

Ingredients

- 2 green onions, sliced
- 3 tablespoons soy sauce
- 2 tablespoons water
- 2 tablespoons white wine or additional water
- 1 tablespoon sugar
- 4 teaspoons vegetable oil, divided
- 1 tablespoon orange juice
- 1 teaspoon grated orange zest
- 1 teaspoon white vinegar
- 3/4 teaspoon ground ginger
- 1 tablespoon quick-cooking tapioca
- 1-1/2 pounds beef stew meat, cut into 1-inch cubes
- 1 pound small red potatoes, quartered

Direction

- In a big bowl, stir the ginger, vinegar, orange juice, zest, 3 teaspoons oil, sugar, water, wine or additional water, soy sauce and green onions. Mix in tapioca and allow to rest for 15 minutes.
- In a greased 11x7-inch baking dish, add the potatoes and the beef. Add tapioca mixture on top. Bake with cover at 350° for around 2 hours, or till meat soften.

Nutrition Information

- Calories: 271 calories
- Total Carbohydrate: 17g carbohydrate (3g sugars
- Cholesterol: 70mg cholesterol
- Protein: 24g protein.
- Total Fat: 11g fat (3g saturated fat)
- Sodium: 512mg sodium
- Fiber: 1g fiber)

894. Potato Corn Casserole

Serving: 4 servings. | Prep: 20mins | Cook: 25mins | Ready in:

Ingredients

- 1 pound lean ground beef
- Salt and pepper to taste
- 1/4 cup diced onion
- 4 medium potatoes, peeled and diced
- 1 can (14-3/4 ounces) cream-style corn
- 1 tablespoon butter

Direction

- Into a shallow 2-quart microwave-safe dish, crumble beef. Sprinkle with pepper and salt. Layer with corn, potatoes, and onion. Dot butter over top. Put cover and set microwave for 9-10 minutes on high; mix.
- Cover, let it heat for 7-9 minutes more or until potatoes are tender and meat is not pink anymore.

Nutrition Information

- Calories: 400 calories
- Protein: 26g protein.
- Total Fat: 12g fat (5g saturated fat)
- Sodium: 380mg sodium
- Fiber: 3g fiber)
- Total Carbohydrate: 49g carbohydrate (6g sugars
- Cholesterol: 77mg cholesterol

895. Potato Leek Skillet

Serving: 4 servings. | Prep: 5mins | Cook: 25mins | Ready in:

Ingredients

- 1/2 pound ground beef
- 2 medium potatoes, cubed and cooked
- 3 large leeks (white part only), cut into 1/2-inch slices
- 1/2 cup water
- 2 tablespoons olive oil
- 1 teaspoon salt
- 1/2 teaspoon pepper
- 1/2 teaspoon dill weed

Direction

- Cook beef over medium heat in a frying pan till not pink anymore; let drain. Put in the dill, pepper, salt, oil, water, leeks and potatoes. Let it boil. Decrease heat; simmer while uncovered for about 5 minutes until leeks become tender.

Nutrition Information

- Calories: 252 calories
- Cholesterol: 28mg cholesterol
- Protein: 12g protein.
- Total Fat: 12g fat (3g saturated fat)
- Sodium: 643mg sodium
- Fiber: 2g fiber)
- Total Carbohydrate: 24g carbohydrate (4g sugars

896.   Potato Sausage Casserole

Serving: 6 servings. | Prep: 20mins | Cook: 01hours05mins | Ready in:

Ingredients

- 1 pound Jones No Sugar Pork Sausage Roll sausage
- 1 can (10-3/4 ounces) condensed cream of mushroom soup, undiluted
- 3/4 cup milk
- 1/2 cup chopped onion
- 1/2 teaspoon salt
- 1/4 teaspoon pepper

- 3 cups sliced peeled potatoes
- 2 cups shredded cheddar cheese
- Minced fresh parsley, optional

Direction

- Start preheating the oven to 350°. Cook sausage in a big frying pan on medium heat until no pink remains; strain and put aside. Mix together pepper, salt, onion, milk, and soup.
- Layer 1/2 potatoes, the soup mixture, and sausage in a 2-quart baking dish coated with cooking spray. Continue layering.
- Put a cover on and bake until the potatoes are soft, about 60-65 minutes. Sprinkle cheese over; bake without a cover until the cheese melts, about 2-3 minutes. Use parsley to garnish if you want.

Nutrition Information

- Calories: 430 calories
- Protein: 17g protein.
- Total Fat: 29g fat (15g saturated fat)
- Sodium: 1130mg sodium
- Fiber: 2g fiber)
- Total Carbohydrate: 25g carbohydrate (4g sugars
- Cholesterol: 77mg cholesterol

897.   Potato Sloppy Joe Bake

Serving: 6-8 servings. | Prep: 15mins | Cook: 30mins | Ready in:

Ingredients

- 1 pound ground beef
- 1 can (15-1/2 ounces) sloppy joe sauce
- 1 can (10-3/4 ounces) condensed cream of potato soup, undiluted
- 1 package (32 ounces) frozen cubed hash brown potatoes, thawed
- 1 cup shredded cheddar cheese

Direction

- Cook beef in a big frying pan over medium heat until no pink remains; strain. Add soup and sloppy joe sauce. In a 13x9-inch baking dish coated with cooking spray, put hash browns. Put the beef mixture on top.
- Put a cover on and bake for 20 minutes at 450°. Remove the cover, bake until fully heated, about another 10 minutes. Sprinkle cheese over.

Nutrition Information

- Calories: 290 calories
- Total Carbohydrate: 30g carbohydrate (4g sugars
- Cholesterol: 47mg cholesterol
- Protein: 18g protein.
- Total Fat: 11g fat (6g saturated fat)
- Sodium: 763mg sodium
- Fiber: 3g fiber)

---

898. Potato And Cabbage Casserole

Serving: 10 servings. | Prep: 25mins | Cook: 01hours30mins | Ready in:

Ingredients

- 5 cups shredded cabbage
- 6 medium potatoes, sliced
- 4 medium carrots, sliced
- 1 small onion, chopped
- 1 teaspoon salt
- 1/2 teaspoon pepper
- 1 pound lean ground beef
- 1 can (10-3/4 ounces) condensed cream of mushroom soup, undiluted
- 1 can (10-1/2 ounces) condensed vegetable beef soup, undiluted

Direction

- Mix the first six ingredients together in a large bowl. Crumble beef over mixture; toss lightly. Place into a greased baking dish of 3 quarts. Spread soups on top.
- Cover up and bake at 350° until the vegetables are tender and the beef is no longer pink, about 90 minutes.

Nutrition Information

- Calories: 228 calories
- Sodium: 677mg sodium
- Fiber: 4g fiber)
- Total Carbohydrate: 27g carbohydrate (5g sugars
- Cholesterol: 33mg cholesterol
- Protein: 13g protein.
- Total Fat: 8g fat (3g saturated fat)

---

899. Potato Stuffed Kielbasa

Serving: 4 servings. | Prep: 15mins | Cook: 20mins | Ready in:

Ingredients

- 1 pound Johnsonville® Fully Cooked Polish Kielbasa Sausage Rope
- 2 cups mashed potatoes
- 2 tablespoons thinly sliced green onion
- 1 teaspoon prepared mustard
- 1/2 cup shredded cheddar cheese

Direction

- Slice sausage into 4 pieces; slice each piece lengthwise no more than 1/2 inch of the opposite side. Flatten the sausage pieces by opening it, put in an 11x7-inch baking dish coated with cooking spray.
- Mix mustard, onion, and potatoes together in a big bowl; put on the sausage in mounds. Sprinkle cheese over. Bake without a cover at 350° until fully heated, about 20-25 minutes.

Nutrition Information

- Calories: 506 calories
- Sodium: 1334mg sodium
- Fiber: 0 fiber)
- Total Carbohydrate: 23g carbohydrate (0 sugars
- Cholesterol: 98mg cholesterol
- Protein: 20g protein.
- Total Fat: 36g fat (16g saturated fat)

---

900. Roast Beef With Chive Roasted Potatoes

Serving: 6 servings. | Prep: 20mins | Cook: 25mins | Ready in:

Ingredients

- 2 pounds red potatoes, cut into 1-inch cubes
- 2 tablespoons olive oil
- 2 teaspoons minced chives
- 3/4 teaspoon salt, divided
- 2 medium onions, halved and thinly sliced
- 1 pound sliced fresh mushrooms
- 1/4 cup butter, cubed
- 1 garlic clove, minced
- 1 teaspoon dried rosemary, crushed
- 1/4 teaspoon pepper
- 1/3 cup dry red wine or beef broth
- 2 cups cubed cooked roast beef
- 1 cup beef gravy

Direction

- Add the potatoes into a greased 15x10x1-inch baking pan. Sprinkle with the oil and scatter with a quarter teaspoon salt and chives; toss to cover. Bake, with no cover, at 425 degrees till soften or for 25 to 30 minutes, whisking once in a while.
- At the same time, in the big skillet, sauté the mushrooms and onions in the butter till soften. Put in the rest of the salt, pepper, rosemary and garlic; cook for 60 seconds more. Whisk in

the wine. Put in the gravy and beef; heat completely. Serve along with potatoes.

Nutrition Information

- Calories: 379 calories
- Sodium: 591mg sodium
- Fiber: 5g fiber)
- Total Carbohydrate: 35g carbohydrate (6g sugars
- Cholesterol: 66mg cholesterol
- Protein: 24g protein.
- Total Fat: 15g fat (6g saturated fat)

---

901. Sausage Potato Medley

Serving: 4-6 servings. | Prep: 25mins | Cook: 45mins | Ready in:

Ingredients

- 4 cups thinly sliced peeled potatoes
- 1 pound Jones No Sugar Pork Sausage Roll sausage
- 3/4 cup chopped onion
- 1 cup shredded cheddar cheese
- 3 tablespoons butter
- 1/4 cup all-purpose flour
- 1/2 teaspoon salt
- 1/4 teaspoon pepper
- 2 cups whole milk

Direction

- Cover potatoes with water in a saucepan; put the lid on, and bring to a boil over medium-high heat. Cook potatoes for 5 minutes. Strain; transfer potatoes to an oiled 2-quart baking dish.
- Sauté onion and sausage over medium heat in a large skillet until meat is no longer pink; drain. Scoop over potatoes; scatter with cheese.

- Melt butter in a large saucepan; mix in pepper, salt, and flour until no lumps remain. Slowly pour in milk. Bring to a boil; cook while stirring until mixture is bubbly and thickened, about 2 minutes. Pour over cheese layer. Bake, covered for 45 to 50 minutes at 350°, or until potatoes are soft.

Nutrition Information

- Calories: 437 calories
- Protein: 15g protein.
- Total Fat: 28g fat (14g saturated fat)
- Sodium: 723mg sodium
- Fiber: 2g fiber)
- Total Carbohydrate: 32g carbohydrate (7g sugars
- Cholesterol: 74mg cholesterol

902.　　Sausage And Potato Pie

Serving: 6 servings. | Prep: 25mins | Cook: 5mins | Ready in:

Ingredients

- 1 pound Jones No Sugar Pork Sausage Roll sausage
- 3/4 cup shredded mozzarella cheese, divided
- 1/2 cup finely chopped onion, divided
- 1/4 cup dry bread crumbs
- 1/4 cup water
- 4 bacon strips
- 1 cup shredded raw potato
- 1/4 cup finely chopped green pepper
- 4 eggs
- 1/4 cup milk
- 1/8 teaspoon salt
- Dash pepper
- 1/4 cup shredded cheddar cheese

Direction

- Mix together water, bread crumbs, 1/4 cup onion, 1/2 cup mozzarella cheese, and sausage. In a non-oiled 9-inch pie pan, press the mixture up the sides and onto the bottom, making a rim along the edge of the pan. Bake at 375° until the juices run clear, about 20 minutes. Then drain. In the meantime, cook bacon in a frying pan until crunchy; transfer onto paper towels to strain. Save 1 tablespoon of drippings. Add potato, cook over medium-high heat for until turning brown, about 10 minutes, tossing sometimes. Add the leftover onion and green pepper. Lower the heat to medium, cook until the vegetables are soft, about 5 minutes, tossing sometimes. Combine pepper, salt, milk, and eggs in a bowl; mix in cheddar cheese. Add to the frying pan, lower the heat and cook until the eggs are a little moist, about 2-3 minutes. Spoon the mixture into the sausage shell. Sprinkle the leftover mozzarella over; crumble over the top with bacon. Put back into the oven until the cheese melts, about 5 minutes.

Nutrition Information

- Calories:
- Protein:
- Total Fat:
- Sodium:
- Fiber:
- Total Carbohydrate:
- Cholesterol:

903.　　Scalloped Potatoes 'n' Franks

Serving: 4-6 servings. | Prep: 25mins | Cook: 01hours40mins | Ready in:

Ingredients

- 2 tablespoons chopped onion
- 3 tablespoons butter

- 1/4 cup all-purpose flour
- 1-1/2 teaspoons salt
- 1/8 teaspoon pepper
- 2 cups 2% milk
- 1 cup shredded Swiss cheese
- 2 tablespoons minced fresh parsley
- 5 medium potatoes, peeled and thinly sliced
- 8 hot dogs, halved and sliced

Direction

- Sauté onion in a big saucepan with melted butter until it softens. Add in the pepper, salt, and flour. Stir till blended. Pour in slowly the milk and stir over medium heat to fully incorporate the ingredients. Simmer the mixture for 2 minutes when the liquid has thickened. Remove from heat. Drop in the cheese, and stir the mixture together until it melts. Toss in some parsley.
- Assemble the dish in a 2 quarter sized baking dish which has been greased. Arrange half of the potatoes as the first layer. Pour in half of the sauce and place on top the hotdogs. Arrange the remaining potatoes on top and pour in the remaining sauce.
- Bake the covered dish for 1 and half hours at 350 degrees in the oven. Cook until potatoes are soft and the dish is bubbly. Remove the cover and allow the top part to brown for another 10 minutes.

Nutrition Information

- Calories: 488 calories
- Total Fat: 32g fat (16g saturated fat)
- Sodium: 1354mg sodium
- Fiber: 2g fiber)
- Total Carbohydrate: 34g carbohydrate (8g sugars
- Cholesterol: 76mg cholesterol
- Protein: 17g protein.

904.   Scalloped Potatoes And Hamburger

Serving: 6 servings. | Prep: 25mins | Cook: 45mins | Ready in:

Ingredients

- 1 pound ground beef
- 6 medium potatoes, peeled and sliced
- 1 large onion, sliced
- Salt and pepper to taste
- 1 can (10-3/4 ounces) condensed cream of mushroom soup, undiluted
- 1 cup milk
- 1/4 cup chopped green pepper

Direction

- Cook beef in a skillet over medium heat until not pink anymore; drain. Layer 1/2 of the potatoes, onion and beef in a greased baking dish (13x9 inches); season with pepper and salt. Repeat layers. Place green pepper, milk and soup together in a bowl; mix well. Drizzle over top. Cover and bake at 350° for 45 minutes. Remove the cover; bake until potatoes are tender, about 15 more minutes.

Nutrition Information

- Calories:
- Fiber:
- Total Carbohydrate:
- Cholesterol:
- Protein:
- Total Fat:
- Sodium:

905.   Smoked Sausage Potato Bake

Serving: 4-6 servings. | Prep: 10mins | Cook: 30mins | Ready in:

Ingredients

- 1-3/4 cups water
- 2/3 cup whole milk
- 5 tablespoons butter, divided
- 1/2 teaspoon salt
- 2-2/3 cups mashed potato flakes
- 1 cup sour cream
- 1 cup shredded cheddar cheese
- 1 pound smoked sausage links, halved lengthwise and cut into 1/2-inch slices
- 1 cup shredded Monterey Jack cheese
- 2 tablespoons dry bread crumbs

Direction

- Place salt, 4 tablespoons butter, milk, and water in a big saucepan; heat to a boil. Take away from heat; mix in potato flakes. Let it sit for half a minute or until the liquid is absorbed. Use a fork to beat until fluffy. Mix in cheddar cheese and sour cream.
- Transfer half into an oiled 2-quart baking dish using a spoon. Top with the rest of potatoes and sausage. Sprinkle Monterey Jack cheese over top.
- Melt the rest of butter, add in bread crumbs and toss. Arrange over top. Bake at 350 degrees without cover for 30-35 minutes or until heated through and edges turn golden brown.

Nutrition Information

- Calories: 662 calories
- Cholesterol: 140mg cholesterol
- Protein: 23g protein.
- Total Fat: 49g fat (26g saturated fat)
- Sodium: 1382mg sodium
- Fiber: 1g fiber)
- Total Carbohydrate: 31g carbohydrate (4g sugars

906.   Smoky Potato Skillet

Serving: 4-6 servings. | Prep: 10mins | Cook: 25mins | Ready in:

Ingredients

- 1 package (16 ounces) smoked sausage links, cut into 1-inch pieces
- 2 celery ribs, chopped
- 1 medium onion, chopped
- 1 tablespoon butter
- 2 cups hot water
- 2/3 cup 2% milk
- 1 package (4.9 ounces) au gratin potatoes

Direction

- Sauté onion, celery, and sausage with butter in a big frying pan until the vegetables are soft. Mix in contents of sauce mix from potatoes, milk, and water.
- Boil it. Mix in potatoes. Lower the heat, put a cover on and simmer until the potatoes are soft, about 20-25 minutes, tossing 1 time.

Nutrition Information

- Calories: 368 calories
- Total Fat: 24g fat (9g saturated fat)
- Sodium: 1294mg sodium
- Fiber: 2g fiber)
- Total Carbohydrate: 24g carbohydrate (5g sugars
- Cholesterol: 56mg cholesterol
- Protein: 12g protein.

907.   Turkey Potato Supper

Serving: 4-6 servings. | Prep: 15mins | Cook: 35mins | Ready in:

Ingredients

- 2 cups water

- 1/4 cup butter
- 1 teaspoon salt
- 2-2/3 cups mashed potato flakes
- 2 eggs, lightly beaten
- 1 can (10-3/4 ounces) condensed cream of chicken soup, undiluted
- 1/4 cup mayonnaise
- 1 teaspoon lemon juice
- 1/2 teaspoon curry powder
- 2 cups cubed cooked turkey
- 3 cups frozen chopped broccoli, thawed
- 1/4 cup slivered almonds, toasted, optional

Direction

- Boil salt, butter, and water in a large saucepan. Take away from the heat; mix in potato flakes. Allow to stand for half a minute. Use a fork to whip. Mix in eggs. Press the potatoes up the sides and onto the bottoms of an 8-inch square baking dish coated with cooking spray to shape into a shell.
- Mix curry, lemon juice, mayonnaise, and soup in a bowl. Stir in broccoli and turkey. Without the cover, bake for 20 minutes at 350 degrees. If desired, dust with almonds.
- Bake until the filling is heated through and potato edges turn golden brown, 15-20 minutes. Before serving, allow to stand for 10 minutes.

Nutrition Information

- Calories: 404 calories
- Protein: 21g protein.
- Total Fat: 22g fat (8g saturated fat)
- Sodium: 1031mg sodium
- Fiber: 3g fiber)
- Total Carbohydrate: 30g carbohydrate (1g sugars
- Cholesterol: 134mg cholesterol

Chapter 9: Turkey Casserole Recipes

***

908. Biscuit Turkey Bake

Serving: 5 servings. | Prep: 10mins | Cook: 20mins | Ready in:

Ingredients

- 1 can (10-3/4 ounces) condensed cream of chicken soup, undiluted
- 1 cup chopped cooked turkey or chicken
- 1 can (4 ounces) mushroom stems and pieces, drained
- 1/2 cup frozen peas
- 1/4 cup 2% milk
- Dash each ground cumin, dried basil and thyme
- 1 tube (12 ounces) refrigerated buttermilk biscuits

Direction

- Preheat oven to 350°. Stir seasonings, milk, peas, mushrooms, turkey and soup together in a large bowl. Spread into a greased 8-inch square baking dish; position biscuits over the top.
- Bake while uncovered for 20-25 minutes, or till biscuits become golden brown.

Nutrition Information

- Calories:
- Total Fat:
- Sodium:
- Fiber:
- Total Carbohydrate:
- Cholesterol:
- Protein:

909. Broccoli Turkey Supreme

Serving: 8 servings. | Prep: 15mins | Cook: 01hours15mins | Ready in:

Ingredients

- 4 cups cubed cooked turkey breast
- 1 can (10-3/4 ounces) condensed cream of chicken soup, undiluted
- 4 cups frozen broccoli florets, thawed and drained
- 1 package (6.9 ounces) chicken-flavored rice mix
- 1-1/3 cups milk
- 1 cup chicken broth
- 1 cup chopped celery
- 1 can (8 ounces) sliced water chestnuts, drained
- 3/4 cup mayonnaise
- 1/2 cup chopped onion

Direction

- Mix all of the ingredients together in a big bowl. Remove into a 3-quart baking dish coated with cooking spray. Put a cover on and bake for 60 minutes at 325°. Remove the cover and bake until the rice is soft, about another 15-20 minutes.

Nutrition Information

- Calories: 0g sugar total.

910. Broccoli Turkey Brunch Casserole

Serving: 6 servings. | Prep: 20mins | Cook: 45mins | Ready in:

Ingredients

- 1-1/2 cups fat-free milk
- 1 can (10-3/4 ounces) reduced-fat reduced-sodium condensed cream of chicken soup, undiluted
- 1 carton (8 ounces) egg substitute
- 1/4 cup reduced-fat sour cream
- 1/2 teaspoon pepper
- 1/4 teaspoon poultry seasoning
- 1/8 teaspoon salt
- 2-1/2 cups cubed cooked turkey breast
- 1 package (16 ounces) frozen chopped broccoli, thawed and drained
- 2 cups seasoned stuffing cubes
- 1 cup shredded reduced-fat cheddar cheese, divided

Direction

- Mix egg substitute, salt, sour cream, milk, poultry seasoning, soup, and pepper in a big bowl. Mix in 3/4 cup cheese, turkey, stuffing cubes, and broccoli. Move to a greased 13x9-in. pan.
- Don't cover; bake in a 350-degree oven for 40 minutes. Sprinkle on remaining cheese. Bake until knife poked in middle comes out clean, 5-10 minutes. Let it cool for 5 minutes before enjoying.

Nutrition Information

- Calories: 303 calories
- Protein: 33g protein. Diabetic Exchanges: 3 lean meat
- Total Fat: 7g fat (4g saturated fat)
- Sodium: 762mg sodium
- Fiber: 3g fiber)
- Total Carbohydrate: 26g carbohydrate (8g sugars
- Cholesterol: 72mg cholesterol

911. Butternut Turkey Bake

Serving: 4 servings. | Prep: 01hours10mins | Cook: 25mins | Ready in:

Ingredients

- 1 medium butternut squash (about 2-1/2 pounds)
- 3/4 cup finely chopped onion
- 2 tablespoons butter
- 2 cups seasoned salad croutons
- 1/2 teaspoon salt
- 1/2 teaspoon poultry seasoning
- 1/2 teaspoon pepper
- 2 cups cubed cooked turkey
- 1 cup chicken broth
- 1/2 cup shredded cheddar cheese

Direction

- Divide the squash into 1/2; remove the seeds. Put the squash into a 15x10x1-in. baking pan, cut side down; pour in 1/2 in. hot water. Bake, uncovered, for 45 mins at 350°.
- Drain the water from baking pan. Flip the squash cut side up. Bake until tender, about 10 to 15 mins more. Scoop out the flesh. Then mash and put aside.
- Sauté onion in a large skillet in butter until tender. Mix in pepper, poultry seasoning, salt and the croutons. Cook until the croutons are toasted, about 2 to 3 mins more. Mix in broth, turkey and squash, then heat through.
- Place into an oiled 1-1/2-qt. baking dish. Bake, uncovered, for 20 mins at 350°. Top with cheese. Bake until the cheese is melted and the edges are bubbly, about 5 to 10 mins more.

Nutrition Information

- Calories: 383 calories
- Protein: 28g protein.
- Total Fat: 15g fat (8g saturated fat)
- Sodium: 828mg sodium
- Fiber: 8g fiber)

- Total Carbohydrate: 37g carbohydrate (7g sugars
- Cholesterol: 85mg cholesterol

912. Cheddar Turkey Bake

Serving: 2 casseroles (4-6 servings each). | Prep: 20mins | Cook: 35mins | Ready in:

Ingredients

- 2 cups water
- 2 cups chicken broth
- 4 teaspoons dried minced onion
- 2 cups uncooked long grain rice
- 4 cups cubed cooked turkey
- 2 cups frozen peas, thawed
- 2 cans (10-3/4 ounces each) condensed cheddar cheese soup, undiluted
- 2 cups milk
- 1 teaspoon salt
- 2 cups finely crushed butter-flavored crackers (about 60 crackers)
- 6 tablespoons butter, melted

Direction

- Bring onion, broth, and water in a large saucepan to a boil. Lower heat. Add rice; simmer, covered until tender, about 15 minutes. Take away from the heat; fluff rice using a fork.
- Distribute rice into 2 greased 9x9-inch baking pans. Sprinkle peas and turkey over the top the 2 pans. Combine salt, milk, and soup in a large bowl; add to turkey. Combine butter and cracker crumbs; scatter over top.
- Freeze, covered one casserole for a maximum of 3 months. Bake the remaining casserole without covering for 35 minutes at 350°, or until tops turn golden brown.
- For the frozen casserole: let defrost for 24 hours in the fridge. Bake without a cover for 45 to 50 minutes at 350°, or until thoroughly heated.

Nutrition Information

- Calories: 387 calories
- Fiber: 2g fiber)
- Total Carbohydrate: 43g carbohydrate (5g sugars
- Cholesterol: 59mg cholesterol
- Protein: 21g protein.
- Total Fat: 15g fat (6g saturated fat)
- Sodium: 810mg sodium

913. Corn Bread Turkey Casserole

Serving: 3 casseroles (8 servings each). | Prep: 30mins | Cook: 35mins | Ready in:

Ingredients

- 3 packages (6 ounces each) crushed corn bread stuffing mix
- 11 cups cubed cooked turkey
- 2 cups shredded cheddar cheese
- 2 cans (10-3/4 ounces each) condensed cream of celery soup, undiluted
- 2 cans (10-3/4 ounces each) condensed cream of chicken soup, undiluted
- 1 can (10-3/4 ounces) condensed cream of mushroom soup, undiluted
- 1 can (12 ounces) evaporated milk
- 1-1/2 cups shredded Swiss cheese

Direction

- Follow directions on package to make stuffing mix. Mix in cheddar cheese and turkey. Mix milk and soups in a big bowl. In three 13x9-in. greased pans, layer 1 cup of the turkey mixture and then 1 cup soup mixture in each one. Repeat the layers. Sprinkle Swiss cheese on top. Place two in the freezer and they can remain in freezer for up to 3 months. For the last pan, cover and bake in a 350-degree oven

until bubbling, 30-35 minutes. Let it cool for 5-10 minutes before eating. For the frozen ones: place in refrigerator to thaw. Take out and let warm to room temperature for 30 minutes before baking. Do not cover; bake in a 350-degree oven until bubbling, 35-40 minutes. Let it cool for 5-10 minutes before eating.

Nutrition Information

- Calories: 377 calories
- Protein: 27g protein.
- Total Fat: 19g fat (9g saturated fat)
- Sodium: 973mg sodium
- Fiber: 2g fiber)
- Total Carbohydrate: 23g carbohydrate (5g sugars
- Cholesterol: 89mg cholesterol

914. Creamed Turkey With Bow Ties

Serving: 6 servings. | Prep: 15mins | Cook: 15mins | Ready in:

Ingredients

- 1 package (12 ounces) bow tie pasta
- 12 green onions, chopped
- 6 celery ribs, chopped
- 1/2 pound fresh mushrooms, sliced
- 2 tablespoons butter
- 2-1/2 cups cubed cooked turkey breast
- 1 can (14-1/2 ounces) chicken broth
- 1 can (10-3/4 ounces) reduced-fat reduced-sodium condensed cream of chicken soup, undiluted
- 1/4 cup fat-free sour cream
- Pepper to taste

Direction

- Following the package instructions, cook the pasta. At the same time, sauté mushrooms, celery, and onions in butter in a large skillet until they become tender. Turn down the heat. Put in sour cream, soup, broth, and turkey; heat them through but don't boil. Flavor with pepper.

- Then drain the pasta; put the turkey mixture on top.

Nutrition Information

- Calories: 391 calories
- Cholesterol: 67mg cholesterol
- Protein: 29g protein.
- Total Fat: 7g fat (3g saturated fat)
- Sodium: 602mg sodium
- Fiber: 4g fiber)
- Total Carbohydrate: 53g carbohydrate (6g sugars

---

915. Crescent Topped Turkey Amandine

Serving: 4 servings. | Prep: 20mins | Cook: 30mins | Ready in:

Ingredients

- 3 cups cubed cooked turkey
- 1 can (10-3/4 ounces) condensed cream of mushroom soup, undiluted
- 1 can (8 ounces) sliced water chestnuts, drained
- 2/3 cup mayonnaise
- 1/2 cup chopped celery
- 1/2 cup chopped onion
- 1 tube (4 ounces) refrigerated crescent rolls
- 2/3 cup shredded Swiss cheese
- 1/2 cup sliced almonds
- 1/4 cup butter, melted

Direction

- Start preheating the oven at 375°. Blend the first 6 ingredients in a large saucepan; heat

through. Place to a greased 2-quart baking dish. Unroll the crescent dough and put over the turkey mixture.

- In a small bowl, mix butter, almonds, and cheese. Scoop over the dough. Bake, without covering, for 30 to 35 minutes, or until the crust turns golden brown and the filling bubbles.

Nutrition Information

- Calories: 895 calories
- Sodium: 1185mg sodium
- Fiber: 4g fiber)
- Total Carbohydrate: 29g carbohydrate (6g sugars
- Cholesterol: 143mg cholesterol
- Protein: 42g protein.
- Total Fat: 67g fat (19g saturated fat)

---

916. Crunchy Almond Turkey Casserole

Serving: 8 servings. | Prep: 15mins | Cook: 35mins | Ready in:

Ingredients

- 2 cans (10-3/4 ounces each) condensed cream of mushroom soup, undiluted
- 1/2 cup mayonnaise
- 1/2 cup sour cream
- 2 tablespoons chopped onion
- 2 tablespoons lemon juice
- 1 teaspoon salt
- 1/2 teaspoon white pepper
- 5 cups cubed cooked turkey
- 3 cups cooked rice
- 4 celery ribs, chopped
- 1 can (8 ounces) sliced water chestnuts, drained
- 1 cup sliced almonds
- Topping:

- 1-1/2 cups crushed Ritz crackers (about 40 crackers)
- 1/3 cup butter, melted
- 1/4 cup sliced almonds

Direction

- Mix pepper, salt, lemon juice, onion, sour cream, mayonnaise, and soup in a large bowl. Stir in almonds, water chestnuts, celery, rice, and turkey
- Place into a 13x9-inch, greased baking dish. Bake with no cover for 25 minutes at 350 degrees. Mix the topping ingredients; scatter on the turkey mixture. Place back into the oven; bake until golden brown and bubbly for an additional of 10 to 15 minutes.

Nutrition Information

- Calories: 678 calories
- Total Fat: 41g fat (12g saturated fat)
- Sodium: 1211mg sodium
- Fiber: 4g fiber)
- Total Carbohydrate: 43g carbohydrate (5g sugars
- Cholesterol: 105mg cholesterol
- Protein: 34g protein.

917. Crunchy Turkey Casserole

Serving: 6-8 servings. | Prep: 15mins | Cook: 30mins | Ready in:

Ingredients

- 2 cans (10-3/4 ounces each) condensed cream of mushroom soup, undiluted
- 1/2 cup 2% milk or chicken broth
- 4 cups cubed cooked turkey
- 2 celery ribs, thinly sliced
- 1 small onion, chopped

- 1 can (8 ounces) sliced water chestnuts, drained and halved
- 1 tablespoon reduced-sodium soy sauce
- 1 can (3 ounces) chow mein noodles
- 1/2 cup slivered almonds

Direction

- Mix together milk and soup in a big bowl. Mix in soy sauce, water chestnuts, onion, celery, and turkey.
- Remove into a shallow 2-quart baking dish coated with cooking spray. Sprinkle almonds and noodles over. Bake without a cover at 350° until fully heated, about 30 minutes.

Nutrition Information

- Calories: 0
- Sodium: 497 mg sodium
- Fiber: 3 g fiber
- Total Carbohydrate: 16 g carbohydrate
- Cholesterol: 57 mg cholesterol
- Protein: 25 g protein.
- Total Fat: 13 g fat (3 g saturated fat)

918. Green Bean Turkey Bake

Serving: 6 servings. | Prep: 10mins | Cook: 10mins | Ready in:

Ingredients

- 2 cups frozen cut green beans, thawed
- 1-1/2 cups cubed cooked turkey breast
- 1 can (10-3/4 ounces) condensed cream of mushroom soup, undiluted
- 1 cup shredded cheddar cheese
- 1/3 cup 2% milk
- 3 cups mashed potatoes
- 1/2 cup cheese-flavored snack crackers, crushed

Direction

- Combine milk, cheese, soup, turkey, and green beans in a 2-quart microwaveable dish. Microwave with cover for 5 to 6 minutes on high power, stirring once, until bubbly.
- Gently scatter mashed potato mixture over turkey mixture; sprinkle cracker crumbs on top. Cook, with cover on high power until heated fully, for 2 to 4 minutes. Rest for 5 minutes before serving.

Nutrition Information

- Calories:
- Cholesterol:
- Protein:
- Total Fat:
- Sodium:
- Fiber:
- Total Carbohydrate:

---

919. Holiday Corn 'n' Turkey Casserole

Serving: 8 servings. | Prep: 20mins | Cook: 25mins | Ready in:

Ingredients

- 1 small onion, finely chopped
- 1/4 cup butter, cubed
- 1/4 cup all-purpose flour
- 3/4 teaspoon salt
- 1/2 teaspoon ground mustard
- 1/2 teaspoon pepper
- 3/4 cup whole milk
- 2 cups frozen corn, thawed
- 1 package (9 ounces) frozen broccoli cuts, thawed and chopped
- 2 cups cubed cooked turkey
- 1 cup shredded cheddar cheese
- 2 large eggs, lightly beaten
- 1/3 cup sliced almonds

Direction

- Sauté onion with butter in a big saucepan until soft. Mix pepper, mustard, salt, and flour together; mix into the onion mixture until combined. Slowly pour in the milk. Boil over medium heat. Stir and cook until thickened, about 2 minutes. Take away from the heat.
- Mix cheese, turkey, broccoli, and corn together in a big bowl. Stir eggs into the onion mixture. Add to the turkey mixture, whisk until blended.
- Remove into a 1 1/2-quart baking dish coated with cooking spray. Sprinkle almonds over. Bake without a cover at 350° until a thermometer displays 160°, about 25-30 minutes.

Nutrition Information

- Calories: 371 calories
- Protein: 25g protein.
- Total Fat: 21g fat (11g saturated fat)
- Sodium: 543mg sodium
- Fiber: 3g fiber)
- Total Carbohydrate: 22g carbohydrate (4g sugars
- Cholesterol: 149mg cholesterol

---

920. Hot Brown Turkey Casserole

Serving: 12 servings. | Prep: 40mins | Cook: 20mins | Ready in:

Ingredients

- 1/4 cup butter
- 1/4 cup all-purpose flour
- 4 cups 2% milk
- 1 large egg
- 2/3 cup grated Parmesan cheese, divided
- 1/4 teaspoon salt
- 1/4 teaspoon pepper
- 12 slices bread, toasted and divided

- 2 pounds thinly sliced cooked turkey or chicken
- 1/4 teaspoon paprika
- 6 bacon strips, cooked and crumbled
- 1 cup tomatoes, chopped and seeded
- 1 teaspoon minced fresh parsley

Direction

- Set the oven at 350° and start preheating. Place a large saucepan on medium heat; melt butter. Mix in flour till smooth; slowly whisk in milk. Allow to boil while stirring constantly; cook for 6-8 minutes till slightly thickened. Take away from the heat.
- Lightly beat egg into a small bowl. Slowly whisk in 1/2 cup of sauce. Gradually put back all into the pan, whisking constantly. Put in pepper, salt and 1/2 cup of Parmesan. Cook while stirring till thickened. (Do not boil.) Layer 6 toast slices and turkey on a greased 13x9-in. baking dish; pour the sauce over. Sprinkle with the remaining Parmesan cheese, bacon and paprika.
- Bake for 20-25 minutes, till heated through. Place parsley and tomatoes on top. Cut the remaining toast slices in half diagonally; serve on the side.

Nutrition Information

- Calories: 316 calories
- Sodium: 472mg sodium
- Fiber: 1g fiber)
- Total Carbohydrate: 19g carbohydrate (6g sugars
- Cholesterol: 117mg cholesterol
- Protein: 30g protein.
- Total Fat: 13g fat (6g saturated fat)

921.   Leftover Turkey Bake

Serving: 4 servings. | Prep: 20mins | Cook: 35mins | Ready in:

Ingredients

- 1-1/2 cups finely chopped onion
- 1/2 cup finely chopped celery
- 1 can (14-1/2 ounces) reduced-sodium chicken broth, divided
- 2 eggs, lightly beaten
- 2 teaspoons poultry seasoning
- 1/2 teaspoon salt
- 1/4 teaspoon pepper
- 3 cups cubed whole grain bread
- 3 cups cubed white bread
- 2 cups cubed cooked turkey breast
- 1/2 cup chopped fresh or frozen cranberries

Direction

- In a big saucepan, heat 1/2 cup broth, celery, and onion to a boil. Lower the heat and let simmer without cover for 5-8 minutes or until vegetables are tender. Take away from heat. Mix in the remaining broth, pepper, salt, poultry seasoning, and eggs until blended. Add cranberries, turkey, and bread cubes; blend nicely.
- With a spoon, transfer to a 2-quart baking dished coated with cooking spray. Put on cover and bake for 15 minutes at 350 degrees. Remove cover and bake for 20-25 minutes more or until thermometer shows 160.

Nutrition Information

- Calories: 290 calories
- Total Carbohydrate: 34g carbohydrate (8g sugars
- Cholesterol: 154mg cholesterol
- Protein: 27g protein.
- Total Fat: 5g fat (1g saturated fat)
- Sodium: 916mg sodium
- Fiber: 4g fiber)

922. Leftover Turkey Tetrazzini

Serving: 4-6 servings. | Prep: 25mins | Cook: 25mins | Ready in:

Ingredients

- 1 package (7 ounces) thin spaghetti, broken in half
- 2 cups cubed cooked turkey
- 1 cup sliced fresh mushrooms
- 1 small onion, chopped
- 3 tablespoons butter
- 1 can (10-3/4 ounces) condensed cream of mushroom soup, undiluted
- 1 cup whole milk
- 1/2 teaspoon poultry seasoning
- 1/8 teaspoon ground mustard
- 1 cup shredded cheddar cheese
- 1 cup shredded part-skim mozzarella cheese
- 1 tablespoon shredded Parmesan cheese
- Minced fresh parsley

Direction

- Cook spaghetti following the directions on the packaging. Drain and transfer to an 11x7-inch baking dish coated with cooking spray. Put turkey on top; put aside.
- Sauté onion and mushrooms with butter in a big skillet until they are tender. Whip in the mustard, poultry seasoning, milk and the soup until blended. Put in cheddar cheese; cook while stirring over medium heat until melted. Pour the mixture on top of the turkey.
- Top with Parmesan cheese and mozzarella cheese (the dish will be full). Bake at 350° without a cover for 25-30 minutes or until heated through. Drizzle with parsley.

Nutrition Information

- Calories: 444 calories
- Cholesterol: 90mg cholesterol
- Protein: 30g protein.
- Total Fat: 21g fat (12g saturated fat)
- Sodium: 685mg sodium
- Fiber: 2g fiber)
- Total Carbohydrate: 33g carbohydrate (5g sugars

923. Mom's Turkey Tetrazzini

Serving: 6 servings. | Prep: 25mins | Cook: 25mins | Ready in:

Ingredients

- 1 package (12 ounces) fettuccine
- 1/2 pound sliced fresh mushrooms
- 1 medium onion, chopped
- 1/4 cup butter, cubed
- 3 tablespoons all-purpose flour
- 1 cup white wine or chicken broth
- 3 cups 2% milk
- 3 cups cubed cooked turkey
- 3/4 teaspoon salt
- 1/2 teaspoon pepper
- 1/2 teaspoon hot pepper sauce
- 1/2 cup shredded Parmesan cheese
- Paprika, optional

Direction

- Set the oven to 375° and start preheating. Cook fettuccine as directed on the package.
- In the meantime, sauté onion and mushrooms in butter until tender in a large skillet. Stir in flour until blended; beat in whine for about 2 minutes until smooth. Beat in milk slowly. Bring to boiling; cook while stirring until thickened. Stir in pepper sauce, pepper, salt and turkey.
- Drain fettuccine. Layer 1/2 of fettuccine, turkey mixture and cheese in a greased 13x9-in. baking dish. Top with the same layers. Scatter with paprika if preferred.
- Bake with a cover for 25-30 minutes or until heated through. Rest 10 minutes; serve.

Nutrition Information

- Calories: 516 calories
- Protein: 37g protein.
- Total Fat: 17g fat (9g saturated fat)
- Sodium: 596mg sodium
- Fiber: 4g fiber)
- Total Carbohydrate: 53g carbohydrate (10g sugars
- Cholesterol: 87mg cholesterol

---

924.   Mushroom Turkey Tetrazzini

Serving: 8 servings. | Prep: 35mins | Cook: 25mins | Ready in:

Ingredients

- 12 ounces uncooked multigrain spaghetti, broken into 2-inch pieces
- 2 teaspoons chicken bouillon granules
- 2 tablespoons butter
- 1/2 pound sliced fresh mushrooms
- 2 tablespoons all-purpose flour
- 1/4 cup sherry or additional pasta water
- 3/4 teaspoon salt-free lemon-pepper seasoning
- 1/2 teaspoon salt
- 1/8 teaspoon ground nutmeg
- 1 cup fat-free evaporated milk
- 2/3 cup grated Parmesan cheese, divided
- 4 cups cubed cooked turkey breast
- 1/4 teaspoon paprika, optional

Direction

- Set the oven at 375° to preheat. Cook spaghetti following the package directions until al dente. Drain, reserve 2-1/2 cups pasta water; then transfer the spaghetti to a 13x9-in. baking dish greased with cooking spray. Next, dissolve the bouillon in the retained pasta water. Over medium-high heat, heat butter in a large nonstick skillet; sauté mushrooms until

softened. After that, stir in flour until well blended. Stir in the seasonings, reserved pasta water, and sherry gradually. Boil; cook and stir until thickened, for about 2 minutes.
- Reduce the heat to low; stir in 1/3 cup cheese and milk until blended. Put in the turkey, stirring constantly, heat through. Pour over the spaghetti and toss to combine. Dust with the leftover cheese and, paprika if desired.
- Cover and bake until bubbly, for 25-30 minutes.

Nutrition Information

- Calories: 357 calories
- Cholesterol: 71mg cholesterol
- Protein: 34g protein. Diabetic Exchanges: 3 starch
- Total Fat: 7g fat (3g saturated fat)
- Sodium: 717mg sodium
- Fiber: 3g fiber)
- Total Carbohydrate: 38g carbohydrate (5g sugars

---

925.   Pastry Topped Turkey Casserole

Serving: 6 servings. | Prep: 45mins | Cook: 20mins | Ready in:

Ingredients

- 2 cups diced red potatoes
- 1 large onion, finely chopped
- 2 celery ribs, chopped
- 2 teaspoons chicken bouillon granules
- 1/2 teaspoon dried rosemary, crushed
- 1/4 teaspoon garlic powder
- 1/4 teaspoon dried thyme
- 1/8 teaspoon pepper
- 1 can (14-1/2 ounces) reduced-sodium chicken broth
- 1/2 cup water
- 3 tablespoons all-purpose flour

- 2/3 cup fat-free evaporated milk
- 3 cups frozen mixed vegetables, thawed and drained
- 2 cups cubed cooked turkey breast
- CRUST:
- 1/4 cup all-purpose flour
- 1/4 cup whole wheat flour
- 1/2 teaspoon baking powder
- 1/8 teaspoon salt
- 4 tablespoons fat-free milk, divided
- 1 tablespoon canola oil
- Paprika

Direction

- Set oven to 400° to preheat. Arrange the first ten ingredients in a large saucepan; bring to a boil. Lower heat; cover and simmer for 10 to 15 minutes, or until potatoes are tender.
- Stir together evaporated milk and flour until no lumps remain; mix into the pan. Bring to a boil; stirring frequently; cook while stirring for 2 minute, or until thickened. Add turkey and frozen vegetables; cook until thoroughly heated, stirring sometimes. Pour mixture into an unoiled 8x8-inch baking dish.
- To make crust, combine salt, baking powder, and flours together; mix in oil and 3 tablespoons milk. Roll the dough to a thickness of 1/8-inch on a lightly floured work surface; slice into short strips, place the strips over filling. Brush remaining milk over the strips; scatter top with paprika.
- Bake without covering for 20 to 25 minutes, or until the filling is bubbling. Allow to cool for 10 minutes before serving.

Nutrition Information

- Calories: 280 calories
- Protein: 23g protein. Diabetic Exchanges: 2 starch
- Total Fat: 4g fat (1g saturated fat)
- Sodium: 696mg sodium
- Fiber: 6g fiber)

- Total Carbohydrate: 38g carbohydrate (9g sugars
- Cholesterol: 39mg cholesterol

926.   Portobello Pasta Bake

Serving: 4 servings. | Prep: 20mins | Cook: 20mins | Ready in:

Ingredients

- 2-1/2 cups uncooked multigrain spiral pasta
- 3 large portobello mushrooms
- 1 tablespoon olive oil
- 1 tablespoon butter
- 3 garlic cloves, minced
- 3 tablespoons all-purpose flour
- 1-1/2 cups 2% milk
- 1/3 cup heavy whipping cream
- 2 cups cubed cooked turkey
- 3/4 teaspoon salt
- 1/4 teaspoon pepper
- 1 cup shredded part-skim mozzarella cheese, divided
- 2 tablespoons grated Parmesan cheese

Direction

- Start preheating the oven to 350°. Cook pasta following the package instructions. Scrape and remove gills from the mushrooms using a spoon, cut the caps.
- Heat butter and oil in a big frying pan over medium-high heat. Add the cut mushrooms, stir and cook until soft. Add garlic, cook for another 1 minute. Mix in flour until combined, slowly add cream and milk. Boil it, stir and cook until thickened, about 2 minutes. Mix in pepper, salt, and turkey until fully heated.
- Strain the pasta, put on the turkey mixture and mix to blend. Mix in 3/4 cup mozzarella cheese.
- Remove into an 8-inch square baking dish coated with cooking spray. Sprinkle the leftover mozzarella cheese and Parmesan

cheese over. Bake without a cover until the cheese melts, about 20-25 minutes.

Nutrition Information

- Calories: 551 calories
- Sodium: 822mg sodium
- Fiber: 5g fiber)
- Total Carbohydrate: 41g carbohydrate (7g sugars
- Cholesterol: 128mg cholesterol
- Protein: 39g protein.
- Total Fat: 25g fat (12g saturated fat)

927.   Rice Turkey Casserole

Serving: 12 servings. | Prep: 50mins | Cook: 25mins | Ready in:

Ingredients

- 4 cups chicken broth
- 1/4 cup uncooked wild rice
- 1-3/4 cups uncooked long grain rice
- 2 cups sliced fresh mushrooms
- 1/2 cup fresh broccoli florets
- 1 small onion, chopped
- 1/4 cup grated carrot
- 1/4 cup sliced celery
- 2 tablespoons olive oil
- 5 cups cubed cooked turkey
- 1 jar (2 ounces) diced pimientos, drained
- 1 teaspoon salt
- 1/2 teaspoon dried marjoram
- 1/2 teaspoon dried oregano
- 5 tablespoons all-purpose flour
- 3 cups whole milk
- 1/4 cup white wine or chicken broth
- 2 cups shredded Swiss cheese
- 2 cups shredded cheddar cheese, divided

Direction

- Boil the broth in a large saucepan; put in the wild rice. Put on a cover and simmer for 25 minutes. Put in the long-grain rice and bring to a simmer until it becomes tender, 25 more minutes.
- Sauté celery, carrot, onion, broccoli, and mushrooms in oil in a large skillet until they become tender. Put in oregano, marjoram, salt, pimientos, and turkey. Mix in the rice.
- Mix wine, milk, and flour in a large saucepan till smooth. Boil; stir and cook until thick, 2 minutes. Stir in a cup of cheddar cheese and Swiss cheese until they melt. Put into the turkey mixture.
- Place into a 13x9-inch baking dish coated with cooking spray. Dust with the remaining Cheddar cheese. Without the cover, bake at 350 degrees until heated through, 25-30 minutes.

Nutrition Information

- Calories: 432 calories
- Protein: 32g protein.
- Total Fat: 18g fat (10g saturated fat)
- Sodium: 744mg sodium
- Fiber: 1g fiber)
- Total Carbohydrate: 33g carbohydrate (5g sugars
- Cholesterol: 89mg cholesterol

928.   Saucy Macaroni Skillet

Serving: 6 servings. | Prep: 5mins | Cook: 20mins | Ready in:

Ingredients

- 1-1/2 cups uncooked elbow macaroni
- 4 celery ribs, chopped
- 1/2 cup chopped green pepper
- 1/4 cup chopped onion
- 1/4 cup butter, cubed

- 2 cans (10-3/4 ounces each) condensed cream of chicken soup, undiluted
- 2/3 cup whole milk
- 2 cups shredded cheddar cheese
- 3 cups cubed cooked turkey or chicken
- 1 jar (4 ounces) diced pimientos, drained
- 1/2 teaspoon salt
- 1/4 teaspoon ground nutmeg
- 1/2 cup sliced almonds, toasted

Direction

- Following package directions to cook macaroni. In the meantime, sauté together onion, green pepper, celery in a big saucepan with butter until softened. Add milk and soup, stir, until combined. Put in cheese, then cook and stir on medium heat until it has melted.
- Drain macaroni, then put macaroni into the soup mixture with nutmeg, salt, pimientos, turkey. Cook and stir until heated through. Sprinkle almonds on top.

Nutrition Information

- Calories: 509 calories
- Cholesterol: 121mg cholesterol
- Protein: 35g protein.
- Total Fat: 30g fat (16g saturated fat)
- Sodium: 975mg sodium
- Fiber: 3g fiber)
- Total Carbohydrate: 24g carbohydrate (4g sugars

929. Secondhand Turkey

Serving: 4 servings. | Prep: 30mins | Cook: 20mins | Ready in:

Ingredients

- 1/2 pound sliced fresh mushrooms
- 1/2 cup chopped celery
- 5 tablespoons butter, divided

- 2 tablespoons cornstarch
- 2 cups 2% milk
- 2 cups cubed cooked turkey
- 2 cups cooked egg noodles
- 1/4 cup chicken broth
- 1 teaspoon salt
- 1/2 teaspoon dried thyme
- 1/8 teaspoon white pepper
- 1/2 cup dry bread crumbs

Direction

- Sauté celery and mushrooms in 3 tablespoons butter in a large skillet until softened. Blend milk and cornstarch until smooth; stir into the mushroom mixture. Boil over medium heat, stirring regularly. Cook for until thickened, 1 minute.
- Stir in pepper, thyme, salt, broth, noodles and turkey. Pour into a greased 2-qt. baking dish. Next, melt the leftover butter and toss with bread crumbs. Dust over the casserole.
- Uncover and bake for 20-25 minutes, at 375°, or until heated through.

Nutrition Information

- Calories: 479 calories
- Sodium: 1038mg sodium
- Fiber: 2g fiber)
- Total Carbohydrate: 36g carbohydrate (7g sugars
- Cholesterol: 126mg cholesterol
- Protein: 31g protein.
- Total Fat: 24g fat (13g saturated fat)

930. Spanish Rice With Turkey

Serving: 5 servings. | Prep: 15mins | Cook: 15mins | Ready in:

Ingredients

- 1 pound ground turkey breast
- 1/2 cup chopped onion
- 1/2 cup chopped green pepper
- 1/2 teaspoon garlic powder
- 2 cans (14-1/2 ounces each) diced tomatoes, undrained
- 2 cups cooked long grain brown rice
- 1 teaspoon sugar
- 1 teaspoon chili powder
- 1/4 teaspoon pepper
- 1/8 teaspoon hot pepper sauce
- 1/2 cup shredded reduced-fat cheddar cheese

Direction

- Combine garlic powder, green pepper, onion and turkey in a large skillet, cook over medium heat until the pink color disappears from meat; drain. Stir in the next 6 ingredients and bring to a boil. Lower the heat and simmer, covered, for 15 to 20 minutes or until mixture is heated through. Add cheese on top.

Nutrition Information

- Calories: 308 calories
- Sodium: 384mg sodium
- Fiber: 4g fiber)
- Total Carbohydrate: 30g carbohydrate (0 sugars
- Cholesterol: 78mg cholesterol
- Protein: 24g protein. Diabetic Exchanges: 2 starch
- Total Fat: 11g fat (4g saturated fat)

931. TLC (Thanksgiving Leftover Casserole)

Serving: 8 servings. | Prep: 20mins | Cook: 01hours05mins | Ready in:

Ingredients

- 4 cups seasoned stuffing cubes

- 4 cups cubed cooked turkey
- 2 celery ribs, finely chopped
- 1 cup frozen peas
- 1 cup fresh or frozen cranberries
- 1/2 cup chopped sweet onion
- 1/4 cup all-purpose flour
- 4 large eggs
- 3 cups 2% milk
- 1 can (8-1/4 ounces) cream-style corn
- 1/2 teaspoon salt
- 1/2 teaspoon pepper
- 2 tablespoons butter
- 1/3 cup coarsely chopped pecans

Direction

- Set the oven at 350° to preheat. In a greased 13x9-in. baking dish, layer the first 6 ingredients. Whisk milk, eggs, and flour in a large bowl until smooth. Put in pepper, salt and corn; mix well. Pour over the top; allow to stand for 15 minutes. Next, dot with butter and dust with pecans.
- Bake, covered, for 35 minutes. Then uncover and bake until a knife comes out clean once inserted in the center, for 30-35 minutes.

Nutrition Information

- Calories: 415 calories
- Sodium: 768mg sodium
- Fiber: 4g fiber)
- Total Carbohydrate: 38g carbohydrate (9g sugars
- Cholesterol: 173mg cholesterol
- Protein: 32g protein. Diabetic Exchanges: 3 lean meat
- Total Fat: 15g fat (5g saturated fat)

932. Tastes Like Thanksgiving Casserole

Serving: 12 servings | Prep: 25mins | Cook: | Ready in:

Ingredients

- 1 pkg. (24 oz.) ORE-IDA STEAM N' MASH Cut Russet Potatoes
- 2 stalks celery, chopped
- 1/2 cup chopped onions
- 1/4 cup butter
- 1-1/2 cups hot water
- 1 pkg. (6 oz.) STOVE TOP Stuffing Mix for Turkey
- 4 cups shredded cooked turkey
- 2 cans (10-3/4 oz. each) condensed cream of chicken soup
- 3/4 cup BREAKSTONE'S or KNUDSEN Sour Cream, divided
- 1 tsp. garlic powder
- 1 pkg. (8 oz.) PHILADELPHIA Cream Cheese, softened
- 1-1/2 cups KRAFT Sharp Cheddar Cheese

Direction

- Put the potatoes in the microwave and cook as the package instructions. Do not mash the potatoes.
- In the meantime, in a big pan over medium heat, cook onions and celery with butter for 4-5mins until the celery is soft. Mix in stuffing mix and water; spread in a 13-in by 9-in baking dish greased with cooking spray.
- Combine garlic powder, turkey, a quarter cup of sour cream, and soup; spread over the stuffing mixture.
- Put potatoes into a big bowl; mash in the remaining sour cream and cream cheese until it reaches your preferred consistency and the ingredients are well combined. Scoop over the turkey mixture.
- Bake for 25mis then sprinkle cheddar cheese on top. Bake for another 10mins until the cheddar melts and the casserole is completely cooked through.

Nutrition Information

- Calories: 400
- Saturated Fat: 12 g
- Protein: 22 g
- Total Carbohydrate: 26 g
- Cholesterol: 110 mg
- Total Fat: 23 g
- Sodium: 960 mg
- Fiber: 2 g
- Sugar: 3 g

---

933.   Tempting Turkey Casserole

Serving: 3 servings. | Prep: 15mins | Cook: 25mins | Ready in:

Ingredients

- 3 ounces uncooked spaghetti, broken into 2-inch pieces
- 1/2 cup process cheese sauce, warmed
- 1/4 cup 2% milk
- 1-1/2 cups frozen chopped broccoli, thawed
- 3/4 cup cubed cooked turkey
- 1/3 cup canned mushroom stems and pieces, drained
- 1 tablespoon pimientos, chopped
- 1/8 to 1/4 teaspoon onion powder
- 1/8 teaspoon poultry seasoning

Direction

- Following package directions to cook spaghetti. At the same time, whisk milk and cheese sauce together in a small bowl. Put in poultry seasoning, onion powder, pimientos, mushrooms, turkey and broccoli. Drain pasta and put into broccoli mixture.
- Turn to a 1-quart baking dish sprayed with cooking spray. Cover and bake at 350 degrees until heated through, about 25 to 30 minutes.

Nutrition Information

- Calories: 313 calories
- Fiber: 3g fiber)

- Total Carbohydrate: 29g carbohydrate (4g sugars
- Cholesterol: 55mg cholesterol
- Protein: 22g protein.
- Total Fat: 12g fat (8g saturated fat)
- Sodium: 838mg sodium

934. Thanksgiving In A Pan

Serving: 6 servings. | Prep: 15mins | Cook: 30mins | Ready in:

Ingredients

- 1 package (6 ounces) stuffing mix
- 2-1/2 cups cubed cooked turkey
- 2 cups frozen cut green beans, thawed
- 1 jar (12 ounces) turkey gravy
- Pepper to taste

Direction

- Follow directions on package to make stuffing mix. Move to an 11x7-in. greased pan. Put pepper, turkey, gravy, and beans on top. Cover; bake in a 350-degree oven until cooked through, 30-35 minutes.

Nutrition Information

- Calories:
- Protein:
- Total Fat:
- Sodium:
- Fiber:
- Total Carbohydrate:
- Cholesterol:

935. Turkey & Spinach Stuffing Casserole

Serving: 4 servings. | Prep: 15mins | Cook: 10mins | Ready in:

Ingredients

- 1 can (14-1/2 ounces) reduced-sodium chicken broth
- 3 tablespoons butter
- 3 cups stuffing mix
- 3 cups cubed cooked turkey
- 2 cups fresh baby spinach
- 1/2 cup dried cranberries
- 3/4 cup shredded cheddar cheese

Direction

- Prepare the oven by preheating to 350 degrees. Place butter and broth in a large pot and bring to a boil. Remove the pot from heat. Stir in stuffing mix until moist. Mix in cranberries, turkey, and spinach. Place mixture in 11x7-in. baking pan sprayed with cooking spray. Take the cheese and sprinkle on top. Bake at 350 degrees, uncovered, until cheese is melted, 10-15 minutes.

Nutrition Information

- Calories: 565 calories
- Fiber: 2g fiber)
- Total Carbohydrate: 43g carbohydrate (15g sugars
- Cholesterol: 125mg cholesterol
- Protein: 42g protein.
- Total Fat: 24g fat (12g saturated fat)
- Sodium: 1259mg sodium

936. Turkey 'n' Stuffing Pie

Serving: 4-6 servings. | Prep: 30mins | Cook: 25mins | Ready in:

Ingredients

- 1 egg, lightly beaten
- 1 cup chicken broth
- 1/3 cup butter, melted
- 5 cups seasoned stuffing cubes
- FILLING:
- 1 can (4 ounces) mushroom stems and pieces, drained
- 1/2 cup chopped onion
- 1 tablespoon butter
- 1 tablespoon all-purpose flour
- 3 cups cubed cooked turkey
- 1 cup frozen peas
- 1 tablespoon minced fresh parsley
- 1 teaspoon Worcestershire sauce
- 1/2 teaspoon dried thyme
- 1 jar (12 ounces) turkey gravy
- 5 slices process American cheese, cut into strips

Direction

- Mix butter, broth, and egg in a large bowl. Add in the stuffing and stir. Press up the sides and on the bottom of a 9-inch, greased pie plate; put aside.
- For the filling: Sauté onion and mushrooms in butter in a large skillet until they are tender. Dust with the flour until combined thoroughly. Stir in thyme, Worcestershire sauce, parsley, peas, and turkey. Add in gravy and stir. Let come to a boil; stir and boil for 2 minutes.
- Scoop into the crust. Bake for 20 minutes at 375 degrees. Place the cheese strips over the filling in a lattice pattern. Bake until the cheese melts, for 5-10 more minutes.

Nutrition Information

- Calories: 511 calories
- Total Carbohydrate: 43g carbohydrate (6g sugars
- Cholesterol: 137mg cholesterol
- Protein: 32g protein.
- Total Fat: 23g fat (12g saturated fat)

- Sodium: 1560mg sodium
- Fiber: 4g fiber)

937. Turkey Asparagus Casserole

Serving: 4 servings. | Prep: 10mins | Cook: 30mins | Ready in:

Ingredients

- 1 package (10 ounces) frozen cut asparagus
- 2 cups cubed cooked turkey or chicken
- 1 can (10-3/4 ounces) condensed cream of chicken soup, undiluted
- 1/4 cup water
- 1 can (2.8 ounces) french-fried onions

Direction

- Cook asparagus for 2mins in a small pot with a small amount of water; drain then arrange in an oiled 11-in by 7-in baking dish. Place turkey on top. Mix water and soup together; spoon on top of the turkey. Bake for 25-30mins without cover in a 350°F oven. Scatter onions on top then bake for another 5mins until it turns golden brown.

Nutrition Information

- Calories: 328 calories
- Sodium: 800mg sodium
- Fiber: 2g fiber)
- Total Carbohydrate: 16g carbohydrate (2g sugars
- Cholesterol: 59mg cholesterol
- Protein: 24g protein.
- Total Fat: 18g fat (5g saturated fat)

938. Turkey Cabbage Bake

Serving: 6 servings. | Prep: 30mins | Cook: 15mins | Ready in:

Ingredients

- 2 tubes (8 ounces each) refrigerated crescent rolls
- 1-1/2 pounds ground turkey
- 1/2 cup chopped onion
- 1/2 cup finely chopped carrot
- 1 teaspoon minced garlic
- 2 cups finely chopped cabbage
- 1 can (10-3/4 ounces) condensed cream of mushroom soup, undiluted
- 1/2 teaspoon dried thyme
- 1 cup shredded part-skim mozzarella cheese

Direction

- Flatten one tube of crescent dough into one long rectangle; secure seams and perforations. Press onto the base of an oiled 13x9-inch baking dish. Bake at 425°, until golden brown, for 6 to 8 minutes.
- In the meantime, in a large skillet, cook carrot, onion, and turkey on medium heat until meat is no more pink. Put in garlic; cook for an extra 1 minute. Drain. Include in thyme, soup, and cabbage. Transfer over crust; spread cheese over the top.
- Flour lightly a surface, and then form the second tube of crescent dough into a 13x9-inch rectangle, securing seams and perforations. Transfer over casserole.
- Bake, without covering, at 375°, until crust seems golden brown, about 14 to 16 minutes.

Nutrition Information

- Calories:
- Sodium:
- Fiber:
- Total Carbohydrate:
- Cholesterol:
- Protein:
- Total Fat:

939. Turkey Casserole

Serving: 6 | Prep: 20mins | Cook: 50mins | Ready in:

Ingredients

- 1 cup diced celery
- 5 tablespoons butter
- 1 onion, chopped
- 1/2 green bell pepper, chopped
- 6 tablespoons all-purpose flour
- 1 (10.75 ounce) can cream of mushroom soup
- 1 (10.75 ounce) can milk
- 1 (6 ounce) can mushrooms
- 3 cups diced cooked turkey
- 1 (4 ounce) jar chopped pimento peppers
- 1/2 cup slivered almonds
- salt to taste
- 1 cup soft bread crumbs
- 1 cup shredded Cheddar cheese

Direction

- Set an oven to 190°C (375°F) and start preheating.
- Boil a large pot of lightly salted water; cook celery in the boiling water for 5-10 minutes, until it becomes tender; drain the celery.
- In a skillet, heat the butter over medium heat; stir and cook bell pepper and onion in the heated butter for 5-10 minutes until they become soft. Beat the flour into the onion mixture until flour and butter form a paste. Put in mushrooms, milk, and mushroom soup; cook and stir from time to time for 5-10 minutes until the mixture becomes smooth.
- Stir salt, almonds, pimento peppers, celery and turkey into the mushroom soup mixture; stir and cook for 5 minutes, until heated through. Add the mixture to a 2-quart casserole dish; put Cheddar cheese and breadcrumbs on top.
- In the prepared oven, bake for 30-40 minutes, until the cheese melts and casserole bubbles.

Nutrition Information

- Calories: 475 calories;
- Total Fat: 28.4
- Sodium: 773
- Total Carbohydrate: 22.7
- Cholesterol: 102
- Protein: 32.2

940. Turkey Day Bake

Serving: 6-8 servings. | Prep: 10mins | Cook: 30mins | Ready in:

Ingredients

- 4 cups cooked stuffing
- 2-1/2 cups cubed cooked turkey
- 2 cups cooked broccoli florets
- 2 cups turkey gravy
- 4 slices process American cheese, halved

Direction

- Press the stuffing on the bottom of a 2 1/2-quart baking dish coated with cooking spray. Put broccoli and turkey on top. Spread gravy over all.
- Without the cover, bake at 350 degrees until the edges bubble, 25-30 minutes. Put cheese on top; bake until the cheese melts, 2-4 more minutes.

Nutrition Information

- Calories: 251 calories
- Total Fat: 6g fat (2g saturated fat)
- Sodium: 1002mg sodium
- Fiber: 1g fiber)
- Total Carbohydrate: 26g carbohydrate (4g sugars
- Cholesterol: 45mg cholesterol
- Protein: 20g protein.

941. Turkey Divan

Serving: 6 | Prep: 10mins | Cook: 50mins | Ready in:

Ingredients

- 2 (10 ounce) packages frozen broccoli spears
- 1/4 cup margarine
- 6 tablespoons all-purpose flour
- salt and ground black pepper to taste
- 2 cups chicken broth
- 1/2 cup heavy whipping cream
- 3 tablespoons white wine
- 3 cups cooked turkey breast, sliced
- 1/4 cup shredded Monterey Jack cheese

Direction

- In a saucepan, put broccoli and 4 cups of water. Boil; lower the heat; simmer with a cover for 5-8 minutes, or till tender. Drain.
- Set the oven at 350°F (175°C) and start preheating.
- In a saucepan over medium heat, melt margarine; mix in pepper, salt and flour, stir properly. Pour in chicken broth; cook while stirring for around 10 minutes, or till the sauce bubbles and thickens. Pour in wine and cream; stir till well combined.
- On the bottom of a 7x12-in. baking sheet, place broccoli. Spread half of the sauce over broccoli. Arrange sliced turkey on top. In the saucepan, mix Monterey Jack cheese into the remaining sauce. Transfer the cheese sauce over the turkey.
- Bake in the preheated oven for around 20 minutes, or till bubbly. Keep broiling for around 5 minutes, or till the cheese sauce turns golden.

Nutrition Information

- Calories: 331 calories;

- Total Fat: 20.1
- Sodium: 218
- Total Carbohydrate: 11.4
- Cholesterol: 85
- Protein: 25.6

942. Turkey Enchilada Casserole

Serving: 10 servings. | Prep: 30mins | Cook: 25mins | Ready in:

Ingredients

- 1 pound lean ground turkey
- 1 medium green pepper, chopped
- 1 medium onion, chopped
- 3 garlic cloves, minced
- 2 cans (15 ounces each) black beans, rinsed and drained
- 1 jar (16 ounces) salsa
- 1 can (15 ounces) tomato sauce
- 1 can (14-1/2 ounces) Mexican stewed tomatoes
- 1 teaspoon each onion powder, garlic powder and ground cumin
- 12 corn tortillas (6 inches)
- 2 cups shredded reduced-fat cheddar cheese, divided

Direction

- Coat a large nonstick saucepan with cooking spray. In the prepared saucepan, combine onion, green pepper and turkey and cook over medium heat until the pink color disappears from meat. Add garlic and cook for another 1 minute. Drain. Stir in cumin, garlic powder, onion powder, tomatoes, tomato sauce, salsa and beans. Bring to a boil. Lower the heat and simmer, uncovered, for 10 minutes.
- Set the oven to 350° and start preheating. Coat a 13x9 inches baking dish with cooking spray. In the prepared baking dish, spread 1 cup meat sauce. Arrange 6 tortillas on top. Spread

over half of the remaining meat sauce and add 1 cup cheese on top. Continue layering with remaining meat sauce and tortillas.
- Bake in the preheated oven, covered, for 20 minutes. Uncover and add remaining cheese on top. Bake for an additional 5 to 10 minutes or until bubbles form and cheese is completely melted.

Nutrition Information

- Calories: 318 calories
- Total Fat: 9g fat (4g saturated fat)
- Sodium: 936mg sodium
- Fiber: 7g fiber)
- Total Carbohydrate: 37g carbohydrate (7g sugars
- Cholesterol: 52mg cholesterol
- Protein: 21g protein.

943. Turkey Garden Medley

Serving: 4-6 servings. | Prep: 25mins | Cook: 30mins | Ready in:

Ingredients

- 1 pound boneless skinless turkey breasts, cut into strips
- 1 garlic clove, minced
- 1/4 cup butter, divided
- 1 small yellow squash, julienned
- 1 small zucchini, julienned
- 1/2 cup each julienned green and sweet red pepper
- 1/4 cup thinly sliced onion
- 2 tablespoons all-purpose flour
- 1/2 teaspoon salt-free seasoning blend
- 1/4 teaspoon pepper
- 3/4 cup low-sodium chicken broth
- 1/2 cup evaporated skim milk
- 8 ounces angel hair pasta, cooked and drained
- 2 tablespoons shredded Parmesan cheese

Direction

- Over medium-high heat, sauté garlic and turkey in 2 tablespoons butter in a large skillet until the juices of the turkey run clear, for 10-12 minutes. Put in the vegetable; cook until crisp-tender; put aside.
- Melt the leftover butter in a small saucepan. Place in flour, the seasoning blend, and pepper; stir until smooth paste forms. Pour the broth gradually, stirring regularly. Bring to a boil; then cook until thickened, for 2 minutes. Next, stir in cream and heat through.
- Pour over the vegetables and turkey; stir until well mixed. In a greased 2-qt. baking dish, arrange pasta. Pour over the top with the turkey mixture. Dust with Parmesan cheese.
- Bake at 350°, covered, for 20 minutes; then uncover and bake for another 10 minutes.

Nutrition Information

- Calories: 199 calories
- Sodium: 227mg sodium
- Fiber: 2g fiber)
- Total Carbohydrate: 14g carbohydrate (0 sugars
- Cholesterol: 47mg cholesterol
- Protein: 23g protein. Diabetic Exchanges: 2-1/2 lean meat
- Total Fat: 6g fat (0 saturated fat)

---

944.   Turkey Hash

Serving: Makes 4 servings | Prep: 25mins | Cook: 1hours | Ready in:

Ingredients

- 1 1/2 pounds medium Yukon Gold potatoes
- 7 tablespoons unsalted butter, divided
- 1 medium onion, finely chopped
- 2 Cubanelle peppers (Italian green frying peppers), finely chopped

- 1 cup shredded cooked turkey (preferably dark meat)
- 4 large eggs

Direction

- Preparation: Generously pour in cold water to cover potatoes, then simmer, loosely covered, until softened, about 20 to 25 minutes. Drain. Let cool slightly, then peel off and use a box grater to grate coarsely.
- While cooling, heat 6 tablespoons of butter in a 12-inch nonstick skillet on medium-high heat; cook pepper and onion, stirring sometimes, until golden brown, about 8 to 10 minutes.
- Include in 1/2 teaspoon of pepper, 3/4 teaspoon of salt, turkey, and potatoes and cook, turning on occasion, until browned in spots, for 15 to 20 minutes. Place hash into plates.
- Fry eggs in teaspoons butter left in skillet over medium heat. Spread on the hash.

Nutrition Information

- Calories: 459
- Protein: 21 g(42%)
- Total Fat: 27 g(41%)
- Saturated Fat: 15 g(74%)
- Sodium: 122 mg(5%)
- Fiber: 5 g(21%)
- Total Carbohydrate: 35 g(12%)
- Cholesterol: 275 mg(92%)

---

945.   Turkey Mushroom Casserole

Serving: 2 casseroles (4 servings each). | Prep: 50mins | Cook: 30mins | Ready in:

Ingredients

- 1 pound uncooked spaghetti
- 1/2 pound sliced fresh mushrooms

- 1 cup chopped onion
- 2 tablespoons olive oil
- 1/2 teaspoon minced garlic
- 3 cans (10-3/4 ounces each) condensed cream of mushroom soup, undiluted
- 3 cups cubed cooked turkey
- 1 cup chicken broth
- 1/3 cup sherry or additional chicken broth
- 1 teaspoon Italian seasoning
- 3/4 teaspoon pepper
- 2 cups grated Parmesan cheese, divided

Direction

- Follow the instruction on package to cook the spaghetti.
- At the same time, in the Dutch oven, sauté the onion and mushrooms in oil till soften. Put in garlic; cook for 60 seconds more. Whisk in 1 cup of the cheese, pepper, Italian seasoning, sherry, broth, turkey and soup. Drain the spaghetti; whisk to the turkey mixture.
- Move into two greased 8-inch square baking dishes. Scatter with the leftover cheese. Place 1 casserole in freezer with cover for no more than 3 months. Bake leftover casserole with a cover at 350 degrees till completely heated or for 30 to 40 minutes.
- To use the frozen casserole: Thaw in fridge overnight. Take out of fridge half an hour prior to baking. Bake with cover at 350 degrees for 45 minutes. Remove the cover; bake till bubbling or for 5 to 10 minutes more.

Nutrition Information

- Calories: 534 calories
- Total Carbohydrate: 55g carbohydrate (4g sugars
- Cholesterol: 63mg cholesterol
- Protein: 33g protein.
- Total Fat: 19g fat (6g saturated fat)
- Sodium: 1286mg sodium
- Fiber: 4g fiber)

946. Turkey Noodle Bake

Serving: 4 servings. | Prep: 25mins | Cook: 45mins | Ready in:

Ingredients

- 2-1/2 cups uncooked yolk-free noodles
- 2 cups cubed cooked turkey breast
- 1 can (10-3/4 ounces) reduced-fat reduced-sodium condensed cream of chicken soup, undiluted
- 1/8 teaspoon garlic salt
- 1/8 teaspoon dried rosemary, crushed
- Dash pepper
- 1 package (10 ounces) frozen chopped spinach, thawed and squeezed dry
- 1 cup (8 ounces) fat-free cottage cheese
- 3/4 cup shredded part-skim mozzarella cheese, divided
- 1/8 teaspoon paprika

Direction

- Cook noodles following the package instructions. In the meantime, mix pepper, rosemary, garlic salt, soup, and turkey together in a big bowl. Mix 1/2 cup mozzarella cheese, cottage cheese, and spinach together in a small bowl.
- Strain the noodles. In a greased 2-quart baking dish, put 1/2 the noodles, layer with cottage cheese mixtures and 1/2 of the turkey. Repeat layers.
- Put a cover on and bake for 35 minutes at 350°. Remove the cover, sprinkle the leftover mozzarella over. Bake until the edges turn light brown, about another 10-15 minutes. Sprinkle with paprika. Let sit before serving, about 5 minutes.

Nutrition Information

- Calories: 357 calories
- Total Carbohydrate: 32g carbohydrate (5g sugars
- Cholesterol: 81mg cholesterol

- Protein: 40g protein. Diabetic Exchanges: 5 lean meat
- Total Fat: 6g fat (3g saturated fat)
- Sodium: 746mg sodium
- Fiber: 4g fiber)

947.   Turkey Noodle Casserole

Serving: 2 casseroles (6 serving each). | Prep: 30mins | Cook: 30mins | Ready in:

Ingredients

- 2 pounds ground turkey
- 2 cups chopped celery
- 1/4 cup chopped green pepper
- 1/4 cup chopped onion
- 1 can (10-3/4 ounces) condensed cream of mushroom soup, undiluted
- 1 can (8 ounces) sliced water chestnuts, drained
- 1 jar (4-1/2 ounces) sliced mushrooms, drained
- 1 jar (4 ounces) diced pimientos, drained
- 1/4 cup soy sauce
- 1/2 teaspoon salt
- 1/2 teaspoon lemon-pepper seasoning
- 1 cup sour cream
- 8 ounces cooked wide egg noodles

Direction

- Cook the turkey in a large skillet over medium heat until it is not pink anymore. Put in onion, green pepper, and celery; cook until they become tender. Stir in lemon-pepper, salt, soy sauce, pimientos, mushrooms, water chestnuts, and soup. Turn down the heat; simmer for 20 minutes.
- Take away from the heat; add noodles and sour cream. Store half in a freezer container; put on a cover and freeze for up to 3 months. In a 2-quart baking dish coated with cooking spray, arrange the remaining mixture. Put on a

cover and bake at 350 degrees until heated through, 30-35 minutes.
- Put in the fridge to thaw to use the frozen casserole. Place into a 2-quart baking dish coated with cooking spray, then bake following the instructions.

Nutrition Information

- Calories: 307 calories
- Total Carbohydrate: 22g carbohydrate (2g sugars
- Cholesterol: 84mg cholesterol
- Protein: 17g protein.
- Total Fat: 17g fat (6g saturated fat)
- Sodium: 760mg sodium
- Fiber: 2g fiber)

948.   Turkey Pie

Serving: 2 servings. | Prep: 20mins | Cook: 25mins | Ready in:

Ingredients

- 1 cup water
- 1/2 cup frozen mixed vegetables
- 2 teaspoons chicken bouillon granules
- 2 tablespoons plus 1/2 teaspoon cornstarch
- 1 cup 2% milk
- 1 cup cubed cooked turkey
- 1/2 cup shredded cheddar cheese
- 2 teaspoons minced fresh parsley
- 1/4 teaspoon salt
- 1/8 teaspoon pepper
- 1 tube (4 ounces) refrigerated crescent rolls

Direction

- Place bouillon, vegetables, and water in a big saucepan, heat to a boil. Lower heat and simmer without cover for 3-5 minutes or until the vegetables are tender.

- Blend milk and cornstarch together in a small bowl until smooth; put into the vegetable mixture. Heat to a boil; stir and cook for 1-2 minutes or until thickened. Add in pepper, salt, parsley, cheese, and turkey. Transfer to an oiled 8-inch square baking dish.
- Spread out crescent roll dough; split into 2 rectangles. Seal perforations and seams. Arrange them by putting the long sides together to make a square; pinch together the edges to seal. Slice into 8 strips; create a lattice crust over the hot turkey mixture.
- Bake at 375 degrees for 25-30 minutes or until top is golden brown.

Nutrition Information

- Calories: 583 calories
- Total Carbohydrate: 44g carbohydrate (12g sugars
- Cholesterol: 100mg cholesterol
- Protein: 36g protein.
- Total Fat: 28g fat (13g saturated fat)
- Sodium: 1877mg sodium
- Fiber: 2g fiber)

949.　　Turkey Sausage Casserole

Serving: 8 servings. | Prep: 15mins | Cook: 20mins | Ready in:

Ingredients

- 1/2 cup finely chopped onion
- 2 teaspoons butter, divided
- 1 pound low-fat smoked turkey sausage, cut into 1/4-inch slices
- 1 package (10 ounces) spiral noodles, cooked and drained
- 1/2 pound fresh mushrooms, sliced
- 1 can (10-3/4 ounces) reduced-fat reduced-sodium condensed cream of chicken soup, undiluted

- 1 can (10-3/4 ounces) condensed cheddar cheese soup, undiluted
- 1 cup fat-free evaporated milk
- 1/2 cup crushed reduced-fat butter-flavored crackers

Direction

- Sauté onion with 1 teaspoon butter in a frying pan until soft. Add milk, soups, mushrooms, noodles, and sausage. Remove into a greased 13x9-inch baking dish. Sprinkle cracker crumbs over, use the leftover butter to dot.
- Bake without a cover at 375° until fully heated, about 20-25 minutes.

Nutrition Information

- Calories: 320 calories
- Protein: 17g protein. Diabetic Exchanges: 2-1/2 starch
- Total Fat: 7g fat (2g saturated fat)
- Sodium: 1018mg sodium
- Fiber: 2g fiber)
- Total Carbohydrate: 48g carbohydrate (9g sugars
- Cholesterol: 29mg cholesterol

950.　　Turkey Shepherd's Pie

Serving: 6 | Prep: 15mins | Cook: 45mins | Ready in:

Ingredients

- 3 large potatoes, peeled
- 2 tablespoons butter, room temperature
- 1/4 cup warm milk
- 1 tablespoon olive oil
- 1 onion, chopped
- 1 pound ground turkey
- 1 large carrot, shredded
- 1 (4.5 ounce) can sliced mushrooms
- 1 tablespoon chopped fresh parsley
- 1/4 teaspoon dried thyme

- 1 clove garlic, minced
- 1 teaspoon chicken bouillon powder
- 1 tablespoon all-purpose flour
- salt to taste
- ground black pepper to taste

Direction

- Boil potatoes for 15-20 minutes until soft. As the potatoes cook, assemble other ingredients.
- Mash potatoes with milk and butter. Use pepper and salt to season to taste. Put aside.
- Start preheating the oven to 375°F (190°C).
- In a frying pan, heat olive oil over medium heat, mix in onion. Sauté the onion for 5 minutes until translucent and tender. Mix in the chicken bouillon, garlic, thyme, parsley, mushrooms, carrot, and ground turkey. Stir and cook until the meat is fully heated and crumbled. Add pepper and salt to taste. Mix in flour and cook for another 1 minute.
- Remove the meat mixture into a casserole dish or deep-dish pie pan. Spread over the meat with mashed potatoes, use a fork to swirl.
- Put in the preheated oven and bake for 30 minutes until the mashed potatoes have turned light brown on top.

Nutrition Information

- Calories: 339 calories;
- Total Fat: 12.9
- Sodium: 342
- Total Carbohydrate: 38
- Cholesterol: 71
- Protein: 18.3

951.   Turkey Spinach Casserole

Serving: 6 servings. | Prep: 20mins | Cook: 40mins | Ready in:

Ingredients

- 1 can (10-3/4 ounces) reduced-fat reduced-sodium condensed cream of chicken soup, undiluted
- 1/2 cup reduced-fat mayonnaise
- 1/2 cup water
- 2 cups cubed cooked turkey breast
- 1 package (10 ounces) frozen chopped spinach, thawed and squeezed dry
- 3/4 cup uncooked instant brown rice
- 1 medium yellow summer squash, cubed
- 1/4 cup chopped red onion
- 1 teaspoon ground mustard
- 1/2 teaspoon dried parsley flakes
- 1/2 teaspoon garlic powder
- 1/8 teaspoon pepper
- 1/4 cup fat-free Parmesan cheese topping
- 1/8 teaspoon paprika

Direction

- Combine water, mayonnaise and soup together in a large bowl. Mix in the next nine ingredients. Using cooking spray, coat a shallow 2 1/2-qt. baking dish; pour in the soup mixture.
- Bake with a cover at 350° till the rice turns tender, 35-40 minutes. Uncover; sprinkle paprika and cheese topping over top. Bake till the cheese is melted, 5 more minutes.

Nutrition Information

- Calories: 323 calories
- Sodium: 669mg sodium
- Fiber: 3g fiber)
- Total Carbohydrate: 28g carbohydrate (0 sugars
- Cholesterol: 54mg cholesterol
- Protein: 23g protein. Diabetic Exchanges: 2 lean meat
- Total Fat: 13g fat (3g saturated fat)

952. Turkey Squash Casserole

Serving: 6 servings. | Prep: 20mins | Cook: 35mins | Ready in:

Ingredients

- 1 pound ground turkey
- 1 tablespoon canola oil
- 2 cups sliced yellow summer squash
- 1 medium onion, chopped
- 2 large eggs
- 1 cup evaporated milk
- 1 cup shredded part-skim mozzarella cheese
- 6 tablespoons butter, melted
- 1/2 teaspoon salt
- 1/4 teaspoon pepper
- 1 cup crushed saltines (about 30 crackers)

Direction

- Put oil in a big frying pan and cook turkey on medium heat until not pink. Add onion and squash. Cook until veggies are tender and crisp; drain excess grease. Mix pepper, cheese, eggs, butter, milk, and salt in a small bowl. Mix into the turkey mixture. Move to an 8-in. greased pan. Sprinkle on cracker crumbs. Do not cover; bake in a 375-degree oven until cooked through, 35-40 minutes.

Nutrition Information

- Calories: 459 calories
- Total Carbohydrate: 17g carbohydrate (7g sugars
- Cholesterol: 177mg cholesterol
- Protein: 23g protein.
- Total Fat: 33g fat (15g saturated fat)
- Sodium: 670mg sodium
- Fiber: 2g fiber)

953. Turkey Stuffing Roll Ups

Serving: 6 servings. | Prep: 15mins | Cook: 25mins | Ready in:

Ingredients

- 1 package (6 ounces) stuffing mix
- 1 can (10-3/4 ounces) condensed cream of chicken soup, undiluted
- 3/4 cup 2% milk
- 1 pound sliced deli smoked turkey
- 1 can (2.8 ounces) french-fried onions, crushed

Direction

- Prepare stuffing mix as directed on package. In the meantime, combine milk and soup in a small bowl; put to one side. Spread each turkey slice with about 1/4 cup of stuffing.
- Roll up; arrange in an oiled 13x9-inch baking dish. Stream soup mixture over the roll-ups. Bake without covering for 20 minutes at 350°. Sprinkle with onions. Bake until thoroughly heated, for 5 more minutes.

Nutrition Information

- Calories:
- Sodium:
- Fiber:
- Total Carbohydrate:
- Cholesterol:
- Protein:
- Total Fat:

954. Turkey Wild Rice Casserole

Serving: 6 servings. | Prep: 60mins | Cook: 60mins | Ready in:

Ingredients

- 3 cups water

- 1 cup uncooked wild rice
- 1/2 cup chopped onion
- 1/2 cup chopped carrot
- 1/2 cup chopped celery
- 1 tablespoon butter
- 1 tablespoon canola oil
- 3 tablespoons all-purpose flour
- 1/2 teaspoon rubbed sage
- 1/2 teaspoon salt, divided
- 1/8 teaspoon pepper
- 3/4 cup reduced-sodium chicken broth
- 1/2 cup fat-free milk
- 2 turkey breast tenderloins (3/4 pound each)
- 1 teaspoon dried parsley
- 1/8 teaspoon paprika

Direction

- Bring onion, wild rice, and water in a small saucepan to a boil. Lower heat; simmer, covered until rice is tender, about 55 to 60 minutes. In the meantime, sauté celery and carrot in oil and butter in a separate saucepan until tender.
- Stir together pepper, 1/4 teaspoon salt, sage, and flour; mix in to carrot mixture until combined. Slowly pour in milk and broth. Bring to a boil; cook while stirring until thickened, about 1 minute. Turn off the heat. Mix in rice. Pour mixture into a 2-quart baking dish greased cooking spray. Arrange turkey atop rice mixture. Mix together the remaining salt, paprika, and parsley; scatter over turkey. Bake, covered for 60 to 70 minutes at 350°, or until a thermometer reaches 170° when inserting into the turkey. Cut turkey into slices; enjoy with rice.

Nutrition Information

- Calories: 313 calories
- Cholesterol: 87mg cholesterol
- Protein: 36g protein. Diabetic Exchanges: 3 lean meat
- Total Fat: 5g fat (2g saturated fat)
- Sodium: 371mg sodium

- Fiber: 3g fiber)
- Total Carbohydrate: 29g carbohydrate (4g sugars

955.   Turkey Wild Rice Dish

Serving: 6 servings. | Prep: 15mins | Cook: 45mins | Ready in:

Ingredients

- 1 package (6 ounces) long grain and wild rice mix
- 3 cups cubed cooked turkey
- 1 can (10-3/4 ounces) condensed cream of chicken soup, undiluted
- 1 can (8 ounces) sliced water chestnuts, drained and halved
- 3/4 cup water
- 1/4 cup chopped onion
- 3 tablespoons soy sauce
- 1 cup soft bread crumbs
- 1 tablespoon butter, melted

Direction

- Cook rice following the package instructions. Mix in soy sauce, onion, water, water chestnuts, soup, and turkey. Remove into a 2-quart greased baking dish. Put a cover on and bake for 30 minutes at 350°.
- Remove the cover. Mix together butter and bread crumbs; sprinkle onto the top. Bake until turning golden brown and bubbly, about another 15-20 minutes. Let sit before serving, about 15 minutes.

Nutrition Information

- Calories: 322 calories
- Protein: 27g protein.
- Total Fat: 9g fat (3g saturated fat)
- Sodium: 1337mg sodium
- Fiber: 2g fiber)

- Total Carbohydrate: 33g carbohydrate (3g sugars
- Cholesterol: 62mg cholesterol

956. Turkey And Dressing Bake

Serving: 4 servings. | Prep: 15mins | Cook: 35mins | Ready in:

Ingredients

- 4 cups leftover cooked stuffing
- 2 tablespoons minced fresh parsley
- 1-1/2 cups cubed cooked turkey
- 2/3 cup condensed cream of chicken soup, undiluted
- 3 tablespoons water

Direction

- Mix parsley and stuffing in a large bowl. Place into an 8-inch square, greased baking dish. Place turkey on top. Mix water and soup; scoop on the top.
- Bake with no cover at 350 degrees until heated thoroughly, for 25 minutes to half an hour.

Nutrition Information

- Calories: 484 calories
- Sodium: 1414mg sodium
- Fiber: 6g fiber)
- Total Carbohydrate: 47g carbohydrate (5g sugars
- Cholesterol: 43mg cholesterol
- Protein: 23g protein.
- Total Fat: 22g fat (5g saturated fat)

957. Turkey And Dressing Casserole

Serving: 4 servings. | Prep: 35mins | Cook: 25mins | Ready in:

Ingredients

- 1 celery rib, chopped
- 1/4 cup chopped onion
- 2 tablespoons butter
- 1 cup coarsely crumbled corn bread
- 1 cup cubed day-old bread
- 2 tablespoons chicken or turkey broth
- 1/4 teaspoon poultry seasoning
- 1/4 teaspoon salt
- Dash pepper
- GRAVY:
- 1/4 cup butter, cubed
- 1/4 cup all-purpose flour
- 1/4 teaspoon salt
- 1 cup chicken or turkey broth
- 1/4 cup milk
- 1 egg, lightly beaten
- 1-1/2 cups cubed cooked turkey
- Dry bread crumbs, optional

Direction

- Sauté onion and celery with butter in a small frying pan until soft. Remove into a big bowl. Mix in seasonings, broth, bread cubes, and cornbread. Remove into a 1-quart baking dish coated with cooking spray.
- To prepare the gravy, heat butter in a big saucepan. Mix in salt and flour until smooth. Slowly pour in milk and broth. Boil it. Lower the heat, stir and cook for 2 minutes. Take away from the heat. Mix a little amount of the hot mixture into the egg, put all back into the pan, whisking continually. Lightly boil, stir and cook for another 2 minutes.
- Spoon over the dressing mixture with 1/2 the gravy. Layer with turkey and the rest of the gravy. Sprinkle bread crumbs over if you want. Put a cover on and bake at 350° until fully heated, about 25-30 minutes.

- Alternatively, put a cover on the casserole and freeze for a maximum of 3 months.
- To use the frozen casserole: Take out of the freezer before baking; about 30 minutes (do not thaw). Bake for 1 1/2 hours at 350°. Remove the cover, bake until fully heated and bubbly, about another 10-15 minutes.

Nutrition Information

- Calories: 385 calories
- Sodium: 980mg sodium
- Fiber: 1g fiber)
- Total Carbohydrate: 24g carbohydrate (3g sugars
- Cholesterol: 141mg cholesterol
- Protein: 21g protein.
- Total Fat: 23g fat (12g saturated fat)

958.   Veggie Turkey Casserole

Serving: 4 servings. | Prep: 10mins | Cook: 30mins | Ready in:

Ingredients

- 3 cups cubed cooked turkey
- 2 cups frozen mixed vegetables
- 2 cups frozen broccoli florets
- 1 can (10-3/4 ounces) condensed cream of chicken soup, undiluted
- 1 can (10-3/4 ounces) condensed cream of mushroom soup, undiluted
- 1/2 cup chopped onion
- 1/4 teaspoon garlic powder
- 1/4 teaspoon celery seed

Direction

- Mix all the ingredients together in a large bowl. Pour into an oil 11x7-inch baking dish. Bake without a cover for 30 to 35 minutes at 350°, or until thoroughly heated. Mix before serving.

Nutrition Information

- Calories: 379 calories
- Total Fat: 13g fat (4g saturated fat)
- Sodium: 1226mg sodium
- Fiber: 6g fiber)
- Total Carbohydrate: 26g carbohydrate (6g sugars
- Cholesterol: 89mg cholesterol
- Protein: 37g protein.

959.   Wild Rice Turkey Dish

Serving: 10 servings. | Prep: 10mins | Cook: 45mins | Ready in:

Ingredients

- 6 cups cooked wild rice
- 3 cups cubed cooked turkey
- 1 can (10-3/4 ounces) condensed cream of mushroom soup, undiluted
- 3 celery ribs, sliced
- 1-1/3 cups sliced fresh mushrooms
- 1 medium onion, chopped
- 1 cup sour cream
- 1/2 cup butter, melted
- 1 teaspoon salt
- 1/4 teaspoon pepper

Direction

- Mix together all of the ingredients in a large bowl. Transfer to a greased 13x9-in. baking dish. Bake with a cover for 45 minutes at 350°. Continue baking without a cover till lightly browned, 15 more minutes.

Nutrition Information

- Calories: 331 calories
- Cholesterol: 73mg cholesterol
- Protein: 18g protein.
- Total Fat: 17g fat (10g saturated fat)
- Sodium: 597mg sodium

- Fiber: 3g fiber)
- Total Carbohydrate: 26g carbohydrate (3g sugars

---

960.   **Zippy Turkey And Rice**

Serving: 8 servings. | Prep: 45mins | Cook: 35mins | Ready in:

Ingredients

- 1 cup uncooked brown rice
- 1 pound lean ground turkey
- 1 large onion, chopped
- 1 can (14-1/2 ounces) diced tomatoes with mild green chilies, undrained
- 2/3 cup picante sauce
- 2 teaspoons chili powder
- 2 teaspoons ground cumin
- 1 can (16 ounces) kidney beans, rinsed and drained
- 1 cup shredded reduced-fat cheddar cheese, divided

Direction

- Based on the instruction on the package, cook rice.
- At the same time, cook onion and turkey on medium heat in a big nonstick skillet till meat is not pink anymore; drain. Mix in cumin, chili powder, picante sauce, and tomatoes; heat though. Take out of the heat; mix in cooked rice, half cup of cheese and kidney beans.
- Move to a 13x9-in. baking dish that's coated using cooking spray.
- Keep it covered and bake at 350 degrees for half an hour. Uncover it; drizzle with the rest of cheese. Bake till cheese becomes melted or for 5 to 10 minutes longer.

Nutrition Information

- Calories: 294 calories

- Total Carbohydrate: 35g carbohydrate (6g sugars
- Cholesterol: 55mg cholesterol
- Protein: 20g protein. Diabetic Exchanges: 3 lean meat
- Total Fat: 9g fat (3g saturated fat)
- Sodium: 593mg sodium
- Fiber: 5g fiber)

Chapter 10: Vegetable Casserole Recipes

***

---

961.   **Beef 'n' Eggplant Pie**

Serving: 4-6 servings. | Prep: 20mins | Cook: 20mins | Ready in:

Ingredients

- 1/4 cup butter, cubed
- 2 cups cubed eggplant
- 3/4 pound ground beef
- 1/2 cup finely chopped onion
- 1 celery rib with leaves, chopped
- 1 garlic clove, minced
- 1 can (8 ounces) tomato sauce
- 1 tablespoon minced fresh parsley
- 1 tablespoon dried oregano
- 1 teaspoon salt
- 1/8 teaspoon pepper
- 1 unbaked pastry shell (9 inches)
- 1/2 to 1 cup shredded part-skim mozzarella cheese

Direction

- In a small skillet, melt butter. Add eggplant; sauté for around 5 minutes until soften.
- In a large skillet, cook over medium heat the onion, beef, garlic and celery until meat is there is not pink anymore; and then drain. Stir in the tomato sauce, eggplant, oregano, parsley, pepper and salt; allow to boil. Take away from the heat.
- Prick pastry shell by using a fork. Mix in beef mixture. Bake at 375° for nearly 20 to 25 minutes. Use cheese to sprinkle. Bake for an addition of 5 to 10 minutes until cheese is melted. Allow 10 minutes to rest before cutting.

Nutrition Information

- Calories: 368 calories
- Total Carbohydrate: 23g carbohydrate (4g sugars
- Cholesterol: 62mg cholesterol
- Protein: 14g protein.
- Total Fat: 24g fat (12g saturated fat)
- Sodium: 857mg sodium
- Fiber: 2g fiber)

962.   Broccoli Beef Supper

Serving: 8 servings. | Prep: 15mins | Cook: 35mins | Ready in:

Ingredients

- 4 cups frozen cottage fries
- 1 pound ground beef
- 3 cups frozen chopped broccoli, thawed
- 1 can (2.8 ounces) french-fried onions, divided
- 1 medium tomato, chopped
- 1 can (10-3/4 ounces) condensed cream of celery soup, undiluted
- 1 cup shredded cheddar cheese, divided
- 1/2 cup whole milk
- 1/4 teaspoon garlic powder
- 1/4 teaspoon pepper

Direction

- Line cottage fries on the bottom and sides of a greased baking dish of 13x9 inches. Bake with no cover, at 400° for 10 minutes.
- In the meantime, over medium heat in a large skillet, cook beef till no longer pink; drain. Layer the beef, broccoli, half of the onions and the tomato over fries. Combine pepper, garlic powder, milk, 1/2 cup of cheese and soup in a small bowl; pour over top.
- Cover up and bake at 400° for 20 minutes. Remove the cover; sprinkle with the remaining onions and cheese. Bake until cheese is melted, about 2 more minutes.

Nutrition Information

- Calories: 420 calories
- Sodium: 529mg sodium
- Fiber: 3g fiber)
- Total Carbohydrate: 40g carbohydrate (3g sugars
- Cholesterol: 46mg cholesterol
- Protein: 18g protein.
- Total Fat: 22g fat (9g saturated fat)

963.   Broccoli Chicken Casserole

Serving: 5 servings. | Prep: 15mins | Cook: 35mins | Ready in:

Ingredients

- 2-1/2 cups uncooked yolk-free noodles
- 2-1/2 cups cubed cooked chicken breast
- 4 cups frozen broccoli florets, thawed
- 1 small onion, chopped
- 1 can (10-3/4 ounces) reduced-fat reduced-sodium condensed cream of chicken soup, undiluted
- 1/2 cup fat-free milk
- 1/2 cup shredded part-skim mozzarella cheese

- 1 teaspoon dried basil
- 1/4 teaspoon salt
- 1/8 teaspoon pepper
- Paprika, optional

Direction

- Follow the package instructions to cook noodles; strain and put into a large bowl. Include in onion, broccoli and chicken. Mix pepper, salt, basil, cheese, milk and soup together in a small bowl. Transfer over the chicken mixture; mix till combined.
- Transfer into a 2-quart baking sheet greased with cooking spray. Bake with a cover at 350° till bubbly, 35-40 minutes. Sprinkle paprika over if you want.

Nutrition Information

- Calories: 284 calories
- Total Carbohydrate: 27g carbohydrate (5g sugars
- Cholesterol: 66mg cholesterol
- Protein: 29g protein. Diabetic Exchanges: 3 lean meat
- Total Fat: 5g fat (2g saturated fat)
- Sodium: 489mg sodium
- Fiber: 3g fiber)

964. Broccoli Chicken Delight

Serving: 8-10 servings. | Prep: 10mins | Cook: 60mins | Ready in:

Ingredients

- 1 package (16 ounces) frozen broccoli cuts, thawed
- 3-1/2 cups cubed cooked chicken
- 2 cans (10-3/4 ounces each) condensed cream of chicken soup, undiluted
- 1 cup mayonnaise
- 1 tablespoon lemon juice

- 1/4 teaspoon curry powder
- 2 cups shredded cheddar cheese
- 1 cup crushed butter-flavored crackers (about 25 crackers)

Direction

- In a greased baking dish of 13x9-inch, layer chicken and broccoli. In a bowl, combine the mayonnaise, soup, curry and lemon juice; pour over chicken. Use cheese and cracker crumbs to sprinkle over.
- Bake with cover at 350° for around 1 hour till heated through.

Nutrition Information

- Calories: 429 calories
- Protein: 22g protein.
- Total Fat: 32g fat (9g saturated fat)
- Sodium: 627mg sodium
- Fiber: 2g fiber)
- Total Carbohydrate: 11g carbohydrate (2g sugars
- Cholesterol: 80mg cholesterol

965. Broccoli Chicken Supreme

Serving: 12 servings. | Prep: 30mins | Cook: 20mins | Ready in:

Ingredients

- 6 cups fresh broccoli florets
- 3 cups sliced fresh mushrooms
- 1 tablespoon butter
- 6 cups cubed cooked chicken
- 3 cans (8 ounces each) sliced water chestnuts, drained
- SAUCE:
- 6 tablespoons butter, cubed
- 1/2 cup plus 1 tablespoon all-purpose flour
- 1-1/2 teaspoons seasoned salt

- 1/8 teaspoon pepper
- 3 cups chicken broth
- 1 cup heavy whipping cream
- 6 egg yolks, lightly beaten
- 3/4 teaspoon lemon juice
- 1/8 teaspoon ground nutmeg
- 3/4 cup slivered almonds, toasted

Direction

- In a steamer basket, place broccoli; place in a big saucepan above 1 inch of water. Let boil; and steam with cover for nearly 5 to 7 minutes till crisp-tender. In the meantime, in a large skillet, sauté mushrooms in butter until soften.
- In a greased baking dish of 13- x 9-inch, layer two-thirds of the mushrooms, 4 cups chicken, 4 cups broccoli and two cans of water chestnuts. In an 8-inch square, greased baking dish, layer the rest of mushrooms, chicken, broccoli and water chestnuts.
- In a large saucepan over medium heat, melt butter. Blend in pepper, seasoned salt and flour till smooth. Add broth and cream gradually. Let boil; cook and stir for around 2 minutes until bubbly and thickened. Take away from the heat.
- Stir into egg yolks a small amount of hot mixture. Return all to the pan; cook and stir till mixture reaches 160° and coats the back of a metal spoon. Take away from the heat; mix in nutmeg and lemon juice.
- Pour 3 cups sauce over the large casserole and the rest sauce over the small casserole; scatter almonds over. Bake with no cover at 375° for approximately 20 to 25 minutes till heated through and bubbly.

Nutrition Information

- Calories: 394 calories
- Cholesterol: 211mg cholesterol
- Protein: 26g protein.
- Total Fat: 25g fat (11g saturated fat)
- Sodium: 569mg sodium
- Fiber: 4g fiber)

- Total Carbohydrate: 17g carbohydrate (3g sugars

966.   Broccoli Rice Hot Dish

Serving: 6 servings. | Prep: 15mins | Cook: 25mins | Ready in:

Ingredients

- 2 cups hot cooked rice
- 3/4 cup shredded reduced-fat cheddar cheese
- 1/2 cup egg substitute
- 3/4 teaspoon garlic salt
- FILLING:
- 3 cups frozen chopped broccoli, thawed
- 4 ounces chopped fresh mushrooms
- 1/2 cup chopped sweet red pepper
- 1/2 medium onion, chopped
- 1 cup egg substitute
- 1/2 cup fat-free milk
- 1/2 teaspoon onion salt
- 1/2 teaspoon pepper
- 1 cup shredded reduced-fat cheddar cheese

Direction

- Mix together garlic salt, egg substitute, cheese and rice in a big bowl. Transfer to a 2-quart baking dish sprayed with cooking spray and press the mixture firmly. Bake at 375 degrees for about 10 minutes.
- In the meantime, put in a steam basket set over 1 inch boiling water in a saucepan with onion, red pepper, mushrooms and broccoli. Bring the mixture to a boil, then cover and steam until tender yet still crisp, about 5 minutes.
- Mix together pepper, onion salt, milk and egg substitute in a big bowl, then stir in vegetables. Pour the mixture over crust, then use cheese to sprinkle over. Bake at 375 degrees without a cover until a knife stuck in the center exits clean, about 25 to 30 minutes.

Nutrition Information

- Calories: 226 calories
- Sodium: 527mg sodium
- Fiber: 2g fiber)
- Total Carbohydrate: 23g carbohydrate (0 sugars
- Cholesterol: 24mg cholesterol
- Protein: 19g protein. Diabetic Exchanges: 2 lean meat
- Total Fat: 7g fat (5g saturated fat)

967.   Broccoli Tuna Casserole

Serving: 8 servings. | Prep: 35mins | Cook: 60mins | Ready in:

Ingredients

- 5 cups uncooked whole wheat egg noodles
- 1 teaspoon butter
- 1/4 cup chopped onion
- 1/4 cup cornstarch
- 2 cups fat-free milk
- 1 teaspoon dried basil
- 1 teaspoon dried thyme
- 3/4 teaspoon salt
- 1/2 teaspoon pepper
- 1 cup reduced-sodium chicken broth
- 1 cup shredded Monterey Jack cheese, divided
- 4 cups frozen broccoli florets, thawed
- 2 pouches (6.4 ounces each) albacore white tuna in water
- 1/3 cup panko (Japanese) bread crumbs
- 1 tablespoon butter, melted

Direction

- Start preheating the oven to 350°. Cook noodles following the package instructions; strain. Remove into a greased shallow 13x9-inch or 3-quart baking dish.
- In the meantime, melt butter in a big greased nonstick frying pan over medium-high heat. Add onion, cook while stirring until soft.

Combine seasonings, milk, and cornstarch in a small bowl; mix into the pan. Mix in broth. Boil it, cook while stirring until thickened, about 2 minutes. Mix in 3/4 cup cheese until melted, mix in tuna and broccoli.

- Add to the noodles, stir thoroughly. Sprinkle the leftover cheese over. Mix melted butter with bread crumbs; sprinkle the mixture over the casserole. Put a cover on and bake for 45 minutes. Bake without a cover until the cheese melts, about another 15-20 minutes. If you want to freeze the casserole: Let the unbaked casserole cool, put a cover on and freeze. When using, slightly thaw overnight in a fridge. Take out of the fridge before baking, about 30 minutes. Start preheating the oven to 350°. Bake the casserole following the instructions; raise the time if needed to fully heat and a thermometer displays 165° when you insert it into the middle.

Nutrition Information

- Calories: 271 calories
- Total Carbohydrate: 30g carbohydrate (4g sugars
- Cholesterol: 38mg cholesterol
- Protein: 22g protein. Diabetic Exchanges: 2 starch
- Total Fat: 8g fat (4g saturated fat)
- Sodium: 601mg sodium
- Fiber: 4g fiber)

968.   Broccoli Tuna Squares

Serving: 8 servings. | Prep: 15mins | Cook: 35mins | Ready in:

Ingredients

- 1 tube (8 ounces) refrigerated crescent rolls
- 1 cup shredded Monterey Jack cheese
- 3 cups frozen chopped broccoli, cooked and drained

- 4 large eggs, lightly beaten
- 1 can (10-3/4 ounces) condensed cream of broccoli soup, undiluted
- 2 tablespoons mayonnaise
- 3/4 teaspoon onion powder
- 1/2 teaspoon dill weed
- 1 can (12 ounces) tuna, drained and flaked
- 1 tablespoon diced pimientos, drained

Direction

- Unroll crescent roll dough out into a long rectangle; arrange in an ungreased 13x9-in. baking dish. Next, seal the seams up and perforations; then press 1/2 in. up the sides and down the bottom. Sprinkle with broccoli and cheese.
- Combine dill, onion powder, mayonnaise, soup, and eggs in a large bowl. Stir in pimientos and tuna; pour over the broccoli.
- Bake without cover for 35-40 minutes at 350°, or until inserting a knife in the center and it comes out clean. Allow to sit for 10 minutes before serving.

Nutrition Information

- Calories: 318 calories
- Total Fat: 18g fat (6g saturated fat)
- Sodium: 738mg sodium
- Fiber: 1g fiber)
- Total Carbohydrate: 16g carbohydrate (3g sugars
- Cholesterol: 134mg cholesterol
- Protein: 21g protein.

969. Cheesy Vegetable Egg Dish

Serving: 10 servings. | Prep: 20mins | Cook: 35mins | Ready in:

Ingredients

- 1 medium zucchini, diced
- 1 medium onion, chopped
- 1 can (4 ounces) mushroom stems and pieces, drained
- 1/4 cup chopped green pepper
- 1/2 cup butter, cubed
- 1/2 cup all-purpose flour
- 1 teaspoon baking powder
- 1/2 teaspoon salt
- 10 large eggs, lightly beaten
- 2 cups 4% cottage cheese
- 4 cups shredded Monterey Jack cheese

Direction

- Sauté green pepper, mushrooms, onion, and zucchini in butter in a large skillet until tender. Whisk in salt, baking powder and flour to blend.
- In a large bowl, stir cottage cheese and eggs. Mix in Monterey Jack cheese and vegetables.
- Pour into a greased 2-1/2-quart baking dish. Bake without a cover, at 350° until a thermometer reaches 160°, 35-45 minutes.

Nutrition Information

- Calories: 407 calories
- Sodium: 759mg sodium
- Fiber: 1g fiber)
- Total Carbohydrate: 10g carbohydrate (4g sugars
- Cholesterol: 287mg cholesterol
- Protein: 24g protein.
- Total Fat: 30g fat (17g saturated fat)

970. Classic Cabbage Rolls

Serving: 4 servings. | Prep: 30mins | Cook: 01hours30mins | Ready in:

Ingredients

- 1 medium head cabbage

- 1-1/2 cups chopped onion, divided
- 1 tablespoon butter
- 2 cans (14-1/2 ounces each) Italian stewed tomatoes
- 4 garlic cloves, minced
- 2 tablespoons brown sugar
- 1-1/2 teaspoons salt, divided
- 1 cup cooked rice
- 1/4 cup ketchup
- 2 tablespoons Worcestershire sauce
- 1/4 teaspoon pepper
- 1 pound lean ground beef (90% lean)
- 1/4 pound Johnsonville® Ground Mild Italian sausage
- 1/2 cup V8 juice, optional

Direction

- Cook cabbage in boiling water in a Dutch oven for 10 minutes, until outer leaves are soft; drain. Rinse in cold water; drain. Take 8 big outer leaves (refrigerate the remainder cabbage for other use); put aside.
- Sauté 1 cup onion in butter until soft in a big saucepan. Put in 1/2 teaspoon salt, brown sugar, garlic and tomatoes. Simmer for 15 minutes, blending occasionally.
- In the meantime, mix the remaining onion and salt with pepper, Worcestershire sauce, ketchup and rice in a big bowl. Crumble sausage and beef over the mixture and blend well.
- For easier rolling, take thick vein from off the cabbage leaves. Put on each leaf about 1/2 cup meat blend; fold in sides. Begin at an unfolded edge, roll up the leaf to fully enclose filling. Position in a skillet, seam side down. Top the sauce.
- Cover and cook for an hour at medium-low heat. If required, put in V8 juice. Turn heat to low; cook for another 20 minutes or until rolls are heated through and an inserted thermometer into the filling registers 160°

Nutrition Information

- Calories:

- Protein:
- Total Fat:
- Sodium:
- Fiber:
- Total Carbohydrate:
- Cholesterol:

971. Classic Cheesy Zucchini Bake

Serving: 12-16 servings. | Prep: 35mins | Cook: 25mins | Ready in:

Ingredients

- 4-1/2 cups sliced zucchini
- 2 to 3 tablespoons olive oil
- Salt and pepper to taste
- 1 large onion, chopped
- 2 tablespoons minced garlic
- 1 can (10-3/4 ounces) tomato puree
- 1 can (6 ounces) tomato paste
- 3 tablespoons sugar
- 1 teaspoon Italian seasoning
- 1 teaspoon dried basil
- 2 cans (2-1/4 ounces each) sliced ripe olives, drained
- 3 cups shredded part-skim mozzarella cheese
- 6 large eggs, lightly beaten
- 1-1/2 cups grated Parmesan cheese

Direction

- Sauté zucchini in oil in a large skillet until softened. Mix in pepper and salt. Pour into an unoiled 13x9-inch baking dish.
- Sauté onion in the same skillet until tender but crisp. Add garlic, sauté for another minute. Mix in basil, Italian seasoning, sugar, tomato paste, and tomato puree. Bring to a boil. Lower the heat; simmer without covering until mixture is slightly thickened, for 10 to 15 minutes. Mix in olives. Stream mixture over zucchini. Scatter top with mozzarella cheese.

- Stir together Parmesan cheese and eggs; pour over zucchini. Bake without a cover for 25 to 30 minutes at 375° until a knife comes out clean from the center. Allow to sit for 15 minutes before serving.

Nutrition Information

- Calories:
- Sodium:
- Fiber:
- Total Carbohydrate:
- Cholesterol:
- Protein:
- Total Fat:

---

972.   Contest Winning Eggplant Parmesan

Serving: 8 servings. | Prep: 40mins | Cook: 25mins | Ready in:

Ingredients

- 3 large eggs, beaten
- 2-1/2 cups panko (Japanese) bread crumbs
- 3 medium eggplants, cut into 1/4-inch slices
- 2 jars (4-1/2 ounces each) sliced mushrooms, drained
- 1/2 tsp dried basil
- 1/8 teaspoon dried oregano
- 2 cups shredded part-skim mozzarella cheese
- 1/2 cup grated Parmesan cheese
- 1 jar (28 ounces) spaghetti sauce

Direction

- Set the oven to 350° and start preheating. In another shallow bowl, place bread crumbs and eggs. Dip eggplant in eggs, then in crumbs to coat. Transfer onto baking sheets coated with cooking spray. Bake until golden brown and tender or for 15-20 minutes, turning once.

- Mix oregano, basil and mushrooms in a small bowl. Mix Parmesan cheeses and mozzarella in another small bowl.
- In a 13x9-in. baking dish coated with cooking spray, spread half a cup of sauce. Layer with 1/3 of the mushroom mixture, 1/3 of the eggplant, 3/4 cup sauce and 1/3 of cheese mixture. Arrange the same layer 2 more times.
- Bake without a cover at 350° until heated through and cheese is melted or for 25-30 minutes.

Nutrition Information

- Calories: 305 calories
- Sodium: 912mg sodium
- Fiber: 9g fiber)
- Total Carbohydrate: 32g carbohydrate (12g sugars
- Cholesterol: 102mg cholesterol
- Protein: 18g protein.
- Total Fat: 12g fat (5g saturated fat)

---

973.   Eggplant Casserole

Serving: 8 servings. | Prep: 20mins | Cook: 30mins | Ready in:

Ingredients

- 4 cups water
- 1 medium eggplant, peeled and cubed
- 1-1/2 pounds ground beef
- 1 medium onion, chopped
- 1 medium green pepper, chopped
- 3 medium tomatoes, chopped
- Salt and pepper to taste
- 1/2 cup milk
- 1 egg, beaten
- 1/2 cup dry bread crumbs
- 2 tablespoons butter, melted

Direction

- Take water to a boil in a saucepan; add eggplant. Boil until tender, about 5 to 8 minutes; drain and put aside.
- Cook green pepper, onion and beef over medium heat in a skillet until the meat is not pink anymore; drain. Put in pepper, salt and tomatoes. Cook and mix until the tomato is soft, about 5 minutes. Take away from the heat. Mix in eggplant, egg and milk; blend well.
- Shift to a greased baking dish of 13 x 9 inch. Stir in butter and bread crumbs; dust over the top. Bake, uncovered, for 30 minutes at 375°, until heated through.

Nutrition Information

- Calories: 278 calories
- Fiber: 3g fiber)
- Total Carbohydrate: 15g carbohydrate (6g sugars
- Cholesterol: 93mg cholesterol
- Protein: 21g protein.
- Total Fat: 15g fat (7g saturated fat)
- Sodium: 151mg sodium

974. Eggplant Parmigiana

Serving: 12 servings | Prep: 25mins | Cook: | Ready in:

Ingredients

- 1 cup flour
- 2 large eggplant s, cut into 1/2-inch-thick slices
- 1/2 cup olive oil
- 1 jar (24 oz.) CLASSICO Four Cheese Pasta Sauce
- 1-1/2 cups KRAFT Shredded Low-Moisture Part-Skim Mozzarella Cheese
- 1/3 cup KRAFT Grated Parmesan Cheese

Direction

- 1. Put the flour in a pie plate. Put 1 slice of eggplant in the flour at a time, flip to evenly coat with flour on both sides. Carefully shake to remove extra flour.
- 2. In a big nonstick frying pan, heat oil over medium heat. In batches, add the slices of eggplant; cook until evenly browned and crisp, 1-2 minutes per side.
- 3. Put 1 cup of pasta sauce in a greased 13x9-in. pan. Layer with 1/3 of each: the eggplant slices, rest of the pasta sauce, mozzarella cheese, and Parmesan cheese. Repeat the layers twice.
- 4. Bake until cooked through, 30-35 minutes.

Nutrition Information

- Calories: 250
- Sodium: 490 mg
- Fiber: 3 g
- Sugar: 5 g
- Total Carbohydrate: 17 g
- Cholesterol: 30 mg
- Total Fat: 16 g
- Saturated Fat: 6 g
- Protein: 8 g

975. Four Vegetable Bake

Serving: 8 servings. | Prep: 20mins | Cook: 20mins | Ready in:

Ingredients

- 3 medium zucchini, cut into 1/4-inch slices
- 1 pound sliced fresh mushrooms
- 1 medium onion, chopped
- 1/2 cup chopped green onions
- 8 tablespoons butter, divided
- 1/4 cup all-purpose flour
- 1 cup 2% milk
- 1 can (14 ounces) water-packed artichoke hearts, rinsed, drained and quartered
- 3/4 cup shredded Swiss cheese

- 1/2 teaspoon salt
- 1/4 teaspoon pepper
- 3/4 cup seasoned bread crumbs

Direction

- Set the oven at 350° and start preheating. In a large skillet, melt 3 tablespoons of butter; sauté in onions, mushrooms and zucchini till the zucchini turns crisp-tender; take away and set aside.
- Melt 3 tablespoons of butter in the same skillet. Mix in flour till smooth. Slowly combine in milk till well blended. Allow to boil; cook and stir till thickened, for 2 minutes. Mix in pepper, salt, cheese, artichokes and the zucchini mixture.
- Place onto a greased 11x7-in. baking sheet. Melt the remaining butter; toss with bread crumbs. Sprinkle over the top. Bake without a cover till bubbly and the topping is slightly browned, for 20-25 minutes.

Nutrition Information

- Calories: 265 calories
- Total Carbohydrate: 22g carbohydrate (6g sugars
- Cholesterol: 44mg cholesterol
- Protein: 10g protein.
- Total Fat: 16g fat (10g saturated fat)
- Sodium: 596mg sodium
- Fiber: 3g fiber)

976.   Golden Broccoli Bake

Serving: 6 servings. | Prep: 20mins | Cook: 35mins | Ready in:

Ingredients

- 1 pound ground beef, cooked and drained
- 1 can (10-3/4 ounces) condensed cream of mushroom soup, undiluted
- 3 cups frozen chopped broccoli, thawed

- 1 large egg
- 2 cups shredded cheddar cheese, divided
- 2 cups hot mashed potatoes (prepared with milk and butter)

Direction

- Blend the first four ingredients in a bowl; stir thoroughly. Mix in 1 cup of cheese. Put to a greased 11x7-inch baking dish.
- Mix the remaining cheese and potatoes together in a bowl; stir thoroughly. Pour over the meat mixture. Bake while uncovered at 350° for around 30 minutes or until lightly browned.

Nutrition Information

- Calories: 391 calories
- Sodium: 861mg sodium
- Fiber: 3g fiber)
- Total Carbohydrate: 19g carbohydrate (2g sugars
- Cholesterol: 123mg cholesterol
- Protein: 26g protein.
- Total Fat: 24g fat (14g saturated fat)

977.   Greek Zucchini & Feta Bake

Serving: 12 servings. | Prep: 40mins | Cook: 30mins | Ready in:

Ingredients

- 2 tablespoons olive oil, divided
- 5 medium zucchini, cut into 1/2-in. cubes (about 6 cups)
- 2 large onions, chopped (about 4 cups)
- 1 teaspoon dried oregano, divided
- 1/2 teaspoon salt
- 1/4 teaspoon pepper
- 6 large eggs
- 2 teaspoons baking powder

- 1 cup (8 ounces) reduced-fat plain yogurt
- 1 cup all-purpose flour
- 2 packages (8 ounces each) feta cheese, cubed
- 1/4 cup minced fresh parsley
- 1 teaspoon paprika

Direction

- To preheat: Set oven to 350 degrees. Put a tablespoon oil in a Dutch oven and heat on medium high heat. Put in half a teaspoon of oregano, half of the onions, half of the zucchini and cook for 8 to 10 minutes till zucchini becomes crisp-tender, remember to stir while cooking. Get zucchini out of pan. Repeat the process with the remaining vegetables. Put previously cooked vegetables back to the pan. Add pepper and salt. Allow to cool briefly.
- Put baking powder and egg in a large bowl, whisk till both are blended, add flour, yogurt and whisk till all are blended. Put in zucchini mixture, parsley, cheese and stir. Grease a 13x9 in. baking dish and transfer the mixture into the dish. Use paprika to sprinkle.
- Bake without cover for 30 to 35 minutes till the mixture is set and becomes golden brown. Allow to sit for 10 minutes before cutting.

Nutrition Information

- Calories: 231 calories
- Sodium: 583mg sodium
- Fiber: 2g fiber)
- Total Carbohydrate: 16g carbohydrate (6g sugars
- Cholesterol: 128mg cholesterol
- Protein: 12g protein.
- Total Fat: 13g fat (7g saturated fat)

---

978. Hamburger Zucchini Pie

Serving: 6-8 servings. | Prep: 35mins | Cook: 60mins | Ready in:

Ingredients

- Pastry for a double-crust pie (9 inches)
- 4 medium zucchini, cut into 1/4-inch slices (about 4-1/2 cups)
- 1/2 pound ground beef
- 1/2 cup finely chopped green pepper
- 1/2 cup dry bread crumbs
- 1/2 cup grated Parmesan cheese
- 1 tablespoon dried minced onion
- 1 teaspoon each salt, dried oregano and dried parsley flakes
- 1/2 teaspoon garlic salt
- 2 medium tomatoes, peeled and sliced

Direction

- Line bottom pastry on a 9-inch pie plate; trim even with the plate's edge. Place 1/2 the zucchini in pastry shell; put aside.
- Cook green pepper and beef in a large skillet over medium heat until meat is no longer pink; drain. Mix in garlic salt, parsley, oregano, salt, onion, Parmesan cheese and breadcrumbs. Spoon 1/2 the mixture over the zucchini; repeat layers. Place tomatoes on top.
- Roll out the remaining pastry to fit the pie's top; put over filling. Cut slits on top. Trim, flute, then seal the edges. Bake at 350° until golden brown, about 60-65 minutes. Allow to sit for 5 minutes before cutting.

Nutrition Information

- Calories:
- Cholesterol:
- Protein:
- Total Fat:
- Sodium:
- Fiber:
- Total Carbohydrate:

979. Herbed Beef Vegetable Casserole

Serving: 10 servings. | Prep: 20mins | Cook: 30mins | Ready in:

Ingredients

- 2 pounds ground beef
- 1 medium eggplant, cubed
- 2 medium zucchini, cubed
- 1 medium onion, chopped
- 1 medium sweet yellow pepper
- 3 garlic cloves, minced
- 1 can (28 ounces) stewed tomatoes
- 1 cup cooked rice
- 1 cup shredded cheddar cheese, divided
- 1/2 cup beef broth
- 1/2 teaspoon each oregano, savory and thyme
- 1/2 teaspoon salt
- 1/4 teaspoon pepper

Direction

- Cook beef in a Dutch oven over medium heat till not pink anymore; let drain. Put in the garlic, zucchini, yellow pepper, onion and eggplant; cook till softened. Put in seasonings, broth, a half cup of cheese, rice and tomatoes; stir thoroughly.
- Put to a greased 13x9-inch baking dish. Top with the leftover cheese. Bake while uncovered at 350° for around 30 minutes or till heated through.

Nutrition Information

- Calories: 257 calories
- Sodium: 434mg sodium
- Fiber: 3g fiber)
- Total Carbohydrate: 18g carbohydrate (8g sugars
- Cholesterol: 56mg cholesterol
- Protein: 21g protein.
- Total Fat: 12g fat (6g saturated fat)

980. Makeover Spinach Tuna Casserole

Serving: 8 servings. | Prep: 25mins | Cook: 40mins | Ready in:

Ingredients

- 5 cups uncooked egg noodles
- 1 cup (8 ounces) reduced-fat sour cream
- 1/2 cup fat-free mayonnaise
- 2 to 3 teaspoons lemon juice
- 2 tablespoons butter
- 1/4 cup all-purpose flour
- 2 cups fat-free milk
- 1/3 cup plus 2 tablespoons shredded Parmesan cheese, divided
- 1 package (10 ounces) frozen chopped spinach, thawed and squeezed dry
- 1 package (6 ounces) reduced-sodium chicken stuffing mix
- 1/3 cup seasoned bread crumbs
- 2 cans (6 ounces each) light water-packed tuna, drained and flaked

Direction

- Set an oven to preheat to 350 degrees. Cook the noodles following the package instructions.
- In the meantime, mix together the lemon juice, mayonnaise and sour cream in a small bowl; put aside.
- Melt the butter in a big saucepan, then mix in flour until combined. Slowly stir in the milk, then boil. Cook and stir for 2 minutes or until it becomes thick. Lower the heat and mix in 1/3 cup of cheese, stirring until it melts. Take away from heat and mix in sour cream mixture. Add tuna, breadcrumbs, stuffing mix and spinach.
- Drain the noodles and put in a cooking spray coated 13x9-inch baking dish. Put the tuna mixture on top and sprinkle with leftover cheese.

- Put cover on and let it bake for 35 minutes. Take off the cover and bake for 5 to 10 minutes more or until heated through and light brown.

Nutrition Information

- Calories: 346 calories
- Total Carbohydrate: 41g carbohydrate (9g sugars
- Cholesterol: 50mg cholesterol
- Protein: 24g protein. Diabetic Exchanges: 2-1/2 starch
- Total Fat: 9g fat (5g saturated fat)
- Sodium: 734mg sodium
- Fiber: 2g fiber)

981. Meatball Stuffed Zucchini

Serving: 8-10 servings. | Prep: 25mins | Cook: 45mins | Ready in:

Ingredients

- 4 to 5 medium zucchini
- 1-1/2 cups soft bread crumbs
- 1 tablespoon minced fresh parsley
- 1/4 cup grated Parmesan cheese
- 1 small onion, chopped
- 1 large egg, lightly beaten
- 1 teaspoon salt
- 1/2 teaspoon pepper
- 1-1/2 pounds lean ground beef
- 1 can (10-3/4 ounces) condensed tomato soup, undiluted
- 1/2 cup water

Direction

- Halve each zucchini lengthwise; remove a thin slice off the bases to have them sit flat. Scoop out the pulp while reserving 1/4-inch shells. Thinly chop pulp.
- Combine the seasonings, egg, onion, Parmesan cheese, parsley, breadcrumbs and pulp in a big

bowl. Crumble beef over mixture, then thoroughly combine.
- Fill zucchini shells with meat mixture. Arrange in a 13x9-inch baking dish. Mix water and tomato soup together; spread over zucchini. Bake at 350° for around 45-50 minutes.

Nutrition Information

- Calories: 172 calories
- Total Carbohydrate: 11g carbohydrate (5g sugars
- Cholesterol: 64mg cholesterol
- Protein: 16g protein.
- Total Fat: 7g fat (3g saturated fat)
- Sodium: 528mg sodium
- Fiber: 2g fiber)

982. Mix 'n' Match Squash Casserole

Serving: 6-8 servings. | Prep: 20mins | Cook: 30mins | Ready in:

Ingredients

- 4 cups cubed summer squash (yellow, zucchini, pattypan and/or sunburst)
- 1 pound Jones No Sugar Pork Sausage Roll, cooked and drained
- 1 cup dry bread crumbs
- 1/4 cup chopped green pepper
- 1/4 cup chopped onion
- 1/2 cup grated Parmesan cheese
- 2 large eggs, beaten
- 1/2 cup whole milk
- 1/2 teaspoon salt

Direction

- In a large saucepan, place a small amount of water and squash; cook with a cover until tender or for 8-10 minutes. Drain. Add the rest of the ingredients; combine well. Place on a greased 11x7-inch baking dish. Bake without a cover for 30-35 minutes at 325°.

Nutrition Information

- Calories: 234 calories
- Fiber: 2g fiber)
- Total Carbohydrate: 15g carbohydrate (4g sugars
- Cholesterol: 80mg cholesterol
- Protein: 11g protein.
- Total Fat: 15g fat (6g saturated fat)
- Sodium: 615mg sodium

983.   Mixed Veggie Casserole

Serving: 4 servings. | Prep: 20mins | Cook: 30mins | Ready in:

Ingredients

- 1 pound ground beef
- 1 small onion, chopped
- 1 can (10-3/4 ounces) condensed tomato soup, undiluted
- 1 teaspoon Italian seasoning
- Salt and pepper to taste
- 1 can (15 ounces) mixed vegetables, drained
- 2 cups hot mashed potatoes (prepared with milk an butter)
- 1 cup cubed process cheese (Velveeta)

Direction

- Over medium heat, cook onion and beef in a large skillet until the meat is no more pink; allow to drain. Stir in the soup, pepper, salt, and Italian seasoning.
- Transfer the mixture to a greased 9-in. square baking dish. Dust with the vegetables. Combine cheese and mashed potatoes in a bowl; then spread over the greens. Bake without cover for 30 minutes at 350°, or until bubbly.

Nutrition Information

- Calories: 480 calories
- Sodium: 1563mg sodium
- Fiber: 5g fiber)
- Total Carbohydrate: 38g carbohydrate (10g sugars
- Cholesterol: 89mg cholesterol
- Protein: 31g protein.
- Total Fat: 22g fat (12g saturated fat)

984.   Mushroom Spinach Bake

Serving: 6 servings. | Prep: 30mins | Cook: 20mins | Ready in:

Ingredients

- 3 tablespoons plus 1-1/2 teaspoons butter
- 1/2 cup all-purpose flour
- 2 cups 2% milk
- 4 large eggs, lightly beaten
- 1 cup shredded Gruyere or Swiss cheese
- 1/2 teaspoon salt
- 1/8 teaspoon pepper
- Dash ground nutmeg
- MUSHROOM SPINACH FILLING:
- 2 cups sliced baby portobello mushrooms
- 1 tablespoon chopped shallot
- 1 tablespoon butter
- 1 teaspoon white truffle oil, optional
- 1 package (10 ounces) frozen chopped spinach, thawed and squeezed dry
- 1 tablespoon all-purpose flour
- 1/8 teaspoon salt
- 1/8 teaspoon pepper
- 1/4 cup heavy whipping cream
- 1/3 cup shredded Gruyere or Swiss cheese

Direction

- Melt butter in a big saucepan. Mix in flour until smooth; gradually pour in milk. Heat to a boil; stir and cook until thickened, or for 1-2 minutes.

- Mix a small portion of hot mixture into the eggs. Bring all back to pan, mixing continuously. Mix in nutmeg, pepper, salt, and cheese; put aside.
- To prepare filling: in a big skillet, in butter and oil if wished, sauté shallot and mushrooms until tender. Put in spinach, cook for 1 more minute. Blend in pepper, salt, and flour until mixed. Gradually pour in cream; heat through (don't boil).
- In a lightly oiled 8-inch square baking dish, put 1/2 of the egg mixture. Top with the rest of egg mixture and the filling. Sprinkle cheese on top. Bake 20-25 minutes at 400 degrees or until an inserted knife into the center comes out clean.

Nutrition Information

- Calories: 349 calories
- Total Carbohydrate: 17g carbohydrate (6g sugars
- Cholesterol: 205mg cholesterol
- Protein: 17g protein.
- Total Fat: 24g fat (14g saturated fat)
- Sodium: 496mg sodium
- Fiber: 2g fiber)

985. Salmon Broccoli Bake

Serving: 4 servings. | Prep: 15mins | Cook: 35mins | Ready in:

Ingredients

- 1 cup chopped onion
- 1 tablespoon butter
- 1-1/2 cups cooked wild rice
- 1 can (7-1/2 ounces) salmon, drained, bones and skin removed
- 1 large egg, beaten
- 1/2 cup mayonnaise

- 1/2 cup grated Parmesan cheese
- 3 cups frozen chopped broccoli, thawed and drained
- 1-1/2 cups shredded cheddar cheese, divided

Direction

- Put butter in a big frying pan, sauté onion until tender. Take off heat; mix in salmon and rice. Mix mayonnaise and egg; mix into salmon mixture.
- Put half into a 2-qt. greased dish; put half the Parmesan and broccoli on top. Sprinkle on 1 cup cheddar cheese. Put remaining salmon mixture, Parmesan, and broccoli on top.
- Don't cover; bake in a 350-degree oven for 30 minutes. Sprinkle on remaining cheddar cheese. Bake until cheese melts, 5 minutes.

Nutrition Information

- Calories: 616 calories
- Protein: 31g protein.
- Total Fat: 45g fat (17g saturated fat)
- Sodium: 942mg sodium
- Fiber: 4g fiber)
- Total Carbohydrate: 22g carbohydrate (4g sugars
- Cholesterol: 147mg cholesterol

986. Saucy Broccoli Beef Bake

Serving: 2 servings. | Prep: 25mins | Cook: 30mins | Ready in:

Ingredients

- 1/2 pound ground beef
- 1/4 cup chopped onion
- 1 cup frozen broccoli cuts, thawed
- 1 block (4 ounces) process cheese (Velveeta), cubed
- 3/4 cup cooked rice
- 1/4 cup chopped green pepper

- 1/4 cup canned mushroom stems and pieces
- 3 tablespoons Homemade Cream-Style Soup Mix
- 2/3 cup water

Direction

- In a skillet over medium heat, cook onion and beef until meat is no longer pink; drain. Take it away from the heat. Put in mushrooms, green pepper, rice, cheese and broccoli; put aside. Whisk water and soup mix together in a microwave-safe bowl. Microwave with no cover on high heat for 90 seconds, whisking occasionally. Add over beef mixture and stir until blended.
- Place into a greased 1-quart baking dish. Bake with no cover at 350° until heated through, about 20-30 minutes.

Nutrition Information

- Calories:
- Fiber:
- Total Carbohydrate:
- Cholesterol:
- Protein:
- Total Fat:
- Sodium:

---

987.   Sausage And Broccoli Bake

Serving: 6-8 servings. | Prep: 20mins | Cook: 30mins | Ready in:

Ingredients

- 3 cups frozen chopped broccoli
- 1 pound Johnsonville® Ground Mild Italian sausage
- 3 cups seasoned salad croutons
- 2 cups shredded sharp cheddar cheese
- 4 large eggs, lightly beaten

- 1 can (10-3/4 ounces) condensed cream of broccoli soup, undiluted
- 1-1/3 cups whole milk
- 1 can (2.8 ounces) french-fried onions

Direction

- Cook broccoli as directed on the package; drain; put aside. Cook sausage over medium heat in a large skillet until meat is not pink anymore; drain. Add cheese, croutons and broccoli.
- Place on a greased 2-quart baking dish. Mix milk, soup and eggs in a large bowl. Top on sausage mixture.
- Bake without a cover for 25 minutes at 375°. Scatter with French-fried onions. Bake until the inserted knife in the center comes out clean or for 3-5 more minutes.

Nutrition Information

- Calories: 532 calories
- Fiber: 2g fiber)
- Total Carbohydrate: 22g carbohydrate (4g sugars
- Cholesterol: 187mg cholesterol
- Protein: 22g protein.
- Total Fat: 39g fat (17g saturated fat)
- Sodium: 1152mg sodium

---

988.   Sloppy Joe Veggie Casserole

Serving: 8 servings. | Prep: 25mins | Cook: 30mins | Ready in:

Ingredients

- 2-1/2 cups uncooked penne pasta
- 1 pound ground beef
- 1 small onion, chopped
- 1 package (16 ounces) frozen mixed vegetables
- 1-1/2 cups water

- 1 can (15 ounces) tomato sauce
- 1 can (6 ounces) tomato paste
- 1 envelope sloppy joe mix
- 1 tablespoon dried parsley flakes
- 1/2 teaspoon dried oregano
- 2 cups (16 ounces) 2% cottage cheese
- 1-1/2 cups shredded Colby-Monterey Jack cheese, divided

Direction

- Following the instructions on package, cook pasta.
- At the same time, cook the onion and beef on medium heat in the big skillet till the meat is not pink anymore; drain off. Put in oregano, parsley, sloppy joe mix, tomato paste, tomato sauce, water and veggies. Boil. Lower the heat; let simmer, while uncovered, till the veggies become tender-crisp or for 7 to 9 minutes. Drain off pasta; whisk into the beef mixture.
- Scoop 1/2 mixture into the greased 13x9-inch baking dish. Put the rest of the pasta mixture, three quarters cup of the Colby-Monterey Jack cheese, and cottage cheese on top.
- Put cover on and bake at 350 degrees for 25 minutes. Remove the cover; drizzle with the rest of Colby-Monterey Jack cheese. Bake till bubbling and cheese melts or for 5 to 10 more minutes.

Nutrition Information

- Calories: 433 calories
- Fiber: 5g fiber)
- Total Carbohydrate: 40g carbohydrate (11g sugars
- Cholesterol: 59mg cholesterol
- Protein: 31g protein.
- Total Fat: 16g fat (9g saturated fat)
- Sodium: 1127mg sodium

989.   Spaghetti Squash Casserole

Serving: 6 | Prep: 20mins | Cook: 1hours | Ready in:

Ingredients

- 3 pounds spaghetti squash, halved lengthwise and seeded
- 1 tablespoon vegetable oil
- 1 medium onion, chopped
- 1 (8 ounce) can sliced mushrooms
- 1 teaspoon dried basil
- 3/4 cup sour cream
- 1/4 cup freshly grated Parmesan cheese
- 3 slices bread, cubed

Direction

- Preheat an oven to 205°C/400°F.
- On baking sheet, cook squash for 40 minutes till tender in preheated oven. Use fork to shred when slightly cooled; put on lightly oiled casserole dish. Discard shell; don't turn oven off.
- Heat 1 tbsp. oil in skillet on medium heat; mix and cook basil, mushrooms and onions till onions are tender and translucent. Mix sour cream and onion mixture into squash till mixed well. Sprinkle parmesan cheese; use bread cubes to cover.
- In preheated oven, bake for 15 minutes till top is toasted and lightly browned and warmed through.

Nutrition Information

- Calories: 211 calories;
- Total Fat: 10.6
- Sodium: 364
- Total Carbohydrate: 25.9
- Cholesterol: 16
- Protein: 5.9

990.   Spaghetti Squash With Balsamic Vegetables And Toasted Pine Nuts

Serving: 6 servings. | Prep: 20mins | Cook: 15mins | Ready in:

Ingredients

- 1 medium spaghetti squash (about 4 pounds)
- 1 cup chopped carrots
- 1 small red onion, halved and sliced
- 1 tablespoon olive oil
- 4 garlic cloves, minced
- 1 can (15-1/2 ounces) great northern beans, rinsed and drained
- 1 can (14-1/2 ounces) diced tomatoes, drained
- 1 can (14 ounces) water-packed artichoke hearts, rinsed, drained and halved
- 1 medium zucchini, chopped
- 3 tablespoons balsamic vinegar
- 2 teaspoons minced fresh thyme or 1/2 teaspoon dried thyme
- 1/4 teaspoon salt
- 1/4 teaspoon pepper
- 1/2 cup pine nuts, toasted

Direction

- Lengthwise, cut squash in half; throw seeds. Put squash on microwave-safe plate, cut side down. Microwave on high, uncovered, till tender for 15-18 minutes.
- Meanwhile, sauté onion and carrots in oil in big nonstick skillet till tender. Add garlic; cook for a minute. Mix pepper, salt, thyme, vinegar, zucchini, artichokes, tomatoes and beans in; mix and cook on medium heat till heated through for 8-10 minutes.
- Use fork to separate strands when squash is cool enough to touch. Serve with bean mixture then sprinkle nuts.

Nutrition Information

- Calories: 275 calories
- Total Carbohydrate: 41g carbohydrate (6g sugars
- Cholesterol: 0 cholesterol
- Protein: 11g protein. Diabetic Exchanges: 2-1/2 starch
- Total Fat: 10g fat (1g saturated fat)
- Sodium: 510mg sodium
- Fiber: 10g fiber)

991.   Spinach Bake With Sausage

Serving: 2 servings. | Prep: 10mins | Cook: 20mins | Ready in:

Ingredients

- 1/4 pound Jones No Sugar Pork Sausage Roll sausage
- 1/2 cup chopped onion
- 1/2 cup chopped celery
- 1 package (10 ounces) frozen chopped spinach, thawed and drained
- 1 egg, beaten
- 1/2 cup dry bread crumbs
- 1/4 cup shredded cheddar cheese
- 1/4 teaspoon salt
- 1 tablespoon grated Parmesan cheese

Direction

- Cook celery, sausage, and onion until meat is not pink and veggies are tender in a small frying pan on medium heat. Drain excess grease; take off heat.
- Mix in crumbs, salt, spinach, cheddar cheese, and egg. Move to a shallow 1-qt. greased dish. Sprinkle on Parmesan. Cover; bake in a 350-degree oven until cooked through, 20 minutes.

Nutrition Information

- Calories: 374 calories
- Sodium: 1056mg sodium

- Fiber: 6g fiber)
- Total Carbohydrate: 31g carbohydrate (5g sugars
- Cholesterol: 144mg cholesterol
- Protein: 19g protein.
- Total Fat: 20g fat (8g saturated fat)

- Calories: 342 calories
- Protein: 19g protein.
- Total Fat: 17g fat (9g saturated fat)
- Sodium: 835mg sodium
- Fiber: 3g fiber)
- Total Carbohydrate: 27g carbohydrate (3g sugars
- Cholesterol: 69mg cholesterol

992. Spinach Beef Bake

Serving: 6-8 servings. | Prep: 10mins | Cook: 45mins | Ready in:

Ingredients

- 1 pound ground beef
- 1 jar (4-1/2 ounces) sliced mushrooms, drained
- 1 medium onion, chopped
- 2 garlic cloves, minced
- 1-1/2 teaspoon dried oregano
- 1-1/4 teaspoon salt
- 1/4 teaspoon pepper
- 2 packages (10 ounces each) frozen chopped spinach, thawed and squeezed dry
- 1 can (10-3/4 ounces) condensed cream of celery soup, undiluted
- 1 cup sour cream
- 1 cup uncooked long grain rice
- 1 cup shredded part-skim mozzarella cheese

Direction

- Brown beef in a frying pan; drain. Add pepper, salt, oregano, garlic, onion and mushrooms. Add rice, sour cream, soup and spinach; combine well.
- Move the mixture to a 2-1/2-quart baking dish coated with cooking spray. Dredge mozzarella cheese over top. Set oven at 350°, bake while covered until the rice gets tender, about 45 to 50 minutes.

Nutrition Information

993. Spinach Skillet Bake

Serving: 6 servings. | Prep: 30mins | Cook: 20mins | Ready in:

Ingredients

- 1 pound ground beef
- 1 medium onion, chopped
- 1 package (10 ounces) frozen chopped spinach, thawed and squeezed dry
- 1 can (4 ounces) mushroom stems and pieces, drained
- 1 teaspoon garlic salt
- 1 teaspoon dried basil
- 1/4 cup butter
- 1/4 cup all-purpose flour
- 1/2 teaspoon salt
- 2 cups whole milk
- 1 cup shredded Monterey Jack cheese or part-skim mozzarella cheese
- Biscuits, optional

Direction

- Cook onion and beef in a 10-in. ovenproof skillet or cast-iron over medium heat until meat is not pink anymore; drain. Mix in basil, garlic salt, mushrooms and spinach. Cover and cook for 5 minutes.
- Melt butter in a saucepan over medium heat. Add in salt and flour until smooth. Slowly pour in milk. Let it come to a boil; cook and stir until thickened, about 2 minutes. Mix in cheese. Pour over meat mixture; stir well.

Lower the heat; cook with a cover until heated through. Serve with biscuits, if desired.

Nutrition Information

- Calories: 351 calories
- Sodium: 872mg sodium
- Fiber: 2g fiber)
- Total Carbohydrate: 13g carbohydrate (6g sugars
- Cholesterol: 85mg cholesterol
- Protein: 23g protein.
- Total Fat: 23g fat (13g saturated fat)

994. Spinach Tuna Casserole

Serving: 2 servings. | Prep: 10mins | Cook: 20mins | Ready in:

Ingredients

- 1 package (10 ounces) frozen chopped spinach, thawed and squeezed dry
- 1 can (6 ounces) tuna, drained
- 1/3 cup seasoned bread crumbs
- 3 tablespoons crushed seasoned stuffing
- 1/4 teaspoon salt
- 1/2 cup mayonnaise
- 1/4 cup sour cream
- 2 to 3 teaspoons lemon juice
- 2 to 3 tablespoons Parmesan cheese

Direction

- Combine the first 5 ingredients in a bowl; blend nicely. Mix together lemon juice, sour cream, and mayonnaise; put into tuna mixture, blend well.
- Move to an oiled 2-cup baking dish. Arrange Parmesan cheese over top. Put on cover and bake at 350 degrees until heated through or for 20-25 minutes.

Nutrition Information

- Calories: 711 calories
- Protein: 32g protein.
- Total Fat: 53g fat (11g saturated fat)
- Sodium: 1457mg sodium
- Fiber: 5g fiber)
- Total Carbohydrate: 25g carbohydrate (2g sugars
- Cholesterol: 69mg cholesterol

995. Stuffing Topped Chicken And Broccoli

Serving: 8-10 servings. | Prep: 15mins | Cook: 45mins | Ready in:

Ingredients

- 1 package (6 ounces) stuffing mix
- 2 cans (10-3/4 ounces each) condensed cream of chicken soup, undiluted
- 1 cup water
- 3 tablespoons sour cream
- 3-1/2 cups cubed cooked chicken
- 2 cups instant rice, cooked
- 2 packages (10 ounces each) frozen broccoli cuts, thawed

Direction

- Follow the package instructions to prepare stuffing mix; set aside. Mix together sour cream, water and soup in a large bowl till blended. Mix in broccoli, rice and chicken.
- Move onto a 3-quart baking dish coated with grease. Place the stuffing on top. Bake with a cover at 350° for 30 minutes. Keep baking without a cover till bubbly, 15-20 more minutes.

Nutrition Information

- Calories:
- Total Fat:
- Sodium:

- Fiber:
- Total Carbohydrate:
- Cholesterol:
- Protein:

- Total Carbohydrate: 25g carbohydrate (7g sugars
- Cholesterol: 43mg cholesterol
- Protein: 17g protein.
- Total Fat: 9g fat (5g saturated fat)

996. Vegetable Beef Casserole

Serving: 6-8 servings. | Prep: 20mins | Cook: 01hours15mins | Ready in:

Ingredients

- 3 medium potatoes, sliced
- 3 carrots, sliced
- 3 celery ribs, sliced
- 2 cups cut fresh or frozen cut green beans
- 1 medium onion, chopped
- 1 pound lean ground beef (90% lean)
- 1 teaspoon dried thyme
- 1 teaspoon salt
- 1 teaspoon pepper
- 4 medium tomatoes, peeled, seeded and chopped
- 1 cup shredded cheddar cheese

Direction

- Layer half the onion, green beans, celery, carrots and potatoes in a 3-quart casserole. Crumble top of vegetables with half of the uncooked beef. Dust with 1/2 teaspoon each of pepper, salt and thyme. Repeat layers.
- Put tomatoes on top. Cover and bake for 15 minutes at 400°. Lower the heat to 350°; bake for about another hour or until meat is no longer pink and vegetables are soft. Scatter cheese over; cover and allow to stand until cheese melts.

Nutrition Information

- Calories: 243 calories
- Sodium: 452mg sodium
- Fiber: 5g fiber)

997. Veggie Casserole

Serving: 6 | Prep: 10mins | Cook: 25mins | Ready in:

Ingredients

- 1 (14.5 ounce) can French-style green beans, drained
- 1 (11 ounce) can white corn, drained
- 1 small onion, chopped
- 1/2 green bell pepper, chopped
- 1 (8 ounce) container sour cream
- 1 (10.75 ounce) can condensed cream of celery soup
- 1/2 cup shredded sharp Cheddar cheese
- salt and pepper to taste
- 1/2 (16 ounce) package cheese flavored crackers, crushed
- 1/4 cup butter, melted

Direction

- Set the oven to 350°F (175°C) and start preheating.
- Combine green bell pepper, onion, corn and green beans in a large bowl. Mix in shredded cheese, condensed soup and sour cream. Add pepper and salt to taste. Stir well and spread into a 2-quart casserole dish. In another bowl, combine melted butter and crushed crackers together. Sprinkle on top of vegetable mixture.
- Bake in the oven until the top is golden brown, about 25 minutes.

Nutrition Information

- Calories: 483 calories;
- Cholesterol: 57

572

- Protein: 10.2
- Total Fat: 30.8
- Sodium: 1263
- Total Carbohydrate: 41.7

---

998. Veggie Cheese Squares

Serving: 4-6 servings. | Prep: 20mins | Cook: 30mins | Ready in:

Ingredients

- 1-1/2 cups fresh broccoli florets
- 1 medium sweet red pepper, julienned
- 2 tablespoons olive oil
- 2 garlic cloves, minced
- 4 large eggs
- 1 cup whole milk
- 1 cup shredded cheddar cheese, divided
- 1/2 teaspoon dried thyme
- 1/4 teaspoon salt

Direction

- Start preheating oven to 350 degrees. Put oil in a big frying pan and sauté red pepper and broccoli. Add the garlic and cook for 1 more minute. Place in a 9-in. greased square pan. In a separate bowl, mix salt, milk, thyme, eggs, and 3/4 cup cheese. Dump over broccoli mixture. Do not cover; bake for 25-30 minutes; sprinkle on remaining cheese. Bake until cheese melts, 5 minutes. Let it cool for 5 minutes before serving.

Nutrition Information

- Calories: 193 calories
- Protein: 10g protein.
- Total Fat: 15g fat (7g saturated fat)
- Sodium: 279mg sodium
- Fiber: 1g fiber)
- Total Carbohydrate: 6g carbohydrate (3g sugars

- Cholesterol: 167mg cholesterol

---

999. Veggie Stuffed Eggplant

Serving: 2 servings. | Prep: 25mins | Cook: 20mins | Ready in:

Ingredients

- 1 medium eggplant
- 1/2 cup chopped onion
- 2 garlic cloves, minced
- 1/2 cup chopped fresh mushrooms
- 1/2 cup chopped zucchini
- 1/2 cup chopped sweet red pepper
- 3/4 cup seeded chopped tomatoes
- 1/4 cup toasted wheat germ
- 2 tablespoons minced fresh parsley
- 1/2 teaspoon dried thyme
- 1/4 teaspoon salt
- 1/4 teaspoon pepper
- Dash crushed red pepper flakes
- 1 tablespoon grated Parmesan cheese

Direction

- Take eggplant and cut it lengthwise in half; remove all the pulp and leave a 1/4-in. thick shell. Cut the pulp into cubes and set both the pulp and the shells aside. Sauté garlic and onion in a big nonstick greased frying pan until the onion is soft. Mix in the eggplant pulp, zucchini, mushrooms, and red pepper; sauté until veggies are tender and crisp, 4-6 minutes. Mix in pepper flakes, parsley, pepper, tomatoes, salt, wheat germ, and thyme; cook for 1 more minute. Evenly divide the mixture between the shells; sprinkle on Parmesan. Put on a cookie sheet; bake in a 400-degree oven until shells are soft, 20-25 minutes.

Nutrition Information

- Calories: 186 calories

- Sodium: 363mg sodium
- Fiber: 12g fiber)
- Total Carbohydrate: 35g carbohydrate (16g sugars
- Cholesterol: 2mg cholesterol
- Protein: 11g protein. Diabetic Exchanges: 2 starch
- Total Fat: 3g fat (1g saturated fat)

1000.   Zucchini Garden Casserole

Serving: 8 servings. | Prep: 20mins | Cook: 01hours15mins | Ready in:

Ingredients

- 4 medium zucchini (about 1-1/2 pounds), sliced
- 1 tablespoon olive oil
- 1 can (28 ounces) diced tomatoes, drained
- 1 cup uncooked instant rice
- 1/4 cup chopped green pepper
- 1/4 cup chopped onion
- 2 tablespoons chopped fresh parsley
- 1 teaspoon salt
- 1/4 teaspoon ground cinnamon
- 1/4 teaspoon ground allspice
- 1/4 teaspoon pepper
- 1-1/2 pounds lean ground beef
- 1 can (8 ounces) tomato sauce
- 1 cup shredded Colby cheese

Direction

- Sauté zucchini in oil in a big frying pan until crisp-tender. In a greased 13x9-inch baking dish, put half of the zucchini. Layer with half of the tomatoes.
- Blend the seasonings, parsley, onion, green pepper, and rice in a big bowl. Crumble the beef over mixture, then stir thoroughly. Whisk in tomato sauce. Spread over tomato layer. Cover with zucchini and the leftover tomatoes.

- Bake, covered, at 375° for 1 hour or until a thermometer reaches 160°. Uncover, then dust with cheese. Bake for 15 more minutes or until cheese becomes melted.

Nutrition Information

- Calories: 291 calories
- Total Fat: 13g fat (6g saturated fat)
- Sodium: 685mg sodium
- Fiber: 3g fiber)
- Total Carbohydrate: 20g carbohydrate (6g sugars
- Cholesterol: 65mg cholesterol
- Protein: 23g protein.

1001.   Zucchini Supper

Serving: 8 servings. | Prep: 25mins | Cook: 35mins | Ready in:

Ingredients

- 1 pound ground beef
- 1 pound Jones No Sugar Pork Sausage Roll sausage
- 4 cups chopped zucchini
- 1 pound process cheese (Velveeta), cubed
- 1 can (10-3/4 ounces) condensed cream of mushroom soup, undiluted
- 1 can (10-3/4 ounces) condensed cheddar cheese soup, undiluted
- 1 package (6 ounces) stuffing mix
- 3 eggs, lightly beaten
- 1 small onion, chopped
- 1/2 teaspoon salt
- 1/2 teaspoon garlic powder
- 1/4 teaspoon pepper

Direction

- In a Dutch oven, cook over medium heat sausage and beef until there is not pink anymore; and then drain. Stir in the rest

ingredients. Stirring occasionally while cooking until heated through.
- Place to a greased baking dish of 13 x 9-inch. Bake while covered at 350° for nearly 30 to 35 minutes until a thermometer reads 160°. Uncover and stir. Bake for an addition of 4 to 6 minutes until golden brown.

Nutrition Information

- Calories: 572 calories
- Cholesterol: 170mg cholesterol
- Protein: 33g protein.
- Total Fat: 37g fat (17g saturated fat)
- Sodium: 2064mg sodium
- Fiber: 2g fiber)
- Total Carbohydrate: 29g carbohydrate (10g sugars

Index

D

E

F

Conclusion

Thank you again for downloading this book!

I hope you enjoyed reading about my book!

If you enjoyed this book, please take the time to share your thoughts and post a review on Amazon. It'd be greatly appreciated!

Write me an honest review about the book – I truly value your opinion and thoughts and I will incorporate them into my next book, which is already underway.

Thank you!

If you have any questions, **feel free to contact at:** _author@ashkenazirecipes.com_

Julia Nedd

ashkenazirecipes.com

Printed in Great Britain
by Amazon